Cecil B. Williams, Ph.D., University of Chicago, is Professor and Chairman, Department of English, Texas Christian University. Formerly, he was Professor and Head, Department of English, DePaul University, College of Commerce. He also taught at the Katherine Gibbs School and Oklahoma State University, and was a Fulbright Lecturer at the University of Hamburg, Germany. Dr. Williams has written numerous articles and several textbooks in the fields of business and English.

E. Glenn Griffin is Associate Professor of English, Purdue University. He is also a Director and Fellow, American Business Writing Association; Director, North Central Reading Association; Associate Editor, *Journal of Communication;* and was formerly President of the American Business Writing Association. In addition to numerous articles and reviews for leading journals and periodicals, Professor Griffin has written books on reading skills and executive improvement.

Effective Business Communication

Cecil B. Williams

Texas Christian University

E. Glenn Griffin

Purdue University

THIRD EDITION

THE RONALD PRESS COMPANY · NEW YORK

Library of Congress Catalog Card Number: 66-21861
PRINTED IN THE UNITED STATES OF AMERICA

Preface

Change is as characteristic of the business communication field as it is of any aspect of life. So in this Third Edition of a textbook whose first two editions have been widely used in colleges and universities throughout the country for almost twenty years, there is change. The title, adapted from *Effective Business Writing* in the first editions, implies a broader perspective of language usage, especially in the part that writing plays in business communication. The entire book supports that implication.

We have added a chapter on general communication, dealing with reading, speaking, and listening as they pertain to business. The subjects of "supervision" and "advancement" are presented from the standpoint of social dynamics that affect competent management. New exercises and problems call for assignments in all components of communication. The end-of-chapter readings reflect the views of psychologists, engineers, social scientists; even the poet's attitude toward business communication is represented. And new illustrative materials throughout the book further show the broadened concept. This fuller look at how we use language is imperative in a society whose business philosophy has become so markedly interdisciplinary.

This Third Edition looks at fundamentals of communication, and specifically discusses the different communications jobs the student will be called on to do in business and industry; it has a reference section on details a person often refers to in communicating, and includes chapter readings from leading publications.

These end-of-chapter readings (about half of which are new) serve as time savers. Having articles pertinent to the different subjects available, the student does not have to search for readings, and the teacher saves the time used in placing books and periodicals on reserve or in reproducing printed materials for class discussion. The readings do not preclude additional reading for other viewpoints; throughout the book, students are repeatedly directed to current publications through the *Business Periodicals Index* and the *Applied Science and Technology Index*.

For this Third Edition, we have borrowed widely from businessmen and industrialists in two ways: (1) The illustrative materials throughout the text and the readings are concrete evidence of our using the thinking practices of people in the field; (2) less apparent, but just as meaningful, are the reactions of leaders in various businesses and industries whose philosophies and practices we know through consulting in firms throughout the country.

The authors wish to express their special appreciation to John Ball, President of the Resources-Development Corporation, co-author of the Second Edition of this book.

In addition, we have an inexpressible debt to associates in professional organizations such as the American Business Writing Association, the National Society for the Study of Communication, the North Central Reading Association, and the Conference on College Composition and Communication. Through holding offices and editorial positions in these organizations and participation in their conventions, we have gained immeasurably from the teachings and advice of some of the forerunners in the field of communication. Through this osmosis, we have garnered the best current concepts for students in our own classes and for users of this book.

Cecil B. Williams

E. Glenn Griffin

Fort Worth, Texas
West Lafayette, Indiana
May, 1966

Acknowledgments

ABWA Bulletin, American Business Writing Association; Advertising Age; American Management Association; C. R. Anderson, Permanent Honorary President, American Business Writing Association; Andover Corporation; Armco Steel Corporation; J. E. Bixler, Duncan Electric Company; William P. Boyd, University of Texas; Harold Brayman, formerly Director, Public Relations Department, E. I. du Pont de Nemours & Company; W. Earl Britton, University of Michigan; Jack C. Carr, State Farm Insurance Companies; Center for Programmed Instruction, Inc.; Champion Paper and Fibre Company; Cincinnati Milling Machine Company; Russell Cosper, Purdue University; William Damerst, Pennsylvania State University; Allen Dibble, National Homes Corporation; Fortune; Charles S. Fries, University of Michigan; Gerald Gammon, Robertshaw Controls Company; General Electric Company; General Motors Corporation; General Petroleum Corporation; Victor E. Gibbens, Purdue University; Harvard Business Review; International Harvester Company; George I. Lambert; Leslie L. Lewis, Dartnell Corporation; Life; Harold L. Martin, Kent McKamy, Business Management; G. & C. Merriam Company; Barriss Mills, Purdue University; William Mumpower, Advanced Management Journal; Administrative Management Society; Newsweek; Charles E. Peck, University of Washington; Robert Perloff, Purdue University; Glenn Perry, E. I. du Pont de Nemours & Company; Prentice-Hall, Inc.; Printers' Ink Publishing Company; Purdue National Bank, Lafayette, Indiana; Random House, Inc.; W. Charles Redding, Communication Research Center, Purdue University; Reporter of Direct Mail Advertising; Royal Bank of Canada, Montreal, Quebec; Rod Serling; Norman G. Shidle; Harry Sholl, University of Chicago Alumni Fund; Donald B. Smith, Sr., First National Bank, Kokomo, Indiana; Donald B. Smith, Jr., First National Bank, Kokomo, Indiana; Society of Automotive Engineers; Society of Technical Writers and Publishers; Time; Leon C. Trachtman, Purdue Research Foundation, Purdue University; Wayne C. Trumbull; Francis W. Weeks, American Business Writing Association; WLW—Television, Cincinnati; Aline Woods.

C. B. W.
E. G. G.

Contents

Part I: The Fundamentals

Part II: Business Letters

Part III: Other Business Writing

Part IV: Appendixes

PART I

THE FUNDAMENTALS

1

The Language of the Market Place

The manager has a specific tool: information. He does not "handle" people; he motivates, guides, organizes people to do their own work. His tool—his only tool—to do all this is the spoken or written word or the language of numbers.—Peter F. Drucker, *The Practice of Management*

To study writing and speaking may never have seemed really practical or very interesting to you. That is understandable, I think.[1] Why should we *study* something that we have been using all our lives—and with a fair amount of success?

After all, not many of us have gone without food, shelter, or other necessities because we couldn't express ourselves. Even before a child learns to talk, he makes his wants and needs known. The bodily movements, the crying, and the nonsense sounds of the infant are just as much communication as words are, as we shall discuss later on. And depending less on writing than on speaking to fulfill desires, as most persons do, only adds to the feeling of futility in studying the written phases of communication. Actually, the chances are fairly good that you have found the study of writing and speaking rather dull.

A different perspective on what really constitutes communication—writing, speaking, reading, and listening—will show that it is practical and that it can be stimulative. The demand from business and industry for

---

[1] To keep the personal tone of the first editions, "I" is used alternately by the authors, who endorse all the principles of the book.

3

those proficient in expressing themselves proves the practicality of the study, because business is practical. Nothing is bought, sold, paid for, given, or obtained without communication. Excitement or stimulation in the subject comes from the person's realization of what he is actually doing and not doing as he studies the four phases of the communicative process. For instance, in English and speech classes a student is not just writing or reading assignments or making or listening to speeches. As he engages in writing or speaking, he is changing some aspect of the world as he informs, persuades, or entertains. As he listens or reads, his own thinking, personality, or needs are being altered to some degree. To make the most of such study, the student will apply what he has learned from other courses and experiences, not just those in writing and speaking.

Information from your technical and scientific courses is most useful in communicating in business and industry; the social and behavioral sciences—sociology, anthropology, psychology, etc.—are basic to communication; the characters, their behavior and thinking, that you have met and will meet in the study of literature can be your allies as you communicate now with your instructors, fellow students, and others. In fact, all the ramifications of your education will be brought into play as you strive to understand and to be understood by those around you.

A course in business communication can be dull and impractical if it is viewed only as dealing with words as used in getting and giving information. However, it will be alive and potent if you make the course a vehicle to use the many other disciplines mentioned above that are vital in getting a job done. That job involves *people* and their *reactions* to words, not just the words as light waves and sound waves in writing and reading, speaking and listening. If you will notice, *people* are mentioned before *words* in the opening quotation of this chapter. The practicality of your studying communication will soon become evident to you. Your first application and interview for employment will be the proving ground. And, in subsequent employment, proficient application of what you have learned will bring rewards, both personal and monetary.

BUSINESS COMMUNICATION AND OTHER COMMUNICATION

Business communication differs from general communication chiefly in being closer to the payoff—in being aimed more specifically at making something happen (usually right away) that otherwise wouldn't happen. If it is my job to get out a sales letter to sell electric alarm clocks, a letter which will be reproduced and sent to ten thousand prospects on a selective mailing list, the thought uppermost in my mind is to make the prospects vividly aware of the advantages of electric alarm clocks—to get them to fill in a coupon and clip a check for $6.95 to it. If they do that, say anywhere from 5 to 10 per cent of them, my letter was a good one. It had a job to do, and it did it. That was its only reason for being, its only justification of the expense involved in sending it out.

Always, the business letter, folder, booklet, or report has a job to do. Perhaps it is to sell alarm clocks or a new kind of paint. Or it may be to induce a series of John Smiths to pay up accounts that are overdue. Possibly it's to give Joseph Jackson, of Abilene, Kansas, an adjustment on a mail-order corn sheller that arrived in damaged condition. You don't want him to be unhappy about it; he worked hard for the money he mailed you, and he is entitled to service; moreover, you have had two hundred dollars' worth of business from him, and you know you can't afford to fiddle with the prospects of getting three hundred more. Or it could be to answer a simple inquiry from Mrs. Alex Kaminski of Youngstown, Ohio. Her request looks more like a plain nuisance than anything else, but it is really a disguised opportunity to introduce your glass coffee makers into a new community and thereby expand your business volume by several thousand dollars a year.

Whether you are a sales manager for Macy's, in the collection department of Tiffany, an adjustment man for Montgomery Ward, assistant general freight agent for the Rock Island Lines, credit manager for International Harvester Company—or simply Henry G. Brown, twenty-two years old, just graduating from Western Springs College and applying for your first position—your letter has a job to do, and it will be a good letter if it does it. And if it doesn't do it, our only interest is in why it didn't—so the next one will.

THE PHILOSOPHY OF BUSINESS COMMUNICATION

By now you must see that the underlying philosophy of business communication is *pragmatism:* a theory is only as good as its results. A letter is good if it works, if it does its job. You don't have to read William James or John Dewey to understand that—though some acquaintance with them won't hurt.

THE NECESSITY FOR STUDY AND PRACTICE

Our first paragraph said something about learning through developing instinctive responses, getting the "feel" for the job. The ability to communicate effectively comes partly that way, true enough, and we hope to get the feel as we go along. But there will be plenty of studying to do too. Although our objective is simple, as, for that matter, is that of the astronaut in his space capsule, nevertheless, like him, we have to deal with some fairly intricate machinery. It is the same machinery we have been tinkering with since grade school, but because we have more interesting and practical uses for it now, we shall get better acquainted with it so as to make it work better.

BUSINESS COMMUNICATION AND ACCOMPLISHMENT

Let's look at the way a modern business letter tackles a tough assignment. Remington Rand wanted to reach thousands of customers quickly and inexpensively to sell filing equipment. From all the media available the company chose direct mail. The selling job was given to a letter—no salesmen, no fancy brochures, no pictures were sent along to help. The success or failure of the sales plan depended on words on a page. Remington Rand mailed 9,951 copies of the letter reproduced opposite.

One proof of the quality of this letter is the fact that it won for its writer, Mr. Charles R. Pope, one of the gold medals awarded in the Dartnell Corporation's annual better letters competition; a better proof is the dollars-and-cents result of the mailing. There were 628 readers who responded, and their response led to orders for over $100,000 worth of filing systems and supplies. The letter paid off, decidedly.

More examples: In Boston, an engineering consultant mailed a sales letter to 250 housewives living near new installations of his firm's storm windows. He received 206 inquiries for information, and 141 sales of the rather expensive installations were made. In Cincinnati, the sales manager of a lumber-supplying firm decided to try reviving 38 accounts which had been "dead" for two years. He wrote a five-paragraph letter to each one and brought back 23 as customers.

In all these situations letter-writing technique proved fully equal to the demand placed on it. There is a feeling of substantial accomplishment in producing a letter that does its job well—in breaking through to reach or exceed your goal through the effective use of language.

THE LANGUAGE OF BUSINESS

The language of the Remington Rand letter is, of course, the business language of today, the kind that well-educated businessmen would use talking face to face, only perhaps a little more formal or dignified. We may wonder, not that it greatly matters, what kind of business language the Greek merchant sailors used when they traded in the ports of Sicily, or the Venetians of the caravans which Marco Polo accompanied to the cities of Kublai Khan when they dealt with the Asiatics. Probably the quarrel over the proper tone of business language went on in earliest times. Some merchants were better in sales and collections than others, not only because their goods were superior, but also because their language was better adapted to selling and collecting.

As long ago as 1599, John Hoskins in his *Directions for Speech and Style* recognized that letters should be written in simple, rather than

Let This FREE Offer Show You How
KOMPAKT FASTENERS Can Cut Office Costs . . .

If you are now using bulky "old-style" file fasteners — the kind
you buy separately and attach to folders yourself — then you
should know about the many economies and profitable advantages
of KOMPAKTS.

Here's a file fastener that not only eliminates all the fuss and
bother but more important — actually saves 25% to 60% of your
filing cabinet space! Organizations of every kind have discovered that Kompakts save up to 90 filing inches for every 1,000
folders in their files — how much salvaged floor space would
that come to in your office?

As you will see, Kompakt Fasteners come to you already installed
in the file folder. Tremendous savings in space are made possible because the folder is specially embossed and the fasteners
are "BUILT-IN" FLUSH WITH THE FOLDER SURFACE. Nothing protrudes
to catch or tear adjoining folders or mar furniture. They stack
evenly, file uniformly. And they have a reinforcing metal ridge
which provides extra strength without extra thickness — an
exclusive Kompakt feature!

Organizations that had never used file fasteners to protect
important papers before, now have assurance of filing security
— and a great saving in executive and clerical time, too.
Papers worth filing can't get lost, out of sequence or damaged.
In the bargain, compared to other fasteners, Kompakts permit a
far faster filing operation — in some cases as much as 25%!
And all because Kompakt Fastener Folders are more easily handled
— both in and out of the files.

And that's where our offer comes in. We'd like to send you,
with our compliments, one of these unique Kompakt-equipped
folders so that you can handle it and judge it yourself — note
too, how it assures security for filed material, the eight
separate "anchoring" points, the smooth "burrless" prongs and
other advantages that can add speed and efficiency to your filing
operation. It costs you nothing to have this Kompakt Fastener
Folder for your personal inspection — and we think you'll like
it a lot. Just drop the card in the mail, we'll send the folder
along to you promptly.

                              Very truly yours,
                              REMINGTON RAND INC.

                              J. A. Grundy[2]

---

[2] Used by permission of Dartnell Corporation.

affected, language. His phraseology seems a little quaint, but his advice is surprisingly close to what we need now:

> Sometimes men make business of kindness, as:
>
>> I could not satisfy myself till I had discharged my remembrance, and charged my letter, with commendations unto you,
>
> or such like words, which go a-begging for some meaning, and labor to be delivered of a great burden of nothing.
>
> Now for fashion, it consisteth in four things, or qualities of your style. The first is brevity. For letters must not be treatises or discoursings, and except it be among learned men, and even amongst them, there is a kind of thrift or saving of words. Therefore are you to examine the clearest passages of your understanding and through them to convey your sweetest and most significant English words that you can devise, that you may the easier teach them the readiest way to another man's conceit; and to pen it fully, roundly, and distinctly, so as the reader may not think a second view cast away upon your letter.
>
> Brevity is attained, by . . . avoiding idle compliments, prefaces, protestations, parenthesis, superfluous and wanton circuits of figures, and digressions; . . . by breaking of sentences. . . . But . . . there is a briefness of parts sometimes that makes the whole long: as,
>
>> I came to the stairs, I took a pair of oars. They launched out, rowed apace, I landed at the Court-gate, I paid my fare, went up to the presence, asked for my lord. I was admitted.
>
> All this is but: *I went to the Court and spake with my lord.*[3]

In 1759 the great Samuel Johnson condemned the use of extravagant language and emphasized the effectiveness of its opposite:

> Advertisements are now so numerous that they are very negligently perused, and it therefore becomes necessary to gain attention by magnificence of promises, and by eloquence sometimes sublime and sometimes pathetic. . . .
>
> There are some, however, that know the prejudice of mankind in favor of modest sincerity.[4]

It is significant that Winston Churchill had not long been Prime Minister when he turned his vigorous hand to simplification of official communication:

> Mr. Churchill has recently invited his colleagues in the Government and all heads of Departments in the Civil Service to join in an effort to save everybody's time by condensing official papers and avoiding official jargon. In this message on "brevity" he says: "To do our work we all have to read a mass of papers. Nearly all of them are too long. This wastes time, while energy has to be spent in looking for the essential points."[5]

[3] *ABWA Bulletin,* October, 1938, pp. 6, 7.
[4] *Ibid.,* p. 6.
[5] *Printers' Ink,* September 20, 1940, p. 67.

That is what matters—wasting time and energy looking for essential points. Business communication, more than any other kind, must be used so that he who runs may understand. It's such an easy and tempting game to hide behind a cloud of words. Mr. Churchill had more to say:

Let us have an end of such phrases as these: "It is also of importance to bear in mind the following considerations . . ."; or "Consideration should be given to the possibility of carrying into effect. . . ." Most of these woolly phrases are mere padding, which can be left out altogether or replaced by a single word. Let us not shrink from using the short expressive phrase, even if it is conversational.[6]

Men in high places in our government, too, have discovered that they must warn employees against piling up words which yield little meaning.

AIM OF THE BUSINESSMAN

The businessman must remember that he is of the people and for the people and that he *must get his message to people*. His aim is not so much to impress them with his personality as to efface himself so that his message may become a disembodied voice speaking and accomplishing its work—to write a letter which will not cause the reader to think, "What a good letter that is," but rather, "That's a good offer; I'll take it right away," or "That's as fair an adjustment as anybody could ask for," or "There's a company that really appreciates the customer's point of view; they get my business from now on."

You recall the story of the ancient Greek orators Demosthenes and Aeschines, who lived in the days when Greece fought constantly against Philip and his Macedonians to preserve her national entity. Aeschines, though not so great a man as Demosthenes, could appreciate his rival's greatness. "When I address the people," he complained, "they always say, 'How well he speaks'; but when you address them, they cry, 'Let us march against Philip!'"

HOW STYLE HAS CHANGED TO GIVE US
THE BUSINESS LANGUAGE OF TODAY

Style changes in business writing have been about what one might expect. Since lawyers wrote most of the first business letters and continue to write a good many of them, business writing has been much influenced by legal language. However indispensable the legal profession may be to business, the influence of legal phraseology upon business expression has been a most unfortunate one. Even the lawyers realize this now, for writers of recent business law books endeavor to express the rules of law in clear and simple language.

[6] *Ibid.*, p. 68.

The malign influence of legal phraseology and the survival of old-fashioned love of bombast are well illustrated in the "Notice" still being printed on some monthly bank statements:

A statement of each account and cancelled voucher are ready for delivery on or before the second business day of each month. Each depositor undertakes promptly to call for and examine the statement and cancelled vouchers and agrees that such statement shall be conclusively deemed correct and such vouchers shall be conclusively deemed correct and genuine in all respects including signatures and endorsements and the bank shall be conclusively deemed without negligence in honoring such vouchers unless errors therein are called to the bank's attention within thirty days after such statement is ready for delivery and within ten days after receipt by the depositor of such statement and vouchers. Delivery to this bank of items for collection or credit shall constitute acceptance of these conditions.

Without worrying too much about the grammatical error in the first sentence, let us see what sense the long second sentence makes. It won't convey anything to the majority of readers, for they will simply "tune out" when they begin to run into the *such's* and *deemed's*. Actually, however, doesn't the passage add up to just, "Depositors should call for statements promptly and call attention to any errors at once"? If legal liability must be fixed, we could add, "The bank will not be responsible for errors not brought to its attention within ten days after receipt of the statement and vouchers by the customer, or at latest within thirty days after the statement is ready for delivery." Our two sentences add up to fifty-three words of simple language against the one hundred and twenty-five words of gobbledygook in the original.

A century ago, in "The American Scholar," Emerson gave the right advice: "Life is our dictionary. . . . Life lies behind us as the quarry from whence we get tiles and copestones for the masonry of to-day. This is the way to learn grammar. Colleges and books only copy the language which the field and the workyard made." If we model our business communication on the best speech of business people rather than on the language of the courtroom or the statute book, we shall be much less likely to go wrong.

THE DEVELOPMENT OF JARGON

About the worst thing that ever happened to business communication style was the popular acceptance in the nineteenth century of model books such as *Webster's Complete Letter-Writer*. The expanding trade of America drew into business many persons without business experience and without much education. As a result, there developed a need for some kind of short cut to good writing: an "easy way" to handle correspondence. Dozens of different model books were published to meet this need.

Each model book contained a hundred or more different letters and claimed to offer a model which could be used for any conceivable business situation. The theory was not that the businessman was to get ideas from these letters, but that he was to copy them word for word, filling in the blanks with appropriate names, dates, or places. Since the publisher hoped to sell the model book to such differing businessmen as a maker of coffins in Indiana, a seller of shoes in Massachusetts, and a planter of cotton in Georgia, he could not be very specific about the kind of product he was writing about in the models. He had to be vague about time; he could not have a model letter promise delivery in two days or in two weeks, but "in due course." The writers of the model books, therefore, developed a kind of language that specialized in saying nothing, in being as unspecific as possible. Here are a letter and reply from one of the model books:

From a country tradesman, containing an order for goods:

Wareham, August 2d, 1805.

GENTLEMEN—*I will thank you immediately to send me the goods, as per order enclosed.*

I must here remark, that in your completion of my last order, several of the articles, especially the paper, was of an inferior quality.

You will be careful to avoid this error in future.

> *I am, gentlemen,*
> *Your obedient servant,*

Messrs. White & Co.   *C. Bailey*

The order to follow here.

Answer:

Boston, August 4th, 1805.

SIR—*We have this day completed and sent off by wagon, your obliging order*

We are greatly concerned at your complaint of some of the goods last received. It must have originated in an error of our packer; but on your returning them, we will credit you the full amount.

Hoping to be favored with your future orders,

> *We are, sir, yours truly,*

With the rise of the educational level of businessmen, and the accompanying emphasis on effective use of language in business, the model books died a natural death. Many thousands were sold in 1880; by 1920 only a few. Several inexpensive letter-writing manuals are sold by retail booksellers today, but their purpose is to improve letter writing, not to serve as a substitute for it.

Unfortunately the influence of the model books is still with us in the old-fashioned jargon that some businessmen still use from force of habit. Such expressions as "your esteemed favor," "trusting our offer may meet with your careful consideration," and "your communication of recent date" may be found in letters now actually in the mails. At their worst they sound something like this:

Yours of the 6th inst. received and contents noted. Beg to state that having given the matter due attention will have to advise that company policy will prevent our taking favorable action on your request. We wish to say that your past patronage has met with our sincere appreciation, and that we are looking forward to a continuation of our favorable relationship. Hoping to hear from you soon, we beg to remain . . .

To realize the absurdity of this letter, read it again, but this time imagine that it is being spoken over the telephone to a customer that the speaker has known for years. Obviously no one ever uses that kind of language in speaking. Yet some businessmen have got so used to hearing these artificial expressions roll off their tongues in dictation that they firmly believe they are good; it would be as hard to give them up as to stop smoking or to install a new filing system.

In spite of oldtimers, jargon is on the way out; the new generation of business writers will do without it and will learn instead to write the language of the market place simply and effectively.

PROGRAM FOR IMPROVEMENT IN BUSINESS COMMUNICATION

As we continue our study of this potentially fascinating and remunerative subject of business communication, let us follow this program:

1. Improve in the fundamentals of writing—grammar, spelling, punctuation, and sentence structure—and achieve a high standard of performance in *every letter, memorandum, or report* which we write.
2. Eliminate from our working vocabularies all trite, hackneyed, rubber-stamp expressions.
3. Build our general vocabularies so that we possess the exact word needed to express our precise shade of meaning, to lend smoothness to our style, and to provide the thought symbols which we require to think imaginatively and creatively.
4. Acquire skill in interpreting communication problems as they come to us so that we can incorporate the proper, and best, solutions in replies.
5. Master psychology so that we can present our material in the way that will cause it to be best received by the person on whose desk it falls.

Outside the classroom, we shall have additional opportunities to improve our written business messages. These will include library reading in such business journals as *Advertising Age, Business Week, Industrial Marketing, Printers' Ink, Dun's Review and Modern Industry*, and *Fortune*, general magazines like the *Saturday Evening Post* or *Life*, and news magazines like *Time* or *Newsweek*. And, though we may have scorned them in high school, we may as well recognize now that Shakespeare and Milton, Addison and Stevenson, Hawthorne and Melville can do much to quicken our imagination and lend something of their word wizardry to our style.

When we make a purchase at a store, pay a bill, or visit the bank, we are carrying on business transactions and thus coming in contact with the language of the market place. Just as it is said that no advertising man can succeed unless he believes in Santa Claus, so also it may be said that no one can succeed in business communication unless he is interested in business people and how they speak and act.

WHAT KIND OF LANGUAGE ARE YOU USING?

Whether you are speaking or writing in the market place or anywhere else, you will do well to be aware of the functions of language, or the reasons for using language.

Misunderstandings occur because someone fails to grasp the meaning of a word, or the thoughts in a sentence. But another major obstacle to communication is the failure of the writer or speaker to understand the *purpose* of language. Is the purpose of the person doing the speaking or writing *informative, persuasive*, or *expressive?* In practice, many persons seem to consider as adequate the simple, schoolboy definition "Language is for telling."

If a message is to inform, then that definition is accurate. For example, a memorandum from a sales manager, stating that sales for a period just ended were up 2 per cent, may be considered mere information. Assume the following one-sentence note to salesmen: "Company sales increased 2 per cent in October." The manager was passing on *information* not known to those receiving the memo.

To add one word to the sentence may change the purpose of the message. Had the sentence been "Company sales increased only 2 per cent in October," the manager's purpose would probably have been to instill in his staff the need for action to increase sales more. The aim, then, would be *persuasive*, or *action-provoking*.

The third function of language, the *expressive* (also termed *affective*), may be injected into the sales manager's memo, using the same words, but adding a typographical detail. Underscoring could be used to reflect the manager's pleasure in the increased business, as follows: "Company sales increased 2 per cent in October." His purpose here would be to have his salesmen feel good—as *he* did—about their showing.

THE IMPLICATION AND THE INFERENCE

No doubt, some of you, in reading these examples, have inferred other meanings in the sentences. For instance, someone could say that the manager stressed "2 per cent" to belittle the amount of increase; he was using irony to stress the point. Such interpretation is quite plausible when we consider a salesman-reader who may not have had a 2-per-cent increase.

In a case of this kind, the salesman would *infer* criticism, but the manager was *implying* pleasure. The *sender* implies; the *receiver* infers.

Misconstrued meanings can result from two other aspects of the communication process that we should be mindful of in using language. One of these is a classification of words as individuals react to them. Words may be thought of as either neutral or emotive—neutral words being generally those that merely convey ideas, such as "desk," "typewriter," "carbon copy," "mail delivery"; and emotive words being those that arouse emotional reactions because of their close association to our attitudes, such as "hate," "delinquent," "good time," "profits." This subject will be discussed more fully in Chapter 6.

THE BASIC FACT OF DIFFERENCE

The second aspect of communication—and the most important, if you are going to get cooperation or be a successful leader—is the constant awareness of the basic differences among individuals. In his book *Is Anybody Listening?* (New York: Simon & Schuster, Inc., 1952), William H. Whyte, Jr., put it this way:

. . . the prime obstacle of every form of communication . . . is the gap in background, experience, and motivations between ourselves and those with whom we would communicate. . . . All the communication in the world is not going to make a coal miner think like a coal operator. . . . But if we cannot close the gap, we must at least acknowledge it. For this acknowledgement of difference is the vital preface to all efforts that follow.

Both the functions of language and the classification of words depend on differences among those we would communicate with. The different interpretations of the three messages in the memorandum discussed just now are apparent. It is different inferences to words that make them neutral or emotive. For example, the word "desk," I daresay, leaves most of you unmoved. However, to an employee recently promoted from a production-line job to a supervisory position, the word could have considerable emotional impact. The office equipment becomes a symbol of his new situation, or status. Likely, after he has been in the new job for a time, he will again react neutrally to the word.

These points on language are discussed fully in later chapters, but, because of their importance to successful communication, they have been mentioned here so that from the outset you will become aware of their importance—if you haven't already considered language in its fuller ramifications—and apply them in any situation of speech or writing, listening or reading.

The Language of Business *

by THE EDITORS OF FORTUNE

Not so long ago, the businessman used to take his language pretty much for granted. He could afford to. His place was respected and his authority unquestioned. And so he bought, he sold, he collected his bills, made an occasional speech perhaps—and if the public, the workers, or the government didn't quite understand what he was up to, well, so much the better for all concerned.

But no longer. Acknowledging the fact—and the necessity—of others' scrutiny, he has made the interchange of facts and ideas with them one of his principal jobs. The house organ, the interoffice memo, the press release, the press conference, the annual report—the range of his efforts has grown enormous. So widespread, indeed, that business has become almost as extensive a publisher as the government itself.

Is the language of business up to the job? The news—and refreshing news it is—is that the American businessman himself has begun to conclude that it is not. Some, in fact, have gone so far as to assert that the pomposity of management prose is the "root ill of our communication troubles." While that may be an overexcited judgment, management's surveys have demonstrated that a large amount of its language has been not only incomprehensible to the people it is trying to reach, but enormously expensive in money, time, and misunderstanding as well. "It is high time the American businessman discovered the English language—it would be very useful to him" . . . "We've turned our offices into paper mills" . . . "We love curt clear correspondence—but damned few of us know how to write it." Everywhere the chorus of self-criticism is growing.

The positive results of this self-examination have been impressive. In company after company, executives have been setting up "writing clinics" to scour management copy, staging correspondence-improvement courses, holding school in conference and public-speaking techniques, and, at the very least, peppering subordinates with "For-God's-sake-won't-you-people-learn-to-use-English-

* William H. Whyte, Jr., former Assistant Managing Editor of *Fortune*, deserves credit for this article, as study of his *Is Anybody Listening?* (New York: Simon & Schuster, Inc., 1952) readily shows. It was published in *Fortune*, November, 1950. Many more recent articles on business communication reflect Mr. Whyte's influence. (By permission of *Fortune*.)

around-here" memos. All of which is clearly to the good. At the same time—
and not so clearly to the good—a school of experts has come forward to help the
businessman by redesigning the language of industry. To accomplish this, the
experts have developed a scientific method that, as we shall see later, has some
disturbing implications. Meanwhile, a look at the anatomy of this language
that is to be redesigned.

First, the written variety—and that infamous jargon, which, for want of a
better term, we'll call businesese. Its signal characteristic, as the reader and
all other critics of businesese will recognize, is its uniformity. Almost invariably, businesese is marked by the heavy use of the passive construction. Nobody ever *does* anything. Things *happen*—and the author of the action is only
barely implied. Thus, one does not refer to something, reference is made to;
similarly, while prices may rise, nobody *raises* them. To be sure, in businesese
there is not quite the same anonymity as is found in federal prose, for "I" and
"we" do appear often. Except when the news to be relayed is good, however,
there is no mistaking that "I" and "we" are merely a convenient fiction and
that the real author isn't a person at all but that great mystic force known as
the corporation.

Except for a few special expressions, its vocabulary is everywhere quite the
same. Midwesterners are likely to dispute the latter point, but a reading of
approximately 500,000 words of business prose indicates no striking differences
—in the Midwest or anywhere else. Moreover, in sounding out a hundred
executives on the subject, *Fortune* found that their views coincided remarkably, particularly so in the matter of pet peeves (principally: "please be advised," "in reference to yours of . . . ," "we wish to draw attention," "to
acknowledge your letter"). The phrases of businesese are everywhere so uniform, in fact, that stenographers have a full set of shorthand symbols for them.

Because of this uniformity, defenders of businesese can argue that it doesn't
make for misunderstanding. After all, everybody knows the symbols, and
furthermore, wouldn't a lot of people be offended by the terseness of more
concise wording? There is something to this theory. Since businesese generally
is twice as wordy as plain English, however, the theory is rather expensive to
uphold. By the use of regular English the cost of the average letter—commonly
estimated at 75 cents to $1—can be cut by about 20 cents.* For a firm emitting
a million letters a year, this could mean an annual saving of $200,000. Prob-
ably it would be even greater; for, by the calculations of correspondence specialist Richard Morris, roughly 15 per cent of the letters currently being written
wouldn't be necessary at all if the preceding correspondence had been in
regular English in the first place.

Where do the terms of businesese come from? Most, of course, are hand-
me-downs from former generations of businessmen, but many are the fruit of
cross-fertilization with other jargons. A businessman who castigates government
bureacrats, for example, is at the same time apt to be activating, expediting,
implementing, effectuating, optimizing, minimizing, and maximizing—and at
all levels and echelons within the framework of broad policy areas. Similarly,

---

* Authors' note: As seen elsewhere in the book, the cost of a letter today is estimated at $2.32.

though he is amused by the long-hairs and the social scientists, he is beginning to speak knowingly of projective techniques, social dynamics, depth interviewing, and sometime soon, if he keeps up at this rate, he will probably appropriate the hallmark of the sound sociological paper, "insightful." Businesese, in fact, has very nearly become the great common meeting ground of the jargons.

Why do people who in private talk so pungently often write so pompously? There are many reasons: tradition, the demands of time, carelessness, the conservative influence of the secretary. Above all is the simple matter of status. Theorem: the less established the status of a person, the more his dependence on jargon. Examine the man who has just graduated from pecking out his own letters to declaiming them to a secretary and you are likely to have a man hopelessly intoxicated with the rhythm of businesese. Conversely, if you come across a blunt yes or no in a letter, you don't need to glance further to grasp that the author feels pretty firm in his chair.

The application of euphemism, a favored device of businesese, further illustrates this status principle. Take the field of selling. At the top of the ladder you will find a great many people in it: *Sales* managers, vice presidents for *sales*, etc. As you go down the ranks, however, it becomes difficult to find people in this line of work. Field underwriters, estate planners, merchandising apprentices, social engineers, distribution analysts, and representatives of one kind or another, yes. But *sales*men? Rarely.

Not only does businesese confer status, it protects it as well, by its magnificent usefulness for buck passing and hedging. "All you have to remember," one executive says, "is the one basis which characterizes all such intracommunication: let the language be ambiguous enough that if the text be successfully carried out, all credit may be claimed; but if the text be unsuccessfully carried out, a technical alibi can be set up out of the text itself."

For this purpose there is a regular subglossary of businesese. Most notable terms: "in the process of," "at this time," "under consideration," "in the not-too-distant future," "company policy," and when one is unable to explain something properly, "obviously." People who have to submit periodic reports to their superiors are particularly dependent on such terms—salesmen, for example, would have a hard time if they couldn't report of some prospects that they were "very impressed." ("I am allergic to that word," says one sales manager. "It results in so few orders.")

The full application of businesese to hedging occurs when more than two heads are put to work on a problem. As the members of top management sit around the table, a relatively simple policy statement is introduced for discussion. This is kicked around a bit, as the saying goes, for though it certainly is a fine statement, couldn't agree with it more, there are just a few little angles and suggestions that maybe ought to be noted. Thereupon each executive, much as a baseball captain grasps a bat in choosing up sides, adds his qualification, until finally the original statement has been at once pointed up, toned down, given more dignity, made more forceful, altered to anticipate possible objections, concretized, amended, and resolved. Now no longer a mere statement but a philosophy, or collection of philosophies, it is turned over to the Public Relations Department to give to the waiting public. There is nothing, as so many people say, quite like what you get when everybody on the team works together.

Besides written businesese, there is another and far more influential category of business English. Generally, it is found in the spoken language of business—in particular, that brand to be heard at the banquet table, the convention, and the conference table.

It might be called *reverse* gobbledegook, for in almost every outward respect it is the opposite of written jargon. Where written jargon is multisyllabic, the other is filled with short terse words; its sentences are short and their construction so much more active than passive that exclamation marks occur almost as frequently as periods. It is English that is on the beam, English with its feet on the ground; in short, *shirt-sleeve* English.

Thanks to reverse gobbledegook, the less you have to say, the more emphatically you can say it. As a result, reverse gobbledegook can be self-defeating; that is, since its whole effect lies in the dynamic quality the words convey, their constant use tends to neutralize them. This can be overcome, however, by adding strengtheners—so that, in a very real sense of the word, it cannot be overemphasized that you sincerely, and unquestionably, meant what you said in the first place.

Like written businesese, reverse gobbledegook also confers status. For this purpose, it provides a sort of slang that, skillfully applied—particularly at the conference table—will impart to the user an appearance of savviness and general know-how.

II

For all its faults, business language is the subject of plenty of good news. Over a third of top U. S. corporations, a *Fortune* sampling indicates, have set up some sort of program to improve it. Monsanto Chemical and Glidden Co. are working on both letters and interoffice memos. "In our campaign to simplify communications," reports Glidden's President Dwight Joyce, "we encourage 'Yes' and 'No' answers, which in turn makes for briefer, clearer questions." Montgomery Ward uses slide films to show its people how to write good-will-building letters. Numerous banks, insurance companies, and department stores have engaged experts to simplify and personalize their letters. And over the past two years the "Cy" Frailey business-correspondence courses sponsored by the Dartnell Corporation in major cities of the U.S. have attracted 25,000 executives.

Public-speaking courses are provided by such companies as SKF, Jones & Laughlin, and Johnson & Johnson. In the last two years General Motors has encouraged 2,000 of its management and supervisory people to express themselves better by taking Dale Carnegie speech courses. Business and management associations (e.g., National Association of Manufacturers, American Management Association, American Institute of Banking, National Association of Foremen) publish material on speech training. In one notable instance, at Bridgeport, Connecticut, an informal group of businessmen became so absorbed in the problem that they chipped in and hired a Yale professor to teach them how to address groups and conduct meetings. And evidently the crusade is more than a nine-to-five concern of businessmen. To judge from recent book sales, they are reading more "practical English" and vocabulary-building books than ever before.

Parallelling these better-business-English efforts has been a movement of even greater significance. It has been called the "plain talk" movement, but it is, in fact, a sort of prose-engineering program, for its core is the use of some newly refined scientific techniques to achieve readability. In only four years it has already produced a measurable effect on the English of business and, if it continues to thrive, it will have a profound effect not only on the English of business but on the English of advertising, journalism, and literature as well.

How did it happen? Such phenomena are usually hard to account for. This one, however, is not.

"My own contribution . . . has been quite modest," readability expert Dr. Rudolf Flesch recently told a convention of P. R. men, "but I think I can truthfully say that it has already had some effect." Dr. Flesch was unduly modest. Rarely have the man and the moment collided so effectively. Almost from the moment in 1946 when he turned his Columbia Ph.D. thesis on readability into the best-selling *The Art of Plain Talk*, Flesch's impact has been tremendous.

The scientific basis was not new; it was evolved by psychologists in the 1920's for the grading and writing of children's textbooks. But as developed by Flesch it gave a new form—and justification—to a movement that had been overtaking American prose. "It was as if," recalls one enthusiast, "we had just been waiting for someone to break the ice."

What Flesch teaches, briefly, is a scientific method of achieving plain, understandable prose. To this end we should write as we talk; eschew irony, rhythm, rhetorical sentences; substitute concrete for abstract words. Equally important, we should surcharge our prose with as much human interest as possible. Then, to measure how we are succeeding, we can apply two formulas. One, based on syllable and sentence count per 100 words, measures the "reading ease" of our writing. The other, based on the percentage of "personal" words and sentences, measures its "human interest." The reading-ease index is tied to the different levels of the U.S. adult population. Thus we can scientifically make sure that we are writing to the level of our particular audience—or better yet, as Flesch advises, somewhat below it.

The first impact of this doctrine was on newspaper writing, but soon it was making itself felt in another field. For years industrial psychologists had been champing to apply scientific methods to employee-management communication material, but, what with cultural-lag troubles, they hadn't been able to get very far. And now here at last was the ideal wedge; "the effectiveness . . . [of] the Flesch formula," as one put it, "forces the issue." Enthusiastically they fell to work measuring house organ prose, reconstructing information bulletins, and in general showing business just how terrible its stuff was and how much better it could be.

Before long another readability expert, Robert Gunning, was making studies for Borden's, the B&O Railroad, and other large companies. John McElroy (formerly head of Gunning's industrial division) set up Readability Associates, and was soon holding seminars on his "fog-count" system for such firms as Ford, Detroit Edison, and American Airlines. General Motors, making a broad attack on the readability problem, has at times employed all three experts, Gunning, McElroy, and Flesch. The Psychological Corporation began four-day workshops, where, at $500 a head, company representatives could be instructed in the readability techniques so that they in turn could go back and teach them to others. Even the military joined in; in the most notable efforts the Air Matériel Command got out an official—and highly readable—manual on the Flesch approach and put psychologist A. O. England to work indoctrinating all hands in it.

What's been the effect of all this? The readability formulas have dramatized, as no subjective critique ever could, the needless obscurity and pomposity of much everyday language. Furthermore, the readability texts have been so full of so much good sense on such matters as grammar and punctuation that they have served to encourage the timid away from outworn do's and don'ts of writing. Wherever the readability doctrines have been taught, there has been not only a decrease in the use of jargon, but a new enthusiasm and respect for the rhythm of colloquial speech.

So far, so good. But how much further, and then how good? The implications of the readability approach warrant careful thought. For if American "functional" English is to be homogenized more and more along these new lines, we should at least, before it all becomes official, have a hard look at what it is leading us to. In purest businesese, is there a danger that we'll jump out of a Pandora's box into a fire?

First, a look at some of the new rules. Most important, the advice that is the core of the movement: to write as we talk. Part of the "secret" of readable writing, we are told, lies in repetition and loosely built sentences—because that is the way we talk. Well, at least that's the way some people talk—haltings, backtrackings, and that sort of thing—they talk on forever sometimes—a lot of excelsior, that's what it adds up to—and it's not difficult at all, because it's certainly easier than the old-fashioned way of organizing your thoughts. In fact, there is only one real question to be raised. Are talk and writing the same thing? They are not—and to say that they should be allows and encourages us to rationalize sloppiness and faulty thinking.

In this colloquializing we are also adjured to make everything into a human-interest story. It is true, of course, that one who describes a problem in terms of the simple love of a man for his dog, a tale as old as time, will have a more *readable* piece than one who tends to somewhat more abstract treatment. But there are quite a number of things that *cannot* be explained by a human-interest tale, and to treat them as if they could be is to mislead the reader by oversimplifying.

Emphasis on the short word, naturally enough, is another feature of the plain-talk movement, and while the readability experts themselves caution people against applying this prescription too rigidly, it has reached a rather extreme point of veneration. Short words, certainly, need no defense. But there are times when the longer one is the *right* word, and if it were not used the writer would have to take up more space saying it another way. And even if the long word were unknown to such and such a percentage of the audience, it might be perfectly clear—or stimulating—to them in a context of sound, lucid English. The Elizabethans knew this well—and so, for that matter, do the pulp writers (e.g., the gibbous moon, the lambent ray, diaphanous dresses, etc.).

By now, if we have followed the above rules, our style should be understandable enough. Just to make sure, however, Flesch has a few more rules.

> *Do not use rhythm (maybe your reader won't catch on).*
> *Do not use periodic sentences.*
> *Do not use rhetorical questions.*
> *Do not use metaphors without an explanation.*
> *Do not use contrast without an explanation.*
> *Do not use irony (half the people won't get it).*

Now we are not to forswear these devices because they are bad; we are to discard them because somebody might possibly misunderstand us. The blood-toil-tears-and-sweat metaphor of Churchill, for example: "The reader gets a vague notion," says Flesch, "that Churchill used a little word picture of three wet things instead of saying *war;* and that's that." Flesch goes on to ask a rhetorical question: would "you must expect great suffering and hard work" have been a better way to put it? "Nobody, of couse," he says, "can answer such a question." Nobody? We'll take a crack at it. NO!

If we have followed these rules, we are now able to talk the level of language the audience will be able to understand "without effort." But even this is not enough. *We must go one step below that level.* We must "shoot beneath the target"; we must "translate down the scale." And for this we don't even need the formulas, for, as Flesch correctly points out, this writing down should by now have become instinctive to us.

Let us imagine that over the next hundred years everyone followed this advice and deliberately wrote beneath the capabilities of his audience. What would happen? Theoretically, we would get ourselves into a sort of ever decreasing circle, and as layer after layer of our language atrophied, eventually spiral our way back to the schoolbook level that got the whole readability doctrine under way in the first place. The "regression" equation would be complete.

And haven't we gone quite far enough as it is? Already we have turned the man in the street into a Frankenstein. We hand him an electric recorder to edit our movies; we watch his radio dial to predetermine what we will put on the air—and now we are to ape him to learn how to write.

We should long since have delivered ourselves of this oaf, for in reality, he does not even exist. He is a self-perpetuating stereotype, the reflection of the lowest common denominators we have been looking for. In creating him we have done not only ourselves but our audiences a disservice, for though they will respond to the tawdry, they will also respond—as many a book, speech, ad, and movie has demonstrated—to the best we give them. But they cannot if we abdicate our moral obligation to give the best that is in us.

So what of the formulas? What do they really measure? Understandability? (And, if so, of what?) Simplicity? Or merely the number of things they are supposed to measure? For a practical experiment, *Fortune* selected thirteen out of a collection of one hundred business speeches. The eight most fatuous of the speeches were put in one group; the five most lucid in another. Each speech was then evaluated by means of the two formulas to find its reading-ease and human-interest scores. The result: there was practically no *significant difference* between the average scores of the two groups. (Average reading-ease score: 61—eighth and ninth grade reading level; average human-interest score: 40—"very interesting.") All, then, represented good "plain talk"—and there was nothing in the scores to indicate the tremendous disparity between the two types.

In thus ignoring the relationship between style and content, the formulas have ignored the fundamentals of language. Language is not something we can disembody; it is an ethical as well as a mechanical matter, inextricably bound up in ourselves, our positions, and our relations with those about us. When a businessman double-talks, for example, it is often for reasons deeper than mishandled prose—hypersensitivity to criticism, fear of the competition, fear of getting out of line with trade-association policy, fear of a government suit, a serious split in corporation policy—or, as is occasionally the case, the lack of any policy to begin with. Is "plain talk" the answer here? It is not. It is a fraud on the listener.

For it is only the illusion of simplicity that the manipulation of language can win for us. Simplicity is an elusive, almost complex thing. It comes from discipline and organization of thought, intellectual courage—and many other attributes more hard won than by short words and short sentences. For plain talk—honest plain talk—is the reward of simplicity, not the means to it. The distinction may seem slight, but it is tremendously important.

Let us not forswear all the richness of our language. Its misuse is not the root ill of our communication problem; it is only the signal of it. And if we make a real effort to win mutual understanding, we need have no fear of the infinite variety of our language—or the ability of our listeners to respond to it. All of which applies to businessmen no less than to everyone else in our society. When businessmen have something to say, and mean it, and feel it, their audience will understand.

Exercises and Problems in Communication

1. Write a letter to your instructor, introducing yourself and stating what you most want to learn in this course. Find out how the instructor should be addressed (by all means, spell the name correctly), and in general try to make your letter correct in all details. (You might preview Chapter 2 for suggestions on letter format.) It is not too soon to learn that *every letter* is its writer's representative.

2. Assume that the division of this course you're presently enrolled in is closed and that the instructor has sole power to admit you to the division. Write the instructor, asking that you be admitted. This is an exercise in persuasion, so you should keep in mind the instructor's attitude toward a larger class. Although he is altruistic and understanding of students' problems, a larger class means more work for him. *Give evidence* of your ability to con-

tribute to the class and of your interest in the course. Increase your chances of getting into the division by making it easy for the instructor to let you know that you have been admitted. Including a return-addressed post card with your request or suggesting that he may let you know by telephone ("Anyone who answers can take the message") is more motivating than a mere concluding expression of hope or appreciation for consideration of your request.

3. Write a criticism of the Remington Rand letter. Which points discussed in this chapter does it illustrate especially well?

4. Write a short business article, prepare a short talk, or prepare for a group discussion on an incident in your life, supporting the statement that "the underlying philosophy of business communication is *pragmatism.*"

5. For discussion or written assignment, read the poem "Money" by Carl Sandburg (in his book *Chicago Poems*). What are the implications of pragmatism in such lines as "Money talk is bigger than talk talk"?

6. To a similar end, read "The Beautiful World of the Utopian Socialists," Chapter 5 in Robert L. Heilbroner's *The Worldly Philosophers.* As you consider the concept of pragmatism, also observe Mr. Heilbroner's sharp ability as a writer. (This is one of a number of exercises throughout this book, encouraging you to read for improvement in writing style. Keep in mind that in a successful career you will probably write much more than letters, memos, and reports.)

7. To get better acquainted with the subject, read in magazines available in your college library that might have articles dealing with the language of the market place. Now is a good time to become acquainted with the *Business Periodicals Index* and the *Applied Science and Technology Index.* For this assignment, refer to headings such as "Communication," "Correspondence," and "Language," in those two guides.

8. Through the *Readers' Guide to Periodical Literature,* find some magazine articles at least twenty years old, about usage in business communication. Then read articles on the subject in current periodicals. How do you account for the frequent appearance of articles on this subject? Does the recurrence imply slowness to break old habits or to accept new principles? What, if any, differences did you find in principles or opinions in the older and the more recent articles?

9. Leaf through an issue of a general magazine (*Life, Look, Harper's, Atlantic Monthly*), a news magazine (*Time, Newsweek*), or a periodical in your particular field of interest (trade journals, professional organization publications). Examine the advertisements of interest to you. Then write a letter to your instructor, reporting what you have discovered about the language of the market place. You may want to justify the usages found in the writing.

10. In one or two of the various volumes of quotations—among them are the standby, Bartlett's *Familiar Quotations;* Robin Hyman, *The Modern Dictionary of Quotations* (London: Evans Brothers, 1962); Burton E. Stevenson, *The Home Book of Quotations* (New York: Dodd, Mead, 1958); Robert Hamilton, *Canadian Quotations and Phrases* (Toronto: McClelland & Stewart, 1952); and John Chapin, *The Book of Catholic Quotations* (New York: Farrar, Straus & Cudahy, 1956)—look up the entries on such concepts as language, words, trade, business, money. The diverse notions and the expressions in the quotations serve a good purpose in expressing philosophies behind business activities throughout the centuries, and thereby helping you to develop your own writing style. Write an informal letter on your reaction to your reading to someone of your acquaintance or to an assumed business associate.

11. In a recent periodical or in a book on education and training for various careers, find a notable person's thinking on the necessity of training in effective communication, spoken and written, for success in those careers. For the sake of argument, find what you consider weak or untenable points in the author's reasoning.

12. Today's emphasis on creativity is reflected in a vast amount of writing. Read some current articles or books on the subject. Adapt some of the principles of "applied imagination" to your own writing, speaking, and study. Write a letter to a younger student, encouraging him to apply some of the principles, in thinking about his career, to improve his grades, or in working on a school committee.

13. To sense differences (if you actually see any) in two styles of writing (textbook and company publication), compare the writing in this chapter and in the end-of-chapter reading. (Note that it is from a business magazine.)

14. Study some advertisements in business magazines—such as *Fortune, U.S. News and World Report, Dun's Review,* and *Business Week*—and compare or contrast these advertisements, as to purpose, presentation, word choice, etc., with the advertisements in the general and news magazines mentioned in this chapter.

15. Select from current magazines examples of persuasive, informative, and affective writing. For class discussion, prepare a list of points in the articles to show how the functions of language are achieved.

16. Make a "collection" of old or current slang or of jargon expressions from your field of interest. Write beside each one the conventional way of saying the same thing.

17. From current business-magazine articles, select examples of emotive words. As an exercise in vocabulary development, substitute neutral words for the emotive ones. Does the change alter the purpose of the writing to make it more informative rather than persuasive or affective?

18. Write a 200-word summary of the reading "The Language of Business."

19. In a manila folder, start saving your returned letter assignments and "correction sheets," those rewritten letters or parts of letters that observe your instructor's suggestions for revision. The much-quoted advice is well taken here: "Good writing is not so much a matter of writing as of re-writing."

20. In another folder, keep your examples of business writing, that is, those letters, memorandums, and reports that you can get through retrieving them from wastebaskets, begging them from relatives and friends, or in other ways that your ingenuity may suggest. The greater the number and variety of the examples, the more practical your knowledge of business communication will be, from your analysis of the writing. Also, your instructor may, later in the school term, ask that such an accumulation of writing be submitted to him as part of an analytical report.

2

What a Business Letter Looks Like

There is a great deal in the first impressions.—CONGREVE,
The Way of the World

Before the reader even begins to consider the content of a letter, before
he has had a chance even to read the first line, he has reacted to the letter
—he has seen the letter, at least momentarily, as a *picture*, and has been
influenced by what he has seen. A favorable or unfavorable instantaneous
first impression strongly influences the later reaction to the letter's contents; hence the importance of considering the external, or stenographic,
aspects of business letters.

BREAKDOWN OF LETTER COSTS

The stenographic cost of the letter is normally the second largest item.
Possibly you have not thought much about total costs, or itemized costs,
of business letters; you are aware, however, I am sure, that the postage
is only a minute part of the total. First-class letters cost over two dollars
each.[1] The figure includes the dictator's and stenographer's salaries, postage and mailing costs, and fixed costs—rent, depreciation, supervision,
taxes, utilities, and insurance. According to Edward M. Ryan, of the
Dartnell Corporation, the cost ($2.32) has risen $1.15 since 1953, the
increase in cost being due to inflation, the shorter workweek, non-pro-
ductive labor costs (time lost by dictators and stenographers in waiting,
illness, and vacations), and increased fixed costs. Form letters range from

[1] *ABWA Bulletin*, May, 1964, p. 27.

about half the cost of first-class letters for small mailings down to less than a tenth for very large mailings.

SIZES OF LETTER SHEETS

The standard business letter sheet is 8½ inches wide by 11 inches long. Most letters are written on this size sheet. The half-size sheet, however, either 8½ by 5½, with the standard heading, or 5½ by 8½, with a half-size reproduction of the same heading, has long been recognized. Recently the 7⅞ by 10½ sheet, sometimes called Monarch size, has been gaining in favor for business use. It had already become popular for social correspondence; and now business firms, especially department stores and mail-order houses, are using it increasingly, particularly for sales and collection letters. Government offices and the military services have standardized a letter sheet slightly smaller than the business sheet, 8 by 10½ inches, and a few business firms have adopted it.

In the sales letter, it has long been recognized that one way of attracting attention to the selling message is to use sizes of letter sheet and envelope that are out of the ordinary. Hence we find everything from slight deviations to the miniatures employed by the *Reader's Digest* and the giant sheet that opens up to four times standard letter size, used as a sales letter by a prominent publisher.

For your own letter writing practice, you should use, unless your instructor directs otherwise, the 8½ by 11 inch sheet.

QUALITY OF PAPER

Cost of the letter sheet and envelope is ordinarily about 1½ per cent of the total cost of the letter. Although economy has usually been important in American business, probably too many firms and individuals have economized on stationery. Use of a good white rag-content, watermarked paper will increase the cost of the letter hardly more than 1 per cent, and will lend far more than this to its effectiveness. The good quality paper presents clearly the printing of the letterhead and the typing of the letter itself. Also, it permits the stenographer to make erasures that will not show, and as long as stenographers remain less infallible than machines there will be the necessity for an occasional erasure.[2] At least part of the added cost of the better paper is retrieved at once, since fewer spoiled sheets reach the wastebasket.

THE PICTURE FRAME LETTER

The *form* of the business letter has become largely standardized. On a sheet of unruled paper, the typing or writing (only a small fraction of

---

[2] Even machines "make mistakes." A number of letters typed on an automatic typewriter in an airlines office had to be discarded when it was discovered that the "a" key had suddenly failed to strike after a "k."

business letters are in longhand) is arranged neatly as a picture in a contrasting frame or mat. The very *appearance* of the letter on its sheet should be pleasing to the reader.

Balance means that writing should be properly placed and spaced. *Spacing* is a special part of *placing*. Advertising copy writers know that they dare not print heavy blocks of writing with insufficient white space for relief. It might seem that the letter writer would wish to insure "daylighted" letters by using double spacing. Actually, the double-spaced business letter is rare; even for short letters the effect is better when we single space within paragraphs and double space between. Examination of representative business letters shows that only 4 per cent are double spaced.

Although substantial agreement has been reached on single spacing, the question of indenting or not indenting the first line of the paragraph remains a matter of preference. Probably most would agree that the modified block form with lines starting flush at the left margin looks neater, but indention provides additional white space. When indention is found, it is not necessarily the five-space or eight-space indention that you were taught in typing, for many writers prefer a deeper indention. Some firms instruct stenographers to indent paragraphs even with the colon after the "Dear Sir" or "Dear Mr. Jones" of the salutation.

Do not forget the lower part of the picture frame if the letter is too long to go on one sheet readily. Use a second sheet, making sure that it is the same size and quality as the letterhead. Never use a letterhead for a second page. Head the second sheet thus:

Mr. John Jones	-2-	March 15, 19

LEADING LETTER FORMS

In general, four styles of setting up letter material are recognized: (1) full block, (2) modified block, (3) indention, (4) hanging indention. Specimens of each type of letter are given in Figures 1 to 4 following. The full block (Figure 1) is slightly the easiest to use, since everything is aligned at the left-hand margin. It can be quite attractive for short letters. A streamlined version of the full block form, the AMS Simplified Letter, is shown in Figure 5. The modified block form is used more than all the others, but the degree of modification varies. It is shown in Figure 2, with inside address, salutation, all lines of the body of the letter, and dictator and stenographic identification aligned at the left margin, and date line and signature material balancing at bottom and top toward the right. It is perhaps gaining in preference, but many firms continue to

5871 Mohawk Drive
Los Angeles, California
November 1, 19

Professor E. Glenn Griffin
Department of English
Purdue University
Lafayette, Indiana

Dear Professor Griffin:

When you said in class last year that former students find their ways
back to teachers' doors, I thought you were quoting some sentimentality.
You did not know that I was having such subversive thoughts as you were
lecturing, of course, but I have to swallow my thoughts--or does a person swallow only words? Anyway, here I am at your doorstep to ask a
favor.

I have had my fling in production work, which I thought I wanted more
than anything else, and now I find that the writing bug is biting me.
I want to apply for some jobs in technical writing out here on the
Coast. May I list your name as a reference to those companies I apply
to? There won't be any more than five or six.

The technical writing field seems to be a good one, as you know. Every
day the local papers carry ads for people qualified in this line, and,
an added attraction, the salaries offered are good. Note that the money
is only an added feature!

I hope that you can find time to write for me, since you know my writing
ability. And I would appreciate hearing from you by the first of the
year, since I will start looking for another job about the first of
February. I want to stay here at Continental for at least a year and a
half. Leaving my first position after graduation sooner than that
wouldn't be fair to the company, I think.

I look forward to hearing from you, whether your answer is yes or no.

Sincerely yours,

Wayne Trumbull

Wayne C. Trumbull

WCT:JBT

P. S. The typist's initials do not mean that I have a secretary. Joan
is a private secretary to a bank president in Santa Monica, and she says
her husband writes as well as her boss does. How is that for a recommendation to a former teacher?

Fig. 1. Full block letter form. In this form, all letter parts begin at the left
margin, including the date line and the signature. (Used by permission of Mr.
Trumbull.)

GENERAL MOTORS CORPORATION

GENERAL MOTORS BUILDING

3044 WEST GRAND BOULEVARD

DETROIT 2, MICHIGAN

March 4, 19

Dr. John Ball
Miami University
Oxford, Ohio

Dear Dr. Ball:

We are glad to know, through Miss Lyda McHenry of Wayne University, of your interest in the GM Information Rack Service. You are welcome to keep the information rack which you now have, and we will be happy to provide the same service for Miami University that we do for Wayne, Notre Dame, Purdue and several other universities.

Your name has been added to our regular mailing list to receive 150 copies of each booklet offered through the Information Rack Service in the future. If this quantity proves to be either too high or too low, we will adjust it accordingly, based upon periodic reports of the booklets picked up from your rack.

An instruction sheet is attached. It explains exactly how the Service operates. Should you need any further information, or additional copies of certain booklets at any time, please do not hesitate to get in touch with me.

Cordially yours,

William H. Lane
Editor, Special Publications
Employe Relations Staff

WHL:atl

Fig. 2. Modified block letter form. Here the date line and the signature are at the right. Open punctuation is used. (Used by permission of General Motors Corporation.)

prefer the indented first line of paragraphs, following this form otherwise (see Figure 3). Full indention, including even the inside address, is not illustrated, for it is seldom used today, since there is general agreement that the effect is unattractive. Hanging indention (Figure 4) is in the

1799 South Seventh Street
Danville, Illinois
April 2, 19

Dr. Hugh A. Templeton
2212 Monroe Avenue
Omaha, Nebraska

Dear Dr. Templeton:

Professor O. L. Ault of the Dairy Department at Purdue suggested that I write you about employment after I graduate in June. Professor Ault told me about your conversation with him at the dairy meeting in Chicago, about your consulting work and your plans for developing your new company.

Since you know Professor Ault as well as you do, I believe that his suggestion that I write you tells you something about the kind of person I am. The development work you are doing with companies is the kind I have prepared for, and I can tell you that starting with a new organization such as yours appeals to me.

The enclosed data sheet will give you a fuller picture of my qualifications, so you may see whether you want to take time for us to talk when you come to the campus in May.

You may write me either at my home address or the Lafayette address. I come to Danville one day a week to work on the analysis I am doing for the Dairy Association here.

I will appreciate it if you will write me before long whether you will want to see me, so I may make any necessary arrangements at work. My class schedule is such that I can see you at some time any day you would be on the campus.

Yours very truly,

George I. Lambert

George I. Lambert

Fig. 3. Indented letter form. Note that the heading and inside address are not indented, as the paragraphs are. More important is the content of the letter. The applicant wrote a different type of letter than he would have, had he been writing without advance recommendation. See "Employment Letters," Chapter 9. (Used by permission of George I. Lambert.)

novelty class, and is restricted to occasional use, chiefly in sales letters, and for tabulating material to heighten the emphasis sought.

Most firms today use the same form for the envelope address as for the letter, though some prefer to use indention for envelope addresses at all times.

Advertising Age
THE NATIONAL NEWSPAPER OF ADVERTISING

PUBLISHED AT 100 E. OHIO STREET, CHICAGO • NEW YORK OFFICE, 330 W. 42nd STREET

Mr. Cecil B. Williams,   April 19, 19
De Paul University,
64 E. Lake Street,
Chicago, Ill.,

Dear Mr. Williams:

        You have not as yet sent us your renewal
subscription to ADVERTISING AGE.

        Why?

It cannot be the price — $ 2 — for you would gladly give
      many times that amount for one news item
      that a single issue of ADVERTISING AGE
      will bring.

It cannot be the want of time — for a few strokes of the
      pen would place your name back again on
      ADVERTISING AGE'S mailing list. We had
      to remove it last week, as we had not
      received your renewal instructions.

It cannot be you are not interested — for you know that the
      advance information we give you thru our
      publication is very vital in these times
      of so many changes.

It cannot be the need of opportunity — for we have written
      you several letters, giving you the oppor-
      tunity and as yet you have not responded to
      any of them.

      So we write once again. Will you give
      yourself a chance to learn what ADVERTISING
      AGE is accomplishing for you even while you
      are keeping it from your desk ? We do not
      want to annoy you; we want to help you.—
      Just fill out the enclosed blank and return
      it to us in the postage paid envelope and
      we will again start service to you with our
      next issue.

               Sincerely,

               I.O. Kebby,
IOK:L   ADVERTISING AGE.
Encl.

"everybody reads the news"

Fig. 4. Hanging indented letter form. In this example of the hanging indention style, close punctuation is used in the date line and inside address. The
purpose of the hanging indention is to focus attention on the successive "It cannot be . . ." sales arguments. (Used by permission of *Advertising Age*.)

31

AREA CODE 215 — HA 4-6703
FAX — FJM

ADMINISTRATIVE
MANAGEMENT
SOCIETY ● WILLOW GROVE, PA. ● 19090

Dated Today

Miss Office Secretary
Better Business Letters, Inc.
1 Main Street
Busytown, U.S.A.

SIMPLIFIED LETTER

There's a new movement underway to take some of the monotony out of
letters given you to type, Miss Secretary. The movement is symbolized by the Simplified Letter being sponsored by AMS.

What is it? You're reading a sample.

Notice the left block format and the general positioning of the letter. We didn't write "Dear Miss ----," nor will we write "Yours
truly" or "Sincerely yours." Are they really important? We feel
just as friendly toward you without them.

Notice the following points:

1. Date location
2. The address
3. The subject
4. The name of the writer

Don't form a final opinion until you've really tried out the Simplified Letter. Why not drop me a note and I will send you the brochure
we have prepared? It offers suggestions for typing and dictating, as
well as a comparison of the chief physical characteristics of the
Simplified Letter with those of the most popular "standard" letter.

Thousands of secretaries and executives are sold on the Simplified
style. We hope you will soon be one of them.

K. H. KOSTENBADER - STAFF ASSOCIATE

cc: D. J. Pierce

Fig. 5. AMS Simplified Letter. (Used by permission of Administrative Management Society.)

"QUALITY-SERVICE"

January 2, 19

To: Mr. H. P. Gaw
           Works Metallurgist
           Middletown Division

From: R. J. Bendure

Subject: A.S.T.M. Nitric Acid Tests -
           Type 304 Sheets

           S.I. 51-455 - Report #2

FOR TIME STAMP

Samples representative of Heat 81761 and Heat 81755 in
the mill annealed condition were previously submitted to
the standard 65% boiling nitric acid test. The average
rates for five periods were 0.0014 and 0.0012 inches per
month, respectively, as reported in S.I. 51-455 dated
December 5, 19 .

While both heats met the required specification, the rates
were somewhat higher than was expected. This was particularly true in the case of Heat 81761.

The coupons which had been tested in nitric acid were
examined microscopically. Electrolytic etching with 10%
sodium cyanide and 10% chromic acid showed no evidence of
grain boundary sensitization.

The higher than expected rates obtained on these two heats
cannot be explained on the basis of carbide or other grain
boundary precipitate.

Reference

Research Record Book 1789, p. 79.

RJB:EF
cc:
W. W. Black
M. E. Carruthers
F. H. Fanning
A. L. Feild
R. P. Hindman
D. S. Holstein
P. E. Ramseyer
G. D. Tranter

R J Bendure
Chemist
Research Laboratories

Fig. 6A. Interoffice communication form. The letter is typed on special interoffice stationery. (Used by permission of Armco Steel Corporation.)

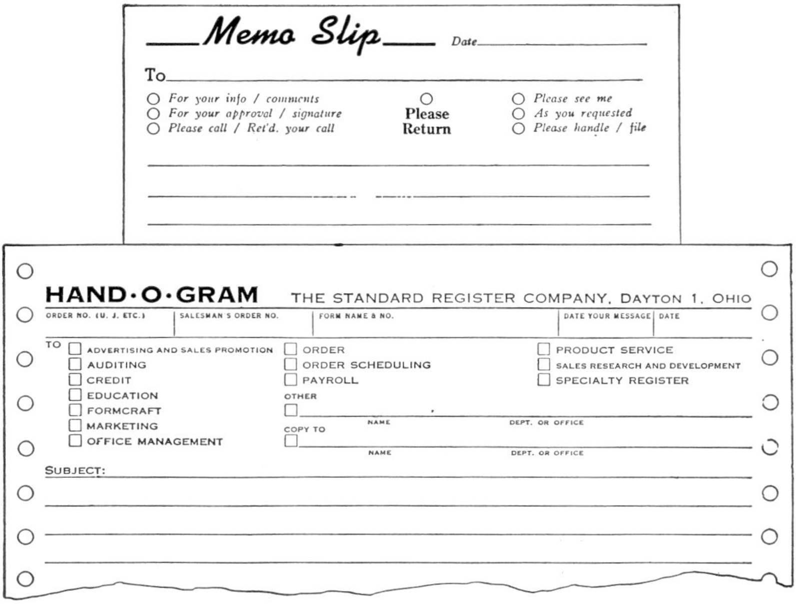
Memo Slip Date
To
For your info / comments
For your approval / signature
Please call / Ret'd. your call
Please Return
Please see me
As you requested
Please handle / file

HAND·O·GRAM THE STANDARD REGISTER COMPANY, DAYTON 1, OHIO
ORDER NO. (U. J. ETC.) | SALESMAN'S ORDER NO. | FORM NAME & NO. | DATE YOUR MESSAGE | DATE
TO
ADVERTISING AND SALES PROMOTION
AUDITING
CREDIT
EDUCATION
FORMCRAFT
MARKETING
OFFICE MANAGEMENT
ORDER
ORDER SCHEDULING
PAYROLL
OTHER
NAME DEPT. OR OFFICE
COPY TO
NAME DEPT. OR OFFICE
PRODUCT SERVICE
SALES RESEARCH AND DEVELOPMENT
SPECIALTY REGISTER
SUBJECT:

Figs. 6B and 6C. Interoffice communication forms. Many firms use memo forms for brief interoffice communications.

Regardless of the style of letter we decide upon, we must follow the style consistently, and in our concern with the left-hand margin we must not neglect the right-hand one. The ideal right-hand margin is one that is fairly straight without having too many hyphenated words. Good stenographers break words only between syllables, according to the rules in Chapter 4, and they try to avoid breaks in successive lines. Ordinarily a satisfactory right-hand margin can be managed by breaking no more than five or six words in a full-page letter. The typewriter bell is intended to facilitate keeping an even margin, but, although it does help, we cannot depend upon it entirely.

When preparing your first assignments, either with pen or typewriter, you should be reconciled to making some trial copies. If you must set up the letter six times before it looks right, the effort is justified, for not until you get a picture frame effect which satisfies you, can you be confident that your letter will strike pleasingly upon the eye of a reader. Here, as elsewhere, practice brings skill and speed.

THE PARTS OF THE BUSINESS LETTER

Most authorities say that a complete business letter has at least *seven* parts, and it may have in addition one or more of at least five occasional,

REPLY MESSAGE

THIS FORM AVAILABLE FROM GRAYARC CO., 662 THIRD AVE., BROOKLYN 32, N. Y.

FROM

TO

ANDOVER CORPORATION
310 NO. EARL AVENUE
LAFAYETTE, INDIANA

SUBJECT:_____ DATE:_____

FOLD ↑

PLEASE REPLY TO ⟶ SIGNED

DATE | SIGNED

SEND WHITE AND PINK COPIES WITH CARBONS INTACT. PINK COPY IS RETURNED WITH REPLY.

GRAYARC CO., BROOKLYN 32, N. Y.

DETACH THIS COPY – RETAIN FOR ANSWER

Fig. 7. The yellow copy from one of a number of composite forms used widely for expediting short messages such as orders, inquiries, and answers. Three identical printed forms (white, yellow, pink) have carbon sheets between them. The originator makes three copies of his message, retaining the yellow copy and sending the original and second carbon. The recipient's reply on the bottom half of the white sheet is duplicated on the pink sheet, which is returned to the originator. The word "FOLD" and the arrow on the left margin indicate that the originator folds back the copies he sends and inserts them in a window envelope, thereby saving a second typing of the recipient's address. (Used by permission of the Andover Corporation.)

or optional, parts. Figure 9 shows all these parts in their preferred positions on the full letter sheet. For clearness and emphasis we shall list them here:

REQUIRED	OCCASIONAL OR OPTIONAL
Heading	File or order number
Inside address	Subject reference
Salutation	Attention line

Required	Occasional or Optional
Body	Enclosure notice
Complimentary close	Postscript
Signature	
Signature identification	

You will find that studying the illustrations is the best way to get a clear idea of how the letter should look with all its necessary parts in order, but a few things should be said about each part.

NATIONAL HOMES CORPORATION

LAFAYETTE, INDIANA

ADMINISTRATIVE BULLETIN

NATIONAL HOMES CORPORATION

LAFAYETTE, INDIANA

SALES BULLETIN

NATIONAL HOMES CORPORATION

LAFAYETTE, INDIANA

CONSTRUCTION BULLETIN

NATION'S LARGEST PRODUCERS OF PREFABRICATED HOMES

Fig. 8. Another correspondence device to speed handling of correspondence. Bulletins on 8½″ by 11″ colored paper (green, yellow, blue) from the designated departments to builder-dealers let the recipient know at a glance whether he should read the message, which of his personnel to forward it to, etc. Colored pages from different departments also facilitate filing and file references. (Used by permission.)

A

PURDUE UNIVERSITY
DEPARTMENT OF ENGLISH
LAFAYETTE, INDIANA 47907
April 24, 19

h

File 9 PR 313

B

Public Relations Department
E. I. du Pont de Nemours & Company
Wilmington, Delaware

i

Subject: Permission to reproduce your paper at PRSA

j

Attention: Mr. Harold Brayman

C

Gentlemen:

I am writing to ask permission to use "Public Opinion: New
Sovereign Power," your talk to the Public Relations Society
of America, in a textbook I am revising.

The book, _Effective Business Communication_, is to be published
by The Ronald Press Company. The first two editions, under
the title _Effective Business Writing_, have been used in universities and colleges throughout the country since 1947.

D

Your talk would be used as an end-of-chapter reading with the
chapter on public relations. There would be no evaluation of
the talk. (This request to use it speaks for my opinion of
the content and presentation.) Along with other questions
about the whole chapter, there would probably be two or three
questions relating to the communicative aspects of your paper,
such as organization, Biblical and historical references, etc.

If you think it advisable, a footnote on tax percentages could
call attention to the date of the talk and the recent changes
in the federal tax structure.

I will be grateful for your considering this request. And
can you please let me know your reaction soon, so I may plan
further work accordingly.

E

F

G

Sincerely,

E. Glenn Griffin

E. Glenn Griffin
Associate Professor

k

EGG:ngm
Enclosure

l

P. S. The enclosed copy of your talk, which I received from
your office, shows the two deletions that would be made in the
text. The reasons are apparent, I believe.

Fig. 9. Required and optional parts of a letter. _Required:_ A. heading, B.
inside address, C. salutation, D. body, E. complimentary close, F. signature, G.
signature identification. _Optional:_ h. file or order number, i. subject reference,
j. attention line, k. enclosure notice, l. postscript.

The Heading

Businessmen and professional men usually write letters on sheets with printed headings for two obvious reasons: (1) There is a time economy in having the company name and address and, where desirable, the telephone number already printed on the letter sheets. (2) There is a prestige value in an attractive heading at the top of the sheet in comparison

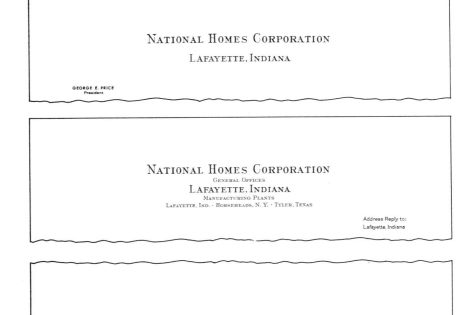

Fig. 10. Modern 8½″ by 11″ letterheads. Many companies use an identifying picture, drawing, or insigne at the bottom of the stationery.

with a mere typed return address. The letterhead also serves to identify the writer with his firm or institution. Many advertisers offering free booklets or samples specify that the individual must reply on his business or professional letterhead.

Since letterheads figure so prominently in the reader's impression of the letter, they are subject to constant change and improvement. Representative modern letterheads are shown in Figure 10. Some concerns like to feature a picture of the parent plant; manufacturers of food products may use appetizing combinations of gay colors to display some of their products. Some firms include officers' names or lists of products along the side of the letter sheet. The variety of forms employed today is shown in the letters used as examples throughout the book.

Fig. 11. Departmental letterheads. Many firms use different letterheads for different purposes or different departments. The letterhead used for duplicate copies is printed on onionskin paper. (Used by permission.)

Individuals who are not professional persons or members of a firm should use blank sheets of good quality typing paper and supply the strictly essential information of the heading, that is, return address and date.

On letterheads the stenographer types in the date, either placing it on the right-hand side so that it balances the signature material, or else centering it under the company name.

The Inside Address

A student will sometimes ask why a letter needs an inside address since the envelope address suffices to get it to its destination. The answer is simple. Since envelopes are usually thrown away, the letter sheet must itself be a complete communication, which can be handled and filed as such. Also, the Post Office Department ultimately looks for an inside address when envelopes are wrongly addressed and show no return address.

An inside address includes typically: (1) name of person or firm alone, or name of person plus the firm; (2) local address, that is, street, avenue, boulevard, or road, with number; (3) city, state, and zip code. It is desirable to restrict this material to three or four lines; seldom is it really necessary to have more. But in general *do not use abbreviations* in the inside address. Sometimes, to be sure, one must choose between abbreviating and having awkwardly balanced lines. Frequently the abbreviation looks worse, or more disrespectful, than the lack of balance.

For clearness, it is of course necessary that the parts of the address be separated. To show separation it was formerly customary to use commas not only within but also at the end of all address lines except the last, which was followed by a period. This is an example of *close* punctuation, shown below. In *open* punctuation the end-of-line punctuation is omitted, except for the period after abbreviations. The trend is toward the open system; a check shows that it now leads at least nine to one.

CLOSE SYSTEM	OPEN SYSTEM
Mr. Robert H. Daly,	Mr. Robert H. Daly
3125 Giddings Street,	3125 Giddings Street
Chicago, Illinois,	Chicago, Illinois
60225.	60225
Dr. W. H. Spencer, Dean,	Dr. W. H. Spencer, Dean
The School of Business,	The School of Business
The University of Chicago,	The University of Chicago
Chicago, Illinois,	Chicago, Illinois
60637.	60637

The Salutation

Some authorities counsel dispensing with the salutation entirely, but in practice most prefer to use it—because talking to a man without in effect saying "Hello" or "Glad to see you looking so well today" seems abrupt. We still use salutations and complimentary closes in business letters for the same reason that we say "Hello" when we meet and "Good-by" when we part.

A generation ago, "Dear Sir" in the singular was nearly standard, with "Dear Sirs" and "Gentlemen" sharing the plural. The salutations most frequently found today are these:

Sir: Madam:	Most formal of all; use to address important persons you do not know.
My dear Sir: My dear Madam:	Slightly less formal; very seldom used in America because to many persons it seems condescending.[3]
Dear Sir: Dear Madam:	Only about one letter in eight uses this salutation today; it apparently is not formal enough for formal letters or cordial enough for letters which seek to convey the personal touch.
Dear Mr. Smith: Dear Dr. Smith: Dear Miss Smith: Dear Mrs. Smith: [4]	This form is now the most popular by far. It seems friendly and personal, and it is in no way discourteous: we say "Mr. Jones" or "Miss Brown" when we meet someone for the first time, or when we speak on the telephone to someone we do not know.
Dear James: Dear Mary:	Informal and friendly; use only to address someone you know well.
Dear Jim, Dear Peg,	Quite suitable for business use if you would use the same form in writing a personal letter to the same person.
Gentlemen:	This form has replaced "Dear Sirs" for addressing a company or group made up of men or of both men and women.
Mesdames: Ladies:	These forms are used to address a group made up entirely of women; "Ladies" is the more modern form. Caution: most firms which have feminine names (such as Elizabeth Arden) are not made up entirely of women.

General descriptive salutations, such as "Dear Friend," "Dear Member," "Dear Customer," "To the Librarian," are gaining in popularity, for better or for worse. In letters of solicitation, "Dear Member," "Dear Friend" or "Dear Fellow American" (more doubtful) have proved satisfactory. A good impression in sales letters to regular customers may attend "Dear Friend" or "Dear Customer."

Some 10 per cent of letters use substitutes for the salutation; wider use of the AMS Simplified Letter should encourage even more substitution. Here is an example from the beginning of an answer to an inquiry:

```
Many thanks, Mr. Ball,

for your interest in Beauty Bonded Formica and its
application to the VANITORY and kitchen work surface
tops.
```

[3] Several other forms are often regarded as condescending, and were therefore omitted from the list: "My dear Mr. Smith," "My dear Smith," "Dear Smith," "My dear James."

[4] Some firms now use "Ms." for all women to avoid guesswork when they have no way of knowing whether the addressee is married or unmarried. There have been strong negative comments to balance the favorable remarks on this new plan. Guessing "Miss" is less likely to offend.

Other substitutes for conventional salutation form in recent correspondence give you an idea of the conversational tone created by their use: "You are right, Mr. Roberts," "We're sorry, Miss James," and "We've been wondering, Mr. Nelcamp."

H. Kohnstamm & Co. Inc.

SERVICE THROUGH
CHEMISTRY
SINCE 1851

SUPPOSE FOUR PROMINENT OPERATORS WALKED INTO YOUR PLANT -

- and one of them said:

    "I have tried every kind of cover cloth on the market and have standardized on THERMOTEX. Twelve weeks on a Tiltor Bosom Press beats anything I know of".

You would listen, wouldn't you?

And the second successful operator said:

    "We have a high-speed production plant and get 40,000 shirts from a THERMOTEX cover on a backer in a Tiltor shirt unit".

As a progressive business man you would be interested, but listen to what the third has to say:

    "We processed 26,983 shirts on a single THERMOTEX cover. This unit makes three lays so this one cover held up under 80,949 lays".

And last, but not least, one of the best laundry production engineers in the country quotes:

    "We operate on a 42½ hour work week. A THERMOTEX cover on a Tiltor Body Press gave 69 days of actual service".

Suppose these four successful laundry operators walked into your plant and made these claims. Would you believe them? Would you try THERMOTEX? Of course you would. These men are real - these quotations are their own. Cover just one of your presses with THERMOTEX and see for yourself. If you do not find it the most economical cover cloth you ever used THE TRIAL WILL COST YOU NOTHING.

Write the size and type of press on the enclosed card. Mail it today and we will send you a THERMOTEX cover for trial.

                              Cordially yours,
                              H. KOHNSTAMM & CO., INC.

                          Per
                              N. R. HOFFMAN

Fig. 12. Effective use of tabulation. (Used by permission of the Dartnell Corporation.)

After the salutation, the colon (the punctuation mark of formal introduction) is practically standard. A few firms who use open punctuation in the inside address reason that it is logical to dispense with marks after the salutation and complimentary close also. The comma, usual after the salutation in personal letters, is seldom used for business. The hyphen following the colon is old-fashioned. The semicolon is entirely wrong; nothing more surely betrays ignorance of basic principles in business writing than using the semicolon with the salutation. The exclamation point is occasionally found with the salutation in sales letters, where it is thought to increase the reader's interest in the sales message.

The Body of the Letter

The body of the letter is more the dictator's headache than the stenographer's—it is harder to think out than it is to set up. It contains the solution to the *problem* of the letter; it presents the major selling point, the collection appeal, the proffered adjustment. Once the decision has been reached on basic letter form (block or indention), and paragraphing is understood, the body of the letter presents no considerable stenographic problem.

But do not forget the idea of the picture within its frame. Have wider margins for short letters and begin the inside address lower. On longer letters, be especially careful not to crowd the signature material—it is better to use a second sheet. *Neatness* is the keynote. Letters containing lists of points gain effectiveness through use of tabulation. When such material is indented a few spaces it is more readily picked up by the eye, and the general effect of the letter is more pleasing.

And don't start the letter with a rubber stamp or close it with a participle! Although the clichés and participial closes are on the way out, there are still too many of both. The following short letter shows how *not to* begin and end.

```
Enclosed herewith please find Endorsement to be attached to your
Jewelry Floater Policy No. 20383 General, transferring same to
cover at 5520 South Shore Drive.

Thanking you to see that same is attached to policy, I am

                                    Very truly yours,
```

The Complimentary Close

Despite the fact that "Yours truly" has become something of a joke, this form of complimentary close has not entirely gone out. The fuller forms, "Very truly yours," or "Yours very truly," have been recommended in business writing books. Recently, however, corresponding to the gain in the salutation "Dear Mr. Jones," the friendlier "Sincerely" and "Cordially" forms are becoming more prevalent. In one hundred recent letters, we find the following distribution:

Yours truly	3	Sincerely (various forms)	29
Very truly yours	25	Cordially (various forms)	14
Yours very truly	21	(Other forms)	4
Respectfully yours	1	(No complimentary close)	3

The complimentary close should match the salutation in tone. (See the Reference Section.)

Signature

Practically never does a business letter go out unsigned, unless by oversight. Form letters, however, are often printed by a photographic or other process which also reproduces the signature, and other form letters are signed with a signature stamp. Individualized letters are signed by the dictator or by someone he has authorized to sign for him. If a secretary is authorized to write letters for her employer or superior and sign them, she should initial below the signature to make the relationship clear, though some firms do not so distinguish such letters. It is definitely discourteous to the recipient to mail him a letter with no signature.

A woman's signature should show her marital status. In America, Jane Kimball marries Robert E. Jones and thereby becomes Mrs. R. E. Jones. Before her marriage, she signed her business letters, if in longhand,

(Miss) Jane Kimball

if typed,

Jane Kimball
Miss Jane Kimball

What does she sign after she is married? She has probably decided to retain "Kimball"; so her *name* is Jane Kimball Jones. Her *title*, however, is Mrs. R. E. Jones, and she will be so addressed. She will sign,

Jane Kimball Jones
(Mrs. R. E. Jones)

If she is a widow, does she sign differently? The question has not been settled. Socially she continues to be Mrs. R. E. Jones unless she remarries, but in the business world she may be Mrs. Jane Kimball Jones. As long as her husband lived, he was probably (unless he had published disclaimers) responsible for her bills, but as a widow she is responsible for them herself. Something of an effort has been made to establish the widow's signature for business purposes as follows,

Jane Kimball Jones
(Mrs. Jane Kimball Jones)

It seems doubtful, however, that the form will be generally adopted. Many widows will disregard it, perhaps some because it is also correct for divorcees, and some married women will use it inadvertently.

The divorcee who does not resume her maiden name may continue to use her former husband's surname, but she should not use his first name or initials.

For company letters, it is sometimes necessary to indicate responsibility by the signature form. Which comes first, company name (typed) or pen signature of the dictator? Whose letter is it? Is the dictator acting for himself or for the company? Since ordinarily he is acting for the company, the company's name should be typed in by the stenographer two lines below the complimentary close. She should then allow four spaces for the dictator's signature before typing his name and his company position, such as "Branch Manager." But if a bank president should philanthropically lend his name and prestige to a local Red Cross or United Fund drive by signing a form letter, the order would of course be reversed:

> John R. Jones
> President, The First National Bank

Signature Identification

Identification of signatures has become standard practice. This identification includes all or part of the following, all typed: dictator's name, dictator's official position, dictator's initials, and stenographer's initials. Position for this material is shown in Figures 1, 2, 4, and 8. The dictator's name typed at the left-hand margin eliminates the duplication in typing his initials.

Pen signatures, although necessary, are often nearly illegible. Perhaps nothing annoys a correspondent more than being expected to reply to a letter with an illegible signature and no typed identification. Even where the signature is legible, the identification serves to make the letter seem more complete and businesslike.

SPECIAL AND OPTIONAL PARTS OF THE LETTER

Placement of the parts on the letter sheet is shown in Figure 9. Traffic and mail-order correspondence, especially, tends to use a *file number* or *order number* to facilitate reference. Less prevalent (outside of military correspondence, where it is regular and has a different position) is the *subject* or "*Re*" reference, which is usually centered like the first position of the file or order number, or lower, on the same line with the salutation. Certain companies such as insurance firms use "*Re*" for quicker reference to a number of identifying details such as policy number, name of the insured, addresses, etc. Most letters include the subject in the opening sentence, and normally that is the best place for it.

One of the most important and least understood occasional letter parts is the *attention line*. It was formerly placed on the same line with the salutation, but now is found usually between the inside address and the salutation, either flush with the left-hand margin or centered. Why should a given letter be marked "Attention of Mr. Henry L. Brown" if it is Marshall Field & Company business and a dozen other men work in the same department with Mr. Brown? The usual reason is to keep the same person working on a particular business transaction until a settlement is reached. If Mr. Brown, for Field's, has sent you a collection letter, you would want your reply to reach Mr. Brown, not someone else. If you are a retail druggist requesting from a wholesaler a replacement on a damaged shipment and your first letter draws a response from C. R. Mitchell requesting more definite information on damage or adjustment wanted, you should mark your reply "Attention of Mr. C. R. Mitchell." Again, suppose you are an old customer of the Famous-Barr Company in St. Louis and you have now moved to a village in the central part of Missouri. You have become acquainted with Miss Roberts in the notions department and would like to have her select and ship some merchandise to you. You would naturally mark your order "Attention of Miss Helen Roberts." Note that the salutation should agree with the first line of the inside address rather than with the attention line.

Some firms insist on the use of the attention line for legal reasons. The letter (but not the right to publish it) belongs to its legal addressee—and that legal addressee is the person or firm whose name appears on the top line of the address. Thus a letter addressed to an employee by name should not be opened by the firm if the employee is on vacation or is with another firm (though in actual practice many such letters are opened). I have been told of an incident wherein a firm lost $1,000,000 worth of orders because of this technicality. The attention line provides a method for maintaining the firm as the legal addressee and at the same time directing the letter to an individual.[5]

The attention line is not to be used for *personal* letters sent to an individual at his business address. These, if it is advisable to send them there at all, should have the individual's name first and the company name second.

[5] Although I have taken considerable space to show the usefulness of the attention line, I should observe that many good supervisors and counselors oppose its use, on the grounds that (1) it seems artificial and pedantic; (2) it treats the individual as a mere fixture about the place when he is really part of the company and proud of it. Chas. R. Riker, in "Our Letters," No. 124 (Westinghouse Company), has marshaled an imposing array of authorities who favor addressing the individual in the company instead of using the attention line.

The *enclosure notice* is placed below the stenographer's initials, to notify the mailing clerk or remind the stenographer of any enclosures that are to be added to the letter before the envelope is closed. Sometimes one or more carbon copies of a letter are mailed; for example, when an individual writes to a manager in response to an agent's solicitations and wants the agent to know what he has written, or when a treasurer writes a letter accompanying a payment and is required to inform the comptroller. When this is done, it is cutomary to notify the person receiving the original by typing "c.c. to R. M. Jones" immediately below the stenographer's initials. However, if a person receiving the carbon copy is to have information not divulged in the original, the sender adds the information to the carbon copy, marking it "bcc" (blind carbon copy). This device saves writing a letter to accompany the carbon copy. It is used considerably between home office personnel and field representatives or salesmen, in cases of three-way corerspondence among the field people, the home office, and customers.

The *postscript*, which in a personal letter is ordinarily an afterthought, might seem to be out of place in business letter writing. Actually, however, the business letter postscript properly used is not an afterthought, but a device for (1) securing special emphasis for a point in the body of the letter; (2) presenting a new point, such as another item in a sales letter, which doesn't fit into the body of the letter but may pay off well in a postscript. About 3 per cent of letters generally (a much higher percentage for sales letters) employ postscripts. Sample postscripts:

YOU'LL HAVE TO HURRY, FOR THIS OFFER WILL BE IN EFFECT FOR ONLY 10 DAYS.

Please address all letters, packages, or boxes to me, personally.

You may inspect a sample copy at any university or public library.

FOLDING AND ENCLOSING THE LETTER

Two sizes of envelope are commonly used in business writing—the letter, or commercial, size, 6½ by about 3⅝ inches, and the official size, about 9½ by 4⅛ inches. The smaller size is always used for half sheets, whichever way the letterhead runs. Most firms prefer the official size for full sheets, especially for letters of more than one page.

When folding the full sheet for either size envelope, remember that the object is to provide for easy opening. For the commercial size envelope, fold the letter from the bottom, bringing the bottom to within a quarter or a half inch of the top, then crease, making sure the side edges are even. Next, fold from right to left, leaving the third and final fold to come from left to right. With this last fold toward you, insert the folded letter in the envelope. The opening of the folded letter will thus be at the top of the envelope. For the official envelope, fold the sheet first from the bottom, taking a little more than one third, crease, bring the top part down, crease and insert in the envelope, also with the last fold toward you and the open part uppermost. When letters are folded and inserted properly, the spring, or resiliency, of the paper makes the sheet open naturally in the reader's hands. A number of firms now use window envelopes to avoid typing the address on the envelope. This necessitates a different letter fold so that the inside address will show through the window.

POST CARDS AND POSTAL CARDS

Post cards may be the picture cards you send back home from Mackinac, Carlsbad Cavern, or Lake Louise to your Uncle Jake or Aunt Martha when you go on your summer vacation. These are social, not business, writing. But government postal cards and other post cards have a considerable business use. In requests for catalogues, acknowledgments of routine orders, and miscellaneous matters, such cards take a fraction of the time to prepare, cost much less to send, and do the job just as well. Double cards are convenient for short sales messages and orders, and for simple inquiries and replies.

Postal cards are a greatly simplified communication form. The face carries the receiver's name and address only, the back the sender's address and the message. It is permissible to write the sender's address and date all in a single line across the top of the card, thus

```
339 E. Chicago Avenue, Chicago 11, Illinois, June 10, 19
```

BUSINESS REPLY ENVELOPES AND CARDS

Since profitable returns on direct mail ventures can be as low as 2 or 3 per cent, it is apparent that there would be much waste in enclosing stamped envelopes or even postal cards. Making action easy, however, facilitates response. Recognizing a need, the Post Office Department has provided for special business reply cards and envelopes. An individual or a firm may secure a permit to use these. For those that are returned, regular postage and a small additional fee must be paid by the individual or firm that employed them, but those which are not returned cost nothing in postage.

AIR MAIL

A great landmark in carrying the mails came when the railroad took over from the pony express or the slower stagecoach. Several genera-

Fig. 13. A modern business reply envelope.

tions thought in terms of train-borne letters almost exclusively. Now, however, thousands of letters daily go winging through the air, and the number is rapidly increasing. Under favorable conditions, the greater the distance, the greater the proportionate saving in time by air. Since the increased postage increases total letter costs only fractionally, the resulting business speed-up may represent greatly increased efficiency.

A lighter paper may be used for air mail letters. It is advisable to use air mail stamps and special air mail envelopes, although this is not compulsory if the envelope is marked "Air Mail." Air mail postal cards are also available.

Fig. 14. A modern business reply card.

THE TYPIST'S ROLE IN EFFECTIVE COMMUNICATION

Even with full knowledge of everything discussed in this chapter up to this point, you might turn out a letter that would fail to make a good impression on a fair-minded reader. If the parts are not attractively arranged on the page, with lettering consistent in touch, with lines even and free of misplaced letters and punctuation marks, and with no evidence of erasures—no matter who receives the correspondence, he will have a negative reaction to untidiness and carelessness. Often good content is adversely affected by that bad first impression. Since business letters often must work rapidly or not at all, the first impression should be favorable.

March 10, 19

Cecil B. Williams
1645 W. 105 th St.
Chicago, Illinois

Dear Mr. Williams

We wish to thank you for your
corteous mailing back to us AUTUMN LEAVES
by June Perlin send to you by mistake.

Enclosed, please find $.09 worth
of stamps as reinbursement for the postage
on the above manuscript. If we have evalueated
your expense incorrectly, please notify us ,
and we will gladly mail you the proper amount.

Very sincerely,

Fig. 15. How bad stenography can be. This letter (reproduced here minus letterhead and signature) somehow got into the mail of a book dealer.

If you do your own typing now, use the machine to its best advantage for perfectly typed work. If another person types your assignments, insist on perfection; if your relationship to that person makes such demands awkward, have him or her read this section. If in the future you are in a supervisory or managerial position, with someone else to type the work that goes out over your signature—and many of you who are using this book will be in such positions—maintain the high standards you set for yourself now.

Effective content plus good stenography equals business writing of distinction.

Effective Letters Are Attractive, Too! *

by ALINE WOODS †

It is indeed a pleasure to be able to talk with the dictators and their hench-men [the stenographers] at the same time. It's not often, I find, that these two groups meet as one. Ordinarily, members of each group get together, and about the only thing discussed is what's wrong with the work of the other group. I think it's going to be pleasant and *profitable* for us to work together these next few weeks, toward seeing how company writing can be made even better than it is now.

When I say that we're going to try to develop some teamwork, I am not intending to say that there isn't teamwork among you now, but, as anyone knows who has driven horses (and at the cost of putting myself in another era, I will tell you I did, as a young girl on a farm), just because two horses are in front of the same wagon doesn't necessarily mean that they are pulling together as well as they might.

I do see the two groups here as a team in good correspondence. Each side has its responsibilities in getting a job done. Yet, the dictation-transcribing job, as I see it, is an inseparable one. Oh, to be sure, there are parts of it that fall specifically to one of you and parts that are the other's responsibility. Obvious examples are the actual dictation and typing. Each one of the team knows that he or she wouldn't do the other half of that job. No manager is going to sit down to type a company letter—that is, the outgoing copy; his time is too valuable. And none of you stenographers, secretaries, or transcribers is going to turn on the dictating equipment and compose a letter, report, or memo. Of course, there are always those who think they can do the other fellow's job better. In every company I work with, I hear a girl as she is transcribing say something like "If I couldn't talk plainer than that, I'd quit." Then there's the other side's complaint. From the dictator as he is reading something back from transcription, we hear, "I didn't know that typist was so smart; she spells in Russian." And so the battle rages.

From your training or experience you know that clearness in speaking, com-plete instructions as to number of copies wanted, identification and spelling unusual terms, and other aspects of general courtesy are a dictator's responsi-

---

* Reproduced from a taped talk, especially for *Effective Business Communication*. This is the gist of Mrs. Woods's introduction of herself in the initial session with com-pany personnel directly responsible for correspondence and other company writing. (By permission of Mrs. Woods.)

† The pseudonym of a successful communication consultant to business and in-dustry.

bility. You who reproduce the spoken word onto paper know (whether you *do* it, or not) that your job is turning out neat pages as far as over-all appearance is concerned, pages free of smudges and smears, and individual components—such as words and the layout of the piece—that are correct and set up according to today's practices.

The correct and conventional is what we will be working on in classes and in individual conferences. And it is sure that I will be repeating some of the points I make here, but I would like to discuss with you now what I see as those phases of your work that are affected by attitudes.

The first of these is an important one because it makes a difference in the way you work with each other. To make the point, I quote a correspondence supervisor in a large company.

Dictators are afraid of their secretaries. Now, don't jump to conclusions—or for the shooting irons. I will explain—and modify—the opinion. What this supervisor has in mind is that person who will not send back a piece of transcribed work for revision or redoing. I am aware that many times such hesitancy is due to the pressure of time, wanting to get the report or letter on its way. However, I have seen enough time ill spent by executives to put some credence in the correspondence supervisor's comment about the dictator's fear of his girl Friday. For example, the head of the technical-literature department of a Detroit company has in his desk pads of foolscap (that's that yellow lined paper, and another term whose use marks my age). He uses this paper to write longhand everything that goes out from his desk—catalogs, his part of the annual report, letters, memorandums. Everything!

When you learn that there is a Dictaphone directly behind his chair and a secretary at her desk across the room from him, you may wonder too why all this time-consuming *hand*writing. Why doesn't he dictate? He says that he doesn't want to create so much work for his girl by having her type something two or three times. Generous and thoughtful though this man may be—if he is motivated by altruism—he is costing his company money. The difference in his salary and his secretary's makes his time worth considerably more to the company than hers is. His time could be spent to better advantage on other things; and his girl's morale would be boosted, in all probability, if she were allowed to use her secretarial training.

Another aspect of correctness, in my book, and a responsibility of both the dictator and the secretary is proofreading. Ideally, this operation should be proofreading for the typist and rereading for the dictator, but too many slips are overlooked by too many for the dictator to take a chance. These two readings of a piece that's going out from an office can be mighty important. We all have heard reports of companies' losing large sums because of misquotations (actually mistakes rather than misquotes) of prices in letters. And there are the jokes that get into newspapers and magazines about misspellings and misapplied phrases from business correspondence. You all have heard or read, I'm sure, of the person who, in writing for a job, said that his *martial* status would be changed in two weeks because he was going to be married. Merely a change of two letters in a word; in this case, one person didn't proofread. It would seem that either the person who dictated the notice said to be on a bulletin board in a Washington department or the one who typed it would have sensed the irregularity—either social or grammatical—in the message. The notice read, "Those executives who do not have secretaries of their own may take advantage of the girls in the transcription pool."

It isn't always a direct unnecessary outlay of money that results from lack of proofreading. One of the best cases I have heard of for proofreading is interesting because it's the sort of thing that happens so innocently, and it is interesting too because it isn't dramatic or colossal like the loss of thousands of dollars because of a misquotation.

The case was one of hiring a young woman, a college graduate. The company involved was United Airlines. The young woman had been invited to the Chicago office for interviews, and apparently she had made quite an impression on those who had interviewed her. A day or so after her visit, the man in charge of recruiting college graduates, who had supervised her visit to the offices, wrote her a short letter. In the letter the writer mentioned that those executives who had talked with Miss M. had liked her very much, that he hoped she was pleased with her visit, and that he hoped she would think favorably of United Airlines when she was ready to make her final decision as to employment. A short letter, friendly and warm. So far, that is. The last paragraph of the letter really threw a switcheroo into the meaning. It was one sentence, and it said, "It was not pleasant to have you visit our office."

The upshot of that three-letter word, which a typist did not see when she proofread (that is, if she did) was a telegram of apology from the director of personnel, a long-distance phone call, and a 100-mile drive for the recruiter to the campus of the prospective employee's college. You see, Miss M. accepted the director's apology in the wire but saw no need for an answer; she was away from school when the long-distance call was made to her at her school; and then some ten days later the recruiter was going across state to another college, and he drove 50 miles out of his way—two ways—to be sure that there were no hard feelings.

If I were to stop right now and ask if there are questions, one of you girls, I'm sure, would ask why I blame the secretary. Why let the director go scot-free, since he had signed the letter. Truth of the matter is, he didn't. The secretary had.

You see, the recruiter, like so many of you men, did a batch of dictation before he was going to be out of the office on a trip. The letter to Miss M. was in the batch. His secretary, as so many of you girls do, signed her boss's name to the pieces requiring it, and, of course, with her initials. That little detail, by the way, was observed by Miss M. when she received the letter with the "not," and, for some reason, the fact that the dictator hadn't signed the letter was her reason for exonerating him.

Now the question is who started all the activity in trying to get the "not" straightened out—maybe I should say, "united." The secretary hadn't proofread to catch the bobble; Miss M. didn't squeal. So who in the company caught the boner? Well, the recruiter—bless his heart—was one of those individuals who regard correspondence highly enough that he makes sure of what goes out of his office. When he gets back from a trip, he goes over the carbons of this dictation, typed while he's away. This he did, and he saw the word that caused so much lost time.

Now, I have used one of the oldest tricks in the hat in dragging out this story of "Will Miss M. go with United?" I have done this because I wanted to make the point of time—time lost.

Since this is the only time during my weeks here that both the "talkers" and the typists will meet together, as we are now, I think it would be helpful if the teammates in this job of better writing know the phases of the work I'll stress with each side. What I'll say will be old hat to some of you; to others, it will be review; and to some, some of what I say will be totally new. Whatever the category you as individuals are in, I look forward to working with you.

To start where the correspondence starts, let's turn to the dictator. I'm going to say that writing is thinking and, until a person has his thinking straight, he can't very well write straight. He has to organize what he's going to say before he utters a sound to the machine. I hope after a few weeks there will be no instance of a girl typing merrily along, only to hear from the disk: "Correction. Cut that last paragraph." As you girls know, in a lot of cases, you don't know just how far back he wants you to cut, because you put in the paragraphs yourself, not having had any indication from the disk about punctuation and paragraphing. Those of you who dictate and have secretaries need not concern yourselves about these mechanical matters, because your girls know your speaking habits in dictation and they are acquainted with the subject matter of your departments; but what if your disks go to the pool? You can bet that you can expedite correspondence a great deal by dictating paragraphs and any out-of-the-ordinary punctuation you may want used. And do, by all means, spell technical terms, foreign words, and the like. This is not to say that those in the typing pool are any less competent than the secretary. It's just that they aren't specialists in certain departments.

I will listen to some disks to see whether and where work has to be done on clearness in speaking. In the dozens of surveys made in companies, there is always—without fail—one complaint. Typists and secretaries criticize dictators for chewing gum, smoking pipe or cigars, lowering their voices, or for making purely unintelligible sounds as they dictate.

I hope we can avert some urges to kill by eliminating from dictation such tidbits as " 'Very truly yours, John J. Jones.' Oh, I'm sorry I omitted something. Can the typist please squeeze an attention line in before the salutation? 'Attention: George M. Cain.' Thank you, Miss Typist." The "thank you" and the "please"—courteous though they may be—do not make up for the time it takes to retype a page-long letter.

How many copies do you want? What particular kind of stationery do you want the piece to go out on? How long is the item to be typed? These are details of instructions that the dictator can and should let the typist have—either through oral directions on the disk or by means of the typist's tab.

Now, what does the typist have to contribute to attractive letters?

First, I think she has an attitude of cheerfulness toward her work—or she should have, if the over-all job of correspondence is to be as good as it should. In three or four good-sized companies, after efficiency analyses have shown employee disgruntlement, estimates have been made that the cost of dissatis-faction to a company can run as high as 15 per cent of salaries.

Just to let you know what my role here is, I will tell you that I'm not here to spread sweetness and light. I am not the lady in the TV commercial that brings sunshine to everybody by showing how to get the housework done in half the time by switching products. I will try to spread light—on how you can make your job as efficient as possible. Tests have shown that efficiency—with both the one doing the work and the one supervising it—brings better morale. You can call that sweetness, if you want to.

The tangible part of the typist's job, of course, is to turn out pages with adequate speed, and pages that don't attract attention to themselves. That's another way of saying that, if your letter or report is well-placed, neat, correct, it will let the person receiving it get right to what it was intended for—his reading it. If the page does not meet these requirements, the receiver takes at least one stop before the reading. It was a German philosopher, I believe, who originally said, "A good beginning is half the battle." Let your job be that good beginning. As has been said so many times, the correspondence out of your department to another one or out from the company *is* your department or company to the person getting it.

On the point of attractive pages, I sometimes wonder whether this thing of using music to teach rhythm in typing hasn't had a bad effect on some students. I'm referring to the evenness of touch in typing. I know one girl whose typing makes me think of a symphonic composition. There's a run of heavy typing that tapers off into words so dim they're actually hard to read. You can almost hear the blare of the brass followed by the soft strings of the violins. I call this crescendo-diminuendo typing—the heavy and the light, the loud and the soft. Whatever it's called, it detracts from a page.

Then there's that matter of erasures. I haven't found a typist yet who doesn't misstrike once in a while. The error is forgivable; an untidy correction isn't. A girl in a company I worked with recently seemed to think that that little puff of breath many girls use to get the eraser dust off the page was all she needed for getting the wrong letter off a page. At least, her typing frequently looks like a silent whistle is the only eraser she has used. The strike-overs look like Greek letters. Maybe it was her work that the boss saw when he said his typist could spell in Russian.

You girls and I will spend some time in classes and in conferences, as is necessary, on taking care of the typewriter. Keeping that machine clean and in working order is just as important as proper care of a piece of $50,000 equipment out in the plant. Yes, I know there's a maintenance department here. But as far as I'm concerned, every person who works with a machine is, in effect, part of maintenance—responsible for his own tools. By the way, I hold to this point to you dictators on care of your dictating equipment, too. Repairs are the job of maintenance; care of equipment to keep it out of mainte-nance is your job.

Well, this is the over-all picture of why I'm here. It has been a general picture, but that was the purpose in getting together here before we start the program of specifics for improved communication.

Back to the team thought I started with, I'd like to add that I am not opposed to making it a team of three now and then. The dictator, the typist, and I. As we talk over the specific aspects of getting out effective correspondence and reports, we'll keep in mind the responsibilities of each person to his or her part of it. Sometimes, it is possible that the three of us will get together for a conference, to iron out wrinkles.

I'm just old-fashioned enough to believe that people can talk over anything that isn't right. We will look at what is right and what may not be so right. Our God-given intelligence is our ticket to learning the right way. And the common sense approach to working with others to improve a situation is our authority to carry out those responsibilities.

Exercises and Problems in Communication

1. The following letter (with names changed), sent from a firm in London to a Chicago packing company, illustrates differences between British and American practice, but it also illustrates bad setting up on the page and otherwise does not represent good British business writing. Set up the material according to approved American practice.

120 & 134 Newcastle Row
London, England
P. Lancaster & Sons.

DM/TD.   16th January, 19
SECURITY PACKING CO.,
Chicago.

Dear Sirs,

Ref. C. B. Brown

Some time ago you expressed interest in our product ESTERICIDE.

The continued expansions in the sales of this product, in the face of trade recession and lower prices, gives added proof of its efficacy and value to the Fat Melter and Refiner, and we would like you to reconsider the question of its adoption for regular use.

If we can be of any assistance to you by submitting further samples, or in any other particular, we shall be glad to be of service.

Trusting to hear from you, we are,

Yours faithfully,

P. LANCASTER AND SONS

2. Make carbon copies of the following letter scoring chart and use the charts to score each of three letters which you have collected.

	Perfect score	This letter
The "picture frame"	20%	_____
The letterhead	15	_____
Inside address	10	_____
Salutation	5	_____
Body (suitable indention, etc.)	10	_____
Complimentary close	5	_____
Signature	10	_____
Signature identification	10	_____
Special letter parts and stenographic detail	15	_____
Total	100%	

3. Paragraph the following material and set it up in each of these four styles: block, modified block, indention, hanging indention. Supply heading, signature, etc.

Dear Mr. Howell:

Thank you for your letter of November 20 and the return of the extra issue of the Service. We are glad to credit your account and cancel the charge. We assure you that it is not our policy to send any of our material beyond the expiration date without authority. As in your case where we have a purchase order for a specified period of time, we do attempt to obtain a renewal subscription, but if not received we would cancel without any further service. However, as most of our accounts are orders which are on an until-cancelled basis, the service clerk neglected to cancel your order and the extra issue was mailed before we received your letter requesting cancellation. We regret this error and appreciate the opportunity of sending you the extra postage you have used.

Sincerely,

4. Set up the following letter in Simplified form. Supply heading, signature, etc.; make as many paragraphs as you think would be appropriate.

HAD YOU HEARD? There's a new movement under way to take some of the monotony out of the letters given you to type. The movement is symbolized by the Simplified Letter being sponsored by AMS. What is it? You're reading a sample. Notice the left block format and the general positioning of the letter. We didn't write "Dear Miss ————," nor will we write "Yours truly" or "Sincerely yours." Are they really important? We feel just as friendly to you without them. Notice the following points: 1. Date location, 2. The address, 3. The subject, 4. The name of the writer. Now take a look at the Suggestions prepared for you. Talk them over with your boss. But don't form a final opinion until you've really tried out the Letter. That's what our secretary did. As a matter of fact, she finally wrote most of the Suggestions herself. She says she's sold — and hopes you'll have great luck with better (Simplified) letters.

5. See the footnote on page 46, regarding use of the "Attention" line. Look through the book for letters with that feature. What are the aspects of the letters that might make for artificiality?

6. What would you say is the purpose of Mrs. Woods's talk (the end-of-chapter reading), according to the functions of language discussed in Chapter 1?

7. In connection with her extended account of the letter with the unintentional "not," she said she was using "one of the oldest tricks in the hat." Do any other devices of public speaking become obvious?

8. Look ahead to Chapter 6, for the discussion on figures of speech. Which of them does Mrs. Woods use?

9. Which of them is she employing in her description of the typist who used the "puff of breath" for easing typing errors? Which one for the "crescendo-diminuendo" reference to uneven typing?

10. Assume you were trying to curtail correspondence costs in a company and you suggested the use of window envelopes to save typists' time in typing the address on the envelope. Another person objected, saying that he didn't want customers to think your company so "cheap" that you couldn't afford the time for that brief operation. What arguments would you use in pursuing your suggestion for cost reduction? Prepare other points for class discussion on the subject of correspondence costs.

3

Psychology in Business Communication

Speech was made to open man to man, and not to hide him; to promote commerce, and not betray it.—DAVID LLOYD, *State Worthies*

Without some dissimulation no business can be carried on at all.—LORD CHESTERFIELD, *Letters to His Son*

Probably the first implication of psychology in business communication is to the writer himself. What is it that makes writing difficult for so many? Of course, many responses to that question will come to your mind immediately as you recall the themes, reports, and term papers you have labored over.

A factor in this "self-analysis" that you might consider is "No one likes to write!" Jan Struther, columnist for the London *Times* and author of best-selling books, said, "If someone tells me he likes to write, I call him a liar. If he says he likes to have written, I believe him." To be sure, this is a generalization, but businessmen and industrialists attest to this reaction to writing. They find writing hard, but, when they "put in the last period" on a piece of writing, there is that glow of satisfaction of a job completed. They like *to have written*.

Asked in an interview shortly before his untimely death whether he found writing easy, Ernest Hemingway said that when you first start writing, it is a lot of fun. But when you learn that you have to write for the reader, the thing you remember about writing is how hard it is.

Many companies have printed intraoffice forms that admonish personnel to put something into writing rather than say it. The pertinence of these forms is reflected in their captions, or headings: "AVO" ("Avoid Verbal Orders"), "Write It; Don't Say It," and "The Spoken Word Doesn't Go." The need for such forms and their application to dislike for writing is well expressed by a representative of the Republic Steel Corporation in Cleveland, who said that one of the hardest jobs in a company is to get someone to put policy statements, orders, and instructions into writing. A person will talk freely and at length about such company details, but getting him to write them is quite another matter.

One way, of course, to diminish this aversion is to learn those principles that make the job of effective writing easier. And, as you are learning, you can be assured that if you find it hard to achieve good writing, you are not alone.

But to more direct applications of psychology in our dealings and associations with others, or the psychology of business. You will see, through examination of successful letters in later chapters, how important psychology is in business communication.

THREE KINDS OF PSYCHOLOGY

Psychology means so many different things to different persons that it is necessary for us to agree on what it means to us before we can talk about it.

Pseudo-psychology

This is not psychology at all, but rather the stock-in-trade of charlatans who have found that psychology has become popular as a cure for personal and corporate ills and who have learned to capitalize on that popularity. Since most of the general public are not trained to tell the difference between fake psychology and the real thing, many of these pseudo-psychologists have gained great popularity and profit from their exploitation. The short cut is the most common selling point of the pseudo-psychologists, since there is nothing more appealing to the public than a new, easy way to success, or popularity, or beauty, or friendship, or peace of mind. The fallacy of the short cuts that are concocted to be sold to the public is that they confuse the symptoms of a thing with the thing itself—friendship, for example, gets all mixed up with such superficialities as the way to shake hands, and the implication is that if you learn to shake hands the right way you, too, will have friends.

Many pseudo-psychologists have entered the field of communication with three short cuts, or six easy ways, or ten simple steps. To a person who really wants to improve his abilities rather than his morale, these short cuts do more harm than good; by oversimplifying the communication process they encourage carelessness and a superficial approach. There are no short cuts to effective writing, reading, speaking, and listening, just as there are no short cuts to good golf, good architectural planning, or good surgery.

Yankee Peddler Psychology

A favorite Yankee peddler story is about the salesman who offered the first unconditional guarantee. He brought a gross of worthless clocks and started out across western Massachusetts, offering to replace any defective clock he sold with a new one, "No questions asked." When he had sold 143 clocks he started back over his route, trading the 144th clock for the first, the first for the second, the second for the third, and so on. In making his guarantee he had not promised that the replacement clocks would work.

This Yankee peddler's psychology was real psychology, all right; there's nothing "pseudo" about it, even though its ethics are questionable. There are many Yankee peddler methods that make money today. If you wish to sell only once to each customer, and are willing to run close to the law, you may choose Yankee peddler methods yourself; many persons will still send 25¢ for "two beautifully colored steel engravings of famous Americans, produced by the country's foremost producer of steel engravings" (a 1¢ stamp and a 5¢ stamp). But if you associate yourself with a permanent business, one that depends on the same customers year after year, you must decide against using Yankee peddler psychology, however effective it might be.

Psychology for the Permanent Business

Business psychology is not yet a well-defined subject, although there are now many books on it, and perhaps the psychology of business communication has been less well worked out than that of business in general. According to W. P. Boyd, a long-time leader in the business-communication field, there are two obvious precepts: (1) be concrete, and (2) adapt the language to the reader. Most other things that need to be said will relate to one or the other of these.

Few persons, if any, would be impressed by, "We have in an attractive case a relatively modern electric alarm clock which is usually found dependable and which we are glad to offer for sale rather inexpensively." Yet the clock in question might be such a good one that it would warrant a description like the following:

> You'll marvel that anything less than human could prove such a welcome messenger of the dawn. With its clear, bell-like, cheerful tones, the Electro-Vox will tell you, at precisely the moment of your own choice, exactly when the new day should begin.
>
> With timekeeping as accurate as the motion of the sun itself, and almost as silent, this new Model 893 Electric Alarm Clock in

its attractive gold trim ivory case (or other combinations if you prefer) will be an ornament to any nightstand or dresser.

And the special introductory price for this pleasant bedroom companion is only $6.95.

Simply fill in the enclosed card and drop it in the corner mailbox—to bring you by return mail the clock you've long been wanting!

Keeping in mind the basic fact of difference discussed in Chapter 1, we must recognize that some prospects hearing or reading these two descriptions of the same product might prefer the first. The second could seem overdrawn to the more staid prospect. Be that as it may, one phase of merchandising is clear: Customers today do not part with their money in return merely for certain goods, gadgets, and machines—any more than they live by bread (or breakfast cereal) alone. They want to be sold on the *aura* of a product as well as the product itself; they want, in addition to the regular use-values, the plus values of distinction, exoticism, or lasting, dependable service. And always they buy because *they* want to buy, not because *you* want to sell; they respond to collection appeals not because you want them to pay but because you have made *them want* to pay; and they are satisfied with adjustments not because you think they should be satisfied but because, somehow, they *are* satisfied.

THE "YOU" ATTITUDE

Most business communication books make the phrase "the 'you' attitude" the keynote in their discussions of business psychology. (The phrase, incidentally, has become hackneyed to many in the business communication field. It is used and discussed here because of its basicness, for you to apply it as a concept rather than to adopt the term for frequent use in writing or speaking.) A popular jingle makes the idea easy to remember:

> To sell John Smith what John Smith buys,
> You must see John Smith with John Smith's eyes.

Another poetic expression of the "I" versus the "you" attitude is by Richard Brinsley Sheridan the eighteenth-century Irish dramatist and political leader:

> You write with ease to show your breeding,
> But easy writing's curst hard reading.

The letter reproduced in Figure 16 makes full use of the "you" attitude, in showing the prospect advantages of using the bank's services. The writing is far from being "curst hard reading."

Just how selfish the average human being is, is a subject of endless debate. Although we are compounded of selfishness and altruism in

FIRST NATIONAL BANK

KOKOMO, INDIANA

DONALD B. SMITH, JR.
SENIOR VICE PRESIDENT

June 16, 19

John Doe
123 South Main Street
Kokomo, Indiana

Dear John:

We are proud of you! Please accept our congratulations on your graduation and add our good wishes to those you are receiving from your many other friends.

Doesn't the check at the top of the page look good? It would look even better with your name on it.

I hope that some day you will be able to write a check for one thousand dollars--or even ten times a thousand. Your success will make it possible to carry an account large enough to pay a check that large. Of course, we'd like the check to be written on First National.

As we've heard so often, in any success, the start is important. We would like to help you make a good start in your finances. To help you start a checking account, First National will give you one year's service free. No service charges on your account for one year. You may deposit any amount and draw on it without charge.

Too, we will have checks printed free of charge with your name and address. All you do is come in, sign signature cards, and make your first deposit.

If you're going to be in college this fall or if you will be working, a checking account will be a real convenience. A checking account is an easy way of keeping track of your finances. It is also a safe way of doing business; you don't have to carry cash with you.

Come in soon. Just bring this letter with you or ask any of the bank personnel about First National's "Graduate's Checking Account". We look forward to meeting you.

Again, congratulations on your graduation and best wishes for a successful future!

Sincerely yours,

Senior Vice President

DBS:mj

Fig. 16. This letter brings a 20 per cent return in new accounts. The conversational tone contributes a great deal for recipients on a high-school-senior mailing list. (Used by permission.)

varying degrees, there can hardly be any question that the person who means most to us looks back at us from the mirror. Perhaps it is better that way, since he is the one we are most responsible for.

Some few goods are bought because the seller wants to sell them. A housewife may buy a magazine from a poor neighbor boy though she knows she will not find time to read it. Hard-headed businessmen have been known to save orders for salesmen with needy families, especially if they or their firms suffered no loss thereby. But altruistic business behavior is oftener the exception than the rule, from the very nature of things. We naturally buy the books which we or our children need; women buy the hat which "does something for them," either in their own eyes or in the eyes of others of their set; Johnny buys a kite because he wants to fly it, not because "a fellow wanted to sell it to me." It is the businessman's job to study how people behave, why they behave as they do, and to adapt his techniques to their behavior.

Just what is this thing called the "you" attitude? The meaning seems fairly obvious from the sound of the phrase, but how can we set about getting this magic touch? Let us look at some aspects of the "you" attitude one by one, so that we will be in a position to make sure that it is never lacking in our letters.

First of all, the person who has learned to work and to like to work has made important progress toward "you" attitude letters. No employer wants grudging, resentful, clock-watching service. An employee who is lazy can hardly hope to be an asset to his employer. One of the most significant of business axioms is, "An employee who works only for money will never have much money." The estimate that nine tenths of a man's satisfaction in life comes from his work is probably not too high, but many persons don't find it out as soon as they should.

For communication purposes, then, acquiring the "you" attitude reduces to two essentials: (1) get into the spirit of your work so that you will both understand what John Smith wants and be able and willing to give it to him; and (2) extend your firm's best service always in the most cheerful, considerate, and tactful way.

Doing any job well carries with it its thrill of accomplishment. You can't afford to forget that, in writing especially, you must be your own severest taskmaster. It is not only the beginner who evaluates his work. On the fiftieth anniversary of her stage career, Ethel Barrymore said that, despite the years, she had never stepped onto the stage without being mindful of the audience, and on her exits, she always wondered whether she had done her best job in interpretation, projection, etc.

Anyone can learn from competent criticism of his work, and in the business communication field you can acquire knacks of writing and speaking that few texts or teachers can impart. Perhaps you can even look forward to producing some day a form letter that will pull a million dollars' worth of business for your company. Setting your standards high is the surest way to make certain that you will one day develop abilities of which you can be truly proud. If you grasp sufficiently well the basic concept of what constitutes effective communication, you will be making real progress toward masterly writing and speaking when you consistently win your *own* approval of what you have composed.

THE SENSE OF BELONGING

In twentieth-century America, we are very much members of society, of groups: churches, schools, families, and business organizations. Morale, *esprit de corps,* is tremendously important. We don't lose our individuality by helping build the institution; in fact, we become more important as our church, our school, or the company employing us grows. The letter writing department of the Armco Steel Corporation has developed such fine techniques, and such pride in them, that it has twice put them in book form, the first edition winning such fame that it had a circulation of 100,000 copies outside the company. There is a certain prestige in working for Swift & Company, Dow Chemical Company, E. I. du Pont de Nemours & Company, Aluminum Company of America, or Johns-Manville Corporation, whatever the anticapitalists may say. These companies didn't build up to their present size and importance without employees who did their job well and at the same time saw beyond it. Your employer may not have such a well-known name, but the first thing for you to do is to identify your interests with his, pride yourself in being a member of the organization, and serve its customers well by having your letters prove that yours is a company of integrity and efficiency.

KNOWLEDGE OF PRODUCTS AND SERVICES

In answering inquiries, and in sales especially, one simply must know his company's products. An inquiry for a certain model of typewriter comes to an employee of a typewriter manufacturer. He knows that this model is no longer being carried; he has many letters to write. Without any research at all, or any recognition that his correspondent may be manager of a one-machine office struggling along for the present with an unsatisfactory rental machine, or an author planning to get started on a new book, he writes back:

Dear Sir:

In response to your inquiry of February 15, we are sorry to inform you that our typewriter Model No. 296813 has been discontinued. Our supply of this model is exhausted, and no more will be available.

Very truly yours,

But, you may say, *you* wouldn't write such a bad letter as that. Are you perfectly sure you wouldn't? What, at bottom, is wrong? Indifference mainly—or a failure to develop any sense of responsibility to the employer, any recognition of *esprit de corps.* This letter simply invites business to go elsewhere—the writer was too busy to be bothered. Let's see what the "you" attitude suggests. Model No. 296813 wasn't discontinued without reason and with no heir apparent. Either it didn't fill any great need or it didn't work well. It has been replaced now by Model 296823, which has several superior features that should be a joy to talk about. The job is to have fun selling the prospective customer on the new model and make him happy at the same time. But the letter writer didn't see it that way. Simmons Hardware Company has made much of the slogan, "The remembrance of quality remains long after the price is forgotten." We can paraphrase this for our purposes: "The satisfaction in a good purchase which has been well sold accompanies its every use."

CUSTOMER STUDY: WHY PEOPLE BUY AND PAY AND COME AGAIN

There are several other things to selling besides knowing your products and services, but this knowledge is absolutely indispensable. Without it, how can you possibly make a customer happy? Even if the product has potentialities, it may wear out before the customer discovers all of them—unless it is sold in a way which makes its values apparent.

On this subject of sales, let's do a little logical reasoning. As was said a few paragraphs back, people buy because they want to buy. They want to buy, for instance, because of what they think the new automobile will do for them—in comfort and convenience and trouble-free operation, in prestige among the neighbors, in satisfying esthetic responsiveness, in the opportunities that it opens up for them to escape the humdrum of the daily round by gliding over glistening trailways to groves of palm or snow-capped mountains. The "you" attitude means that the salesman or letter writer must not only be *willing* to see from the other person's point of view, but be *able* to visualize what will bring satisfaction, or joy, to the other person, and get that into his message.

MAKING ACTION EASY

It is not enough merely to make the person *want* what you have to sell, or desire to pay overdue accounts. You must make action easy by concentrating on one line, or at most two possible lines, of action. Enterprising magazines like *Time, Newsweek,* or *Reader's Digest* solicit subscriptions by means of appealing sales letters, but they also enclose cards which are easy to fill in and envelopes which are addressed and postage-free—often the kind that go air mail, not because the recipient couldn't possibly live another week without the magazine but because the advertisers realize the value of making the transaction *seem* urgent, businesslike. A man who cannot meet account payments as he has agreed to may feel that it is not worth while to pay anything at all. You may be able to show him a simple plan of easier payments that will save or restore his credit standing without being a burden. Always, customer *service* is the keynote.

In adjustments it is not enough merely to grant what the claimant is entitled to, or to refuse what would be unjust to your company and to other customers. Think the matter through. If your company has to stand a loss in making an adjustment, as it often will, how can it be reimbursed? Through future business, of course, from the same customer. By making him happy, you may more than make up for the adjustment loss in a few weeks. If you must refuse him, bring him around to your side of the counter, to see that in your place, out of fairness to other customers or to keep company policy constant, he'd naturally do just what you are doing.

Application letters have their psychology too. If a person is employable (and his first task is to develop his abilities, skills, and general character so that he will be), he must convince an employer that he would be an advisable addition to the payroll. He is partly caught, he realizes, in a vicious circle. With a good record of employment behind him he could get a job readily; but he can't have this record until he has somehow managed to hold at least one job. He can skilfully show, however, that he has been *preparing* for employment, that he has been educating himself according to a plan, that he has been expecting to work in the future for just such an employer as the one to whom he is applying. The ideal, it has been said, is to write an application letter that shows such familiarity with a business and such a spirit of cooperation that the employer feels that he is reading a memorandum for someone already in his employ. Then his next move is to give directions for further work to be done; the applicant is in!

Although each kind of business transaction has its special psychological problems (they will be discussed in later chapters), we must never forget the two guiding principles: be concrete, and adapt what you have to say to the reader. No matter how powerful the sending facilities of a radio station or how entertaining its programs, nothing is accomplished unless the broadcasting is on a wave length that radio owners can tune in.

One businessman calling on another who wrote many letters was surprised to see an empty picture frame hanging in plain sight of the man at the desk. In the frame was a white sheet of paper, but nothing else. The visitor asked for an explanation. "Oh, that is the picture of the man I write my letters to. Until I can see in that frame a clear picture of the man who is to get my letter, I know I'm not ready to write to him."

PSYCHOLOGY AND STYLE

Style, the *tone* of the writing, has a great deal to do with the way it is received. Shakespeare, in his sketches of the seven ages of man, makes speech tones play an important part in showing character: whining school-boy, sighing lover, soldier speaking in strange oaths, justice pronouncing his judgments in tones appropriate to his important position, the pantaloon, doddering toward old age, his voice changing to childish shrillness, piping and whistling in his speech. Just as man's different ages and positions have their characteristic ways of speech, so also business writing has its appropriate tones. Two businessmen speaking face to face would be able to show what they meant by the tone of the voice, bringing down a fist on the counter, or shrugging the shoulders. Business writing has a more limited repertory, or tool kit, but it can be appropriate in style.

CHARACTERISTICS OF THE BUSINESS STYLE

We have already said that the language of business is concrete and adapted to the reader. Also it is positive, constructive; not negative, planless. You have often heard persons express their willingness, "I'll do anything you say." Business writing must suggest, present constructive plans: for financing a new landscaping job, explaining how a record player can operate through the speaker of the family radio, getting service out of a balky washing machine, showing how an undercapitalized business can build up to a basis for full credit rating.

The following is the first paragraph of a letter sent out by a chemical rubber company to buyers and users of laboratory supplies:

```
We find that you failed to take advantage of a single piece of
laboratory equipment listed in our Supplement "D-1." Hundreds
of laboratories in industry and education have benefited through
the service afforded by this book.
```

Notice the querulous, scolding tone, and especially the use of the word *failed*. The whole approach is negative. Compare the following positive revision:

```
I am sending this just as a reminder of the items of laboratory
equipment listed in our Supplement "D-1," since your order
hasn't reached us yet.
```

Negative Expressions	Positive Expressions
Because of a heavy run on our stock we will be unable to ship before	Although the demand has been unexpectedly heavy, we can get your order to you by
Don't suppose you could	Feel sure you will find
If you have any regard for your credit standing	You know the value of an A-1 credit rating
Mistakes are bound to happen	Shall exercise even greater care to prevent
Sorry to inform you	Glad to report

Negative Expressions	Positive Expressions
Such an unusual request	Such a discriminating choice
The inconvenience and undependability of an old-fashioned toaster	The modern magic of a toaster that delivers every slice the exact shade you like best
We assure you it will never happen again	We appreciate your giving us this opportunity to improve our service

Not only must business writing be positive; it must also be *concise*. This does not mean, as some students think, that every letter must be as brief as possible, but it does mean that there shouldn't be waste verbiage. This question was argued at a national convention of the American Business Writing Association. One college professor spoke against the wordiness in student letters. A businessman rose to defend long letters; he'd rather have a two-page letter that did its job, he said, than an interchange of short letters that got nowhere. Other professors and businessmen spoke, with the professors tending to talk *against wordiness* and the businessmen *for completeness*. Eventually, of course, the argument was ruled no contest, since it became apparent that what everybody wanted was efficient, result-producing letters, whatever the needed length might be. We may say that conciseness is not so much brievity as an *efficiency quotient* derived by dividing the size of the job to be done by the length of the letter. If there are two hundred word-units of work in the problem and the letter does the job fully in two hundred words, its conciseness is 100 per cent. If it uses more words—or if it doesn't fully do the job—it lacks conciseness.

We all have to guard against going around Robin Hood's barn to get to Grandma's front gate. "We can" is usually better than "we will be able to"; often "so" will express as much as "in such a way that." The piled-up phrases, the meaningless words, are in the way. They are bound to annoy the reader who has learned to value his time. Such expressions have been aptly labeled "thought-cloggers." A few examples may serve as a reminder to anyone addicted to verbosity and as a warning to anyone who thinks that efficient writing is long-winded. Contrast the entries in the two columns for quickness of thought.

in the event that	if
in the neighborhood of	about
along the lines of	like
for the purpose of	for
in the manufacture of	making

PREJUDICE WORDS AND PREPOSSESSIVE WORDS

Psychology of tone means also that prejudice words must be avoided. A bull probably doesn't know why red maddens him, but it is to the interest of everyone having any dealings with bulls to know that it does make him see red. The language of business has its red rags: prejudice words, we call them. No good adjustment letter says "you claim" or mentions the word "complaint" to a customer. No good mail-order correspondent tells a customer that she "failed" to give size or color. No experienced collection writer tells a customer he has "neglected" to send in a payment.

Homely people are said to avoid mirrors, harsh-voiced persons to be uninterested in song. You could probably name exceptions, but you'll agree that a person in a jam or possessing a fault is already sufficiently unhappy; he doesn't want the thing thrown in his face. Rather, he'll be grateful to you if you can help him restore his self-esteem by enabling him to meet payment due dates, fill out order forms correctly, or get such use from a machine as he expected when he bought it. Avoiding prejudice words is just another way of showing human courtesy and consideration.

Words with Unfavorable Associations

(to be avoided in business)

appeaser	fail	nonsense
aristocrat	failure	nouveau riche
artificial	fellow traveler	obligated
bureaucrat	frogeater (Frenchman)	obstructionist
capitalist	greaser (Mexican)	politician
city slicker	hayseed	predatory rich
claim	insinuation	radical
communist	international banker	strikebreaker
complain	labor racketeer	unfair
complaint	misinformed	Yankee
conservative	misled	(used by a Southerner)
crackpot	misrepresented	you agreed
dead beat	money-changers	you promised
dictator	must	your carelessness
	neglect	your ignorance

Words with Favorable Associations

American	genuine	new
American-made	grandmother	only
Beverly	hand-dipped	original
brotherhood	home	Raleigh
champagne	homemade	tea rose
citizen	honor	unique
democratic (in America)	league	vigorous
dependable	liberty	vital
established	modern	Windsor
federation	mother	youthful

JARGON; RUBBER STAMPS

Perhaps the most glaring, or at any rate the most prevalent, offense against psychology of tone in business communication is the use of rubber-stamp terms. Chapter 1 discussed the unhappy influence on business phraseology of legal writing and of the nineteenth-century model letter books. Although it is almost universally agreed that business jargon is out-dated and ineffectual, many persons in business continue to use rubber-stamp terms. Apparently (1) they want to save time; (2) they mistakenly believe the expressions are good business form; or (3) they are too apathetic to avoid using them.

1. It is quicker to throw a few rubber stamps together than it is to think out an equal amount of original language. And businessmen are hurried, though many of them are like Chaucer's Man of Law, who "seemed busier than he was." The first reason is the most nearly excusable of the three, but seldom really excusable since the rubber-stamp is so ineffectual, and hence the saving in time is a net loss in humanness. Compare the following letters, used by different companies for the same job.

Dear Sir:—   Re— Mich. Fire and Marine 3166

Our records indicate that the above-mentioned policy covering your automobile for fire and theft comprehensive insurance in the amount of $450.00 expires on September 20th of this year.

We would greatly appreciate your order to renew this coverage for you and trust that we may hear from you in this regard.

Thanking you for past favors and hoping for the continuance of your patronage, we are,

                    Your very truly,

Dear Sir:

The Comprehensive Fire and Theft Insurance we wrote last year on your 1960 Oldsmobile will expire August 13, 1964.

The cost to renew this insurance for the same term is, as before, $16.00.

We shall be pleased to take care of this for you.

                    Yours very truly,

To which company would you pay insurance fees more cheerfully? Doesn't the first letter sound as if it were written simply because it was something that had to be cleared off a desk, while the second sounds natural and human? Here the rubber stamps probably didn't actually save any time, for the second letter is shorter and would be quickly and readily written by a person with the right kind of attitude toward his job.

2. Resorting to rubber stamps is a form of autointoxication; the writer has developed a kind of perverted appetite for them. He thinks, mistakenly of course, that they sound businesslike. It is true that language styles have changed a great deal. There is some excuse for an elderly businessman who has made a success of his business to continue dictating "in this regard," "trusting this will meet with your approval." But the present generation doesn't wear side whiskers; there is no reason why it should subscribe to business writing fashions that are going out of date and should go out even faster. Business language isn't a jargon of telegraphic style, clichés, and rubber stamps.

3. Many persons indulge in rubber stamps simply because they haven't learned any better, or are too careless or indifferent to take the trouble to learn better. It is much easier to use rubber stamps that might mean almost anything, and usually don't mean anything at all, than to think of accurate, unambiguous terms. Often the careless writer is like the man in the anecdote about a government bureau in Washington. A harried worker asked a fellow worker whose desk was always clear before quitting time for the secret of his efficiency.

"That's easy," replied the second. "In such a large organization I figure that there must be someone named Smith; so when anything hard comes in, I just mark it 'Attention of Mr. Smith,' and pass it on."

"So that's it," said the first man, wearily. "My name happens to be Smith."

Using rubber-stamp expressions is frequently a way of tossing the problems sooner or later onto Mr. Smith's desk, for unless a person thinks hard enough on the problem to say what he means in clear, simple language, the chances are that his message—written or verbal—won't really do its job. Instead it will result in wasteful crisscrossing, in lost or disgruntled customers, or at best in diminishing that precious business asset called good will.

Throwing away the offensive rubber-stamp expressions is not too difficult; in fact it is simply being considerate of the customer, and in the long run protecting our own business interests. If we are answering a specific letter, we can say "February 15" quite as readily as "recent date"; if we have "consulted our records," we can say "our duplicate of the bill of lading," "a carbon copy of our letter of February 12." If something is "enclosed," common sense says it must be "herewith"—why waste space and block traffic? And instead of "thanking in advance," let's concentrate on securing the action that in future will give us cause for thankfulness. In other words, let's work at our job of dispatching business in a style which is up to date and efficient, which gets immediate results and builds good will for the future.

GLOSSARY OF JARGON [1]

(These expressions sound worse in some contexts than in others)

according to our records
acknowledge receipt
advise
as per
assuring you of our . . . in the future
at hand
attached
attached hereto
be advised
beg to remain
beg to state
contents duly noted
early date; earliest possible moment
enclosed herewith
enclosed please find
enlarge upon this opportunity
esteemed favor
esteemed patronage
even date
favor us with your patronage
feel free to
for your information
hoping to hear from you
in regard to the same
in settlement thereof
in this connection
instant
it has come to my attention

kind indulgence
kindly
matter; this matter
meets with your approval
noted the contents
permit me to say
personal interview
recent date
referring to your letter
replying to your letter
said order
thank you in advance
thanking you for past favors
the above-mentioned
this day
to hand
trusting the above will be satisfactory
under separate cover
valued order
we have your letter
we remain
will find enclosed
wish to advise; wish to say; wish to state
writing in regard to
your earliest convenience
yours of the 15th received

SUMMARY OF THE PSYCHOLOGY OF BUSINESS COMMUNICATION

Since even the psychologists haven't yet found every answer to why human beings behave as they do, we can't draw up all-inclusive rules on what to say and write in business, but must treat each transaction to some extent as a separate problem. We can, however, make good use of what has been found out. We know now that there is an enormous difference between the results in psychologically-right and psychologically-wrong communication. We know that customers buy not merely goods but also the atmosphere which can accompany them, and that this atmosphere may last as long as the goods. We know that good business communication is concrete and that it is adapted to the customer—that the "you" attitude is fundamentally important. We know that *service* is a keynote

[1] See also the Glossary, p. 545.

of American business—that he profits most who serves best, and that a feeling of service rendered is important to a businessman's happiness. We know that we should like our jobs and deal with patrons in such a way that our own approval will be the highest award for performance.

That different dealings—inquiries, sales, collections, adjustments, applications, and reports—all have their special psychologies, we recognize, and we intend to study them more fully later. Since we have also found that there is a psychology of tone, or style, we must strive to be positive, not negative; tactful, not prejudicial; original, not imitative. If we do this, we may not frequently achieve $5,000 selling sentences, but we shall at least contribute materially toward keeping the wheels of business smoothly and efficiently turning in the production of goods and services which contribute to the American standard of living and the general welfare of society. At the same time we shall individually be climbing the business ladder because we have what business needs.

Writing Better Letters *

Ours is an age of high-powered communication. Telephones link continents, radio broadcasts to every country, television brings events into our living-rooms, wire services function at split-second speed.

We are all trying to express and explain ourselves one to another. In our contacts internationally and nationally, and in our business and social dealings, our customary instrument is the written or spoken word.

Perhaps, since words are free as air and just as much taken for granted, we don't place enough value upon them. But when we remember that without words we could not communicate, not even with ourselves, they become our most precious possession.

Words are important, then, and they are powerful. Are we realizing their full worth and potentialities? And just how much of all we write and speak really reaches the other person?

Rudyard Kipling tells in one of his *Just So* stories a fascinating tale of what might have happened to the first letter. The small daughter of Tegumai, a Primitive Man, sent a letter—the first letter—written on birch-bark, asking by means of a series of pictures for a new spear for her father to use carp-hunting. The letter was received, read, and thoroughly misunderstood by her mother, who thought it told of a great and terrible battle, and she rallied the whole tribe to the rescue of her husband.

On the other hand we have the true story of the famous composer, Tchaikovsky, and his correspondence which lasted for many years with the wealthy Madame Nedejda von Meck, who became his influential patron and his best

---

* Practical applications of psychology are readily apparent in this reading. The fine writing and the pertinent comments are characteristic of *The Royal Bank of Canada Monthly Letter*. This one appeared in April, 1951. (Used by permission of The Royal Bank of Canada.)

friend. The composer exchanged hundreds of letters with her, but they never once met.

Somewhere between the failure of Tegumai's daughter and the success of Tchaikovsky come most of our efforts in the field of communication. We are aware of the necessity to express ourselves clearly and to understand other people better; we are trying to communicate—but the universal state of misunderstanding testifies to a need for improvement of our methods.

What Is Communication?

Let's look at business. Business men are more and more aware of the vital importance of communication. Before the war the word "communication" was not in general use except as a term for a system of communication such as telegraph, telephone or post. Today there is hardly a business speech in which the word is not used—and used in its basic dictionary meaning: "The interchange of thoughts or opinions."

Smooth operation of every business organization is dependent to a large extent on the ability of business men to communicate intelligently, effectively and swiftly with other people. This includes not only their customers, but their employees and their colleagues. The man who can explain himself may command what he wants; he who cannot convey his desires in an understandable way is left to his own personal resources.

The persuasive tongue or typewriter is, therefore, among the primary assets which an individual and a business must have in order to attain any real success.

Before the Beginning

A letter seems a simple thing; it has a beginning, a middle and an end. But between the beginning and the end lie many dangers.

We really have to begin *before* the beginning. We must copy the architect, who first drafts his plan and designs every detail.

The authors of the long-lived play, *Life with Father*, found that the time taken in planning paid dividends. They spent two years in working out a plan, and then wrote the play in seventeen days. An article like this may take only a few hours to write, but before the first key is struck there were years of reading and an intensive three or four weeks of research.

Business men are not in the playwriting profession, time is short, and business letters are not intended to be pieces of deathless prose. But a few minutes, well-spent in thinking of what you are going to say, how you are going to say it, and to whom you are going to say it, will help to lift your letters out of the routine class and into a more informative, inspired and *effective* sphere. There can be more "punch" in a short, well-thought-out and well-composed letter than in a far more effusive, gushing and lengthy letter.

How to Say It

After you have planned your beginning, middle and end—sounding the main theme at the beginning, echoing it at the end, and developing it by natural steps in the middle—how are you going to say it?

Sir Arthur Quiller-Couch, whose *Art of Writing* we have often quoted, says that the first aim of speech is to be understood, and that the more clearly we write the more easily and surely we will be understood. That seems like a self-evident truth, and doubtless is, but the purpose of this article is not to discuss truths but who does what about them.

Most good writing is simple; the natural quality of good prose is simplicity. A man who thinks that long words and the use of abstractions are symbols of superior writing is quite wrong. The long words may be quite correct, and their attributes may be admirable, but this article deals with making communications understandable. To refer to a man as "envoy extraordinary and minister plenipotentiary" may flatter him in the standing and sanctity of his profession, but if you wish to communicate an idea of his position you will call him "Minister."

Simplicity is an elusive thing; it must be sought after. It is a complex thing; discipline and organization of thought, as well as intellectual courage, contribute to it.

The allurements of elegant variation, as they are called by H. W. Fowler, the distinguished compiler of the Oxford English Dictionary and author of several books on good English usage, do not attract first-rate writers, and quite often such attempts to be picturesque and different are strained and unnatural.

In this dangerous class falls the use of foreign words. This is a weakness to which some of us are inclined, thinking perhaps that they inject a piquancy into our writing. (If we were really honest, we might find that our love for them stems from a pride in our superior knowledge!) A good rule to follow is that all words not English in appearance are, in English writing, ugly and not pretty. They are, however, justified if they afford much the shortest or clearest, if not the only, way to the meaning—or if they have some particular appropriateness of association or allusion in the sentences wherein they are used.

The same is true of technical terms. When they are being used in speech or writing for the general public, or for customers who are not experienced in their use, such terms should be translated into more familiar language.

Short words (and usually, though not always, they are familiar words) help to achieve clarity of expression. They are not only easier to use, but more powerful in effect; extra syllables reduce and do not increase, vigour. And you are not losing beauty of expression. Shakespeare, in his sonnets, those lovely and lilting pieces of literature, used short words almost exclusively. More than 96 per cent of their language consists of words of not more than two syllables.

Habitual use of long words may lose you the confidence of your reader. As the Eaglet said in *Alice in Wonderland:* "Speak English! I don't know the meaning of half the long words, and what's more, I don't believe you do either!"

Short sentences, like short words, strengthen our writing. The average written sentence in Queen Elizabeth's day ran to about 45 words; the Victorian sentence to 29; ours to 20 and fewer.

Write About Things

Concrete words are the basis of a vigorous style. They are words that correspond as closely as possible to what we feel, see, think, imagine, experience and reason. Such words are more easily pictured, and as a result more easily understood by your reader. Look at the Parables. They speak only of things which you can touch and see. "A sower went forth to sow seed"; "The kingdom of heaven is like unto leaven, which a woman took." These are not abstractions. They bring the great principles of conduct and belief to the people in familiar pictures.

A French philosopher said the same thing in this way: "An abstract style is always bad. Your sentences should be full of stones, metals, chairs, tables, animals, men and women."

All these faults—use of long words, use of technical or obscure words unnecessarily, use of lengthy sentences, and use of abstract terms instead of concrete images—all these seem to find their natural home in jargon.

Jargon loves abstractions, far-fetched words, obscure constructions, false prestige and cloudy phrases. It confuses, but it also protects. It is useful to employ this ambiguous language, it has been said, so that if the text be successfully carried out, all credit may be claimed; but if the text be unsuccessfully carried out, a technical alibi can be set up out of the text itself.

But it is not good, honest English, and what's more, your readers won't understand it.

And Now: Style

What about style? It has been said that style is much the same as good manners in other human intercourse. It grows out of trying to understand others, of thinking of them rather than yourself, and of thinking with the heart as well as with the head.

Cardinal Newman, a great master of style, denied that style is a kind of extraneous ornament laid on to tickle the taste. Dean Swift, another authority, said that proper words in proper places make the true definition of style. Style has also been defined as that use of words by which they convey more than their dictionary meaning—the personal and artistic use of language.

To those who wish to improve their writing style, here is a word of advice: when you feel you have perpetrated a specially fine piece of writing, look at it impersonally and even ruthlessly—then delete cold-bloodedly, particularly the superfluous adjectives.

Style may be said to be the power to touch with ease, grace, and precision any note in the gamut of human thought or emotion.

Dr. Rudolf Flesch tells us in *The Art of Readable Writing* that your language differs from that of anybody else. It's part of your own unique personality. It has traces of the family you grew up in, the place where you came from, the people you have associated with, the jobs you have had, the schools you went to, the books you have read, your hobbies, your sports, your philosophy, your religion, your politics, your prejudices, your memories, your ambitions, your dreams and your affections.

This adds interest in life for those of us who write business letters, because in communicating with others on behalf of our company we have a double responsibility; to express our own personality and that of the company we are representing. Our letters can be a happy union of our own character and that of our organization, its friendliness and its wish to serve. When you stop to think it over, the best letters are of this sort.

This thinking of your reader and his feelings is just another evidence of good manners. In our intercourse with readers we should strive to satisfy Newman's famous definition of a gentleman as one who never inflicts pain: we will always try to be good company, to make our readers at home and at ease and pleased with themselves. Even the most difficult tasks of communicating ideas may be approached in this urbane spirit.

If we succeed, all our communications with others will be received with a remark similar to that expressed by George Eliot: "I never before met with so many of my own feelings expressed just as I should like them."

Get to Know People

The letter-writer has many obligations. He must put aside his own feelings and thoughts and consider first those of the other man. He must fit the proposition to the reader and he must never give the impression that he thinks the reader is ignorant or in any way inferior. He must never *write down*.

In our personal, face-to-face contacts, we do not like people who are condescending. In a letter, this quality seems worse, because somehow we think of written words as being so premeditated and planned.

The great authors, as Emerson said, never condescend. To write down to our readers is a denial of our whole way of life, and a negation of the philosophy that every one of us is on the way up. Our readers are not unintelligent, although they may be uninformed, which is a totally different thing. Our job, in all our communications with others, is to supply information that may be useful to them.

If we study our audience, we will be less likely to make mistakes. Let us make sure we know for whom we are writing. Let us talk to our prospective readers and customers, if we can, and find out what they know, what they don't know, and what they would like to know. Then we can incorporate the results of our findings in our own minds, and write for our readers. We will be writing not to Man, but to a man.

Writing cannot have the same personal impact as speech; it has been said that spoken language is the primary phenomenon, and writing is only a more or less imperfect reflection of it. But, by aiming for clear, correct, thoughtful written communications full of fellow-feeling, we can approach a reasonable facsimile of it. At the same time we can avoid the occasional rambling vagueness and careless thinking that sometimes characterizes our talking selves.

The more we know of people, their likes and dislikes, their ways and habits, their hopes and fears, the better all our communications with others will be This is itself a reflection of the fact that the more human, the more sympathetic. and the more understanding we are, the better persons we will be not only in our own inner lives but in our dealings with others.

Reading Is Essential

There is a second way of attaining what we seek. Association with others teaches us about human nature; there is also wide reading, which introduces us to the minds and experiences of great writers in their observations of people and events. The world of literature lies open to all of us.

Reading extends our experience, increases our interests; it adds to our knowledge and our pleasure. The more extensive our acquaintance is with the works of those who have excelled, the more extensive will be our understanding and our powers of communication. Right reading makes a full man—a man not replete, but complete.

Being human, we can all find excuses for not reading as we know we should. Time is short, days are full, the mass of written material is enormous, and selection is difficult.

In one of his lectures on English literature given at Cambridge in the earlier part of this century, Sir Arthur Quiller-Couch recommended the reading of three books: The Bible, Shakespeare and Homer.

Now we may not have a copy of Homer at hand, or even a volume of Shakespeare, but all of us can probably find a Bible on our bookshelves.

We cannot aspire to prose such as we find written there; but it will be something if we become fully aware that such writing exists. One who wishes to improve his style and clarity and expressiveness will lose himself in the beauties of a great book just because it is a masterpiece, but at the same time he will absorb the goodness of it.

Read as widely as you can; read the classics, for they are doubly permanent. They remain significant and they also acquire new significance in succeeding ages. Read books by modern authors, don't overlook magazines and the daily newspaper, but be selective. Choose the best, and by that we mean the best for you. There are doubtless legitimate occasions for indulging in "escape" literature—the kind of book that uses up an evening after a hard day at the office. Next day you don't remember the plot of it, and not a phrase is worth repeating. As a steady diet that is too thin fare for an ambitious youth or a grown man.

Are there "Tricks of the Trade"?

When you come down to the hard facts of writing, how are you going to make sure you are communicating your ideas?

By gadgets? There is one made of celluloid, on which you dial certain facts about what you have just written: things like syllables and affixes. There will pop out at you from one of the little windows a verdict ranging from "easy" to "very hard."

By semantic devices? Well, there is a book on our desk which shows the number of times certain words are used in 1,000,000 words. From it we find that "gadget" was used two times, and "word" more than 100 times. Does that help? Somehow, we can scarcely fancy a business man (two times in 1 million) leafing through a book while dictating to his stenographer (six times in a million) a letter asking someone to pay his bill (more than 100 times in a million).

By books of similes? Well, one such book gives 88 *pages* of words which may stand for "very" in certain circumstances. But picking the right circumstance is still the writer's problem.

When it comes to choosing between two words, a common plan is for the business man dictator to jump at one, and then ask his stenographer, "Does that sound all right?"

That these aids, if aids they be, to readable writing exist, is proof that improvement is needed, and that there is a void to fill.

Good writing is not achieved by rules and devices. It is an art to be practised. To wait for inspiration is fatally inefficient, although it is a common-enough alibi. The secret of success is solid daily practice.

Armed with a few ideas; a genuine concern and interest in our readers; a reverence for and knowledge of our language; a background, constantly expanding, of good reading; and perhaps a reminder in our diaries to check our correspondence periodically, we shall be well equipped.

At the Reader's End

The business of communication demands two—the author and the reader. We have spoken solely of the duties and responsibilities of the writer in this matter of communication. What about the reader?

In the creation of works of art, literature, poetry and drama, the responsibility of communication laid upon the artist is great. He has obligations to fulfil, for his is the great gift, the great thought, expressing itself to an audience. He is the expert. But in business life the roles of writer and reader are largely interchangeable. At one moment we are the writer, and at the next we are the reader. Much of what we have said about one holds true for the other.

The reader who puts aside prejudice and brings an understanding spirit and an open mind to a piece of writing is co-operating wholeheartedly with the writer, who, in turn, has been thinking mainly of the recipient. A meeting of minds takes place, and a closer understanding is reached.

As the General Manager of this bank said not long ago in introducing a collection of our Monthly Letters on *The Communication of Ideas:* "No greater good could be achieved by humanity today than the ability to communicate ideas. If we know what others are thinking, and if other people—in business and social life, nationally and internationally—understand what is in our minds, what we are striving for, what we hope for, many misunderstandings will be avoided."

After all, there are few gifts that one human being can give to another in this world as rich as understanding.

Exercises and Problems in Communication

1. Read in some of the several books on the subject of psychology in business. Discuss the principles, in either a written or an oral assignment, as directed by your instructor. You will find some provocative material for class discussion in *Practical Business Psychology*, by Donald A. Laird, and *Psychology in Business*, by Leslie R. Beach. Since most college graduates who go into business and industry are soon in management positions, you may find of interest the following: Roger M. Bellows, *Psychology of Personnel in Business and Industry;* Mason Haire, *Psychology in Management;* and Loren Baritz, *The Servants of Power.* Although the stress in the "management" books is on intra-

company communication, you will find many of the principles applicable to our more major concern in this course: the customer and the public.

2. Following is an actual copy of a business letter sent from a trucking company to a large mail-order house. Allowing for the somewhat technical nature of the subject matter, comment on its clearness and conciseness. Do you think you could write a satisfactory answer to such a letter?

Dear Mr. Muntwyler:

Our tariff is now in the process of being composed by the
Wisconsin Traffic Bureau. In order to handle your goods on
the same basis, in the future as in the past, we are asking
that the following commodity rates, exception to the classi-
sification, be entered as far as our points are concerned.
Merchandise, when the shipper reconsigns to the same company,
subsidiary or branch store, rated third-class or higher,
providing not over 40% is higher than third-class rate from
Chicago, Minneapolis, and St. Paul to all points at 60% of
first-class.

Merchandise, when the shipper reconsigns to the same companies,
subsidiary or branch store, and rated third-class or higher and
over 40% is merchandise classified higher than third-class rate
from Chicago, Minneapolis and St. Paul to all points, 80% of
first-class.

This is protecting fourth-class merchandise and lower at the
class rates. The reason for the 40% notation is that we are
informed that a commodity rate cannot be placed on all classes
of merchandise unless each and every article handled is named.
We were further informed by wording in this manner that same
would be accepted by the Interstate Commerce Commission.

If you have any suggestions or help in regard to this we would
be glad to have your comments by return mail. Thanking you,
I remain

                                    Yours very sincerely,

3. From the editorial page of a newspaper (name the paper and date) collect at least ten prejudice terms. Give enough of the context to show how they were used.

4. From the advertisements in a general or news magazine collect at least ten words or terms with favorable associations. Name the products with which they were associated.

5. From your file of letters written for this course, make a list of the rubber-stamp expressions you have used so far. Opposite each term, write a fresher expression, one that you would prefer in a letter for a less sterile, less mechanical tone.

6. Revise this letter, avoiding jargon completely:

It has come to my attention that this is the first time you have
seen fit to favor us with your valued patronage. May I enlarge

upon this opportunity to offer you a sincere and heartfelt
welcome to our happy circle of customers.

Your letter of October tenth has been received and contents duly
noted. The articles you ordered are being sent under separate
cover and should reach you at an early date. Please favor me
with a reply by return mail if there should be anything which in
any way does not meet your expectations.

As per the white shirt, permit me to say that the type you
mention is still out of stock. For your information, however,
please be advised that your name has been added to our mailing
list. We wish to call your attention to the fact that you will
be notifed at the earliest possible moment when the shipment of
shirts is at hand.

Enclosed please find a check for three dollars and twelve cents
($3.12), which according to our records is the balance due you
from your money order. Thanking you for your order, and assuring
you of our prompt attention to any of your valued orders in the
future, we remain,

Very truly yours,

7. Write three sentences about each of the following concepts: book, class session, employer, work, food, piece of writing, pipe (for smoking), office party, teacher, house, office, student, effort, regard (for a person). Let the synonyms you use reflect three attitudes: the neutral (as discussed in Chapter 1), the prejudicial, and the prepossessive; for example, sentences with synonyms for *automobile* might be

> The company bought a *car* yesterday for the transportation pool.
> We got rid of our *junk heap.*
> We rode to the party in a *limousine.*

8. As an exercise in implication versus inference, discuss your choices of words in the preceding exercise with someone (your roommate, classmates, instructor). As you know, there are no *right* or *wrong* answers (except in word meanings), but your discussion will probably point up the fact of differences in reactions to language.

9. Rewrite the following letter sent from a bank to new residents in the town. Although the stress on *we* may be inferred as appeal in pointing at what the bank can do for its customers and what Lincoln has to offer residents, see if you can't reduce the use of that word, putting the strong appeal on the services. (Names of those receiving this letter, incidentally, were taken from "Say Hello to—," a column in the local daily paper, which listed names of newcomers.)

To the new resident:

Welcome to Lincoln. We are always glad to have fine people
choose Lincoln as home.

We think there are many advantages to living in Lincoln. Our
per capita income is high. We have some of the best schools in

the state. There are many cultural advantages for our citizens, and we have some of the finest recreational facilities in this section of the country.

We would like to welcome you to First National Bank too. We have prompt service of all kinds. Our Loan Department is convenient for either short-term or long-term loans. Our Safety Deposit Box service is fine for protection of valuable papers and possessions. A checking account in our bank is inexpensive and convenient for shopping; and a checking account is a good way for a person to keep personal accounts up-to-date.

We are proud of our bank, which we moved into just last year. The pleasant surroundings are a pleasure to our customers. We think that a bank no longer has to be "cages" and drab colors just because our chief commodity is money.

We are proud of our courteous service. Our employees, from the highest to the lowest, know that courtesy is one of the most rewarding experiences of a day's work. Our customers are our most prized possessions.

We would like to have you visit us soon.

Yours sincerely,

President

10. For effective use of the pronoun "we" in communication, read the short essay "The 'We' Approach," in *Instincts in Action*, by Norman Shidle (New York: Publishers Printing Co., 1961). This 160-page book of one-page essays, taken from the Society of Automotive Engineers *Journal*, has much to recommend it to anyone interested in business communication.

4

The Mechanics of
Effective Communication

Grammar, which knows how to control even kings.—MOLIÈRE,
Les Femmes Savantes

*Knowing any language imperfectly is very little better than
not knowing it at all.*—LORD CHESTERFIELD, *Letters to His Son*

"No chain is stronger than its weakest link" is a proverb so old we don't
know its source, though we can easily enough recognize its truth. When
the writer of a text on business communication debates whether or not
he should include a chapter on the fundamentals of writing and reluctantly decides to do it, he may still be a little uneasy in his mind. He
feels like talking for a few sentences before going on to discuss grammar
and other terms which many persons form a permanent prejudice against
in the grade schools. "The poor always ye have with you"; so also the
problem of how to put English words together correctly and effectively in
order that they can best get jobs done.

It is just possible, though according to the law of averages improbable,
that you don't need the kind of review material that follows. In an early
American sentimental novel, there is one tear-dripping chapter which the
author warns "the reader devoid of sensibility" not to read. If you can
prove that you don't need the remainder of this chapter, you may pass
it up.

In any case, what we are attempting here is not a complete review, but
a kind of insurance that you won't waste time trying to write business

letters before you are ready to do so. Our purpose is twofold: (1) to cover the general field sufficiently to provide an adequate review for the well informed and basic instructional material for those who need it; (2) to highlight matters that have come up in our years of teaching so as to give you the benefit of short cuts, reasons why, and learning devices which we have found helpful.

HOW BAD BUSINESS WRITING CAN BE

Following is a copy (except that some proper names have been changed) of a business letter—one that was actually sent through the mails.

```
                 FIRST STATE CORPORATION
                 I n v e s t m e n t s
                 496 Fulton Building
                 Any City, Any State

                 March 25th 19--

Mr. R. N. Jones
342 East Madison St.
Chicago, Ill.

Dear Mr. Jones:-

   Wish to acknowledge reciept of your letter also Post Card
which got mislaid it was with a bunch of cards which recieve
each day on price quotations.

   The Any City Sports Center Inc. is still going fine and can
see no reason why they should not continue doing so as the league
Bowling is contracted for at least another year ahead [written
in] and they just got Contract for the Any City Edison league
which takes up all available time.

   We have disposed of some shares from holders who needed funds
and have little trouble of doing so, so far we have purchased
them at $90.00 and sell them at $100.00 they should be worth this
much more and according to statement they should be worth more
and as time goes on and Loan is paid off they should have a
property with value of at least $100,000.00 and for which less
than $60,000.00 Stock has been sold.

   As you know Dividend has been paid and at a good rate and see
no reason why this rate should not be maintained if not bettered.

                 Yours very truly,

                 FIRST STATE CORPORATION

                 [Illegible pen signature]

Glad to have you write us any time and will try to be of any
service that Can.
```

You don't need to be told that this is a bad letter. I counted twenty-seven errors of detail in it (not including the bad sentences and poor planning), and am not sure that I got them all. Yet the letter is trying to do a business job—sell investment shares—and it is on a rather impressive-looking letterhead. I have often wondered whether any copy of this letter did any selling; I know the one in my files did not.

THE FUNDAMENTALS OF GOOD BUSINESS COMMUNICATION

The thread we spin from when we weave the business message is our knowledge of the fundamentals of good usage: grammar, punctuation, capitalization, spelling, and, of course, vocabulary and sentence structure. Just as no chain can be stronger than its weakest link, so also no business message can be sure of effectiveness, or safe against the risk of making a bad impression, unless the materials it is made from are good.

Business is a race, and most goods are sold competitively. If you sell Mr. and Mrs. Jones an encyclopedia, they won't go to the store this month for the television set they have been talking about; or John and Susan will wait a little longer for the new clothes they were planning to buy. It has to be that way in the kind of economic society we have in America. Where advertising is a highly developed and widely practiced art and incomes are limited, most people will *want* to buy much more than they can afford at any one time. They pick and choose. The best presentations get the best results; yours must be of the superior sort to keep the pace. Twenty years ago an automobile might run a thousand miles between trips to the repair shop; today's models frequently do ten times this well. The difference? Several things—better materials, better machining, better design. The important thing for us to remember is that design and workmanship are largely thrown away when good materials are lacking. Let's look briefly at our materials, that is, our basic knowledge of English fundamentals, to make sure that they are good enough for good business communication.

THIS THING CALLED GRAMMAR

You've probably had an aversion to grammar ever since you learned to spell the word. Lots of students can't even spell it. Still more can't define it. Can you? *Grammar is the rules we've decided to follow in putting words together so that we will each understand what the other fellow means.* This should do for a working definition.

What are some of the rules we've decided on? A subject and a predicate must agree in number. "His firm delivers orders promptly; we also deliver promptly." With *firm* the verb is *delivers;* with *we* it is *deliver.* Why? We've agreed that that's the way it is—that's all—so we can understand each other. Because we must all mean the same thing by our thought signs, knowledge of grammar is indispensable.

Let's look at some of the other rules. The case of a pronoun is determined by its use in its own sentence or clause. "You are the kind of man whom we want on our board of directors." "You are the kind of man who is wanted on our board of directors." Why *whom* in the first sentence and *who* in the second? Because *whom* is the objective case form and *who* the nominative. You might give that for an answer and be quite right, as far as you went. We need to know also, however, that subjects are in the nominative case, and *who* is the subject of *is wanted;* and that objects are in the objective case, and *whom* is the object of *want*.[1]

A pronoun must agree with its antecedent in person, number, and gender. "Every user of our new model refrigerator says *they* are more than satisfied." Why is *they* amiss? Both *user*, the antecedent, and *they* are in the third person; hence there is no disagreement in person. But there is in number; *user* is a singular noun, and *they* is plural. What pronoun should be used? In a general letter, *he* (*man* embraces *woman*); in a letter to women only, *she*. Since the antecedent, *user*, could be in either gender, we adjust the gender here in terms of the job the letter is to do.

A *modifier* is a word, phrase, or clause that limits, changes, or explains the meaning of another word, phrase, or clause. In general, it should be placed as close to what it modifies as possible, and always the connection must be clear. "The packing was so faulty that five bottles were broken on your consignment of two dozen bottles of Sloan's liniment." What is wrong? It is easy to see that something is. "On your consignment of two dozen bottles of Sloan's liniment, the packing was so faulty that five bottles were broken." Although both sentences have the same words, the first is confusing and the second immediately clear. "Having tried in vain to reach you by telephone, this letter is resorted to instead to notify you of the expiration of our offer." As it is written, the statement is that the letter has tried to telephone. "Having tried in vain to reach you by telephone, we are resorting to this letter" is clear—that is, it is *grammatical;* the participial modifier is written the way we have agreed to use participles.

Many writers are very unsure of the *tense*, or time, of their verbs. This may be because they never took the trouble to learn verb conjugations and so do not know the possibilities. The new filing clerk says, on completing a job, "Mr. Brown, I finished this file." Why is this wrong? Because *finished* is the simple past tense; action begun in the past and just completed wants the present perfect, *have finished*. Or the clerk says,

[1] An illustration of the prevalent misuse of *who* and *whom*: A large chain store organization catering to a well-educated clientele has this closing sentence in an elaborate four-page folder, "Please pass this circular to whomever else might be interested." Since the pronoun is the subject of *might be interested*, the nominative *whoever* would be correct. Of course not all recipients of the folder spotted the error, but some of them did; and the advertising manager who signed it must have been embarrassed when it was brought to his attention.

DUNCAN ELECTRIC COMPANY, INC.

WATTHOUR METERS · DEMAND METERS · METER MOUNTING EQUIPMENT

LAFAYETTE, INDIANA

August 18, 19

Professor E. Glenn Griffin
Department of English
Purdue University
Lafayette, Indiana   47907

Dear Professor Griffin:

      You asked my opinion about effective letter writing. It
always is essential, of course, for the writer to use good English
and know his subject well enough to discuss it naturally, correctly
and clearly.

      Another fundamental is brevity. Just as few souls are saved
after the first twenty minutes of a sermon, so do readers usually lose
interest after the first page. Use short words, short sentences and
short paragraphs.

      A long time ago, an esteemed boss suggested to me that a
helpful letter writing habit was to put yourself in the reader's place
and always keep his viewpoint in mind. This is not natural for most
people, but the more the trait can be acquired, the greater the likelihood of the writer's getting the response he hopes to achieve.

      The ability to write effective and understandable letters and
memoranda has become an increasingly valuable skill in commerce and
industry. It is far more important for a letter or message to be easily
read and easily understood than to be considered a literary gem. When a
person can write in a brief, sincere, and straight-to-the-point manner,
he has an effective letter-writing formula.

      Sincerely,

      JCBixler

      President

Fig. 17. Formula for effective letter writing. Note the stress on correctness of detail. (Reproduced by permission.)

"I worked so fast that before three o'clock I finished the filing." She should say *had finished* for action completed at or before a past time. "Your request for quotations on Early Richmond cherry trees in the five-foot size has been received by us." "We have received your request for quotations on Early Richmond cherry trees in the five-foot size." Why is the second sentence better? Because having the main verb in the active voice makes the meaning clearer and stronger. The passive voice is useful in general writing to secure variety, or sometimes to prevent statements from sounding egotistical, but the active voice is nearly always preferable in business writing.

If you honestly feel that your grammar is weak, the only sensible thing to do is to get out your old grammar, if you still have it, or your Freshman English handbook and work on the subject. Study the rules and the numerous examples until you can be sure of your grammar in your business letters. You have to remember that although many recipients of business letters will not notice any but the worst errors in grammar, others will pounce with delight on any errors they detect.

These purists, as such adherents to usage are labeled by some less conventional authorities and practitioners, have turned down more than one otherwise likely applicant because of some violation of rules in his application letter. The fact that many who pounce on the other fellow's "mistakes" have usage lapses of their own [2] won't mitigate the misfortune if you should be turned down because of some slips. So the only philosophy to apply in writing and speaking is "Know, to be safe."

"PUTTING IN THE POINTS"

Almost as vexing as grammar is punctuation. We have what looks like a fairly complicated set of marks, which are sprinkled here and there in our writing. Most of us have not given much thought to why which one goes where, or why we use them at all. I remember an incident connected with an impromptu theme assignment in a freshman composition class. When the bell had rung, there was the usual scramble among the slower students to get their papers finished and turned in. One of them snatched back his theme exclaiming, "Oh, I forgot to comma it." Evidently he thought punctuation marks were something like salt or other seasoning in cooking; at some stage in the process it was necessary to sprinkle in about so much, in order that the stuff would taste right.

Actually, as most of us must realize by now, *punctuation marks are the road signs of composition.* They enable the reader to follow the pathways of thought with maximum efficiency, without taking wrong turns and having to back up, after possibly wandering around very uncomfortably. It isn't that we couldn't read without punctuation marks. Scholars have managed to settle rather satisfactorily the meaning of the poet of *Beowulf,* even though there is no punctuation in the one surviving manuscript, written by two scribes about A.D. 1000. In most cases we could puzzle

---

[2] An excellent example of this sort of paradox is the president of a Midwestern company who was a speaker at a teachers' convention. For some twenty minutes, the man lashed a group of college teachers for what he called their failure to teach their students (his prospective employees) basic grammar rules as he had been taught them. During the question-and-answer period, he was asked by a member of the audience whether he would hire an apt college graduate who pronounced *nuclear* "nucular" (as a man then high in federal government pronounced the word on radio and television). The company president, sensing the implication that a deviation is hardly a measure of a man's total ability, replied sharply, "That don't make any difference."

out the meaning in unpunctuated writing. But certainly it would be highly inefficient to do so, just as traveling over our frequently intersecting paved highways would be less satisfactory if there were no signs to direct us straight along any particular route.

Following an unmarked highway would be difficult enough, but suppose we had become accustomed to *depending on* highway signs, and then someone—perhaps as a Halloween prank—changed the signs so that they were at the wrong places, or the arrows pointed in wrong directions? In effect, that is what happens when writers use commas and semicolons inaccurately, or when they insert unnecessary marks. They are misleading trusting drivers along the highways of thought. Let's make sure that we know which signs go where and always place them right so that we will make it *as easy as possible* for our readers to understand *exactly what we mean.*[3] We cannot afford to forget that millions of dollars have sometimes hinged upon the placing of one comma.

PERIOD AND COLON

In reviewing the punctuation marks, it is best to proceed from those simplest in their use to those that are more troublesome. The *period* gives us little difficulty. It has basically just two uses: as a stop and as a sign of abbreviation. As a stop, it follows declarative and imperative sentences. If we misuse a period, we do so usually through carelessness, not ignorance, but in practice one is as bad as the other. The reader often can't tell which is which, and there is no reason why he should try to.

The *colon* also is simple enough in its uses. It is always a look-ahead sign, a hand pointing forward to something coming. It precedes a list and is the standard mark after salutations in business letters. A century ago it was used with some frequency in compound sentences where the coordination was better without a conjunction, but in this it has been largely replaced by the semicolon. It retains a linking use in expressions of time (4:15 p.m.) and in chapter-verse combinations (Acts 4:13).

INTERROGATION AND EXCLAMATION POINTS

The *question mark*, or interrogation point, follows all direct questions, but not indirect questions such as "Jones asked Smith if he had any lots for sale." It also has a small amount of use, in parentheses, to indicate uncertainty in a date or choice of word—but usually in business communication we can and should be certain.

The *exclamation point* in ordinary writing merely marks an excited statement, as its name would imply. In business writing, it is used rather

---

[3] J. N. Hook, in *Hook's Guide to Good Writing: Grammar, Style, Usage* (New York: The Ronald Press Co., 1962), gives excellent direction for punctuation.

more than in general writing; for instance, it can help lend an artificial note of excitement to a selling message. It is frequently found after the last sentence in a sales letter, whatever the sentence form. There is some tendency to have it replace the question mark where excitation to action is worked for, as in "When a magazine which almost a million subscribers know is a bargain at the regular rate can be had at half price on this special introductory offer, don't you agree that this is an opportunity which you can't afford to miss!"

PARENTHESES AND BRACKETS

Parentheses ( ) and *brackets* [ ] have only a limited use in business writing, but it is important to know their proper use, especially to prevent confusing them. Parentheses, in effect, are special commas; that is, they enclose a statement or other material that helps the reader's understanding but would overload or otherwise disturb the sentence if handled in any other way. What is enclosed is parenthetical to what the writer himself is saying. Brackets are an *editor's mark;* that is, a bracketed expression is inserted, for instance, in a long quotation to explain a set of figures or something else that might not be clear to the reader. For example, an editor lets the reader know the year referred to in the following sentence: "The speaker said, 'Last year [1963] per capita income in the United States hit an all-time high.'"

SEMICOLON

Although the *semicolon* is employed extensively, its uses are not too numerous or too complicated to be understood. It has three main uses: (1) to connect independent clauses in a compound sentence where a conjunction does not connect the clauses; (2) to introduce an independent clause beginning with a formal conjunctive adverb, such as *however* or *therefore;* and (3) to serve as a "heavy comma" in complicated lists where commas do the smaller jobs of separation, as in city-state and month-year lists, and also in compound sentences where a conjunction is used but the clauses are long or have commas within themselves. Learning the first two rules is the best insurance against that serious fault called the "comma splice" (see Chapter 5), and mastery of the first, particularly, gives the writer a very effective construction.

COMMA

It is not surprising that the comma is the most troublesome of marks. It is employed more than all the others put together, and its uses vary from those that are required to those that are optional, or nearly so. "The report was submitted March 17, and the plans were ready April 3." "The report was submitted March 17 and approved March 24." Why is there a comma before *and* in the first sentence and not in the second? The first sentence has two complete statements, two subjects; the second has a compound predicate, two actions but only one subject. The comma is used in the first sentence to let the reader know, in time, that he is shifting to a new subject and a new complete statement. Without it he might first misread and have to back up, with resultant delay and annoyance. A comma is not needed in the second sentence, but in some compound predicates the comma is used for clarity or emphasis.

Although careful study of the rules for the comma will help us a great deal in the use of this mark, we may as well recognize that complete uniformity does not exist and is not desirable. Ordinarily descriptive and narrative writing and simple expository writing do not require as much pointing as the lawyer's brief or the scientist's treatise, where clearness and precision are more requisite than smoothness and ease.

In general the comma is used: (1) to *separate,* so that sentence parts will not be misread; (2) to *enclose* parenthetical or explanatory material; and (3) to *indicate omissions.*

Since there are so many variations within the three basic uses of the comma, it will be necessary to leave most of the illustrations to the exercises at the end of the chapter. Here we shall note the newer trends in the rules for commas. We find fewer commas today than in nineteenth-century writings and, as we have observed, fewer in business writing than in some other kinds. The general rule (not to be relied on thoughtlessly) is "If in doubt, don't." Short introductory expressions can usually get along, and better, without commas. Close appositions, as "his friend Mr. Johnson," do not need them. On the other hand, we now place them rather regularly before the coordinating conjunctions *and, but, or, for,* where these introduce independent clauses. Also, we have decided that it is advisable to use them before conjunctions in what we call the a, b, and c series of words, phrases, or clauses—as in the expression just concluded. Frequently the series requires them for clarity, as in "The college bookstore has sections for books on literature, science, mathematics, economics, and history." With the comma before *and,* we know at once that five sections are involved; without it we might be puzzled to know whether or not economics and history books are shelved separately. Since the comma is frequently required for clearness in the a, b, and c series and never does any harm there, it seems simpler to use it regularly than to decide each time whether it is needed or not.

Those who think the comma is inconsequential might consider a situation in British litigation. Three persons were named to share part of an estate, as follows: "The remainder of the estate will be divided among A, B and C." Despite the "among," denoting more than two, A came into one-half, and B and C got one-fourth each. The ruling was that the absence of a comma after B's name indicated that the testator had not intended equal shares among the three persons named.

DASH AND APOSTROPHE

Your composition teacher probably denied you the use of the *dash* (double hyphen in typing). He may have called it a lazy person's mark, since it could take the place of any of the other marks, but allowed its use in abrupt shifts and before a summary statement following a list of some length. Your business writing teacher will be more liberal. It is true that the dash substitutes for commas, semicolons, and even periods. But since in business writing we work frequently for the effect of lightness and speed, and judicious use of the dash tends to produce such effects, we should use more dashes in business letters than elsewhere—but not too many.

The *apostrophe* has three uses: (1) to show possession; (2) to take the place of omitted letters in contractions and abbreviations; and (3) to form plurals of figures, letters, and words referred to as words. The important caution is: do not confuse these functions. For instance, in the statement, "It's necessary that its importance be stressed," the first word is contracted from *it is;* the fourth is merely a possessive adjective like *his* or *our.*

QUOTATION MARKS

Quotation marks are used: (1) to enclose the exact words of another; (2) to label technical terms or slang when these are at variance with the context and quoting would help the reader (but do not quote unnecessarily); and (3) to designate titles of book chapters or magazine articles. Since it is easier to type quotation marks than to indicate italics by underlining, quotation marks are employed in business writing for book titles also, although there is some risk of confusion in employing them for both the chapter and the book title. For typing efficiency common business communication usage today allows for capitalizing all letters in a book title, thus avoiding underlining.

Using quotation marks alone may not be troublesome, but many students have difficulty in combining them with other marks. American practice, though not altogether logical, is relatively simple. The comma or colon preceding the start of a quotation is placed outside the quotes.

Periods and commas following a quotation are always inside the quotation marks, colons and semicolons outside, question marks and exclamation points inside or outside depending on whether they refer to a quoted part of a sentence only or to the sentence as a whole.

> Brown said to me, "Do you intend to sell by Thursday?"
> Did Brown say to you, "I intend to sell by Thursday"?

For quotations within quotations, the same rule applies. It is the rule to precede a quoted sentence by a comma, but where the thought flows smoothly, this comma may be omitted.

ITALICS

Italics are not frequent in business writing, partly because they are troublesome to indicate on the typewriter; also, underlining does not look well when used extensively. They should be used for titles of magazines, for names of ships, and are preferable to quotation marks for book titles. (But see above, under "Quotation Marks.") In literary works some authors resort to italics freely for emphasis. Italics are still properly employed for emphasis in business writing, but it is easy to overuse them—to the impairment of the appearance of the letter. Besides, the use of any device for emphasis is like putting seasoning in food: enough is good; too much spoils everything.

ELLIPSES

Ellipses are the series of periods used to show an ellipsis, or omission: three for omissions within a sentence, four to include the period at the end of a sentence. They may be either single or double spaced. Ellipses have considerable business utility. It is frequently desirable in quoting to skip parts of sentences or even whole sentences, informing the reader by ellipses that something has been left out. Since judicious omission frequently adds liveliness to the effect, sales writers have found that they can get an illusion of speed by frequent dotting with ellipses. This use is common in advertising copy and has some sanction in direct-mail selling.

CAPITAL LETTERS

Capitalization, like punctuation, has evolved gradually and has not become completely standardized. It, too, owes its development to the writer's desire to make his meaning as clear as possible. Like punctuation points, capital letters in certain positions serve as signposts, making it easier to follow the paths of thought. We use capitals in three main situations: (1) to mark beginnings; (2) to label nouns used in a special way (proper nouns); and (3) to emphasize important words in multiple-word names and titles.

Capital letters mark several kinds of beginnings. The most important is the beginning of a sentence. Another is the beginning of a line of poetry; still another, the first word in a quotation when the quotation, although incorporated in another sentence is really a sentence in itself.

(If, however, the first word of the sentence being quoted is omitted from the quotation, the introductory word is not capitalized; for example: The customer said that he was aware that "fair adjustment practices are part of Linden's operation.") The first word in a formal list (introduced by a colon) may also be capitalized.

Nouns (name words) tend to be especially important to the understanding of what is written. To emphasize this fact, the Germans have made it a rule to capitalize all nouns. English practice has been to capitalize some nouns and not others. Although it is more in conformity with the general rule of capitalizing for clearness or emphasis to capitalize only the nouns used in a special sense, it is frequently difficult to distinguish between proper and common nouns; hence the central difficulty in capitalization. Names of particular places and things are capitalized: Robert Jones, Mrs. Jones, John and Mary, Professor Wilson, J. Edgar Hoover, Director of the Federal Bureau of Investigation, Marshall Field & Co., the *New York Times*, The American National Bank. With none of the foregoing should you have any difficulty, except possibly the last. Some newspapers do not capitalize *bank*, and *the* is not always capitalized even when part of the name. It is, however, advisable to adhere strictly to the style shown on the letterhead or other communication of each particular business organization when using its name in a business letter or a publication. Points of the compass are capitalized if they represent specific geographical sections (East is East and West is West; cotton grows chiefly in the South), but not otherwise. Seasons of the year are not capitalized unless they are personified. For example, "Grass turns green in the spring," but, "The gentle spirit of Spring breathed life into the flowers."

There are several kinds of multiple-word names including titles of books, articles, pamphlets, and the like that have the first word and all the important words capitalized, that is, all words other than conjunctions, prepositions, and articles. Thus: *The Last of the Mohicans*, "The Airplane of the Future," "Crop Rotation in the Southwest." Names of ships, buildings, firms, and educational institutions come under this rule.

The words for many articles named for countries, cities, and persons have become so common that they no longer require capitals: chinaware, para rubber, astrakhan, maltese cat, graham flour, arabic and roman numbers. But it is still Idaho potatoes and Florida oranges, and this usage applies when referring to a product named for any state regardless of where the article is produced. The tendency is toward fewer capitals. Remember this rule, "Be sure if you can, but if in doubt, don't." [4]

---

[4] The exercises at the end of the chapter will enable you and your instructor to cover capitalization more thoroughly. For a fuller discussion see *Webster's Seventh New Collegiate Dictionary*, p. 1204, or a good composition handbook.

SPELLING (RIGHT WRITING)

The learned term for *spelling* is the Greek word *orthography*, which means *right writing*. Early writers in English used this term in discussing the subject, but were divided in their opinions as to how important uniformity in spelling was. There are still some who feel that complete standardization is unnecessary; even the dictionaries allow an occasional variant form. Although educators assure us (a comfort to poor spellers) that there is little correlation between ability to spell and general intelligence, we must realize that bad spelling in business letters is not good business. At best, it risks distracting the reader's attention from the message of the letter to the letter itself, and this violates our basic rule that the business letter should get, not attention, but results.

Some persons become fatalistic about spelling. They make the excuse, "I was always a poor speller." They are not altogether to be blamed; spelling is much harder for some than for others, for reasons which we shall briefly consider. But let's not give up. Anyone who seriously wants to achieve "right writing" can do a lot about it.

Persons who spell easily are endowed with good visualization, or mental photography. They see words clearly and retain a good image; hence they are able to speak or write them correctly. But some persons' minds won't photograph clearly, and nothing seems to make them fully dependable, although cultivating a habit of looking at difficult words more carefully when reading, then glancing away from the page to see if the image is clear, will help enormously.

There are a number of ways to improve one's spelling, besides this basic way of reading with spelling in mind. Training of the *ear* ranks perhaps next to training of the *eye*, though English is so far from phonetic that anyone who spells by sound alone will make numerous errors.[5] Nevertheless, careful attention to the sounds of words will help a great deal.

[5] In the early days of our nation, such patriotic Americans as Benjamin Franklin (1706–90) and Noah Webster (1758–1843) gave much thought to the idea of a distinct American language, characterized especially by a highly phonetic spelling. Webster is known today chiefly as the "father of the dictionary," the first complete edition of which appeared in 1828, but he was better known in the nineteenth century for his "blue back speller," of which more than 75,000,000 copies have been sold. At one time he advocated the following kind of spelling: "I very early discuvered, that altho the name of an old and respectable karacter givs credit and consequence to hiz ritings, yet the name of a yung man is often prejudicial to his performances. By conceeling my name, the opinions of men hav been prezerved from an undu bias arizing from personal prejudices, the faults of the ritings hav been detected, and their merit in public estimation ascertained." Quoted in F. L. Pattee, *The First Century of American Literature* (New York: Appleton-Century-Crofts, Inc., 1935), p. 176. Later, however, he decided to settle for such mild, and plainly sensible, reforms as dropping the *u* from words like *favour* and *honour,* and using *er* instead of *re* in *center* and *theater.*

Of the numerous rules for spelling, at least a few are worth learning, especially if one thinks them through to see *why*, as well as *how*, they work. Everyone has met the jingle

> *i* before *e* except after *c*
> or when sounded like *a*
> as in *neighbor* and *weigh*.

It is well worth knowing, for it should prevent misspelling such common words as *receive* and *relieve*, and it has only a few exceptions, notably *seize*, *weird*, and *leisure*.

Useful too are some rules involving pronunciation. Most of us learn pronunciation chiefly by imitation; that is, we hear the words spoken by persons who presumably know how to sound them, and then we say them the same way. How do you make sure of sounds if you have no opportunity to hear the word? You have learned, probably, that good dictionaries print a key at the bottom of each page, where common words illustrate the sounds of letters with the various markings. By comparing the sound in the key with the marking on the doubtful word, you can usually figure it out. It would be more efficient of course to know the meaning of the marks; and this you can learn by studying the key at length, or better still, the discussion of pronunciation in the front of the dictionary.

For good spelling it is particularly important to know certain facts and rules about sounds, which oddly enough most persons are never really taught. An open syllable is one ending with a vowel, as *la* in *la-bel*. A closed syllable ends with a consonant, as *lat* in *lat-tice*. In an open accented syllable the sound of the vowel is normally long, in closed syllables short. But if only one consonant follows the vowel and another vowel then follows (including final *e*), the vowel is still long, as in *fate*. Why? The philologists know, but the explanation is complicated. All that matters to us is that our language *works that way*, and that knowledge of this fact helps us in spelling when we come to learning and applying the following long but very useful rule:

> Words of one syllable or accented on the last syllable, ending in one consonant preceded by one vowel, double the consonant before adding an ending beginning with a vowel.

Why do we add an *r* before the *ed* in *occurred?* Because to be logical, with only one *r*, we would have to pronounce the *u* as in *cured*. That is, we complicate spelling to keep pronunciation as simple, or consistent, as possible. Why do we not double the *r* in *secured?* The *u* was already long in *secure* because of the final *e*. Why has *traveled* replaced *travelled?* Because since the word is accented on the first syllable, pronunciation of the first *e* is not affected by the ending. Most persons can remember rules much better when they understand the reason back of them.

Here's another useful rule involving pronunciation:

> In words ending in *ce* or *ge*, the *e* is dropped before endings beginning with *i* or *e* and retained before endings beginning with *a*, *o*, or *u*.

To apply this rule, we must know that *c* is soft (sounds like *s*) before *i* or *e*, and hard (like *k*) before *a*, *o*, or *u*. And *g* before *i* or *e* is sounded like *j*; before *a*, *o*, or *u*, like *guh* (as in *gate*). So we have *servicing*, but *serviceable; encouraging*, but *courageous*.

Perhaps the trickiest of all letters in spelling is *c*. As the final letter of a syllable it is regularly sounded *k*; at the beginning, it is either *s* or *k* as indicated in the preceding paragraph. Only in combination with *h* (as in *church*) does it have something of an independent sound. Suppose you heard a word which sounded like *flăk-sĭd*. How would you spell it? How do you pronounce *succeed*? Isn't it *sŭk-sēd*? The first *c* is the final *k* sound; the second the *s* sound before *e*. The new word, then, you rightly guess, is spelled *flaccid*. And what do you do if you want to use *traffic* or *picnic* as a verb in the past tense? You could add a *k* to keep the sound unchanged before the *ed* ending. And of course that is exactly what is done.

Students who have taken courses in vocabulary building or the history of the English language know that etymology can be of great aid in the spelling of some words. If one knows that *tele* in *telephone* or *telegraphy* was a Greek root meaning *far*, he will have no trouble with the fourth letter of these words. Knowing *sacrilegious* comes from *sacrilege*, not *religious*, prevents misspelling this frequently troublesome word.

There are many other rules for spelling, but I doubt that it is worth while to introduce any more here. We do need to say a word about hyphenation and syllabication, although for full discussion of these points it is best to go to the dictionary.

HYPHENATION AND SYLLABICATION

The hyphen is occasionally used in long compound nouns as a sort of intermediate stage in the transformation from two short words to one longer one. Some few complicated words continue to be hyphenated, for example, the "in-law" words like *mother-in-law*. Words like *lifeboat*, *baseball*, and *businessman* are now written solid. The majority of nouns pass directly from the two-word to the one-word stage. Hyphens are preferably used, however, in compound adjectives preceding nouns: *well-turned* phrase, *hard-working* student, *dark-colored* glasses. But, "His phrases were well turned." Compounds including *self* regularly use the hyphen: *self-educated* man.

The hyphen is also the mark used in words broken at the end of a line, to let the reader know at once that the word is unfinished (*far* is a word, also the first syllable in *farther* and *farrow*). Break words only *between syllables* (consulting the dictionary if necessary). Also, do not leave a one-letter syllable alone at the end of a line, and preferably not a two-letter one; and avoid breaking words in successive lines, as this gives the letter a displeasing appearance.

WHAT MAKES GOOD USAGE?

The grammar books do not make good usage; the college professors do not make it. Good usage is the language appropriate to the job of communication that has to be done: appropriate to the subject, to the audience, to the speaker or writer. What might be good usage in one situation might be very poor usage in another; a college student who used meticulous "literary" English in a lively discussion of the pennant race at his fraternity house, for instance, would seem as out of place as an ungrammatical article in the *Atlantic Monthly*. The kind of good usage we talk about in writing classes is the language of letters and reports, of articles in *Life* and *Fortune:* the careful language of well-educated men and women who are trying to communicate clearly and precisely. It is necessary for you to learn to use that careful language well, for you will need to use it daily in your work and in many important ways outside your work.

GOOD USAGE CHANGES

Good usage is not something you can learn once and forget about; it changes constantly. For the rest of your life you will need to keep a watch on usage so that your language will not become dated or old-fashioned.

RÉSUMÉ ON IMPORTANCE OF THE FUNDAMENTALS

Into the good business letter must go good grammar, correct punctuation, proper capitalization, and correct spelling. The ideal, of course, is to learn these fundamentals sufficiently well that you can face business writing problems as jobs, with all your mental energies free to dispatch them properly and efficiently. Even when you progress to where you are dictating your letters to stenographers or dictaphones, it will still be a great satisfaction, and a necessary precaution, to be able to check the details before attaching your signature.

If you still have trouble with these fundamentals after studying them more or less systematically for many years, you may wonder whether mastery of them is possible for you. The answer is here: *There is no rule in grammar, punctuation, capitalization, or spelling, that you cannot learn, and learn to apply, in twenty minutes.* And since most persons are troubled by only a few rules, they need make no systematic review of grammar from beginning to end; they need only to come to a showdown with the rules that bother them, one at a time, until they have learned them all. There is no short cut, no way to learn them all at once.

A Poet Speaks to Businessmen *

by BARRISS MILLS

In this article I hope to show that poetry has something useful and practical to say to the businessman. I shall not argue that reading poetry will necessarily make him a better businessman, or enable him to make more money, although this may well be true. I *will* argue that anything which helps us, as men and women first and businessmen or poets afterward, to live more fully, with greater awareness of what it means to be alive, is useful and practical in human terms. This is precisely what poetry can do.

At this point, I am going to forget the businessman, except to realize that he is reading this article to see just what poetry does mean, and that he can make his own judgment as to whether he can draw from it. And I am going to deal with poetry as specifically as possible, avoiding vague words, such as "culture," which poets distrust at least as much as businessmen do. Such words may mean much or little, depending on what they refer to, and poets try to be as hardheaded about the meanings of words as businessmen are supposed to be about their dollars and cents.

In fact, the main thing poets have to say to us concerns words and the ways of looking at experience which are reflected in them. For the poet is primarily a user of words. Everything he sees and hears, everything he thinks and feels, is filtered through the words that make up his poems. As a result, he has an almost religious respect for words and the human values they represent.

The poet knows that words have power to shape men's minds—to give meanings, whether false or true, to what men see and hear. But others know this, too, and use the language to shape men's thinking in ways that the poet cannot condone.

What Do We Live For?

The dominant motives of our time seem to be economic, political, and technological. Money power, political power, and the power of science and technics loom largest in the nation and the world today, and the men who are listened to by society are the men who manipulate such power successfully.

Perhaps this has always been true. But in our society a new power has been added, or an old power strengthened incredibly—the power of mass communications, through newspapers, magazines, radio, and television, to make men's minds, and their very lives, conform to these dominant motives.

* This article from the *Harvard Business Review*, September–October, 1960, pp. 103–106, is used here by permission of the author and the publisher.

Dr. Mills's poetry has appeared in numerous literary magazines. His two volumes of poetry, *The Black and White Geometry* (1955) and *Parvenus and Ancestors* (1959), were published by The Sparrow Press. A translation of *The Idylls of Theokritos* (1963) was published by Purdue University Studies.

If money and status have always been the measure of successful living for many men, they seem now, to judge from the advertisements, the commercials, and most of the editorials and magazine articles, to have become the measure of life for all men and women—attainable in some degree by everyone in the impending earthly paradise where everyone has a new house, a new car, a new washing machine, and a solid place in the New Suburbia.

But the poet has always rejected the notion that money and status—or cash balances, referendums, and production curves—are the real measure of living. He considers them at best peripheral and at worst antithetical to the essential human experience. Business, politics, technology are ways of dealing with men and things en masse. Men and things become units rather than individuals. They lose their identities in vast manipulations that become more and more impersonal as they grow in size and importance.

For the poet, these mass manipulations of men and things, and particularly the growing tendency to consider such manipulations the norms or even the goals of human existence, are genuinely shocking.

To the poet, each individual life should be an adventure—a succession of discoveries—from the day we are born into this fascinating world till the day we leave it. The poet insists we should experience life over again daily—seeing, hearing, touching, and savoring life as it is lived in all its moods and weathers.

He may find more to interest him, as a poet, in the way a patch of sunlight settles in a winter tree, or the way a child takes its first steps along the earth, or the way dogs bark at an old woman carrying groceries home in a basket, than in summit meetings, or steel strikes, or the race for the moon.

We might almost say the poet ignores the "larger" issues in favor of significant *moments* in the human experience as it is lived and has always been lived since man became man.

In the Beginning the Word

The chief means by which the poet tries to uphold the eternal human verities in the face of society's preoccupation with substitutes for living is the preservation and extension of the ordinary language of men and women. This point needs emphasis because of the common misconception that poetry uses a special language of its own—something called "poetic diction." It is true that poetry does not use language in the same *way* as ordinary speech. Poetry is heightened language—a rigorous selection of words intensified by rhythms, sound patterns, metaphors, and by other formal elements. But the basic ingredients are the words of everyday speech, and the advent of an artificial "poetic diction" marks the loss of vitality in poetry. Almost every new poetic movement begins with rejection of "poetic diction" and a return to the everyday speech of men and women.

In working with the ordinary language of society, poetry differs from science, which has created its own language of mathematics and its own technical vocabulary.

The method of science is to abstract from experience its least common denominators—the qualities which are general, measurable, and predictable. Thus science arrives at truths for which a kind of universal testimony can be given, based on exact and impersonal measurement or controlled experiment. Water always flows downhill, at a rate determined by the slope of the incline, subject to certain variations in the depth or width of the riverbed. The color of the water, the setting of the stream, the sunlight dancing on the ripples, the mood of the observer—these have no interest for the scientist because of their idiosyncratic nature. But they are the chief concern of the poet.

Mathematics and the technical vocabulary of science are language purged of the richness and color of the senses, the complex associations of history, the irrationalities of the individual human experience. As such, they are tremendously powerful instruments for certain purposes—so very powerful they seem almost to have got beyond human control.

The Language of Poetry

Poetry does not use "purified" language, but rather the words we all use more haltingly, with more of a sprawl, to muddle through whatever we have to say. The words are no different; it is the form into which they are put that distinguishes poetry from ordinary prose.

The reason the words are the same is that the truths the poet is seeking are humane truths—truths about the total human experience, and the ordinary language is the richest, the most subtle and sensitive expression of that experience. Thus, the words of science, or of business and politics, are by no means excluded from poetry, for they are part of the total human experience, too.

It is this humanness of the language—the essential honesty and vitality with which it reflects the human condition—that the poet tries to preserve against the corruption of dead and dishonest usages which tend to dehumanize it.

The dead usage of language is the cliché or stereotyped image—jargon and gobbledygook of all kinds, in business, in government, in education, and even in most talk about poetry. The dishonest usage is double talk—the half-truths of propaganda and advertising, of slick politicians and the hard sell.

The cliché and double talk are *not*, for the most part, the language of men and women in everyday life. Poets have always listened carefully to the talk of people in the streets or in their homes: the survivals of ancient speech patterns in their diction, syntax, and pronunciation; their earthy and often original swearwords, vulgar words, and expletives; and especially their slang—new words and new metaphors in the making. It is not so paradoxical as it may seem that most innovations in the language occur either among the poets or among the people. And it should be no surprise that clichés and double talk flourish most among the bureaucrats and promoters, organizations and campaigns, where the human use of language is most obscured.

The assaults of the cliché and double talk on the language are continual and unending, till not only the readers and listeners, at whom they are aimed, but even the perpetrators themselves can be taken in by them. Or the perpetrators may convince themselves that means are justified by ends, and that half-truths (which are of course half-lies) serve the "cause," whatever it may be—the sale of toothpaste and thereby the "economy" and thereby the "national welfare" —better than whole ones.

Truth Is Beauty

The poet believes that corruption of the language is corruption of man's mind and spirit. To the propagandist and adman, words and images are mere counters, to be manipulated for whatever ends the propagandist and adman have in view. But to the poet, words have a character of their own. He loves honest words, hates lying ones. He feels strongly his own commitment to use words only to tell whole truths, or as nearly whole truths as his vision and his skill with words will permit. This commitment is voluntary and "free"; no one pays him for his work, and no one can tell him how to do it.

His quarrel with the propagandist and the adman is that they prostitute language and metaphor—the fundamental image-making quality of poetry—to base purposes. Yet their motives are clear enough. They quite frankly use words as means to ends, and they share society's easy conscience about language. Perhaps, in the poet's view, theirs is a venial sin.

The cardinal sinner is the false poet, or the pseudopoet, whose uses of language and metaphor pass for poetry, and hence for whole truths, though they are really clichés and half-truths after all. People used to ask: "Why isn't Edgar Guest as good a poet as Shakespeare?" The answer is that Guest and others like him are not poets at all, but false poets. They do not even try to get at whole truths.

On the contrary, their purpose is to confirm the clichés and half-truths—the preconceptions and complacencies—which their readers have already come to accept. The false poet's stock in trade is sentimentality—the easy, comfortable smile and the easy, comfortable tear. The false poet seems to deny that man is born to sorrow, that man is bound to die, that we have only one life to live and usually manage to bungle it somehow.

The real poet does not beguile us. He plants new seeds of doubt to undermine our complacency. He urges us to sharper visions of reality and more difficult resolves. He is not a moralist, in the usual meaning of that term. He is almost never an ascetic, and is likely to take a nearly pagan delight in the life of the senses. He is not even an idealist, as a rule, being more likely to trust in people and things than in abstract ideas. Yet he *is* a moralist in his conviction that language must be used to seek the whole truth about the human experience—its terrible as well as its beautiful aspects.

Telling the whole truth—even the small part of it any of us is able to comprehend—is very hard. Perhaps it is impossible. And it engenders in the poet a paradoxical attitude toward language and toward poetry itself. He is both a conservator of old uses of language and an experimenter with new ones.

Fusing Past and Present

The poet loves the color and taste and feel of old words—the common words worn smooth with the rubbings of everyday use, and the uncommon words encrusted with centuries of human history. But he needs new words, or new meanings for old words. The language as he receives it is a marvelous heritage.

But he cannot merely spend it, like a prodigal, or hoard it, like the servant in the parable of the talents. He must use it and add to it by discovering new ways of getting at the rich, varied truth about the human enterprise.

Poets are on the cutting edge of language as it reaches out to include new things, or new ways of looking at old things. This is a paradox. Nothing is more essentially conservative than language or poetry. Nothing of the past is really lost to the language. New meanings and new metaphors are piled, like geological strata, on old meanings and metaphors. Even the literal, dictionary meanings of words are, for the most part, fossilized metaphors. And words are constantly being formed into new metaphors, which shape men's ways of looking at experience.

New poetry does not supersede old poetry. Homer, Sophocles, the poets of the Bible, and Shakespeare are still the greatest poets. No new poet hopes to equal them, much less surpass them. But the greatest poets of the past are not enough. Their language is not quite our language; their experience not quite our experience. We live in the present, on the cutting edge of time—and we need *our* poets to shape the language to present needs.

Out of the poet's use of words and metaphors come larger images, sometimes called myths, which attempt to catch the essential character of present-day experience, and to relate that to the past and what the myths of the past tell us about the human venture. And when the poet is prophetic, he creates myths of a better life, or a fuller one, than now seems possible to us.

Finally, the poet pits his images or myths against the countermyths of business, or politics, or technology, or whatever are the dominant motives of society —to expose the hollowness of those slogans and shibboleths which misdirect our energies or lull us into complacency. Thus the poet tries to make us alive to all the possibilities of living as a human being, not merely the prospects that society's spokesmen, official or self-appointed, hold up to us.

The poet will always fail to attain the completeness of vision and thought and feeling which is his goal. The bad poet may fail utterly. But the better poet will put together a few words, a few images which will enable us to see our lives in a new way.

And if the poet is very good, his words will be listened to not only in his own time but afterward. Those bits of the real truth he manages to utter will never die.

Because of their pertinence to the editorial philosophy of one of the better business magazines, two "editors' notes" that accompanied the foregoing article are included here. Although brief, the comments also serve as examples of style that you may well study.

The most recent prescriptions for remedying the ills of business education, as embodied in the Ford and Carnegie reports, call for heavy doses of the humanities, and of the language arts in particular. These studies decry the narrow, vocational orientation of the traditional business school curricula. Both hold that the modern businessman must be a person of broader outlook and culture than his predecessor in the commercial world of yesterday. Thus do the humanities enter, like the Marines, to save the situation.

Perhaps in the long run such a shift in business education will create an average businessman who is interested in poetry and the other arts. Perhaps greater leisure, coupled with broader education, will foster in our nation, as it has in other times and places, a cultural renaissance. In the meantime, the businessman born the proverbial thirty years too soon may ask himself what he has been missing, and whether an art such as poetry has something of value to offer him today.—*The Editors*

From time to time in coming issues, HBR will ask men who have distinguished themselves in the various fields of religion, medicine, politics, science, law, and art to tell us quite frankly what they think of business and businessmen. In these messages drawn from unique experiences and differing viewpoints, there will be sharp criticism as well as praise for HBR readers to think about, accept, or reject.—*The Editors*

Exercises and Problems in Communication

1. Rewrite the letter of the First State Corporation (page 85), correcting all errors of detail. You may be dissatisfied with your results, since the letter is so badly planned that correction of structural faults will still not fit it for the mails, but we must first concentrate on fundamentals, reserving general planning and sentence structure until later.

2. In the following sentences choose the preferred form:

A. 1. The manager, as well as the president, (feel) (feels) sure that he knows which plans are best.
2. Each one of the clerks (was) (were) asked for an opinion.
3. Every one of the copies (has) (have) been proofread.
4. None of the employees (was) (were) allowed at the meeting.
5. There (is) (are) always a large number of orders at this time of year.
6. Jones is one of those department heads who (is) (are) a pleasure to be associated with.
7. (Are) (Is) either of the vice-presidents going to be here?
8. A number of employees (is) (are) on the policy committee.
9. The number of employees on the committee (is) (are) negligible.
10. The majority of the officers (is) (are) in favor of the change.

B. 1. The card was sent to the secretary and (me) (I).
2. Every employee may move ahead as fast as (they) (he) can.
3. Give the message to (whoever) (whomever) answers.
4. Give the message to (whoever) (whomever) you see.
5. Every one of the officers sent (their) (his) best wishes to the retiree.
6. The bonus was given to (us) (we) employees (who) (whom) had put in overtime.
7. He and (I) (myself) were the winners in the sales contest.

8. Please return the forms to her and (me) (myself).
9. Do you object to (his) (him) having charge of the office?
10. Did you think of (me) (my) walking out as a breach of office etiquette?

C. 1. Orders (that come in by ten o'clock) will be filled by noon (that come in by ten o'clock).
2. (Only) (The) (the) personnel manager (only) knows who is being considered for promotion.
3. Having got behind in their schedules, (the orders could not be handled by the shipping clerks) (the shipping clerks could not handle the orders).
4. (Not) (All) (all) employees are (not) eligible for these benefits.
5. If she had (laid) (lain) the memo on the desk, the manager would have found it.
6. The secretary became ill and went to the ladies' lounge to (lay) (lie) down.
7. She (lay) (laid) there for a short time and came back to her desk, feeling better.
8. The foreman (just) asked (just) for (just) a week's leave.
9. I realized that the typist had finished the letters and (went) (had gone) for the day.
10. When he came back from our new plant in Germany, he told us that the country (is) (was) very progressive.

3. Supply all necessary punctuation marks and capital letters:

dear mr bookseller

here is good news the tribunes famous literary supplement book week is now available for separate subscription at the low rate of $2.00 per year 52 weekly issues

originally conceived as a means of supplying tribune readers with truthful reporting in the field of book news book week caught on from its first issue enthusiastic readers spread the word that here was something new and different in the way of book reviews much better than the two we have here in new york its honesty and midwestern approach are unbelievably refreshing at last we are no longer dependent upon the east for our basis of criticism

in a short time book week which had started out just as another service to tribune readers found itself being regarded far and wide as a major contribution to the nations culture

and so despite many selfish reasons for not doing so we are now offering book week as a separate publication at a price that puts it within easy reach booksellers will find ample use for its truthful informative reports on current books as they are released thats why we are writing you now to suggest that you send us your check today for your copies of the next 52 issues of book week or we'll bill you later if you prefer

book week will save you time help you to keep informed about all
fields of literature provide you with the kind of reading you
will personally enjoy subscribe now

> sincerely

> for book week

p s if there are literary or discussion groups in your community
please send us the names and addresses of the leaders we
should like to make this same offer available to them thank
you

4. The following list of words was used recently in a spelling contest for public-school children. It eliminated all but 8 of 95 entrants. Many of the words are used in business communication. Master them for future use.

antique	noticeable	foursome	sieve
crochet	occurrence	celluloid	conceive
hoping	grievous	rivalry	menagerie
plunging	glossary	initial	eighth
collar	camouflage	annual	optician
abscess	lovable	treacherous	icicle
pageant	syllable	croquet	irrigate
feasible	smoky	martyr	seceded
curable	leopard	dirigible	parallel
privilege	heifer	shriek	reservoir
scheme	cozily	leisure	neuter
molasses	durable	assessor	column

These seven words gave the most difficulty: curable, camouflage, foursome, hoping, smoky, noticeable, and feasible. Note that three of the seven come under pronunciation rules discussed in this chapter; hence they should give you no further trouble.

5. Write a letter to the editors of the *Harvard Business Review*, agreeing or disagreeing with Barriss Mills's thesis that, as the editors wrote, "advertising, public relations, and propaganda conspire to tarnish man's greatest achievement —his ability to communicate honestly and sincerely."

6. Examine six magazines—general, business, and technical—to find advertisements using poetry as an attention getter. Report orally to the class your reactions to the effectiveness of the usage. Keeping in mind the advantages of concreteness, use specific examples from the ads to maintain your audience's attention and to support your opinions.

7. From Mills's article, do you think he would approve of using poetry in advertising? Discuss the point, according to your instructor's assignment.

8. Examine several issues of *Vital Speeches,* to see how speakers use literary references to support points in their presentations. Report your findings in either written or oral form, according to your instructor's assignment.

9. Discuss Mills's use of those figures of speech mentioned in Chapter 6 in connection with development of a business vocabulary.

10. In this list of "spelling demons," or words frequently misspelled, notice how many of the difficult words offer no trouble to the person who has related spelling to pronunciation and word origins. Study the words for mastery, according to your instructor's assignment.

accommodate	benefited	arctic	parliament
occasion	grievous	misspelled	advice
diphtheria	maintenance	prairie	pneumonia
laryngitis	trafficked	thereabouts	villain
professor	impromptu	acknowledge	Philippines
divine	personnel	rheumatism	supersede
beginning	separate	pachyderm	outrageous
hypocrisy	achievement	battalion	ecstasy
sacrilegious	chloroform	embarrass	dictionary
restaurant	hullabaloo	laboratory	surprise
accumulate	permissible	criticize	pursuing
necessary	mischievous	February	
guardian	capillaries	recommend	

5

Business Sentences
and Paragraphs

True ease in writing comes from art not chance,
As those move easiest who have learn'd to dance.
'Tis not enough no harshness gives offence,
The sound must seem an echo to the sense.—
ALEXANDER POPE, "Essay on Criticism"

For good business writing, it is absolutely necessary that sentences be correct in form and appropriate in effect. And every college teacher knows that a student may accumulate the credits necessary for graduation from high school, or even college, without being able to write clear, pleasing, and vigorous sentences.[1]

WHAT IS A SENTENCE?

Composition texts tell us something like, "A sentence is a group of words in which a predicate is combined with a subject to express a single complete thought." If you have never learned such a definition it will be well worth your while to memorize this one.

Checking the derivation of the word helps too. *Sentence* comes from Latin *sententia,* meaning opinion or maxim. We may think of it as the changing of a little fragment of thought material into an impulse, which can be moved as a thought from one mind to other minds. Chaucer and

---

[1] For excellent discussions of sentence structure, longer than can be given here, see Norman G. Shidle, *Clear Writing for Easy Reading* (New York: McGraw-Hill Book Co., 1951), Chapter 8; or Rebecca Hayden, Aurora Haggard, and Dorothy Pilgrim, *Mastering American English* (Englewood Cliffs, N.J.: Prentice-Hall, Inc., 1956).

Shakespeare spoke of "high sentence," signifying expression weighted with meaning.

Still another way to think of sentences is to visualize them as portions of the wires in an armature or an electrical transmission line. If they are made of good material, well drawn to a good pattern, and well connected, there will be a good circuit; the electricity will pass without burning out the connections and causing fires, and without a high loss of potential resulting from resistance. Thought, like electricity, must travel a good circuit, and without good sentences there cannot be a good circuit.

"Connection failures" in writing are caused by many different oversights, a number of them discussed in Chapter 4. Circuits are broken within sentences by such carelessness as (1) danglers, (2) vague reference, (3) inaccurate tense, and (4) misplaced modifiers. The following examples will illustrate these shortcomings:

1. Being self-curing, and needing no heat or pressure for solidification, you can readily see Quikmont's great convenience and time-saving factors.
2. The manager said that Mr. Lyon discussed the problem with Mr. Coran and that he asked them to consider other aspects of it before making the report.
3. We sold the last copy of *The Boom Years* before we received your order.
4. We only want a few hundred bushels.

Good sentences are spoken of also as the sinews which give effective writing its liveliness, its bounce and speed. One of the great masters of English, Henry David Thoreau, said of clarity in sentences, "A sentence should read as if its author, had he held a plow instead of a pen, could have drawn a furrow deep and straight to the end."

You may not see the content of the four sentences just discussed as being "deep," but you will probably see the thoughts as being straight in the following suggested revisions:

1. You can readily see that Quikmont, being self-curing and needing no heat or pressure for solidification, is convenient and time saving.
2. The manager said that Mr. Lyon had discussed the shipping problem with Mr. Coran, who asked Mr. Lyon and the manager to study the problem further before making a report.
3. The last copy of *The Boom Years* had been sold before your order came.
4. We want only a few hundred bushels, *or*
   Only we want a few hundred bushels.

In addition to these four sentence faults, there are the stringy short sentences, which betray the juvenile or immature writer. Some writers misinterpret simplicity for brevity, getting an unevenness into their writing, as in the following, from a "sick report":

The employee became ill. He went to the plant infirmary. Then he was taken to the city hospital.

Although a series of short constructions can be effective, combining the elements here would make for fluency. How would you recast them for ease of reading?

Almost as bad as stringy sentences are the sentences with monotonous or faulty coordination. The writer who uses a larger number of compound sentences in which two clauses again and again are connected by *and, but,* and *for* is only a little more advanced mentally than the one who cannot get beyond a simple sentence. Subordination, however, is more difficult; hence when the writer first graduates into it, he is liable to experience considerable difficulty and make some mistakes. "When we decided not to accept his offer, we had just heard that property values were almost sure to decline in that neighborhood." What is the main idea? What influences what? *When* belongs with the other part of the sentence: "When we heard that property values were almost sure to decline in that neighborhood, we decided not to accept his offer." Sentences should transmit the thought current smoothly, with no breaks, no unnecessary friction.

BASIC SENTENCE FAULTS

Before we talk more about good sentences, it will be advisable to spend a little time making sure that we haven't been writing positively bad sentences. That is, let's look at some of the worst faults in sentence writing so that if we are committing any of these faults, we can proceed to eliminate them.

Although sentences can be of almost any length (from the Biblical "Jesus wept" to John Ruskin's ponderous 300-word creations) as long as they do not violate any of the rules of sentence structure, it is of utmost importance that each should be long enough to accomplish its purpose and no longer.[2] A sentence must contain at least one subject combined with one predicate (except in elliptical sentences like "Close the door," or "Who went?" "John."). If they contain less than this, or if they are introduced by a subordinating connective, we call them fragments, or *period faults:* "while we were considering the offer," "looking for a new filing clerk," "expecting to hear from you before the fifteenth." A form

---

[2] The following intelligible 132-word sentence appeared in a critical review of a television show featuring Barbra Streisand: "But to lose her in a maze of frou frou scenery through which she came flying on gossamer skirt panels—past violins and horns, until she stopped to sing a ballad to a drummer who delicately tapped a series of kettle drums—to have her speak an involved and uninspired piece of dialogue about a button she picked up in a thrift shop—to have her finally settle down before a microphone to offer a bouquet of ballads in the Streisand manner and after one song, to walk her across stage to a stool where she sat for another song only to rise and return to her microphone—all these, among many other devices to alleviate the monotony of a one-woman show, create no milestone in TV entertainment." *Saturday Review,* May 22, 1965, p. 28.

letter of solicitation which I received recently closed with "Appreciating your interest and help in the past and counting on you for this new fiscal year." It is too bad to spoil an otherwise good letter with such a fragment. Most fragments result not so much from ignorance as from carelessness—but the effect on the reader is the same, whatever the cause.

The sister fault of the fragment is the run-on sentence, or *comma splice*. It is perfectly permissible to write compound sentences in which two or more independent clauses are joined, but the joining must be according to the rules; there must be no illicit wedlock. Consider this example: "The first lot was sold June 5, the entire block was gone before the end of the month." What is wrong? This sentence is taken from a passage describing "land office business" in real estate sales. The two clauses are related; they really belong together. The fault is that the comma may not be used alone to join independent clauses (with rare exceptions, which are discussed in composition handbooks). We should use (1) semicolon, or (2) comma plus conjunction, or (3) semicolon plus conjunctive adverb. In the quoted sentence the semicolon alone would probably be best, but notice that *but* plus comma could be used, also semicolon plus *however.* There is also the possibility that a complex sentence, in which the first clause is subordinated through introducing it by *although,* leaving the comma after June 5, might be better than any form of compound sentence. The good writer knows that in many places in writing there are several possibilities and that it takes delicate discrimination to know which is best. First of all, however, the writer must learn *not to break the rules;* if he wants to combine independent clauses, he must learn how the thing can or cannot be done.

BASIC GRAMMATICAL FUNCTIONS IN SENTENCES

Getting a clear conception of the grammatical parts of a sentence and their functions is much more helpful than an ability to recite glib definitions of the eight parts of speech (nouns, pronouns, verbs, adjectives, adverbs, prepositions, conjunctions, interjections).

Functionally there are four, not eight, parts of speech:

    I. The name words (nouns and pronouns—substantives)
        A. The nominative case
            1. Subjects of verbs
            2. Predicate nominative (subjective or attribute complement)
            3. Miscellaneous functions (appositives, direct address, nominative absolute)
        B. The objective case
            1. Direct objects of verbs, prepositions, gerunds, infinitives, and participles
            2. Indirect objects

3. Some appositives
4. Subject of infinitive
II. The action words
A. Verbs
B. Verbals (participles, gerunds, infinitives)
III. Modifying, or limiting, words
A. Adjectives (modifying nouns, pronouns, or their equivalents)
B. Adverbs (modifying verbs, adjectives, other adverbs, or equivalent phrases or clauses)
IV. The linking, or joining, words
A. Conjunctions (the link words, phrases, or clauses)
B. Prepositions (they join a noun or pronoun, called the object, to something else in the sentence, the resulting phrase functioning as a noun, adjective, or adverb)

It is apparent from the foregoing outline that the four functional parts of speech—name words, action words, modifying words, and linking words—include seven of the eight classes of words that are traditionally listed as parts of speech. They do not include interjections because these have no real grammatical function.

Our best devices for analyzing words and phrases are the two following questions: (1) Is one word functioning separately, or is it part of a group of words functioning as one? (2) Which of the four functional parts of speech am I dealing with?

THE THREE BASIC PRINCIPLES OF COMPOSITION

Sherman Perry, in *Let's Write Good Letters*, rephrases the old terms *unity, coherence,* and *emphasis.* I like his way of putting it:

> Make your letter have *oneness.*
> *Make it stick together.*
> Make it have *thrust.*

Whether you call it unity or oneness, you should apply the principle to every sentence you write. Each sentence must have only *one main point;* there is seldom room for two different kinds of ideas in one sentence.

You can make your sentence stick together by putting the words in logical order and by showing how the parts of a sentence are related to each other. Coordination, subordination, and parallelism are the result of applying logic to sentence building; all three may be aids to coherence. In addition, coherence helps to warn the reader of unexpected changes in the direction of your thought. If you say, "I don't believe we should have lower taxes, and I think the tax should be removed from gasoline," your reader will feel that you are contradicting yourself; replacing "and" by "however" would establish the relationship for the reader.

Emphasis or thrust can be obtained by using simple, straightforward sentence structure and readable words that the reader can take at full stride. The traditional means of emphasis include repeating key words, using contrast, building to a climax, and building suspense. Use of these four devices for emphasis is illustrated in the sentences below:

Repetition: Buy now! *Buy* now for the cold months ahead! Buy *now* before stock is limited! *Buy now* at reduced prices!

Contrast: This insecticide is highly effective, yet safe.

Climax: The stock in one case was damaged slightly, but a second case was worse, and the third—even the case was ruined.

Suspense: Successful management—and many managers overlook this point —depends on sympathetic attitude toward employees.

THE LOGIC OF SENTENCE CONSTRUCTION

Ideas do not always come to a person as sentences, logically constructed, arranged in proper order. Rather, ideas tend to come at random, useful ones mixed in with quite irrelevant ones, important ones and unimportant ones mixed together, some rather fully expressed and others merely snatches of thought, some not concepts at all but merely pictures or impressions. Sentences and paragraphs are quite literally "constructed" from these random ideas.

Suppose I begin to write a note to cancel an appointment. As I pick up pencil and paper the following pictures and concepts come into my mind:

I won't be able to meet you this afternoon . . .

I should give the reason . . .

I'm going to meet a friend . . . (visual image of Mr. X, carrying a brief case).

How is it going to sound if I cancel an appointment with one friend just to meet another friend?

I'll have to show that it is business . . .

It's urgent because Mr. X is leaving town tonight . . .

I wonder whether I should offer Mr. X dinner . . . (visual image of rushing to catch a train, impression of confusion).

No . . .

Which of these ideas can I use in my note? Unconsciously I discard most of them as irrelevant, evaluate the rest, and write, "I won't be able to meet you this afternoon because I have to see Mr. X on business before he leaves town tonight."

This process of sorting out and evaluating ideas should be almost automatic; it is so basic and so easy. Yet most of us do a kind of half-way job of it—the kind of half-way job of brick-laying I would do if I mixed some mortar in a bucket and started to build a garden wall in my strictly amateur way.

If we were to stop to figure out sentence construction by ourselves we could readily recognize that all the ideas which go into sentences are not of equal importance: they couldn't be. And since they are of unequal importance, it might be helpful for us, as we study them, to tag each one mentally with a name or code of some kind to show their relative importance. We might call the most important idea in a group of ideas "A"—an "A" idea. The least important ideas which are still worth keeping would be "D" ideas, and the ones in between would be "B" and "C" ideas.

Now, the type of structure that we have available in the sentence to give to each idea can also be rated in order of importance; the most important, of course, is the independent clause.

"A" structure:	independent clause
"B" structure:	dependent clause
"C" structure:	phrase infinitive
	participial
	prepositional
"D" structure:	word modifier adverb
	adjective

Reduced to its basic principle, good sentence structure means that in order to show the reader that the "A" idea is the most important, we give it the "A" structure in the sentence, and so on down to "D" structure for the "D" idea.

In following this principle logically we will, when we have an "A" idea and a "B" idea, give the "B" idea subordinate structure in the sentence; we will give it "B" structure to show that it is less important than the "A" idea. And in so doing we will be using *subordination*.

When we have two "A" ideas or two "B" ideas, it would be only fair to give them equal structure: in other words, to use *coordination*. The coordinate conjunction which joins two ideas of equal importance serves as an equals sign to the reader to establish the relationship of the ideas.

CLASSIFICATIONS OF SENTENCES

Grammatically, sentences are classified as simple, compound, complex, and compound-complex, on the basis of the number of independent and dependent clauses they contain. Rhetorically, sentences are classified generally as loose and periodic. Rhetoric, the art of writing, also concerns itself with such special structures as parallelism, the balanced structure (antithesis), and climax (ascending and descending order).

I don't know why we haven't another term instead of loose sentence, for the word *loose* is so generally used unfavorably (loose nuts or connections, loose discipline, loose morals) that nine persons out of ten instinctively think of a loose sentence as a bad sentence. Actually, a *loose sentence* is merely one that is substantially complete, or makes sense, at one or more places before the end, as in "The sales manager talked with me while his secretary looked for the new-product file." That the *periodic sentence* has no complete meaning until the end, or period, is shown in "When the sales manager's secretary came back, I left the office." Although in normal writing most sentences are loose, since the periodic sentence tends to be an emphatic form, the average writer should use more periodic sentences than he does.

Sentences are said to have *parallel structure* if the same or similar grammatical structures are used for logically equivalent thought elements; that is, phrase against phrase, clause against clause, consistency in voice and tense. "Harry Greene is our best collection letter writer, and some good sales letter writing jobs have also been turned out by him" is not parallel. You will agree that the shift in the second part to passive voice is awkward and ineffective. "Harry Greene is our best collection letter writer, and he has also turned out some good sales letters" is more natural and effective, hence better rhetoric. Stricter parallelism would require the use of *has been* instead of *is* in the first clause, but strict grammatical parallelism is less to be insisted on than substantial, or logical, parallelism.

When parallelism is especially neat, we get the *balanced structure:* "We learn to drive automobiles, but we forget to enjoy our walks." Where contrast rather than comparison is implied, as here, we call the balanced structure *antithesis.* Parallelism has a limited amount of use in either general writing or business writing; too much of it hammers on the ear and becomes tiresome or annoying. In business writing, especially sales writing, however, its judicious use is highly effective. It is well to remember that some of the greatest masters of English prose, notably Edmund Burke, Thomas B. Macaulay, and Abraham Lincoln, used a great deal of parallelism, including balance and antithesis.

SOME POPULAR MISCONCEPTIONS

Before concluding our discussion of sentences, we should deal briefly with certain misconceptions that you may have cherished because your earlier teachers had to simplify some of the rules, knowing that you weren't yet ready for the exceptions.

Is it wrong to end a sentence with a preposition? Most of the time it is, but for rhetorical rather than grammatical reasons. Most prepositions are small words, with little more than a linking function. Since we know that the emphatic spots in a sentence normally are the beginning and the end, we know we should have at the end something more important than a preposition. The best writers, however, recognize that it is sometimes desirable to emphasize prepositions, and they do not hesitate to put them at the end if rhetorically they belong there. Observe these examples:

What do we educate for?

Is it the nearness to the school that you object to?

The soil out of which such men as he are made is good to be born on, good to live on, good to die for and to be buried in.[3]

Another grade school rule which we have outgrown is that sentences should never begin with the coordinating conjunctions *and, but,* and *for.* Grade school teachers often forbid children to begin sentences thus, but this is simply because children are addicted to stringing thoughts together loosely with these conjunctions. Although mature writers do not frequently begin sentences with them, they feel at liberty to do so whenever a smoother or more firmly knit structure results. This you can readily check by examining articles in the *Atlantic Monthly, Harper's,* or the *Saturday Review.* Occasionally it is even desirable to begin the first sentence in a new paragraph with a conjunction, especially *for,* as the best transition from what has been discussed to what is to follow. Consider these examples: "But when these 200 suits are gone, we can get no more; so . . ." "And you will exclaim too when you taste the crispy goodness of . . ." "For the lasting satisfaction of our customers is our watchword at all times."

Much disputed is the use of the split infinitive; that is, the insertion of a modifier between *to* and the verb in such a sentence as, "In order to successfully meet competition, we must reduce our prices on these two items immediately." This sentence would be smoother and at least as effective if *successfully* were placed after *competition.* Very seldom is there either necessity or advantage in splitting an infinitive, but there is no logical reason why the construction is wrong, and some good modern writers occasionally use it when there is a gain in either clearness or emphasis.

A final point in our discussion of misconceptions is the use of *repetition.* Repetition is either good or bad. It is bad when one word is repeated simply because the writer is too careless or word-poor to supply a synonym which will be more pleasing or do the job more exactly. It is good when it is intentional and hammers home an idea. And it is well to remember that it is always better to repeat than to be misunderstood.

APPLYING THE RULES

Although in college we come to realize that something of the irresponsible enjoyment of childhood is gone forever, it is a satisfaction to grow up. Similarly it is good to learn that the rules of writing are more

---

[3] The last example is from Lowell's address on President Garfield. You will scarcely need to be told to avoid such a piling up as "What did you bring that book for me to be read to out of for?" See Porter G. Perrin, *Writer's Guide and Index to English* (Chicago: Scott, Foresman & Co., 1962), p. 710. This book has an excellent discussion of prepositions, including their use at the end of sentences.

for apprentices than for experts. If Robert Penn Warren or John O'Hara occasionally uses a fragment instead of a sentence, it isn't that he doesn't know better, but that he is an artist who knows that here for once the fragment is right. In other words, after we have thoroughly mastered the rules, we can safely apply their principle rather than strictly their letter. By now you should have so assimilated these rules that they will not be in the way of your writing precisely what you mean. The reader of quantities of business letters may work crossword or jigsaw puzzles for diversion, but he doesn't want to solve puzzles when he faces what purports to be a business letter. The letter as a whole must be clear; the clarity and effectiveness of the whole are to a very large extent a matter of what the sum of the sentences adds up to. More than most writing, business letters must be written so that he who runs may read—and be certain of what he has read.

Paragraphing the Business Letter

We have been saying all along that business English is pretty much ordinary good English adapted to business purposes. The following discussion will be devoted partly to paragraphing in general and partly to the adaptations of paragraph structure to serve the special purposes of business writing.

DEFINITION OF A PARAGRAPH

What is a paragraph? The oldest manuscripts don't have paragraphs, just as they are without punctuation and capitalization. The paragraph is a device to facilitate reading. The word *paragraph* (Greek *para*, beside, *graphein*, to write) meant originally a sign written in the margin to show thought divisions. Composition books still define a paragraph as "a group of sentences which develops a thought." [4]

PARAGRAPH LENGTH

Today paragraphs are not so long as they were in the nineteenth century, when they largely ran from one hundred to three hundred words. In modern magazine writing they are perhaps half that, but in business letters they are usually shorter. The same rules apply to business letter paragraphs as to paragraphs in general, but certain allowances are made in their application. The paragraph may be regarded as a device which has three purposes: (1) to break up the material into units that are logical from the nature of the material itself and from the writer's natural style; (2) to break the material so that it will appear as units readily grasped by

[4] Helpful discussions of paragraph structure and types of paragraphs are found in Williams and Ball, *College Writing* (New York: The Ronald Press Co., 1957), Chapter 7.

the reader; and (3) to break the lines of writing into typographical units that will present a good appearance on a page.

In ordinary writing the first purpose is considered most important. Philosophical material is developed by philosophers in rather long paragraphs; descriptive materials will usually be best in long paragraphs. Mathematical discussions and explanations of scientific materials need, and get, short paragraphs. Seldom in a business letter does the nature of the material suggest a very long paragraph, though one will occasionally still see a two-hundred-word letter written as a single paragraph—but not by a successful business person. Business reports may call for fairly long paragraphs.

The second purpose, consideration of the reader, is a fundamental matter in business writing, as indeed it should be in all writing. The lower the general educational level of readers, the shorter and simpler paragraphs must be, and many business letters go to persons of little education. Newspapers, which cater to all readers, from doctors of philosophy to persons who can barely read at all, always use short paragraphs.

It is apparent that our first two purposes suggest that paragraphs in business letters should be rather short. The writer's task is to present relatively simple material so that the reader can grasp it quickly. Typographical considerations also dictate that the business paragraph be brief. To provide the necessary white space for quick, easy reading, business paragraphs are usually no more than from two to six lines long. Businessmen who read a great many letters learn to take in the contents practically at a glance, but they can do this readily only if the letter is written in brief paragraphs.

CLEAR STRUCTURE IN THE PARAGRAPH

Business paragraphs must be *clear*. Securing clarity is largely a matter of remembering our old friends Unity, Coherence, and Emphasis. If everything in the paragraph clearly belongs there and the thought is developed; if the order of sentences is right, with modifiers correctly placed and pronoun reference clear; and if stress falls where it should, the paragraph is practically certain to be a good one. Topic sentences will usually be the first sentences. When the topic sentence alone makes the thought sufficiently clear to the reader, he can skip to the next paragraph. The successful businessman has assimilated Franklin's "do not squander time." He appreciates your helping him conserve it and holds it against you if he has to puzzle through your paragraphs.

SEQUENCE OF PARAGRAPHS

Strangely enough, even in well-planned letters paragraphs sometimes do not at first fall into the right order. I have composed a draft of a letter that I thought was going nicely, only to discover later that the last or next to the last paragraph would constitute my best opening! Direct-mail firms report that transposing the second and third paragraphs in a letter can make the difference between loss and profit.

As will be more apparent later, in certain types of letters paragraph order is fixed by the nature of the letter. A sales letter, which follows the psychological steps to the sale, must have its attention-getter at the beginning, its action-impeller at the end. Letters acknowledging orders start with a form of "thank you for your order"; application letters may begin with a statement about the job—the position the applicant is applying for, how the applicant knows of an opening, etc.; they end with the request for an interview. The problem of securing effective paragraph sequence in business letters, then, is partly a matter of knowing to what extent sequence is fixed by general requirements, partly a matter of determining a logical development for the individual letter. The idea which must not be missed is that order of paragraphs is extremely important and that even with relatively logical thinkers, it doesn't altogether take care of itself.

HOW GOOD PARAGRAPHS VITALIZE LETTERS

Vitality, or briskness, is characteristic of good business letters. Part of the snappy movement comes from clear, or even clever, transitions between paragraphs. Observe these opening words of the several paragraphs in a letter successfully selling neckties by mail: The young men . . . The original . . . Since I was a boy . . . So, why pay . . . We enclose pictures . . . Wools are also . . . We proudly repeat . . .

Or consider these in a department store letter selling women's shoes: Here's timely . . . Next Monday . . . Here, however . . . Every pair . . . Choose a pair . . . This advance selling . . . You can see that the letter writer is staying awake throughout, and that his paragraph openings prove it to the reader. Always something is happening; the letter has movement; it doesn't go dead. An elaborate list of transitional expressions is not required: the conjunctions *and, but, for;* the demonstratives *this, these;* connectives like *here, next, since, so.*

Sometimes repetition of beginnings with different material following is good. *Time* magazine has these paragraph beginnings in a letter soliciting subscriptions: This year, the news . . . And the news . . . The news is big at home . . . The news is big abroad . . . The news is big in medicine . . . The news is big and exciting . . . And that is why . . . TIME will tell . . . TIME will make . . . Try TIME for . . . Try TIME under . . . Eight months of . . . Won't you Air-mail . . .

Paragraphs should end firmly, just as they should begin challengingly. Often the beginning picks up a word or phrase from the previous ending to help the transition, to keep the thought circuit open and productive.

SPECIAL POINTS IN PARAGRAPHING

Opening and closing paragraphs are nearly always brief; the longest paragraphs come in the middle of the letter. In sales letters the paragraphs are sometimes rather long but are broken up by use of ellipses, which give an illusion of movement and also serve to let daylight into the copy.

We may conclude our discussion of paragraphs with the statement that paragraphing, like capitalization, punctuation, and sentence structure, has always one object: to enable the reader to get the meaning as easily and as certainly as possible. Paragraphing which does this is good; any other kind is not.

Efficient Writing

by W. EARL BRITTON *

Efficient and effective writing depends, in part at least, upon the proper performance of their particular functions by the various parts of speech. The writer who would express himself directly and tersely must decide which of his ideas should be conveyed as nouns, which as verbs, and which as modifiers. Although nouns commonly become verbs, and verbs become nouns or even adjectives—and certainly our language is more flexible as a result—illogical or careless shifts of this sort can be not only ineffective but even obstructive. It is particularly evident that when verbs assume the role of nouns or adjectives, expression often becomes wordy and indirect.

This general notion can be illustrated by the following sentences:

A. Comedy appeals to the intellect.
B. The appeal of comedy is to the intellect.

If context permits the use of either form A or form B, the first has decided advantages over the second. Sentence A, using five instead of eight words, is nearly 37% shorter than B. But the principal advantage of A lies in its subject and verb. Since the writer is talking about *comedy*, it is properly the subject; and since he is saying that it appeals, *appeals* is properly the verb. In B, however, *comedy*, which is the subject of A, is taken out of play and buried in a prepositional phrase, which modifies *appeal*. And the verb *appeals* is sacrificed by conversion into a noun, subject of the sentence; consequently, the sentence must be completed with the ineffective verb *is*, which means little more than the "equals" sign in mathematics. Although context will often require sentences of type B, the greater the proportion of sentences of type A in a manuscript, the more efficient the communication.

* The principles in this reading are basic to all effective communication—speaking, reading, listening, as well as to writing. Dr. Britton, of the Department of English of the University of Michigan since 1936, has consulted with industries on report writing and served as General Editor of *Scientific Writing*, Meta R. Emberger and M. R. Hall (New York: Harcourt, Brace & World, Inc., 1955). The piece, from the *TWE Journal* (Spring, 1956), is used here by permission of Dr. Britton and the Society of Technical Writers and Publishers.

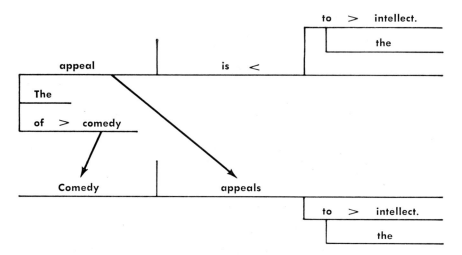

We can focus this principle more sharply by declaring that efficiency of expression depends very largely upon the verb; indeed, as the verb goes, so goes the writing. Ballard says, "The verb is the grammarian's idol. It is to him the light and life of the sentence. . . . The predicate itself—the predicate par excellence—is the verb. And the more meaning the grammarian finds crowded into the verb, the happier he is." [1] A fundamental task of a writer, then, is to protect the verb; in particular, he must be sure that the idea best suited to the verb is expressed in the verb and not lured away into some less effective grammatical form. In the sentence

> Stabilizing a road is performed in different ways

the writer evidently is discussing roads, and means to say that they are stabilized in different ways. But the idea of *stabilizing* looms so large and significant in his thinking that he places it at the beginning of his statement, where it can be only a noun. Having sacrificed this verb idea, he must complete his sentence with the unsatisfactory "is performed."

Sometimes, though less frequently, in shifting to a noun, a verb becomes not the subject, as in the preceding sentence, but the object, as in the statement

> Yet each places a different interpretation on the word *optimism.*

Here *interprets* can be a verb and *different* an adverb, as in the revision

> Yet each interprets optimism differently.

But the most remarkable distortion of a verb is its conversion into an adjective, as in this statement:

> Whenever declining business visited the merchant, he was inclined to give up and seek his fortune elsewhere.

[1] Philip Boswood Ballard, *Thought and Language* (London, 1934), pp. 86–87

The sentence can be more direct by changing the adjective *declining* into a verb, as follows:

Whenever business declined . . .

A writer must be particularly alert to the effects of certain rhetorical forces that can impair or completely destroy the verb. Among these are many of the common small verbs, including most of the verbs in Basic English. Writers long have combined verbs with other parts of speech to create unique expressions. It is difficult if not impossible to find replacements for terms like *get away with* and *get by*. But all too many writers combine verbs and nouns to the point of inefficiency, for when these built-up verbs displace available, single-word verbs, the writing is likely to become indirect and wordy. These combinations may be grammatically acceptable but they are not always effective. This fact is evident in certain combinations in which the following verbs are involved.

1. *Make* can weaken a verb by converting it into a noun as in the sentence

He never makes any attempt to broaden his culture.

2. *Get* is widely used in combinations that force a verb into the form of a past participle. Why write

Women spend less time in their kitchens today but get more accomplished,

when, by converting the participle into a finite verb, we can say

Women spend less time in their kitchens today but accomplish more.

3. *Have* can be objectionable on two counts. Often it is simply superfluous.

The wholesome attitude that she has toward her father represents her attitude toward everyone.

can be phrased more directly by omitting *she has*:

Her wholesome attitude toward her father represents her attitude toward everyone.

In the second place, *have* can change a verb into another part of speech, usually a noun.

He has an intense dislike for Math

is more directly expressed as

He dislikes Math intensely.

4. *Do* also converts verbs into nouns. In the sentence

Tonight I must do some studying

the verb *study* has been converted into a noun by *do*, and has become its object. *Do* is unnecessary, as can be seen in the revision

Tonight I must study.

In the dependent clauses of the following sentences, what could have been effective verbs have become the subjects of *do:*

> There are two methods by which plant decentralization can be done,

and

> The subsidiary plants ship parts to the main plant where assembly is done.

The verb of the first can, and, I think, should be not *do* but *decentralize;* of the second not *do* but *assemble.* These statements are far more direct when reconstructed around these verbs:

> There are two methods by which a plant can be decentralized,

and

> The subsidiary plants ship parts to the main plant which assembles them,

or, simpler still,

> The subsidiary plants ship parts to the main plant for assembly.

5. *Exist* also can distort verbs. The sentence

> A distrusting sentiment exists toward federal control

provides another fascinating example of an adjective expressing a notion that could be expressed more efficiently by a verb. *Distrust* could be an effective verb; here it serves, rather, as a modifier of the word *sentiment,* which is the subject but is not essential to the meaning of the sentence. The writer is compelled to complete his statement with the inadequate verb *exist.* The statement is more direct when *distrust* is the verb, in a revision like this:

> Many Americans distrust federal control.

Other verbs that combine with other parts of speech to displace single-word verbs are *give, use, hold, come, feel,* and *take.* We shall pause only for an example of each.

6. *Give*

> To the primitive man, religion gave explanation of things unknown

may be rhythmical but is hardly a direct way of saying

> Religion explained the unknown to primitive man.

7. *Use*

> If a writer wishes to express an idea clearly, he must use a wise choice and arrangement of words

can be improved by eliminating the verb *use* and converting *choice* and *arrangement* into verbs as follows:

> To express an idea clearly, a writer must choose and arrange his words wisely.

8. *Hold*

> She held a complete disregard for her household duties

is more direct in the revision

> She completely disregarded her household duties.

9. *Come*

> He was glad that there had come an end to their acquaintance

becomes

> He was glad that their acquaintance had ended.

10. *Feel*

> Fielding expected his reader to feel admiration for Tom Jones

becomes

> Fielding expected his reader to admire Tom Jones.

11. *Take*

> Take a look at the dictionary

becomes

> Look at the dictionary.

12. Finally, there is the verb *to be*, which, though indispensable, can lead to wordy and indirect expression when it forsakes its normal functions. The alert writer will scrutinize carefully the verb *to be* in four constructions. First, there is the familiar fault of inexact equating, which is still with us. In the statement

> Patriotism is where you love your country

patriotism is not a where but a devotion to or love of one's country. In the second place, the verb *to be* encourages lazy writing by combining with particles to form expressions for which the writer is too indolent to locate an exact verb. *Is for* and *is against* are normally weak substitutes for more precise terms. Third, the verb *to be* is sometimes objectionable in the expletive, especially when it forces potentially modifying ideas into noun form, as in this sentence:

> It seemed that there was a scarcity of jobs at this time.

Here *scarcity* can be more effective as a modifier than a substantive. It is properly a substantive in the statement

> The scarcity of jobs worried the graduating seniors;

but the first sentence becomes more efficient if *scarcity* is made into an adjective, *scarce:*

> It seemed that jobs were scarce at this time.

The expletive can also produce illogical and needless subordination. In the sentence

> There are portions of his writing, however, where his personal feelings are injected into the story

the superflous "There are . . . where" construction is superimposed upon the basic idea. The meaning of the sentence is obvious enough:

> In portions of his writing, however, his personal feelings are evident.

And finally, the most serious objection to the verb *to be* is that it facilitates the shifting of a verb into a noun form, as in this sentence:

> The expected completion of this reactor will be sometime in 1958.

Up to this point we have been concerned with the necessity of expressing in a verb the idea that is most effectively expressed by that form. But the converse of this notion is of equal significance. It is just as essential to know when to avoid as when to employ a verb. The verb is too precious to be wasted on non-verbal matter. Moreover, indiscriminate use of the verb to convey any and all matter may obscure or at least detract from the verb of a clause or sentence. In the statement

> The floor is lighted only when an operation is being performed

the second and rather clumsy verb is not required. The sentence is more efficient when the verb is replaced by a prepositional phrase as follows:

> The floor is lighted only during an operation.

The statement

> Women want to be up-to-date when it comes to fashions and manners

likewise improves when the little word *in* replaces the awkward clause "when it comes to." That is,

> Women want to be up-to-date in fashions and manners.

So much, then, for selecting the proper verb with which to communicate an idea. We now turn to the task of managing the verb after it has been selected.

Efficiency of expression requires that a suitable idea be conveyed not only in the verb but also in the appropriate form of that verb. To achieve this efficiency it is necessary to prevent the major and minor forms of the verb. As the names imply, the finite forms are explicit; they have person, number, tense, and mood. The indefinite or infinite forms, that is, the verbals, are not as precise as the finite forms; in a sense they may be regarded as defective because they do not communicate as much information as the finite forms. They do not indicate person or number, but only tense and mood.

The significant distinction between definite and indefinite forms of the verb lies in the notion that the use of these forms must be determined by the meaning that is to be conveyed. In order to select the appropriate verb form the writer must differentiate between the major and minor elements of his communication. Since the finite forms are complete and precise, they usually perform the heavy-duty work of clauses and sentences. In fact, sentences conventionally cannot exist without finite verbs. The indefinite forms, on the contrary, are not complete and precise and are not used as verbs of sentences. They perform, instead, the lighter or unstressed tasks of phrases; they are particularly serviceable when the writer wishes to tuck into a sentence certain associated notions which would unbalance his construction if expressed in finite form.

Of the three verbals, the infinitive and the gerund pose practically no difficulty in composition. But the present participle can cause serious problems for the writer because of its nature and its tendency to usurp the function of the main verb.

Winston Churchill's style is remarkable for its dependence upon finite verbs. His verbals are pretty much limited to the infinitive and the gerund; he uses the present participle sparingly. The more present participles in a piece of writing, the less direct and efficient it is likely to be. And that is to be expected, since the relationship between the participle and the word it modifies is very loose. In fact, the relationship is so loose that sometimes the participle drifts away completely from the associated word.

I am not concerned here with the common faults like dangling or misplaced modifiers, but with the more basic matter of assuring that the participle does not encroach upon the role of the main verb. I happen to know that the student who wrote

> The naturalist examines life dispassionately, presenting all the facts but drawing no conclusions

intended that *presenting* and *drawing* should be of equal significance with *examines*, and therefore should have written

> The naturalist examines life dispassionately, presents all the facts, but draws no conclusion.

It would be interesting to discover why this writer shifted from a first order verb form to a second order verb form, although presenting three coordinate notions. I suspect that such writers assume that the only function of the different verb forms is to provide variety rather than precision of expression, and therefore carelessly shift from one form to another without regard for meaning.

Stylistically, use of the participial phrase to conclude a sentence can be weak and anticlimactic. This practice is at its worst when inexperienced writers launch a sentence with a vigorous, finite verb, and then nudge it along by tossing in a participle whenever it shows signs of slowing down, as in:

> As these roads are built new and generally not along previous right-of-ways, they are well graded, eliminating sharp curves and large rises and dips providing both a safer and more comfortable ride.

But a more serious result of concluding sentences with present participles is confusion in meaning. I think that technical writers are particularly given to this construction. In the sentence

> The liquid metal will be pumped through the pile, absorbing the heat generated and carrying it to the heat exchanger

the meaning is not precise. Are the *absorbing* and *carrying* of heat the purpose of the pumping, the result of the pumping, or merely activities associated with the pumping? Observe the loose relationship between the participial phrase and the main verb in this sentence:

> An inspector should be well grounded in the elements of good workmanship, understanding the problems of the mechanic and the engineer.

Does the writer mean that

> An inspector should be well grounded in the elements of good workmanship and understand the problems of the mechanic and the engineer,

or is he saying that

> An inspector should be well grounded in the elements of good workmanship in order to understand the problems of the mechanic and the engineer?

The present participle is highly useful when it performs its proper functions; but when it is handled carelessly, and especially when it encroaches upon the work of the finite verb, it can weaken and confuse communication. I have suggested in this paper that the most direct and efficient style is governed by the meaning that is conveyed. When meaning determines the pattern of the sentence, there is little waste motion in the rhetoric. That is why one needs to fix upon his subject, for that is what he is talking about; but most of all he needs to know what he is saying about that subject, for that is his verb. Efficient writing depends very largely upon expressing in a finite, active, single-word verb the idea that can be conveyed most effectively in the verb form.

Exercises and Problems in Communication

1. Correct period faults and comma faults in the following entries:
a. Concerning the proposal mentioned previously.
b. He knew what you wanted he was not open to suggestion.
c. Having given your claim carefully review.
d. First we will study the whole area of credit, then we will consider claims problems.
e. Mr. James is no longer with our company, however Mr. Johnson can answer your inquiry.
f. The same offer will apply in January, you may submit an order then.
g. The plan which we have followed for over twenty years.
h. When the offer does expire.
i. Not knowing the approved methods.
j. Although every possible solution has been considered.

2. Rewrite the following sentences, correcting danglers, poor pronoun reference, or misplaced modifiers:
a. Considering the disadvantages of the job, it seems to be a risk you do not want to take.

b. Entering the office, my eyes were attracted to the extravagant furnishings.

c. Anticipating the fluctuations of demands in the clothing business is one of the great challenges.

d. The shoe salesman told Smithson that he had heard about the foreclosure from one of his friends.

e. Mr. Thomas leaned back against the desk and put his foot up on the open drawer and ran his hand through his hair.

f. The superintendent told John that he would have to catch the train at 8:15.

g. Whenever one is going to have a personal interview, you should be suitably dressed.

h. No one in the office keeps their desk drawers locked.

i. Coming into the office late once a week the boss is critical of your tardiness.

j. Between dictating to a stenographer and using the machine, you will find the latter easier.

3. Revise the following sentences from application letters sent by college seniors. Change the structure and any other features to vitalize the sentences for a better approach to getting a job.

a. I am very interested in the field of chemical engineering.

b. I was graduated from Ohio University, and my major field of study was in Political Science.

c. Your new sales trainee who you are about to select will be a college graduate.

d. When I graduate at the end of August, I will be qualified to fill the position of electronics technician.

e. Although in my apprenticeship I did not fill the capacity of pharmacist, I had the drug department experience that is invaluable to me.

f. Your advertisement in the *Post-Dispatch* interested me exceedingly because I know I can fill the position.

g. Experience during summers in selling heightened my interest.

h. My major study at Wisconsin was based on work on textiles.

i. Everyone of my professors liked me.

j. Because of the distance when coming to your personnel office I would like to take an aptitude test you wrote of and have a personal interview.

4. Reconstruct the following sentences, improving parallelism, to help a potential reader get the meaning more quickly:

a. We had three objectives in mind for the coming year: (1) to increase production, (2) raising wages, and (3) educating office employees.

b. The accountants, typists and the punch-card operators are to receive a wage increase.

c. Three requisites for a good writing style are: (1) an attitude of consideration for others, (2) think clearly, and (3) knowledge of correct mechanics of writing.

d. This model has three drawbacks; they are, it has a limited use, and the customer will have to learn a new operation, and why does it have to cost so much?

e. The disadvantages of my work as an assistant in a retail organization include the usual red tape of large concerns; and repetitive work: the continuous typing of hundreds of memos and reports is very uninteresting in many cases. A third fault is of poor communication between various related areas in our company.

5. Applying principles of coordination and subordination for strength in sentences, revise these sentences:
   a. He had two older brothers, who were outstanding executives both in mercantile and manufacturing companies, and they had a great deal of influence on his career.
   b. Sales to universities dropped off and was caused by poor relationships with their administrations.
   c. Lime is another important raw material and is procured by our suppliers.
   d. She is a woman of strong constitution, and she was determined to manage the business by herself.
   e. The report you asked for is not finished. The Purchasing Department has not sent in estimates yet but a copy will be on its way to you by next week.
   f. As you see by the memorandum, the meeting should last about two hours and is scheduled for Thursday, June 30.
   g. The containers for the mailings were cardboard cartons made by the Stratton Company. Also the slick finished, colorful 9 × 12 folders, with the Company's story, were very attractive using black for the background and a picture in color of the Company's mascot in the corner.
   h. Meredith Cones was injured as he was crossing the loading dock and he has been dismissed from the infirmary.
   i. It is apparent of course that there has been a decline in Company stock and we hope this report will be of value to you.
   i. Your account for April is still unpaid, which brings your total amount due to $45.63, and we will have to ask you to remit this amount by July 1.

6. Make sentences with the following phrases, changing any nouns or adjectives that have verb forms to verbs:
   a. held no liking
   b. felt respect for
   c. gave help
   d. got an award
   e. made two attempts
   f. had to make a choice
   g. do some letter writing
   h. is dependent on
   i. use a little economy
   j. there is a popular desire

7. Rewrite the following letter to get effective coordination and subordination:

We would like to ask a few questions about your last order to us, and thank you for it, and it will be shipped as soon as we hear from you about the answers to these questions.

We see by your letter that you say "One dozen styles B and C." Do you want that we should send one dozen of each or to send one dozen of both put together? This we did not understand, also method of payment. No method of payment given. You do not have a charge account due to the fact that you never asked for one therefore we cannot charge the merchandise unless you ask for a charge account to be opened, which if you want to be done, we will do and charge this order to it. Will you tell us do you want it done?

We again want to thank you for your order, and we apologize for the delay in sending it, and we hope to serve you better in the future, and best wishes. Thank you.

8. The following was a good sales letter before the paragraphs were disarranged. Rewrite the letter, restoring proper paragraph sequence—making no other changes.

Dear Mr. Smith:

You will find this book one of the most fascinating stories on home comfort you have ever read.

In order to avoid a repetition of this condition next winter, we suggest you learn now, how Johns-Manville Rock Wool Home Insulation can save up to 30% of your fuel and in addition, make your home up to 15 degrees cooler this summer.

If you will return the enclosed card, I will be glad to see that you receive a complimentary copy.

I wish it were possible for me to tell you the complete story of Johns-Manville Rock Wool Home Insulation in this letter. But since this is not practical, why not let me send you a free copy of our twenty-four page book entitled "Comfort That Pays for Itself"? This book illustrates and describes how more than 500,000 American home owners are now enjoying the year 'round advantages and fuel economy of Johns-Manville Home Insulation.

You are probably aware that responsible authorities hold out no hope that the fuel situation will be better for the coming winter.

Fortunately, a great part of your problem can be solved by home insulation and we urge you to start thinking about next winter NOW! Here's why. Because of the unprecedented need for home insulation during the past Fall and Winter, we could not keep up with the demand, and many home owners were not able to obtain the fuel saving benefits as early in the winter as they would have liked because they delayed in placing their orders.

Like thousands of home owners, you no doubt had trouble keeping your home comfortable this past winter.

9. Assume that, at a conference of business correspondents, you are to be one of three panel members to discuss paragraphing in business writing, each member to take about five minutes for his comments. Prepare an outline sum-

marizing the material on paragraphing in this chapter. Your outline should direct you for a talk of about 750 words, since the average speaker's rate is around 150 words per minute.

10. Do a similar exercise of outlining the end-of-chapter reading, as if you were invited to speak to college-bound seniors in your high school. Which of Mr. Britton's points did you find easiest to work with in organizing your thoughts? Analyze your reaction to see whether the more difficult points for you may need attention in your own writing.

6

Building the Business Vocabulary

To communicate is our passion and our despair.—WILLIAM GOLDING, *Free Fall*

Although a positive approach is preferable to a negative one, to avoid possible misunderstanding, I would like to inject a negative note at the outset of this discussion. The chapter title does not imply the acquisition of a special vocabulary; as mentioned in Chapter 1, the language of business does not differ from general usage, except for those terms peculiar to a particular art, science, profession, trade, or industry. Nor am I encouraging you to become a disciple of the "big-word" school, which is the concept the very word "vocabulary" connotes to many persons. The mother of an undergraduate friend of mine reflected the attitude of a goodly number of persons when she said that her son would never become a successful author (the son had been encouraged in writing by his teachers and friends), because he did not "know enough big words."

To state it positively, this chapter deals with aspects of effective usage and the means of developing the tools that any speaker or writer will work with, whatever his career. In short, we are discussing approaches to a *large* vocabulary, not to *big* words.

IMPORTANCE OF A LARGE VOCABULARY

In the field of business communication we knew that words were important even before colleges added vocabulary-building courses. A representative of the Caterpillar Tractor Company reported that, in a study of the company's salesmen, one factor was consistent; there was a significant correlation between sales ability (as shown in individual sales records) and scores on one of the most difficult vocabulary tests of that time. Although the information may seem obsolete, you would get some food for thought—and debate—from Johnson O'Connor's celebrated, and controversial, series of tests showing the startling correlation between the size of vocabulary and success, especially success in business.[1]

Why is a large vocabulary important? There are at least three reasons: (1) to enable the writer to get exactly the right word to express the precise shade of meaning and have it fit smoothly into its context; (2) to insure avoiding ineffective repetitions which more than almost anything else testify to slovenliness of thought and poverty of expression; (3) to provide the business person with the proper thought symbols so that he can think clearly and creatively.

When writers begin drawing pay for magazine articles, for advertising copy, or for books, you can be certain that they have learned to choose their words with skill. Compare the following sentences:

In every business *deal*, we *attempt* to keep *paramount* the *utter contentment* of our *clients*.

In every business *transaction* we *try* to keep *uppermost* the *complete satisfaction* of our *customers*.

The second is an acceptable business sentence; the first would at once label its writer as incompetent for business correspondence—yet every misused word in the first sentence is a synonym of a word correctly used in the second. Professional writers know that just any synonym isn't good enough, and they know too that however well a given word may express a meaning, it isn't satisfactory unless it fits both the tone of the writing and the rhythm of the passage. To be pleasing and effective, writing must be smooth as well as accurate. The feeling for words is a subtle thing, something like the skill that enables a person to drive successfully on slippery streets, play the piano with virtuosity, or swing a golf club "like a pro." One must know words well and practice using them with some of the devotion that a connoisseur might devote to sampling rare wines.

Effective word use is a *skill*, a characteristic way of doing a thing, possessed only by those who have worked for mastery, and achieved it. Developing a deep *feeling* for words seems a necessary preliminary to understanding word relationships, and ultimately acquiring a large working vocabulary.

It isn't that we want the biggest, the most learned word. The best educated people in the majority of instances will choose the simpler rather than the rarer or more polysyllabic word. L. E. Frailey, long recog-

[1] See *Johnson O'Connor English Vocabulary Builder* (Boston: Human Engineering Laboratory, 1948).

nized as a leading authority on business writing, says that no business letter is likely to do its job unless its one-syllable word content is at least 70 per cent. We study vocabulary, just as we study everything in business communication, not for display, but to enable us to accomplish business assignments more successfully.

Frequently in writing we find that we must substitute one word for another for no other reason than that we've used the same word in the preceding sentence and its repetition would be displeasing. We don't try to avoid all repetitions; some of them are distinctly good, but accidental repetitions from poverty of vocabulary are to be avoided.

The third point, the importance of vocabulary in achieving constructive thought, is hard to discuss in other than general terms. Everyone who has studied elementary psychology knows that the *imagination* is circumscribed by experience. You can easily test yourself. Try to imagine an animal, or flower, completely different from any you have ever seen. Your make-believe animal still has legs, hasn't it? Maybe an unusual number. Hair? Eyes? How many? And the flower grows on a stalk or vine and has petals.

What the imagination can do is to effect new combinations, or applications. Thus the inventor watches the bird in flight and plans the airplane; the scientist reasons from the properties of chromium and steel that mixing them might have useful effects, and *chrome steel* is the result. But both the inventor and the scientist must have *symbols to think with:* terms such as *plane, suction, buoyancy, thrust, malleability, tensile strength, cohesion.* If he has the right symbols, then a man's desire to advance knowledge and his mastery over his environment may achieve tangible results in the form of a computer or a satellite. Similarly, the business person needs symbols to make his plans and decisions: to think over possibilities involved in buying that lot on the corner and building on it, the pro and con of a business partnership with Henry Jones—or planning the Monsanto Chemical works or the G.E. jet plant. We can't travel the railways of thought unless the rolling stock is there.

HOW VOCABULARY EXPANSION TAKES PLACE

Granted that the speaker or writer wants a bigger and better vocabulary, how can he get it?

1. He must have the desire to build his vocabulary, and the stick-to-it-iveness to add thousands of words to his word hoard.

2. He must make a resolution that will be harder to keep than most of the resolutions we make for New Year's: "I will never again let a word pass by without learning its meaning."

3. He must follow that resolution through hard reading and light reading, even in listening to speeches and conversations. It helps to note

down the words on an index card so that they can all be looked up even if there is no dictionary handy when the words are encountered. Collecting new words in this way can become a kind of game.

4. He should learn to use the full resources of a good dictionary, and should keep one constantly available for reference.

5. He may add to the enjoyment and success of his vocabulary-building project by studying language history—how our words were first used and how their usage developed.

6. Through learning a foreign language or studying etymology he will learn that knowledge of roots and affixes gives us new words without our having to learn each one separately.

7. He may receive special help from a book of synonyms or a thesaurus.

The person who follows the first four steps of the vocabulary-building process will find that at the end of six months his vocabulary will be definitely, measurably larger, and that his ability to express himself will be correspondingly greater. The last three steps make vocabulary building easier and more interesting.

Apart from the sort of special study he may have made in vocabulary building and history of the language courses, the average person hasn't very full opportunity to study the influence that *a word's history* has on its present-day use. Most of what he can do will be in connection with the large dictionaries. *Webster's Third New International Dictionary* quotes a number of illustrations of a given word as it was used perhaps centuries ago. The *Oxford English Dictionary* and the *Dictionary of American English,* prepared "on historical principles," show how a word has been used from early to modern times. Knowing that Celtic inhabitants of Britain used *slogan* as a battle cry might help the advertiser advance in his *campaign* (French *campagne* from Latin *campus,* field) with greater *courage* (French *cour,* heart, plus *age,* relating to) to *ultimate* (from Latin *ultimo,* last, final) *triumph* (from Latin *triumphus,* signifying to the Romans a celebration of glorious success, especially military victory).

The point is of course that knowledge of word history enlivens the imagination; we use a word with greater assurance when we know that important Greeks, or Romans, or Frenchmen, or Anglo-Saxons used it to express their accomplishments as human beings. It is interesting, too, to note how words change in meaning. A *steward* was once the keeper of the *pigsty;* a *dean,* a soldier, the leader of ten; a *minister,* a servant; *precocious* meant half-baked.[2] When the Normans invaded England, the French *catel* gave us our word *cattle.* Later from Parisian French we got *chattel,* meaning the same thing. But we "specialized" *cattle* to mean live-

[2] J. C. Hixson and I. Colodny, *Word Ways* (New York: American Book Co., 1939), p. 105.

stock, later bovine animals, and used *chattel* to mean personal property as distinguished from real estate. In Shakespeare's time *nice* meant foolish, and a *clown* was a country person, while a *fool* was a clown.

Closely related to cultivating acquaintance with word history is the study of etymology, the science of the original form of words, which enables us to discover how the parts of words have combined to give us the familiar symbols which we use. If we can learn certain roots of words and certain prefixes and suffixes, we discover that we can understand the meaning of a great many words without going to the dictionary.[3]

If we know that *volente* comes from Latin *volens*, wishing, and that *bene* means good and *male* bad, we can easily understand the meaning of *benevolence* and *malevolence*.[4] Similarly, if we know Latin *dicere*, to say, we can use our same prefixes and be sure that *benediction* means blessing and *malediction* a curse. If we know that Greek *bios* means life and that *logy* comes from *logos*, word or science, we easily deduce that *biology* is the science of life. Adding *graphy* from *graphein*, write, to *bios*, we know that *biography* is "life-writing." Or if we use *logy* again and combine with it *philos*, friend or lover, we know that *philology* is love of, or understanding of, words. And since *sophia* is wisdom, we can use *philos* again and get *philosophy*, love of wisdom, which has come to mean understanding of how to live, or knowing the way to wise living. If we have learned that the Greek prefix *mono* means one, we know that *monologue* is talk by one person, and we can easily understand how *monotony* came to mean what it does.

Some persons find that they can't seem to get into the spirit of pursuing historical meanings of words or engaging in word building with roots and affixes. These persons may prefer to follow the notebook method. When they encounter a new word, they write it down, preferably with a few words of context. Then they look it up in the dictionary at the earliest opportunity, continue vigilant for its reappearance in their reading, and, at the first chance, work it into their own writing and speaking. George Herbert Palmer in *Self-Cultivation in English* says that a word slips freely off the tongue—and I would add, the pen—the third time it is used.

For twentieth-century business, we need not only to improve our stock of standard, established words, but also to watch the language growing, and grow with it. Many words in general business use have come to us by *antonomasia;* that is, they have been made from names of persons or places. Thus we have *watt, bendix, boycott, china, roman* (type or nu-

[3] An excellent book for learning root words, prefixes, and suffixes is *Words in Context*, by A. A. De Vitis and J. R. Warner (New York: Appleton-Century-Crofts, Inc., 1961).

[4] As in the sentence "We may well have reached the point where the benevolence of the automobile is being nullified by its malevolence." (From "Our Highways and Our Traffic," *The Royal Bank of Canada Letter*, January 1965, p. 1.)

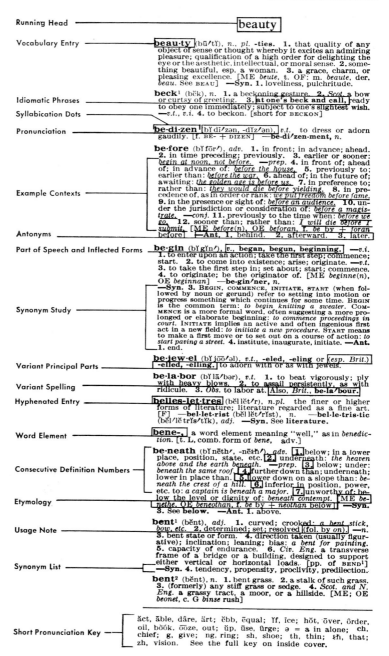

Running Head

Vocabulary Entry

Idiomatic Phrases

Syllabication Dots

Pronunciation

Example Contexts

Antonyms

Part of Speech and Inflected Forms

Synonym Study

Variant Principal Parts

Variant Spelling

Hyphenated Entry

Word Element

Consecutive Definition Numbers

Etymology

Usage Note

Synonym List

Short Pronunciation Key

beauty

beau·ty (bū′tĭ), n., pl. **-ties.** **1.** that quality of any object of sense or thought whereby it excites an admiring pleasure; qualification of a high order for delighting the eye or the aesthetic, intellectual, or moral sense. **2.** something beautiful, esp. a woman. **3.** a grace, charm, or pleasing excellence. [ME beute, t. OF: m. beaute, der. beau. See BEAU] —Syn. **1.** loveliness, pulchritude.

beck¹ (bĕk), n. **1.** a beckoning gesture. **2.** Scot. a bow or curtsy of greeting. **3.** at one's beck and call, ready to obey one immediately; subject to one's slightest wish. —v.t., v.i. **4.** to beckon. [short for BECKON]

be·di·zen (bĭ dī′zən, -dĭz′ən), v.t. to dress or adorn gaudily. [f. BE- + DIZEN] —be·di′zen·ment, n.

be·fore (bĭ fōr′), adv. **1.** in front; in advance; ahead. **2.** in time preceding; previously. **3.** earlier or sooner: begin at noon, not before. —prep. **4.** in front of; ahead of; in advance of: before the house. **5.** previously to; earlier than: before the war. **6.** ahead of; in the future of; awaiting: the golden age is before us. **7.** in preference to; rather than: they would die before yielding. **8.** in precedence of, as in order or rank: we put freedom before fame. **9.** in the presence or sight of: before an audience. **10.** under the jurisdiction or consideration of: before a magistrate. —conj. **11.** previously to the time when: before we go. **12.** sooner than; rather than: I will die before I submit. [ME before(n), OE beforan, f. be by + foran before] —Ant. **1.** behind. **2.** afterward. **3.** later.

be·gin (bĭ gĭn′), v., began, begun, beginning. —v.i. **1.** to enter upon an action; take the first step; commence; start. **2.** to come into existence; arise; originate. —v.t. **3.** to take the first step in; set about; start; commence. **4.** to originate; be the originator of. [ME beginne(n), OE beginnan] —be·gin′ner, n. —Syn. **3.** BEGIN, COMMENCE, INITIATE, START (when followed by noun or gerund) refer to setting into motion or progress something which continues for some time. BEGIN is the common term: to begin knitting a sweater. COMMENCE is a more formal word, often suggesting a more prolonged or elaborate beginning: to commence proceedings in court. INITIATE implies an active and often ingenious first act in a new field: to initiate a new procedure. START means to make a first move or to set out on a course of action: to start paving a street. **4.** institute, inaugurate, initiate. —Ant. **1.** end.

be·jew·el (bĭ jōō′əl), v.t., -eled, -eling or (esp. Brit.) -elled, -elling. to adorn with or as with jewels.

be·la·bor (bĭ lā′bər), v.t. **1.** to beat vigorously; ply with heavy blows. **2.** to assail persistently, as with ridicule. **3.** Obs. to labor at. Also, Brit., be·la′bour.

belles-let·tres (bĕl lĕt′r), n.pl. the finer or higher forms of literature; literature regarded as a fine art. [F] —bel·let·rist (bĕl lĕt′rĭst), n. —bel·le·tris·tic (bĕl′lĕ trĭs′tĭk), adj. —Syn. See literature.

bene-, a word element meaning "well," as in benediction. [t. L, comb. form of bene, adv.]

be·neath (bĭ nēth′, -nĕth′), adv. **1.** below; in a lower place, position, state, etc. **2.** underneath: the heaven above and the earth beneath. —prep. **3.** below; under; beneath the same roof. **4.** further down than; underneath; lower in place than. **5.** lower down on a slope than: beneath the crest of a hill. **6.** inferior in position, power, etc. to: a captain is beneath a major. **7.** unworthy of; below the level or dignity of: beneath contempt. [ME beneth, OE beneothan, f. be by + neothan below] —Syn. **3.** See below. —Ant. **1.** above.

bent¹ (bĕnt), adj. **1.** curved; crooked: a bent stick, bow, etc. **2.** determined; set; resolved (fol. by on). —n. **3.** bent state or form. **4.** direction taken (usually figurative); inclination; leaning; bias: a bent for painting. **5.** capacity of endurance. **6.** Civ. Eng. a transverse frame of a bridge or a building, designed to support either vertical or horizontal loads. [pp. of BEND¹] —Syn. **4.** tendency, propensity, proclivity, predilection.

bent² (bĕnt), n. **1.** bent grass. **2.** a stalk of such grass. **3.** (formerly) any stiff grass or sedge. **4.** Scot. and N. Eng. a grassy tract, a moor, or a hillside. [ME; OE beonet, c. G binse rush]

Fig. 18. What the dictionary tells. (Reprinted from *The American College* House, Inc.)

brunch

bi-, a prefix meaning: **1.** twice, doubly, two, as in *bilateral, binocular, biweekly.* **2.** (in science) denoting (in general) two, as in *bicarbonate.* Also, **bin-.** [t. L, comb. form of *bis* twice, doubly, der. L *duo* two] ──── Prefix

Bi, *Chem.* bismuth.

B.I., British India. ──── Abbreviation

bi·son (bī′sən, -zən), *n., pl.* **-son.** *Zool.* a large North American bovine ruminant, *Bison bison* (**American bison,** or buffalo), with high, well-haired shoulders. [t. L, t. Gmc.; cf. G *wisent*] ──── Illustration

American Bison, *Bison bison*
(10 to 12 ft. long,
ab. 6 ft. high at the shoulder) ──── Caption

blood·mo·bile (blŭd′mə bēl′), *n.* a small truck with medical equipment for receiving blood donations.

Bos·ton (bôs′tən, bŏs′tən), *n.* **1.** the capital of Massachusetts, in the E part: the largest city and seaport in New England. 697,197 (1960). **2.** (*l.c.*) a game of cards, played by four persons with two packs of cards. **3.** (*l.c.*) a social dance, a modification of the waltz. **─Bos·to-ni·an** (bŏs tō′nĭ ən, bôs tō′-), *adj., n.* ──── Geographical Entry / Run-on Entry

bot·tle (bŏt′əl), *n., v.,* **-tled, -tling.** **─***n.* **1.** a portable vessel with a neck or mouth, now commonly made of glass, used for holding liquids. **2.** the contents of a bottle; as much as a bottle contains: *a bottle of wine.* **3. the bottle,** intoxicating liquor. **4.** bottled milk for babies: *raised on the bottle.* **─***v.t.* **5.** to put into or seal in a bottle; esp. in England, to can or put up fruit or vegetables. **6. bottle up,** to shut in or restrain closely: *to bottle up one's feelings.* [ME *botel,* t. OF: *m. botele,* g. LL *butticula,* dim. of *buttis* BUTT⁴] **─bot′tler,** *n.* ──── Homograph Numbers

bot·tle (bŏt′əl), *n. Brit. Dial.* a bundle, esp. of hay. [ME *botel,* t. OF, dim. of *botte* bundle]

bou·fant (bōō fän′), *adj.* [*French.*] puffed out; full, as sleeves or draperies. **─bou·fante** (bōō fänt′), *adj. fem.* ──── Foreign Word Label

brain washing, systematic indoctrination that changes or undermines one's political convictions. **─brain-wash,** *v.* ──── Two Word Entry

brain wave, 1. (*pl.*) *Med.* electroencephalogram **2.** *Colloq.* a sudden idea or inspiration.

brass (brăs, bräs), *n.* **1.** a durable, malleable, and ductile yellow alloy, consisting essentially of copper and zinc. **2.** a utensil, ornament, or other article made of brass. **3.** *Mach.* a bearing, bush, or the like. **4.** [*Music.*] **a.** a musical instrument of the trumpet or horn families. **b.** such instruments collectively in a band or orchestra. **5.** [*Brit.*] a memorial tablet incised with an effigy, coat of arms or the like. **6.** metallic yellow; lemon, amber, or reddish yellow. **7.** *U.S. Slang.* **a.** high-ranking military officers. **b.** any important officials. **8.** [*Colloq.*] excessive assurance; impudence; effrontery. **9.** *Brit. Slang.* money. **─***adj.* **10.** of brass. **11.** using musical instruments made of brass. [ME *bras,* OE *bræs*] **─brass′-like′,** *adj.* ──── Subject Label / Geographic Label / Usage Label

brig·and·age (brĭg′ənd ĭj), *n.* the practice of brigands; plundering. [Also, **brig′and·ism.**] ──── Variant Form

Bron·të (brŏn′tĭ), *n.* **1. Anne,** (*Acton Bell*) 1820–49, British novelist. **2.** her sister, **Charlotte,** (*Currer Bell*) 1816–55, British novelist. **3.** her sister, **Emily Jane,** (*Ellis Bell*) 1818–48, British novelist. ──── Biographical Entry

brown·ie (brou′nĭ), *n.* **1.** (in folklore) a little brown goblin, esp. one who helps secretly in household work. **2.** *U.S.* a small, highly shortened chocolate cake, often containing nuts. **3.** [(*cap.*)] a trademark for a type of inexpensive camera. **4.** any inexpensive camera. **5.** [(*cap.*)] a member of the junior division (ages 8–11) of the Girl Scouts or (*Brit.*) the Girl Guides. **─Syn. 1.** See **fairy.** ──── Capitalization

Brum·mell (brŭm′əl), *n.* [See **Beau Brummell.**] ──── Cross Reference

brunch (brŭnch), *n.* a mid-morning meal that serves both as breakfast and lunch. [b. BREAKFAST and LUNCH]

b., blend of, blended; c., cognate with; d., dialect, dialectal; der., derived from; f., formed from; g., going back to; m., modification of; r., replacing; s., stem of; t., taken from; ?, perhaps. See the full key on inside cover. ──── Short Etymology Key

Dictionary [Copyright 1947, Copyright © 1964], by permission of Random

merals), *arabic, millinery, sherry, diesel,* and *derrick.* And we are building new words constantly, especially in the field of applied science, or technology. "The Greeks had a word for it," we say, and thus compliment the Greeks on their learning, for of course they had words for only what they knew. Today, however, we use many Greek words which the Greeks themselves never knew. By using Greek roots, we have built words to cover the need of an ever-expanding application of science to our daily living. Among the neo-Greek words are *astronaut, telephone, telegraphy, biochemistry, thermometer, dynamo, hydrometer.* Other languages too, especially Latin and German, have been levied on to help us keep pace with what emerges from the laboratory and the proving ground.

By now it must be apparent how centrally the dictionary figures in any campaign to improve the business, or general, vocabulary. The *dictionary* (*diction* plus *ary,* a place for) is itself a *vocabulary,* but a larger one than you or I can ever hope to acquire. *Webster's Third New International Dictionary* has 450,000 entries, *Webster's Seventh New Collegiate* more than 100,000. Shakespeare achieved immortality with 15,000; you have probably got along thus far on many fewer than that. We need to remember that the great object in word study is not in any case the building of the biggest possible vocabulary so much as increasing our familiarity with those words which have a great deal of use, so that we will always choose the right ones for a particular job.

The dictionary is indispensable, then, to the student who would get more words, but even more to a writer or speaker who needs to check his use of particular words. A successful businessman told me recently that he had two secretaries, a good one and a poor one. The difference was that the good one used the dictionary freely; the poor one seemed to have an aversion to it.

In using the dictionary, it is naturally of the greatest importance that one choose a really good work. For study purposes, one of the best of the college-size dictionaries is most suitable; [5] for office use, the unabridged dictionary, since it gives fuller information. The reproduction of a page from *Inside the ACD* in Fig. 18 illustrates graphically the resources the *American College Dictionary* places at the reader's disposal.

SYNONYMS, ANTONYMS, HOMONYMS

If we decide to enlarge our vocabulary so that we can use words more exactly, with better rhythms, and with avoidance of ineffective repetitions, it follows readily that a part of our word equipment should be familiarity

---

[5] *Webster's Seventh New Collegiate Dictionary,* the *American College Dictionary,* Funk and Wagnalls' *Standard College Dictionary,* or *Webster's New World Dictionary.*

with *synonyms*.[6] Although frequently the writer is at a loss to find any word for his meaning, sometimes his embarrassment is of the opposite sort: he has so many words to choose from that, like the centipede that forgot which leg came after which, he is stopped, unable to go on. The very fact that English is made up from so many other languages accounts in part for the duplicate words. Thus we have *will* and *testament, to help* and *to aid,* the first in each pair an Anglo-Saxon, the second a French, term.

An almost random opening of Funk and Wagnalls' *Standard College Dictionary* reveals terms with numerous synonyms. *Acumen* has *sharpness, acuteness, insight, perception, cleverness, perspicacity. Strike* has *hit, tap, slap, cuff, clout, swat,* and *smite.* We must realize that, although synonyms are words enough alike in meaning that they can sometimes substitute, not all are suitable in any given spot. Part of their meanings they hold in common, but not all. For example, among the synonyms for *noise* are *sound, clamor, hubbub, racket, uproar, tumult, outcry,* and *din.* Suppose that in a sales letter we want to say that the product, an electric refrigerator, operates *quietly.* We may say, "It is so quiet that, even if you are in the room, you will not be aware of any noise." But *noise* is a slightly offensive word in this connection.[7] Certainly we won't choose *racket, din,* or *clamor.* The least displeasing word seems to be *sound,* which we may choose, or we may decide to recast the sentence so as to use an adjective instead of a noun, *soundless* or *noiseless* or *silent.* Observe that some synonyms of the noun *noise—sound, clamor, din—*also have verb forms; the others do not. The English language is so rich in possibilities of expression that saying exactly what one means can become a most fascinating game.[8]

[6] Probably the most often quoted opinion on this subject is the comment of Mark Twain, who said, "The difference between the right word and almost the right word is the difference between lightning and the lightning bug."

[7] The word can be used to good effect. David Ogilvy, of the Ogilvy, Benson and Mather advertising agency, says, "The best headline I ever wrote contained *eighteen* words: *At Sixty Miles an Hour the Loudest Noise in the New Rolls-Royce comes from the electric clock.*" In a footnote, Mr. Ogilvy adds that "When the chief engineer at the Rolls-Royce factory read this, he shook his head sadly and said, 'It is time we did something about that damned clock.'" Mr. Ogilvy's book *Confessions of an Advertising Man* (New York: Atheneum, 1963) is referred to again in Chapter 15.

[8] A quotation from James Branch Cabell, one of the most polished stylists among modern novelists, is interesting. "In this world, wherein no fervour endures for a long while, and every clock-tick brings the infested tepid globe a little nearer to the moon's white nakedness and quiet, the wise will play while playing is permitted. The playthings will be words, because a man finds nowhere any lovelier toys." From *The Lineage of Lichfield* (New York: Robert McBride & Co., 1922), p. 45.

Of course the business person does not play with words as toys; rather, he uses them as building bricks or paving stones, but he too learns to fit them together smoothly and securely.

Not only do we need thorough familiarity with words of similar meaning; also, we frequently need a word which means just the opposite of another. These words are called *antonyms* (Greek *anti*, opposite, plus *onoma*, name). For *noble*, the dictionary gives as antonyms *narrow, small, insignificant, obscure*. Suppose you found occasion to say, "I should call his attitude far from noble; in fact to me it seems——." You would see that *obscure* or *insignificant* would not fit; *narrow* or *small* might do. A longer list of antonyms would include *mean* and *petty*, which are also possibilities.

From our brief discussion of synonyms and antonyms it must now be apparent that although dictionaries and special books of synonyms [9] or a thesaurus [10] will be helpful, nevertheless we must get a great deal of our familiarity with words by closely observing their use in their *contexts*. This suggests the importance of reading, not only such classic masters as Shakespeare, Milton, Addison, Ruskin, Stevenson, Irving, Emerson, and Lowell, but also the best writers of our own day. To get the precise flavor of the language as you will need to use it in both speaking and writing, you should read the newspapers, especially the signed articles by established writers, and the advertising copy in newspapers and magazines.

You have been doing this anyhow, you may say. But from now on you will do it from a new point of view, that of the writer studying his craft. When you reread Shakespeare, you will attempt to discover what has made him "not of an age, but for all time." As you read articles in the business journals or your favorite magazine, you will do so not merely for information but also with the close attention of the apprentice learning his craft. And you will look more closely at the advertisements which confront you everywhere, not to learn what is for sale, but to discover how the anonymous copy writer makes words reveal the flavor of soup, the glamour of perfume, the comfort of shoes, the elegance of tablecloths or silver, or the convenience and comfort of a shining new automobile.

Homonyms, or *homophones*, are another class of words to which we must give special attention. It isn't so much a matter of learning to use homonyms as of becoming sufficiently familiar with them that we won't accidentally misuse them, for they are words which sound alike but have distinct meanings. Common homonyms are: *there* and *their, see* and *sea*,

[9] *Webster's Dictionary of Synonyms* (Springfield, Mass.: G. & C. Merriam Co., 1942), with its excellent introductory discussion of synonymy, is the best treatment of synonyms.

[10] *Roget's Thesaurus of the English Language in Dictionary Form*, revised by C. O. Mawson (Garden City, N. Y.: Garden City Publishing Co., 1951). This is an improved edition of the standard "treasury of words." Here words are arranged by classes and indexed. Many writers have found this work very helpful. *The Comprehensive Word Guide*, by Norman Lewis (New York: Doubleday & Co., Inc., 1958), can also serve well for study to strengthen vocabulary or for spot use in selecting individual words.

deer and *dear, fair* and *fare, beat* and *beet, seed* and *cede, brood* and *brewed, write* and *right*. Fortunately most homonyms are such short, simple words that one is not likely to misuse them except through carelessness, a failing which most of us have to be on guard against at all times.

SELECTING FROM THE WORD HOARD

Everyone knows that a diamond loses some of its precious weight when it is cut and polished; in the cabinetmaker's shop we see blocks and shavings lost from pieces of wood that go into furniture. Similarly everyone has a vocabulary somewhat larger than he can use in ordinary writing and speaking, including business communication. Some expressions may be heirlooms, still employed in his family although they are generally out of date. Others may be provincial, that is, used in his neighborhood but not throughout the nation. Still others he may have heard in conversations or in reading modern novels including "low life" characters. To admit words to general written and spoken use, authorities set forth three requirements: they must be in (1) present, (2) national, and (3) reputable use.

We say that our language is based on Anglo-Saxon, and yet a person who knows American English well may look on Anglo-Saxon as a foreign tongue. *Beowulf* in the original Anglo-Saxon is harder to read than a poem in modern French. Chaucer, who wrote in the fourteenth century, requires much special study for the average person, and even Shakespeare, who wrote three centuries ago, used many words that modern editors change in school editions of his plays. It is not enough that a word should have been in good use once; it must be in *present* use. Language is flexible, and changes to meet changing needs. Just as adherents of the theory of the divine right of kings were willing to say "The King can do no wrong," so we hold that the best writers in a given period commit no offense; that is, words are in good use if the good writers employ them, writing in their own persons (of course, in a play or a novel a writer suits the language to the characters he presents). Shakespeare used *thou, doth, privily, assay, hark,* and *prevent* where we say *you, does, secretly, test, pay attention,* and *anticipate.*

Words must also be in *national* use. This point, a matter of much concern in the books of four decades ago, is no longer very troublesome, since the same magazines are read in Boston, New York, Macon, Fort Worth, Tucson, Fresno, Spokane, Cheyenne, and Fond du Lac; the same radio and television programs and announcers are heard and seen from coast to coast; and graduates of the University of Alabama teach English at the University of Minnesota, or vice versa.

Reputable usage, however, gives us more difficulties. The chief menace

Brobdingnagian accomplishment
(Chesapeake Bay Bridge-Tunnel is amphibious colossus)

Inception of the alternately elevated and submarine automotive procession across the seventeen and a half mile Chesapeake Bay Bridge-Tunnel will signalize consummation of one of the modern world's most Brobdingnagian engineering accomplishments. Approximately a month subsequent to the vernal equinox, when inauguration ceremonies transpire, the operational intelligence

 of this amphibious colossus will already have been functioning for a considerable period in the Administration Building contiguous to the northern extremity. Significantly, the interior of the structure will remain within one degree of desired temperature, under governance of an advanced and comprehensive Robertshaw Environmental Controls System. Thus Bridge-Tunnel directive personnel will be assured of ambient and optimum atmospheric conditions for efficient cerebration.

P.S. The last word in "automatic control" is still

Fig. 19. Vocabulary in business communication. The ad is one of a series appearing in some dozen national magazines. The company calls it the "sesquipedalian" series. (Used by permission of the Robertshaw Controls Company.)

to reputable usage is *slang*. Slang comprises a large group of expressions, many of them ungrammatical or inelegant, which are coined from time to time and come to enjoy a certain vogue. But it is dangerous, and wrong, to condemn all change in language, for the general law of evolution applies to language as to all other human activity.

Even before Jonathan Swift issued his *Proposal for Correcting the English Tongue* in 1712, efforts had been made to standardize language. Since Samuel Johnson finished the first great English dictionary in 1755, dictionaries have tended to keep language changes more orderly and within bounds. But language continues to change every day, chiefly for two reasons, into one of which slang enters. Not only must language expand as knowledge does (we must have a word for telephone when we make the invention; if we discover and use duraluminum, we must name it), but also we must cater to the human love of color and novelty. "Something there is that doesn't love a wall" applies to more than fences between neighbors. Vigorous minds don't like to be shut in by conventional language; hence arises a great deal of experimentation.

Slang is chiefly of two kinds: (1) the word or phrase that tries to cut through and achieve more color and vigor (*pep, phony, in the groove, cooking with gas, on the beam, super, way out*); (2) the word or expression that merely seeks novelty, to be different, or is a lazy substitute for established language (*hot stuff, hock* meaning pawn or mortgage, *whole ball of wax, swell, lousy, it's the berries*). The chances for survival are much greater in slang of the first kind.

In general, a slang expression will survive and rise to respectability (1) if it serves a useful language function—that is, fills a language gap— and (2) if it is not inelegant or offensive in any way. *Mob*, which in Swift's day was slang, is now in good use to describe a noisy, unruly crowd. Similarly *on the beam* (from aviation, where it is not slang) is now slang for proceeding correctly and speedily but promises to rise above the slang level in this sense. *Enthuse* in verb formations has not yet won general acceptance, not because there is no need for it, but because most educated persons somehow don't like the word, preferring the adjective and noun forms, *enthusiastic* and *enthusiasm*. *It's the berries* never won general acceptance and has dropped out of use now because it is ambiguous in meaning and undignified in tone. Words like *swell* and *keen*, which have recognized uses, become slang when they are used as lazy substitutes for almost any adjectives, but the slang use normally runs its course in a short time.

If an educated person wishes to use slang in a formal context, he may prefer to enclose it in quotation marks, though this practice is becoming less common. Standard words used as slang have most need to be quoted, for they have become in effect technical terms.

We will save ourselves some worry and confusion if we recognize that colloquial, or spoken, usage is much less strict than written usage; the average person uses more slang in speaking than in writing. Business writing tends to be somewhat conversational in tone, but like all good writers, the business writer should use slang sparingly.

GENERAL AND SPECIFIC, ABSTRACT AND CONCRETE WORDS

It is necessary that the language should include general terms, like *house, wood, animal;* and abstract terms, like *quality, justice,* and *honor.* In business, however, the preference should be given to specific and concrete words: *trim bungalow, commodious two-story colonial residence, fumed oak, dark mahogany, fat yearling steer, bacon-type Berkshire gilts.* We do not say the electric refrigerator has high quality, that our guarantee involves justice for all customers, or that the delinquent debtor's honor requires that he meet his account payments promptly. Instead we say the refrigerator has a precision motor built by General Electric and modern fiberglas insulation which keeps in the food-preserving cold, that our guarantee is "satisfaction or your money back," or that we believe that a person who appreciates the quality of an RCA stereophonic phonograph must recognize that its reasonable price can be maintained only if customers pay their monthly installments promptly.

FIGURES OF SPEECH

Closely related in language effectiveness to choosing specific and concrete words is the employment of figures of speech. A *trope,* or *figure of speech,* is an expression which manages to double up on meaning, in effect to say a thing two ways at one time, once directly and once indirectly. The business person will not use figures of speech very much except in sales letters and advertising copy, but he should know the commoner kinds and their possibilities.

A *simile* is a direct comparison, identified by the presence of *like* or *as.* "This gleaming glassware on your table will be like the bride's bouquet, the final touch in a perfect picture." The glassware isn't like a bouquet in general; the resemblance is in its beauty and in its being the perfect final touch.

A *metaphor* is an implied comparison, calling one thing something else to show resemblance. "Our modern vacuum cleaner will prove the maid-of-all-work which you have always wanted." The cleaner isn't a maid, but resembles the maid in the one respect of helping efficiently with the housework.

Hyperbole is an exaggerated comparison for effect. Except for the exaggeration, it might be a simile or metaphor. "These fluffy woolen blankets will keep you warm with hardly the weight of a feather." The lightest woolen blanket is heavier than a feather, but the exaggerated comparison emphasizes the lightness.

Metonymy is the use of a substitute expression instead of the literal one, the former being naturally or customarily associated with the latter. "With one of our tender, farm-fed turkeys, you can make your Thanksgiving table the envy of all your guests." Of course, it will not be the table, as a piece of furniture, that will be envied, but your resourcefulness as a host or hostess.

Closely related to metonymy is *synecdoche,* naming the part to represent the whole. "Three hundred hands will be needed as soon as the plant is ready to operate." Obviously what is meant is that three hundred employees (possessing six hundred hands and other bodily parts to match) will be needed.

Personification is the attribution to lower animals, inanimate objects, or abstractions, of qualities really possessed only by human beings. "It is ambition, and no other mistress, that whips and urges a man up the ladder of success." Actually the wielding of a whip is associated with persons, but we make our point more vivid by presenting ambition as a woman compelling reluctant man to go where his own quiet inclinations might not lead him.

Two final words need to be said on using figures of speech: (1) nearly all effective writers use them, at least occasionally; (2) you must learn to use them through cultivating the imaginative approach to life that will make them come to you spontaneously. Don't try to drag them into your writing and speaking by main force, for if you do this they are more likely to sound awkward and unnatural than striking and effective.

DIVISION OF LABOR AMONG VARIOUS KINDS OF WORDS AND PHRASES

Division of labor is an accepted term in the business world. In a shoe factory one workman prepares the welted sole, another stitches uppers, a third puts in eyelets for laces. In an automobile factory the worker who is responsible for the connecting rods has nothing to do with differential gears. In an office the receptionist and the filing clerk do not have similar duties. But in shoe factory, automobile factory, or office, all workers contribute to the output, or result. In our sentences we divide the labor among name words (nouns and pronouns), action words (verbs and verbals), modifiers (adjectives and adverbs), joining words (conjunctions and prepositions), and interjections.

It is an accomplishment to be able to combine nouns, verbs, and modifiers to express thoughts. It is even more of an art to have a faculty for using adjectives to supply color and vividness in description. The great artist in writing, however, is the one who is a master of *division of labor.*

He will not overwork his adjectives, because he can contribute to the descriptive effect through choosing the specific concrete noun and the precise, image-making verb. If you say "The bashful young boy entered the room," you have presented something of a descriptive image, but "The timid youth sidled furtively into the kitchen" is far more pictorial and effective. Instead of *boy*, you can say *youth, stripling, youngster, lad;* instead of *enter*, you may use *sidle, slink, bustle, dart, rush, sneak, dash, saunter.* Again, compare "We should like to show you what neat, skillful, and attractive work we can do in reproducing all kinds of form letters" with "Wouldn't you like to see how our method of form letter reproduction looks on your own letterhead?" The second sentence is from an actual business letter.

IDIOM

Another aspect of word usage that the business writer must pay some attention to is *idiom.* This term (from Greek *idioma,* a peculiarity) means an expression peculiar to a language. Idioms are in general of two kinds: (1) those combinations of words, frequently ungrammatical, which mean something which could not be deduced from the separate words (such idioms cause much difficulty in translating from one language to another); and (2) combinations which are arbitrary, that is, correct one way and not another simply because usage has established one way. In the first class we find: *pick a quarrel, done for, beside himself, all in, had better, many a man, every other day, give something to boot, if you please, get rid of, get angry, ten-foot pole, ran into, time and again, bailed out* (speaking of a pilot).

Idioms of the second class include *how do you do* (compare the French *how do you carry yourself* and the Spanish *how are you*), *good-by* (French *au revoir,* "until seeing again"; Spanish *hasta otra vez,* "until another time"), and the use of certain prepositions with certain nouns and verbs: *at* (not *to, in, with*) *home* (German *nach* or *zu Hause,* "to home"), *comply with* (not *to* or *in*), *acquiesce in* (not *with,* or *to*), *pay up* a debt, *pay to* a person.[11]

Most of us have no great difficulty with idiom since we learn idioms as we learn the language as a whole, but it is well to know where grammar leaves off and idiom begins. Also, where grammar is not involved, a well-developed feeling for the idiom of our own language improves the effectiveness of our writing.

[11] For a good, relatively brief discussion of idioms and a list of words with correct prepositions, see pages 409–413 in *The Harper Handbook of College Composition,* by George S. Wykoff and Harry Shaw (New York: Harper & Row, 1962). Idiom, like slang, changes. A number of idiomatic expressions are included in the Glossary of *Effective Business Communication.*

RELATION OF THE INDIVIDUAL'S VOCABULARY TO HIS SUCCESS IN BUSINESS

Building the business vocabulary is an important part of achieving success in business. Just as business requires capital in order that wheels may turn and production lines move, so also business requires that the speaker and writer have a good word hoard from which to draw in order to think business thoughts and devise sentences and paragraphs that will carry the business message so as to do the business job.

Usage Levels and Dialect Distribution *

by Charles C. Fries

Even a very superficial examination of the language practices of native speakers of English will reveal many differences in those practices from person to person. A hasty glance at the materials gathered for the *Linguistic Atlas of New England* not only will confirm the impression one receives from casually listening to the speech of those who talk English but will furnish convincing evidence that the differences of usage among native speakers of English are much greater and much more intricate than is usually believed. These differences of English usage occur not only in matters of vocabulary but also in matters of grammar and especially in matters of pronunciation. It is these differences in the practices of those who speak English that give rise to the many discussions concerning our language and often send students and others to our dictionaries for the information necessary to understand these differences. Ever since the publication of Samuel Johnson's *English Dictionary* in 1755 the "dictionary" has been looked to and consulted as the "authority" concerning the acceptability of words and the proper use of word meanings. "What does *the* dictionary say?" occurs as the common question in all our disputes concerning our language—as if there were but one dictionary with ultimate authority and as if the statements recorded in any dictionary were valid for all time. Those who ask "What does the dictionary say?" practically never inquire concerning the publication date of the particular dictionary consulted or the qualifications of those who have produced it. The desire for an easily accessible "authority" on the part of the general public has created an enormous market for many cheap dictionaries, often produced by unscrupulous publishers who have achieved cheapness by reprinting old dictionary materials upon which the copyright has expired—adding, of course, a few of the well-known new words in order to give the appearance of being up to date.

---

* This piece appeared first as part of the introductory material in the *American College Dictionary*. It is reprinted by permission of Harper & Row, publishers of the text edition, and Random House, Inc., publishers of the trade edition. Dr. Fries, one of the outstanding linguistic scholars in the world today, has written many important books; they include *The Inflections and Syntax of American English, What Is Good English?* and the *American English Grammar*.

Attitudes Toward Usage Differences. Part of the difficulty lies in the common and traditional view of the differences of English usage. Often it is assumed that there exist in any language only two kinds of words, word meanings, and pronunciations: those that are correct and proper and those that are incorrect or mistakes. The "mistakes" are thought to be derived by ignorance and carelessness from the correct or proper uses. It is assumed also that the separation and labeling of the mistakes is a simple process and that grammarians and lexicographers have long ago made the proper decisions and the results of their work need only be preserved and made known to succeeding generations. It is assumed that all dictionaries will incorporate these "accepted" decisions and therefore there is no reason to inquire concerning the qualifications of the editors of a new dictionary or even the means employed to make the assignment of usage labels valid.

Necessity of Recording Usage. From the point of view of modern linguistic science these common naïve assumptions concerning the differences of usage in English must be discarded. They belong to a prescientific period in the study of language—to an age that still believes the earth to be flat and denies the circulation of the blood. The modern dictionary editor who is aware of the principles and methods of the modern scientific study of language and of the accumulations of knowledge concerning our language built up by the patient study of many scholars cannot in honesty follow the easy path of copying the usage labels as they are attached to words and word meanings in former dictionaries. He cannot, as Samuel Johnson often did, condemn words and word meanings in accord with his special prejudices. Johnson, in spite of the fact that his quotations show that the word *excepting* is used by Dryden and Collier, condemns it with the label "an improper word." In similar fashion he attaches the label "low words" to *budge, fun,* and *clever,* although his own quotations give examples of these words from Shakespeare and from Moore, from Addison, Pope, and Arbuthnot.

Constant change—in pronunciation, in grammatical structure, in word meanings, and in the words themselves—is, as far as we know, the normal condition of every language spoken by a living people. The careful study of these changes by the rigorous techniques developed by linguistic science has given us linguistic history. A hundred years of scholarly work has gone into establishing the details of the history of the English language and has forced us to turn away from the methods of "authority" as they are represented in Samuel Johnson's *Dictionary* and its successors. It has demanded the patient recording of the facts of usage as the language is and has been employed by the hosts of speakers of English in this country and in the other countries where English is the language in which the major affairs of the people are conducted. The editor of a modern dictionary is thus confronted with a wide range of constantly changing differences in English usage that cannot be easily separated into correct and proper forms on the one hand and mistakes on the other. These changes in usage render the older dictionaries inaccurate and make necessary continually new examinations of the status of the words and word meanings in English. A dictionary can be an "authority" only in the sense in which a book of chemistry or of physics or of botany can be an "authority"—by the accuracy and the completeness of its record of the observed facts of the field examined, in accord with the latest principles and techniques of the particular science. Older "authorities" in the uses of words are thus superseded by those which incorporate the latest results of the more scientific investigations in the English language.

Regional Differences. In the matter of English usage it is not always possible to define precisely the boundaries within which a word or a word meaning is used or recognized. The facilities of travel have so developed in modern times that many speakers of English hear constantly the language of those from other geographical areas. And the radio has brought into even the most secluded communities the speech of all sections of the country. This mixing of speech forms from various geographical areas is not by any means limited to the upper classes.

"I knowed you wasn't Oklahomy folks. You talk queer kinda—That ain't no blame, you understan'."

"Ever'body says words different," said Ivy. "Arkansas folks says 'em different, and Oklahomy folks says 'em different. And we seen a lady from Massachusetts, an' she said 'em differentest of all. Couldn' hardly make out what she was sayin'."

(John Steinbeck, *The Grapes of Wrath*, p. 168.)

In the great mass of differences of usage that appear in the practice of English speakers, however, some words and word meanings and some pronunciations are in common use in special parts of the English-speaking world and appear much less frequently or never in other areas. For these this dictionary marks the geographical areas of special use. Some of the areas thus indicated within this country are New England, the old South, and the Southwest for such words as the following: *selectman, sharpie, levee* [1] (def. 1), *granny* (def. 4), *corn pone, alamo, chaps, chuck wagon* (see the definitions of these words).

British usage differs from the usage of the United States in such words as *lift* (def. 21), *navvy, lorry* (def. 1), *petrol* (def. 1), *gorse* (see the definitions of these words, and the preface by A. W. Read on "British and American Usage," page xxviii).

And Australia has its particular words and word meanings, as *paddock* (def. 3), *swag* [2] (def. 2), *billabon, billy* (def. 3) (see the definitions of these words).

Many words and word meanings are characteristic of certain fields of human activity. Each trade and occupation and sport has its technical vocabulary. Some of this technical vocabulary consists of special words used only in science, art, trade, or sport, such as *Binet test, electrode, binnacle, chiaroscuro, silo, forward pass* (see the definitions of these words).

Much of these technical vocabularies, however, consists of special meanings and uses of words that are employed generally in the language. The *field* in baseball has a special sense, as does *sacrifice, run, hit, out, plate, pitcher.* In the preparation and marketing of alcoholic beverages, the words *proof, dry, mash,* and *smooth* are used with special meanings.

"Levels" of Usage. Most frequently, however, discussions of language center upon what are often called the "levels" of usage. Some words and word meanings are frequently called "slang." The term "slang" has suffered such a wide extension of its signification and has been applied to so many varieties of words that it is extremely difficult to draw the line between what is slang and what is not. The difference between slang and not-slang does not rest in the meanings of the words themselves. To say that a man is "recalcitrant" is using an acceptable and somewhat learned word; to call him a "kicker" in the same situation is using slang, although the meanings are similar. Some clipped words, as *gent,* are often regarded as slang; others, such as *piano, phone,* and *cello,* are not slang. Slang cannot be defined in terms of either the forms or the strict meanings of the words themselves; it can, however, be characterized in terms of the suggested feelings accompanying certain words—their connotations rather than their denotations. Flippant humor marks the expressions we call slang. Some examples are *Java* (def. 3), *ice* (def. 8), *croak* (def. 4) *hangout, corking* (see the definitions of these words).

Some expressions appear only in poetry. They suggest then those circumstances in which they usually occur. Others are now found only in the written material of books. To mark them *"Poetic"* and *"Literary"* serves to record the special areas in which they are commonly used. Some examples are *gloaming, e'er, lidless* (def. 3), *naught* (def. 2), *scarce* (def. 4) (see the definitions of these words).

Many expressions occur primarily in conversation rather than in formal writing. The occasions for their use are chiefly conversational situations. These are marked *"Colloq."* Even teachers of English frequently misunderstand the application of the label *Colloquial* in our best dictionaries. Some confuse it with *localism* and think of the words and constructions marked "colloquial" as peculiarities of speaking which are characteristic of a particular locality. Others feel that some stigma attaches to the label *"Colloquial"* and would strive to avoid as incorrect (or as of a low level) all words so marked. The word *colloquial,* however, as used to label words and phrases in a modern scientifically edited dictionary, has no such meaning. It is used to mark those words and constructions whose range of use is primarily that of the polite conversation of cultivated people, of their familiar letters and informal speeches, as distinct from those words and constructions which are common also in formal writing. The usage of our better magazines and of public addresses generally has, during the past generation, moved away from the formal and literary toward the colloquial.

Some words and expressions occur primarily in the language of those without much conventional education. These expressions are often called "illiterate" or "vulgar English," and are considered "incorrect." As a matter of fact, many of these expressions are survivals from an older period of the language and are "incorrect" only in the sense that they do not occur in the usage of standard English—the practice of the socially accepted, those who are carrying on the important affairs of English-speaking people. Much of the language spoken by the uneducated is the same as that of the polite conversation of cultivated people and also duplicates the expressions of formal literary discourse. The usage labels in a dictionary attempt to mark only those expressions that are peculiar to a particular type or dialect of English. If one ignores the differences that characterize the various geographical areas and the differences of the separate fields of human activity, of trades and vocations and sports, the situation may be roughly represented by the following diagram:

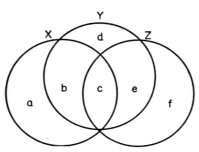

The three circles X, Y, Z represent the three sets of language habits indicated above.

X formal literary English, the words, the expressions, and the structures one finds in serious books.

Y colloquial English, the words, expressions, and the structures of the informal but polite conversation of cultivated people.

Z illiterate English, the words, the expressions, and the structures of the language of the uneducated.

b, c, e represent the overlappings of the three types of English.

c that which is common to all three: formal literary English, colloquial English, and illiterate English.

b that which is common to both formal literary English and colloquial English.

e that which is common to both colloquial English and illiterate English.

a, d, f represent those portions of each type of English that are peculiar to that particular set of language habits.

The following is a list of some of the other usage labels used in this dictionary with typical examples under each of the particular words and expressions to which each label is assigned.

Archaic: impose (def. 8), hugger-mugger (def. 2), glister (def. 1), lief (def. 2), angle [2] (def. 3).

Colloq.: angel (def. 6), brass tacks, fizzle (def. 2), flimflam, goner.

Humorous: celestial (def. 5), human (def. 4).

Obs.: loblolly boy, lust (def. 5), flittermouse, murther, drugget (def. 2).

Obsolesc.: saloon (def. 6), regimen (def. 5).

Rare: image (def. 17), impassionate, faulty (def. 2), instancy (def. 2), genial [1] (def. 3).

Scot.: chap [1] (def. 5), laird, hag [2] (def. 1), icker.

Scot. and N. Eng.: unco, kirk (def. 1), *ilk* (def. 2), *braw, bairn.*

South African: laager, kraal (def. 3).

U.S.: chain lightning, challenge (def. 14), biscuit (def. 1), boss (def. 2), quilting bee.

Exercises and Problems in Communication

Because you feel that you have "made it fairly well" so far with your present word supply, you may be somewhat apathetic about following through on these exercises. I encourage you to develop a word-consciousness as you go through the course. Analyze your vocabulary power, so that you may synthesize your writing and speaking power.

1. To get the sensation that comes from acquiring knowledge and to get started on a systematic program of increasing your vocabulary, look up every new word you hear or read for the next three days. As you look up the words, use the labels on the reproduced page from the dictionary (pages 138 and 139 in this chapter) as a guide to help you get all the information pertaining to the words.

2. Study the diagram near the end of the chapter reading and classify the new words you are learning, according to the levels of usage: formal, colloquial, or illiterate.

3. Analyze the situation in which you heard the new words or the context in which the words were used in your reading. As an exercise in distinctions in usage, label or group the words according to Dr. Fries's "a" through "f" classifications. Discuss your results—supporting your grouping—either in a short paper to your instructor or in a brief talk to your class.

4. To sense general public dependence on a dictionary, consult the *Reader's Guide to Periodical Literature,* Volume XXIII, to see journalistic and scholarly reaction to the publication of *Webster's Third New International Dictionary.* You can get into the debate (it's still going on) as to the function of a dictionary: Is it an authority, or is it a report of language (words) as used by a people? Present your opinion in a paper or a talk.

5. You will find, among the references in the *Reader's Guide,* two that present both sides of the argument on "Webster's Third." The academician's view is given in "But What's a Dictionary for?" by Bergen Evans, in the *Atlantic Monthly,* May, 1962; the professional writer's, in "The String Untuned," by Dwight MacDonald, in *The New Yorker,* March 10, 1962. For the business implications, read "Webster's way out dictionary," in *Business Week,* September 16, 1961. Which functions of language, as discussed in Chapter 1, are the three authors exercising?

6. From a daily newspaper or news magazine (such as *Time* or *Newsweek*) copy twenty words or phrases that modern business and modern applied science have added to the vocabulary within your own memory. Copy enough of the context to make clear the meaning of the term.

7. Look into a business magazine (such as *Business Week* or *Dun's Review,* or a professional journal in your field—chemistry, accounting, home economics, etc.), and make a list as you did in Exercise 6. What differences did you note in style and usage between the general and the more specialized publications?

8. With the same objective of checking words and phrases recently added in American usage, read an issue of *Vital Speeches*. As you look for words, also analyze the style as you did in Exercise 7. What differences, if any, did you detect between written and spoken presentations? (Of course, you will have to imagine hearing the *Vital Speeches* pieces.)

9. To test people's attention to conventional usage, in conversation with fellow students, mispronounce a word (for example, "fakāde" for *façade*, "preform" for *perform*, "jimmick" for *gimmick*), or use a "second" pronunciation (such as *precedence*, with the accent on the second syllable; *rationale*, with the final "e" pronounced; *interesting* or *interested*, accenting the third syllable). Use these pronunciations often enough to get listener reaction. (Although this exercise may require some daring, the procedure can be effective in developing word-consciousness.)

10. Read "Semantics and Its Implications for Teachers of Business Communication," by H. R. Jolliffe, in *The Journal of Business Communication*, March, 1964. The article has applications of semantics for students in writing as well as for teachers.

11. Make a list of seven synonyms and three antonyms for each of the following words: *bright, early, generous, clever, fast, honest, beautiful, cheerful, bitter, lustrous.*

12. Open your dictionary at random, and begin reading about the origins of the words your eyes stop on; you need not concern yourself with the definitions. Write down ten words whose origin seems to you unusual or interesting.

13. For another look at word origins, read *Why You Say It,* by Webb Garrison (New York: Abingdon Press, 1955). Make a written or oral report on those terms discussed in this entertaining, informative book that have business applications.

14. You can become better acquainted with dictionaries and their ramifications through the following books:

Kenneth G. Wilson, R. H. Hendrickson, and Peter Alan Taylor. *Harbrace Guide to Dictionaries.* New York: Harcourt, Brace & World, Inc., 1963.
William and Mary Morris. *Dictionary of Word and Phrase Origins.* New York: Harper & Row, 1962.
Frank Gaynor. *International Business Dictionary in Five Languages.* New York: Philosophical Library, 1946.

Read and report on the various uses these books can serve for the student in business communication.

15. Read an article in *Harper's Magazine, The Atlantic, Fortune,* or the *New York Times Magazine.* Write a brief analysis of the author's use of vocabulary; discuss how word usage contributed to the effectiveness or ineffectiveness of the article. Cite specific word usages to support your evaluation.

16. (a) Make a list of ten slang words or phrases that you have heard from college classmates, relatives, or other associates. (b) Check these expressions in *Webster's Third New International Dictionary.* How many did you find there? Were these all labeled as slang?

17. Make a list of ten idioms commonly employed in the business world. Use each in an original sentence.

18. Read the advertisements in a general magazine (*Life, Look,* or the *Saturday Evening Post*) for examples of each of the following: simile, metaphor, hyperbole, metonymy, synecdoche, personification.

19. For a description of writing techniques unfamiliar to many persons, read about "audio-scriptics" in *The Orchestra of Language*, by Ernest M. Robson (New York: Thomas Yoseloff, 1959). The term, according to the author, includes "the techniques for the writer to make written language more effective with patterns of the tone, timbre, time, and power in the sounds of speech." From your knowledge of derivations, coin a more "common" phrase for "audio-scriptics."

20. Check your ease with words by taking the following test, marking the word in each group that most closely defines the italicized word. (The test grows progressively more difficult. The first 10 words appear in a 7,000-word vocabulary; the last 10 are beyond the 30,000-word level.)

1. *semblance* (1) pretension (2) appearance (3) disturbance (4) concealment
2. *prone* (1) unwilling (2) inclined (3) joyful (4) tense
3. *posterity* (1) success (2) descendants (3) aftereffect (4) determination
4. *parch* (1) dissect (2) freeze (3) dry (4) remove
5. *myriad* (1) proverb (2) colorful (3) great many (4) very few
6. *interpose* (1) come between (2) change (3) inquire (4) stand fast
7. *hale* (1) large (2) round (3) dark (4) robust
8. *grotesque* (1) ghastly (2) huge (3) bizarre (4) minute
9. *compassion* (1) inhumanity (2) sympathy (3) memory (4) difficulty
10. *censure* (1) count (2) condemn (3) debate (4) burn
11. *vestige* (1) contract (2) payment (3) major portion (4) trace
12. *transient* (1) permanent (2) temporary (3) helpful (4) pale
13. *stigma* (1) mark (2) wagon (3) reward (4) kindness
14. *stark* (1) complete (2) bare (3) sharp (4) gray
15. *relinquish* (1) seize (2) reject (3) maintain (4) leave
16. *parasite* (1) hanger-on (2) city-dweller (3) pioneer (4) unrefined metal
17. *latent* (1) dormant (2) tardy (3) immense (4) noisy
18. *inert* (1) foolish (2) lifeless (3) active (4) natural
19. *farce* (1) concealment (2) compulsion (3) mockery (4) battle
20. *cadence* (1) enclosure (2) rhythm (3) radiance (4) cowardice
21. *swarthy* (1) soft (2) grassy (3) dark (4) boastful
22. *sanguine* (1) pessimistic (2) indifferent (3) sane (4) confident
23. *respite* (1) postponement (2) shame (3) ill-will (4) profit
24. *mien* (1) claim (2) exclamation (3) appearance (4) cruelty
25. *deign* (1) delay (2) scorn (3) condescend (4) suspect
26. *dearth* (1) scarcity (2) uncleanness (3) value (4) abundance
27. *category* (1) class (2) mixture (3) dwelling (4) review
28. *blanch* (1) injure (2) hurry (3) whiten (4) salt
29. *articulate* (1) divide (2) respond (3) invent (4) express clearly
30. *arid* (1) cold (2) scented (3) humid (4) dry
31. *tiers* (1) thirds (2) rows (3) windows (4) walls
32. *primeval* (1) vicious (2) important (3) worthless (4) primitive
33. *peremptory* (1) angry (2) uncertain (3) hasty (4) positive
34. *nominal* (1) trifling (2) humble (3) hostile (4) nameless

35. *motley* (1) impure (2) fashionable (3) diverse (4) pretty
36. *insidious* (1) internal (2) sly (3) tasteless (4) aggressive
37. *illicit* (1) improper (2) sickly (3) legal (4) unfinished
38. *evince* (1) bounce (2) avoid (3) invite (4) demonstrate
39. *copse* (1) encounter (2) plenty (3) thicket (4) reaction
40. *anterior* (1) frontal (2) outside (3) additional (4) elevated
41. *whimsical* (1) fanciful (2) noisy (3) stubborn (4) ornamental
42. *sedentary* (1) strange (2) exhausted (3) inactive (4) foreign
43. *petulant* (1) peevish (2) obsequious (3) compliant (4) amorous
44. *medley* (1) mixture (2) tune (3) curiosity (4) middle
45. *innately* (1) innocently (2) stationary (3) naturally (4) foolishly
46. *inertia* (1) sluggishness (2) injustice (3) vigor (4) equity
47. *indigenous* (1) outraged (2) unhealthy (3) native (4) scarce
48. *facetious* (1) serious (2) facial (3) fractional (4) humorous
49. *evoke* (1) destroy (2) call forth (3) develop (4) eject
50. *elicit* (1) bring out (2) mix (3) choose (4) neglect
51. *reticent* (1) gregarious (2) reserved (3) courteous (4) negligent
52. *recalcitrant* (1) depressed (2) reckless (3) disobedient (4) indifferent
53. *querulous* (1) complaining (2) subdued (3) inquistive (4) cheerful
54. *premonition* (1) anger (2) threat (3) forewarning (4) disaster
55. *meticulous* (1) lazy (2) heedless (3) careful (4) small
56. *irrelevant* (1) sacrilegious (2) unreasonable (3) unrelated (4) questionable
57. *invidious* (1) undecided (2) hateful (3) secret (4) exact
58. *innocuous* (1) harmless (2) immune (3) unrighteous (4) innocent
59. *incarnation* (1) imprisonment (2) communication (3) embodiment (4) agitation
60. *homily* (1) ugliness (2) sermon (3) regret (4) lie
61. *scurrilous* (1) desperate (2) abusive (3) frantic (4) diseased
62. *omniscient* (1) forgetful (2) powerful (3) gloomy (4) all-knowing
63. *onerous* (1) lonely (2) exclusive (3) honorary (4) burdensome
64. *intrusive* (1) exceptional (2) retiring (3) abusive (4) encroaching
65. *integument* (1) honesty (2) kindness (3) covering (4) quarrel
66. *consanguinity* (1) health (2) rivalry (3) kinship (4) community
67. *furbish* (1) dismantle (2) remove (3) polish (4) supply
68. *flamboyant* (1) flammable (2) showy (3) up-lifting (4) inconspicuous
69. *enervate* (1) soothe (2)invigorate (3) excite (4) weaken
70. *nostrum* (1) exuberance (2) remedy (3) charity (4) legislature
71. *recrudescence* (1) disappearance (2) forgetfulness (3) revival (4) omission
72. *pragmatic* (1) idealistic (2) practical (3) cruel (4) unofficial
73. *relevancy* (1) pertinency (2) unimportance (3) wastefulness (4) memory
74. *friable* (1) strong (2) breakable (3) edible (4) loose
75. *effulgent* (1) bulging (2) radiant (3) extravagant (4) revolting
76. *devolution* (1) development (2) holiness (3) deprivation (4) degeneration
77. *marquetry* (1) inlaid work (2) canopy (3) drapery (4) salesmanship
78. *peripatetic* (1) sad (2) exclusive (3) hard-working (4) itinerant
79. *proem* (1) long verse (2) preamble (3) temple (4) conclusion
80. *prosy* (1) dull (2) colorful (3) strong (4) fancy

81. *somnolence* (1) loneliness (2) literacy (3) sleepiness (4) good fortune
82. *salacious* (1) humorous (2) religious (3) obscene (4) tasty
83. *sacrosanct* (1) invisible (2) altar (3) dedicated (4) church vestibule
84. *pyriform* (1) shapeless (2) pyramidal (3) blown glass (4) pear-shaped
85. *paradigm* (1) example (2) separation (3) serious defect (4) thick-skinned animal
86. *marmoset* (1) disciplinarian (2) citizen (3) monkey (4) dictator
87. *imbricate* (1) involve (2) overlap (3) occupy (4) survive
88. *excoriate* (1) denounce (2) remove core (3) pull away (4) ease
89. *decrement* (1) decrease (2) damage (3) burial (4) measurement
90. *canard* (1) hoax (2) duck (3) patent (4) coward
91. *coruscate* (1) sparkle (2) whirl (3) injure (4) corrode
92. *gnomic* (1) dwarfed (2) nameless (3) aphoristic (4) silent
93. *hedonistic* (1) willful (2) regretful (3) pleasure-loving (4) top-heavy
94. *impudicity* (1) prudence (2) reluctance (3) immodesty (4) pride
95. *indurate* (1) impermanent (2) tolerant (3) hardened (4) faded
96. *minacious* (1) lying (2) threatening (3) precious (4) vivacious
97. *natant* (1) living (2) watching (3) rejoicing (4) floating
98. *neoteric* (1) internal (2) difficult (3) ancient (4) new
99. *nimiety* (1) worry (2) faithfulness (3) excess (4) deficiency
100. *patronym* (1) surname (2) nobility (3) assistance (4) preference

21. Look up the etymology of the following words in your dictionary, and observe how a knowledge of their origins aids in understanding and remembering their meanings: *amalgamate, aristocracy, barometer, community, consolidate, democracy, entrepreneur, episcopacy, ethereal, lawyer, luminous, monarchy, oligarchy, pathology, plutocracy, psychology, sacrament, speedometer, surgeon thermometer.*

PART II

BUSINESS LETTERS

7

Basic and Utility Letters

*I know a firm that received 137 inquiries from one advertisement, but the reply did not bring in one single order. How inefficient can a firm get?—*RICHARD H. MORRIS, *"Letters That Lose the Business"* [1]

"EVERYDAY LETTERS"

One communication consultant calls the correspondence we will look at in this chapter "everyday letters"; he says that terms such as *basic* and *utility* are grand terms. Although letters regarding credit, adjustments, and collections are an everyday part of most businesses, orders and inquiries and handling of them can take on a rather commonplace aspect.

But there are many companies that let the routine nature of the letters belie their importance. In many instances, an order or inquiry is a first contact between the writer and a company. Too many times, the contact is a short one because of the company's response—or lack of it. In the article from which the chapter-opening quotation is taken, Richard Morris reports that of 100 companies getting inquiries about various products, only 8 per cent answered within ten days, most of the companies took four to eight weeks, and 4 per cent did not reply at all. Each of the 100 was a large company and advertised regularly in national magazines at rates of $15,000 to $25,000 a page. When such sums are spent on promotion and advertising, it would seem that a company would invest $2.32—the average cost of a letter—tor follow-up.

But many letters do not cost two dollars. Relatively simple, they may be dictated in a minute and perhaps signed (properly initialed) and dispatched by the secretary herself. Some involve nothing more than clip-

[1] *Sales Management*, March 20, 1959, p. 52.

ping and filling out a coupon and addressing an envelope. A great many inquiries, answers to inquiries, and order acknowledgments are of this sort. Obviously, such letters as the following would not cost two dollars:

Gentlemen:

Please give us printing quotation on 1,000, 3,000 and 5,000 lots like sample of ledger sheet enclosed.

Yours very truly,

Gentlemen:

May I please have an examination copy of your text BETTER WRITING, which I wish to consider for my class in Freshman Composition.

Very truly yours,

It is business efficiency, of course, to keep down the cost of such letters, in so far as economy is compatible with satisfying the persons who get them; but we should be very careful here, as elsewhere in letter writing, to distinguish between short-term and long-term economy. That is, we must make sure that even our simplest letters will perform satisfactorily the communication job which is to be done, and we must always be ready to write a more elaborate letter whenever the situation calls for one.

REQUESTS AND INQUIRIES

Retailers write to jobbers and manufacturers for price quotations or for descriptions of articles which they are interested in adding to stock; college professors ask publishers about prospective texts for courses; the general public wants samples of products advertised in magazines, or names and addresses of local dealers where the articles can be obtained. Letters of request or inquiry should nearly always be brief, but they should state clearly what is wanted and, usually, why. The reply should be much fuller than the inquiry, for the replier can be expected to assume cheerfully the burden of his labor and expense when the inquiry opens the way to a business transaction. Many requests and inquiries, however, call for favors to the writer without recompense to the replier: a member of a college debate team asks a lawyer or a banker for information or a statement to be used in a debate, or a beginner in the business world asks an established businessman of his acquintance for advice. In such cases, courtesy and expediency suggest that the utmost care and tact be used in wording the letter, and that a stamped, addressed envelope be enclosed for the reply.

The following actual letter (and from a business publication house!) is an example of how *not* to word a request:

Dear Dr. Wilson:

In order that we may justice in our reports on your talk, we will appreciate your sending us a copy of your talk on "Consumer Relations" that you will give Friday night, March 23 at the Business Relations Conference of the University of Chicago.

Yours very truly,

ANSWERING REQUESTS AND INQUIRIES

Here is the method used by the International Harvester Company to handle the thousands of inquiries received each year by the Consumer Relations Department.

1. The face of each inquiry is marked in red with the location of the International Harvester branch office in the inquirer's own territory.

2. The inquiry is classified for more efficient and personalized handling into one of three categories and one of eighteen subcategories (see below).

3. The home office Consumer Relations Department prepares and mails an appropriate acknowledgment or reply. Whenever possible the reply shares with the branch office at least part of the opportunity to help the consumer. For some categories a printed form letter or card can be used; for others (A-3, A-4, B-1 through B-5, for example) a special letter is required.

4. The home office Consumer Relations Department forwards the inquiry to the proper branch office, along with the following information:

(branch office location)
. . . .
This inquiry was received in the Consumer Relations Department.

Acknowledgment card . . . . . . A-1 . . . .

and printed material requested
mailed . . . . April 15, 19-- . . . . .

See Consumer Relations Manual No. 1 for instructions on further handling.

If a special letter was sent to the customer, a copy of that letter is sent to the branch office along with the inquiry. Consumer Relations Manual No. 1 is a 24-page booklet called "Handling Inquiries." It reproduces typical replies to inquiries in all categories and subcategories.

5. The branch office answers the inquiries that have been referred to it for handling and sends supplementary or follow-up letters to persons whose inquiries have been answered by the home office.

CLASSIFICATION OF INQUIRIES

International Harvester has set up the following categories into which all inquiries are divided for most efficient handling:

Category A: (Prospects)
1. Individuals requesting information which can be completely answered by available printed material.
2. Prospective purchasers who desire information on equipment and prices.
3. Prospects who require specific information with regard to equipment capabilities and adaptability to do a specific job.
4. Prospects who require information, in addition to equipment information, with regard to farm practices.
5. Prospects who desire printed material and information on equipment not yet in production.
6. Individuals who request information on equipment not planned or built by the company.

Category B: (Influential Individuals)
1. Government officials.
2. County agents.
3. Magazine and newspaper editors.
4. Educational institutions and educators.
5. Others.

Category C: (Miscellany)
1. School children.
2. Hobbyists and collectors.
3. Individuals requesting information and printed material to gratify their own curiosity.
4. Complaints.
5. Questions on Company policy.
6. Requests to be placed on our publications mailing lists.

The helpfulness of such a classification system is obvious: each inquiry can be routed to the individual or department best able to handle it. Some of the subcategories involve sales; some involve public relations; one involves adjustment. Some of the questions can be handled by a clerk in the Consumer Relations office; others will have to be sent to agricultural engineers with degrees from A & M or State; some will go to top management.

STANDARDIZED FORMS

The General Electric Company used the printed post card illustrated on page 171 to acknowledge requests for a free booklet offered in an advertisement.

Montgomery Ward and Company sent this form letter to "Dear Customer":

Full information about the merchandise you have inquired about is given in the Catalog we are sending you.

Care has been taken to describe and picture the goods just as they are. You may make your selections with the same confidence you would have in purchasing over the counter.

Not only will you save money by ordering your needs from our Catalog, but you will be getting dependable merchandise, sold under our guarantee of satisfaction or your money back.

A publication granted a permission to Mr. Jones:

Thank you for your kind letter of June 28 requesting permission to reprint material contained in the American Journal of Philately.

We are perfectly willing to grant you this permission, and appreciate your writing to us.

SPECIAL INQUIRIES

The cost of such forms is very low, and each does its job adequately. It is important, however, to distinguish between routine requests and inquiries and special ones. A distressing number of replies to such letters are almost unbelievably inadequate. For instance, a college professor offering a new course in American Ideals and Traditions has on hand a book which looks good, but it was published in 1950 and is a little out of date. His inquiry about its availability brought this reply from the publisher:

Thank you for your letter of April twenty-eighth concerning our publication AMERICA SEEKING HERSELF, by F. R. Fortune.

There has been no new edition of this book since that of 1950, which you mentioned.

Very truly yours,

Such a letter leaves the inquirer worse off than he was before. When he wrote, he had a hope; now he hasn't even that, for the publisher hasn't taken the trouble to make any suggestion, or even express regret. The only feature that speaks for the letter is the "Thank you" with which it starts. And the tone of the letter as a whole is such that even the "Thank you" has a hollow ring, leaving the impression that the writer begins all correspondence with that expression. Although courteous, "Thank you" as an opener should be used sparingly. Overuse has made it almost a stereotype. Other expressions of gratitude such as "I appreciate . . . ," "It was good to hear . . . ," etc., should be in the letter writer's repertoire of openings. Not only overused, "Thank you" is misused. A letter answering a customer who had written that she was not accepting merchandise she had ordered, opened with "Thank you for telling us you can't accept your Sharp-Brite Cutlery Set."

Suppose you had been given the professor's letter about the 1950 book. Would you have recognized that he was in a dilemma? The answer is yes, no doubt. You would have recognized first of all that Professor Smith is a potential and valuable customer with a problem. Next you would have asked yourself, "What can I do about it?" You think of three possibilities: (1) Since he is interested in the 1950 book, which is a good one, and admits that he probably won't find exactly what he is looking for, you may give him sales material on this book, and endeavor to relate it to his prospective course. (2) If you decide that it is not suitable, you could suggest anything you know of, for even if he does patronize a competitor, he will at least continue to think well of you. (3) Finally, if you find that you cannot make a positive suggestion, you will at least extend courtesy and leave him with the impression that you have sympathetically considered his problem and done your best to be of service.

The writer of the following letter from an electric razor manufacturer leans over backward to answer the reader's questions clearly:

Dear Mr. Brubeck:

This is an answer to your recent postal card inquiring about the possibility of purchasing a case for your model "R" Shavemaster.

We are not sure just which part you require so we are attaching a copy of our parts list covering the model "R." The bakelite housing on the Shavemaster itself is sometimes referred to as a case, and then there are also listed the leather carrying case and a Deluxe Gift Case which is made of metal and is leatherette covered.

All of the parts listed on the attached sheet are readily available, and we can mail them to you as soon as we have your order.

Yours very truly,

The keynote of this letter is helpfulness; the writer successfully anticipates and avoids misunderstandings which would cause delay and confusion.

Following are three examples of good replies to inquiries:

B. Altman & Co., New York

Dear Mr. Baker:

Thank you for your order which has been forwarded. We can
furnish the following Peek Frean Biscuits:

> Martini cracker biscuit, 1 pound 1¾ ounces, priced at $1.35;
> Afternoon tea assortment, 1 pound 11½ ounces, priced at
> $2.25; Playbox assortment, 1 pound 2¼ ounces, at $1.29;
> English assortment, 1 pound 15½ ounces, at $2.00; and Scot
> assortment, 1 pound 15 ounces at $1.89.

Your further wishes will receive our careful attention.

Very truly yours,

Department of Commerce, Washington, D.C.

Dear Mr. Brown:

Your request of March 11 for a copy of the <u>Report to the Nation</u>
has been received and a copy will go forward to you. We are, of
course, pleased to know that the information contained in this
publication is of use to you, and are adding your name to a list
of those to receive future releases from this Department.

Thank you for writing us.

Sincerely yours,

A Courteous Reply to an Absent-Minded Professor

Dear Professor Jones:

Thank you for your letter of October 7. We appreciate your
interest in Jackson and Hart: THE SOUL OF POETRY, and should
like very much to have you examine it with a view to possible
use in your Freshman English Course.

May we remind you, however, that a copy of this book went to you
from here on publication last May. Won't you kindly look over
your shelves to see whether this is at hand? If a search does
not bring it to light we shall be glad to send another copy.
The list price of the book is $1.50.

Professor Madison King of the University of Temple Beach says
of the above book: "I should like to say that I know of no book
of anywhere near comparable merit for the subject."

Sincerely yours,

Observe that in each of these four letters, the "you" attitude is present.
The writers are all trying either to extend to the inquirer a service or to
explain matters from his point of view.

In response to a simple letter of inquiry concerning the pronunciation of the name of the author of a text, one publisher made a lasting friend of a department head by writing a chatty, two-page letter in reply, discussing pronunciation quirks and other linguistic matters which he had rightly guessed were of mutual interest. Be businesslike, yes, but to be businesslike is not always to be brief.

A classic example of the longer letter of response to requests and inquiries is the following, written by that master letter writer, Abraham Lincoln, to his stepbrother, John D. Johnston, January 2, 1851:

Dear Johnston: Your request for eighty dollars I do not think it best to comply with now. At the various times when I have helped you a little you have said to me, "We can get along very well now"; but in a very short time I find you in the same difficulty again. Now this can only happen by some defect in your conduct. What that defect is, I think I know. You are not lazy, and still you are an idler. I doubt whether, since I saw you, you have done a good whole day's work in any one day. You do not very much dislike to work, and still you do not work much, merely because it does not seem to you that you could get much for it. This habit of uselessly wasting time is the whole difficulty; it is vastly important to you, and still more so to your children, that you should break the habit. It is more important to them, because they have longer to live, and can keep out of an idle habit before they are in it, easier than they can get out after they are in.

You are now in need of some money; and what I propose is, that you shall go to work, "tooth and nail," for somebody who will give you money for it. Let father and your boys take charge of your things at home, prepare for a crop, and make the crop, and you go to work for the best money wages, or in discharge of any debt you owe, that you can get; and to secure you a fair reward for your labor, I now promise you, that for every dollar that you will, between this and the first of May, get for your own labor, either in money or as your own indebtedness, I will then give you one other dollar. By this, if you hire yourself at ten dollars a month, from me you will get ten more, making twenty dollars a month for your work. In this I do not mean you shall go off to St. Louis, or the lead mines, or the gold mines in California, but I mean for you to go at it for the best wages you can get close to home in Coles County. Now, if you will do this, you will be soon out of debt, and, what is better, you will have a habit that will keep you from getting in debt again. But if I should now clear you out of debt, next year you would be just as deep in as ever. You say you would almost give your place in heaven for seventy or eighty dollars. Then you value your place in heaven very cheap, for I am sure you can, with the offer I make, get the seventy or eighty dollars for four or five months' work. You say if I will furnish you the money you will deed me the land, and, if you don't pay the money back, you will deliver possession. Nonsense! If you can't now live with the land, how will you then live without it? You have always been kind to me, and I do not mean to be unkind to you. On the contrary, if you will but follow my advice, you will find it worth more than eighty times eighty dollars to you.

Affectionately your brother,[2]

[2] In Louis Wann, *The Rise of Realism* (New York: The Macmillan Co., 1949), pp. 146–47.

ORDERS AND ACKNOWLEDGMENTS

Order blanks and requisition forms now take care of most of the correspondence involved in ordering goods. Such forms are made as nearly foolproof as possible, and some of them are marvels of ingenuity and typography. Nevertheless, a considerable quantity of goods is still ordered by letter, and companies especially welcome order letters, since they frequently represent new customers, or opportunities for building good will.

Every business person should have a clear picture of the essentials of the order letter. It must give clearly the following information:

1. Name and address of customer.
2. Consignee and address when these are not those of the person placing the order.
3. Mode of shipment (freight, express, parcel post).
4. Time of shipment (all immediate, part immediate, part or all deferred to a specified date).
5. Complete description of article (quantity, name, size, color, style, price, and shipping weight).
6. Terms of payment and kind of remittance, if this accompanies the order.

Irregular and special orders are most likely to require a letter. The following three letters transacted business in a satisfactory way:

Letter of Inquiry to Mail Order Company

I need some replacements for a Jefferson cleaner, which is about eight years old. The parts to be replaced are metal, but plastic could be used as long as they fit.

The parts needed are a rubber hose 6 ft. long, a floor brush, and the long thin, narrow piece for cleaning around upholstery.

Will you let me know the prices on these pieces. And can they be mailed to me at my address, since I don't have a car to drive to Winchester to your catalogue store.

The Mail Order Company's Reply

I am glad to tell you that we can fill your order for the parts for your Jefferson cleaner and that it will not be necessary for you to go to a catalogue store. The order will be sent parcel post to your address.

You will notice that the hose is 7 feet long; it is vinyl rather than rubber. Many sweeper companies are equipping their new sets with vinyl hoses. The attachmment for use on upholstery is a crevice tool. I have listed two types of floor brushes; you can let us know which you want.

When you send your order, will you please use the numbers for the items you want. That information will help us get your order to you in a short time.

12 F 398	7-foot Sweeper Hose	$4.95
12 F 397	Wide Floor Brush	1.89
12 F 396	Combination Rug-Floor Brush	3.69
12 F 391	Plastic Crevice Tool	.49

Parcel post for the hose, a brush, and the crevice tool will be $.38.

We appreciate your writing us about this merchandise.

The Customer's Order

Please send me by parcel post the Jefferson cleaner parts I have listed. The money order for $9.51 covers all expenses.

12 F 398	7-foot Sweeper Hose	$4.95
12 F 396	Combination Rug-Floor Brush	3.69
12 F 391	Plastic Crevice Tool	.49

That was a nice letter your company sent me about this order.

Acknowledgment of orders is established business courtesy, even when the merchandise may arrive approximately as soon as the acknowledgment. Mail order companies regularly acknowledge orders with a printed postal card form. The invoice accompanies the goods or follows later by mail. Order letters are frequently of a nature requiring an acknowledgment by letter in return. Here are examples of such acknowledgments:

Gentlemen:

Thank you for your order No. 7448 dated May 10, 1965, which has been entered on our District Office requisition No. 418 and has been forwarded to our Company's main office. This order is of course subject to acceptance at the main offices. After acceptance of this order, a shipping schedule will be established and you will be immediately notified.

You can be certain that we will give your order our careful attention and that we appreciate this opportunity to serve you.

Very truly yours,

Dear Mr. Smith:

We gratefully acknowledge your order for 32 copies of the December issue of HARPER'S MAGAZINE. The order has been duly entered, and magazines, including your own desk copy, should be in your possession by this time.

Under separate cover we sent you a copy of the December "Suggestions for Teaching."

Cordially yours,

These are satisfactory acknowledgments in two important essentials: each shows appreciation for the order, and each describes the order unmistakably.

GENERAL ELECTRIC COMPANY

Radio, Television and Electronics Department, Schenectady, N. Y.

Your RESPONSE to our offer to mail you the new Electronics book is appreciated. A great deal of care has been taken to make this book of exceptional interest and value—something you will want to keep.

We expect it to be off press in the latter part of November, at which time you will be included in the first mailing.

H. J. DEINES

Advertising Manager

Fig. 20. Printed post card used as a business acknowledgment.

DEFERRED, UNFILLED, AND PARTIALLY FILLED ORDERS

Even under the most stable business conditions, unexpectedly large demands or other factors make it necessary for firms to write letters explaining a lack of ability to serve the customer to the fullest extent. The keynote of letters explaining delays, substitutions, and cancellations is cheerfulness and emphasis upon *what can be done.* Tact is necessary.

As in any complaint situation, it is a temptation to "answer in kind" when a disgruntled customer writes critically and peevishly of his dissatisfaction and inconvenience. A professor who had received his order with an explanation that one item had been back-ordered wrote a nationally known photographic-supply firm that delay in filling orders was going to "ruin the company's good name." Seemingly to add weight to his disgust, the professor's letter was written on his university-department stationery. The reply courteously explained the delay. Copy for national advertising had had to be prepared ahead of the company's receiving the merchandise from a foreign supplier, and only a partial order had been sent from the supplier. Customers' orders for the advertised item had been filled according to the date they were received. The last two paragraphs of the reply were devoted to "answering" the professor's forecast of the company's survival. The last sentence was "If the millions of

customers we serve continue to buy from us as they are, it would seem
that you are rather short-sighted in thinking that one back-order is going
to ruin our Company." The company representative "took the bait"; he
didn't resist the temptation of talking back. The advice to a business
person is "Stay in command of the situation by being courteous."

Examples of letters canceling or deferring orders:

Bookstore

Dear Dr. Thomas:

I'm afraid I must report that PAT THE BUNNY is out of print;
I am unable to fill your order now.

We do have dozens of books for very young children: stiff
stand-up ones, limp cloth ones, washable plastic ones, big colorful ones, priced from 25¢ to $2.00.

Would you like me to send one (I suggest the TALL BOOK OF FARM
ANIMALS, $1.00) for Bonnie to read until PAT THE BUNNY is in
print again?

I will let you know the minute I can fill your original order.

Sincerely yours,

*From the International Harvester Consumer Relations
Manual No. 1, "Handling Inquiries" (post card)*

We thank you for your recent inquiry, but regret that there
will be a delay in sending you the literature.

Demand for many items has been high and our stock is temporarily exhausted. As soon as this material is available it will
be mailed to you.

It is possible that if you will call at the nearest International Harvester dealer, you can get the information you desire
without delay.

INTERNATIONAL HARVESTER COMPANY

The variety of merchandise sold through correspondence is almost
unbelievable, as the letter in Fig. 21 suggests. Through personable
writing, the company has maintained a friendly relationship with its
customers, making the salutation fitting.

REMITTANCES

Letters accompanying remittances are usually brief, but should include
the kind and amount of the payment and what it is for. If a statement is

Dear Friend:

Thank you for requesting information concerning Davis Seafoods. I do welcome this opportunity to send you a list of the many products offered our customers. On it you will find your favorite Seafoods together with just about every other variety of good fish that can be put up in a keepable manner.

Over the years customer-friends from all over the country have learned how easy it is to have good fish sent right to their doors from Gloucester. You may have Ocean Fish that is so appetizing and delicious that no matter where you live, the seashore treats we enjoy in Gloucester are yours for the asking.

Plan now to make a selection of the seafoods you want, choosing the items you wish in whatever quantity you desire. Have in mind the convenience of keeping a supply of these selected quality Seafoods on hand ready to use at a moment's notice. It just isn't possible to obtain better Seafoods anywhere so, unhesitatingly, I guarantee my products to please you in every respect.

I can send you your order promptly--delivery fully prepaid so let me know right away the Seafoods you need.

Thank you for your inquiry.

The Gloucester Fishman

Fig. 21. A friendly reply to an inquiry has sold many an order. "The Gloucester Fishman" has been remarkably successful in selling by mail. (By permission of the Dartnell Corporation.)

returned with the remittance, the letter may be omitted. All remittances except those made by check should be acknowledged. The following are the chief forms for remittances:

1. *Personal or company check.* The most widely used and generally best form, especially for larger amounts and where the remitter has an account or a previous buying history. Convenient, safe, receipts itself.

But where the dependability of the buyer is unknown, it may delay filling the order.

2. *Cashier's check.* The remitter pays with a check drawn on the bank's own funds and signed by the cashier. Safe, relatively inexpensive for moderate amounts, acceptable without delay. The certified check operates similarly, with the bank guaranteeing the remitter's check, usually for a small fee.

3. *Bank draft.* Another safe form, less used by the general public than the cashier's check. Really an order on the remitter's bank to another bank to pay a stated amount to a specified person or firm. Requires a fee.

4. *Postal money order.* A preferred form, especially for sending small amounts, since it is easy to obtain and always acceptable. Express company money orders are similar.

5. *Telegraph money order.* An especially speedy means of transmittal. Relatively expensive, but useful in emergencies or other situations where speed is important. Accepted and paid through telegraph offices. If the receiving office is small, payment may have to await banking hours.

6. *Stamps, currency, coins.* Use of these methods of payment is discouraged, but they are still used for small remittances. They are unsafe, and give no receipt. The chief advantage is convenience. Many firms refuse to accept stamps. Magazine publishers are usually willing to take a chance on a dollar bill for a trial subscription.

INVITATIONS

Formal invitations and replies are matters for Emily Post and Amy Vanderbilt, but informal invitations figure in business writing. Although telephoning has become more the rule for local communications, informal written invitations are often used to arrange luncheons, lectures, and a miscellany of other business or partly business functions. These communications come under the general rules for conversational writing and the "you" attitude. You might write a note to a business acquaintance as follows:

Dear Mr. Jones:

Could you have lunch with me next Tuesday, October 15? I shall be in Akron on that date, and you know it's quite likely that we can find things to talk about and perhaps stir up a little business.

I'll show up at your office at 12 o'clock if this will be all right.

Cordially,

To this, Jones might reply:

Dear Mr. Smith:

I shall be delighted to have lunch with you at 12 o'clock on Tuesday, October 15.

I'll expect you at the office, or, if it is more convenient, just phone and I'll meet you wherever you suggest.

Cordially,

Or, if the date is not available:

Dear Mr. Smith:

Thanks a lot for asking me to lunch Tuesday, October 15. I'm extremely sorry that I won't be able to make it that day, for I've already made plans that I can't change.

Won't you call the office when you get to town, and we'll see what we can do.

Cordially,

For messages of a personal nature such as the following, some businessmen have note paper with an inconspicuous printed notation such as "from the desk of Robert J. Stone," "from Bob Stone," etc. A pleasant gesture on the part of firms is sending a printed card—appropriate to the occasion—personally signed by the firm's personnel who know the recipient well enough to extend personal greetings.

CONGRATULATIONS

Letters or notes of congratulation are in order to business friends who have received promotions, have married, become parents, received honorary degrees, or done anything else which will make a word from a friend seem the whipped cream on the dessert. In earlier chapters we have spoken of the importance of being warm human beings in our business relations. Such letters, although it may be a little difficult to find time to write them, are the natural expression of zest in living. And they contribute more than is realized toward building the good will which is the business equivalent of bread cast upon the waters.

CONDOLENCES

Harder to write, but no less essential and appreciated, are the notes of condolence when there is a death or a serious illness. The keynote here is sympathy and consideration. The classic letter of condolence is Lincoln's letter to Mrs. Bixby on the death of her sons in the Civil War. In expressions of condolence, which are briefly stated in most instances, it is well to keep in mind that, in times of reversals and bereavement, a person probably prefers not to be reminded of his loss or sadness, or (in case of death) how much he is going to miss association with the deceased. Keep the tone of the letter positive, encouraging the recipient to look, not back, but forward.

LETTERS OF APPRECIATION

Another voluntary, but nevertheless important, form is the letter of appreciation. Observe this brief note from Charles Dickens to William Makepeace Thackeray:

My Dear Thackeray,

I have read in The Times to-day an account of your last night's lecture, and I cannot refrain from assuring you in all truth and earnestness that I am profoundly touched by your generous reference to me. I do not know how to tell you what a glow it spread over my heart. Out of its fulness I do entreat you to believe that I shall never forget your words of commendation. If you could wholly know at once how you have moved me, and how you have animated me, you would be the happier I am very certain.

Faithfully yours ever,
Charles Dickens [3]

The tone of a hundred years ago now seems a bit quaint, but the spirit of appreciation in this letter from one of the most human of all writers is as timely now as it ever was.

A retired executive who has considerable correspondence through his company magazine uses an informal note paper with the inscription: "I use this paper to write those who have pleased me."

INTRODUCTIONS

Many business situations call for letters of introduction. A new traveling salesman carries a letter from his company to make it easier for him to meet the retailers on whom he must call. A visitor in Washington takes a note to his Congressman from a prominent citizen back home. A college student wishing to obtain privileges in a private or strange university library brings an introduction from a professor.

The letter of introduction, though subject to abuse, can be very useful. Like all business communications, it should be written simply, clearly, considerately, and to the point. The following examples are worthy of study. The first is a letter from James Russell Lowell to Nathaniel Hawthorne, introducing William Dean Howells. The second is a letter from Benjamin Franklin to a friend in America.

---

[3] *Nineteenth Century Letters*, ed. B. J. Rees (New York: Charles Scribner's Sons, 1919), p. 380.

Cambridge, Aug. 5, 1860.

My dear Hawthorne,—

    I have no masonic claim upon you except community of tobacco, and the young man who brings this does not smoke.

    But he wants to look at you, which will do you no harm, and him a great deal of good.

    His name is Howells, and he is a fine young fellow, and has written several poems in the Atlantic, *which of course you have never read, because you don't do such things yourself, and are old enough to know better.*

    When I think how much you might have profited by the perusal of certain verses of somebody who shall be nameless—but, no matter! If my judgment is good for anything, this youth has more in him than any of our younger fellows in the way of rhyme.

    Of course he can't hope to rival the Consule Planco *men. Therefore let him look at you, and charge it*

                          To yours always,
                                J. R. Lowell [4]

                             Paris, April 2, 1777.

Sir:—

    The bearer of this, who is going to America, presses me to give him a Letter of Recommendation, tho' I know nothing of him, not even his Name. This may seem extraordinary, but I assure you it is not uncommon here. Sometimes, indeed, one unknown Person brings another equally unknown, to recommend him; and sometimes they recommend one another! As to this Gentleman, I must refer you to himself for his Character and Merits, with which he is certainly better acquainted than I can possibly be. I recommend him however to those Civilities, which every Stranger, of whom one knows no Harm, has a Right to; and I request you will do him all the good Offices, and show him all the Favour that, on further Acquaintance, you shall find him to deserve. I have the Honour to be, etc.

                                [B. Franklin] [5]

    Both letters are excellent. Lowell's introduction presents a person who deserves to have the way smoothed for him; Franklin's refuses to jeopardize the standing of the writer or raise hopes in the reader, when the bearer of the letter has no real claim to a letter of introduction.

RECOMMENDATIONS

    Closely related to the letter of introduction is the recommendation, which, since it is used chiefly in job seeking, will be discussed in Chapter 9.

---

    [4] *Letters of James Russell Lowell,* ed. Charles Eliot Norton (New York: Harper & Bros., 1894), I, 305–6.

    [5] *Benjamin Franklin: Representative Selections,* ed. F. L. Mott and C. E. Jorgenson (New York: American Book Co., 1936), p. 389.

NOTIFICATIONS

Appointments and elections to offices, boards, and committees also call for simple, adequate, tactful letters. The following is a letter from a pastor to a layman newly chosen to the board of his church:

Dear Mr. Brown:

It is my pleasure to inform you that after proper nomination by our Committee you were elected a member of the Official Board of Trinity Church.

The Official Board is the governing body of the Local Church. The business and program of the Church must have the vote of this Board. It is the court of final appeal for all that affects the life and work of the Church.

Election to the Official Board is an honor which I am sure you will appreciate.

Congratulations and best wishes,

Note that the letter endeavors to impress the reader with two facts: (1) that membership on the board is an honor, and (2) that the honor carries with it an important responsibility.

BASIC AND UTILITY LETTERS AS AMBASSADORS OF GOOD WILL

In this chapter we have considered letters which, generally speaking, take the least time and thought to write. But many five-minute letters have proved tremendously important. The fact that a messenger is quickly and easily dispatched does not mean that his mission is trivial or that he should go forth with his hair unbrushed or his shoes not tied. Every letter should be a worthy representative of the person who signs it or the firm he represents, both in what it says and in the kind of picture it makes upon the page.

Anyone Can Write Letters! *

by C. R. ANDERSON

"Anyone with ordinary common sense can write letters!" With that blasé attitude, business for years has tossed the important job of letter writing to Tom, Dick, or Harry—often the poorest prepared person in the office. In small offices the task frequently falls to anyone who happens to be able to type.

* That the attitude sardonically expressed in this title is still held by all too many has helped make this piece a classic. It first appeared in *Opinion and Comment,* August 24, 1943, pages 1–7, and is reprinted here by permission of the author. Professor Anderson's being made permanent honorary president of the American Business Writing Association testifies to his influence in his field. His writing, referred to throughout *Effective Business Communication,* includes *Writing for Business* (Homewood, Ill.: Richard D. Irwin, Inc., 1960), which he coedited with J. H. Menning and C. W. Wilkinson.

Ponderously the elected grinds out the routine "Your recent letter received and in reply will say——" all the time thinking that he is imitating business style, or at least company style. "Business letters must be formal—success is judged by how well personality is hidden" becomes his goal. Too often letters are taken as a challenge and are answered defiantly as in a debate rebuttal, leaving only the writer thoroughly pleased. Occasionally the fact that he has a secretary sets up an importance complex in the mind of the dictator, and he parades his feeble style for her admiring pencil. After a time, the very volume of mail handled gives to the correspondent such a false sense of ability that he spurns mere simple rules.

Unfortunately, common sense is not ordinary nor is it sufficient for the modern correspondent. He is handling a phase of business that costs millions of dollars. The average dictated letter costs about a dollar,* which soon pushes the expense total skyward. Did someone say that figure was too high? All right, let's do some estimating. You know how many letters are usually written each day or week. Now allocate the salaries of the dictators, the stenographers, the file clerks, the mail boys, the messengers, the mail sorters. Add the cost of letterheads, envelopes, special printing, carbon paper, file copies. Then there is the equipment item: typewriters, ribbons, stenographers' supplies, dictating machines and cylinders, furniture, mailing appliances. Of course there is the direct cost of stamps and affixing machines. Since the correspondence work requires space, allocate additional funds to cover extra rent, light and power, fuel, taxes, and insurance. Perhaps part of the salaries of supervising executives belongs here. And of course there is always a little waste—spoiled stationery, lost stamps, and returned mail. Some of these are small items in themselves, but when added, subtracted, and divided they make the letter cost of a dollar or more come to life.

But although the financial argument for making each letter carry its full load is potent, it is not so important as the final results achieved. The crux of the matter is how well it does its job with the customer. The correspondent is really the point of contact between the company and the customer. When a correspondent wrote a customer, "Keep your shirt on. Other people want our products, too," he *was* the company, and it took a high-paid man almost three years to get that customer back into the fold. No matter how much fairness and altruism permeates the management, the customer judges only by his own contacts, which are usually letters.

A petulant, cold, we-attitude, or domineering letter has ended many a happy business relationship. Even a careless word or phrase may be enough to damn an entire letter. To ask an enthusiast whether he "tinkers" with radios will ruffle his pride in achievement and send him to a shop where his ability is recognized.

Most correspondents are relatively harmless in real life, but with a typewriter they often become caged ogres, writing fussy little notes beginning:

We cannot understand why you haven't answered.
We know you are honest, but—(or however).

---

* Author's note: Today's figure on the cost of a letter—$2.32—adds significance to Professor Anderson's assertion of the need for competence among correspondents.

Your *complaint* has been received. We are *sorry* that you *failed* to *cooperate* by keeping the machine oiled.

Surely you do not expect a donation of that $6.80.

Of course, it is *entirely out of the question* to send the information.

Because all these thoughtless, negative expressions indicate that the reader is at fault, they will cause the adrenalin to flow until he sputters in rage, and there can be no meeting of minds under favorable conditions. Obviously the correspondent deals with the subtlest of intangibles—the human mind—and he seeks to influence it by using a tricky medium—language. With such complexities, perhaps it is equally obvious that "everyone cannot write letters," and that those who can usually require training and constant study. Perhaps no one with a bad stomach, no one who thinks everyone is out to gyp him, and no one who cannot see the comedy in human life should attempt to represent his company on paper.

Good letter writing is primarily a problem in adaptation—adapting ideas, organization, and diction to the individual reader and situation. To analyze all these in detail is not within the scope of this discussion. But to point out the necessity for specific adaptation to people, to products, and to conditions may suggest in passing some of the answers to organization and diction.

If money permitted, movie scenes would offer the best way to teach correspondents the principles of adaptation. Let them see and hear the reactions in the office when an incomplete order arrives. Watch the customer's face as he reads the letter that accuses him of being too dumb to oil the machine properly. Peep around the corner and view bitter disappointment while the family—father, mother, and children—enthusiastically open a box, only to find the wrong merchandise, or to find it broken. Present on the screen the inquirer who asked for information and reads a curt rebuff indicating that he had no business asking for it. See the relief and pleasure of the customer who reads the first sentence of a letter granting his requested adjustment. Go into homes and show dozens of these human interest scenes, because these letters are intricately bound up with the lives of human beings.

No correspondent with ability and imagination enough to represent a company could handle new situations without remembering those scenes, and it would be a poor dolt indeed who would not try to adapt his letter to meet those reactions—who would not change his creed from "Business is Business," to "Business is Human." He would follow Professor George Burton Hotchkiss' definition of Business English, "It isn't a language, it is a point of view." When the point of view—adaptation to the reader—is firmly established, he will find that many of the minor problems of organization and diction will solve themselves.

Instead of beginning with, "We received your letter of August 10. We are very glad to give you the information requested," the correspondent would try to wipe the anxiety from the face of his reader with a first sentence such as, "Our Model 4A portable schoolhouse, seating 100 pupils, will care for your overflow now and probably for the future." He can hear the reader breathe a sigh of relief and say, "That is just what I want," while he continues reading from a favorable point of view. In the process of saying first what the reader wants most to hear, the writer has not only adapted his ideas and his style to the needs of the customer, but by forgetting self he has automatically abandoned the old-fashioned, rubber-stamped beginning and has streamlined his approach, thus gaining directness, vividness, and economy.

Adaptation to the reader's interest alone changes the negative, we-attitude idea, "Two per cent will be added if your bill is not paid by the tenth of the month," to the positive you-attitude, "You may deduct two per cent if this bill is paid before the tenth of the month," thus holding before the horse the more effective ear of corn rather than using the penalty whip.

Moreover, emphasis is gained by sincere adaptation to the reader's interest. "We are in receipt of your letter of July 20 enclosing your annual report for which we thank you" selfishly exults over finally getting the report in our clutches, and merely says "thank you" as an afterthought in a subordinate clause. With the proper picture in the writer's mind, he would look at the reader, realize that he would like a pat on the back for a job completed, and immediately say, "Thank you for the annual report in your letter of July 20."

To the man who complains when he does not get a free booklet which as a result of his illegible writing was sent to the wrong town, the correspondent may begin wtih a defensive explanation. But if he has absorbed the "you-attitude," he will greet the reader with something like this: "A second copy of your Blank booklet has just been mailed special delivery." Now the customer knows immediately that he is getting what he wants; the "second copy" indicates that the first request was not ignored and causes him to suspend judgment until he can read the facts; the "special delivery" begins to establish the promptness idea that the writer will undoubtedly emphasize in the last paragraph because this customer, who has had difficulty getting a simple booklet, will have to be convinced that merchandise ordered will reach him before he leaves for his vacation. After this positive presentation of what the company *can do*, the writer can back up with comparative safety and in the less important second paragraph explain succinctly what was *not done*. Incidentally, the writer who has studied the psychological adaptation of unpleasant news will not only refuse to lead with it, but, after making his explanation complete and clear, will not follow his natural inclination to return to it in the last paragraph, thus ending on the most unpleasant note in the entire letter.

Adjustment letters, especially those in which the claim is not granted, need careful adaptation because they deal with people who are in uncertain emotional states. All the principles of attention, conviction, and action are present but they are focused *against* the writer. Something unpleasant has happened. In viewing the scene, the dictator realizes that he cannot erase the picture entirely, but he can adapt to the situation by seeking to implant a new, more pleasant picture, such as something that the company can do, and to focus attention on it. Again he emphasizes what the company *can do* instead of what it *cannot do*, and he handles the pleasant before the unpleasant. He follows another principle of adaptation by writing in detail, which means a fairly long letter so that the reader will feel that adequate attention has been given to his complaint, thus salving his ego. Even the sentences are adapted by being longer and hence more soothing than the short, staccato sentences of quick, pleasant news.

Business letter writing is purposive composition. Letters are not written for the sake of letters, as is the case in art for art's sake, or song for song's sake— wholly for the joy of performance. As Charles A. Beard * says: "Some ends, clear or sublimated, lurk in all discussion of human affairs above the level of gossip and babble." The purpose of a letter is evident, but to achieve that end one must adapt to the emotions and intelligence and experience of the reader. This is no easy task, for people's backgrounds are widely divergent, and to adapt to our compatriots may require almost as much study as to adapt to a foreign people. Unfortunately the psychology of writing in business is scantily studied. Only a few companies provide training and supervision for their correspondents. Some of these correspondence supervisors are doing an excellent job, and the correspondents, when they realize the importance of the work, are ready to work for improvement.

Since everyone speaks a common language (this may be debatable!) the attitude persists that "anyone can write a letter." But the United States is a big country, and there are innumerable differences in sectional, racial, occupational, and class likes and dislikes that require constant study if letters are to be effective. Therefore, the need for adaptation of various kinds is as essential as in writing to foreign countries. Obviously a correspondent writing to Latin America will spend much time studying: first, the language, second, business organization and methods, and third, the psychology of the Latin American businessman.

Much failure in Latin American business relations can be traced to our lack of study and of adaptation to another culture. We write to businessmen in those countries as to our own people, although their psychology is vastly different and requires a big dose of our theme-song—adaptation.

A concrete illustration of this point is found in an incident reported in the *KVP Philosopher*.†

A Michigan firm cabled a Cuban customer, "Quotation eighteenth best can do." That seems a perfectly clear, well-worded message. Hundred like it are exchanged in this country every day. But to the Cuban it was almost as insulting as if he had been called names. The cable was reworded to read, "Regret very much that increasing cost of materials makes better quotation impossible." "But what is the difference?" you ask. "The first said the same thing and took fewer words. It costs money to cable." The answer is adaptation.

Here is the Cuban's reply: "I must show this cable to my customer. Had I shown him the first one, he would have thrown me out of his office. You see, we folks down here pride ourselves on being gentlemen before we are businessmen. We are almost as flowery as the Chinese in matters of courtesy. In every simple conversation, we do what you Americans call 'spreading the oil.' We say 'please' in a hundred different ways, and 'thank you' in a hundred more.

* *The Discussion of Human Affairs*, p. 12.
† Kalamazoo Vegetable Parchment Co., Vol. 9, No. 12, pp. 3–5.

"Take that wire, for example. We know that American mill quoted us its best price the first time. Americans, on the whole, are one-price outfits. Down here, we bargain. But even when we know that the quoted price is the best we can hope for, we still want you at least to pretend you are sorry you can't do better. We want you to give some reason, too.

"When I get the reworded cable, I can take it to my customer and say, 'Look, Mr. Machado, I have done the best I can for you, but as you can see, these people have mounting costs and consequently are extremely sorry they cannot give us lower prices.'"

"I tell you honestly, most Latin Americans will pay higher prices to a supplier who understands the language of courtesy than to another who has the same goods for less money but offers them on a 'take it or leave it' basis."

Considerable adaptation in letters is going to be necessary to implement the Good Neighbor policy in business. United States standards will not suffice, just as New England standards will not suffice in the Deep South. These prospective new customers have different emotions and reactions, and in order to adapt our game to the new rules we shall have to make a thorough and systematic study of those rules.

Adaptation to the reader, whether foreign or domestic, leads to that intangible quality in letters known as personality. The man in the drawing room who talks fluently on subjects of interest to his listeners is said to have a "pleasing personality." The letter whose tone, diction, and content are adapted to the reader is also said to have "personality," which is usually a synonym for "effectiveness." A good letter presents a picture of the writer which is better than a photograph because it shows vividly his mental processes. A man's background, English, knowledge of human nature, and observance of business principles stand out in bold relief when reduced to words and sentences. The letter becomes an index rather than a cloak to his personality.

Often we hear the slogan, "Write as you talk." Like all slogans, this should not be taken too literally. It is designed to focus attention on naturalness of expression, which is desirable, but little conversation is effective when reduced verbatim to writing. Actual conversation usually moves slowly—even crab-wise —is full of interruptions and false probings. The speaker's "I mean" is the signal for repetition. Good writing has certain qualities that make it better than most conversation in that it is more concise and direct and saves the time of the reader. A twenty- to thirty-minute conversation can readily be reduced to three to five minutes of reading. Modern letters should combine the *ease* of conversation with the *precision* of business, giving a tone that might be called *semiformally conversational*.

Adaptation to people and products is often influenced by economic and political conditions. Defense preparations may mean orders, regimentation, and dictatorial tone. As a result, many correspondents are intolerant of others' opinions and reactions, and see no need of persuasion, even enough to make palatable a bitter message. But the man who has been trained in the psychology of letters will realize that the customer has been pushed around constantly these days—told that he can't have this and he can't have that. In imperious language he has been told that "economic disturbances have made it impossible to supply merchandise" when he wants to know in words of one syllable adapted to him *why* he can't get the gadget now, *when* he can get it, or *whether* there is a satisfactory substitute.

Recently a local merchant received a letter from a company explaining in considerable detail why it could not fill his order. By most standards, it was a good letter—thorough and considerate. *But* it was a form letter with a bad fill-in. This dealer had been an old customer—in fact was one of the first customers of this manufacturer. His pride was hurt by receiving a form letter from that company. As he said, "They needn't have written all those reasons, but at least they could have sent me a personal letter." Doubtless the company had many such letters to write and it was economical to prepare a form letter (although the sloppy fill-in was inexcusable) but the adaptation to this old, preferred customer was definitely bad.

Wartime letters are adapted to many new uses. They are called upon to replace salesmen who are no longer available or who cannot get the gasoline to travel. Companies that now have nothing to sell write letters discussing service, repairs, substitutes, general war work, and future plans, partly to help customers keep in business and partly to keep in touch with them. In 1918, many companies forgot to maintain their customer contacts, and after the war found that the customers had forgotten them. The best postwar planning is to do something right now.

Some companies must adapt to new war products sold in new war markets. Others promote more efficient use of goods and services, explain shortages and price increases, emphasize long-term values—and send regular letters to employees in the service.

Important in adapting to the changed human factors is the need to educate new classes of buyers who have the money to buy in a new stratum, to cater to more women who have increased their buying power through war jobs, and to deal with people who have developed hair-trigger tempers because of tension and overwork.

Adapting the business message to people, products, and conditions requires more than a typist. Not just anyone can write good letters. But almost anyone *can* improve. Unfortunately neither business nor the school has developed an effective system of testing correspondents before placing them in the important position of talking directly to the customer. Although some companies have developed excellent training courses for correspondents already selected, there is considerable lost motion because many of the trainees never should have been chosen. If some personnel man will construct an adequate test to use in hiring future correspondents, he will serve business by changing "Maybe this fellow can write letters" to "Here is a person qualified to talk to our customers."

And when that person is selected you may be sure that he will be capable of learning and using the principles of adaptation. He will realize that business writing is democratic writing—writing that recognizes the dignity and worth of the individual, and that wields a strong social weapon. He will write to his customers as human beings and not as names on the mailing list. He will study their likes and dislikes, their needs and wishes, and adapt his message to them.

And in so doing, he will broaden his own life, enlarge his sphere of influence, and become a better citizen, father, friend, and neighbor. He will use the you-attitude in ever-widening circles.

As Arnold Bennett said, in discussing the power to put oneself in the place of another, "The faculty will grow just as a muscle will grow; also it will wither as a muscle will wither; and for the same reason." *

Exercises and Problems in Communication

1. Read the article "Letters That Lose the Business," *Sales Management*, March 20, 1959, p. 52, for discussion—written or oral—of apparent company indifference to letters of inquiry.

2. Compare or contrast the two following letters for tone (they are from personnel directors of two companies):

Dear Mr. Williams:

This will acknowledge your recent request for a contribution to the West End Church fund. It has been carefully considered by our Committee on Contributions and we regret to inform you that the Committee did not recommend taking any action at this time.

Dear Mr. Williams:

I am writing about your recent letter soliciting our support of the West End Church fund.

While we appreciate desirability of helping worthy organizations, we are at the present time so completely deluged with appeals coming from every type of organization and group, that we have been temporarily compelled to withdraw from such participation.

I hope you will understand our position in this situation.

3. Write ten opening sentences expressing gratitude. Use "thank you" in no more than one of them.

4. Throughout the book, I suggest that you talk with businessmen and industrialists about effective communication. During such a visit, ask about company practice in sending letters or notes of congratulations, condolence, etc. If the company uses this sort of good-will correspondence, get a description of the correspondence or ask to see a copy. If the company hasn't used "personal" letters, you might suggest that they try the approach to personalizing business. What strategies would you use in order not to appear presumptuous to an executive in making such a suggestion? Discuss this question with the class.

5. As manager of a clothing store in Laurel, a county-seat town of around 50,000, you receive a letter from a customer in a nearby community. He has always paid cash for the $100 to $150 worth of merchandise he has bought from your store each year. Answer his letter which asks whether "you are

---

* *How to Make the Best of Life*, p. 36.

going to have your semi-annual sale before long." The customer's point in asking, he explains, is that circumstances demand that he buy clothes for three members of his family within the next two weeks; the circumstances also demand that he spend as little as possible. Your clearance sale is scheduled for four weeks from the time of his letter.

6. Write the customer's letter to the clothing dealer, in the preceding exercise.

7. Prepare a questionnaire of ten to twelve items to be sent to 50 persons. The questionnaire should contain both fact and opinion questions. Some possible topics are

a. Communication Problems in Business
b. Preparedness of High School Graduates for College
c. Preparedness of High School Graduates for Employment
d. Insurance Rates for Drivers 16 to 25
e. Qualities Looked for in Applicants for Managerial Jobs
f. Effective Letters of Application for Employment
g. The Individual and the Corporation

Some of the considerations in this problem are (1) to analyze the questions, to be sure that fact and opinion questions are proportionate to the use you will put the answers to; (2) to select a mailing list of persons most likely to be informed on, and interested in, the subject you are dealing with; (3) to learn persons or departments in companies or schools to direct your inquiry to, so you can get early replies.

8. Write the covering letter to accompany the questionnaire described in Exercise 7.

9. In preparing for assignments on report writing later in the course, outline your plan in Exercise 7 to include a report for some group interested in the subject of your survey.

10. Write a letter of condolence to a business associate who has experienced some ill fortune or sadness. You learned of his experience when you read the morning paper.

11. Write the same kind of letter to an associate about whose experience you learned two weeks to a month after it occurred.

12. Choose three or four companies in the kind of work you want to engage in after you graduate. (Look up these companies in the various directories discussed in Chapter 9.) Write a letter to the personnel departments, asking for advice on how you can best prepare yourself for employment with the particular company to which your inquiry is sent.

13. Comment on the following form letter sent to customers of a leather-processing company. It had no inside address. The facsimile signature was mechanically reproduced with the rest of the letter. The letter was dated and mailed five days after the assassination of President Kennedy.

Friend:

At a time such as this . . . words are trivial, inappropriate.

We have lost a great leader and friend of humanity.

Yet, life must go on.

May all of our hearts be so blessed of love and Thanksgiving
that there is no room for hate or violence.

Deepest Respect.

Market Research Director

14. As manager of the Personal Shopper department in a department store,
write a *form letter* to be sent to customers when their orders can be only
partially filled.

15. A college classmate of yours ten years ago, now a casual business acquaintance, has just been elected president of the bank where he has been
working since his college days. Write him a letter of congratulation.

16. Comment on the following letter of appreciation, written voluntarily by
a large city laundry:

Dear Mrs. Smith:

Your laundryman, John Roberts, informed us of your kindness in
returning the article sent to you in error. Every safeguard
known to this industry is used to prevent such mistakes, but no
matter how hard we try they still occur now and then.

Mrs. Smith, we want you to know we are sincerely thankful for
your honest action. You most certainly proved you are a customer
we want to serve for a long, long time.

In the future we will double our efforts to make your laundry
and dry-cleaning service smooth and worthy of your recommendations.

Very truly yours,

CLEAN CLOTHES LAUNDRY

17. Comment on the following responses to inquiries to Edinburgh firms
specializing in materials for Scottish clans:

Sir,

We have received your letter for which we thank you, and we write
to advise you that we shall have pleasure in sending our Spring
Mode to you when we receive it from the printers.

We are sorry we have not a Catalogue in circulation at the
moment.

Assuring you at all times of our best services,

We are, Sir,

Yours faithfully,

Dear Sir,

We thank you for your esteemed enquiry, and regret we have not
published our usual catalogue this season, but enclose leaflet

```
showing our skirts and kilts.  We have over 200 different
tartans-Rugs, Ties, Scarves and piece goods.  Enclosed are a
few patterns including the Reid.  Assuring you of our best
attention always,
```

Yours faithfully,

18. Mrs. Robert Terrill, 8 Park Drive, Birmingham, Alabama, saw an ad in a magazine offering a free folder, "Window Beauty." She sent her name to the Andersen Corporation, makers of Andersen Windowalls, Bayport, Minnesota, and is now waiting for her folder to arrive in the mail. A printing strike, however, has tied up the company's printing contractor, and it may be several months before the folder will be ready. Write the Andersen Corporation's letter to Mrs. Terrill.

19. Comment on the following letter of appreciation for business service:

```
Gentlemen:

In June, 1958, we purchased our first INTERNATIONAL Electric
Writing Machine, since we required more copies than the machines
we were using in our office at that time would supply us.  Since
that time, we have purchased five additional machines, making a
total of six Electric Writing Machines used by us at this time.

All of these machines have operated in a splendid manner, giving
us the additional copies we required.  In addition, your Company
has given us splendid service for any adjustments required.

May I say that all of our dealings with your Company have been
satisfactory, prompt, and pleasant.
```

Yours truly,

20. Answer orally or in writing, as your instructor directs, the following questions based on C. R. Anderson's "Anyone Can Write Letters!"

    a. In offices, what is the too frequent method of choosing the person who writes the letters?

    b. Comment on the incident of the correspondent who said, "Keep your shirt on."

    c. What is that subtlest of intangibles with which the correspondent deals?

    d. Why would movie scenes, if money permitted, offer the best way to teach corerspondents the principles of adaptation?

    e. State George Burton Hotchkiss' definition of Business English, and comment on its significance.

    f. How does the principle of adaptation influence letter beginnings? The wording of sentences?

    g. What is the best position in the letter for the unfavorable part of the message?

    h. In the light of your experience with different national, ethnic, or geographical groups, comment on the incident of the cablegram from the Michigan firm to the Cuban customer.

    i. To what extent should business correspondence be conversational?

    j. Why is the provision of correspondence supervisors not the whole solution for the problem of poor correspondence in an office?

8

Sales Letters

Competition reduces us all to size.—WILLIAM FEATHER, *The William Feather Magazine* [1]

If a questionnaire could be devised to produce valid results, it would be interesting to know how widespread is the opinion that "Competition is in the sales department," to quote the superintendent of the blast furnace department in a National Tube plant. The executive's comment pertained to the free exchange of information among competing firms. Representatives of competing companies tour each other's plants and departments for suggestions on methods and practices in planning and production; at lunch and golf, they swap ideas on marketing and promotion. (As in all matters, there are exceptions here. In its open-house invitations to members of a management club, a large midwestern firm asked that club members employed in competing companies not accept the invitation.) If competition does rest mainly in the sales department, salesmen and sales writers are susceptible to the reduction Mr. Feather speaks of in the chapter-opening quotation.

Whatever the wished-for questionnaire on competition in sales would reveal, there is a favorite point of view in the business world that *every letter is a sales letter.* This is true in that all the letters of a company represent its business policies and can contribute toward building good will for the company and thus promote its growth and prosperity. All business letters are sales letters in this general way, but, of the billions [2] of letters that go through the mails annually, certainly more than half are avowedly sales messages of some sort.

[1] Copyright, September, 1963, by the William Feather Company.
[2] According to *The Wall Street Journal*, July 1, 1964, 18.4 billion pieces of third-class mail were sent in 1963. Of this volume, 85 per cent was advertising.

The sales letter may sell goods directly, open doors for salesmen, bring back wandering charge account customers, cash in on magazine advertising, or build good will for future business—in short, perform all sorts of selling jobs. No one would claim that the sales letter is the only, or always the best, means of inducing people to buy. No one would deny that many sales letters go into wastebaskets unread, or merely glanced at.

Just the same, sales letters are tremendously important. Through sales letters the *Reader's Digest* has grown from most humble beginnings until it now has a circulation of over 14 million in the United States, and more than a dozen international editions. Sales letters, more than anything else, have made possible the success of the *Time*, *Life*, and *Fortune* group of magazines and the Book-of-the-Month Club. They enabled the Haband Company, Paterson, New Jersey, to make selling neckties by mail a large business. These are only a few of the enterprises which have been built up chiefly through skillful use of sales letters—not just through *use* of sales letters but through their *skillful use*. Perhaps in no other field of written communication has there been more improvement than in the composition and circulation of sales letters.

WHAT MAKES SALES LETTERS SELL?

Fortunately we know a lot more about what makes sales writing tick than we did a century ago. Many letters and series of letters have been sent out under data measurement controls. We know the job that was assigned to them, how much they cost, and the results. We can't always discover why one letter succeeded where another that looked equally good failed, but we can profitably analyze some of the successful ones.

Consider the Gold Medal [3] letter on page 191. This was sent as a form letter to 1,502 prospects with the hope of adding 500 customers. But, with the other letters in the series, it brought 801 customers, 160 per cent of quota, more than half of all to whom it was sent—a phenomenal record for a form letter mailing.

Why was this letter exceptionally successful? There are several reasons. The mailing list was unusually selective. Since the wiring was already installed, the job was only to sell the prospect on the desirability of using it. But the wiring had been there for some time unused; so there remained an actual selling job to be done. Let's analyze the letter in detail to see what good sales techniques we can discover:

1. The point of contact brought about by the opening of the letter is excellent. The anecdote of the horse and buggy has a humorous quirk that tends to amuse, and hence to interest, so that the recipient reads on.

---

[3] The Dartnell Corporation, Chicago, publishes annually a portfolio of Gold Medal Award letters, chosen from many thousands examined.

NO SALESMEN AVAILABLE, THESE LETTERS WENT OUT AND SOLD 160 PER CENT OF QUOTA

Of interest not only as examples of effective sales letter writing, but also because more companies are today using mail selling to a greater extent than ever before, these letters are illustrative of a series used by Carolina Power & Light. In territories where there is no sales organization, the letters were sent to 1,502 prospects as a means of adding 500 rural customers. When the activity ended, 801 customers, or 160 per cent of quota, had been added. Note that letters are addressed to the housewife.

Carolina Power & Light Company
Raleigh, North Carolina

GOLD MEDAL

Dear Madam:

Many years ago, one of my uncles bought a brand new buggy from a Chicago mail order house but, for some strange reason, he never bought a horse; consequently, he failed to get any pleasure or satisfaction from buggy riding!

And I'm wondering if you are not in just about the same fix — you've had your house wired, but you've never had the pleasure and satisfaction of Electric Service in your home.

Your neighbors, lots of 'em, went right ahead after their homes were wired and let us furnish them with Electric Service -- for a very few cents a day, they've been getting the benefits of CHEAP Electricity -- yes, they've had plenty of light and most of them have a percolator, hot plate, iron or other useful electrical appliances -- many of them have electric refrigeration and running water.

Now, you can enjoy these same things just as cheaply as they do -- and your family will get the same kind of pleasure and satisfaction.

Winter is on the way, and NOW is a good time to put your house wiring to work -- it will stay there until your house falls down without helping you a bit unless you make up your mind to enjoy Electric Services.

Let's talk this matter over. We will answer any questions you may want to ask and give you all the facts about Electric Service in your home. Just mail the enclosed card today!

Very truly yours,

DISTRICT MANAGER

Fig. 22. A successful sales letter. (Used by permission of the Dartnell Corporation.)

The anecdote has a further suitability that the letter writer may have had in mind. Note that the letter is addressed to women. How many of these housewives, through their own recollections or stories told by their mothers, associated a horse and buggy with courtship days? Most of them, the writer could be certain, and he knew that a woman cherishes her romance. But horse and buggy courtship days are gone, and nonelectrified homes are out of date.

2. The letter arouses desire through skillful incorporation of the age-old motive of keeping up with the Joneses. "Your neighbors, lots of 'em." You are as good as your neighbors any day, and if you must have your house electrified to prove it, well, you can afford this too.

3. Adroitly blended with the keeping up with the Joneses appeal is persuasion through concrete description of advantages to be gained: light, convenient appliances, refrigeration, running water.

4. Conviction is brought about through reference to approaching winter, and the hinted, though not expressed, point of the horse and buggy story—you won't ride until you get hitched up.

5. Action is made easy through the cheerful offer to answer questions —note that nothing is said about spending money—and reference to the convenience of mailing the enclosed card.

The letter succeeded, and deserved to, for it was planned according to proved sales psychology and written with originality and skill.

It is said that there is no commodity that isn't sold by mail. To many, the validity of the statement is fixed when they know that over a million dollars' worth of fish was sold by a Massachusetts company by continuing to use a single long and interestingly written letter, with an enclosure. Other successful selling by mail involved the Sonnenfield store in St. Louis. A series of four simple, friendly letters mailed by the company to 3,500 charge customers brought in $241,000 of traceable new business.

Generally speaking, form-letter mailings are profitable if they bring in 2 per cent or more of orders. Many mailings fail to do even this, but direct mail, once considered the problem child of the selling family, promises to develop into the most consistently successful member of the family.

THE SALES LETTER AS A COMPOSITION

Whatever else is true of letters, we must not forget that the business letter is still a composition. It must conform to the principles of unity, coherence, and emphasis, and it must be clearly and correctly written.

First of all, to be a successful composition, a letter must have the right keynote, or what has been called the "core thought" or "sizzle" by Elmer

Wheeler, one of the pioneers in successful sales writing. Suppose you have perfected a new type of electric mixer and are starting to manufacture it on a large scale. If you write a sales letter to interest housewives, you can center it around the fact that the mixer will help the housewife to whip up quickly and economically all sorts of exciting new dishes for the family table, to delight the man of the house, the children, and guests.

If, however, your job is to sell heating equipment to the management of a skyscraper, your composition problem is very different. You will expect the salesman to do a large part of the selling job, but by mail you can simplify his task greatly if you prepare a letter and accompanying folder that will show convincingly that your equipment will (1) save money and (2) be more dependable than any other on the market. The "sizzle" then is economy.

But suppose you are to get out a letter for an old, established maker of rugs or building materials. Your core thought would probably be the firm's leadership in its field and all the advantages that such a position entails: superior manufacturing processes, economy resulting from modern machinery and processing, and quality production by loyal employees of proved skill. Institutional prestige thus becomes the selling point, and association of the name with the product increases the purchaser's confidence and satisfaction. These three brief examples tell us that no one keynote is always best.

As in practically all business communication, the sales-letter writer must use *imagination, humanity,* and *common sense* in planning and writing every letter. Consider the resourcefulness in the following stories, told by Lorin E. Deland. One Saturday afternoon in spring, two bootblacks were soliciting trade on a crowded street. One got more than twice as much business as the other because instead of using the unimaginative cry "Shine your boots here!" he was calling "Get your Sunday shine!" As two street peddlers were selling dolls, one was getting the better of his competitor until an experienced businessman suggested the other peddler hold up his dolls in pairs and cry them as "The Heavenly Twins." The new approach made such a difference that the first peddler soon gave up and went to another street.

Humanity comes into play in sales writing in that we must understand people; *we must know what makes people buy.* With this knowledge, we must adapt our selling message to their needs, their desires, and even their whims—for there are many persons like the wife of the late Oliver Herford, who, according to her spouse, had "a whim of iron."

But even with a strong sales appeal, a letter may still fail if it contains errors in grammar, spelling, or sentence structure that will shock or annoy readers. The *rhetoric* of the letter must be right. Starting the letter with a happy phrase, repeating a pleasing note here and there, or making a point with an appropriate anecdote may be what is needed to turn the trick.

Applicable to letter writers in general, but especially to the sales-letter writer, is the advice of Edward H. Gardner—successful writer, teacher, and advertising man: "For the letter writer who seeks to produce results, no study is nearly so essential as the study of logical plan. He must know how to manage it and subordinate it; his machinery must not creak and groan and obtrude its cogs and levers in our faces . . . but his train must run on the rails." [4] Thus, Mr. Gardner summarized the requirements of the good sales letter after an analysis of 5,000 letters. He found that these letters successfully employed seven plans of organization. They are the old, old plans of rhetoric and composition: general to particular, particular to general, cause to effect, effect to cause (predicament to remedy), argument from resemblance (analogy), testimonial, and argument from expert authority. Any one of these plans may be a good one, depending on the product.

A good sales letter, then, must have the right keynote, or core thought, and be well written; over and above these requisites, it must have a *magical ingredient* about which we know little more than that it is produced by the intelligent application brains to the letter-writing job. A component of the magical ingredient may be a frame of mind, described by one of today's leading advertising men: "A salesman knows that his objective is to sell a product, not win an argument, and that his aim is best accomplished in a harmonious atmosphere. So he sets about establishing it." [5]

CHARACTERISTICS OF GOOD SALES LETTERS

The "you" attitude, discussed in Chapter 3, is the life blood of any writing to sell a product, a service, an idea, qualifications to a prospective employer—anything. In orders, requests—in all utility letters—reader involvement is important, as pointed out in the preceding chapter, but it is not imperative. Letters refusing credit *can* be stated flatly, without explanation; collections *can* be made by threats and coercion; and claims letters *can* "pound the counter," and adjustments *can* be refused without effort to retain customer good will. In these cases, the customer-reader may do what is suggested, requested, or demanded, but his action is a

[4] Edward Hall Gardner, "What Makes a Good Letter Good," in A. G. Saunders and H. L. S. Creek, *The Literature of Business* (4th ed.; New York: Harper & Row, 1937), p. 335.

[5] Arthur E. Meyerhoff, *The Strategy of Persuasion* (New York: Coward-McCann, Inc., 1965), p. 60. (Mr. Meyerhoff heads Arthur Meyerhoff Associates, Inc., with offices in Chicago, Toronto, Montreal, and Zurich.)

second choice, not a preference. The motivation may be fear of an ultimate consequence rather than the pleasure of self-gain. In brief, it is debatable whether the writing itself prompted the action.

In selling, however, there are no outside forces, demands, or coercions on the buyer. As has been indicated, the customer must *want* to buy; and the seller, in many situations, must supply the motivation for the sale. If our *letters* are going to sell, we as letter writers must always furnish the motivation, because the customer doesn't come to us; we "go" to him. To motivate the customer, we must have a knowledge of man's basic drives and desires; this knowledge must be coupled with an awareness of what people are doing and thinking currently. John Murphy, of the Public Relations Department of the Pennsylvania Railroad Company, said that the best way to know what a town is thinking is to talk with the taxi driver, the barber, and the corner druggist. Obviously, Mr. Murphy does not mean that persons in these three businesses can give us the pulse of the nation's economy or merchandising trends. But a cross-section of local thinking can be had from talking with *people*. Personal contacts and the information from well-known national indexes, surveys, and studies—the Institute of Motivational Research, the Alfred Politz Company, Dun and Bradstreet, the A. C. Nielsen Company, and the various governmental and publishing organizations' periodic reports—are indispensable to the sales writer.

George H. Smith states the case well for the sales writer's "knowing" his prospects:

The usefulness of behavior studies in writing copy is apparent. When the writer knows the details of washing dishes, for example, he may speak to the housewife in terms of her own experience. "Before you get your dishpan from under the sink," this soap keeps its suds "right down to the last piece of silver," etc., are statements that make her feel "they're really talking to me." [6]

In addition to knowing people's attitudes and activities, the writer should know the product he's selling. Without a working knowledge of the product, sales writers have many times failed, by trying to sell to the wrong market.

THE FACTORS IN SELLING

Whatever his basic information about his prospect and his product may be, the salesman will approach his job with definite steps in mind. The steps vary slightly, according to authorities, but basically there are four: (1) attention, (2) desire, (3) conviction or proof, and (4) action.

[6] George H. Smith, *Motivation Research in Advertising and Marketing* (New York: McGraw-Hill Book Co., 1954), p. 41.

Attention

Because of the very nature of a seller's job, he must get a prospect's attention. Merchandise on display, headlines and pictures in advertisements, opening sentences or pictures in letters, or statements of contents on envelopes—all of these are efforts to "start a sale."

From your theme-writing days, you recall the analysis of opening paragraphs to ascertain what gets a reader's attention. We can call those devices thus discovered into use again as means of getting attention in letters—sales letters in particular: (1) a startling statement, (2) a question, (3) an anecdote, (4) a quotation, (5) a sentence fragment, (6) a news item, (7) a "pun." All of these are used, as you will see in the examples.

The Statement

468 people will die on the highways this weekend! [from a service-club safety committee]
Your Home May Burn Tonight! [from a fire-extinguisher manufacturer]

The Question

Are You Tongue-Tied at Parties and in Business Meetings? [from the publisher of a vocabulary-improvement book]
Can You Sleep at Night . . .
    knowing that 40,000 children are cold and hungry? [from a philanthropic organization]

There is general wariness of opening questions that can be answered "No," the reason being that the possible negative answer creates no interest on the part of the reader, and he quits reading. With that point in mind, review the preceding question-openers. Which of them, would you say, is most likely to arouse curiosity in the reader?

The Anecdote. An *applicable,* brief story can get attention in a letter just as it can in "warming up an audience." A clever, fitting application of the anecdote-opener was used by a specialty company selling babies' bibs by mail:

Papa Bear, Mama Bear, and Baby Bear were at supper when their doorbell rang. Papa Bear and Mama Bear went to the door.

When they came back to the kitchen, Papa Bear said gruffly, "Somebody's been eating my soup. And Mama Bear said, "And somebody's been eating my soup."

And Baby Bear said, "Burp!"

The desire step of the letter opened with "Three bowls of soup and a burp, but Baby Bear's jacket was spotless. He had on his Babee Bib."

The Quotation. Despite the notion that people generally think of quotations as erudite or stilted, considerable use is made of sayings from statesmen, the Bible, poets. Lincoln and Shakespeare are probably quoted more often than any other political and literary figures, because of the public's familiarity with their ideas.

Well-known proverbs—"A stitch in time saves nine," "A rolling stone gathers no moss," and the rest—are still used (perhaps more frequently than successfully).

The Partial Sentence, or Phrase. The obvious purpose of the partial sentence as an opener is to upset the reader's train of thought, to make him curious, and to lead him into the desire step of the letter. Proverbs are used in part, as in "For want of a nail . . ." or "Birds of a feather. . . ." Garbled sayings have been used with some success. According to some authorities, openings like "Birds of a feather gather no moss" and "Don't do today what you can put off until tomorrow" attract attention because the reader thinks, on first glance, that the writer has unknowingly misquoted, giving the reader the sense of gratification in "being right."

The News Item. The timeliness of a current happening can in itself be an attention-getter. The more select the mailing list, naturally the more applicable a news item can be in creating initial interest in a letter. A forward-looking livestock-feed company wrote a letter for mailing during the International Livestock Exposition. Although written days before the opening of the show, to allow time for processing, the letter was mailed first class. There was no trickery or guesswork in the plan, because the company was assured of the event described in the mailing. The letter began: "Just yesterday at the International Livestock Show in Chicago. . . ."

The "Pun" Opener. This device is called a "gimmick" by some because of the use of a novelty—miniature tools, flowers, animals of plastic, metal, or wood—attached to the page. The opening sentence refers to the object, making a pun, usually serving the sole purpose of arousing interest. A men's clothing store in Memphis has a ten-letter series in which are letters containing a miniature plastic hammer, a pair of pliers, and a pair of scissors. The respective openings are "We keep hammering away at you, Mr. Pless" (each letter bears the recipient's name, stamped in); "Don't pinch yourself, Mr. Pless; you're not dreaming"; and "We've cut prices to an unbelievable low."

A letter from a ladies' shop opened with "A feather from an angel's wing couldn't be softer than a Lady Jane cashmere sweater." A delicate pastel pink feather attached to the page bore out the comparison.

Hardware Mutuals

Insurance for your AUTOMOBILE...HOME... BUSINESS

MUTUAL CASUALTY COMPANY • HARDWARE DEALER MUTUAL FIRE INSURANCE COMPANY

PATTERSON AVENUE • P.O. BOX 8748 • RICHMOND 26, VIRGINIA • PHONE ATlantic 8-2878

GOLD MEDAL

JURY AWARDS $80,000 VERDICT IN AUTO INJURY CASE AGAINST LOCAL CITIZEN!

Couldn't happen to me, you say? Let's hope not. However, each day brings higher jury awards in bodily-injury cases. Few of us could afford to pay a large sum out of our own pocket. However, low limits and high judgments mean just that.

Take a look below. Surprised to see how cheap it is to double or even triple your present limits?

Why wait -- check the limits you want and return this letter. We will do the rest.

Yours very truly,

Sales Correspondent Manager

To increase your limits from $_____, the additional cost per year is:		
INCREASED LIMIT	ADDITIONAL COST	CHECK LIMITS DESIRED
$25,000 per person - $50,000 per accident	$_____	_____
$50,000 per person - $100,000 per accident	$_____	_____
$100,000 per person - $300,000 per accident	$_____	_____

NATIONALLY KNOWN NATIONALLY OPERATED NATIONALLY ADVERTISED

Fig. 23. The news item used as an attention-getting device. Notice that the letter brought 30 per cent returns. (Used by permission of the Dartnell Corporation.)

Desire

It is at the desire point in making a sale, according to some sales managers, that *selling* begins. The salesman or sales writer, having the prospect's attention, applies that knowledge of man's behavior patterns in general and his individual attributes such as ethnic or national qualities, mentioned earlier. The seller appeals to the prospect's emotions or his intellect, or both.

In person-to-person selling, the seller can know when and how to appeal to these two facets of the buyer. In sales writing, since we haven't the advantage of a prospect's questions and innuendoes, we must consider our product in the light of the desires of the persons or the group that makes up our mailing list. The question to be answered for a successful sales letter is "Why would the person I'm writing to buy what I have to sell?" A more general question on this point would be "Why do people buy?"

Among the many lists of answers to that question, there is a marked similarity. The Greeks had one broad, encompassing answer: the desire for comfort and all that it implies in our efforts to attain the good things of life and to avoid all that is annoying and bad. Psychologists have analyzed this comprehensive statement to produce lists of as many as 300 basic reasons for people's buying. More manageable and diagnostic lists comprise ten to twenty-five sources of motivation. Consider the following reasons for buying, as summarized by the Direct Mail Advertising Association, and supply other examples from your acquaintance with sales writing that illustrate the desires.

To Make Money

Your spare time can be turned into earning time.

Retailers are writing us about their increased profits.

To Avoid Effort

The new Servi-Center makes all kitchen sinks obsolete . . . puts everything you need for cooking, washing, and cleanup right at your fingertips.

Sending a list of local dealers' names (part of the easy-action step) with the letter is an application of this appeal.

For Comfort

The Calker air-conditioner brings year-round comfort into every room of your home.

To Save Money [7]

This is your invitation to our August furniture sale. In comfortable, air-conditioned salesrooms, you can save 40% to 60% on nationally advertised merchandise.

This semi-annual event will not be advertised publicly for two weeks. For widest selection and more individual service, come in before July 26.

---

[7] A realistic, paradoxical feature of the desire to save money is reflected in the words of Paul Ramadier, France's former Minister of Finance, when he said in an official speech, "Gentlemen, we must save—no matter how much it costs."

A DIRECT SALES LETTER THAT
UTILIZES CARTOON, COLOR,
AND TYPOGRAPHY

A versatile and prolific sales-
letter cartoonist, M. W.
Finkenbinder, here ties cartoon and copy together in a
direct sales letter. A second
color—pink—was used in the
original cartoon and on the
letterhead, to give added attention value.

Fig. 24. Analyze the appeals. Note the effective use of questions that require quantitative responses. Humor as an attention-getter is shown in both the
drawing and the headline. (Used by permission of the Dartnell Corporation.)

Notice that the letter appeals to comfort and the avoidance of effort in
the very act of shopping for merchandise "to save money."

To Save Time

The No. 1 trans-Atlantic airline welcomes you to a magic world of travel.
Fly New York to London in 6½ hours.

The Necktie Workers Organization letter (Figs. 24 and 25) accentuates
this appeal while stressing the saving of money.

CHOOSE FROM ANY OF THESE FOLLOWING GROUPS:

1. Top quality cottons, acetates, silks and blends....
   $1.25 each or your choice of 6 for only $6.75.

2. For the man with a bow tie taste....
   $2.50 will bring you a group of three.

3. And for the most luxurious taste of all, these all silk....
   $2.50 each or 4 for $8.95.

IDENTIFY YOUR CHOICE
by giving the catalog numbers shown with
each tie on the descriptive color brochure.

MAIL BACK TO US THE FILLED IN ORDER
BLANK IN THE POSTAGE PAID REPLY ENVELOPE.

Fill in the information clearly. In a few days you will
RECEIVE from your postman a neat package
containing your crisp, new neckties.

INSPECT them immediately.

COMPARE them for quality. . . .styling. . . .attractive patterns, and finally for

. . . . bargain prices.

If you are not completely satisfied in every way, send them back. At no time are you taking
a chance on misrepresentation, because we make every sale on an....

ABSOLUTE SATISFACTION GUARANTEE.

That is how confident we are you will give us the nod on this order and continue with us as
a regular, steady customer.

Thank you for your time and for your prompt reply.

Cordially,

Scott Brokaw

Fig. 25. The reverse side of Figure 24. Open space contributes to quick reading, for further appeals, conviction, and action. (Used by permission of the Dartnell Corporation.)

For Cleanliness

CMC keeps cotton garments clean longest. It makes garments easier to wash because the CMC-coated fibers shed dirt quicker.

For Health

This new-formula tablet has been proved fully as effective as barbiturates in clinical tests. It is so safe in bringing sound, restful sleep that it can be made available without a prescription.

Here is a double appeal to health: physical health (adequate sleep) and mental health (safety in using the product).

For Enjoyment

Children are *happier* in a home that has a Hammond Organ.

A telephone visit adds that warm, *personal* touch that can make the folks you call—and you—feel good all over. Anniversaries, birthdays, or any day, your voice is always welcome.

This type of appeal is used widely for many varied products. Even advertising for medicinal products makes appeals to enjoyment, with such reminders as "You can have more fun when you feel good."

To Conserve Possessions

Cuprinol Wood Preservative preserves wood for good! Stops Rot! Kills Termites!

To Protect Family

Taxi fleets equipped with Goodyear's new Captive-Air Steel-Cord Safety Shields drove 5 million miles with only 4 roadside delays. That's only *one* tire change for the equivalent of 30 trips around the world . . . Aren't they the tire for your car—especially if your wife or children drive?

Take your youngsters NOW for their booster shots at your family doctor's. And get *your* booster shot at the same time. [A local club's part in the national drive for polio immunization.]

To Emulate Others

Q. Why do 9 out of 10 stock car winners use Champion spark plugs?
A. Champions give *full-firing* power. Put new Champions in *your* car every 10,000 miles. You'll get an *immediate* boost in horsepower . . . and save gasoline, too!

To Avoid Trouble

When you travel, carry your money in American Express Travelers Cheques. Spendable anywhere, good until used, prompt refund if lost or stolen. NEVER CARRY MORE CASH THAN YOU CAN AFFORD TO LOSE.

To Be Individual

Inimitably ORREFORS glassware

For Beautiful Possessions

Heralding a new era in furniture design!
An intuitive blending of traditional Oriental and contemporary influences.

To Attract the Opposite Sex

Ten Tan gives your skin that smart look that men admire.

To Take Advantage of Opportunities

When your competition is keen, you've got to look as good as you are. DRESS RIGHT—you can't afford not to!
American Institute of Men's and Boys' Wear

For Safety in Buying

Brand Names make wise buying easier!
To get the most for your money *buy by Brand Name and be sure!*
Brand Name Foundation, Inc.

To Avoid Pain

The aftermath of over-indulgence can be distressing and painful. Don't let today's discomfort ruin last night's party.

To Avoid Criticism

Welcomes are warmer when travelers TELEPHONE AHEAD.

To Be Popular

The smart hostess has a supply of Party Pick-Up Puzzles around the party room or on the picnic tables. Follow suit, and you're a popular hostess because your guests enjoy themselves as they act naturally.

For Praise

The last time grade cards came out, Jimmy, our eighth-grader, told me he makes good marks because I had helped him to like to read. I was mighty pleased, of course.
Having books around from the Juniors' Book Club helped.

To Protect Reputation

Does your home speak well for your family and your company? Your local representative of Better Homes Institute can help you maintain it economically.

To Gratify Curiosity

How far is it from Earth to Saturn? What is the Whirlpool galaxy? How do hydrosphere, stratosphere, and ionosphere differ from each other? Maybe you will never *need* the answers to these questions. But wouldn't it be satisfying just to know? Read "What's Outer Space Like?" in next Saturday's *Star*.

Do any of the above examples seem static to you? Analyze them to see what, in your opinion, makes for that condition. Look at word choice, sentence structure, and verb forms, as discussed in Chapters 5 and 6, to see how you would improve those that strike you as less dynamic than they could be.

"THE HIDDEN PERSUADERS"

Because of its currency, *motivational research*—a controversial phase of advertising, marketing, and selling—needs a brief look before we leave the desire factor in sales writing.

Simply stated, M.R., to use the trade label, is a psychological approach to research on human behavior; it exceeds the limits of statistical research, in getting to the *why* of buyers' behavior, rather than the *how many*. An account of one of the first commercial applications of motivational thinking cursorily supplies some details and terminology and shows the personal nature of the concept. The study involved Ivory Soap. According to Ernest Dichter, head of the Institute for Motivational Research, who conducted the study,

The new idea involved was that effective copy appeals and some answers to the problems posed by the advertising agency might be arrived at by letting people talk at great length about their use of this soap. I decided to talk to people about such things as daily baths and showers, rather than to ask people various questions about why they used or did not use Ivory Soap. I personally conducted a hundred non-directive interviews where people were permitted to talk at great length about their most recent experiences with toilet soap. The consequent analysis of these hundred interviews revealed that taking a bath before a date, before a special or festive occasion, seemed to have a greater significance than the daily routine bath. I also found that people bathed more carefully, stayed longer in the tub or shower, in their preparations for such an occasion. I also found that people did not judge soaps so much by their price, appearance, lather, or color, but by a combination of all these factors plus an additional intangible element which I called the personality of a soap. Ivory Soap, I found, had at that time more of a sombre, utilitarian, thoroughly cleansing character than the more glamorous personalities of other soaps such as Cashmere Bouquet, for example. This study was conducted in 1939, and it was here that I developed the concept of the "personality" or "image" of a product.[8]

In 1957, a best-selling book[9] brought motivational research to public attention. In its report of successful applications of motivational research in influencing buying habits, the book disturbed many persons and gave rise to considerable argument in the press and professional circles on moral, as well as psychological and commercial, implications of the concept.

That depth analysis does not produce conclusive information about unconscious drives is shown in depth analysis itself. In a study on motivation in buying air conditioners, Weiss and Geller, a marketing agency, found that *some* people need to feel protected and enclosed and must keep the windows closed at night while they sleep so that nothing "threatening" can enter. But, in *others,* a latent claustrophobia makes a threat of the air conditioner. In a study of "selling the 'sense of power,'" the Institute for Motivational Research found in depth studies that complications arose. The deep-seated sense of power that motivates man's buying is not going to mean sales for the manufacturer of the most powerful car to the exclusion of the less powerful. The Institute discovered that the ultrapowerful machine may arouse guilt feelings in a person about indulging himself with power that might be regarded as needless. These examples illustrating differences could be multiplied many times.

In other words, depth research is not developed to the stage that an individual can be definitively categorized as a "type of buyer." Groups of various natures—social, economic, ethnic—may reflect certain buying

[8] Ernest Dichter, *The Strategy of Desire* (New York: Doubleday & Co., Inc., 1960), pp. 33–34.
[9] Vance Packard, *The Hidden Persuaders* (New York: David McKay Co., Inc.), 1957.

habits, but individuals within those groups will continue (for the present, at any rate) to challenge salesmen and sales correspondents. To reduce the alarm that the public is at the mercy of a band of manipulating tradesmen, as implied in some of the literature, we should keep in mind that only successes are generally reported in accounts for popular reading. Simon O. Lesser, formerly of the Institute staff and now with Louis Harris and Associates, points out that there are still enough uncertainties in depth research to preclude applying the label "miracle" to it.

Transcience of appeals also adds to the inconclusive nature of motivational thinking. George Horsley Smith, a Rutgers University psychologist, writing for the Committee on Motivation Research, states that

. . . needs and their gratification cannot be seen as static? Brands differ in their appeal. Motivation often differs for subgroups in the population, despite the universality of some human drives. The way in which appetites are satisfied varies from time to time and place to place. New tastes and new ways of satisfying old ones emerge as invention and advertising show the way. Every new product (witness television and home air conditioning) creates new problems in motivation research.[10]

Despite the dispute on limitations and virtues of depth analysis, the sales correspondent should be aware of its findings and procedures. Social scientists generally accept motivational research in its present stage. They also foresee that perfecting techniques will make it a standard part of marketing and advertising.

Conviction or Proof

At this point in the sales presentation, the salesman or sales writer says in effect to the prospect, "You're not making a mistake in making this purchase," or "You need not hesitate in buying these goods." He adds, "And here are the reasons." Facts for the prospective buyer's reasoning, to convince him that the appeals, or motivations, are valid, are chosen to fit the particular selling situation. In a personal situation, the salesman decides from his knowledge of the customer before him the points of proof he will use. The sales writer will be guided by his mailing list.

The following nine points of conviction are familiar to almost all readers. Familiarity with them may possibly arise from their violations or misuses; however, used with discrimination and veracity, they are bona fide steps in selling.

Commendations of Users

A. E. Ott, president of Ott Management Development Corporation, endorses Anchor Precision products. "My company has found over the past ten

[10] G. Smith, *Motivation Research in Advertising and Marketing,* p. 12.

years," says Mr. Ott, "that Anchor products give better performance more consistently than other competitive equipment. I might add that we try most all of them in our hundreds of contacts with our clients."

This type of evidence, generally called "testimonial," is the account of product performance in the form of letters, statements, or records of the experiences of typical users. Because of negative reaction to the widespread use of quoted endorsements without names, some advertisers quote endorsements and add "Names of customers given on request" or some similar statement offering identification of users whose endorsements are quoted.

Background of the Seller

No wonder Hicks has been in business for 75 years.

This is our Golden Anniversary year.

Although some marketing authorities feel that the public is not interested in company history, a company's reliability can be shown through brief accounts of its experience. Reputation, financial standing, research and production facilities, capabilities of executives and workers can be pertinent information to buyers.

Official Recognition

Longines—The World's Most Honored Watch
10 World's Fair Grand Prizes—28 Gold Medals—
Highest Observatory Honors—Official Watch, World's Leading Sports and Contest Associations

Demonstration

With Macon Soundproof Walls, it took only three hours to change one room (pictured left) to three private offices (pictured right) at the Morton Insurance Company Headquarters in Los Angeles.

A well-worded description of a demonstration can illustrate how and why the product can bring the advantages claimed, as shown in Fig. 26.

Expert Evidence

This world-famous hairdresser tells why . . .
    why you should use a special colorfast shampoo if you
                    color or lighten your hair.

This type of evidence that a prospect may buy with assurance runs the gamut from the signed statement (the hair stylist is named) and the American Dental Association approval of a dentifrice to the unsupported statement and implied commendation that we see on all sides: "Hospitals the country over use Perfection products," "This is only one reason that doctors recommend Lowden's aspirin," and so on, ad infinitum.

SAMPLE HELPS SELL
MULTITHOUSAND-DOLLAR
SHOP EQUIPMENT

A simple bit of hardwood, enclosed with this letter, served as a see-for-yourself stimulant in bringing requests for further data, E. A. Clevenger reports. Over 10 percent of recipients asked for further details on gang-saw machinery involving $20,000 to $50,000 per sale.

Fig. 26. As indicated in the second paragraph of this letter, a sample serves well as a proof step in sales writing. (Used by permission of the Dartnell Corporation.)

Dramatic Performance. Wide use of dramatic performance as proof is found in automotive-equipment advertising. After the various test-runs and races—the Indianapolis 500-Mile Classic, especially—advertisements and sales letters are rife with the performance records of equipment and parts used in the winning cars.

Sales Records

We are pleased to report that last year we moved into the Top Ten merchandising firms in the U. S. We are grateful for the employee abilities and customer loyalties that make this classification a reality. Our expansion plans indicate that we intend to stay in the Top Ten—moving on toward first place.

Statistics offer a buyer proof of both the increasing popularity of the product and the demand for it. Facts or figures proving consumer satisfaction are frequently given in contrast to sales figures for competitive brands.

Discriminating Outlets

Sold only at the better stores.

Used also as an appeal to emulation of others, this point is intended to bring conviction by emphasizing the success and reputation of outlets stocking the product and implies "no risk" in buying.

Guaranty. A bona fide guaranty is evidence of a manufacturer's or dealer's willingness to let the quality of the product speak for itself. Describing the word "guaranteed" as an "almost classic example" of misrepresentation through lack of precision, I. W. Digges, of the New York Bar Association, lists three conditions that validate a statement of guaranty. Digested from Federal Trade Commission decisions involving representations of guaranty, the conditions can be stated as follows:

1. The test of fairness in a guaranty is what the average consumer has a right to believe from the wording of the guaranty and not what the manufacturer has in mind when he states it.
2. A guaranty, to be fair to the public, must evidence its exact scope. (What is guaranteed? Material? Workmanship? How long is it guaranteed?)
3. A guaranty, to be fair to the public, must show the penalty the advertiser expects to pay if the guaranty is breached. (Does the advertiser pay shipping charges on defective merchandise? Is he liable for any consequences arising from using the merchandise? Does he refund the purchase price or furnish new merchandise?)[11]

Action

The sales manager of a national firm that sells exclusively house-to-house described one of his staff as a "three-storey salesman in a four-storey building." "He never fails to get in," the manager said; "ninety-five per cent of the time, he gets the prospect to handle or use the merchandise; in eighty-five per cent of his calls, he gets virtual acceptance of the product; but his sales record is less than five per cent of his calls. He can't get all the way to the top; he can't ask for the sale." (The company president modified the sales manager's epithet for the salesman. The president said he was a "three-storey *man*"—no *salesman* at all.)

[11] I. W. Digges, *The Modern Law of Advertising and Marketing* (New York: Printers' Ink Publishing Co., 1948), p. 174.

In sales writing, as in direct selling, you must ask for action. A member of the Schwab and Beatty advertising agency says the writer must get "the reader to translate into some sort of action the interest, desire, and conviction [that have been] created." If this step is not accomplished, the admonition continues, "the hard-won ground already gained in the advance toward a sale is allowed to be lost by natural, human inertia." [12]

Even a cursory examination of ten sales letters and direct mail advertisements chosen at random will show the common use made of the three general approaches in sales writing to closing a sale.

"Go to Your Dealer." This "closer" is generally used on "impulse" items, foods, drinks, and other less expensive products in everyday use. The meager bid for action is often tacked on without any tie-in with the rest of the letter. For strength, it needs closer linkage with the reasons given in the copy as to why the reader should go to his dealer, what advantages he will gain if he goes quickly, and what he will lose if he delays.

The action step frequently makes use of a "national" week or month observed in marketing. For example: "July is National Picnic Month. Dealers all over the country are featuring Gardner Picnic Supplies. Visit your local dealer today for those exclusive Gardner pieces shown at the left."

Suggest an Action To Involve the Reader with the Advertiser. This "action" form, used frequently in magazine advertising, can be applied effectively in sales letters. Common examples are the check lists of uses of electricity or ownership of electrical appliances, seen in utility-company advertising. This might be described as "delayed reaction to action." It is intended to induce the reader to do *something* that helps impress upon him more fully the name and advantages of the product. Here again, the action asked for should be associated with the presentation of appeals and conviction.

Get a Direct Response from the Reader. The letter asks for an immediate action. It invites orders. It solicits requests for a free booklet, a sample of the product, a free trial; it announces a contest; or it offers a gadget, novelty, or game that relates to the product. This third form has distinct advantages over the first two, less direct, action steps. It can be used for testing the "pull" of a letter. It provides leads for salesmen. It gives the advertiser a second chance to describe the merits of his product, by getting something into the prospect's hands that will carry a further sales message with it.

[12] *How To Write a Good Advertisement* (New York: Schwab & Beatty, Inc., 1942), p. 45.

The advice to *make action easy* is heard so often it is almost a cliché. But it needs repeating. A realistic view of the competitive market tells us that prospective consumers are not anxiously awaiting our sales messages; therefore, to "get to the fourth storey," by inducing action, the sales writer must make the action *simple, easy,* and *specific.* (See Fig. 27.) One professional sales-letter writer concisely advises beginners to "Ask yourself: 'What do I want people to *do* when they finish reading my copy? How, where, and when do I want them to do it?'"

SALES PROMOTION LETTERS WHICH AVERAGED 5 PERCENT RETURNS

On a mailing of 91,000 pieces in a series of 12 letters, Gold Medal Winner Leslie White, Sales Officer for British European Airways (Special Campaigns) averaged 5 percent returns. An example (7 percent returns from this one) is shown here.

BRITISH EUROPEAN AIRWAYS

Dorland House, Lower Regent St., London SW1   GERrard 9833. Telegrams BEALINE LONDON

GOLD MEDAL

Dear Sir,

There's No Accounting

On checking your account with BEA it was noticed, with regret, that very little direct business has been carried out in the last year. In fact, there's just no accounting!

I sincerely hope that now you have been reminded of your BEA account we shall again have the pleasure of handling your passenger reservations and cargo shipments.

BEA's extensive network of Viscount services to all parts of Europe, North Africa and the Middle East provides ample scope for full use of your BEA Account.

If there is a specific reason why you are not using your account, do please let me know.

It would be of considerable help to us if you would kindly complete the form below and return it in the reply paid envelope.

Yours faithfully,

Leslie White

LESLIE WHITE.

BRITISH EUROPEAN AIRWAYS
Dorland House, Lower Regent Street, S.W.1

FROM ....

ADDRESS ....

....

Please retain our account   ☐

Please cancel our account   ☐

Please arrange for a representative to call   ☐

Mark Here

BEA

Ref. CS.PS/1254/W

Fig. 27. Not only does the writer of this letter make action easy and specific, he also allows for a negative reaction to further business. (Used by permission of the Dartnell Corporation.)

One of the optional parts of a letter, as described in Chapter 2, can be used advantageously in sales letters. A well-planned *postscript* can repeat the desire, conviction, or action step of the sale and serve as that final little nudge that prompts the reader to act. Many excellent sales letters contain postscripts. Why? There are two chief reasons: (1) to remove from the body of the letter something which would violate the central unity but is nevertheless relevant, such as an alternative offer (sometimes an item offered briefly in a postscript outsells the main item); (2) to place greater emphasis on a point than it could otherwise get. Note that *these are not postscripts in the sense of afterthoughts,* and that they are not always introduced by "P.S." Frequently they are placed below the signature, either with no introduction at all or preceded by something like "N.B." (*nota bene,* note well, take notice). The following are representative "selling" postscripts.

From a manufacturer, in a letter accompanying advertising circulars:

P.S. We will be very pleased to see you at our Booth, No. 62, at the National Chemical Exposition, Sherman Hotel, Chicago, Illinois, November 24-29.

From a department store advertising an annual clothing sale:

Special Credit Terms Can Be Arranged.

From a manufacturing laboratory specializing in termite extermination, to help out the action close:

P.S. The notation "send the termite inspector," on the enclosed prepaid post card, will bring him promptly and without obligation on your part.

CONCLUSIONS ON WRITING SUCCESSFUL SALES LETTERS

How much difference is there between a good letter and a poor one? How long does a good letter remain a good one? Neither question can be answered completely. But we can say in general that the difference between a good letter and a poor one is the difference between success and failure, and that a good letter remains a good letter for a long time. Identical letters are not infrequently sent, intentionally, more than once to the same mailing list. I have received the same letter at intervals as many as three or four times—and been impressed each time. And adaptations of an exceptionally good letter are almost unlimited.

Selling by letter is not the only way to sell goods, nor as yet the leading one, but you have learned from this chapter that it *can be* highly successful. Good sales letters sent to the right persons are of increasing importance in supplying a rich variety of articles and services to a multitude of eager buyers and satisfied users.

The Work of the Industrial Psychologist in Relation to Consumers and the Public *

by ROBERT PERLOFF

The activities or operations of industry are, simply put, (1) manufacturing or production and (2) distribution and sales. Industrial psychologists have concerned themselves generally with the manufacturing function, including the selection of workers and their training, the adaptation of machines and equipment to the limitations and abilities of their human operators, and the fusion of social and organizational processes with the objectives of business and industry.

These activities, however, are concerned with what goes on behind the counter, with the people who make the product, with how it should be made, with the social and organizational fabric interlacing worker with work.

But what about the public, that body of individuals that is tied in more explicitly with the distribution and sales functions? In the next decade or two, how can we marshal our technological resources to keep pace with and ourselves add to the state of knowledge of distributing and consuming goods and services, while at the same time benefiting the public? It is to this objective—the industrial psychologist's concern with the consumption function and with the public at large—that this paper is addressed.

What is known about consumers? About the public? What kinds of problems has the industrial psychologist helped to solve? His experiences in this domain appear to have stemmed from three sources: 1. Consumer behavior and preference studies, 2. Data gathering techniques and apparatus for observing and codifying market-place behavior, and 3. Advertising research. Let us view briefly each of these three sources, in order to perceive with some credence and optimism our capacity for shaping a new era of industrial leadership, conspicuous as much for its potential benefits to the public as for its economic contributions to industry.

1. *Consumer behavior and preference studies.* In this rubric we include the multitude of distinct and continuous studies by government agencies such as the Department of Agriculture and the Quartermaster Food & Container Institute, by several universities, and by or on behalf of numerous manufacturers and media of mass communication; dealing with what I would call man-product systems, that is the achievement of some harmony of product development and package design with the consumer's sensory and esthetic tastes, or with problems involving buying intentions and economic forecasting, or with

---

* Reprinted from pre-publication copy by permission of the author. Professor Perloff, currently editor of *The Industrial Psychologist,* is in the psychology department at Purdue University. This paper, somewhat revised, appeared in *Business and Society,* Spring, 1964, under the title "Potential Contributions of the Consumer-oriented Psychologist."

The reading gives some insight into the marketing and production of consumer goods, the planning and work that precede the sales writer's work, with its psychological implications discussed in Chapter 3.

demographic factors which describe the various audiences of communications media. Studies like these have been of incalculable value for determining production schedules, inventory controls, as guides in the matter of reader or viewer interests and for helping describe parameters of audition, gustation, olfaction, and vision. Therefore, it seems fairly clear that industrial psychology's heritage substantively is more than an adequate springboard for continuing to make contributions in the decades ahead.

2. *Data gathering techniques and apparatus for observing and codifying market-place behavior.* Included here are sampling, questionnaire and other instrument construction, identification and control of interviewer bias, the tachistoscope, eye cameras, scaling techniques. Even if we were not to add to these and other available tools and techniques we would probably have a sufficiently versatile portfolio of devices with which to investigate hundreds of new and important questions.

3. *Advertising research.* We know something about color preferences and color effects; about type-face and its associations, at least crudely, with certain product classes or psychological dimensions, such as emotion; about copy-testing or pretesting advertisements; about some of the processes involving the perception and recall of advertising messages; something about buying motives; about the characteristics of purchasers and markets; and some alert, mathematically sophisticated advertising researchers are even beginning to study the problem of evaluating advertising effectiveness. The increasingly important positions occupied by psychologists in the advertising business attest to the reasonably solid foundations from which the psychologist in advertising is being encouraged to launch new programs of research into, and pay-off for, the advertising process.

So where can this heritage of consumer behavior studies, of methodological achievements, and of advertising research . . . lead us? There are two platforms from which one can proceed to help assure for industrial psychology a profitable berth in industry and perhaps even an honored niche in the family of science. These platforms are: 1. The scientific and technological, and 2. The social and psychological.

First, let us look at the scientific and technological milieu and its implications for the industrial psychologist's contributions to his employer and the public, via consumer-oriented channels.

a. *Advances in hardware—telemetering devices, for example.* If a man's physiological changes during an orbital flight are recorded instrumentally on earth, it is possible certainly to record practically the full spectrum of physiological measures of individuals while they are watching television or reading the newspaper, while listening to an experimental stereophonic recording of Bach, while driving an automobile over a treacherously safe turnpike, or while scanning the canned goods on the shelves of supermarkets. Hence we are no longer justified in making that once comfortable retreat from our responsibilities by saying that consumer behaviors during the process of consumption are incapable of being observed.

In a word, we are now able to allow the experimental subject, say a consumer, to behave more or less naturally, in his consumer habitat or environment, shaving with a new or an experimental electric shaver or being swooshed in a rocket-like elevator to the heights of a new skyscraper—while in the researcher's control room, possibly miles away, the consumer's pulse rate, galvanic skin response, and photographic and other records are being stored. Here is a vast new field of research and service opening up, making possible more valid behavioral inferences because implicit in our observations are the operations and behaviors of people as they are manifest in life, not in the artificial and frequently distorted confines of the laboratory.

b. *Advances from within psychology—programed learning, for example.* Beyond the implications of programed learning for selection and training, what is its relevance for the vast area of communications, including advertising and public relations communications, between industry and the consumer or between industry and its various publics? There is mounting evidence, both in educational institutions and in industrial training programs (IBM and Kodak, to name two), that information presented systematically, a frame at a time, utilizing the benefits of reinforcement, and allowing the individual to proceed in accordance with his own abilities and readiness to learn, is absorbed and retained with a degree of efficiency equal to or exceeding that achieved using more conventional methods. With some modification, there is no reason other than indolence why we cannot program for consumers how to assemble home phonographic systems, or how to maintain in proper working order power mowers (along with keeping intact the individual's fingers and toes while operating the mower), or how to repair punctured plastic kiddie pools.

Programed instruction is no panacea for the learning process, nor should it be used necessarily in helping the individual learn *everything*, but on the other hand it would be irresponsible for the consumer-oriented industrial psychologist to overlook its potentialities for communications with and making more lasting impressions upon the consumer and the public.

c. *Advances in medical science—longevity, for instance.* There are many things that senior citizens can do with their time, besides buying cottages in Florida, or subscribing to bigger and better hospital or insurance plans, or feeding the pigeons in the park. Many older people, for instance, are willing and able to eat candy, to buy fashionably new dresses, or even to do some skin diving. However, it seems that, like people, psychologists in industry abide by certain antediluvian stereotypes, among which is the myth regarding the older person's passivity or frailty or his lacking the normal esthetic and physiological appetites. When we think about this, not to mention look at the data (and data do indeed exist on this topic), we are immediately struck by how ridiculous is our exclusion of the older person from these consumer behaviors. It would seem to be apparent, then, that a contribution, not only to the public, but obviously to the marketing interests of industry as well, can and should be made in the direction of considering actively the senior citizen as a consumer for most products and services typically directed to those of us who are less "senior" agewise. Specifically, what I am proposing is that advertising or promotional literature be directed explicitly to the aged as well as to other groups and, too, that wherever this is practicable products be designed in such a way as to be attractive to and consumable by the aged. Moreover, a munificent by-product of a more explicit consideration of the older person as a consumer would be his reawakened interest in useful and relaxing ways of spending his time.

Next, let us examine suggestively the social and psychological platform or milieu, and its implications for the industrial psychologist's contributions to his employer and the public, via consumer-oriented channels.

a. *First, the matter of tastes, standards, or values.* As our tastes and preferences change, as mores take on new dimensions, the public's needs will assume new forms and its perceptions of industry and its products will become more or less favorable as the way that industry and its products become more or less similar to the modes of the day. I am suggesting, to be concrete, that if beards no longer appear to be viewed as peculiar or affected, then any policies against beards, either in the company's advertising or promotional literature, or in its hiring policies, should be recognized as prejudices that need to be eradicated. One may say that beards and such matters are trivia over which we should not be concerned. In themselves, perhaps, they may be trivia, but I suspect that they are symptomatic of the moods of the times through which we travel and that some sensitivity to these moods could bring us a step closer in our understanding of the people who make the product and those who buy it and use it. The matter of taste—what people consider to be in good taste or what might be considered offensive—should be explored by the psychologist in industry to a far greater extent than this subject is being probed currently.

To industry, the benefits of such investigations are obvious and possibly staggering. To the public, the benefits of such investigations include principally, not only learning more about this particular component of behavior, but also the results of such investigations should direct us to change our characterizations of ourselves and of our products, to be less irritating and more palatable to the public. For instance, in some very preliminary work we are doing there are some emerging suggestions in the data that with respect to taste, males find the advertising of female products more distasteful than they do of male products—and the same thing appears to be true for females; that advertisements featuring human ailments such as itching and hemorrhoids appear to be more offensive to people not afflicted with these conditions than to those who are afflicted; and that claims or representations that insult the intelligence, rather than those that are merely whimsical, may be viewed with some disdain.

b. *Next, what are the effects on industry's distribution and sales of such sweeping changes in our society as, to name but two, (1) the larger proportion of people attending college, and (2) early marriages?* Assuming that there is some positive correlation between education and behavior, industry should begin representing itself more rationally to its publics. Perhaps the policies of a company could be explained in its various pieces of literature more critically and less superficially. The second illustration, early marriages, is rife with implications for the psychologist in industry. One very obvious one is in the realm of plant-community relations—say in housing, schools, parks, and zoning problems. Without going further the point here is that if industry is unable to anticipate social and psychological changes such as these, it should at least keep up with them.

c. *Next, there is a kind of "extra-curricular" item that should be thrown in the hopper—the matter of civilian defense, fallout shelters, and the like.* In many communities the plant or building occupied by a company or institution is the only large solid structure, or structures, around for miles. What happens in case of some catastrophe—nuclear, gaseous, or otherwise? Is there a plan? Do people know where to go? What to do? Is there a procedure for medical aid, for sustenance, for rebuilding? Pessimistic or fatalistic as one might be, the optimal strategy is to have a plan and some sufficiently large shelter to accommodate the employees at least, or perhaps even the entire community if provisions for the community are not available in the municipality. Now what does the industrial psychologist have to do with all this? Just this: modest as we might claim our facts to be, certainly we know more than others in the organization about the conditions that make for apathy and the conditions needed to transform apathy to action.

d. *Finally, there are enormous opportunities for industry to benefit the community educationally.* Notwithstanding the National Defense Education Act and the funds the Act makes available to schools, it is probable that the laboratory equipment and research facilities of industry will far outstrip the apparatus and scientific materials available in the schools. Speaking about plant-community relations, here is a relatively easy way to render a vital service and establish some good will simultaneously. I refer to the working out of schedules, which already exist on a limited basis in a handful of communities throughout the land—in Niles Township, Illinois, for one—whereby selected groups of youngsters, mainly of high school age, could under technical supervision and in deference to sound safety precautions, conduct experiments or otherwise become more enduringly aware of the tools and the products of science and of scientific thinking.

✿   ✿   ✿   ✿   ✿   ✿   ✿   ✿   ✿   ✿   ✿   ✿

In conclusion, I have tried to sketch a few of the kinds of contributions the consumer-oriented industrial psychologist has the capabilities of making, stemming from both the technological and the social frameworks in which we will be operating during the coming years. Although these contributions may require some aggressive behavior, possibly even risks, on the part of the industrial psychologist, the outcomes would be not only of immense value to industry, but also extremely rewarding to us as behavioral scientists and as human beings.

Exercises and Problems in Communication

Since, for most students, periodical advertising is more plentiful than sales letters, some of the exercises direct you to observe the first form of sales writing and to read about advertising copy. As you have already decided in reading this chapter, the principles of effective advertising can be generally applied in writing sales letters, and vice versa.

1. Study the regular feature "Which Ad Pulled the Best?" in a number of issues of *Printers' Ink*. (Two advertisements for the same product are shown with discussion of the results.) Analyze the more successful ads, to see what features characterize them.

2. Choose five advertisements from magazines or newspapers. Rewrite the text (copy), deleting adjectives and using stronger verbs.

3. Write startling statements as openers for five sales letters. Avoid using exclamation points or underscoring. Let meaningful, powerful words carry your message.

4. Read Chapter 1 in *Motivation Research in Marketing and Advertising* (footnote on page 205). Distinguish among the psychological factors in motivational research. Report your opinions.

5. Applying the principles discussed in the chapter mentioned in Exercise 4, write five paragraphs containing appeals for a household appliance. Your mailing list is the roster of names of women who have attended a two-day demonstration course sponsored by a utility company. You are a home-appliance dealer.

6. Make a list of products that might satisfy needs, as described in *The Hidden Persuaders:* emotional security, reassurance of worth, ego gratification, creative outlets, love objects, sense of power, sense of roots, desire for immortality. In submitting your list, write brief explanations of how the less common items on your list would satisfy the particular needs.

7. In preparation for writing a sales letter for a specific commodity (your choice), try to sell the product orally to another student. The purpose here is to analyze "prospect resistance" to your approach and to develop the "you" attitude for your letter. Be cautious of "aiming" your letter at your student-prospect; he may be atypical of those on your mailing list.

8. Under the headings "Advertising," "Marketing," and "Commercial Correspondence" in the *Business Periodicals Index*, choose two or three articles on current ideas on these areas of selling. Apply the principles to products in your particular field of interest, and write a sales letter, using the principles.

9. Read "Ads for Eggheads," pages 41–42 in *Sales Management*, April 17, 1964. And see Figure 19 in *Effective Business Communication* for Robertshaw Controls advertising, the subject of the article. Discuss the point made in the article about the lack of noticeable increase in sales and the marked amount of correspondence regarding the "sesquipedalian" advertising, as the company labels the campaign.

10. Read Wm. J. Tobin's article "What Do You *Really* Sell, When You Sell Our Product?" in *Printers' Ink*, February 13, 1955, page 56. In the light of Mr. Tobin's reasoning, write a letter to sell a yard game (e.g., a badminton set). Use appeals that will serve as a "solution . . . to a social problem." Your mailing list is made up of young married couples.

11. Write a letter to be sent to this year's seniors in your high school, "selling" them the idea of enrolling in your university. Don't start to write until you have considered the varied "typical" personalities, interests, and abilities among those on your mailing list. Make an outline of the traits.

12. Get *Applied Imagination,* by Alex F. Osborn (New York: Charles Scribner's Sons, 1955). Read the Preface and Chapter 1, and report, orally or in writing, on creativity as it applies to sales writing.

13. Write a four-line jingle to be used as a sales-letter opener for each of the following: a nursery-rhyme book, a barbecue grill, a resort vacation, used cars.

14. Write five sales-letter openers, using quotations. Consult the books of quotations (Chapter 1, Exercise 10).

15. Acting as secretary of a campus service organization, write a letter to be mailed to automobile owners in the community, urging careful driving on a football weekend. Avoid overused points concerning the number of highway deaths, the consequences of highway accidents, etc.

16. Write openers for a ten-letter series (for two-week-interval mailings), selling any product. Let each opener tell or remind the reader that the letter is one of a series.

17. As part of a campaign to introduce a new line of furniture, write a letter using three appeals: to protect reputation, to emulate others, and to avoid effort. Coordinate your letter with a television program being sponsored by your company as part of the campaign. The hour-long program will have top talent.

18. Write the script for three one-minute television demonstrations of the furniture mentioned in Exercise 17. Do not repeat the appeals or conviction steps used in the letter. Vary the sales points in each of the two-minute periods, directing them to (1) women, (2) men, (3) children.

19. Write two letters announcing the opening of a crafts-supply store in a town of 40,000. Mailing lists for the two letters include (1) 200 charge-account customers of an exclusive clothing store for men and women and (2) 500 charge-account customers of a department store.

20. Look for the following words in the end-of-chapter reading, in the order of listing here: fusion, credence, rubric, parameters, demographic, audition, gustation, olfaction, tachistoscope, panacea, milieu, eradicated, palatable, rife, optimal, apathy, deference. Can you define from context those you did not know beforehand? Look up in the dictionary any of the terms you are not sure of. Use at least ten of them in sentences.

21. Refer again to the expression "hardware" in Section 3a of Professor Perloff's paper. What is the meaning of the term in its use here?

22. How would you label the paper, according to the functions of language? Is it predominantly persuasive, informative, or affective?

23. In the *Business Periodicals Index*, as in Exercise 8, find references to articles having to do with the work of psychologists, engineers, and social scientists in business. You may start by looking under the heading "Psychology." Read the articles to sense the scope of getting a new product marketed and to see how the sales writer can improve his part in that process by knowing the parts others play. Make a report on your reading, as directed by your instructor.

24. Assuming it is the end of the semester, write a notice (a 3″ × 5″ card is all the space you have) advertising your bicycle for sale. The notice will be posted on the bulletin board of your housing unit, occupied by more than 100 students, few of whom you know. Be attentive to the action step, assuming that during "regular" study hours, when most students are in, you're away at work or occupied with extracurricular activities. Keep in mind that, in most selling, the prospects are not anxiously awaiting the advertiser's announcement.

25. Assume you had no inquiries from your bulletin-board ad (see Exercise 24). It lacked adequate information or appeals. Write a letter advertising the bicycle, to be put into the dormitory mail boxes. Because you must type the letters, you want a specific prospect list. How will you get names of the most likely prospects? Make your action step easy, your "in" hours being the same as described in Exercise 24. Use at least one appeal other than economy.

26. The Providence Manufacturing Company, 4400 Hartford Avenue, Providence 12, Rhode Island, has just put on the market a new kind of stainless steel tableware which closely resembles sterling silver. The quality construction and craftsmanship make it possible for the company to make the following guarantee: "PROVIDENCE is guaranteed 50 years. If any piece becomes defective in materials and workmanship within this period, return it and we'll replace it without charge." The knives are fitted with shaped, forged steel blades and are guaranteed "never to leak, rattle, come loose, or pull apart." The knives have hollow handles; the tines and bowls of the forks and spoons are fully tapered in thickness. The tableware comes packed in the following sets:

24 pieces	(6 teaspoons, 6 knives, 6 forks, 6 dessert spoons) in cardboard display box...........................	$18.50
32 pieces	(8 of each instead of 6) in cardboard display box...	22.95
51 pieces	(16 teaspoons, 8 knives, 8 forks, 8 salad forks, 8 dessert spoons, 2 serving spoons) in hand-rubbed hardwood cutlery block............................	42.75
75 pieces	(24 teaspoons, 12 knives, 12 forks, 12 salad forks, 12 dessert spoons, 2 serving spoons) in mahogany finished wood chest.............................	59.50

Open stock and special purpose pieces are available. The design is SIMPLICITY, a modern style with smooth curved lines and no ornamentation of any kind.

Write a sales letter to be sent to jewelry stores and department stores which might stock this new tableware.

9

Employment Letters

If you were in business for yourself, would you hire YOU, *or would you look for somebody younger, more talented, more personable, more cooperative, better dressed, more sales-minded?*— WILLIAM FEATHER, *The William Feather Magazine* [1]

Look again at the quotation and consider the qualifications listed. You can probably ignore the reference to age, since most of you using this book will be competing within an age group for employment. Also, you may want to substitute for "sales-minded" a term applicable to your field of interest, such as *research-minded* or *teacher-oriented*. After the second look, answer the question, putting it into the first person: "Well, would I hire ME?" Better yet, make the question "Why would I hire ME?" With that change, you sense, I am sure, that you have created a selling situation for yourself.

In selling, as pointed out in Chapter 8, we must keep our attention on the customer; in the job application, the customer is the prospective employer. In other words, in trying for the *position that you really want*, you are likely to be more successful if you put your mind to persuasion, rather than to informing, according to the discussion of functions of language in Chapter 1. The end to which you will use your words in getting employment depends upon the times, of course. In the "fat years," or those periods when jobs are plentiful and the employee is in demand, your bid for employment—by letter, telephone call, or interview—*can* be to inform that you are "in the market for work." However, in the "lean years" or in the case of your wanting one particular job or employment with one particular company, you need to persuade. But to persuade

[1] September, 1963, p. 12. Copyright by the William Feather Co.

someone, we must present conditions to justify, in his estimation, the action we wish him to take. In the case of getting employment, those conditions are the applicant's qualifications.

ESTABLISHING BASIC EMPLOYABILITY

The applicant for a position can to a great extent choose the qualifications that he will be able to put into his application letter—if he begins soon enough. I have long felt that there is dishonesty in trying to write a good application letter before one has anything good to sell. The very first step, then, in writing good employment letters is *building basic employability.*

What is basic employability? In a word, it is *character,* but since character includes many traits, we shall go into some detail. Can you get up in the morning at the time you set the night before, or do you argue with the alarm clock? Do you feel sorry for yourself when you discover that someone who made no higher grades in school than you did gets promoted sooner or is paid higher wages? Do you have to be given the same instructions more than once? Are you able to see what needs to be done without being told minutely? Can you carry responsibility, or do you let the other person get the credit or the blame, as the case may be? Are you lazy? Most persons are, at some time or other in their lives; but can you, now that you are looking for a job, be depended on to work steadily, hour after hour, day after day? If you can, even for a short period, you have the industry needed for business; for a short period of steady application will usually result in building enough interest in the job to provide momentum for increasingly spontaneous activity.

Persons who are lazy, flighty, or self-pitying do not have basic employability. Before applying for a job, they should lay the foundations for business usefulness. It is good advice to strive first for employability and then to seek suitable employment.[2]

THE EMPLOYMENT LETTER AS A SALES LETTER

Basically, of course, the employment letter is a *specialized sales letter.* It works for the sale of the writer's services (which utilize his skill, education, and physical strength) in exchange for a weekly or monthly salary. Like any other sales letter, the employment letter follows the four psychological steps: attention, desire, conviction, and action. Unless the opening attracts favorable attention, the letter will go into the wastebasket, and the applicant will be among the 80 or 90 per cent who will not get even as far as the interview. A good opening will at least secure an

---

[2] Reading, or rereading, Elbert Hubbard's *Message to Garcia* is still a good idea. This brief essay, first published in 1899, has had a total circulation of more than 40 million copies.

interested reading for the remainder of the letter, which should induce the necessary desire, conviction, and action.

The psychology of the employment letter is essentially the same as that of other sales letters. The "you" attitude is central. An applicant may *want* employment and *need* employment, but as a rule he will not be hired for reasons of want or need. Rather, he must fit into the machine of the employer's organization. He may help or enable a manufacturer to build a larger business through discharging the duties of an accountant; or he may be of great assistance to an industrial chemist because he is equipped to discover new formulas and processes; or he may be valuable to a department store because he has the abilities for selling across the counter or for handling correspondence in the credit department. The employee wants *pay, progress,* and *satisfaction;* the employer wants *performance, dependability,* and *loyalty.* The tactful applicant will emphasize the employer's wants rather than his own.

The marksman who fixes his eye on the target is more likely to hit it than the one who does not. The target here is satisfying the prospective employer's requirements for the position. One formula for securing employment is, "So familiarize yourself with the employer's business and work routine that your interview will bring about in the employer the illusion that he is talking not to an applicant but to an employee. Then instead of asking himself, 'Can we use this man?' he will say, 'What work can we put this man on now?' "

HOW THE EMPLOYMENT LETTER IS UNIQUE

In what important respect does the employment letter differ from other business letters? It differs in that it must first of all pass scrutiny *as a letter,* whereas other letters succeed better when they are not thought of as letters at all. That is, the regular sales letter focuses attention on the electric razor or the set of books for sale; the collection letter on the balance of $16.23 that is three months overdue; the adjustment letter on the broken lawn mower and how to get it to run again. The reader of these letters is likely not interested in their quality, because he is not interested in the person who wrote them. The employer, however, *is* interested in the person who wrote the application letter—if the letter succeeds. He actually reads character in the letter; its very correctness and neat appearance tell him about the writer. Some employers place such stress on the revealing quality of the letter that they still require applications to be in longhand. In any event, the applicant must never forget that his letter will be judged first *as a letter.* It is not merely a device for getting a business job done, but is his personal sales representative.

Just as he would not think of presenting himself for an employment interview without dressing neatly in every detail, so also the applicant must make certain that his letter presents a proper appearance. Its arrangement must be of the very best; words must not be misspelled; punctuation must be in order. Vocabulary is important, since the choice of words reveals character and education. Arrogant or egocentric language must be avoided on the one hand, and timidity and obsequiousness on the other. Your employer wants you to respect both him and yourself. You believe yourself to be employable, or you would not be applying, but tact will suggest that you will be more likely to secure conviction by presenting the evidence in a clear and orderly manner than by making general claims. Your application letter should be the best letter you are capable of turning out, in both appearance and composition, even if this involves painstaking writing and rewriting.

PRODUCT ANALYSIS

Since in your application letter you have a product to sell, here you will, just as with other sales letters, make a careful analysis of both the product and the market.

The product, of course, is yourself, or, more properly, your *employability*. Many individuals look in the mirror several times a day without forming a clear conception of the sort of business person who looks back at them. Just what does he possess that will enable him to earn money—to get business jobs done? The employable qualities and training have been in process of development for years; now it is time to see what they add up to; we don't want to undersell ourselves. In general, employability is discussed, or offered for sale, under five headings, which are either stated in the letter or application form, or implied. These are:

1. Personal characteristics—age, sex, health.
2. Education and specialized training.
3. Activities—athletics, journalism, forensics, class and organization membership and offices.
4. Experience.
5. Reputation.

"Know thyself" is a rule of fundamental importance to any applicant. The *personal* characteristics, however, require only brief discussion. Most of us have the physical qualifications for the majority of jobs, and recent advances in the sciences of medicine and dietetics enable us more readily to achieve and maintain good health—an asset which is more important in vocational activity than is commonly realized. Personal characteristics are usually stressed less in the application than in the interview. Many applicants, however, include with an application a small-size photograph ($2'' \times 3''$ is a common size) pasted to the upper right-hand corner of the data sheet.[3]

In pursuing our *education,* we should follow the line of aptitude as much as possible. It is important to recognize that it does indeed take all kinds of people to make a world and that a given individual can be happier and more successful in some positions than in others. Although college advisers, parents, and successful business and professional men may be willing to help a person determine the fields in which his best aptitudes lie, he himself is the best judge of what gives him that enthusiasm and satisfaction which he wants and will need in his work. Preparing for exactly the right kind of position is taking a long step toward securing it.

For certain occupations, journalism or politics for example, extra-curricular *activities* may be fully as important as the work accomplished in the classroom. Qualities of leadership are frequently developed in athletics or in holding class offices; the ability to meet people may come through working on school papers or participating in debates. Membership in fraternities (especially honorary ones) and in professional associations, and, in some cases, the pursuit of hobbies, also count as activities.

Experience will also help the applicant to determine the kind of work for which he is best fitted. Success in either education or employment will enable the individual to know himself better and will at the same time supply him with further credentials.

Reputation represents the sum of the impressions one has made upon others—in school, church, and the world of affairs. In the application letter, reputation is indicated by *references,* who are usually the applicant's friends, teachers, and former employers.

How to present the several kinds of credentials most effectively in the letter will be discussed further on.

MARKET ANALYSIS

The market consists of all your prospective employers. Remember that although it may be necessary for you to compete with a number of other applicants for a job, it is also true that employers are potential competitors for your services. If you intend to be a secretary, you have thousands of prospective employers in every state in the Union and possibly some abroad. If you are trained as a chemist and wish to teach, hundreds of high schools and colleges are prospective employers. If you want to be a research worker, numerous institutes and industrial chemical manufacturers may be needing your services.

[3] Some state antidiscrimination laws forbid an employer's requiring or requesting a photograph in connection with employment applications.

Since in America the individual is largely free to choose his vocation, there are many avenues to employment. How, then, can we proceed? The following are some of the chief resources at our disposal:

1. *Newspaper and magazine classified advertising columns.* Thousands of positions are filled annually through this means. It works both ways; that is, the applicant may advertise for the position or the employer may advertise for the employee. In general, this means is more useful for the relatively uneducated and unskilled employee, but it is not limited to this type. Blind ads, which do not give the advertiser's name and address but only a post-office or newspaper box number, are used by both employers and persons seeking jobs.

2. *College, university, and special school employment bureaus and placement services.* For the educated younger employee, these constitute one of the best sources of satisfactory positions. They help the employee to find congenial employment. They are efficient, for they learn what certain employers want, and can send the right type of employee, and to some extent they learn what kind of positions the applicants want and refer them to such positions. And they are usually free.

3. *Commercial employment agencies.* There are a number of commercial agencies in every large city. They fill a great many positions in such professions as teaching and advertising, also among office workers and unskilled laborers. They charge a fee, usually a deduction from wages for a certain number of weeks or months.

4. *Civil service examinations.* Competitive examinations are held at intervals for a wide variety of government positions. Watching post-office bulletin boards or inquiring at information windows will enable the applicant to learn of the kinds of openings available and the dates for the examinations. One can also write to federal, state, and local governments for information about government positions; or buy publications that list Civil Service jobs.

5. *Direct contact, friendly tips, etc.* Not infrequently a friend or relative can apprise the applicant of a suitable opening. This is a good source of employment, but should be used carefully so as not to jeopardize the position of the informant or injure the chances of the applicant.

6. *Unaided resourcefulness of the applicant.* Many good jobs are secured through the simple expedient of applying for them for no other reason than that the applicant wants to work for the company. In times of normal employment, many large firms never advertise for employees, being able to fill all openings satisfactorily from unsolicited applications. Consult the classified telephone directory, business directories, trade journals, and company ads, and make inquiries—then send letters to firms you think you would like to work for. One of them may have, or make, a place for you.

7. The annual guide to business opportunities *Careers for the College Man* is distributed without cost to college placement services by Career, Inc., Chicago, Illinois. It contains useful employment information about many of the country's largest firms; for some of the firms it lists the exact name and address of the personnel director.

A fact that seems to surprise some beginning applicants is that a number of applications may be made simultaneously, or in close sequence—to let employers compete for one's services or give the law of averages a chance to work. The following "pedigreed" letter, published in the *ABWA Bulletin,* is an example of a successful unsolicited letter.

Dear Sir:

For the last three years I have been interested in the field of Enamels, and with graduation from the University of Illinois this month, should like to work for your company. In preparation for this line of work, I have majored in Ceramics, specializing in Enamels, with special courses in Enamels and Microscopy. My university training also includes a wide range of Chemistry, Physics, Mathematics, shop and laboratory work, with some public speaking and Engineering Economics.

Under the direction of Professor C. B. Jones, I worked on two problems: (1) the removal of enamel from defective ware, which would institute a great saving through the recovery of metal that is otherwise irredeemable; and (2) the perfection of a strength test for enamels. This test would give a numerical value for the tensile strength of enamels.

I am a member of Keramos, national honorary and professional ceramic fraternity which requires grades above average and promise as a capabale ceramist. I take an active part in the activities of the Student Branch of the American Ceramic Society and devote a large part of my spare time to the reading of technical literature on Enamels. I am now compiling a bibliography of the literature on Refractories for the years 1926-35, besides having already abstracted and indexed the available literature on Microscopy.

Through my reading, I have been impressed by the progress your company has made in the improvement and perfection of enameled products.

I would prefer to work in the research department, or in the control or inspection departments. If my qualifications interest you, I shall appreciate an interview at your convenience.

References and a data sheet are enclosed.

Sincerely yours,[4]

[4] The history of this letter was supplied by C. R. Anderson, who calls it a good example of playing up college work and observes that the selling points refer to class assignments.

Observe that the applicant does not have very unusual qualifications, but that he does reveal specific interests and has made the best of what he had to offer. He planned to send out seventy-five copies of his letter, as he got them typed, but by mailing only three, he landed a suitable job.

STRUCTURE OF THE EMPLOYMENT LETTER

As was stated on page 223, five kinds of information usually go into the makeup of the application letter: personal data, education, activities, experience, and reputation. Formerly all the information was incorpo-

324 North Salisbury Street
West Lafayette, Indiana
March 23, 19

Mr. Clayton R. Johnston
Personnel Director
Campbell & Jones, Inc.
445 South Seventh Street
St. Louis 5, Missouri

Dear Mr. Johnston:

I would like to apply for a sales position with your company, as described in the notice in the Placement Office for Men here at Purdue University.

My major work at the University has been a combination of sciences and business courses. Putting the two fields together will help me to understand your products and to represent your company in selling those products. My extracurricular activities have given me pleasure and diversion, but they have also broadened my thinking about working successfully with others, especially in directing the work of groups.

Professor Liston, whose name is listed as a reference, will tell you of my personal traits and my business ability in connection with activities in my fraternity. Professor Pooler will speak for my work with him on two special projects in chemistry this school year.

Although "like fathers, like sons" does not prove anyone's abilities, my father is in saleswork, and my grandfather was, before him. Selling is in my blood, I believe.

I would like to talk with you about my qualifications and how they would fit into your company. I can come to St. Louis at your convenience, but Thursday and Friday would be the best days of the week for me, since my schedule is lightest on those days.

I am planning to come to St. Louis when I have heard from my applications to companies there. I would like to visit you at such a time. Will you please write me when you have considered my application, so I may plan my time most economically.

I will appreciate your courtesy.

Sincerely yours,

Harold L. Martin

Harold L. Martin

Fig. 28. An unsolicited application for employment. Note the order and spacing on the data sheet, allowing for ease of reading. (Used by permission of Mr. Martin.)

PERSONAL DATA SHEET

Name: Harold Leslie Martin

Address: 324 North Salisbury   Phone: RIverside 3-9458
           West Lafayette, Indiana

Home Address: 824 Cleveland Street Phone: VAn Dyke 7-6543
               Taylorville, Illinois

Birthplace: St. Louis, Missouri
Birth Date: February 19, 1942
Marital Status: Single
Height: 6' Weight: 180
Physical Condition: Excellent   Glasses for reading

Father's occupation: Sales Manager

Education:
 Clayton High School, Clayton, Missouri 1956-1960
 Purdue University B.S. in Chemistry   1960-1964
     (including two summer sessions)

Extracurricular Activities:
     Kappa Psi (social fraternity)
          Treasurer   1962-1963
          President   1963-1964
     Playshop (student theatre)
     (cast and crew work in two plays,
     each of 3 years)   1962-1964

Applicable Courses
     General Chemistry   10 hours
     Organic Chemistry   8 hours
     Physical Chemistry   6 hours
     Principles of Biology   6 hours
     Introduction to Microbiology 12 hours
     Molecular Biology   4 hours
     Principles of Economics   6 hours
     Business Statistics   6 hours
     Managerial Economics   3 hours
     Personal Finances   3 hours
     Psychology   6 hours

Grade: 4.74 (highest possible - 6.00)

Experience
     Hopper Paper Company, Taylorville, Illinois, Summer–1963
     Worked in production as a vacation substitute
     Immediate superior: Norvel B. Mullen

     Singer Sewing Machine Company, Truman, Arkansas, Summer–1961
     Worked in production as vacation substitute
     Immediate superior: A. K. Burton

Fig. 28 (continued).

During high school:
   The usual jobs of paper-carrier, grocery store stock
   boy, and mowing lawns (saved enough for first year's
   college tuition)

References

Professor J. L. Pooler
Chemistry Department
Purdue University
Lafayette, Indiana

Professor David C. Liston
History Department
Purdue University
Lafayette, Indiana
   (Fraternity Advisor)

Mr. Anton Burdall
Economics Department
Purdue University
Lafayette, Indiana

Mr. J. A. Toohey
2348 Lindell Avenue
Clayton, Missouri
   (Attorney, and family
   business advisor)

Fig. 28 (continued).

rated in a regular letter, which usually took only one page, except for the experienced employee, who might require a second page. The plain application letter may be used by young employees of relatively limited education or experience, but the tendency now is to employ the two-part application consisting of (1) a short letter emphasizing highlights and salient points, and (2) a résumé containing all the factual material in neatly tabulated form. When this double form is used, the letter itself is no longer unwieldy; hence the applicant is free to use it to express his own personality and to stress the points in his qualifications that fit him especially for the job applied for.

On pages 227–29 is an example of the modern letter of application with résumé.

The letter shows the "you" attitude by answering the employer's unspoken questions:

"What does this person want?"	(paragraph 1)
"Why should I hire him—what does he have to offer my organization?"	(paragraphs 2, 3, 4, 5)
"What am I supposed to do about it now?"	(paragraph 6)

Another example of the "you" attitude is the accurate and complete inside address. It can be a difficult research job to secure the exact name and title of an employer; as a result most applicants write to "Personnel Director," "Editor," or "Head, Psychology Department" and let it go at that. However, according to Leonard R. Brice of the Black & Clawson Company, the use of the exact name and title shows courtesy and thoughtfulness, resourcefulness and initiative.

Among the numerous directories listing names of executives and officers of companies are *Dun & Bradstreet Middle Market Directory, Poor's Register of Corporation Directors and Executives,* and the Moody Manuals. The Moody publications are classified under the following headings: Public Utility, Industrial, Transportation, Bank and Finance, and Municipal and Government. Annual reports are also a source for names of company personnel. The diligent applicant will probably learn the name of an individual in the appropriate department in the company, to whom he can direct his letter.

THE DATA SHEET

A résumé should be neat, attractive, and thorough. It should include the essential personal details and at the same time build an objective picture of ability against a background of accomplishment. It should be arranged logically to show the planning and organizing skill of the applicant. There is room for individuality in the choice of a title and of subtitles as well as in the design of the résumé. Entries should be arranged to allow for easy reading, even if a second page is required. If a picture is included to help the employer visualize the applicant, its placement on the page is determined by good page-layout principles. The unretouched picture should show the applicant in "working costume."

All needless listings should be avoided; entries which would require the answers "same" or "none" should be omitted. The data sheet is not an application form with blanks to be filled in, but a volunteered outline of information which the applicant considers relevant.

"Physical condition: excellent" means that an applicant would not expect to miss more than two workdays a year because of illness. "Good" indicates an estimate of from three days to a week; "fair" means from one week to two weeks. "Average" indicates that the applicant would probably miss the whole two weeks that most firms allow for sick leave. If the applicant would be likely to miss more than two weeks or if he has a handicap that would be a real hindrance on the job, he should explain.

Education and experience listings should include all necessary information and be arranged in chronological order (if the applicant prefers, he may list them in reverse chronological order so that his most recent accomplishments will appear first).

School and college affiliations are generally listed under Education; only permanent professional or professionally related affiliations should be listed in a separate section (a good test of permanence is to ask yourself whether you would continue to list the affiliation ten years from now). Most college students do not need a separate affiliations section.

The references should be identified (attorney, professor, family physician, sales manager, etc.) so that the employer may choose the ones he wishes to write to.

The letter and the résumé should be a unit of information. If unity is achieved, there will be no annoying duplication of information in the two pieces. If in the letter you want to stress facts from the résumé, allude to them. Instead of stating, "I will graduate from New York University this June," subordinate the point: "When I graduate in June, I would like to . . . ," or, instead of repeating résumé information with "My grade average is 2.5 out of a perfect 3.00," use the detail for a selling point by referring to it. An example: "My over-all grades indicate adaptability as well as scholarship." The bald, oft used "I have enclosed a résumé" can be eliminated by entering "Enclosure" on the letter.

APPLICATION FORMS

Many firms use a printed application form, which must be filled out even when the applicant has already sent a letter and data sheet containing all, or most, of the same information. Although application forms are much used, never merely send for the application form as a means of opening your bid for employment. Assume that the letter and data sheet will be satisfactory. You can always fill in the application form later if it is wanted.

THE FORMAL VS. THE INFORMAL APPLICATION

Most applications for employment are *formal;* that is, the letter makes a straightforward bid for attention by means of a factual statement, such as, "When I read your advertisement for a research assistant in last night's *News,* I felt that you would be interested in my qualifications for the position," and then goes on to submit qualifications according to the plan which has been outlined.[5]

Unless the applicant has learned from the wording of the Help Wanted ad or otherwise that the employer has a sense of humor, it is usually safer to apply formally, especially if he isn't sure of the effectiveness of his own humor. Occasionally, however, humorous or playful applications are highly successful, just as humorous collection letters are. An applicant describing himself in a Positions Wanted ad as "lazy, undependable, unwilling to work except for high pay, not interested in advancement," got a good response—because he showed originality and because the employers rightly suspected that he was burlesquing the conventional appeals.

An interesting case is that of the Massachusetts Institute of Technology senior who encased his applications in bottles and tossed them "overboard" in the mails. He received many replies in sea lingo, such as "altering course to pick you up," "glad to have you aboard for a talk," and eventually took a job with a Philadelphia advertising agency. The letter follows:

Stranded!

On an island in Cambridge, Mass., a college graduate-to-be in June. Will work like (—) for passage into port. Gold stored here with me (training in arts, sciences, business—including marketing and advertising. Past experience in newspaper office, summer theater, steel mill. Best references). You're going ahead and I'm going your way. Have you room in the hold for a man who can prove he's worth his salt?

THE EMPLOYMENT INTERVIEW

Since ordinarily the employer insists on seeing and talking with the applicant, most application letters do not ask for the job itself but only for an interview. The follow-through is as important in seeking employment

---

[5] In answering Help Wanted ads, applicants frequently paste the ad in the upper left-hand corner of the letter sheet above the inside address. Perhaps it is better to type the ad in the same space—the letter will look neater, and the writer can keep the original ad for reference.

as in the golf swing. The impression made by the best of application letters can be muffed in two minutes if the applicant does not put his best foot forward in the interview. Once more, our best approach is through the "you" attitude. What does the employer want to know about you that he could not learn from the letter? He wants to know what you look like, how you use the English language, how you modulate your voice, what perspective you have on the field you are seeking to enter. He wants assurance that the interest you professed in the job is genuine and well based. He wants to observe your attitude—will you be cooperative and fit well into his organization?

It all comes back pretty much to your *proving* the employability that your application letter claimed. Genuine high employability is always in demand; that which is merely claimed or counterfeited is not. But included in employability is a certain amount of poise and self-control. Do not make the mistake of thinking that you are under observation only while you are being talked to. Your conduct before the interview or while the interviewer has briefly excused himself may count quite as heavily as what occurs during the interview itself. In a word, be *businesslike* in preparing for the interview and in carrying it through.

FOLLOWING UP THE INTERVIEW

According to the personnel director of a machine tool company, 95 per cent of the applicants who are interviewed by his firm go home, sit back, and wait to be notified of the result. The other 5 per cent write letters thanking him for the courtesy extended at the interview and making some pertinent comment on what they learned or saw while at the plant. In his firm the 5 per cent who write stand a much better chance of getting the job; the applicants who write show the kind of courtesy and the public relations sense that he wants his employees to have. Certainly a thanks-for-the-interview letter can do you no harm; it may arrive just at the right moment to secure the position for you under very favorable circumstances. Timing is important here, too. A letter should be sent reasonably soon after an interview. To wait weeks to say "Thank you"—especially until you've heard from the company or until you write about another subject—can make the gratitude seem empty or forced.

Here is an example of a letter used by a student to follow up an interview:

Dear Mr. Lewis:

I enjoyed meeting you and Mr. Black this afternoon. During our tour of the plant I learned a great deal that I had not known about the policies and accomplishments of the Goodstone Company; I am more than ever certain that I want to build my future with the future of your company.

I had expected, frankly, that I would feel nervous and ill at
ease during our interview, but you made me feel at home immediately. Thank you, Mr. Lewis, for your thoughtfulness and
courtesy.

Sincerely yours,

Again, suppose that you receive a courteous acknowledgment of your
application letter but no appointment for an interview. It may be that
your letter will go into a "dead" file and stay there, but there is always
the possibility that chances will be better a little later. You can write a
follow-up soon, extending thanks for the consideration and introducing
further sales material (a school achievement, such as editing a special
issue of the school paper or serving as circulation or advertising manager
for the school magazine with outstanding financial results, some accomplishment during previous employment, an offer to submit specimens of
advertising copy you have prepared). Thus your second letter is in effect
a follow-up sales letter. If it shows freshness of approach and offers
worth-while new evidence, it may be successful.

There are those tenacious individuals who want a particular job badly
enough to write again even after being told there is no position in the
company available to them. The writer of the following letter [6] is such a
person:

Dear Mr. _____:

Thank you for the letter telling me of the disposition of my
application. Frankly—and I believe I hardly need say this to
you—I was disappointed.

I would like to ask a favor of you. In our interview in
Indianapolis you said that when you do not promote an employee,
you make it a point to tell him why he was not promoted. The
favor I am asking involves that very relationship. Will you
tell me what, in your opinion, my inadequacies are? Please
understand that I am not asking this question because of selfish
curiosity; your answer will be used to the end of self-improvement.

I would like to bring to your attention once again that all my
experience and educational training has been focused towards
aviation and my marks in air transportation subjects have been

[6] The applicant, an average student scholastically, had two interviews on the
campus with the company recruiter. About two weeks later, he received a letter
saying he was not accepted for the training program, the position he had applied for;
he was offered a position as an agent, which he did not want. Three days later, the
letter, reproduced here without names, was sent; within two days, the applicant was
notified by wire to fly to New York the following day for a further interview. He
went, with the result that he was offered and accepted the one remaining vacancy
in the training program.

well above average. Because of your company's outstanding
success in the field of air transportation, I have taken particular interest in studying your operations and procedures.
One week ago I made a trip to your offices in Chicago where I
had a long talk with Mr. Vellers and further familiarized myself
with your operations. My training and experience coupled with
my enthusiasm make for a combination which, I repeat, would make
a desirable candidate for your Program. Furthermore, I am sure
you would be aware of my constant growth in aviation by my
participation in the Program.

I would like to ask also if I were to accept a position as an
agent with the expectation of eventual placement on the Special
Trainee Program and correct my inadequacies, how long might I
expect to wait?

I have one other favor that I would like to ask of you. I
realize that you are busy; but, as you probably know, many of
us students must make other commitments by May 31. Therefore,
I would appreciate your writing me at your earliest convenience.
I have enclosed a self-addressed airmail special delivery
envelope. Again I would like to thank you and Mr. Hann for the
consideration you have shown me.

                    Sincerely yours,

The end-of-chapter reading gives specific details of the follow-up, from
a survey among personnel directors. The exercises also deal with some
factors of communication in this phase of getting employment.

LETTERS OF RECOMMENDATION

Nothing succeeds like success, and nothing proves employability like
past employment, or the impression one has made on different individuals.
Consequently *references* have become a fixture in applications, and letters
of recommendation may figure largely in the success of the application.
There are three procedures in an applicant's use of persons (who may
represent companies or institutions) as references: (1) He may name
them in the application, leaving it to the employer to get information from
them. (2) He may solicit them for general letters of recommendation
"To Whom It May Concern" or even particularized letters to accompany
the application. (3) He may request them to send letters of recommendation to such and such prospective employers.

The military services still accept "To Whom It May Concern" letters,
but in general these are now looked upon with disfavor because they tend
to prove the friendliness of the one recommending rather than the employability of the applicant. The first and third procedures are those
most followed, the first when numerous applications are sent, the third

when the applicant is going "all out" in applying for one position, or at most is sending only a few applications.

All recommendations should be voluntary or they may do more harm than good. Few persons will refuse outright a request for a recommendation, but it is all too true that the vague, lukewarm, or reluctant recommendation "damns with faint praise." Whether or not he solicits the letter for immediate use, the applicant should always notify the persons he intends to use as references, for two good reasons: (1) to show common courtesy, (2) to allow the person a chance to adapt his recommendation to the situation; that is, to recommend the applicant for the kind of a job he is seeking. The number of references is usually from three to five. Preferably there should be one personal reference (family physician, pastor, friend), one academic (preferably the department head or a professor in one's major field or his dean), and one business (former employer, ordinarily the most recent or most important one).

Thomas A. Clark, long-time, venerable dean of men at the University of Illinois, said that every year he received dozens of letters asking for statements about students who had listed his name among references on application forms. Every inquiry was answered, to avoid possibly hurting the applicant's chances for employment; but in case after case, the answer to the inquiry could be little more than nothing because the student's file in the dean's office contained no information pertaining to his qualifications for the job. One wonders why a student would list a dean's name, knowing the sparseness or lack of information obtainable from his office. Perhaps those who would do so read the newspaper columnists who, every spring about graduation time, tell graduates how to go about getting jobs. All too often, the advice is seen in those columns to "List references, and use names of the biggest people you can." It seems to me, the writers forget to add, "who can write knowingly about you." Incidentally, if you ask a person's permission to use his name as a reference and he hesitates, it may be well for you to thank him for his time and look further.

The letter requesting permission should be carefully written; I was once unable to recommend a student whom I had thought well of some years earlier because her note showed that she had become unpardonably careless in her work.

A "thank you" note for the recommendation is also in order. Although a teacher or employer is glad to recommend worthy persons, one should not forget that he is busy and that he likes to feel appreciated.

The following letters are the request of a firm (Federal Reserve Bank of Chicago) to a college professor for information about an applicant and the professor's reply. The request was a multigraphed form letter with the applicant's name typed in.

Dear Sir:

Re: Mary Jane O'Brien

The above-named person has applied for employment in this bank and has given your name as a personal reference.

We shall appreciate receiving an expression from you regarding her integrity, industry, marital status, and general standing in the community, together with any other information or comments you may wish to make concerning her.

For your convenience in replying we enclose a stamped, addressed envelope.

Very truly yours,

Assistant Cashier

Gentlemen:

I am glad to respond to your request for information about Miss Mary Jane O'Brien, applicant for a position in your institution.

I have known Miss O'Brien as a student in my classes in Business Correspondence and Advertising Copy Writing, and as my office assistant in English during her senior year at De Paul University.

In both courses she made high grades. My recollection is that she showed as much potential ability in letter writing and copy writing as any student I had, and the general level of her performance on assignments was very high. She is alert and quick, and should require the minimum of instruction to produce satisfactory performance.

As student assistant she performed assigned tasks dependably and efficiently.

In person, Miss O'Brien is of pleasing, responsive disposition. In short, all that I know of her indicates that you should find her a highly satisfactory employee.

Very truly yours,

Miss O'Brien got the job. It is evident that a person's application may be greatly strengthened by letters of recommendation—when the applicant deserves good recommendations.

The following letters illustrate a request for information and reply that were used *after* the applicant had been hired by the company.

Dear Dr. Ellis:

We have selected Mr. John Small as a Vick Advertising-Sales Trainee. In fairness to him and to the Company, we wish to obtain a detailed picture of his strengths and weaknesses as he begins his business career with us.

You, as a long-time acquaintance, have a more intimate knowledge of his background and abilities which will aid us immeasurably in helping him get the successful start he should have. We would appreciate it if you would supply us with answers to the questions set forth below. Needless to say, your reply will be kept in secret confidence.

Does he have the makings of a successful business executive?

What would you say are his ambitions? Can you give evidence of these ambitions?

Would you give us your comments on his personality and mental equipment in terms of his drive, stick-to-it-iveness, maturity, common sense, and any other factors bearing on his employment in such a position?

Answering these questions for us, we realize,is not a small undertaking, and you may not be able to answer all of them. However, by assisting us in this matter, you will be rendering Mr. Small a service in his employment with us.

Yours very truly,

REPORT ON JOHN SMALL

Since I place little trust in abstract terms, I shall be as specific as I can. As I see it, a "successful business executive" must do three things well: he must plan and organize a program to be carried out; he must delegate the work of that program to the persons best able to carry it out; and he must supervise and integrate their work. The most difficult of the three, I believe, is the second.

Mr. Small has proved to me that he can do all three. The success of his publishing venture was due directly to his executive ability in planning, delegating, and supervising the work involved in preparing and printing his booklets of party plans. In addition, Mr. Small's personality will make him a popular executive as well as a good one.

Many college students have the ambition to retire to a shady Country Club porch as soon as possible after their graduation. Mr. Small is not one of these. From my talks with him as well as from observing the many difficult projects he tackled during his years in college I have learned that he wants to get things done, to go as far as he can. I would say that accomplishment and more accomplishment is his ambition.

I believe I have already commented indirectly on Mr. Small's drive—he is the driving type, and I would hate to be the man who (40 years from now) had to convince him that he should

```
retire.  What I have said so far indicates also, I believe,
Mr. Small's maturity and perseverance.  In the years I have known
him I have found him conscientious and dependable.  He is willing
to ask advice if he needs it, and to learn from his mistakes.
He keeps his promises, and he puts his work first.

I am glad to answer questions about a man like Small, for he
will be a credit to his college and his firm.
```

[pen signature]

Many firms have abandoned the practice of checking character references, because, they say, so few who write letters of recommendation know how to evaluate and to write objectively. In these firms knowledge of the character of the applicant is determined from special credit-bureau reports. Even in firms that check references diligently, there is a tendency to pick and choose: Information is weighted most heavily if it comes from a personnel man from another company, from a man who has had training in scientific evaluation of evidence (a physician, a chemist, a teacher), or from a man whose work requires constant objective judgment (a judge).

Some business executives and school administrators express a preference for college teachers as sources of information about applicants. If the teacher has known the student well (and the applicant should not list him as a reference otherwise), the teacher can help a prospective employer, since (1) he has dealt with the applicant recently, (2) he knows something of the student's mental characteristics, (3) he ordinarily writes objectively, there being no pressures to write favorably, such as family or business pressures, and (4) he writes candidly, in protection of his own reputation for good judgment and that of the university.

HONESTY IN EMPLOYMENT LETTERS

There is often a great temptation for the applicant to falsify some of the data in his letter, or even to copy the letters of others. That "honesty is the best policy" is nowhere truer than in preparing the application for employment. The adage is strongly supported by returns in a survey [7] among 392 companies. The number-one item of ninety-nine factors that irritate employment interviewers was "is caught lying." The responses showed that 344 "would not employ," 41 had a "prejudice against," and 7 found an applicant's lying "somewhat irritating." No respondent answered the item "not irritating." Do not yield to any temptation to give incorrect age or greater proficiency that you possess; do not claim edu-

[7] Charles S. Goetzinger, "An Analysis of Irritating Factors in Initial Employment Interviews of Male College Graduates" (unpublished Ph.D. dissertation, Purdue University, 1954).

cational distinctions that you have not won or experience that you have not had. In your new position you want to be free to concentrate on your work without being distracted by the necessity of maintaining a deception.

And, above all, do not *copy* anyone else's application letter, however good it may be. Apart from the ethics of this procedure, there are two excellent arguments against it: (1) No one else's letter will fit you well enough to do justice to your own personality, and (2) another applicant might send the employer a plagiarism of the same letter, thus queering you both. You may study good application letters for what you can learn about techniques, but when you come to writing, write your own letter, and make it the best possible *individualized sales presentation* of your general and special qualifications for the particular job for which you are applying. That is, adapt your plan both to yourself and to the job.

INFLUENCE OF AGE, EMPLOYMENT STATUS, AND ECONOMIC CONDITIONS ON EMPLOYMENT LETTERS

A person just out of high school may write more briefly than the college graduate, the college graduate more briefly for his first position than later when he has had several years of experience. The seasoned employee will frequently include specimens of work—booklets, magazine articles, or advertising campaigns. An applicant with long experience may spend weeks or even months in preparing the elaborate portfolio which will eventually win for him a coveted position with good pay and opportunities for maximum expression of his best aptitudes.

Of course the general employment situation influences results from application letters, good and bad. In the early months of World War II, with the war draining away millions of employables, one evening-school student assured me that even if I hadn't thought much of her application letter, it had got her an interview and job offer without even being mailed! As she was composing it on the train a man had looked over her shoulder and seen the qualifications she was listing, and that was enough.

In striking contrast is the situation during a recession, when the want ad section is a fraction of the size it was during prosperous times, and an answer to one of those ads will bring hundreds and sometimes thousands of letters to an overworked and understaffed personnel department which has long since lost its resilience and probably its sense of humor. In writing a letter of application under such unfavorable circumstances, you must GET THERE FIRST—WITH THE BEST letter in the whole stack. Perfection is a high standard, but one can strive for it: It means *no* possibly disqualifying flaws of any kind in mechanics, grammar, structure, or appearance *plus* the "you" attitude and something extra, a note of sincerity, a spark of life, a *je ne sais quoi* that makes all the difference.

It should be almost needless to stress in conclusion that imagination is creative. When the applicant visualizes himself applying his aptitudes industriously in employment for which he is fitted, he goes a long way toward the ultimate securing of the job of his choice; *to want it concretely* helps to make it an actuality. And we can do a great deal about developing our character and aptitudes into high employability—the foundation upon which good employment must ultimately rest.

Don't's and Do's for Employment Letters

Don't try to base good employment on poor employability.

Do recognize that to deserve good employment, you must deliver good service.

Don't think that an employer is interested only in your qualifications and that you can neglect neatness and polish in your application.

Do bear in mind that the application letter is the one kind of business letter that must always stand examination *as a letter.*

Don't take references and recommendations for granted.

Do realize that persons who recommend you are doing you a favor. Remember to be courteous and appreciative. Their reputations are at stake also.

Don't think that the job is as good as won when you have composed a model application letter.

Do remember that most application letters result in no more than an *opportunity* to get the job, which must be actually won during or after the interview.

Don't overlook sending the follow-up letter, especially when your application and interview were unsolicited.

Do recognize that the follow-up letter offers opportunities to show courtesy and to present further selling material. It is, in effect, a follow-up sales letter.

Don't forget the importance of personalizing your letter, of adapting your qualifications to the position, in so far as possible.

Do recognize that the good salesman always studies his prospects and sells to them as individuals.

Don't overlook the possibility of securing favorable attention through novel, original openings and styles.

Do adapt the style of your letter as well as its content to the person or firm addressed—but be formal unless informality is directly indicated.

Don't use worn-out phraseology, ineffective repetitions, vague and colorless language in application letters.

Do remember that your letter represents a live human being; make it breathe vitality in every phrase.

The Follow-up Letter in the Job Presentation *

by CHARLES E. PECK

One phase of job presentation that many recent college graduates overlook is the voluntary follow-up letter to their application letter or interview. Those who do follow up oftentimes weaken their chances because they include too little or too much material, give the wrong impression, send the message too early or late, or disregard the mechanics of writing.

Because there is no evidence of any research having been made on this type of letter, a three-page questionnaire with a covering letter was mailed to one type of retail store that has many employees—the department store. The purpose of the study is twofold: to inform personnel men how others in the same field evaluate this kind of communication and to help college graduates improve their job presentation.

This article is based on the analysis of 99 usable returns [1] and is concerned mainly with the follow-up letter that a recent college graduate makes on his own initiative. Tabulation of the questions by number of employees permits discussion of noticeable comparisons within seven classifications.[2] Coverage first shows the relative importance of a follow-up by phone, letter, and in person and gives the personnel men's reasons for their preferences. The second section discusses the ideas that the message should include, the importance of mechanics, and major weaknesses in this type of message. Finally the terminal section summarizes.

Importance of the Follow-up

The majority of the responding personnel men in department stores throughout the United States say that a recent college graduate strengthens his chances for the job he has applied for if he follows up in any way his application letter or interview. Of the 99 participants in the survey, 69 said "yes"; 7, "no"; and 23, "depends." More than half (60%) of those who checked "yes" commented that a follow-up shows added interest—either in the job or the company. The remaining 40 per cent gave as reasons the following in order of frequency: displays determination, indicates courtesy, serves as a reminder, permits better understanding of applicant and his qualifications (through observation and submission of additional information), and shows sincerity of purpose. In each of the seven classifications of stores by number of employees, there were more "yes" replies than the combined total for the other two choices.

* Reprinted from the *ABWA Bulletin*, March, 1963, by permission of the author. Professor Peck, of the University of Washington, was formerly in personnel work in business and industry. He has done a great deal of research in communication, chiefly in effective employment applications.

[1] Questionnaire was mailed to 300 department stores in the 150 largest cities in the United States.

[2] The figure following each of the seven employee classifications indicates the number of returns: 300 or less—15; 301 to 500—22; 501 to 1000—20; 1001 to 2000—16; 2001 to 3000—11; 3001 to 5000—10; more than 5000—5.

The 23 respondents who qualified their replies said a follow-up strengthens a graduate's chance depending on the following: his qualifications, possibility of an appropriate opening, instructions given during the interview, and the content of the letter. Only in the classification of 301 to 500 employees was there a noticeable frequency of conditional answers. In that group 45 per cent of the personnel men checked "depends." Most of the seven "no's" stated that they form their opinion of the candidate during the interview; therefore any follow-up is unnecessary.

If personnel men think a follow-up in any form helps the job presentation, which do they prefer? As the table below shows, first choice is the personal visit; a close second choice, the letter; third choice, phone.

	1st Choice	2nd Choice	3rd Choice	Weighted Total [3]
In person	40	12	15	159
Letter	34	18	18	156
Phone	14	30	16	118

In each of the seven store classifications, the combined total of second and third choices for each of the three types of follow-up exceeded the total of first choice except for the following:

1. Stores with 300 or fewer employees gave equal preference to the personal visit and the follow-up letter.
2. Stores with 301–1000 employees preferred the personal visit.
3. Stores with more than 5000 employees preferred the phone follow-up.

Those who commented on their choice of follow-up gave the following reasons:

Personal Visit
For: 1. Shows interest and a willingness to put forth additional effort to get the job.
      2. Keeps applicant's appearance and personality fresh in interviewer's mind.
Against: 1. Form of pressure and an encroachment upon personnel man's time.
      2. Irritating.
      3. Upsets a busy schedule when applicant comes in without an appointment.

Letter
For: 1. Gives the executive officer an opportunity to analyze the situation at his convenience.
      2. Easier to handle a larger number of applicants.

Phone
For: Saves time of personnel manager.
Against: Interrupts.

The two main kinds of follow-up letter are (1) correspondence following an interview and (2) the inquiry when an applicant sends his application letter

---

[3] To help in interpreting these choices, an arbitrary weighing is used: 1st choice, 3 points; 2nd choice, 2 points; 3rd choice, 1 point.

and does not receive a reply. The majority of personnel men react favorably to both kinds [4]—87 per cent for the follow-up to the interview; 68 per cent for the inquiry. Only 2 per cent of the respondents said they react unfavorably—and that is to the inquiry. The rest of the respondents stated they react in a neutral way when they receive a follow-up letter. The greatest percentage of replies that checked neutral reaction toward a message following the interview was found in the stores with 300 or fewer employees.

Because personnel men regard favorably follow-up letters, one might reason that many applicants use this type of correspondence to strengthen their chance for the job. But this is not true. Of all recent college graduates who mailed an application letter to department stores or applied in person, 80 per cent of the stores who participated in the survey said that 10 per cent or less of these candidates sent a follow-up on their own initiative. Over half the stores (58%) receive no more than 5 per cent of follow-ups. Furthermore the trend does not seem to be changing when 54 per cent of the stores report no change within the last five years; 11 per cent, a decrease; only 13 per cent, an increase; the rest, do not know.

Writing the Letter

Because no one has attempted to research the follow-up letter for a job, it is only appropriate to find out what should and should not go into the message. This section discusses ideas to include, importance of mechanics, major weaknesses in the follow-up, "pet peeves" of personnel men, and suggested time of mailing.

Ideas To Include

In a follow-up to an interview, personnel men are especially interested in job identification, applicant's attitude toward the firm, and new material that will help determine the individual's qualifications. In the list below the frequency indicates the preference of the suggested ideas submitted to the stores for consideration:

77—Thanks for the interview
77—Mentions how applicant feels now relative to the firm
68—Identifies the job applicant seeks
68—Adds new materials that may be helpful in determining applicant's qualifications
47—Mentions date of interview
44—Gives applicant's favorable reaction to points covered by the interviewer
35—Highlights applicant's qualification(s) discussed during the interview
35—States that applicant has completed an assignment given to him by the interviewer (such as read a brochure or seen someone)
2—Other

When a graduate does not receive a reply to the application letter he had previously mailed, he should beware of repeating the same information he

[4] Assumption is that the letter is neat and well-written.

mentioned before. For example, 60 per cent of personnel men do not want the applicant to enclose his data sheet when he has sent another one previously with his application letter. Another 14 per cent said they do not care whether the candidate includes this enclosure. Because 73 per cent of the stores retain the original application letter and data sheet for six months or longer, an identical enclosure duplicates material already at hand and clutters the files.[5]

Especially important ideas to include in this type of follow-up are (1) adequate identification so the recipient can locate the applicant's application file and (2) a request for an interview. In the list below the frequency again appears before the suggested ideas:

77—Identifies job sought
69—Gives date of application letter previously sent
64—Requests an interview (if distance is not a limitation)
46—Expresses interest in the job sought
46—Tells when applicant is available
46—Offers to send additional information upon request
45—Includes applicant's telephone number
45—Adds new material about his qualifications for the job
44—Gives reason(s) for wanting to work for the company
34—Inquires about the status of his application
33—Briefly mentions major qualifications already given in application letter.
5—Other

Importance of Mechanics

Not only must one pay attention to the ideas he includes in a follow-up but also to mechanics. As the table below shows, much weight is attached to the first three of the five following kinds of mechanics:

	Much	Some	None	Total
Spelling	91	5	0	96
Neatness	81	9	0	90
Composition	72	19	0	91
Punctuation	43	47	2	92
Placement	17	62	8	87

The majority of stores in all seven classifications put much weight on spelling, neatness,[6] and composition. Although punctuation and letter placement are less significant, at least 90 per cent stated that these two factors carry either much or some weight.

The following comments are typical of personnel men's attitude toward a graduate's mastery of writing mechanics. In a nutshell, these men expect col-

---

[5] One personnel manager submitted a complete file for one candidate who mailed to the store his application letter and two follow-ups—each with the same seven-page résumé.

[6] When asked whether the follow-up should be typewritten or in longhand, 50% of the respondents said it should be typewritten; 45%, does not matter; 5%, longhand. The plurality of the stores with 2000 or fewer employees do not care whether the follow-up is typewritten or in longhand—as long as it is legible. The majority of those exceeding 2000 employees want typewritten letters.

lege people to be thoroughly grounded in these mechanics and believe there is a positive correlation between writing fundamentals and over-all ability.[7]

1. An educated person should produce a letter that is precise, neat, and correct in every detail. The right letter can be an informal re-introduction and create the image of a confident, well-poised individual.
2. By college age, a student should certainly be thoroughly familiar with the mechanics of writing a business letter.
3. These five factors indicate the writer's intelligence, judgment, and writing ability.
4. Any job requires a well-organized and accurate person. These factors indicate his attention to detail and to the way he works.
5. Letters reveal a sense of order or self-organization.
6. A letter tells a great deal about an applicant's education, development potential, and work habits.
7. The ability to communicate in writing is one of the more important requirements for success in business.

Major Weaknesses in the Follow-up Letter

The respondents not only told what should be in a follow-up letter, but also mentioned what they consider major weaknesses in this type of message. Of the 171 points mentioned, 132 [8] (77%) fell into the four following categories:

Mechanics	37
Missing information	32
Wrong tone	32
Wordiness	31
	132

Criticism of mechanics centered around two factors discussed previously—composition and spelling mentioned 15 and 12 times respectively. Others with much lower frequency included illegibility, lack of neatness, letter form (use of form letter or mass produced), and incorrect name and title of recipient or interviewer(s). Although 32 people mentioned missing information, the highest frequency for any category was only 4. Those mentioned more than once included degree of interest in the position, strong point of background, and interest in the firm. All three of these indicate a need for salesmanship in the letter. Wrong tone ranks alongside missing information as the second greatest weakness in a follow-up. Over half (56%) of the comments centered on the following: emphasis on advantages to the applicant rather than for the firm (5); formal, stilted, stereotyped style (5); flattering, flowery, gushy comments (4); and insincerity (4). Wordiness, a close third, included rambling (poor organization) 10 times, lengthy letter 9 times, and repetition 5 times.

When asked to list "pet peeves" for each of the two main types of letter follow-up, the respondents again included entries that fell into the same cate-

---

[7] Other replies pointed out personnel men's dissatisfaction with the writing ability of college graduates: (1) The inability to communicate, whether written or oral, is a major weakness in business today. (2) These five factors (spelling, composition, etc.) and mathematics seem to be lost arts among college graduates.

[8] The other 39 weaknesses were grouped as follows: None—21; little imagination or originality—8; vagueness—6; other—4.

gories as those for previously discussed weaknesses. But the order of the 134 remarks fell into the following five areas:

Wrong tone	43
None	26
Wordiness	22
Mechanics	16
Missing information	16
	123

The outstanding complaint is wrong tone or attitude of the applicant toward the recipient. Ten of the forty-three comments made indicated disgust with a flattering or flowery approach. Others with a frequency of two or more included presumptuousness (4),[9] persistency (4),[10] pressure (3), emphasis on advantages to applicant rather than to the firm (3), over-aggressiveness (3),[11] annoyance (2),[12] demanding (2),[13] and stilted writing (2). The fact that only 26 personnel men said they had no "pet peeves" obviously shows they are in the minority. Within each of the other categories—wordiness, mechanics, and missing information—the ranking of factors parallels those mentioned for weaknesses.

For a follow-up to an application letter when the graduate does not receive a reply, one can come to two conclusions:

1. The majority of the executives do not dislike this type of letter. The reasoning back of this statement is twofold: 32 of the 99 said they had no "pet peeves," 12 of the 48 who did not answer directly added that mailing an acknowledgment to the applicant practically eliminates receiving this type of follow-up.
2. A minority have "pet peeves" about this follow-up letter. Of the 39 mentioned, 19 fall into the category of wrong tone.[14] Those factors with a frequency greater than one include flattery (3), presumptuousness (2), assumption that application is being ignored (2), and pressure (2).

Suggested Time for Mailing

About half (48%) the personnel men believe that a graduate should send his follow-up to an interview within one week. A total of 92 per cent suggest that this type of letter be mailed within two weeks. Probably the reason for this promptness is that the job might be filled if further time elapses. For a follow-up to a letter to which the applicant has no reply, most of these store executives (61%) say that an applicant should wait at least two weeks before writing. In the latter instance this timing no doubt permits the personnel man to circulate information about the individual before acknowledging.

[9] Implication that company is obliged to give further consideration; applicant asks company to pay his expenses.
[10] Including letters from people to whom company indicated a lack of interest.
[11] Including "you can't exist without me."
[12] Including resentment for not having heard from the company.
[13] Including name dropping.
[14] The remaining group themselves as follows: mechanics—6, wordiness—4, missing information—3, and other—7.

Summary

The majority of participating personnel men in department stores through-out the United States say that a recent college graduate strengthens his chances for a job he has applied for if he follows up his application letter or interview. Of the three kinds of follow-up—in person, by letter, and by phone—first choice is the personal visit; a close second, by letter; a distant third choice, by phone.

Over 50 per cent of the 99 respondents react favorably to the two main kinds of follow-up by letter—87 per cent for the follow-up to the interview; 68 per cent for the inquiry when an applicant has not received a reply to his application letter. Yet 80 per cent of the stores which participated in the survey receive 10 per cent or less follow-up letters from applicants who had an interview or sent an application letter.

In a follow-up to an interview, personnel men are especially interested in job identification, applicant's attitude toward the job, and new material that will help evaluate the individual's qualifications. In the other kind of follow-up (inquiry following the application letter) the writer should beware of repeating the same information he mentioned before. Important ideas to include are adequate identification (job sought and date of application letter) and a request for an interview.

Personnel men put much weight on spelling, neatness, and composition. Furthermore these executives react unfavorably when the applicant omits important facts, uses the wrong tone, or writes a wordy letter. In addition, timeliness of mailing the follow-up is important. Over 90 per cent suggest mailing a follow-up to the interview within two weeks. On the other hand 61 per cent say that a graduate should wait at least two weeks before mailing an inquiry following his application letter.

Exercises and Problems in Communication

1. In keeping with the concept of establishing basic employability, write 300 words analyzing your abilities and temperament. Titles such as "Why I Want This Particular Position," "What I Can Contribute to _____ Company (or School)," or "What Kind of Person Am I?" appear as the last entry on some company application forms. Use one of them as the title of your analysis.

2. Prepare an employment portfolio, using the following procedure: Choose three or more companies (if you are training for business or industry), school systems (if your career is to be teaching), or graduate schools (if you are planning to go on for advanced work). Look up these organizations and institutions in the various directories, catalogs, and registers in your university library and placement office, to learn which of them you can work for, teach in, or study at to the best advantage. In this project, you are naturally looking for benefits to yourself; however, more important is the synthesis of what you and the organization have to offer each other. Look at your personal and academic attributes in the light of the company's or school's features and benefits. Write your reactions and decisions (if you truly feel that you can decide) for your

instructor, in the form that he indicates. If you can decide on the one job you want, support your conclusions in the report. If you are at sea about your future plans, you may investigate companies, school systems, and graduate schools, to find the direction you may wish to take. Follow the same assignment in writing your findings.

3. Write a person in your hometown, asking permission to use his name as a character reference. Be sure that the person can write about you in the light of the position you are applying for.

4. Suppose that a prospective employer wrote the person mentioned in Exercise 3. Assume the identity of the person, and write the character reference about yourself to the company.

5. After an interview with the company or school that you want most to work for, you receive a letter from the personnel director. He writes that your qualifications are good but that there are other applicants better suited for the present openings. He wishes you luck in whatever you choose to do in the future. Answer his letter, asking for reconsideration of your application. This exercise requires persuasive writing of the highest order; care must be taken to avoid sheer repetition of your application letter or a tone of pleading or of criticizing the company. Your qualifications as they would apply to the company should be the chief topic of your letter. Observe Professor Peck's findings in the end-of-chapter reading.

6. After an interview in which a person interviewing you referred casually to the high opinion one of your references has of you, write the referent, mentioning the interview incident. The point of your letter is to thank him; you must observe caution in avoiding the implication that his comments were divulged to you.

7. Write a letter to the personnel department of an organization with which you have accepted employment, asking for information about housing, the city, or any phase of your life in the town not related directly to your work.

8. Select from the "Help Wanted" ads in the classified section of a daily newspaper a job that appeals to you, and write your application in the form of a single-page letter. Paste the ad at the top of your lettersheet.

9. For the ad chosen in Exercise 8, write your application in two parts, the short letter and the résumé.

10. Write to one of your former professors, explaining your application (Exercise 8) and asking him to send a letter of recommendation. Tell him enough about the position so that he can write, matching what he knows about your qualifications to the requirements of the job.

11. You eventually receive the position mentioned in the three preceding exercises. Write a "thank you" note to the professor for the helpful recommendation.

12. Examine the treatment of employment letters in a college English text other than this one, and compare the treatment there with the material in this chapter. Evaluate the discussions according to principles set forth in this chapter.

13. Assume that you were offered two jobs by different companies. Write a letter refusing the least advantageous one.

14. Assume that you have been offered a position that is your second (or third) choice in a company. Write the company, to try to get the position you prefer.

15. As a member of the personnel department in a company you have applied to, write a letter to yourself, saying there is no opening. See if you

can keep a positive tone in the letter. Do not use the words *but* or *however.* Oscar Hammerstein II said that *but* is the saddest word in the English language, because it so often reverses a positive attitude or notion to a disappointment.

16. Read *Applied Imagination,* by Alex Osborn, to see how you can make your approach to employment more creative. Report Mr. Osborn's theories either orally or in writing.

17. Study the following letter in connection with the letter on page 234. (The one that follows, incidentally, is the first draft of the letter that the student ultimately sent.) Is there a difference in tone in the two drafts? What effect do sentence length and paragraphing have on tone? Does greater length make for better tone in the final draft? (Although brevity is an admirable feature in communication, if length contributes to tone, sacrifice brevity.) Do the obvious statement in the opening clause, overuse of "I," and sameness in sentence structure establish an argumentative tone for the whole letter?

Dear Sir:

    I received your letter of May 17 today and was disappointed to find out that you could not consider me for Eastern's Special Trainee Program.

    Although I have had two other good offers for jobs, I had hoped that I would have the opportunity to be on your Program. I have always thought quite high of Eastern because of their outstanding success in the air transportation field. I have taken particular interest in studying and learning Eastern's operations and procedure. One week ago I made a trip to Eastern's offices in Chicago where I met Mr. Vellers and further familiarized myself with your operation.

    In our interview in Indianapolis you said that when you do not promote an employee for a position you make it a point to tell him why he was not promoted. I would like to know what you considered was lacking in me so that I can correct my faults for my own self improvement.

    If I were to accept a position as an agent how long would it be before I would be able to get on the Special Trainee Program?

    I must make other committments [sic] by May 31. I would appreciate your writing me at your earliest convenient time. I would like to thank you for the consideration that you have given me in the past.

    Enclosed is a special delivery stamp for you to use on your letter.

                      Sincerely yours,

18. React to the objectivity and applicability of the following excerpts from letters of recommendation:

    a. I know that his work will be satisfactory.

    b. As a student Mr. Shehan has a definite ability, but in a course he is not particularly interested in, his lack of application keeps his grade from being the high grade of which he is capable. I justify this, however, since

I feel he does apply himself to that which he is interested in, which, of course, is important. I mention all this since Mr. Shehan's grades do not represent his true ability as a student.

c. His father, a retired fire department employee of the city of Dayton, and his mother are close friends, and I feel as if Mr. Peyton is a member of the family.

d. The fact that his father is an engineer for a Chicago company gives John the technical sense and logic needed by an engineer.

e. I hope that you may be satisfied with Mr. Carl, and will give him this opportunity to work for you.

19. Rewrite that following unsigned form letter sent from a nationally known company, with an application blank and three tests. Can you relieve the negative tone? Can you rationalize the negative aspect of the writing?

```
Enclosed in this envelope are the following:

                    Sales Application blank
                    Bernreuter Personality Inventory
                    Strong Interest blank
                    Otis, Form A

If you are sure you want to sell _____ _____, complete the
application; it may be handwritten or typewritten.  Then fill
out the three tests after reading the instructions carefully.
Remember to give your own reactions to these questions without
discussion with anyone.  Don't try to give us answers you think
we may want.  Return all of this material in the envelope pro-
vided, along with a letter of application stating why you want
to sell our products and listing any other information you feel
might be helpful.  Also include a recent photograph of yourself.

If you decide you do not want to apply for a sales position,
do not complete the application or other material.  Be sure to
write letting us know your decision.

We appreciate your interest in _____ and hope to hear from
you soon.
```

[Person's name and position typed]

```
                    Personnel and Office Adm.
```

[Company name and address]

20. Rewrite these sentences from application letters, making them specific and positive:

a. I had considerable experience in radio while in college.

b. I took all the marketing I could get while in college.

c. I like journalism. In college I always took a great deal of interest in the college paper.

d. I shall soon be in a position to accept a position with your firm.

e. I don't want to intrude on your valuable time, but I thought you might not mind taking a few minutes to read my letter.

f. Your company needs a salesman who knows how to handle people. I am that man, because I took part in every extracurricular activity I could in high school and college.

g. Are you willing to take a chance on a man who will knock his brains out to make your company the best ever?

h. Incidentally, when you answer will you please tell me what kind of products your company makes.

10

Public Relations

Though man a thinking being is defined,
Few use the grand prerogative of mind.
How few think justly of the thinking few!
How many never think, who think they do!
—JANE TAYLOR, *Essays in Rhyme (On Morals and*
Manners. Prejudice.)
Damn the public.—GEORGE BERNARD SHAW, *The Intelligent*
Woman's Guide to Socialism and Capitalism

As a considered function of business communication, public relations is relatively new; as a condition of any communication situation, public relations has always existed. Despite the absence of documented records to support the supposition, we can well imagine that with the original trade, swap, or barter, there were thoughts or comments such as "He's not a bad one to deal with" or the opposite view: "I don't see how that one does any business at all; he's the cold kind, all right."

Less remote than prehistoric man but perhaps as far removed from our thinking on public relations were the circumstances surrounding acceptance of our own Constitution, as discussed in the end-of-chapter reading.

When we think of public relations as defined by William Gruver, vice-president of Hal Marlowe Associates, public relations counsel, we see all of history as little more than public relations. Mr. Gruver describes the phenomenon as "taking an idea or a concept, a company or an individual and relating it or communicating it to a specific part of the public."

The definition is well illustrated in the experience a few years ago of a food manufacturing company, which we shall call Company A. The company decided to test its public relations by finding out how its employees and the people of the small midwestern city of its location felt about the company, its policies, and its community service. Everything seemed rosy on the surface, but Company A wanted to be sure. It sent a crew of questioners to the city to ask questions. The answers to four of the questions are shown in the chart below.

	The townspeople answered		The Company A employees answered	
	Co. A	Co. X	Co. A	Co. X
	(per cent)		(per cent)	
1. Which of these companies contributes the most to making a good city to live and work in?	10	61	40	22
2. What is your opinion of the officers or department heads of these companies that you know personally?				
Above Average	84	89	79	86
Average	12	10	16	13
Below Average	4	1	5	1
3. If employed, how do you like your work?				
Excellent	47		21	
Good	47		57	
Fair	3		20	
Poor	2		2	
No Opinion	1		0	
4. Do you believe your company is fair in its promotions?				
Yes			54	
No			28	
No Opinion			18	

In these four questions and eleven others Company A took a real beating. Company A management went into a huddle and agreed that the company was not meeting its community responsibilities, that its communications with employees and the community were lousy (that's the word the Public Relations Director used), and that its employee policies and practices had to be overhauled.

Here are some of the steps management took in its intensive public relations campaign:

All supervisory personnel from foremen to the vice-president were invited to join a new Management Club. The club held informal social and discussion meetings, often inviting the wives and families of members to take part and get to know each other better. Some of the wives were surprised to learn that their husbands were executives or supervisors in the largest plant of its kind in the world; they learned to be proud of the company and its policies. The supervisors themselves learned a great deal about company history, practices, and policies; many had not known, for example, that the company's pay scale was the highest in the industry. The discussions included a study of human relations under such topics as "How to Build Employee Morale" and "How to Handle Problems."

The company developed a speakers' bureau, encouraged participation in community affairs, increased its use of radio time, and published an employee newspaper every two weeks on a half-page of the city's daily paper.

The company performed a major operation on policies and practices; it added a full-time public relations man to the local plant payroll, revised its promotion system, and undertook a long-run study and revision of all personnel policies and practices.

The suppliers of the company, the members of the community, and the general public in the surrounding areas were invited not just once but continuously to visit the plant, use the company's facilities, ask questions, make themselves at home because the plant was theirs. Samples of the product were distributed generously. A big one-day anniversary celebration brought thousands of guests and much favorable publicity.

The sales and advertising departments conducted special intensive drives in the area, increasing sales 400 per cent and at the same time increasing community recognition of the importance and quality of the product.

Under the leadership of the new public relations man, the company took stock of its communications of all types and on all levels; it set out on a continuing program of communications improvement.

That is just part of the broad and well-rounded program the company developed. "In everything we did," the public relations director reported, "we saw to it that employees led the parade." After two years the crew of questioners was sent around again to ask the same fifteen questions. Here is what happened:

	The townspeople answered		The Company A employees answered	
	Co. A	Co. X	Co. A	Co. X
	(per cent)		(per cent)	
1. Which of these companies contributes the most to making a good city to live and work in?	35	51	75	23
2. What is your opinion of the officers or department heads of these companies that you know personally?				
Above Average	92	65	95	74
Average	8	30	5	20
Below Average	0	5	0	6
3. If employed, how do you like your work?				
Excellent		55		51
Good		34		40
Fair		8		9
Poor		1		0
No Opinion		2		0
4. Do you believe your company is fair in its promotions?				
Yes				71
No				18
No Opinion				11

The company, in short, showed real improvement all down the line, with important jumps of as much as 350 per cent on vital questions. In addition, its output per man-hour increased and its employee turnover decreased. We have already noted the increase in sales in the area. As the public relations director put it, "We're still far from perfect. We still have problems and we're sure we'll always have problems. . . . But from a public relations point of view, we have a wonderfully satisfying situation: We have an alert and aggressive management that wants to do a job, not only for the company, but also for our employees and the community we live and work in."

THE PUBLIC RELATIONS FUNCTION

You have just read a case study showing the need for a public relations campaign, the methods used to build good public relations, and the results of the campaign. The case study of Company A may already have defined the public relations function for you: it is the development of understanding, of friendship, and of a rapport based on trust between the company and all of its many publics. Stated a bit differently, it is the interpretation of the company to its publics—to the stockholders, to the employees, to the families of the employees, to the members of the community who sell to and deal directly with the company, to the community itself, to the company's customers (retail, wholesale, all levels), and to the general public. Public relations should not be confused with publicity, one of its subdivisions. The letter in Figure 29 illustrates the difference. Public relations is a matter of policy and approach; it is the relationship between the company and the world. Publicity is a tool or method of that approach, but its goal of keeping the company name before the public in print and on the air falls far short of and involves only one aspect of the public relations goal of understanding and rapport.

Just as every individual, whether he wants to or not, has a personality, a group may collectively have a personality. A family may have a personality, though we may not call it just that: when we talk about the impression made on us by a family group we are talking about that group's personality. A fraternity or sorority may have a distinctive personality; a college may have a personality.

In order to achieve the public relations goal, according to a pioneer in public relations, Bennett Chapple of Armco, a company must recognize the existence of the *corporate personality*.[1] The corporate personality

---

[1] The term *image* is much used for this concept. Companies, products, institutions, professions—almost all phases of human activity—are referred to as having an image. This application of personification to organizations and things is quickly exemplified by reference to motivational research, discussed in Chapter 8. Writing of a research study for the Chrysler Corporation, shortly after the Plymouth car was introduced, Ernest Dichter speaks of "the personality, the image of the car." He says, "Plymouth had held up the image of difference."

Using Original Art to Enliven Invitation

Lisle Ramsey and his "ranch hands" invite you to enjoy an old-fashioned WESTERN BUFFET SUPPER at 404 South Fourth Street in St. Louis on Wednesday evening, September 10. We are assuming the DMAA Convention will bring you to St. Louis then (September 10 - 11 -12).

The Convention Program Committee has specially planned Wednesday evening as an "on the town" night, with no convention conflicts. Why not budget enough of your time between 6:30 P.M. and 9:30 P.M. to drop in for a real western treat...

    WESTERN COOKING -- WESTERN MUSIC -- WESTERN HOSPITALITY --

Come when you wish. Browse through our plant...eat when you wish ...stay as long as you like...leave when you choose. To make it an extra easy "must" for you, just call a cab and direct the driver to 404 South Fourth. Our doorman will take care of the cab fare. The elevator will take you to the fifth floor.

May we "set a plate" for you? Just check the RSVP card and head it back, today. The cook will appreciate it, and so will Mr. Ramsey.
                  Cordially,

MWF:bb   M. W. Finkenbinder

Fig. 29. Warmth makes this an *invitation* rather than an *announcement*, which so many such letters become because of stiltedness. (Used by permission of the Dartnell Corporation.)

is built from millions of impressions based on millions of contacts, direct or indirect, between the company and the publics. If the company wants to improve its corporate personality, it must find how these impressions are made and improve its handling of the contacts on which the impressions are based. This inclusive and far-reaching job is the job of public relations.

IMPORTANCE OF THE PUBLIC RELATIONS FUNCTION

From time to time someone will say that the public relations function is growing more important in business and industry year by year. That is not exactly true; it has been of fundamental importance all along. What is happening is that more and more firms are recognizing that importance and trying to do something about it. However, it is not enough for them to hire a public relations director, give him an office and a secretary, and then sit back and say, "Now we have public relations too." Public relations cannot be tacked on somewhere at the edge of a company the way the blacksmith modernized his sign:

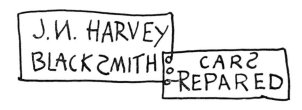

Public relations builds the future of the company; it is not going too far to say that today's public relations *is* tomorrow's plant expansion, tomorrow's production records, tomorrow's satisfied and cooperative labor union, tomorrow's good will, tomorrow's sales. In order to incorporate public relations at a level appropriate to its real importance, management must rethink the basic policies of the company, revise them if necessary, and starting from them instill good public relations all the way through the company organization, from top to bottom.

Here are some quotations from the booklet "Armco Policies," showing the points of view upon which the corporate personality of Armco is based:

Introduction

ARMCO STEEL CORPORATION was organized to provide a permanently profitable investment through the manufacture of special grades of iron and steel required in the fabrication of such finished products as might, from time to time, be demanded in an ever broadening field.

To secure such a result in the largest measure, its organizers believed that it would be necessary to adopt and to practice such policies as would bring about a condition of mutual confidence and create a spirit of sympathy and of real cooperation between the members of its working organization, its customers, its stockholders, and the citizens of the communities in which its plants would be located.

Armco Policies

> *First:* To do business guided and governed by the highest standards of conduct and ethics, striving always for that sort of an ending in all things affecting the conduct of the business as would make "reputation" an invaluable and permanent asset.
>
> *Second:* To adopt "Quality and Service" as a slogan. Quality, the highest attainable, to be represented in Product, in Organization, Plant, Property and Equipment. Service, the best possible, to be rendered to Customers, to Stockholders, to City, State, and Nation.
>
> *Third:* To make every possible effort to develop and maintain a contented, efficient, loyal, aggressive organization, who believe in their Company, to whom work is a pleasure, and to whom extraordinary accomplishment is a personal ambition. . . .
>
> *Seventh:* To do everything possible and practicable on the creating and maintaining of a working partnership between industry and the community. . . .
>
> *Tenth:* In the treatment of Customers, to always be fair and fully considerate of their need. . . .

Organization

> From its very inception *Armco* has pinned its faith to men; has believed that any worth-while success in modern enterprise can only come through cooperative effort. . . .

Cooperation Between the Community and Industry

> *First:* We believe that to whatever extent National Industrial Stability or Instability exists it simply reflects the sum of the average conditions in individual communities.
>
> *Second:* That with the exception of great national disasters, it is the responsibility of the community to create such conditions as will eliminate human unrest and unhappiness and to deal sympathetically and helpfully with the emergencies and tragedies of life.
>
> *Third:* That industrial stability is largely influenced by local civic conditions.
>
> *Fourth:* That industry should, therefore, not only keep its own house in order, but should support every sound constructive agency established in the community, in an effort to make civic conditions respond to the highest needs of its citizens. . . .[2]

EVERY EMPLOYEE HIS OWN PUBLIC RELATIONS DIRECTOR

Every company employee is a company representative and in that position every employee is in a sense a member of the public relations department. He is responsible for building the future of the company in every way that he can:

1. He must know what good public relations is, and recognize its importance to him and to his company.

---

[2] The Armco Board of Directors approved "Armco Policies" in 1919. Excerpts are printed here by permission of Armco Steel Corporation.

2. He will want to accept the responsibility for the public relations involved in the contacts that he has with the company's publics—to *earn* his share of the company's future.

3. He should himself handle nearly all situations involving public relations as he encounters them from day to day, using what might be called the public relations state of mind as an approach and building tactical public relations skill through practice as he goes along.

4. He should, however, recognize his limitations, and ask the Public Relations Department for help on problems that are too tough for him to handle.

He should develop a kind of community consciousness, an awareness that as he works, relaxes, or participates in community activities he is always, in the eyes of the public, a part of the corporate personality of the company where he works.

LETTERS AND PUBLIC RELATIONS

Since every letter written by a company on every level is a direct expression of the corporate personality, it is natural that one of the concrete results of the increasing awareness of public relations is better correspondence. This awareness has prompted many companies to institute correspondence-improvement programs among all levels of their personnel. In these educational programs, as in any company activity, there is an interesting facet of employee relations. Quite often, employees show higher regard for a course or workshop when they know that personnel higher in the echelon have had or are taking the same instruction. For this reason, some companies start "at the top," if the training is applicable to personnel at various levels. Company philosophy back of correspondence-improvement programs is distinctly expressed in *Let's Write Good Letters*, the famous Armco manual for correspondence, by Sherman Perry:

In the eyes of the reader, the person that signs a letter is the company. He is Armco.

The impression made by that letter, words and how they are put together, determines the reader's opinion of us. So, look upon your letter not as just another letter that has to be written but rather as an opportunity to contribute to the sum total of the favorable impression the company desires.

We want the reader to feel that this is not just another company. Rather do we want him to understand that here are thousands of men and women working together as one, working day after day with one compelling motive. And that motive is this: to create and market a worthy product and to conduct ourselves in a way that deserves confidence.

So, you see, it is up to the man at the desk to help shape the reputation of Armco. Obviously, the better he knows Armco, its products, its principles and policies, the more effectively he can do his work.

One must first know and understand before one can determine what to do and how to do it.

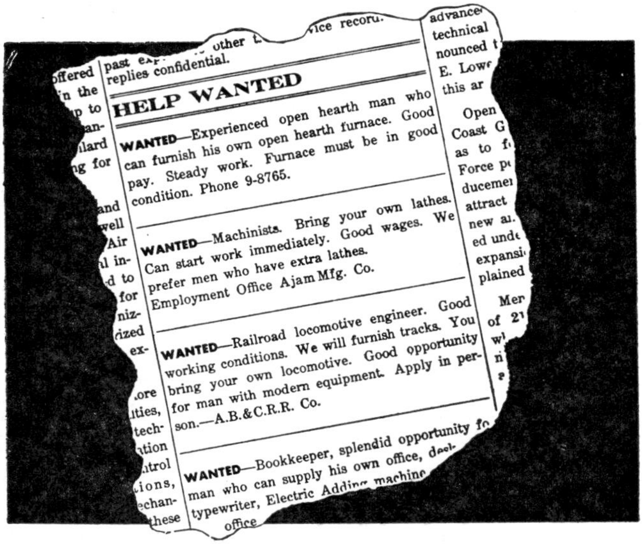

WOULD <u>YOU</u> WANT ONE OF THESE JOBS?

IT'S NO WONDER we never see ads like these in our newspapers! What steel worker could supply his own open hearth furnace? That would cost millions! What machinist owns his own lathes; what engineer has his own locomotive? These things cost more than any of us can afford. Supplying our own individual machines and buildings and offices isn't the way we in industry work.

AND YET—we must have these things to do our job. We must have furnaces and plants and huge and costly machinery to earn a living for ourselves and our families. . So how DO we get them?

THAT IS WHAT our Stockholders do for us. Not just one stockholder, or a few; it takes many. Armco has 44,000 Stockholders. Most of them have ordinary incomes; but they saved some of their money, and invested it in shares of Armco stock. Their savings started our company, equipped it, got it going. From them, and from the profits we re-invest in our business each year, we get the money to buy the tools for our jobs—the tools we couldn't afford to buy ourselves.

WHAT do Stockholders expect in return for risking their savings? They expect a fair share of the profits. Last year (it was a good year) they received 2½ cents in dividends from each dollar of Armco's sales. Armco employees received 30 cents.

STOCKHOLDERS ARE PART OF OUR ARMCO TEAM

Fig. 30. This ad emphasizing the importance of stockholders in our economy first appeared on the back page of the Armco employee magazine. It builds public relations by increasing understanding within the Armco family. (Used by permission.)

Make your letters clear—make them complete—make them go straight to the mark without wasting the reader's time—make them courteous, kind, understanding, sympathetic. Make them so good you are proud of them.

ATTRACTIVENESS, ACCURACY, TONE

By this time, you are aware, I am sure, of the part that attractiveness plays in the impression that a letter makes in reactions to the company it comes from. The importance of accuracy in correspondence to reflect accuracy in other, or all, company operations was poignantly stated by a sales manager with whom I once found myself discussing grading standards in college. He told me that all letters sent out under the famous letterhead of his machine tool company were A letters. One flaw of any kind made them unsatisfactory. "To prepare letter-writers to work for me," he said, "you would have to revise your standards so that D letters, C letters, and B letters were all F—not good enough to send." He went on to explain the reason for his rigid standards. "Some of our machine tools take weeks to make; they sell for enough to buy a good-sized retail business. They are the best of their type in the world. They have no flaws at all. To give the right impression of the kind of company we are we apply the same standards of flawlessness to our correspondence."

Along with appearance and accuracy, the tone of a letter is important in creating the right kind of impression of the company. "I like the way this company does business"; "I like their attitude"; "They certainly are doing all they can to be helpful"—these reactions to letters show that the kind of corporate personality they reflect is the right kind, the kind that builds for the future.

LETTERS TO STOCKHOLDERS

In the past twenty years letters included with the annual report to stockholders or with dividend checks have shown a noticeable change for the better. Their former routine, matter-of-course attitude has been replaced by a cordial interest in the stockholder's point of view and by an understanding of his real concern with the policies and problems of the company. They now consider the stockholder a member of the corporate family, and an important member at that; they take him into the confidence of management without condescension and without reserve.

Some companies send special letters to stockholders at holiday seasons or at company anniversaries to build good will. Some companies take into account the stockholder's interest in strikes, shutdowns, floods, and government regulations affecting his company and his investment; they keep him informed through letters of new developments and of management's point of view.

THE STANDARD REGISTER COMPANY

DAYTON 1, OHIO

M. A. SPAYD
PRESIDENT

TO EACH NEW SHAREHOLDER:

I welcome you as a new shareholder of our company. Founded in
1912, Standard Register had been a privately owned, closely held
organization until our public offering late in 1956. In the
relatively short period since then, it has been a pleasure to
welcome the large number of folks who, like yourself, have become
associated through share ownership.

As a publicly owned corporation, it is now our policy to keep you
informed through quarterly and annual reports and by other timely
mailings of pertinent information. Moreover, we want to extend
an invitation to visit our plants or our sales offices, the latter
located in 1,'5 principal cities.

The business of our company is broad in its concept of service to
business, industry and government. For many years, in many ways,
we have promoted a modern approach to Paperwork Simplification.
We are recognized as a leader in this field.

With a market of great breadth, augmented by revolutionary recent
developments such as Integrated and Electronic Data Processing,
the field of opportunity for our products and services continues
to enlarge tremendously. We believe our organization ready and
ably qualified to capitalize on these opportunities.

In a few days you will receive a copy of our ▬▬▬ Annual Report,
together with the latest interim report for the current year ▬▬▬
and an issue of our PS. Magazine, all of which we are sure you
will find to be of considerable interest. We have other pieces of
literature which should help give you a better understanding of the
company's business and which we shall be glad to send if you desire
it, in which case let us hear from you.

It is our fervent hope that your purchase of shares marks the beginning of a long, pleasant and profitable association with our
company.

Sincerely,

M. A. Spayd

President

Fig. 31. Letter to a new shareholder. (Used by permission of the Dartnell
Corporation.)

LETTERS TO EMPLOYEES

In addition to company magazines, annual reports to employees, bulletin boards, and a wide range of direct-participation activities, nearly all companies use letters to build employee relations. Rather generally, letters to employees have been distinguished by the impersonality that characterized correspondence to stockholders. As in the case of the latter, the intracompany letters are also being improved. Suggestions such as the following, applied where feasible, can bring further improvement.

Eleven Hints for Letters to Employees [3]

1. Write letters only when there's something to talk about; don't make them periodical, or they become routine.
2. Make the letters friendly but not familiar or patronizing.
3. Be specific and be brief.
4. Letters sent to the employee's home are generally more effective than those distributed at the plant or office.
5. Letters should be personalized at least to the extent of being signed by an officer; company names as signatures are cold and impersonal.
6. Letters should be sent by first-class mail, so as not to be confused with advertising matter.
7. Every letter should say something of importance and of interest to the employee and his family; otherwise it is better not to write at all.
8. Check now and then with supervisors or other selected employees to find out how the workers react to the letters.
9. Letters should be written so that they will be easily understood, but without a tone of talking down.
10. Don't let the letters fall into a pattern; make each one as distinctive as possible.
11. Subjects that may be used as "pegs" on which to hang such letters include

   a. Special occasions (holidays, anniversary of company founding, etc.)
   b. The business outlook
   c. Wage and hour matters
   d. Labor-management relations
   e. Job security
   f. Company benefits
   g. Product information
   h. Competition
   i. Future plans

1. Welcome to New Employees. To some, it may seem that the letter below, signed by the president of a company of about 2,500 employees,

[3] Adapted from *The Business-Letter Deskbook*, by Gerald W. Weston (Chicago: Dartnell Corp., 1961). (Used by permission of the publisher.)

stresses work excessively, but the person who, as the new employee (a first-line supervisor), received the letter did not feel that way. He reasoned that the common denominator between him and the head of the company was the job and that by staying with that subject, the president made his letter credible. The recipient also interpreted the reference to selfishness as candidness, contributing to the writer's earnestness. What is your reaction to the letter?

```
To the new employee —

    I wish that I could get into all parts of the plant and
offices to welcome each new employee.  But the company is growing
so rapidly that such personal contacts are impossible.

    I do want to encourage you, however, to become acquainted
with those people you work with.  I hope that you will talk with
your immediate superiors about your work, both the pros and the
cons.  As you will learn, we depend a great deal on suggestions
and recommendations from our employees, no matter what their jobs
are.  For many reasons, not all employee suggestions are adopted,
and not all of them receive cash awards—also for various
reasons.  But it is our thought that a job of work is pleasanter
when a worker looks for ways to improve the job.

    We also think that a happy worker is a better worker.  And
selfishly I hope for happy workers because they make a better
company.

    I'm sure you want to work for as good a company as possible.
As a part of Zenith, you can work toward that goal.

                    My good wishes to you,
```

2. CONGRATULATIONS AND CONDOLENCES. Management is of course not required to take notice when Joe Jones gets promoted to foreman, or when he has a new baby, a birthday, or a death in his family. That is why an expression of management's interest is particularly welcome to Joe: it is something extra, something he hadn't really expected. It makes him proud of his job to be complimented on his work; talking about his family reaches through his barrier of reserve. Albert A. Douglas reports that after he, as editor of the Alcoa *Aluminator*, published the picture of one employee's baby grandson he was swamped with pictures of grandchildren. It is good for the employee's pride to be congratulated in print in the company magazine, so that his fellow-employees can read; a letter from management, however, gives him a far greater sense of accomplishment. There is no reason why both media should not be used.

3. POLICY LETTERS IN EMERGENCIES. Strikes, floods, layoffs, friction in the plant, production slumps, national emergencies—any of these may occasion a letter or a series of letters to the employees. Such letters re-

quire extreme care in preparation, particularly if union trouble is in the wind. It is not a good plan to single out one group of employees for a letter about a labor dispute; management should address itself to all members of the company family rather than to union men, nonunion men, or men of a certain union. Management cannot keep the confidence of its employees if it enters recklessly into factional disputes. Management cannot afford to have or to hold a grudge against any of its employees. On the other hand, a clear and *objective* statement of management's point of view is always of interest to all employees, even if some disagree; and if management does not infringe upon the disagreeing employee's right to hold his own point of view, he will not take it as a personal offense that management does not agree with him. Probably management's best course is to show a frank, forthright picture of its policy on the issue and to emphasize a long-run policy of cooperation and good will; of all types of letters, however, labor policy letters are about the hardest to be sure of.

It is important to give workers advance notice of layoffs; Lawrence Stessin, writing in *Mill and Factory*, says, "The process of laying off workers is a delicate business. The 'shock' method—a cold announcement on a bulletin board, a pink slip—is now widely recognized as a sure way to lose worker and community good will." Mr. Stessin quotes the letter below as an example appropriate to a long-term or indefinite layoff. Note that the reason for company action is given in the second paragraph. Also observe the tone of "openness" that permeates the letter.

```
To:                    Richard Green
Dept.:                 Grinding
Clock No.:             G-116
```

Dear Mr. Green:

The company regrets that it is necessary to place you on layoff status at the end of your shift on December 17. We do not at this time know how long this layoff will last, but we will notify you to return to work as soon as conditions permit.

This temporary reduction is made necessary by the fact that sales have decreased during the last three months. However, we anticipate new orders after the first of the year that will enable us to operate on our former basis.

We think you would like to know the following facts about your status while on layoff:

1. You are carried on the company's books as an employee and your seniority continues to accumulate for all purposes (including vacations) during the layoff period.

2. You will be recalled to work before any other laid-off employee in your department who has less seniority.

3. During your layoff period, you are entitled to unemployment compensation. We suggest that you report immediately after your layoff to the State Unemployment Insurance office, which is located in this city at 327 Market Street. This office will tell you about your rights under the state law.

4. At the present time, under this company's policy, you are entitled to four days' accrued vacation pay. In your case, this amounts to $48 less the usual tax deductions.

We are very interested in utilizing your services again as soon as we are able, and we trust that any temporary employment you obtain elsewhere during the layoff period will be such that you can return to us as soon as we notify you.

If you have any questions, don't hesitate to talk to your foreman. He'll be glad to fill in any gaps.

Sincerely yours,

[Signed] James Strong

Plant Superintendent

P.S.: Please let us know about any change in your address during the layoff period.

4. INCENTIVE LETTERS. Here is a letter sent by an aircraft manufacturer to give recognition to an employee who had dropped a note in the suggestion box.

Dear Mr. Laughton:

We wish to thank you for your suggestion for refueling the fuel nozzle stands.

Your suggestion was thoroughly investigated with the following results:

We wish to commend you for your idea; and although there is a definite savings, we regret it cannot be adopted. Your idea is against the safety rules of the Company and of the Fire Underwriters.

We appreciate your interest in the suggestion system and hope that you will continue to offer suggestions when you feel there is a need for change or improvement.

Yours truly,

After reading this letter the employee knows that his suggestion has been studied; he knows why it will not work; he knows that it is appreciated; and he feels encouraged to try again.

A General Motors employee (a die tester) proves the point. In 17 years, the die tester has made 134 suggestions to the company. For the 35 accepted, he has received $41,905.

Major U. S. corporations, in 1963, paid $19 million to some 500,000 employees for suggestions. The highest award was $25,000, to a Kennecott Copper accountant for a suggested change in a sales contract.[4]

THE *Novelty Advertising* **COMPANY**

Commercial and the Calendars, Business Gifts, Adv

GOLD MEDAL

COSHOCTON, OHIO

Dear Scott:

Yesterday, we had to lay Joe off. You don't know Joe but he has been a faithful employee of our company for many years and has a family of four children.

When he was told that there was no work for him at the present time, he wondered when he would be called back. It was necessary to inform him that some of our salesmen who could be producing a lot of business right now have been lying back, and until they started working again, we just didn't know when we would need him.

Now I know, Scott, that you wouldn't want to prolong Joe's layoff. But, frankly, that is exactly what you are doing, when you are not selling orders every day. Not only do Joe and his family suffer, but all of the manufacturers of materials which go into making up our products. In fact, when you consider the whole matter, our whole business economy is based on sales. It would be horrible to think what would happen if every salesman tomorrow decided he was not going to sell for the next month.

Let's get Joe back on the job at once, Scott, as he needs the work. You are the man that can give him the work--not us.

Sincerely yours,

R. E. Lightell, Vice President
saw

Fig. 32. An incentive letter to a slack salesman. (Used by permission of the Dartnell Corporation.)

The incentive letter in Figure 32 is an outright attempt to build sales. The forthright implication of "man's responsibility to man," that employees are dependent on each other, brought results.

5. LETTERS IN THE COMMUNITY INTEREST. It might seem that for management to ask for money from employees is bad policy, but if the cause

[4] *Time,* June 19, 1964, p. 86.

is right and the tone is right such a request can build employee relations. The following letter is signed by the president of a machine tool company; notice that he considers himself a "fellow employee" and that he talks about "us" (including himself in the employee family) as though he means it.

Dear Fellow Employee:

Most of us have had the blessings of life that come from devoted families, good schools, religion, and opportunity for jobs we like. Some are not so fortunate. The handicapped, the ill, the aged poor, and the homeless child need special help to achieve a position of independence from charity. The agencies of the Community Chest are dedicated to provide that help.

The once-a-year campaign by volunteer workers for the Chest, avoiding the costly effort of fund-raising by each of these many worthy agencies, is the kindling of the spirit of working together in an important undertaking. It is the mobilization of community good will. Without the Chest there would not be the same friendly, helpful, solid American feeling that makes us so proud of this community. There would not be the same wholesome atmosphere in which to live, to work, to raise a family.

Our past record of support for the Chest has been fine, and knowing the people at the Mill is to know the record will again be among the best. All of us will want to give generously to help our needy fellow-citizens when our coworker-volunteer contacts us next week.

                    Sincerely yours,

6. SEASONAL LETTERS. Thanksgiving, Christmas, company anniversaries—these offer an opportunity for a greeting or a word of thanks that will rise above the cliché and strengthen employee good will. Such greetings will enter the employee's home and be read by the whole family; they offer a chance for the company to speak to the employee's wife and children directly and to make them proud of the employee's contribution to the company. Mr. Ginn avoids the cliché of the usual seasonal letter, principally by appealing to curiosity; psychological studies show that very few persons bypass simple riddles and puzzles in reading material. A further strengthening device in Mr. Ginn's letter (Fig. 33) is his asking (in the next-to-last paragraph) for acquiescence to the thought in the coded message.

7. LETTERS TO "SEPARATING" EMPLOYEES. Following the policy of keeping doors open for future contacts, some companies say "good-by" and

F. E. MYERS & BRO. CO.

STEMS • PUMPS • WATER SOFTENERS • SPRAYERS
;E STREET • ASHLAND, OHIO • TELEPHONE 21544

GOLD MEDAL

To all employees:

There are many expressions of good will at Christmas time.

We receive many of these in Holiday cards sent to us by our family and friends and we exchange them personally.

To me there is one expression of good will which stands out above all others. It isn't used much at Christmas, perhaps because it is applicable throughout the ENTIRE year, in everything we do.

This expression is true of our relationship with members of our family . . . of our association with our friends . . . of the part we play in community living . . . of us and our religion. It is equally true of our relationship with our Company.

Rather than reprinting this expression, I am going to give it to you as a coded message. (Not for the purpose of keeping it from you, because the code is easy to work out. Rather, if you spend more time with it, by working it out, it will stay with you more easily.)

Here's the coded expression:

$$\overline{\ 7\ }\ \overline{\ 9\ }\ \overline{\ 22\ }\ \overline{\ 5\ }\ \ \overline{\ 1\ }\ \overline{\ 14\ }\ \overline{\ 4\ }\ \ \overline{\ 25\ }\ \overline{\ 5\ }$$

$$\overline{\ 19\ }\ \overline{\ 8\ }\ \ \overline{\ 1\ }\ \overline{\ 12\ }\ \overline{\ 12\ }\ \ \overline{\ 18\ }\ \overline{\ 5\ }\ \overline{\ 3\ }\ \overline{\ 5\ }\ \overline{\ 9\ }\ \overline{\ 22\ }\ \overline{\ 5\ }$$

The code is simple. The number "1" stands for letter "A". Number "2" stands for letter "B". Number "3" stands for letter "C" and so on.

Have it figured out?

Don't you agree it's a thought that would make the world a much better place if we all lived by it?

Our best wishes for a very Merry Christmas and Happy New Year.

Sincerely,

C J uinn Jr.

President

Fig. 33. A seasonal letter that may "stay with" the reader a little longer than the usual Yuletide greeting. (Used by permission of the Dartnell Corporation.)

"thank you" to certain employees as they leave the company. The good will fostered in these letters, like the following one, is readily apparent.

Dear Bob:

I appreciated very much your letter outlining your plans. Mr. Schoenberger informed me a while ago that you were planning to go to other work in the summer as soon as the semester is finished.

It has been a pleasure working with you this past winter, and your work has definitely been a help to us. I am sure that you will find the American Machine and Foundry Company a very interesting and progressive organization, and that your work with them will be interesting.

I know you will get along well in the future, Bob, because you are willing to work. It is my hope that I will meet you again.

Very truly yours,

[signed]
Manager, Product Development Deparement

LETTERS TO THE COMMUNITY

Good community relations may be built in hundreds of ways, from inviting everybody in town to a barbecue all the way to sending a man to talk at the invitation of a group of Boy Scouts. When Southern States Iron Roofing Company opened a new plant at Nashville it "shot the works."

Here is the letter of invitation to the citizens of the city of Nashville:

Remember how, as a boy,
you liked to take a look
at the new kid on the block . . . ?

Well, there'll be a new kid on your "business block." "Southern States" is coming to Nashville with its newest factory warehouse, located at Harrison Street and 7th Avenue . . . and we'd like for you to take a look at us.

The official opening will be at 9:30 Thursday morning, February 20. Civic and business leaders of Nashville are being invited to attend the opening and meet Southern States officials and representatives. We hope that you will be there.

Our Nashville warehouse—number eight in a rapidly growing Southern chain—will operate as a mail-order branch office, retail store, and distributing warehouse. It contains ample floor space for us to add manufacturing equipment.

After the opening at 9:30 Thursday morning we will hold "open house" for two days—Thursday and Friday. Over 150,000 friends and customers of Southern States in Tennessee and the surrounding trade area have been invited. Charlie Foster, known as the man with the million friends, will be on hand. Small gifts, moving pictures, and a buffet luncheon are a few of the features.

If you cannot attend the opening Thursday morning, please try to come sometime during the two-day "house-warming." I know you'll enjoy yourself, and we are looking forward to having you with us.

Sincerely,

All letters to local schools, churches, charities, civic organizations, newspapers, radio and television stations, utilities, government agencies, and suppliers of services or goods involve public relations and offer an opportunity to create for the company an impression of community consciousness and cooperativeness. Sometimes, however, special letters outside the ordinary demands of business are used to build good will. A department store designed a four-color coat of arms for its suppliers and sent it out with this letter:

Dear Mr. Lane:

Of course it isn't customary for one organization to design
a coat of arms for another. However, our happy association with
you has tempted us to have a fling at expressing the noble
lineage of your company in the traditional way.

Certainly, your organization is entitled to the motto—"Deeds
not words." From you we've had performance and merchandise, not
just promises, during these past difficult months.

As we celebrate our 95th year, we are deeply conscious of the
part our suppliers as well as our customers have played in the
growth and prestige of this store. May the future bring ever-
strengthening bonds of friendliness and cooperation between your
organization and ours.

[signature]

Occasionally a firm will write a letter to the members of the community or to a selected group of the general public (newspaper editors, teachers, other professional groups) to explain company policy or the company point of view on an issue. For example, as president of Inland Steel Company, Clarence B. Randall notified a large number of persons he thought would be interested about a broadcast presenting the steel industry's case against a recent steel strike. On the theory that facts are better than rumors, a manufacturer in a small town wrote to every adult member of the community explaining the reasons for a long shutdown. And one of the most difficult public relations problems I have ever encountered required a letter of explanation to residents of a group of company-owned houses which a company had decided to tear down to permit plant expansion.

LETTERS TO CUSTOMERS

It is said that all letters are sales letters; all letters are also public relations letters. An adjustment letter, a letter granting credit, a letter notifying an applicant that he has been accepted for a position, a letter selling a new product, a reply to an inquiry—they all belong in this chapter. In addition, good public relations will require that many of the

The Champion Paper and Fibre Company

MILLS AT HAMILTON OHIO, CANTON N.C., HOUSTON TEXAS

REUBEN B ROBERTSON President
REUBEN B ROBERTSON JR. Exec Vice Pres
H W SUTER Vice Pres & Gen Sales Mgr
CLARKE MARION Vice Pres
HERBERT T RANDALL, Vice Pres
JOHN P OSBORNE Vice Pres

Hamilton Division

W. H. BENZING, Vice Pres.
DWIGHT J. THOMSON, Vice Pres
SCOTT ZOLLER, Secy & Treas
W. J. DAMTOFT, Asst. Secy. & Asst. Treas
CHARLES W. DABNEY, Jr., Asst. Secy
HOMER L. DILLARD, Controller

Hamilton, Ohio

Welcome to Champion:

Within the next two hours we will endeavor to show you the processes and machinery needed to manufacture paper, and the finishing processes required before it is ready for use by the customer. In the display area you will see some of the many uses made of the paper and will recognize how paper fits into our daily lives.

Papermaking is an art that had its beginning in the dim historic past and has reached its present high state of development and perfection in mills like Champion. This was possible only through the constant efforts of the employees, research, and expansion. We at Champion are proud of the many contributions made to the paper industry by employees of Champion.

Members of various committees who are familiar with the operations in their area will be stationed along the route. Feel free to ask them any questions you may have.

For your protection the route has been well marked and attended by present and past members of the Accident Prevention Committee. We earnestly request that you stay on the route as it is marked. If you have any doubt, ask any committee member for proper directions.

We sincerely hope you will enjoy your visit.

Leo Geiser
Mill Manager

Fig. 34. Letter to visitors at manufacturing plant. This letter is handed to each visitor to the Champion plant. The visitor also gets samples of Champion paper and of the food in the Champion cafeteria. (Used by permission of the Champion Paper and Fibre Company.)

types of letters already discussed under "Public Relations Letters to Employees" be written also to customers. The welcome to the new customer is similar in tone to the welcome to the new employee. Cus-

FIRST NATIONAL BANK

KOKOMO, INDIANA

DONALD B. SMITH
PRESIDENT

June 16, 19

Mr. John Doe
123 South Main Street
Kokomo, Indiana

Dear Mr. Doe:

It is a pleasure to say "thank you" for the account you opened with us recently.

Although protection of customers' funds is a bank's first consideration, we like to extend extra personal services to our depositers. Our pleasant staff is well trained to handle customers' accounts, and our officers can give you complete information about any financial transactions.

Since we are especially interested in rendering outstanding service to you, we will always welcome your advice and constructive comments.

For customer convenience, our banking hours are 9 a.m. to 5 p.m. except on Wednesday and Saturday, on which days we close at 12 noon. You may bank at any of our six locations:

KOKOMO MALL BRANCH--Kokomo Mall Shopping Center

WEST SIDE BRANCH--Forest Park Shopping Center

MAPLE CREST BRANCH--Maple Crest Plaza

NORTH SIDE BRANCH--1601 N. Davis Road

SOUTH KOKOMO BRANCH--1135 S. Main

MAIN OFFICE--Main at Taylor

I speak for my associates, as well as for myself, in welcoming you to the ever-growing circle of First National friends. We are glad to have you with us.

Sincerely yours,

President

Fig. 35. Letter to a new account, offering services that "the company is not paid for." (Used by permission.)

tomers like to be congratulated on promotions, new branch stores, high sales records—yes, and on new babies and new wives also. New York Life builds good will with birthday cards from local agents to clients. One department store I know writes letters of congratulation to all new city officials when they take office. Letters from a bank good-naturedly remind married-men customers that their wives' birthdays are imminent. A congratulatory note to a married couple near anniversary time also may "help the man to remember."

Kroch's & Brentano's, Inc.

BOOKSELLERS (K&B) **STATIONERS**

29 South Wabash Avenue, Chicago 3, Illinois

DEarborn 2-7500

Thank you!

   . . . for helping us make the year just closed the most successful year in our first half-century of business.

   . . . for helping make possible the opening of our second suburban shop. Now, in addition to our three Loop locations, we can serve you directly in both Evanston and Old Orchard in Skokie.

   . . . for being our customer. We hope you will continue to be just that. On our part, we will continue to give you the service you expect from Kroch's & Brentano's--the largest possible selection of books serviced by a friendly, thoroughly trained sales staff.

Should we at any time fail to live up to your expectations, please let us know. Your goodwill is our greatest asset and we will do our best to keep it.

Sincerely,

Carl A. Kroch
President

Fig. 36. New Year's appreciation letter. The special indented form is used to good advantage, avoiding repetition of the key phrase, "Thank you!" (By permission of the Dartnell Corporation.)

Customers may also receive policy letters explaining price increase, shutdown, change in policy, or some other special problem. For one such letter see page 278.

Holidays serve as a good time to express appreciation for patronage. The Kroch's & Brentano's letter in Figure 36 thanks the customer at New Year's time and asks for customer reaction to the bookseller's services.

Recognizing customers' letters of commendation to company personnel for outstanding or unusual service is another means of maintaining good customer relations. The company's saying "You are welcome" to a customer's "thank you" can further good will. Although the following letter deals with an order, the personal aspects of the customer's letter are obviously the first concern of the message.

Dear Miss Johnson:

I must apologize for our delay in answering your letter of September 18 and do not understand why it has taken so long to reach my desk.

It was very thoughtful of you to take the time and trouble to commend the services of Mr. Weldon of our Special Service Department. The manager of this division has shown him your letter and I know both of them were very pleased.

We have also taken care of the merchandise you ordered in this letter and, as you probably know, it has been sent by now.

Thank you again for writing.

                    Sincerely yours,

Quite the antithesis of the foregoing letter is another from the same department of the same midwestern department store. The writer of the following letter seemed definitely unconcerned about customer relations (or sales, for that matter) as he answered Miss Lally's inquiry. The young lady had written asking about the possibility of buying a skunk she had seen in one of the store's display windows, a merchandising feature the company is noted for.

Dear Miss Lally:——

We are sorry but the skunk you inquired about in your letter of March 25th, has been sold.

Thank you for the interest in the matter.

                    Sincerely,

                    [signed]

March 30, 19--

rm:JT

Improper punctuation, improper typing, and improper letter mechanics add to what the recipient called the "disdain" of the message.

A special public relations problem is the refusal of requests for favors or contributions, particularly when such requests come from good customers. The following letter, from the Dunham Brothers Company, Brattleboro, Vermont, holds good will and also maintains the firm line of company policy.

Dear Mrs. Stuart:

This is an answer to your letter of January 18 regarding a contribution to your Hampden County Women's Rod and Gun Club.

Dunham Brothers Company certainly would like to cooperate with you in donating some article of merchandise in connection with your banquet on February 10th but, frankly, we have been obliged to formulate a policy to turn down requests of this nature — and we will try to tell you why. We have nearly six thousand accounts on our books and, as you can well imagine, almost every mail brings us a solicitation of some nature. Our policy is, of course, to treat all of our customers alike and if we were to respond to one request, we would be obligated to respond to all of them. You can easily see that such action would soon lead to a very serious situation and, therefore, we have tried to write courteous letters explaining the situation and, in most cases, these have been accepted with a full understanding as to our policy.

Members of the firm are always most generous in responding to local benefits but we have really had to "draw the line" on expanding such action throughout our territory, which covers not only New England but most of the states east of the Mississippi River.

We feel confident that you will understand our position — and we wish you every success for your banquet in February.

                                        J. L. Dunham
                                        President

THE PUBLIC RELATIONS POINT OF VIEW: A CONCLUDING CASE STUDY

There are two ways for a manufacturer or a supplier to consider his dealers: he can think of them as intelligent, trustworthy persons, interested in his company policies and deserving his full confidence; or he may consider them a sort of necessary nuisance, useful but a constant source of irritating problems. In other words, he can build for the future, or he can fail to see the forest for the trees on the edge.

Such nearsightedness is reflected in the following letter, which really had a generous new returns plan to offer to dealers, but is likely to build ill will rather than good will because of the caustic language used. How would you revise the letter to stress the generosity of the returns plan, diminishing the negative tone of the announcement?

ANNOUNCING:

A NEW COMPANY Z PROTECTION PLAN

Effective on all books purchased through the Trade Division

Company Z offers to retail booksellers in the United States the following protection plan:

ANY BOOK purchased from the Trade Division of Company Z for resale to the general public may be returned for credit ONLY (not for refund) three months after invoice date, and not later than six months after invoice date.

This return privilege applies only to the latest purchase of any given book.

Returns will be credited at full purchase price, without any penalty or premium payment for the privilege.

Books returned must be in new condition, and not contain dealer's marks or labels.

No more than one return shipment may be made in any one month. A packing slip must be included. Returns must be prepaid to our warehouse at (address).

CAUTION: No return will be credited if it is made in under three months or after six months of invoice date on the latest purchase. No exception will be made.

Returns of books before three months or later than six months will not be credited; in such case the customer will be advised that the books will be returned to the customer at his request and his expense. But under no circumstances will credit be allowed.

NO Exceptions will be made to the above rule. And we mean—

NO EXCEPTIONS

If the above requirements are met, permission to return, labels, publisher's lists or other correspondence is unnecessary.

This liberal policy is offered to the bookseller as full protection for his stock up to six months from the date of his invoice, but the bookseller is not, of course, under obligation to return any purchase.

May we suggest that the exact observance of the conditions of this new protection plan will save us all time and expense.

[no signature]

Public Opinion: New Sovereign Power *

by Harold Brayman

The challenges facing us in the years ahead are formidable indeed and will impose upon us all the necessity for energetic effort, much wisdom, and steadfast resolution. For one thing is clear: We can preserve our freedom of enterprise only if it fulfills the aspirations of our society.

And these aspirations, great as they have been in the past, must be considered as modest murmurings when contrasted to the insistent clamor of the demanding future.

This demand will apply with equal force to business and industry, labor, agriculture, the professions, education, and all the rest.

It cannot be evaded, circumvented, by-passed, or ignored, for, as a result of the widespread growth of popular government since World Wars I and II, and of the replacement of most of the colonial dependencies by independent governments based on the will of the people, public opinion has become a dominant world force. With our vastly improved communications and a higher level of public education, the ordinary people in large parts of the world have found a new instrument of authority in their hands—control over governments.

This authority they will wield inexorably to obtain what they want. Today in the United States public opinion dominates the government because public opinion determines who shall govern us, and it is no new untried theory that "he who pays the piper calls the tune."

Not only has popular control of governments become much more direct, but governments are also getting larger and larger, stronger and stronger, and have more influence over the lives of people and corporations. This trend is established and is unlikely to be quickly changed, no matter how strongly those argue who say it shouldn't be so.

A New Character

Therefore, the problem of challenges to the freedom of enterprise takes on a new character. It is not a problem of government. It is not a problem of law. It is not a problem of foreign ideology. It is a problem of public opinion.

I speak to you today as a representative of business, it is true. But I hope no one will misunderstand and think that I speak for business alone. For if the freedom of enterprise disappears from our world, so also will disappear the freedom of the press, the freedom of the pulpit, academic freedom, freedom of thought, and the freedom of action. For all these are intertwined, and it is as imperative for the men of the pulpit, of the press, of the universities to support the freedom of enterprise, as it is for the men of business to support the freedoms of pulpit, press, and the academic community. If one is ever lost, it will not be long before the loss of the others will follow.

* A talk at the opening keynote session of the Sixteenth National Conference, Public Relations Society of America, in San Francisco, November 18, 1963. (Used by permission of Mr. Brayman, formerly director of public relations, E. I. du Pont de Nemours & Company.)

Therefore, the problem, all the way out, becomes a problem of public opinion, and the question naturally follows: What should we do about it?

Clearly to ignore it, to do nothing, to let things take their uninterrupted course, is not likely to lead to the results that most of us would like to see.

What do we do about it?

The answers to this question are not simple, but there are certain fundamentals without which we will never have success.

First, businessmen and others must develop a more widespread understanding of how public opinion is made.

For I emphasize that public opinion does not just develop amorphously, without order; public opinion is made by people, by events, by developments, and by the people who interpret these things.

Understanding of the Communicators

But the point is that, in the business and professional life of our day, the methods of the formation of public opinion are not as widely understood as they ought to be for prompt, effective action.

The first thing that we need is a more widespread understanding by businessmen of the communicators, the people who make a profession and a living out of conveying ideas or information to others.

These break down loosely into three groups: newspaper, magazine, and book writers, including the highly important group of Washington correspondents; television and radio commentators and writers, and the script-writers of movies; and the academic group, which influences not only the classrooms and our future leaders, but also exercises wide influence through research projects in the social science field, and through writing, speaking, and consulting, particularly consultation to government.

These three groups, plus the people in public life, constitute the real power in America today; and until the businessmen, the lawyers, the professional people, and all the makers of news who deal with these groups understand this better than many of them do at present, we shall make little progress.

Leadership for Sound Opinion

Please do not misunderstand me. I am not suggesting that business people, or any of the other classifications, should merely ascertain what public opinion is and then conform to it. Supinely bowing before the public will is neither necessary nor desirable. I do not mean surrender—far from it. What I do mean is leadership to guide public opinion along sound constructive ways.

If we would not be forced into surrender, we must learn to adapt ourselves to the conditions that exist.

One cannot fight in the jungles of Viet Nam with battleships; nor counter atomic bombs with the equipment one should use in Viet Nam. Nor can one select weapons carelessly in the conflict of ideas.

My point is we must adapt to the world we live in, so that we can fight effectively for the principles we believe in. This means not that we give up our ideas, but rather that we reconsider them carefully, make certain they are in line with the public interest, revise where revisions are necessary—yes, even abandon where abandonment may be necessary—but go ahead with renewed determination to bring about the acceptance of those ideas that are sound and those that are fundamental.

Then, secondly, we must develop more leaders than we have at present who understand fully the forces with which they are dealing. We must develop leadership with determination, leadership with an understanding of the strategy of conflict in the field of ideas, and leadership capable of firing public imagination.

Plan the Programs

Then, as the third step, we must attack the individual problems one by one with well-planned programs. Diffuse, sporadic, blow-hot, blow-cold, start-stop, on-again, off-again, unplanned, undirected action will not succeed.

We must make changes where changes are needed so that we can be sure our programs are both practical, sustainable, and in the public interest, and then we must try to build in this country a body of public opinion which will sustain and support sound action to bring about the solution of the problems that exist.

For example, let us look at the problem of technological unemployment, or, as some people prefer to call it, automation. All of us in this room, I am sure, understand that technological development is the key to future prosperity and that, with the tremendous world population growth, it offers the only possibility of a continued rising standard of living for all.

But it is quite apparent that there are more people who do not understand this problem than there are who understand it, and that this situation has been brought about very largely by the displacement of men by machines without proper regard for the problems of the men displaced.

This has built up widespread distrust of technological advance. We see the results very noticeably in the railroads. For many years railroad managements have been required to keep and pay firemen, although the conversion to diesel engines eliminated the necessity for firemen. Similar resistances to savings in costs are spectacular in the newspaper industry in the setting of bogus type, and are spread more widely than is generally known throughout all industry.

Possible to Avoid Obstacles

But it is possible to avoid many of these obstacles to understanding with proper planning. At the Du Pont Company, while we have not been able to avoid layoffs in times of economic decline, or where obsolescent plants have been closed, our executives have been able, in many cases, to plan for the simultaneous introduction of new facilities on the same sites where technological advance was eliminating substantial numbers of men.

In this way, and by undertaking retraining programs for the men involved, the technological advance was not only accepted, but accepted with enthusiasm.

As long as men are going to be thrown out of work by technological advance, they are bound in their own self-interest to resist it.

The solution to the problem of technological unemployment consists of two things: one, planning and retraining programs to eliminate the casting-off of people; and, two, more widespread understanding of the desirability of tech-nological advance for the general public good.

For another example, we shall never have a satisfactory situation for business until there is widespread public and political understanding of the function of profits. As long as profits is a dirty word, and many people look up them as something taken away from the people by exploiters, economic progress will be more difficult than otherwise.

The function of profits is basic to our whole liberty. Our system uses profits as a carrot to produce the incentives for progress. The average human being will not strive hard to do his best without some incentive. If the carrot is not present, then the alternative is the whip—in other words, authoritarian government.

An understanding of profits as a carrot, and also as an automatic regulator of our economy—an encourager of production in items which are in oversupply and low-priced—is vital to the development of sound taxation and sound fiscal policies. This calls for a program of economic education which can only be carried forward under the leadership of American business, and without which political handicaps to the realization of a profit and toward the keeping of a realistic portion of it for future investment and development cannot possibly be overcome.

Modern Attitude

For a third example, we need great improvement in the problem of the relationships with government. Too often government is looked upon as the enemy of business, and too often there has been justification for this attitude. Too often business has been looked upon as the enemy of government, and too often there has been justification for this attitude.

The whole system of business against the government and the government against business must necessarily be supplanted by a more modern cooperative attitude.

For the government itself is dependent upon business. A very large proportion of the government's revenues comes from three sources:

1. Fifty-two per cent of all business profits.
2. Of the remaining 48 per cent, personal income taxes from 20 to 91 per cent on all of that portion which is paid out in dividends.
3. Income taxes at rates varying from 20 to 91 per cent on all payments of the corporation to its employees.*

And business is equally dependent upon government which provides and enforces the rules of conduct, which determines the business climate, and which exercises final control over business operations.

And it is true that political power is destroying the market place as the governing mechanism in our economy.

* Author's note: Though early in 1964 these percentages were lowered by the revision of the federal tax structure, Mr. Brayman's point on government dependency is still apposite.

New Methods of Attack

This calls for new methods of attack. The old antagonisms—both ways—must be supplanted by a more modern cooperative attitude if our highest national aspirations are to be realized. However, this does not mean a cessation of resistance to further government encroachment upon the field of enterprise, but rather it does mean that we must create the conditions so that such encroachment will not have widespread public support.

This means some changes must be made, both ways. For example, businessmen can no longer hire other people to do their job of communication with government for them. This they must do themselves. They will need advisers, and there is no reason why they should not have them in this field any more than in the field of law, labor relations, or any other field.

But it is important that the advisers be sophisticated people who understand modern political thought and methods. Assuming good advice, the businessman can be far more effective for himself than anyone else can be for him.

The old lobbying system—the hired professional—is passé. Already several of the more enlightened companies have abandoned it. It is distrusted by everyone and brings disrepute upon those who continue it, as well as sometimes additional trouble.

I remember a case a few years ago in a state legislature where a leading business in the state found itself faced with a proposed measure which would have been very costly to it. It poured on the heat through an intense lobbying campaign and managed to beat the bill, which never had any sound justification in the first place.

The next year when the legislature met and its session had continued for a month or so, there was a somewhat unhappy lobbyist, for he had only a modest retaining fee and no work to do. Much to his disappointment, no one had even introduced the controversial bill.

But he was a resourceful lobbyist, and it didn't take him long to find a friendly legislator who could be persuaded to reintroduce the bill that year so that he could again milk the big corporation to fight this pernicious idea.

Direct Action

Instead the modern techniques consist of direct and cooperative action with government carried on by the top group of people in any business organization. This involves knowing and being on a friendly basis with the people from all levels of government with whom one deals, or is likely to deal.

It involves open and direct advocacy of one's point of view where direct interest is involved.

It involves welcoming opportunities to testify before Congressional or legislative committees on appropriate subjects, and very careful preparatory work when so testifying.

It involves making capable business people available for government service on a short-term basis where their services are needed and requested.

It involves, above all, a spirit of cooperativeness and understanding, both ways: of recognition on the part of business that big government is here to stay and will continue to be an important factor in our lives, and the adoption of a genuinely cooperative attitude toward it; that a stable and prosperous level of business is vital to the well-being of our people; and that demagogic and ill-founded attacks on business, designed primarily to get votes, can be no longer tolerated by the American public.

In the Middle

I have mentioned but three problems. These problems must be solved, and I have great confidence in the American business community to solve them. Businessmen have met serious problems before and found solutions. They will meet and solve these.

Because the problems we have discussed all involve public opinion to a great extent, public relations practitioners are in the middle of all these controversies, and in a position to have great influence for good on future events. And let me point out in passing that the reaction to public relations people in the future will be determined very largely not by how loudly we shout, or by how we are depicted in movies and television, but rather by what kind of results we get.

The problems of business seem overwhelming in many instances, I know, perhaps almost impossible of solution in some cases; and we of business, struggling with them, often seem like little Davids struggling against Goliaths.

But let us not forget that great changes have been brought about in public opinion in the past; and that given a just cause, intelligent effort, and persistence in that effort, who can say that opinion cannot be changed in the future?

I often wonder what kind of results a research project on the sampling of public opinion would have produced in the early days of the American experiment.

Public Opinion Can Be Changed

Based on a highly unscientific glance at history, for example, we might suspect that a public opinion survey in 1760 would have found a heavy negative vote on the question, "Do you favor a war for independence?"

The less dramatic proposal of a complete severance from Great Britain, even if it could be done without war, would have had a mixed reception.

If the Opinion Research Corporation had existed in 1803 and conducted a survey of public opinion at the time, I'm sure it would have found little interest in the idea of paying $15,000,000 to purchase from Napoleon a vast tract of Louisiana wilderness which everyone knew would take centuries to settle.

The distinguished historian Allan Nevins in his Foundation lecture before the Public Relations Society of America in 1962 pointed out that, when the Constitutional Convention at Philadelphia adjourned, there was little hope that the new constitution would ever be ratified by more than a few states, to say nothing of the nine required to make it effective.

Then he recounted, as so many of you will remember, how Hamilton and Madison, then 30 and 36 years of age, respectively, put it over by a brilliant campaign to change and lead public opinion—a campaign based on the *Federalist Papers* as the basic argument for ratification.

Universal suffrage was an idea that took many years to become well established. A poll taken in John Adams' day would probably have supported the practice of confining the ballot to landowners, and even in Grover Cleveland's Administration such a poll would have made it eminently clear that woman's place, wherever else it might be, was certainly not in the polling booth.

Hideous Institution

The institution of human slavery, hideous as it seems to history, was not regarded with disfavor in the late Eighteenth Century. Washington and Jefferson owned slaves and suffered no disparagement thereby. Even the victims of such injustice were inclined to accept the situation as inevitable. The abolitionist movement, powerful as it was, encountered hard going and surely would have failed without the dedicated eloquence of its leaders.

The practice of avoiding military service by hiring a substitute aroused no public indignation whatever until after the Civil War. The researchers would have demonstrated that such behavior was the will of the people. Lincoln saw nothing out of the way in keeping his son "out of the ranks," as he said, and Grant, reflecting the conventional notion of the times, was happy to oblige with a staff appointment. The voice of protest did not find approval until much later.

The inventions and technical innovations which led the country to growth and prosperity were almost universally introduced amid distrust and apathy; the market researcher would have established very quickly that the steamboat was doomed to failure, the telephone a silly passing fad, and the automobile dangerous because it scared all the horses and made horse and buggy travel hazardous.

The significance of this frivolous bit of retroactive research is not that the majority was frequently wrong. The important conclusion, it seems to me, is that great ideas and great movements survived against heavy opposition or monumental indifference and eventually won wide acceptance.

They did not do so automatically. They prevailed because someone, somewhere, assumed the role of the advocate and joined another voice to the national chorus. In the beginning the voice may have been weak and scarcely audible; in the end, if the cause was just, its cry carried the full-bodied resonance of public acclaim.

Whole, Coherent Force

The goals American seeks—economic growth, full employment, extended educational opportunity, control of our physical environment, triumph over the ancient enemies of man—will not be achieved by any single element of our society. To the extent that we gain our objectives, it will be because the national effort is a whole, a coherent force.

Cohesion and cooperation can be achieved only when each of our many communities—business, labor, agriculture, public service, and education—participate seriously and eloquently in the national debate. Only then, as Hamilton and Madison and others foresaw in reaching for the modest goals of the early years, do we find the most suitable accommodation, the grand design that offers us maximum opportunity and minimum restriction.

The fundamental qualification is that no participant, be it business, labor or whatever, remain silent and unresponsive, that no idea be too new—or no idea too old—to seek consideration.

I know of no greater responsibility for the public relations profession than to guide and to lead this expression of the public will, to the end that public policy may evolve with understanding and with wisdom.

The many institutions who are our clients have much to contribute to the formation of a wise national policy. Let us do our utmost to assure that each voice is effective and persuasive, and that it harmonizes, in tempo and pitch, with the anthem of America's greatness.

So let us not be deterred by the difficulties and complexities of the problems we face. That this assignment is not an easy one, we know. We have the discouraging knowledge that never, in the world, has representative democracy managed to survive for more than a comparatively short span of centuries the penalties exacted by the apathy and selfishness of human beings, both individually and in the mass.

But the fact that it never has happened does not mean that it never can happen. Improved communication and education provide the facilities for creating the understanding that alone can save us from going the way of all the democratic societies that preceded ours.

Let us of business recall that Hamilton and Madison and others have faced problems as great or greater than ours and succeeded.

So let us take courage; let us renew our dedication; let us go forward with determination and zeal. And let us remember always that in Florence there stands, as a symbol to all who strive against odds, the great Michelangelo statue of David; I know of none anywhere of Goliath.

Exercises and Problems in Communication

1. Make simple line graphs to illustrate the improvement shown by the second survey of the public relations of Company X. Which of the factors tested showed the most improvement? Which showed the least? What might account for the difference?

2. Write a set of basic company policies for a company in your area. To what extent is your set of policies influenced by public relations?

3. Find at least four letters in your collection that show the public relations point of view; bring them to class for discussion. If possible, bring a letter or two in which the public relations point of view is noticeably absent.

4. Study the annual report of a corporation; write the corporation's letter to the stockholder to accompany the report.

5. Write a letter of welcome to a new employee in a company where you have worked or where you have made purchases. Assume that you are writing as president of the company.

6. As president of the company, write a letter congratulating an employee on his election as president of the local Rotary Club.

7. As public relations director of a company, write letters to all local schools offering to supply guided tours of your buildings to any classes which would be interested.

8. Using the Company Z book returns letter as a source of material, write a letter on the same subject for a better impression on the reader.

9. Write a Thanksgiving or Christmas letter of greeting to your customers. Assume that you are a manufacturer of machine tools, a dealer in farm equipment, or a retail dry cleaning firm.

10. A strike has closed down your printing plant for six weeks. Since the strike was about a jurisdictional dispute you have been powerless to settle it. Today the men are coming back to work, and you are so far behind on orders that you would like to increase the production rate. Write a letter to the returning employees.

11. Write a letter to the customers who have been waiting for their printing orders, telling them that production is about to begin again. (You may assume that they have been notified earlier that a strike was causing the delay in their orders.)

12. Write a letter to your stockholders announcing the return to production and the results of the strike: a loss of 37 working days, an outright loss of orders totaling $65,000.00, and the establishment of a strong union unfavorable to management in place of a friendly union.

13. Write an analysis of the differences that would be necessary in the three letters above.

14. The registrar of Eastern College must refuse admission to the student who wrote the letter which follows. His high school record is so poor that he would certainly fail most of his college courses. Only if the student made an exceptionally good record in postgraduate work at a preparatory school could Eastern College admit him.

106 Lawnville Road
Terrace Park, New Jersey
July 8, 19--

Registrar of Eastern College
Andover, New Hampshire

Dear Sir:

I would like to come to Eastern College.

My father went to Eastern for two years and played on the team. My father in an insurance business. I am interested in journalism as a career. I have always been intrested in newspaper work. I never did much good in English in high school but am willing to learn.

Am sending along a transcrip of my highschool work. I would like to live in State Hall. Can you help me find a garage to rent for my car?

Yours truely,

Jack K. Jarvis

Obviously, Eastern must refuse Jarvis admission. Write the letter from the Eastern admissions director, to whom Jack's letter was forwarded and to whose office he should have sent it. As admissions director, you will offer him some constructive advice.

15. Read the chapter "Sweet Are the Uses of Publicity," in Bennet Cerf's *Try and Stop Me*. Discuss the practices described, in the light of present-day concepts of public relations.

16. Assume that on the campus there is a rumor of adverse criticism involving some group you are a member of—your housing unit, a church group, a professional club. You know that there is some truth in the rumor. Write a letter to the editor of the campus newspaper, clarifying the charges.

17. Discuss Mr. Gruver's and Mr. Brayman's definitions of public relations on pages 253 and 279, respectively. Are there any basic differences in the two. What is the aim of Mr. Brayman's talk: informational, persuasive, or affective?

18. Write a brief paper—two or three paragraphs—to remove the prejudice of stereotyped notions (the "image") on each of the following: profits, lobbyists, boss, business, union.

19. As in other chapters, to develop your word store, check in the end-of-chapter reading the following words: *circumvented, inexorably, amorphously, supinely, diffuse, sporadic, fiscal, encroachment, pernicious, advocacy, demagogic, disparagement*. Use those you are not sure of in sentences.

20. Under "Stockholders" in the *Business Periodicals Index*, look up some of the articles on shareholder meetings of various companies. Write brief character sketches of the individuals described as playing prominent parts in the proceedings.

21. Write five other analogies that might be used for the David-Goliath comparison that Mr. Brayman brought into his talk.

22. Read "Communications Seen as Big Business in 1980," in *Editor & Publisher*, August 17, 1963, page 24. What phases of public relations practices today point to future conditions described in the article?

23. Read (or reread) accounts of three or four incidents of some period of history you are especially interested in, to see what part public relations may have played in the outcomes. Describe the implications orally to the class, according to your instructor's assignment.

24. Assume you are applying for a position in public relations and have been directed on the company application form to write 200 words on your qualifications for the position. On the basis of Mr. Brayman's discussion, what points would you make? Write the qualifications statement.

25. Rewrite the "skunk" letter on page 276, explaining to Miss Lally that window-display materials are not for sale. Keep in mind, however, that your store does have a large toy department.

11

Claims and Adjustments

Give a customer a square deal, and he will never stop saying nice things about you and your business.—GERALD W. WESTON, *The Business-Letter Deskbook*

An account supervisor of a fairly large company once said to me he wished that the adjustment phase of the business day could be automated; then the matter of claims would be the easiest operation in business, rather than the most vexing, as he saw it. Briefly, the plan in my friend's wishful thinking was as follows: Any defective materials, parts, or equipment would automatically slip out of place, either from installation or from storage, and be conveyed "in some way" across a town, or to another city, or even the width of the nation, to the original source of its manufacture. At its destination, the defective merchandise would nudge its replacement out of stock, and the replacement would make the return trip to ease into position, and whatever process depended on it would be resumed. More realistically (and tritely) the supervisor philosophized that the human element in claims and adjustments is the troublesome element.

No one would take issue with him, I'm sure. It is a truism that gains in the physical sciences far exceed successes in the social and behavioral sciences. But strides are being made in the people part of business. Common-sense attitudes are bringing about changes in all areas of relationships; in business, some of the changes are already apparent.

The two extremes in adjustment policies—the chilling *caveat emptor* ("Let the purchaser beware") and the impractical "The customer is always right"—although still in evidence in certain quarters, are being replaced by the reasonable policy of allowing adjustment according to the circumstances of the individual claim.

289

Application of the first of these extremes was common enough so that it now plays a prominent part in the melodramatic fiction about commerce a few decades ago; and the hazardous position of the customer throughout mercantile history is alluded to frequently in Miriam Beard's definitive, readable account of *The History of the Businessman*. In general today, the announcement of "all sales final, no returns, no refunds" is as near as a company would come to stating that the buyer should beware in contemplating purchases from that company. The antithetical customer-always-right philosophy, attributed to pioneer merchant John Wanamaker, *is* attached to company names; however, in the final analysis, it is more slogan than statement of policy.

The old attitude toward adjustments was that the adjustment was a tax on business, partly inescapable, but something of a headache or nuisance at best. With such an attitude, it is understandable that the department taking care of it would be called the Complaint Department, and that its atmosphere would be heavy with gloom. Some of us can remember seeing the department stores change the name of the department to Adjustment Bureau, Adjustment Desk, Customer Service Department, Service Desk, or simply Customers' Service.

THE REAL CHANGE IN ATTITUDE TOWARD CLAIMS AND ADJUSTMENTS

The changes in department designation are of little consequence, of course, without a change in thinking. New names and the same old policies in adjustments have justifiably given rise to satirical jokes and cartoons. One such *Saturday Evening Post* cartoon pictured a customer studying a rope ladder dropped from a hole in the ceiling to about three feet from the floor. On the wall near the rope a sign with an arrow pointing upward announced "Customer Service—Tenth Floor."

The real change in attitude on adjustment is, as mentioned, in the view of the individual, and is well expressed by Kenneth E. Clair, account supervisor of Allied Radio Corporation in Chicago. Mr. Clair points out that the mass-communications techniques available in working with customers, stockholders, employees, and other publics are of little value "when you are confronted with a man with a problem he thinks you caused him." Toll charges on a phone call to an Allied Radio customer sometimes exceed the amount of the order involved in the adjustment. Someone asks, "Does this kind of business pay off?" and Mr. Clair answers, "Yes, emphatically!" [1] With such attention to serving customers, it is easy to see why the company processes over 8,000 individual orders daily.

[1] "Customer Complaints: Problem or Opportunity?" *Public Relations Journal*, May, 1962, p. 25.

RELATION BETWEEN CREDIT AND COLLECTIONS AND CLAIMS AND ADJUSTMENTS

Adjustment letters are very closely tied in with credit and collection letters. The adjustment department turns over many letters to the credit department, or at least goes into consultation with the credit department about them. You can easily see how this would be necessary. Mrs. Anson Brown is having trouble with an electric ironer which she bought from a retail store of one of the mail-order companies. She wants to return the ironer, trading it in on a more expensive model which she says is probably what she should have bought in the first place. When the adjustment man receives this letter for disposition, he will have to check the condition of the account. If he finds that Mrs. Brown has paid all her installments promptly, he may allow the exchange, offsetting the larger profit on the new ironer against the loss on the old one, which will have to be disposed of as used goods. If, however, she has been slow pay, he will not approve the exchange, or not until she has brought her payments up to date. In other words, adjustment policy toward a particular customer is affected by the volume of his buying and by his previous credit and collection history.

Another point at which collection and adjustment letters come together is in the basic rule governing their composition. Chapter 12 points out that the good collection letter must collect the money in such a way as to keep the customer's business. Similarly, the good adjustment letter must make the adjustment with that object in mind. The good adjustment leaves the door open for future pleasant—and profitable—business relations. But since making adjustments which will please cantankerous customers—and there are some—can be prohibitively expensive, we must make a further qualification. We must not empty our shelves to keep the customer happy; we won't be able to give service, either good or bad, if we go bankrupt!

The basic rule for adjustments, then, is "Make the adjustment in such a way as to satisfy the customer—but at reasonable expense to yourself." Your only direct way of recouping an adjustment loss is through the customer's future business; indirectly you may gain through increased good will and the new business the well-made adjustment will bring you from the customer's friends. Suppose a particular customer's annual business volume is $200 and your net profit from this business is 10 per cent. You could grant this customer four $5 adjustments before you ran a loss, but the chances are that he will not require more than one, if any.

RELATION BETWEEN CLAIMS AND ADJUSTMENTS AND SALES

Contrary to being a tax on business, as they were once considered, adjustments can be instruments for getting additional business. A leading merchant states the point thus: "Complaints, returns, and collections are on the boundary line of business, where customers can be won or lost. When puzzled about where new business is to come from, we remind ourselves that in addition to good merchandise and low prices, we have those border-line sources of new business."

Today manufacturers and merchandisers welcome customer reactions to their products; their great fear is that the customer will say nothing but take his business elsewhere. As the direct-mail advertising men have pointed out to us, a customer is so hard to get in the first place that it is worth while to take great pains to keep him. On the average an old customer is more valuable than a new one, for the new one may be merely shopping around; nevertheless, many firms spend liberally in advertising while literally driving customers away in their adjustment department.

Robert E. Johnson, senior vice-president, marketing and services, of United Air Lines, illustrates these principles in speaking of his company's attitude toward customers' reaction to service: "An irate customer may be difficult to sell, but let me tell you, he is certainly easier to see." In 1963, 2 million of United's 13½ million passengers were using the airline for the first time. In discussing the economics of new customers, Mr. Johnson says: "If we apply the total cost of our advertising, sales promotion, training and marketing to these 2 million, we would be spending $10 on each to get them to fly United. The average profit on a fare is 88¢. So you see, the idea is to keep your new customers as well as get them." Of the 100,000 letters United Airlines gets in a year, "some of them are complaints." These, United salesmen are trained to regard as "the best sales leads they can get." [2]

Compare the following letters, both from mail-order companies:

Dear Sir:

We were sorry to learn from your letter of March 12 that you are having trouble with your mower.

The Matchless Mower has proved successful in every state in the Union when it has been taken care of, but naturally it sometimes has to be cleaned and the oil changed.

If you will consult the instruction booklet which was sent with your mower, you will find adequate instructions for the cleaning and oiling. Please follow these simple instructions and you will have no more trouble with the machine.

                    Your truly,

Dear Mr. Wilson:

You will find enclosed with this letter the amount due you.

[2] *Advertising Age,* December 16, 1963, p. 84.

We appreciate hearing from you about your orders, as the comments of our customers help us to improve our merchandise and service.

Whenever we can be of service in the future it will be a pleasure indeed to hear from you.

Yours very truly,

REFUND $9.34

Suppose you are the customer in both cases—which letter would affect you the more favorably? Probably you would bristle as you read the first one, which practically calls you a nincompoop. In a way, you probably are at fault. Perhaps you mislaid the manual of instructions and never thought of cleaning or changing the oil in the machine. Customers have been guilty of such carelessness. But in any case, the mower is not giving service, and the seller doesn't care—merely takes the occasion to try to make you feel like a fool. You don't like it; few people would. The second letter is much better. It refunds the money which you wanted back in place of the unsatisfactory merchandise, and it even thanks you for presenting the store with an opportunity to improve its goods and service. Which store will you feel like trading with in the future?

THE LANGUAGE OF CLAIM AND ADJUSTMENT LETTERS

In Owen Wister's novel, *The Virginian*, the title character says, "When you call me that, *smile!*" to an enemy who has just called him an offensive name. *Smile*, or gun play will follow. In adjustment letters, the smile in the language may make all the difference in the world in the results. The English language is rich both in fighting, chip-on-the-shoulder words and in words that smile. Here are some examples:

WORDS AND PHRASES THAT OFFEND	LANGUAGE WITH A SMILE
You won't be able to	It is likely that we can help
There is no possible way	Perhaps the following would help
It is unreasonable to expect	Even in unusual cases
You waited too long to write	The discount period, I am sorry to say, has passed
You misread the guarantee	
You claim	If you will re-read the guarantee
Your complaint	Thank you for your letter
You failed to	We were pleased to receive
You neglected to	Of course you were right in
You overlooked	You may be sure that
You should have realized	You can expect right away
We never had any such trouble before	We want you to know that
You are the only one who has found fault	You may be assured that
We can hardly believe	We want you to be one of our many satisfied customers

"When you call me that, *smile!*" in adjustment writing means that we should always treat the recipient of our letter as a friend, not an enemy, and that our immediate job is to transform him from an unhappy customer into a happy, satisfied—and permanent—one.

REQUIREMENTS AND STRUCTURE OF A GOOD CLAIM LETTER

Good claim letters follow a three-point outline:

1. Present the situation—the basis for the claim.
2. State the adjustment wanted.
3. Express business courtesy and use the action-easy close.

Observe how the three points are incorporated in the following letter:

Gentlemen:

My order No. B76934 of January 20 for two dozen boxes of face powder and six cartons of toothpaste arrived today. The shipment was so badly damaged that the merchandise cannot be used.

I am accordingly shipping it back to you by express C.O.D., expecting you to send a duplicate shipment at once. You will be able to determine whether the damage was due to faulty packing or improper handling by the express company.

Such accidents are bound to occur occasionally, and I am not finding fault with your usually excellent service; but since I want this merchandise for my Saturday sale on February 2, I shall appreciate your letting me know whether or not I can expect the new shipment not later than January 30.

                                        Very truly yours,

In presenting the situation, the customer assumes that the seller means to give good service, ordinarily does, wants to know it when he doesn't, and welcomes the opportunity to straighten out what went wrong this time. It is important to state the adjustment wanted, for the seller may not be much of a mind reader even at close range, and at letter-writing distance he is certainly handicapped in ascertaining what is wanted when he isn't told. Many claim, or complaint, letters reveal little more than that the customer is unhappy—has a sense of not having been done well by. Does he want to return the merchandise and get his money back, exchange the merchandise for something else, or what? If he can decide *what he wants* and say so clearly and courteously, he will in all probability get it—if the claim is reasonable. And the close of the letter should confirm the business relationship and, where possible, suggest how the expected action in satisfying the claim can most readily take place.

The claim letter which follows is exceptional in tone; it is friendly, yet it is firm in its request for adjustment.

Gentlemen:

I present: THE CASE OF THE COURTEOUS CUSTOMER.

On November 16, 19--, Mr. K. L. Watson of 216 East Withrow
Avenue, Oxford, Ohio, ordered

    2 years   Harpers Bazaar
    2 years   New Yorker
    1 year   Saturday Review
    1 year   Newsweek

I included this order with orders from four other customers in
my November 16 order to you. The magazines for all five customers came to $62.20. I included my check for $62.20; you
cashed it.

The magazines for all the other customers came as ordered, and
Mr. Watson has been receiving Newsweek regularly.

What he did not tell me until today, however, is that he has
not in all this time received a single copy of any of the other
three magazines he ordered. You would expect him to be angry or
at least upset; instead he is friendly and apparently too understanding and cooperative for his own good.

Please check into Mr. Watson's Harpers Bazaar, New Yorker, and
Sat Rev as quickly as possible so that he will have no more
delay. He deserves some kind of reward for being so patient.

Sincerely yours,

You will find the ending to the story, the magazine agency's reply, on
page 300.

REQUIREMENTS AND STRUCTURE OF A GOOD ADJUSTMENT LETTER

Adjustment letters tend to be longer than claim letters [3]; but their
structure is much the same. The following outline serves for most adjustment letters:

1. Affirm the customer's mood or express appreciation.
2. Tell the good news.
3. Review the situation and give the basis for the adjustment.
4. Supply customer education (if it is in order) and build good will
   for future business relations.

If the claim letter is reasonable in tone, the adjustment letter begins
with an expression of appreciation for bringing the matter to the recip-

---

[3] This condition prevails especially if the adjustment letter is explanatory to the
point of being persuasive; as pointed out, the claim letter is usually informative, telling what happened and what is expected. The letter on page 303 shows length used
to advantage in an adjustment letter.

ient's attention. Frequently, however, the claim letter is so angry and abusive that the recipient is tempted to reply in kind—if *he* likes *his* brand of sarcasm, *I* like *mine* even better. But this won't do. Whether the complainant has a genuine grievance or not, he nearly always *thinks* he has, and for practical purposes this is the same thing. Probably by the time he gets the reply, he will have cooled down considerably, and it would be a mistake to rekindle him. Don't argue with him; instead, affirm his mood with such expressions as "In your circumstances I should feel just as you do about the damaged goods which you received," or "I don't blame you for being out of sorts when you got a carpet sweeper instead of an electric mixer—no one could make cakes with a carpet sweeper," or "We'd feel like shooting someone too if we got someone else's order instead of our own." When the customer finds you aren't excited, he (or she) will usually be rather calm in reading what you have to say.

And when there is good news, tell it early, not later than the second paragraph; in some letters it should be in the opening sentence. Since the only way you are going to be able to recoup the expense of the adjustment is through good will and future business, don't close the door to this possibility by forcing your reader to read three or four paragraphs before he discovers that you are, after all, going to give him what he wants. And don't begrudge the customer the adjustment or you might almost as well not grant it at all. Tell the good news quickly and cheerfully. Observe the following letter, from an electric appliance sales agency, as an example of how not to grant an adjustment:

```
Dear Sir:

We were surprise to learn of your difficulty with the Model
1175-A All-Purpose Tester.  We practically never have any com-
plaints on this item.

On consulting our service man, I learned that trouble such as
yours is usually due to misusing the instrument through over-
loading.  This destroys the copper oxide in the rectifier.

When an instrument has been damaged in this way, the only way
it can be put back in service is through supplying a replacement
rectifier.  If you will consult page 2 of the enclosed tester
catalogue, you will see that the cost of a new rectifier is
$4.50 in the U.S.A., plus shipping charges.

Although the trouble you have had with your tester was through
your fault and not ours, we have decided in this instance to
send you a replacement rectifier at our expense.  We hope that
you will take better care of this one, as you need not expect to
get another one free.

                                          Yours very truly,
```

Fig. 37. Clarity, length, and a disarming opening make this an effective response to a complaint. (Used by permission of the Dartnell Corporation.)

The general tone of this letter is annoyance with the customer and reluctance to extend service. There is a possibility that the customer is at fault, but there is no certainty of this; and since the adjustment is being granted anyway, the letter writer should make the most of his opportunity to build good will for the company. Notice that with similar subject matter but a better psychological arrangement and a more cheerful tone, the letter gives an entirely different effect:

Dear Mr. Jones:

Your Model 1175-A All-Purpose Tester can be put into first-class working order with the replacement rectifier described on page 2

of the enclosed catalogue. We are sending you a new rectifier
at our expense, and it should reach you within three days of the
arrival of this letter.

Although the Model 1175-A Tester usually gives excellent service,
the copper oxide in the rectifier can be deactivated by an overload of current. Probably the rectifier in your tester was
accidentally overloaded. With careful use, the new rectifier
should last indefinitely.

As our catalogue shows, the replacement rectifier is priced at
$4.50, plus shipping charges. The terms of our guarantee would
not require us to assume this expense, but we intend our merchandise to give superior service, and we want our customers to
be satisfied.

We predict a long and useful life for your tester.

                    Cordially yours,

In the revised letter the situation is reviewed in such a way that the
customer learns that his difficulty is possibly due to his own fault, and
the principle of self-interest will tend to impel him to use the repaired
tester with greater care. But first he learns the good news that his tester
can be repaired and that the replacement part will cost him nothing. He
is not scolded, and the emphasis in the letter is where it belongs—on the
willingness and competence of the seller to help the customer out of his
difficulty as efficiently as possible.

A CLAIM LETTER AND THE ANSWER, BOTH WORTHY OF ANALYSIS

The following claim by a Chicago shoe dealer seems to exude frustra-
tion. Note the effect that letter mechanics (one long paragraph) has;
this feature seems to accentuate the sarcasm, depicting a flushed-faced
customer pounding on the counter. Even the careless typing (reproduced here) adds to the frenzied tone. The letter is to a New York
supplier.

Gentlemen:

We have just received a case of black suede loafers #S4305X
at #4.35 plus 21/2%. I have never seen a worse looking suede
in my life. How you could even ship this type of merchandise
at any p rice is beyond our understanding. It looks like they
took a bunch of blotters soaked them together and used them for
uppers. Also whoever lasted the t ips should last one more
pair and then die. Yes, that is how disgusted I am with these
shoes. You are getting this case back. I have showed same to
your Mr. Stover ad he quite agrees with me. I am also returning
some very bad Buckler shoes as I wrote you a few days ago. and 1
am also returning the balance of Nos. 4590 X, patent plastic
wedgie as fast as we sell this shoe they come back, crackedand

with nai ls sticking up in the soles. You people may as well
understand that the time has come when the merchanss and the
public want to receive somewhere near value for a dollar. These
shoes aren't worth .50¢ on the dollar. Upon examination of
these shoes returned I know you will agree with me. I can only
say this in closing I hope you have better values for sp ring,
than these.

                    Yours very truly,

Letter lay-out and typing (except in the salutation) in the supplier's
sales manager's response are satisfactory. But tone is another matter.
Credibility seems to hit a new low when the warmth and cordiality expressed in the last two paragraphs are coupled with the denunciation of
the earlier part of the letter. Question: How inconsistent can a person be?

Dear Mr. Anhorn:

You recently wrote us on November 14th a very childish and
nasty letter.

We are accustomed to dealing with business firms on a business
basis and have no respect for a "smart alec". If you desire to
work on this basis, we can work with you, otherwise, we have no
desire to do so.

If you have a specific problem which you have relating to any
particular shoe which you have purchased from us, we are always
glad to discuss it with you and we are reasonable people to work
with.

We will examine the shoes referred to in your letter and any
that are defective, we will adjust properly.

We hope you will take this letter in the spirit it is written,
and that we will maintain a cordial relationship in the future.

Kindest regards.

                    Very truly yours,

To know that a "cordial relationship" *was* maintained between these
two firms seems only to support that oldest of all adages that it takes all
kinds.

THE FOUR ADJUSTMENT SITUATIONS

There are various ways in which the business machine can slip a cog;
more than one party to the transaction can cause it to be unsatisfactory.
For discussion purposes we can say that there are four general adjustment
situations, each requiring its own kind of handling.

1. Seller at fault—grant cheerful adjustment at once.

2. Second person (usually the carrier) at fault—grant the adjustment for the convenience of the customer, to keep his good will.
3. Fault mixed or seller at fault under extenuating circumstances—grant the adjustment, or compromise.
4. Buyer at fault with no extenuating circumstances—refuse the adjustment as tactfully and constructively as possible.

Seller at Fault

With the best of intentions, the seller is often at fault. Although *caveat emptor* is not applicable to American business in general, in many transactions the customer does not receive the goods and services that he pays for until he notifies the seller of what has gone wrong. Shipments may be improperly packed and arrive damaged. A packer may omit some vital part of the order. A mail-order company may send the wrong size of automobile tires or the wrong color of paint. Occasionally a machine is made with a defective part that causes it to fail in operation long before the normal time.

It is unfortunate when any of these failures to serve the customer occur. Often he is seriously inconvenienced. The least that the seller can do in such cases is to exert himself to remedy the fault as promptly and courteously as possible. A customer can stand disappointment; he will not tolerate lack of appreciation.

If, then, you are the seller at fault, spare no pains to extend the best possible *service* in the situation. Don't think that a cheerful letter *alone* will make the customer happy. Tell him the good news in a clear, considerate way. You don't need to grovel; adjustment letters could do with fewer "sorry's" and "regret's." Here, as elsewhere, actions speak louder than words. And don't tell him "It will never happen again." Lightning *does* strike more than once in the same place; so it could happen again. But if you handle this time well, he won't worry about the future.

The following letter is the magazine agency's reply to the letter of claim on page 295.

Dear Mr. Childs:

    In connection with your letter of April 27th we agree that Mr. K. L. Watson is certainly a courteous customer and we may also add that you are too!

    On your order of November 16th you included

        HARPERS BAZAAR — two years
        NEW YORKER   "
        SAT REV   one year

for Mr. Watson, but these items were all on the reverse portion of the order form and due to an inexcusable error on our part

these three items were not copied off and submitted to the
publishers at the time your order was received. Of course, we
have now properly entered all three items and you may assure
Mr. Watson that after a reasonable length of time has been
allowed for the publishers to enter these subscriptions he will
receive service regularly for the full period of time originally
ordered for each magazine.

We also agree that Mr. Watson deserves a reward for his
courtesy, and therefore, we are entering in his favor with our
compliments a subscription to READER'S DIGEST for eight months.

If necessary to refer to this transaction in the future,
simply make mention of our order #97406. Thank you.

Cordially yours,

Carrier or Agent at Fault

If there is many a slip between the cup and the lip, so also there are
many possibilities of mishap to goods before they reach the intended
users. In the majority of instances in which the fault is with neither seller
nor buyer, it is with the carrier—the railroad, trucking or express company, air carrier, water carrier, or postal service. Technically, the seller
discharges his responsibility when he sees that the merchandise is properly packed and loaded. In practice, however, the seller assumes responsibility up to safe delivery, for he is ordinarily in a much better position
to secure redress than is the buyer. For goods lost or damaged in transit,
then, the seller normally makes the adjustment cheerfully, and takes the
opportunity to build further good will thereby. As a rule, he will eventually collect from the carrier, but he is extending an accommodation to
the customer, who should appreciate this fact if he phrases his letter well.
The following is a typical satisfactory exchange of letters:

Gentlemen:

We were very much concerned when our Receiving Department
reported that upon unpacking your recent shipment, Order No.
38923, they found one box contained four VT-227-B Amplifier
Tubes which apparently had been broken in transit.

The Receiving Department has called this matter to the attention
of the express company by noting on the receipt that the box
containing the tubes was received in a damaged condition. The
rest of the shipment arrived in good order.

Since our company does not carry a large stock of these particular tubes and the present supply is low, we will appreciate
your making a duplicate shipment and taking up the matter with
the express company.

Very truly yours,

Dear Mr. Smith:

Four VT-227-B Amplifier Tubes have been sent to you by prepaid express to replace those broken in transit on your Order No. 38923.

We appreciate your letter of September 22, bringing this mishap to our attention, also your thoughtfulness in having the damage noted on the express receipt.

Doubtless the new tubes will arrive promptly to take their place on your shelves. We are always happy to hear that our merchandise is in such good demand, and you can be sure that we will do everything possible to enable you to keep it in stock.

Cordially yours,

Buyer and Seller Both at Fault

Sometimes in unsatisfactory transactions the fault is uncertain or divided between the buyer and the seller; or the buyer may be at fault but in such a way that he is not wholly to blame. In such situations the seller exerts himself to make the customer happy, but usually does not shoulder heavy replacement expenses. The customer may have mistakenly or accidentally ordered the wrong article or the wrong size or color. Mail-order companies have had so much trouble on this point that they take extra space to make their catalogue descriptions as foolproof as possible—tie not included with shirt, tubes with tires, hat with dress, etc. Or the customer may have broken a machine by putting it to the wrong use. However he got there, he is in trouble and needs to be helped out; as a rule he will be grateful for any assistance that is given to him.

The following letter grants an adjustment where the buyer is probably at fault.

Dear Mrs. Campbell:

We are sending two beaters to replace those for your mixer, which you wrote about on December 22. There will be no charge, although there usually is in cases of such claims.

Your record with us prompts this action in making the adjustment; and I hope that you will continue to find our merchandise and service at the standards you spoke of in your letter.

I hope, too, that your mixer will again give you as much pleasure as you mentioned. With proper care and use, it will, I'm sure.

Yours very truly,

Buyer at Fault

The final adjustment situation is the one where the customer is so clearly at fault that no adjustment can be granted. The customer may try to return for credit goods that have already been used and damaged;

he may want a monetary adjustment where none is due; he may want goods replaced outside the terms of the sales agreement or guarantee. Unfortunately, there are some persons in the world who deliberately try to take advantage. These are equivalent to the dead beats with whom the collection man must deal. They must be handled with comparable firmness, though they are less of a problem, for they are often merely trying to get something to which they are not entitled, whereas the dead beat already has it and refuses to pay for it. Reply firmly to the customer who makes an unwarranted complaint, and stress company policy and the necessity of being fair to all.

The letter below from the assistant manager of a large mail-order retail store is to a customer who had made a purchase only to learn that her neighbor got the same item two weeks later as a "premium" with a larger purchase. Mrs. D. apparently obeyed the not uncommon impulse to ask for a refund after buying an item at regular price just before a sale.

Dear Mrs. Dobson:

Your letter of April 15th has reached me and I would like to justify your writing it with this reply.

We appreciate your patronage as one of our good customers. I feel that you have enjoyed the merchandise which you have purchased here in the past. It is probable that you feel that you have had good results with what you have purchased and have received values in relation to what price you paid for this merchandise. It is our sincere desire to continue our relationship with our customers on such a basis.

In all the history of the retail business it is found that from time to time "Special Promotions" are used to entice people to decide to buy at certain times items which they have been considering for some time. This is the general practice of all retail concerns and ours is no exception. Such advertising promotions have proved to be successful.

We regret that you have not been fortunate enough to purchase from us at some time which would have given you the benefit of greater values through premium gifts made to you with your purchase, however, we will from time to time, in the future, offer occasional premiums and we hope that you may be able on one of these occasions to accept one or more of our combination offers.

Thank you for your letter and, believe me, we are here for the purpose of serving you, if and whenever we can do so. Please call on me at any time for assistance in any problem which you may have.

                    Very sincerely yours,

Had the assistant manager foregone the platitudinous and inappropriate offer of help in his final sentence, he would have done a commendable job. The letter—long, for a purpose—says "No" without using the word. Note that there is only one negative used in the entire explanation.

ADJUSTING THE ADJUSTMENT

Although the foregoing principles should be kept in mind constantly by the adjustment writer, he must remember that even the adjustment policy must be adjusted to fit individual cases. Large customers tend to get more consideration than small ones; old, established customers, more than new and occasional ones. Conversely, chronic "kickers" are dealt with more firmly and receive less consideration than the customers who complain only now and then. A great many claims are so typical that simple form letters will take care of them, but there are many others that must be dealt with individually as special problems. The adjustment man can never afford to forget the great painter's reply to the novice who wanted to know how the master mixed his paints: "I mix them with brains."

FORM LETTERS FOR ADJUSTMENTS

For simple, routine adjustments, form letters represent both economy and efficiency. A skillfully written form letter which fits the situation will be much better than an individual letter badly written by an incompetent person. A variant of the form letter is the letter made up by assembling form paragraphs. In my discussion I have assumed that forms would be used for routine adjustments; consequently most of the discussion has been devoted to letters that handle the numerous adjustments which are individual problems.

CHECKING ON ADJUSTMENTS

It is not safe for a company to *assume* that its adjustment policy is satisfactory. Not all aggrieved customers make their dissatisfaction known. Correspondence supervisors need to check periodically the carbon copies of adjustment letters that the various correspondents send out. Sometimes a few positive suggestions will improve the adjustment policy amazingly. Again, field work may be done to check the results—to learn whether the adjustments have actually given satisfaction. Double postal cards may be sent out to make the customer's reply easy, or traveling salesmen may be instructed to check up. A good adjustment policy is less created than *achieved* over a period of time through tempering good principles in the light of actual business practices.

THE PRINCIPLE OF RESALE

Like the collection man, the adjustment letter writer should never forget that he is dealing with a person who *once wanted the article*. Probably he still wants it and you have only to help him get it delivered in satisfactory condition or learn to operate it well. If he thinks he no longer wants it, you may choose between giving him an exchange or a refund or reselling him on the original article, basing your decision, as a matter of course, upon what will be best for him if he can only be brought to see it; that is, upon *business service*.

The letter which follows was written by a pen manufacturer in answer to a letter from a dissatisfied customer. The customer was pleased by the reply, particularly by the tone of the beginning and the courtesy shown throughout the letter.

Mr. Schuyler Van Rensselaer Mellen
116 East Vine Street
Toledo, Ohio

Dear Sir:

We are happy that our recent advertisement on our new Seamanette Lighter has prompted you to write to us of your experience with your "68" pen. Yes, you have every right to expect the utmost in writing pleasure from a Seaman "68" pen, and you may be assured we do want you to receive your full share of enjoyment.

If you wish, you may wrap up your pen and return it to us, insured, with the attached brown mailer. One of our service experts will be happy to examine it and put it through a series of laboratory tests. Of course, if any defect is detected in material or workmanship, you will receive a brand new pen with our compliments. If the pen can be put in like-new condition with a few adjustments, this service will be rendered with our compliments, providing there are no damaged or missing parts.

No doubt you have been filling your pen properly, but we find it is the answer to so many pen problems that we believe it is worth while reviewing with our customers.

A "68" pen should be filled step-by-step with the attached rules, twice a week. If you have our plunger-type "68" pen, be sure to hold the plunger down on the 11th stroke until the pen has been removed from the ink. When properly filled, a "68" pen should hold approximately 28 to 32 drops of ink and write continuously from 4 to 10 hours, depending upon the grade of the point and the adjustment of the flow of ink. You will want to give your pen one more chance.

We shall be on the lookout for your parcel, and you may be assured it will be given our most sincere interest. Thank you again for bringing this to our attention.

Very truly yours,

BUSINESS BUILDING THROUGH A GOOD ADJUSTMENT POLICY

As we have already mentioned, many authorities hold that every business letter is a sales letter. Practically speaking, this is true; certainly adjustment letters present the best of sales opportunities. The courtesy and consideration extended to customers by the adjustment man can make lifelong friends.[4]

Don't's and Do's for Claim and Adjustment Letters

Don't resent the customer's claims or statements of grievance.

Do welcome a customer's reaction, for it is thus that you can learn to serve him.

Don't return the customer's anger, irritation, or sarcasm with your own brand—however well you like yours.

Do remember that "A soft answer turneth away wrath," and that you must be a gentleman whether you are dealing with gentlemen or not.

Don't be gloomy or pessimistic about your inability to grant the customer all that he asks for.

Do remember that "Half a loaf is better than no bread," and that a little with good cheer may be better than much with surliness.

Don't withhold the positive aspects of the adjustment until the end of the letter; the customer may be so disheartened by then that even good news won't be welcome.

Do tell the good news at once; this is the natural, human way to bring good news. Once the customer is in a good mood, it will be relatively easy to keep him so.

Don't try to treat all customers by simple rules of thumb.

Do remember to adapt the adjustment policy to the special situation; circumstances do alter cases.

Don't treat the adjustment situation as a burden and a tax upon business.

Do regard the adjustment situation as an unparalleled opportunity to increase business through building good will.

[4] Although it never got into the mails, what might strike many a disgruntled customer as the acme in public relations was written by a secretary. The young lady's superior, having carried on a two-month correspondence in an adjustment question, asked her to try her hand (for a fresh approach) at getting the customer to see the unreasonableness of her request. The secretary's letter opened with "Dear Madam: It's a damned dirty shame the way our company has treated you."

Don't regard the customer as someone far away and remote from your interests and concerns.	*Do* consider that the customer is a man "of like passions with you," and you will be more likely to accord him treatment that will make him happy.
Don't say "our records show that."	*Do* say "the carbon copy of our invoice (letter) dated June 17."
Don't use negative, querulous terms in your adjustment letters.	*Do* choose always the positive, cheerful words. "Thank you," "glad," "happy" are good news in any language.

How to Turn Complaints into Extra Sales

by TED POLLOCK *

They can take any of a hundred forms: "THIS BILL IS OUTRAGEOUS." "Your service is terrible." "DELIVERIES ARE LATE." "The last one I bought broke down." "*Your company doesn't keep its promises.*"

Every salesman in your company runs into complaints like these. And, depending on his ability to handle them, such complaints can be shattering, frustrating, costly experiences—or positively priceless opportunities to sew up a customer's allegiance and business.

Which they shall be, say the men who have learned to turn them to advantage, is largely determined by four factors—the salesman's:

- Attitude and approach.
- Capacity for "discovering the villain."
- Ability to find solutions.
- Knack for cashing in on complaints.

In that order.

Attitude and approach

"The real McCoy salesman sees a complaint for what it really is," says Ralph Shamah, district sales manager for A. Schreter & Sons Co., men's wear manufacturers, "a chance to be of service to a customer when that service is most wanted, a golden opportunity to prove to a buyer that his problem is the salesman's problem.

"But you can't expect a customer to believe you care unless you show him that you do. This means, first of all, *taking the complaint seriously.*

"Whether your customer thinks you're giving him the evil eye or grumbles about defective merchandise is immaterial. The point is, as far as he's con-

* Mr. Pollock, who holds a Ph.D. from Columbia University, has written innumerable articles from interviews with hundreds of salesmen and their managers. This one is from his book *Professional Salesman's Guide* (West Nyack, N.Y.: Parker Publishing Co., 1964). The selection appeared originally in *Management Methods,* January, 1960, pp. 56–58. It is reprinted here by permission of Prentice-Hall, Inc.

cerned, he has a legitimate beef. Minimize it in any way and you immediately compound his grievance because you are, in effect, challenging his judgment.

"Besides, a man with a gripe is in no mood to be reasonable. Not at first, anyway. Above all, he craves an audience, someone to whom he can pour out his tale of woe. Therefore, the smart salesman makes it a point, at the first hint of trouble, to *get to his customer.*

"If it isn't possible to put in a personal appearance, call him up. But *get there.* It's the very best way to show a man how highly you value his business.

"Once there, *listen.* Look interested. Display concern. Get all the facts. Don't speak until you're certain that he has nothing more to say. A talked-out customer is the easiest one with which to deal.

"Then *summarize,* in your own words, his net valid complaint. This serves two purposes: it disarms the complainer by showing him how closely you have followed what he's been saying. And it helps you keep his points straight in your own mind."

Adds a salesman for a fuel distributor: "Next to letting off steam, what the disgruntled customer wants most is satisfaction. If his complaint is justified, be quick to admit it—but be sure to explain *why* things went wrong and *why* a recurrence is all but impossible. Otherwise, your assurance that 'It won't happen again' may sound like a hollow promise."

The sales director of a paper products company has found the phrase, "Now that we know the problem . . ." followed by a specific remedy for the complaint, can be a most valuable good-will winner.

In his own words: "A customer who raises Cain frequently feels a little sheepish after wading into a salesman. 'Now that we know' helps him save face. It's a way of thanking him for pointing out an error or shortcoming. At the same time, it's a promise—that any future complaints will receive the same prompt attention. For a short phrase it does a whale of a job."

Welcome complaints

Summing up, David Colen, president, Fotomart Inc., photographic supplies wholesalers, advises: "Welcome complaints as voluntary tip-offs to what you can do to cement relations with your customers. It's the man with the silently nursed dissatisfaction who should worry you, for you'll never know how you can be of maximum service to him. The most skillful doctor in the world can't treat a patient who refuses to say where it hurts."

"Discover the villain"

According to Walter Hardy, vice-president in charge of sales, Radio Division, North American Philips Co., the biggest mistake a salesman can make in handling a complaint is to pin the blame on "someone in the front office."

"Avoid that approach like the plague!" he warns. "Passing the buck can only arouse suspicion, as if the salesman were saying, 'It's not my fault, but I'll help you anyway.' Rather than dig up excuses, ask your customer, 'What happened?' That way, you boil the whole issue down to *what* went wrong rather than *who* is to blame. You ally yourself with him in a search for the common enemy—the cause of his complaint. When you find it, get rid of it."

Sometimes, the grievance is based on error. When that's the case, a calm review of the circumstances may divulge the culprit.

The chief adjuster for a large metropolitan department store cites the lady who bought several copper-bottomed cooking utensils, only to call back in a few days with fire in her eyes.

"She complained that the copper had 'burned off' after a few days' cooking," he recalls. "When we asked her whether she had tried polishing the utensils, it turned out that the salesman who originally sold them to her neglected to explain how to care for them. When we showed her how, she was satisfied—and bought some polish to boot. Of course, if the salesman had done the job properly in the first place, that complaint would never have been filed. But a little detective work uncovered the reason—and suggested the remedy—for it."

While all complaints are not so easily settled, many do fall under certain broad categories. Next time your salesmen find themselves facing a complaint, suggest that they consider these possibilities as the cause. This could save a lot of sound and fury:

- *Improper use of product or service.*

Even the simplest gadget in the world that is used incorrectly won't operate effectively or measure up to the claims of the manufacturer. The soap recommended by a washing machine manufacturer, for example, will obviously do a better job of washing clothes in *his* machine than the soap that the customer chooses indiscriminately. The advertisement written for a trade audience won't have the same kind of impact on the consumer public. The truck built to carry a 10-ton load may well buckle under a 15-ton burden.

Check on your customer's handling of your product or service. The villain could be simple misuse.

- *Improper diagnosis.*

A buyer complains about a machine's sputtering performance. The salesman investigates and finds—faulty wiring. An irate customer descends on a retailer because of spotty reception on his new TV set. The culprit? A diathermy machine in a nearby hospital.

Sometimes an outside factor, one you have nothing to do with, is the cause of the complaint. Find it if you can—and make a friend.

- *Misunderstanding.*

Many complaints are based on lack of information. The man who doesn't get a discount because he pays in six weeks instead of 30 days . . . the customer whose policy has lapsed . . . the buyer who misreads your guarantee—each bases his complaint on a different frame of reference from you.

Such "emotional static" can lead to a verbal free-for-all. A few well placed questions and some patient answers can clear the air.

But suppose the customer's complaint is justified? What then?

Finding solutions

The main reason for investigating a complaint is to undo some kind of damage—to profits, products or peace of mind.

Easier said than done?

Of course! But well within the salesman's power—provided he learns how to find solutions that are mutually acceptable to his customer and company.

The salesman's first step toward finding such solutions is to familiarize himself with his company's facilities and adjustment policies. Precisely what guarantees does it offer? Who is responsible for deliveries . . . maintenance . . . billing? How soon can parts be replaced? What departments are especially geared to help customers with offbeat problems? Where is your nearest warehouse? How far does his own authority to make adjustments extend?

The answers to such questions will automatically set limits to the kind of redress he can offer—but the result will be *proposals that he knows you can live up to.*

Once you know what you can do for your customer, tell him—precisely, concretely, honestly. If you cannot give him an immediate answer, tell him you will take it up with your firm and give him the answer within a few days. Whenever possible, give him just a little more than he expects or demands by way of allowance or replacement.

For example, if your customer's demands are unfair—but not costly—make no charge for repairs or service. If his complaint is filed three days after the expiration of a 90-day guarantee, honor it—if you can. In short, don't win the argument and lose the customer.

The second step toward finding mutually acceptable solutions is to ask your customer, after telling him what you will do to rectify the error, "Is that acceptable to you?" Encourage his comments on the justice of your plan, for such encouragement pays a double dividend. It indicates your confidence in the fairness of the proposal and it proves that your only interest is his total satisfaction.

"If you, your company or merchandise are at fault, settle the complaint on the spot," says a retail specialist for a large appliance manufacturer. "People are generally reasonable. What they want—and have a right to expect—is fair play. Erase the *cause* of a complaint and, in nine cases out of 10, you will hear no more about it. But it's a good idea to take the initiative later and check back on the situation."

Cash in on complaints

It is one thing to "take care" of a complaint, quite another to turn it into what every salesman craves—extra sales.

Yet, it's done every day, in a wide variety of ways. Here are the most important ways:

1. Self-improvement. In those cases where the salesman is personally at fault, a complaint can be a blessing in disguise. For example, if investigation shows that product performance is poor because the salesman neglected to explain its operation clearly, he can take steps to sharpen future demonstrations.

If the difficulty centers about lack of service, he can re-assess—and improve—his current methods of keeping in touch with customers. Even if a personality quirk is alienating customers, he can work on eliminating the cause of the friction. The important thing is to learn to look on every form of criticism— spelled out or implied—as a springboard to better performance.

2. *Company feedback.* "I get some of my best ideas from complaints," reports an office furniture salesman. "For instance, a customer once lodged a protest with me over the construction of our desks—the way they were built, a lot of unsightly wires hung over one side. I wrote up the complaint and passed it along to our production people. The result was the addition of interior conduits that kept telephone and other wires out of the way. That feature turned into one of my most potent selling points." If your customer's gripe is legitimate, examine the possibilities of eliminating its cause by bringing it to the attention of your own company. Anything you can do to improve your firm's product or service is bound to improve your over-all sales.

3. *Your other customers.* Some time ago, the Electrolux Corp. received several complaints about the malfunctioning of a certain part of a new vacuum cleaner. Tests indicated that there *was* something wrong with it. Rather than hope for the best and attending to complaints as they came in, the company replaced the part on some 50,000 machines already in use. The result: 50,000 customers mightily impressed by Electrolux's desire to keep them happy.

The moral? Customer A's complaint could be an anticipation of customer B's, C's and D's. After attending to A, why not hurry over to the others and show yourself off as a *voluntary* trouble-shooter? Neat. Impressive.

4. *When you're innocent.* Here's a chance to win the gratitude of your toughest customer. Even if his problem has nothing to do with your product or service—*help him solve it.* There is no better way to clinch a business relationship than to prove yourself a friend in need.

Have another customer who solved the dilemma? Find out how he did it— and pass along the information. Can any of your company's experts come to the rescue of a customer? Get their help. Know how your customer can reduce his inventory . . . save money . . . be more efficient? Tell him.

The salesman who snaps into action when his customer bellows loud and clear is not one-tenth as rare as the one who takes his cue from a casually mentioned problem.

5. *Complaints about the competition.* Not all the gripes you hear will refer to *your* product. Some at least will be leveled at your competitors. Take them for what they're worth—million dollar tips that can be put to work for you. Not for knocking the competition—but as a clue to how you can make your product more desirable than ever to customers and prospects.

6. *Future reference.* Once you have a disgruntled customer, you also have his pet peeve out in the open. You know precisely what irks him most. What a bonanza! From that moment on, you can see to it that the circumstances that brought on his complaint are never allowed to build up again. Given enough complaints, a dedicated salesman ought to be able to turn himself into the perfect salesman—so sensitive to customers' needs he knows them before they do.

When you must say "NO."

Not every complaint can be adjusted to the customer's complete satisfaction. When he wants more than you can give him, try this four-step approach:

- Explain why you cannot do what he asks.
- If possible, draw a parallel with his own line of business.
- Hammer away at the benefits of your product or service.*

Exercises and Problems in Communication

1. Assume that you are a correspondence supervisor in an insurance company and you see the carbon copy of the following letter to a claimant (not one of your policyholders). What corrections on letter form would you suggest to the correspondent who wrote the letter? More important, how would you describe the tone of the letter to the writer, for correction? What part do first-person pronouns play in the writing?

```
Mrs. J. S. Schneider
3040 Winston Drive
Lexington, Kentucky

                          Re: Brown, J. E., the insured
Gentlemen:                    Schneider, J. S.

    We have given careful consideration to the facts as presented
to us in the above captioned case.

    Our policy is to settle claims promptly and fairly.  We must
be guided by our duty to our policyholders to make payment for
only those claims for which they are responsible.

    A review of the facts in this case reveals our assured is not
responsible for your loss and in view of this decision, we must
respectfully decline payment in this instance.

                          Very truly yours,
```

Discuss this letter from the standpoint of implication of the writer and of inference of the receiver.

2. As head of the public relations department in a meat-packing firm, you receive a letter from a consumer who has found a fly in one of your company's canned products bought in a retail store. Write the consumer a letter, making the fly a villain which got into your plant (you have no notion how) and hid away in the particular container the customer bought. The point of your approach is to point up the sanitary conditions in the factory. Such a letter was written in this circumstance by an employee in an Indiana company. The letter showed such finesse on the part of the writer that the customer practically took oath in her reply to the "villain" story never to buy products processed by the firm's competitors.

3. Answer the following letter written by a college student. "Club 15" mentioned in the letter was a radio program on which the redemption offer was

---

* This advice appeared as a headnote with Mr. Pollock's article in the *Management Methods* version.

made. If you think, after reading Mr. Klein's letter, that he would enjoy having an answer in the tone of his letter, write one. Whatever approach you take, make every effort to avoid the stereotyped thank-you-for-taking-advantage-of-our-offer response.

```
Crandall Specialty Foods
Advertising Department
Camden, Iowa

Gentlemen:

We have just finished supper which consisted in part of a can of
your pork and beans.  Shortly afterwards, we heard your offer on
the Club 15 show to redeem at double money, the can of your pork
and beans if we didn't think it was the best we had tasted.

Sorry, gentlemen, it is not the best I have ever tasted.  As a
matter of fact, I don't think much of it at all.

I am enclosing the lable [sic] of this dead soldier for which
I paid 13¢.  Therefore, I will be glad to have the 26¢ in the
near future which you have guaranteed over the radio.

Thank you very much.

                              Yours very truly,

                              K. O. Klein

P.S. As soon as I receive the check, I will go to the store
     and buy two more cans of your pork and beans as my two
     roommates think it's the nuts.
```

4. You have been called in as consultant to a mail-order firm to consider revision of company form letters. What would you do with the three following claim pieces used by the company? Can you get rid of the businessese?

(1)

```
                              Re: Your Cl. #_____
                                  Our Cl. #_____

Gentlemen:

_____1.  Claim has been cancelled, Please close file and return
           our supporting papers.

_____2.  Attached is a statement from your agent acknowledging
           receipt of salvage merchandise.  Please remit amount
           of claim promptly.

_____3.  Please consolidate the attached detail with the balance
           of our claim file and arrange to allow us prompt
           settlement.

                              Yours truly,

                              Auditor
```

(2)

Gentlemen:

Re: Our Claim #_____

Our above numbered claim filed on _____ in the amount of $_____ has never been acknowledged. To date we have not received the merchandise shortage, if any, for which our claim was filed.

Since sufficient time has lapsed in which to conclude an investigation, we request your check in settlement or information as to the current status of our claim.

Yours truly,

Controller

(3)

Re: Our Claim #_____

Our above numbered claim filed on _____ in the amount of $_____ has never been acknowledged. To date we have not received the merchandise shortage, if any, for which our claim was filed.

On _____ we wrote in part as follows: "Since sufficient time has lapsed in which to conclude an investigation, we request your check in settlement or information as to the current status of our claim".

We do not understand why receipt of our claim has never been acknowledged, why the claim still remains unpaid, or your apparent disregard for our follow-up letter.

In view of the above we request your check in settlement or your reasons in full as to why your payment cannot be submitted by return mail.

Yours truly,

Controller

5. Consider the next three letters. The April 20 letter, referred to in the first one, was a two-page claim letter telling of the customer's extreme dissatisfaction with the reupholstery (charge, $50 to the customer) on a three-piece sectional (purchase price, $300) after one year's use. The repair was necessary because of what the customer deemed inferior material in the original furniture. Her complaint is about material and especially workmanship in the repair. The key sentence of her April 20 letter: "The 'before' and 'after' look is so obvious our family and friends who are regular callers at our home who once remarked 'What a beautiful sectional!' now ask 'What in the world HAPPENED to your beautiful sectional?' "

June 7, 19--

Mr. Telston
Carver Manufacturing Company
Carterville, Illinois

Dear Mr. Telston:

I received an acknowledgment to my letter of April 20 to the effect that you were out of the city and were to return some time after May 1, at which time my letter would be given your attention.

It is now June 7 and I have heard nothing. This I do not understand, nor can I appreciate.

May I please have the courtesy of a reply.

Very truly yours,

Mary Telczewski

Mr. Telston is vice-president in charge of sales.

June 12, 19--

Mrs. Mary Telczewski
2838 Cantor Drive
South Bend 28, Indiana

Dear Mrs. Telczewski:

Please excuse the delay in answering your letter regarding your complaint. In some way your letter was filed without an answer being given to you.

According to the reports I have received from our representatives, Mr. Ely and Mr. Osborn, your sectional was not altered in any way from its original dimensions and there is no real basis for your feeling that it has not been reupholstered properly.

Both of these men are experienced and I must rely on their report to me in determining our responsibility in the matter. In view of the information I have, therefore, it appears to me that your complaint is not justified.

Yours very truly,

[Signed]

Vice President

Mr. Telston's letter was signed and initialed by his secretary. Does this detail affect a customer's reaction to the tone and message in a letter such as the one you've just read? Do you think it contributed to the "indignity" referred to in Miss Telczewski's response, below?

June 25, 19--

Mr. Ted F.Telston, Vice President
Carver Manufacturing Company
Carterville, Illinois

Dear Mr. Telston:

Your reply of June 12 to my letter of complaint in which I
outlined the multiple discrepancies in the sectional your
company reupholstered for me is totally unacceptable.

And I do not appreciate having my integrity impugned with the
inference that I do not speak the truth. Neither do I appreciate your flat dismissal "your complaint is not justified."
It is justified!

The sectional IS altered from its original dimensions, and there
IS a real basis for my feeling that it has not been reupholstered
properly. Your relying on the "experience" of Mr. Ely and
Mr. Osborn notwithstanding, I can prove the rework is defective.
I will oppose opinion with fact. I am prepared to prove it with
photographic evidence and material witnesses who will attest
to the present condition of the sectional as compared to its
original condition at the time I purchased it. Naturally, your
men will try to do a selling job to make Carver come out smelling
like a rose.

This sectional was of sub-standard quality in the first place
or the reupholstering would not have been necessary. I paid out
$300 of quality money but I do not have $300 of quality merchandise in return. This loss has been compounded by a botched up
rework job.

For a sales executive, Mr. Telston, I am truly amazed at your
attitude. Customer good will is one of the most valuable assets
a company can own. Customer ill will is one of the most costly
liabilities. Money poured into the coffers of advertising media
is of no avail if it is negated by bad customer relations.

To have to submit to the indignity of this level of action is
completely foreign to me and I find it most distasteful, to say
the least. This is without parallel in all our combined experiences. This is a matter of record with the Credit Bureau,
where the Telczewski credit rating is A1.

I am totally within my rights to demand recovery of the damages
I have sustained. What further avenues of recourse I pursue
depend on Carver and Talbott's [the local merchant from whom
the sectional was bought].

I shall await your reconsideration of this case.

Very truly yours,

(Miss) Mary Telczewski

Assume Mr. Telston's role in this exchange and answer Miss Telczewski's letter. Incidentally, his letter should not offer replacement. That adjustment was not reached for about a year, in this case.

6. As Creighton Publishing Company, 110 Fifth Avenue, New York City, reply to this letter from one of your retail bookdealer customers:

We received your shipment of <u>Report Writing</u> by Thomas and Hymer —and how!

We ordered 30 copies, and you sent 300. We can't possibly use more than 35.

What do you want us to do with all these books? We don't have nearly enough storage space as it is.

Very truly yours,

7. A customer pays an account with a trust company before it is due with the understanding that part of the finance charge will be refunded. Disappointed with the amount of the refund, he asks for an explanation, and receives in reply the following letter. Does it fulfill the requirements of a good adjustment letter? In the form of a letter to your instructor, write a brief criticism.

Mr. Rufus D. Wilson
3920 East 103rd Street
Chicago, Illinois

Re: Account Number 441-33-17528

Dear Mr. Wilson:

In reply to your letter of March 11 we wish to state that although your total charge on the account was $57.69, of this amount $8.40 was paid by us to the Federal government, which amount is not returnable as they do not rebate. On the remainder of the charge, which was $49.29, we base our rebate on the fact that the heaviest charges are earned in the early portions of the note, since that is the period during which the greatest amount of money is outstanding.

We will not attempt in this letter to break this down in detail but will merely say that it is figured on a pro rata basis of the net charge.

Your promissory note will be marked "paid" and forwarded to you within a week to ten days.

Yours very truly,

8. In a letter to your instructor, criticize the following railway passenger traffic adjustment letter. Rid it of business jargon.

Dear Sir:

Having reference to your claim for adjustment on B&O and IC RR rail transportation which you presented with your form letter of October 21st, file T. W. F.

In connection with the IC RR ticket, we wish to advise that as
it is customary for originating carriers to arrange adjustments
on their own transportation we are today forwarding that ticket
to Mr. J. J. Herron, AP&SA of the IC RR at Chicago, requesting
him to communicate direct with you in regard to matter of
adjustment.

You will no doubt hear from him in due course of time.

In regard to the B&O ticket we are pleased to attach hereto our
draft in your favor in the amount of $65.00, which we trust will
satisfactorily adjust this claim.

Yours very truly,

Assistant Passenger Traffic Manager

9. Mr. Harold Lambert, 24 University Place, Detroit, Michigan, bought a
$399.50 radio-record player combination at Hudsons'. After using the com-
bination for two weeks he wrote that he is unable to get the record-changing
mechanism to work properly and asked that the store pick up the player. The
department manager reports that the mechanism of that particular changer is
unusual and somewhat hard to learn to operate, but that otherwise it is the
best and surest mechanism made. Write Hudsons' letter.

10. About six months ago the Fischer Hardware Company, Evansville,
Indiana, offered a shipment of surplus house paint, not guaranteed, at $2.25 a
gallon. George Burris, a painting contractor who lives at 542 S. Ninth St.,
bought fifty gallons of this "bargain" paint and began to use it on jobs around
town. Today Fischer Hardware received a letter from Burris requesting adjustment:

That paint isn't any good; it is flaking off the houses I used
it on. My customers are asking me what I am going to do about
it. But I think you should be the one to do something about it.

Refuse adjustment; the paint was clearly advertised "Not Guaranteed." But
remember that Burris buys hundreds of gallons of paint from you each year,
and that he is in a bad spot. The paint loss is small; the labor of repainting
the houses is the major item of cost to him. Keep him as a customer without
bribing him in any way: no free paint, no free brushes, no discounts beyond
the 10% he already receives.

11. In a letter to your instructor criticize the following actual reply to a
customer's letter of complaint. Rewrite it with improved tone, being careful
not to talk down.

Dear Miss Dobson:-

We are in receipt of your letter of Jan. 17th, in regard to the
knobs of your Harmony Radio.

In regard to this you just pull the knobs off the radio and
the knobs will come off.

Thanking you for your patience in the matter, we remain

Yours very truly,

12. The recipient of the following letter had asked for an adjustment on a battery which had failed within a week of his purchase of a Class A used car. He lived at a considerable distance from the sales agency. Criticize the letter.

Dear Sir:

We are in receipt of your letter with regard to trouble you experienced with your car. Inasmuch as our warrantee on the bill of sale states that the car must be returned to our service department for any repairs that are to be made, we feel that we are under no obligation to make this refund.

Hoping this trouble has been eliminated and that the car will continue to give you satisfactory service, we remain

                    Yours very truly,

13. Seven months ago Mrs. Leslie Hilton, 411 Orchard Avenue, bought four pairs of draperies after reading this ad:

THE DRAPERY SHOP'S ANNUAL SALE OF FINE DRAPERIES
VALUES UP TO $35, ONLY $12.95 A PAIR
DRY-CLEAN-ONLY TAPESTRIES   NO MAIL OR PHONE ORDERS

Today you received this letter:

Gentlemen,

At your annual sale I bought four pairs of maroon tapestry draperies at $12.95 a pair. Yesterday I laundered them for the first time, and the colors all faded and ran together.

Since the draperies are no good to me the way they are, I am sending them back to your store for adjustment.

                    Very truly yours,

Refuse adjustment to Mrs. Hilton. The draperies were plainly tagged "Dry Clean Only—Do Not Launder;" the ad emphasized the "Dry Clean Only."

14. Here is a letter of claim that was actually written to a mail-order house. Discuss the effectiveness of its appeals. What function does the "basic premise" paragraph serve? Why did Harrison make the fourth paragraph so short? Is the claim letter too long?

                              414 Larchmont Avenue
                              Union City, Indiana
                              May 16, 19--

Adjustment Manager
Sears, Roebuck and Company
Chicago 7, Illinois

Dear Sir:

Let me begin by establishing a basic premise. It is possible to buy from a great mail-order house good, new merchandise, competitively priced, merchandise that mail-order house will stand behind. Right? Of course it is; Sears' whole business is based on that premise.

Well, my wife and I have been having trouble getting a new Kenmore vacuum sweeper from Sears by mail. We sent you our order and our check (for the Kenmore DeLuxe tank type cleaner) on April 16. A little over a week later one came. It had been insecurely packaged, and it had obviously fallen out of the box onto some hard surface before it was delivered to us. The result: a marred, dented sweeper. We returned it promptly with a letter explaining that since the sweeper was intended for a gift we wanted a new, perfect one.

Another sweeper arrived today. It had not fallen out of its box; it was wrapped carefully. But it had been used--not just once, but often--enough to scratch the switch handle, scrape the paint off the belly, dent the intake, and bend the intake head so that it does not fit the sweeper body tightly. Perhaps it has been a demonstrator; perhaps it had been out on "ten day trial" (though if it got that much use in ten days it was pretty rough use). One thing is certain: it is a used sweeper.

I am returning the sweeper with this letter.

Now, here is where we get back to our basic premise. We want a Kenmore DeLuxe tank-type sweeper. We read about it in CONSUMER REPORTS; we like what we read. But we want a new sweeper, not a damaged one or a second-hand one. Is that too much to ask?

Of course we can buy a new sweeper down the block; we could have such a sweeper delivered yet today. But we are still sold on your product and on your company; we don't want a Hoover-- we want a Kenmore. But we do want it soon. Will you send us one soon, or will we be forced to accept a second-choice brand?

Sincerely yours,

James Harrison

James Harrison

15. In the *Business Periodical Index* look under "Complaints," "Customer Relations," and "Adjustments" for articles showing current thinking on the advantages and disadvantages of adjustment policies.

16. Collect a number of adjustment letters, analyze them for tone, and report orally to the class on effective tone in claim and adjustment dealings. Keep in mind that in speaking, as in writing, examples help clarify points and hold interest; so cite and quote from the letters you discuss.

17. Assume that the class is the customer service department of a retail company and *you are a relatively new member of the department.* Adjustment policies, you feel, are fair, but the tone of letters and telephone conversations is grudging. Basing your comments on "How To Turn Complaints into Extra

Sales" (which you heard as a convention talk), present your views for a more rational attitude toward adjustments.

18. Prepare a three-minute debate presentation on either side of the premise that the customer is always right.

19. As the manager of the "Complaint Department" in a firm prepare an entertaining eight-minute after-dinner talk on adjustments and claims. Your audience is college seniors majoring in retailing. For this assignment, draw on your own experience in selling, if any, and get ideas from personnel in local stores for incidents to relate in your talk. Since your purpose is affective, keep in mind that "all art is exaggerated," and that to speak artfully, you may need to "embroider" a bit. Hyperbole and vivid words are important tools in this assignment.

20. Some company magazines and newspapers have columns or pages featuring letters from customers complimenting personnel for courteous service and treatment. As company president or vice-president in charge of personnel, write an editorial to head this page in one issue. You will laud the personnel of the customer service department and also intimate that the exemplary service is the result of effective training of the persons receiving the compliments.

12

Credit and Collections

*So far as my coin would stretch; and where it would not, I have
used my credit.*—WILLIAM SHAKESPEARE, *King Henry IV, Part I*

"*Your last check has bounced again.*" [1]

In the two quotations above lies the basis for the discussion in this
chapter. The first is clear enough; it is the hub of today's business,
whether the transaction involves the youngster charging his daily ice
cream cone until he gets his allowance on Saturday or the financier who
"buys" the Empire State Building. Credit is used, where and when the
coin does not stretch. The second quotation reflects an attitude still
prevalent in collection writing. Because money is the lifeblood of a
business, many persons say we must be "business-like" in dealing with it.

Let's look momentarily at the meaning of "business-like." If the term
signifies that moneys owed should be paid, then there is no argument. If it
means, as was described in the preceding chapter, on adjustments, that
an air of gloom, suspicion, and unpleasantness should permeate the
operations of credit and collection departments, then there is need for
discussion—if not room for argument.

I borrow the expression "business-like about collections" from a credit-
collection manager of a large department store, who reached his present
position through his real ability in counseling customers and, in turn, in
collecting accounts. But he came into the position in the years when
credit played a smaller, more "person-to-person" part in the business than
it does today. Talking with a customer at his desk or on the telephone,
he is still the soul of understanding and compassion; but his correspondence is quite another matter. New employees in the department

---

[1] The opening sentence of a collection letter from a manufacturer.

who have attempted to inject into collection letters the very feeling that the manager displays in person are thwarted. Any appeal deviating from threat, command, or compulsion is considered unbusiness-like. The manager's blind spot precludes his accepting the fact that understanding can be shown in writing as well as in personal conference.

Although we are dealing with both oral and written communication, more attention will be given in this chapter to the written, because credit and collection matters are conducted generally through correspondence. There will be discussion later in the chapter about use of the telephone in collections.

To allay possible fear that the next pages are to be a plea for pity, an admonition for "sweet talk," or encouragement to give customers unlimited time to pay, I will summarize the teachings of the chapter at the outset: Collect the money, and keep the customer—if he is good for the company—to help make a profit.

Part of a company's *raison d'être* is service—service to its customers (in merchandise paid for), to the community (in contributions to organizations, city projects, etc.), to its employees (profit-sharing plans, scholarships to employees and their relatives). But without profit, these services are not possible, of course.

CREDIT—WHAT IT IS

In general, "credit" is the transaction of business in terms of promises to pay instead of immediate payment. The word comes from the Latin *credo*, meaning "I believe" or "I trust." In any satisfactory credit transaction this element of belief, or faith, must exist on both sides: the buyer must intend to pay and believe that he can pay; the seller must believe that the buyer can pay and that he will, within the terms of his agreement.

VOLUME AND NATURE OF CREDIT BUSINESS

For the most part, credit transactions are highly satisfactory in American business. More than 99 per cent of payments promised in credit transactions are paid ultimately, from 30 to 40 per cent with no prodding or difficulty whatever. It has been estimated that more than 90 per cent of wholesale business (manufacturer or jobber to dealer) and 60 per cent of retail business is done on credit.

Why do purchasers prefer to pay later rather than at once? There are numerous reasons. The retailer makes a direct financial gain through being able to operate on less capital. If the average value of goods on his shelves is $10,000 and his monthly turnover is $5,000, he can, by using his thirty days' credit, operate on $5,000 capital instead of $10,000. You can see that credit enables him to double the volume of his business. And if he sends a dozen orders a month to one supplier, it is much more convenient and economical to remit once than to do so a dozen times. Or, if he pays within the discount period of ten days, as well-established businesses tend to do, even the short period is a great convenience.

The retail customer who maintains one or more charge accounts derives many advantages. By credit purchases he *establishes credit*. The cash purchaser is largely anonymous, whereas the charge customer leaves a complete record of his purchases and his business habits. The charge customer receives notices of sales that are not advertised to the general public, or not until a later date. His credit enables him to take advantage of these sales, whether or not he has the cash in hand. Moreover, purchases bought on credit can be returned for credit more conveniently than cash purchases can be returned for cash. Stores esteem their regular charge customers and accord them the best of treatment.

KINDS OF CREDIT

Thus far we have spoken chiefly in terms of direct credit relations between seller and buyer: mercantile credit and retail credit. There is also the large volume of intermediate credit business handled by the banks, which cater both to businessmen and to retail purchasers. Banks regularly supply a great deal of working capital for businesses, from large manufacturers all the way down to small retailers. But the bank does not create credit. The banker must judge whether the borrower can be trusted to pay as agreed upon; that is, whether or not he possesses *actual credit*. In making loans, banks ordinarily require security, usually in the form of accommodation indorsers on a note, or a mortgage on real or personal property. The Federal Government also grants credit; for example, to banks and companies through the Reconstruction Finance Corporation and to individuals through such agencies as the Agricultural Adjustment Agency of the Department of Agriculture.

A borrower's credit may be either *potential* or *actual*. Anyone who has the ability to meet obligations at a later date has potential credit, which varies with the measure of his ability to pay. When a person establishes a credit relationship with a jobber, store, or bank, he begins to translate at least part of his potential credit into actual credit. If he has a department store charge account which entitles him to charge $100 worth of merchandise monthly, his full potential credit is $100. If, say, by the twentieth of the month he has charged $70, his actual credit is then $70, and his potential credit is the difference between $100 and that figure, or $30. But when he pays his bill at the beginning of the next month, his potential credit returns to the original amount, or that amount less any new purchases he has made up to the date of payment. Thus, potential credit, in normal credit relationships, is constantly being translated into actual credit and back again.

THE THREE C's OF CREDIT

Authorities are in agreement that credit may be most conveniently measured in terms of Character, Capital, and Capacity. The meaning of these three terms is partly self-evident, but each will be discussed briefly.

Character is defined by psychologists as the sum total of an individual's characteristics. In relation to credit, character is the individual's tendency to make good on his financial obligations. This is partly the recognition of the binding quality of contractual relations, which is simple honesty, and partly a matter of habits. First, of course, comes the *intention,* the recognition of the obligation. Next in importance, after intention, or honesty, are business-like *habits.* Vague and general intentions to make payments when promised are worth little if the borrower is not systematic enough to make the promises good, but the intent to do right is fundamental. Once he is sure of the borrower's character, the credit man can ordinarily cope with bad business habits and to some extent with unpredictable misfortunes.

For business purposes character includes associations and appearances. When J. P. Morgan wanted to assist a deserving young man, he walked across the floor of the New York Stock Exchange with him. Thereafter the young man's credit was much greater than before. In his famous *Autobiography* Benjamin Franklin tells how as a young man he took pains to rise early and begin work ahead of others, making sure that those whose business favor he needed saw him on the streets and in his shop.

Capital is defined as the amount of property owned by an individual or company at a given time. But credit is not always high where there is much property although the chances favor it. If a widow has been left a $50,000 home and a half million dollars in cash and bonds, her credit will be good until she proves it otherwise. A retail hardware merchant with enough working capital to keep his shelves filled and his bills paid regularly within the discount period is more highly esteemed as a credit risk than one who can barely pay within the net period.

Capacity has a less definite meaning. In general it refers to the individual or company as a going concern rather than as a fixed entity. It is compounded of current income, business ability, occupational stability, health, and other factors, not disregarding common sense. Many persons spend a great deal of money without ever acquiring any considerable amount of capital. This is true especially of professional people—teachers, doctors, and some lawyers—and of salaried persons generally. A salary of $10,000 a year equals the earnings on $200,000 of capital at 5 per cent; hence, so long as the continuance of the salary is reasonably certain, the salaried person has a business worth comparable to that of the individual with $200,000 of invested capital and no earned income. The risk in deal-

WOodlawn 3-3460

The Esterbrook Pen Company

Delaware Avenue and Cooper Street, Camden 1, New Jersey, U.S.A.

Cable Address · Esterbrook, Camden

GOLD MEDAL

Gentlemen:

W - h - o - o - s - h !

Every day news reports are filled with satellite launchings
and projected world plans for outer space travel.

Thank heavens, I don't have to look to the skies nor conjure
up dreams of things to come. Esterbrook has its own shining orbit . . .
our prompt paying accounts.

These are down to earth folks, real business persons who
reach their pinnacle of success by hard work, high principles of
financial responsibility and an excellent record of remittance consistency.

People like you are the stars of my credit firmament.
Your brilliant acumen and clear operation have guided me to a
celestial appreciation of how luck my star is . . . in having you as a
customer.

Sincerely,

B. E. Van Dyke
Credit Manager

Esterbrook

A M E R I C A ' S   O L D E S T   P E N   M A K E R

Fig. 38. A "thank you" credit letter using current news interest for attention.
(By permission of the Dartnell Corporation.)

ing with the salaried person is of course somewhat greater, since it is
possible to collect from capital as well as income. Nevertheless, it is
apparent that the man who spends freely to maintain a high standard
of living is a more desirable customer, as long as he can meet his bills,
than the wealthy person who spends less. And the small retailer who
does a thriving business on small capital may be a better risk than the
large retailer with three times the capital and one third the turnover.

Are all the three C's present in every satisfactory credit risk? Analysis will show that where character is present, one of the other C's may be largely dispensed with. Character and capital can make a good risk if the capital is well invested; character and capacity are enough provided employment is stable and business conditions are good. This is the formula: Character plus capital and capacity, or character plus either capital or capacity, equals business credit. Preferably, of course, both capital and capacity should be found combined with character, but character is practically indispensable.

CLASSES OF CREDIT RISKS

Credit customers are classified according to how they handle their obligations. The seller divides them into three groups: (1) good pay, (2) good-but-slow pay, and (3) poor pay.

Roughly one-third of all retail charge customers pay within the regular period (by the 10th or 15th of the month following purchases) with no urging of any sort. Another third pay in full with relatively little urging. Of the remaining third, the poor-pay group, all but about 5 per cent will pay under the pressure of a good collection system. Even most of the stubborn 5 per cent, who resist payment strongly (they represent the credit department's bad guesses), will eventually pay, but so slowly and so reluctantly that their business is usually not worth retaining.

The good-pay customers are of course the most profitable. Then why bother with the others? The competitive situation is such that most stores could not get sufficient volume of business from the good-pay class alone. The good-but-slow-pay group is well worth having too, and even the better part of the poor-pay group. The credit policy varies, even within the same store, with the group dealt with. The better stores usually cater to the higher type of risk, hence they maintain more liberal credit terms. Credit jewelers and certain credit clothiers maintain very strict credit and collection policies.

ESTABLISHING THE CREDIT RELATIONSHIP

The credit relationship is established in three ways:

1. The customer requests credit.
2. The customer sends an order without remittance, expecting the seller to take the initiative in establishing credit relations.
3. The seller invites the buyer to establish credit relations.

All three ways are used a great deal. In retail transactions the customer usually requests credit. He is given a credit application form to fill out, on which he is asked to state his occupation, the name of his employer, previous credit dealings, and banking and personal references.

Then the store conducts such credit investigations as it deems necessary by means of credit inquiry letters. The following was used by one large department store:

Dear Mr. Smith:

We shall appreciate any information which you may give us on the financial responsibility and promptness in meeting obligations of Mr. John Robinson, 1932 East Ohio Street. Mr. Robinson has informed us that he is employed by Midwestern University, 1634 East Randolph Street. Your reply, which may be made below, will be held in confidence.

Yours very truly,

For mercantile transactions (manufacturer-dealer, jobber-dealer), it is common practice for the dealer merely to send in an order. Then the seller consults commercial credit rating associations (Dun & Bradstreet or local credit associations), and if necessary sends a credit application form, which may call for the name of the dealer's bank, a record of his previous credit dealings, and a statement of his assets, liabilities, net worth, and profits. When it is necessary to ask for credit information, the writer must exercise tact to avoid reflection on the customer's credit standing. The following letter embodies good procedure:

Dear Mr. Crawford:

Thank you for your order of May 9. It is a pleasure to welcome you into the Clothes Clean family.

While we are anxious to forward the washing machines without delay, it is our company policy to make the usual inquiries regarding credit. Will you, therefore, please furnish the names of several firms you have done business with recently?

You of course realize that it will take a little time to check the references. Therefore, if the units are needed right away, may we ship them C.O.D.? They will be sent the same day your letter is received and the full cash discount will be deducted in advance.

We sincerely hope that this is the beginning of many years of pleasant and mutually profitable business relations.

Very truly yours,

CLOTHES CLEAN COMPANY

Credit Manager

The seller may invite the buyer to purchase on credit. This is done especially in retail business with cash customers of long standing or with selected groups who are thought to be good risks. One Chicago department store issued credit cards to all faculty members of a university. Not all took advantage of this implied compliment to their profession, but for a number it was the beginning of charge account relations that continued indefinitely. The enterprising seller will not always wait for the buyer to take the initiative. Consider the following letter soliciting the opening of a charge account:

Dear Mrs. Jones:

Have you realized the convenience of saying, "Charge it, please"?

Our Credit Department takes the position that a customer who has shown that he deserves credit should enjoy the great convenience of a Charge Account. You have been making cash purchases in our store now for five years. Don't misunderstand us—we're glad to have you as a cash customer—but we thought you'd like to know that you have established credit with us that is waiting to be used.

A charge account has a number of advantages. Charge customers receive notices of bargain merchandise which is in lots too small for newspaper advertisement, and they receive letters announcing other sales several days before the public is informed through general advertisements. Ready cash is not needed for taking advantage of sales. Unsuitable merchandise may be conveniently returned for credit. Finally, by using your credit, you improve your credit standing—your credit record with us is available for transfer elsewhere.

At the beginning of each month, you receive your itemized statement of the previous month's purchases. You have until the 15th to make your payment, and you retain a permanent record of each item purchased.

Exciting new shipments of merchandise are coming in every day, and our buyers are scouring the country for styles and qualities to please you—and at prices that you will like.

To open a charge account you need only fill in and sign the enclosed simple form. As soon as we receive it, we will send you your charge-plate, which will enable you to make purchases as quickly as with cash. Then you too can say, "Charge it, please."

Very truly yours,

CREDIT DEPARTMENT

A few years ago the Shell Oil Company had a "noticeable" increase in charge-account customers through mailing credit cards to automobile owners who were not Shell customers. Prior investigation into the prospect's credit rating reduced risk. A direct approach to more charge accounts is in retail companies' conducting drives, with prizes to sales-people getting the most credit applications from cash customers. The J. C. Penney Company recently used this device.

RULES FOR CREDIT LETTERS IN DIFFERENT SITUATIONS

When the investigation indicates that the customer is an excellent credit risk, the credit man writes a letter congratulating the customer on his fine credit standing and stating that the account is ready for use. The alert credit man will also (1) describe one or more articles available for immediate purchase and (2) state the credit terms and policies concisely and clearly. Study the following letter from a manufacturer to a new dealer:

Dear Mr. Strawbridge:

Thank you for mailing us your Order No. 4632, and welcome to the vast family of Electro dealers. Your order is being filled and will be shipped today by express.

It is a pleasure to extend the convenience of an open account to you. Our terms are 2 per cent discount for cash within ten days and net for payment within thirty days from the normal delivery date.

Hoping to make our relationship pleasant and profitable for you, we have included advertising and display material with your order. These materials have been used to advantage by others of our customers.

I am also sending our current Catalogue No. 38, with the thought of its simplifying your stock needs. We take pride in our policy of filling orders within 48 hours and would look forward to your availing yourself of that service.

We shall serve you so as to merit your continued good will and patronage. And we invite your suggestions at any time that our service does not meet your expectations.

Yours very sincerely,

When the investigation leaves the customer's credit status doubtful, the credit man will ordinarily work for immediate cash business and hold out the hope of credit later. If the doubtful factor is the lack of capital in a small business, the customer's credit situation might conceivably improve within a short time.

If the investigation brings only negative results, credit is, of course, out of the question, and all that can be done is to refuse courteously and leave the door open for cash business. The next letter, also from a manufacturer to a dealer, shows judicious treatment.

Dear Mr. Byers:

We appreciate very much your interest in a business association
with our company, as indicated by your order and application
for credit sent on May 31.

Since we would like to establish a continuing account with your
company, I am sorry that the information immediately available
seems not to warrant approving the application.

I would, however, like to send you the material that you
selected, so may we send the order to you on a C.O.D. basis?
If you wish to send cash, we can ship it the same day we receive
word.

We welcome your business and, in turn, any comments for better-
ing what is already considered good service by our many satisfied customers.

Cordially yours,

CREDIT AND SALES

Credit and sales are closely related in industry, where credit policy
is generally based on salesmen's reports and collection strategy is often
suggested by salesmen who know the customers. The industrial credit
manager is sales-oriented in another way also: he recognizes that each
customer's potential credit is an important sales opportunity. He therefore attempts to persuade each customer to use his potential credit to
the limit. He may write the customer that by failing to put his potential
credit to work he is not making full use of his assets; usually, however,
he sends a message through the salesman inviting the customer to "buy
up to $——" without reservation, on the basis of his record.

Some alert retailers also attempt to increase the use of their customers'
untapped potential credit by inviting their charge customers to buy more,
to come in oftener, or to come to special sales for charge customers only.

Both of these letters were used by department stores:

Dear Friend:

There's much ado about Christmas at Mabley's these days. Our
shops and counters are filling with the most wonderful gift
items ever, and we're ready to ring the bell with our Yuletide
store decorations.

It has been a while since we have seen you, and we can't think
of a better time for you to pay us a visit. This is the time
of the year when the "Spirit of Christmas Towers High" at
Mabley's, and over one thousand cheerful employees are looking
forward to seeing you soon.

So, put your Charga-Plate in your purse or pocket and come on
down to Mabley's. Your charge account hasn't had its usual

calls lately—and we want you to know that it is still in good
working order, that all of us here at Mabley's are ready to
serve you.

                              Cordially,

                    (Printed on a blank monthly statement form)

                    My job is a pleasure
                    with customers like you—

                    Those who pay their bills so well
                    Are far between and few.

                    Yet—I have a problem—
                    And little problems mount.

                    Life will be more pleasant
                    If you'll use your charge account.

                              Yours very truly,

Collections

RELATION BETWEEN CREDIT POLICY AND COLLECTIONS

Just as a good mailing list makes for successful direct-mail selling, so
also a good credit policy makes for relatively easy and satisfactory collections. The credit man ordinarily cannot make or destroy credit; it is
his job to *recognize* it. We say that credit is *granted* or *refused.* In effect
this means that the credit man decides either that credit exists or that it
does not. He must scrutinize the three C's of credit carefully and add
them to ascertain whether or not the sum equals useful credit for his employer. Overcautious credit men make enemies in the sales department,
which works for volume; too liberal credit men invite trouble in the
collections department.

C. J. Martin, at one time Secretary of the National Consumer Credit
Reporting Corporation, said that a well-managed credit department
keeps its bad debt losses at .5 per cent. If losses are more than one-half
of 1 per cent, the policies are lax; if they are less than that, the policy
is too strict and loses business for the company. Of those people, Mr.
Martin said, whose accounts are 30 days past due, 17 per cent will trade
elsewhere; 53 per cent of those owing bills 60 days overdue will not
come back; and 71 per cent of the 90-days-overdue group will buy from
competitors.

It is apparent that credit and collections must go hand in hand. If
all people were honest, if no one ever yielded to the temptation to buy

beyond his means, and if no one were subject to misfortune, there would be few, if any, collection letters. But since these conditions won't be found outside Utopia, many collection letters have to be written. The better the credit policy, the fewer the letters, but there will always be some, and in large businesses a great many, because of the competitive situation already discussed.

The cost of letters leads some people to "write off" bad accounts; but indebtedness should be collected insofar as possible. Even if collection of the most stubborn accounts—those listed in Class 3 (poor pay)—leaves no net gain for the seller, the collection is warranted, for it has a salutary effect on the business as a whole. Going after the stubborn accounts discourages delinquency, and it encourages the man who pays his debts through relieving him of any fear that he is helping pay for the purchases of "dead beats."

THE BASIC RULE IN WRITING COLLECTION LETTERS

The writer of collection letters must do more than merely collect delinquent accounts; *he must get the money without offending the customer.* The old-style collection letter, which "burst into tears in the first sentence and screamed for the law in the second," is now definitely out of fashion. A considerable percentage of the firm's business volume is with the slow-pay customer; if he is worth having at all (and for the most part he is), he is worth keeping. When you write your collection letters, then, remember that your job is twofold: to get the money, and to keep the customer.

PSYCHOLOGY OF COLLECTIONS: THE APPEALS

Practically no one likes to part with money, especially for something already used. Even the spendthrift would rather make a new purchase than pay for an old one. Why, then, do certain customers pay under collection pressure when they fail to pay on their own initiative? There are many reasons, but the following six are the important ones:

1. Having the attention prodded
2. Recognition of seller's need
3. Fear
4. Pride—self-interest
5. Honor—fair play
6. A favorable mood, perhaps induced by humor

For the good-but-slow-pay customer, prodding the attention tactfully is usually all that is required. The fuel company notice shown in Figure 39 has the additional advantage of making action easy.

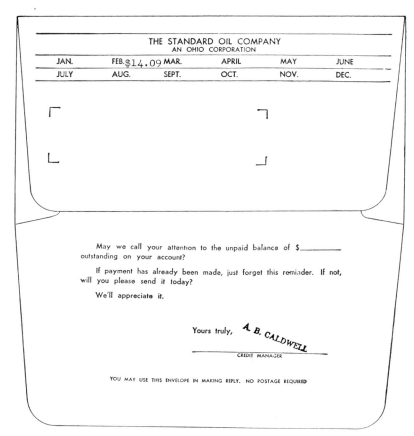

Fig. 39. Reminder, printed under the flap of a business reply envelope. (Used by permission.)

This form notice was used by a wholesaler:

Gentlemen:

"The wheel that squeaks the loudest gets the most grease," they say.

But I don't like to listen to squeaking, and neither do you.

Will you help me disprove the adage by sending your check for $287.75 today?

Cordially,

These two form letters were used by department stores:

Dear Customer:

We have always felt that any letters to our customers regarding their accounts with us, to be successful, should be both brief and friendly.

This letter is brief, and there should be no question regarding its friendliness.

Won't you make it successful by sending us your check covering the payment currently due on your account?

Simply detach this letter at the perforation and enclose with your remittance in the attached envelope. If your payment has been sent to us, please accept our thanks and disregard this letter.

                              Yours very truly,

Dear Mr. Smith:

We haven't received payment of your account, $30.84.

If there is any question about the amount, please let us know. Otherwise, your remittance at this time will be appreciated.

                              Yours very truly,

Perhaps the oldest form of collection letter was some variation of "We need the money." This is basically the weakest of all appeals for a number of reasons; among them, the three outstanding ones are (1) it violates the principle of the "you" attitude; (2) it easily offends the average intelligence, because the debtor *knows* that a firm needs to collect accounts, to stay in business; and (3) it is negative psychologically, in that the appeal tends to suggest that the company is in straits. People identify with success; they do not like to be associated with failure.

Among expressions that imply, or state, these three conditions, in the order named, are: (1) "We want . . ." (2) "Surely you understand that we have to have our money." This offensive statement was used for about six months by a new credit manager in a lamp manufacturing concern, until salesmen and other representatives began reporting to the home office the customers' unfavorable reaction to such collection practices. (3)"We appeal to you in a sense of fairness. We have filled your orders, but we cannot restock until we have received payment on

ERSAL MATCH CORPORATION
STITUTION KEYED TO LEADERSHIP AND DEDICATED TO SERVICE
urers of ADVERTISING BOOK MATCHES AND ALL TYPES OF WOOD MATCHES

GENERAL OFFICES
SAINT LOUIS 3, MISSOURI

It is a pleasure to bring an overlooked invoice to your attention.

You always handle it immediately.

November 8   #11069 $74.00

                          Appreciatively

                          UNIVERSAL MATCH CORPORATION

ED MEIRINK:EHA   Credit Manager

FACTORIES AND SALES OFFICES COAST TO COAST

Fig. 40. A brief collection letter from the Universal Match Corporation, using pride as the appeal in a most positive manner. (Used by permission of the Dartnell Corporation.)

Dear New Subscriber:

It's good to know you want to see things ...

to see life; to see the world; to

eyewitness great events; to watch the faces of the

poor and the gestures of the proud; to

see strange things -- machines, armies, multi-

tudes, shadows in the jungle and on the moon;

to see man's work -- his paintings,

towers and discoveries; to see things

thousands of miles away, things hidden behind

walls and within rooms, things

dangerous to come to; the women that men love

and many children; to see and take

pleasure in seeing; to see and be amazed;

to see and be instructed. Thank you for your order!

Cordially,

NE The Editors of

From David Wells, Credit Manager:
   Sorry to add a commercial P.S. to this letter in the form of
the enclosed bill -- but you asked us to charge you for your
subscription. And it would be most considerate of you if you
would send us your remittance today (returning the enclosed
bill so we can properly credit your account). Thank you!

Fig. 41. A picture-story letter. This *Life* letter used bright colors—reds, yellows
—and it got results. (Used by permission of *Life*.)

our many outstanding accounts." It is not difficult to see how a customer might, in cursory reading of the loosely stated appeal, visualize a "sinking ship."

A number of companies do use the need approach in humor in early letters in a collection series. One example, which is still used although many younger customers are not familiar with one of the terms, is a form letter with a small feather attached to the page. The message opens with "Have you ever lifted a feather? Wasn't heavy, was it? But have you ever carried a featherbed? That's the situation we're in right now. Your account is a feather, but our total accounts are like the featherbed."

Since *fear* is a powerful instinct, and perhaps partly because some human beings like to see others squirm, many collection letters include a threat of some kind. The trend, however, is to use threats much less than formerly. Remembering that his job is not only to collect the account but also to keep the good will and future business of the customer, and knowing that people tend to keep away from what has made them afraid, the collection man is cautious about appealing to fear. As education improves and knowledge of business methods becomes more generally known, people are less easily scared, anyway.

An interesting question discussed with credit men is whether the "you" attitude is possible when the fear appeal is used. Of course, fear is an emotion of the debtor, and we cannot ascertain his reaction to a proposed action to collect his overdue account. But we can refrain from a negative appeal; we can stress the positive. For example, many letters contain such expressions as "If you do not . . . , we will be forced to . . . ." Customer reaction would be more healthful, were the writer to inform the customer that "If you do . . . , we will not need to . . . ." The same action is to be taken, but the negative is in the company's step, making possible the power of *positive* suggestion for the customer's action.

Because they affect credibility in communication, two widely used "scare" expressions need looking at. "We will be forced to . . ." and "You leave us no alternative but to . . ." have long appeared in connection with "next-step" action in collection writing. In most instances, these statements involve more bristling of the creditor than bustling of the debtor. These appeals are incredible because there are other alternatives. Ridiculous though it may sound at first thought, one company alternative is to write off the account. This is not to be done, of course; but a writer can state the action to be taken without hiding behind a façade. Let the company take action it is legally and morally justified in taking; but let it do so in the spirit of "this is our right and responsibility," rather than "you are causing this."

The following is the text of a final-step letter used by a large furniture store:

Dear Customer:

If you wish to avoid having your account charged with a finance fee, it will be necessary that you immediately remit the arrears, which now amount to _____.

The charge mentioned above, at the present writing, amounts to _____, and increases the longer the account is unpaid.

We sincerely trust that immediate arrangements will be made to bring your account up to date.

Respectfully yours,

The letter on page 341 "says" the same thing as the preceding one, but in a quite different tone. Suppose that you received both of these letters and compare your reactions.

Pride was included by the medieval scholastics as one, and sometimes the chief, of the seven deadly sins. It can be a fault, but functioning within bounds it is a powerful urge to constructive action. Certainly pride in credit standing is one of the most powerful collection appeals. A large department store sends this letter to long-time customers whose accounts remain unpaid for a period of time:

Dear Sir:

You usually pay your bills promptly; the present bill must have been overlooked. May we expect payment within the next two weeks?

Yours very truly,

The following more urgent letter combines appeals to pride and to fair play:

Gentlemen:

In checking recently with Mr. Harry Wilson, Treasurer of the Wesley Men's Bible Class, on the accounts which I solicited for the annual <u>Directory</u>, I learned that your account of $3.50 for 1/8 page advertising space was unpaid, the only one of my accounts of which this was true.

The Delcliff Grocery and Market, if it is the kind of business that I have thought of it as being, does not want local advertising space which it has contracted but not paid for.

There must have been an oversight or slip of some sort. Won't you please give the matter your immediate capable attention?

Very sincerely yours,

THIS DOES THE JOB EXCEPT WHEN HOPELESS

The frank, cordial, but firm tone of this letter has made it successful and frequently used. The third of a series for delinquent accounts, it manages to convey a feeling of urgency without antagonizing the debtor. Gold Medal awarded to G. J. Gonord, copywriter.

GLOVERS ADVERTISING

Incorporated Practitioners in Advertising

MARK LANE · BRISTOL 1

TELEGRAMS 25483 · DIRECTORS: C. GLOVER, A.I.P.A., F. GLOVER, G. SHERIDAN-SHEDDEN

Don't you find that "overdue account" letters are difficult to write - especially when to a client whose business you value and whom you respect?

We've written you twice now, and frankly don't know how to word this one.

Won't you help us out by sending your cheque today - please.

Yours faithfully,
for GLOVERS ADVERTISING.

G. J. Gonord

GOLD MEDAL

Fig. 42. A collection letter using the appeal of a problem common to the creditor and the debtor. (By permission of the Dartnell Corporation.)

(Dartnell File: L-4, CREDIT AND COLLECTIONS)

Gentlemen:

You will probably wonder why this rubber band is fastened to this letter. It has been put there to illustrate a rather important business principle.

If you will take this rubber band and stretch it just as far as you can, you will observe that the more it is stretched, the more resistance it offers to be stretched. You will also find that when a certain point is reached, it will snap and break. That point is known as the "breaking point".

Your credit and this rubber band have much in common. Once it breaks, the most important asset in your business is lost—your reputation for paying bills promptly.

Why not get out your check book and send us a check for at least a portion of your account. It is tremendously important so far as your good name is concerned. Do it now.

Yours very truly,

HUBER SLIPPER CO., INC.

L.F.Huber

Secretary

LFH:R

Comfort for Busy Feet and Leisure Hours

Fig. 43. Compare or contrast the tone in this letter and the one regarding finance fee on page 339. (This letter used by permission of the Dartnell Corporation.)

This letter collected the small sum that had been long unpaid after a personal call on the store manager had failed. It provides a natural transition to the next point, the appeal to honor or fair play. Although there is a great deal of chicanery in the world, most men *intend* to play fair and respond amazingly when put on their honor in a tactful way.

Samuel Sewall, a leader among the colonial businessmen who made coastal New England one of the great trading centers of the world, realized the value of appealing to the debtor's honor. The language is quaint, but the collection psychology is up to date.

Dec. 3d, 1700

To Mr. Jn' Williams of Barbadoes

Sir, I presume the old verse 'If knocking thrice, no one comes go off', is not to be understood of creditors in demanding their just debts. The tenth year is now current since I lent you ten pounds, merely out of respect to you as a stranger and a scholar: you having then met with disappointment by the loss of effects sent for your support. You have written to me that you would not let my kindness rot under the clods of ingratitude. But there has been hitherto vox *and* praeterea nihil *[a promise and no pay]. I am come again to knock at your door to enquire if any ingenuity or honor dwell there. Not doubting but if there do I shall reap benefit by it and that you will pay to my order the money which I sent you gratis July 23d 1691, of which I have not received one penny.*[2]

The following letter from a credit clothier is more in the modern manner:

Dear Mr. Smith:

We again find it necessary to remind you that payments on your account are past due.

Most surely you meant it when in making your purchase you agreed on certain terms.

Kindly send your remittance according to the terms of the con-tract. It should not be necessary to write each time a payment is due.

Very truly yours,

QUALITY CLOTHING COMPANY

Credit Manager

Still another kind of appeal in collection letters is that which induces action through promoting a *favorable mood*, or state of mind. The individual devoid of a sense of humor is fortunately rare. When the corners of his mouth are tilting up, a person will part with money more

[2] N. H. Chamberlain, *Samuel Sewall and the World He Lived In* (Boston: DeWolfe, Fiske & Co., 1897), pp. 93–94.

readily. The success of the "piece of string" letters (based on Mother's device of tying a string around Johnny's finger so he won't forget his errand) used by many firms, especially magazine publishers, is due more than anything else to the homely humorous touch. In general, the humorous collection letter works best with the well-educated and well-to-do customers whose non-payment is due chiefly to carelessness, and when amounts due are small.

The next letter is almost a classic from long use in various versions:

```
A few weeks ago we sent a letter to several hundred readers
reminding them that their subscriptions were in arrears and
gently hinting that an early remittance would be appreciated.

A percentage of them promptly paid up.  Some replied that they
would pay "next week" or "next month" but two of these died
within the week.  Another said he would pay the "next time" he
saw us.  He went blind.  And yet another telephoned that he
would "run down and pay sometime."  He has rheumatism now and
can't even walk.  Jim said he would "see us in h—— first."
He got religion that night and will not be able to keep the
appointment.

We have had no word from the others and you happen to be one
of them.  We have not taken your name off the list as yet
because it seems "sorter" natural to see it there.

We have been pretty good sports to leave it there all this time.
Won't you be an equally good sport and see that it stays "put."
We can't carry you indefinitely.[3]
```

Extraordinary politeness, as exemplified in the following letter used by a commercial tire and supply company, also ranks high in producing a paying mood. This appeal is perhaps especially satisfactory with women customers:

```
Dear Madam:

You know—

    —how hard it is to ask for money

    —and say just enough to get it

    —without offending

Your check may be on its way.  If not, we know you will send it
immediately.

In either case, thank you.

                    Cordially yours,

Balance $12.35.
```

[3] *ABWA Bulletin,* September, 1939, p. 4. Reprinted from the London *Free Press.*

540 N. MICHIGAN AVE. • CHICAGO 11 • ILLINOIS

Dear Subscriber:

　　These four little dogs from Africa are called
Basenjis --

　　-- and I am sending you their picture because
they never bark nor yelp, but only softly "grooo".

　　TIME never barks either, about overdue bills
like this one -- nor are we as worried about your
account as these four little Basenjis seem to be.

　　But I would like to mark this bill "Paid" --
and stop "groooing" to you about it in the mails.

　　So please will you attach a check to it and
return it to me today?

　　　　　　　　　　　　　Cordially,

　　　　　　　　　　　　　Charles Mason

CM-H   Credit Manager

Fig. 44. This collection letter brings a smile. A former employee of Time,
Inc., reported that one *Time* subscriber wrote that he enjoyed the *Time* collection
letters so much that he was not going to pay until he had received the entire
series, whereupon a member of the correspondence department sent him the
series at one time. The subscriber sent his check. (By permission of *Time*.)

We have discussed six kinds of appeal, but it is apparent that some of the best collection letters *combine* two or three appeals. The *Time* letter on page 344 combines humor with reminder; the letter of Sam Sewall, humor and honor; the Huber Slipper Company letter, humor and pride (self-interest); and the Delcliff Grocery and Market letter on page 339, reminder and honor. For best results, then, decide upon the logical dominant appeal, and, if advisable, combine other appeals with it to make the strongest possible letter. Somehow, the collection letter must create the *urge to pay*, must make the tendency toward payment achieve dominance over any kind of natural tendency to withhold.

And whatever the appeal, or appeals, employed, the letter as a whole must be specific. A keynote here, as elsewhere in business, is *definite-*

When Unearned Discount Is Taken

Gentlemen:

Pennies make dollars—in profits or losses. Results at year-end are merely an accumulation of these minor amounts.

Cash discount contributes to this profit factor and as such is of mutual interest. To you it represents added profit on your sales of Lily products— to us, the prompt return of our capital invested in goods shipped.

We feel it is only good business for our customers to take advantage of this opportunity for added profit. This discount, however, is only offered on payments mailed within the discount periods as shown on our invoice. Payments not mailed within the dates specified in our terms do not earn maximum discount.

In applying your Check #8097 mailed May 20, we notice you have taken full 2 per cent discount, although in referring to the dates of the invoices being paid, this maximum discount period expired prior to the mailing date of your check.

Perhaps these invoices could not be paid within the discount period because of some omission on our part. If this is the case, please tell us and we will cancel the enclosed debit. Thank you.

Cordially yours,

Fig. 45. Unearned discount letter. (By permission of the Dartnell Corporation.)

ness. The credit man emphasizes date and terms of payment; the collection man must do the same. "Soon," "within a short time," "within a reasonable period," are far less effective than "by June 15," "within ten days," "not later than July 14, two weeks from today." And the amount due should be given in each letter.

A final point to remember is that many people just don't know how to manage their affairs well; their ability to see into and plan their financial future is limited. Often it is not enough to put pressure upon these people to pay; one must also *show them how to pay,* help them plan their budgets, arrange the terms of payment—do everything except make the money for them. With such customers, the first necessity is to get a frank response from them, even if it is unaccompanied by any

Requesting Payment of Unearned Discount

Dear Mr. Jones:

Thank you for your check for $61.50, but it was rather surprising to find that you took the 2% cash discount ten days after the time limit.

As you of course know, for many, many years standard merchandising terms have been 2% cash within ten days from date of invoice, or net thirty days. Cash discount is a reward for prompt payment. Buyers, therefore, have the choice of the cash saving or the longer time to use their money. But I am sure you will agree that no one is entitled to <u>both</u> the discount <u>and</u> the extra time.

That 2% is a highly desirable saving. To many firms it amounts to about one-fourth of their net profits. That's why we always try to discount our own bills. But only as our customers pay promptly can we do this, and then pass on to them the benefits in low prices and good merchandise.

I am sure you realize the justice of this and will OK the enclosed invoice for payment. We appreciate your business and feel sure you will understand our position.

Cordially,

Fig. 46. Unearned discount letter. (By permission of the Dartnell Corporation.)

payment, and then to help them plan. Often they will be most grateful for your help in enabling them to pay their debts and regain their self-respect. Less troublesome, but somewhat in the same class, is the person who suffers temporary financial embarrassment because of family illness, say, or business reverses. Since he is already unhappy, your collection letters must be extraordinarily cheerful, considerate, and helpful.

Another step often necessary in the collection process is a letter after payment has been received. A discount customer sometimes remits payment, having taken the deduction, after the discount period has expired. Such irregularity requires a reminder of the credit policy. The letters in Figures 45 and 46 handle this situation with fairness, forthrightness, and reasoning.

HOW DIFFERENT BUSINESS SITUATIONS AFFECT COLLECTION PROCEDURE

Although the psychology involved is much the same throughout, collection procedure differs considerably with the business situation. The jobber's relation to the retailer is not the same as the department store's to the retail customer; installment selling has its special problems, as does direct mail.

Since the manufacturer or jobber has a relatively large volume of business with a relatively small number of customers, he investigates each credit situation with great care. Terms of sale have an important influence on prompt payment, for the retailer who discounts his bills gains a worth-while business advantage over his more lagging competitor. It is apparent that the appeal to pride and self-interest will be most successful in these mercantile situations, with fair play, fear, and simple prodding following, perhaps in that order.

A great number of collection letters are written by department stores and other retail establishments to their customers. The volume of business with each customer is usually small, but the total is important. Large department stores have worked out elaborate series of collection notices and letters. In some cases the collection writer has fifty or more form letters to choose from; nevertheless, for the more difficult, or more important, situations he will compose original, personalized letters. A typical department store sequence will run somewhat as follows:

1. Monthly statement (not considered a bill) mailed the first of the month following purchases
2. Second statement, sometimes including a stamped notice to show that the payment is overdue
3. Brief printed notice, calling attention to charge account terms
4. Short letter inquiring whether there has been dissatisfaction with purchases or any question concerning the amount of the bill

5. Longer letter of discussion reviewing the situation and asking for immediate payment or an explanation
6. Letter applying firmer pressure through threat to turn the account over to a collection agency or resort to legal action
7. Ultimatum letter, giving the customer a specified number of days to pay in order to avert legal action

An example of the ultimatum letter from a manufacturer shows that collections can be made without a nagging or quarrelsome tone to the customer:

Gentlemen:

It seldom becomes necessary for us to turn an account over to an attorney for collection. On those few occasions when circumstances warrant, we consider it only fair to tell the customer exactly what we intend to do.

We have made every effort, I believe, to be fair and patient in requesting that you settle your December account of $109.30. We have written several times, asking that you let us know how we could cooperate with you in straightening out this indebtedness.

Because of your continued silence, we shall refer your account to our attorney for collection— a step that we sincerely regret. So won't you respond to this final appeal for your cooperation, and thereby avoid a procedure that can only mean embarrassment, inconvenience, and additional expense to you.

Unless we hear from you by February 22nd, we shall transfer your account to the office of our attorney. Please use the enclosed reply envelope to let us hear from you.

                              Cordially,

                              THE ESTERBROOK PEN COMPANY

                              B. E. Van Dyke

                              Credit Manager [4]

Not all sequences will include both Nos. 6 and 7. A telephone call may be substituted for No. 4, 5, or 6, and a telegram for No. 6 or 7. When the account is actually turned over to a collection agency, or a lawyer, at least one letter will ordinarily be sent (on an impressive letterhead) before final action is taken.

The *spacing* of the items in a collection series will vary greatly. Old, established accounts will not be dunned until the account is two or three

[4] Adapted from a letter from The Esterbrook Pen Company, which won a Gold Medal award for Mr. Van Dyke. (Used by permission of the Dartnell Corporation.)

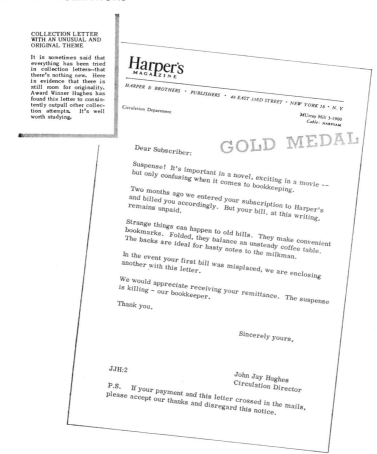

COLLECTION LETTER
WITH AN UNUSUAL AND
ORIGINAL THEME

It is sometimes said that
everything has been tried
in collection letters—that
there's nothing new. Here
is evidence that there is
still room for originality.
Award Winner Hughes has
found this letter to consistently outpull other collection attempts. It's well
worth studying.

Harper's
MAGAZINE

HARPER & BROTHERS · PUBLISHERS · 49 EAST 33RD STREET · NEW YORK 16 · N. Y.

Circulation Department

MUrray Hill 3-1900
Cable: HARPSAM

GOLD MEDAL

Dear Subscriber:

Suspense! It's important in a novel, exciting in a movie --
but only confusing when it comes to bookkeeping.

Two months ago we entered your subscription to Harper's
and billed you accordingly. But your bill, at this writing,
remains unpaid.

Strange things can happen to old bills. They make convenient
bookmarks. Folded, they balance an unsteady coffee table.
The backs are ideal for hasty notes to the milkman.

In the event your first bill was misplaced, we are enclosing
another with this letter.

We would appreciate receiving your remittance. The suspense
is killing - our bookkeeper.

Thank you.

Sincerely yours,

JJH:2

John Jay Hughes
Circulation Director

P.S.   If your payment and this letter crossed in the mails,
please accept our thanks and disregard this notice.

Fig. 47. Another example of a collection letter to "jog" a subscriber's memory. (Used by permission of the Dartnell Corporation.)

months in arrears, and the entire sequence may take from six months
to a year. Stores dealing with low income groups, or any store dealing
with refractory accounts, will begin applying pressure almost immediately, running through the sequence (not always all of the seven items)
in from six weeks to three months.

The collection policy for installment selling does not differ greatly
from that for charge accounts, much installment selling being done by
stores which also use charge accounts—for large purchases which go
over the customer's established charge account limits, or for customers
not maintaining charge accounts. The credit situation may be more
strained, since purchases are often large and frequently purchasers have

relatively little credit; hence the tendency is to be somewhat stricter. Strictness would be still more necessary were it not for the fact that title to installment-bought merchandise ordinarily rests with the seller until the last payment has been made. Auto finance companies have developed extremely successful collection techniques, including actual repossession of a considerable number of cars. In general, installment selling uses the appeal to fear more than charge account selling, and is less elaborately polite, though tact here, as in all business dealings, is important.

Direct-mail selling depends to an extraordinarily large extent on effective collection letters. Some direct-mail business, to be sure, involves cash in advance or cash on delivery, but it includes also much installment buying and a considerable number of trial-offer and deferred-payment sales. The magazines particularly, notably *Time* and *Newsweek*, flourish through the effectiveness of their subscription-extension letters, which may be classified as collection letters rather than sales letters, though they are something of both.

ECONOMIC CONDITIONS AND COLLECTION POLICY

As long as the wheels of industry are turning smoothly, it is easy to see that tomorrow's income is practically as good as cash and that it is logical to buy things with it. Not until recession comes do we realize that future income is really an intangible and that credit may mean debt.

Look at Joe Jones, making $85 a week, paying $15 on his car, $5 on his refrigerator, and $5 on his television set. He owes $60 to a furniture dealer, $50 to a grocer, $45 to the coal dealer. Yet there is money for everything he needs. He is sitting on top of the world—until he loses his job. Then he finds himself with no income except unemployment compensation. He has an installment obligation which he will be unable to meet if he is to buy food and shelter. When he reads the small print he will find that the installment contracts become due and payable all at once if a payment or two is skipped.

How would you advise the coal dealer to collect that $45 coal bill from Joe? The dealer finds that almost everyone in town shares Joe's predicament. He himself will be unable to get more coal to sell unless he can make payments on his own bills to his suppliers. Obviously he can't sue his customers for his money and keep the good will that he needs to stay in business. There is only one way open to him:

He must get there FIRST with a PLAN.

He must talk it over with Joe, by letter or in person, and show him that coal is important to him, so important that he will want to pay off the bill at $1 or $2 a week in return for the dealer's promise to make sure the house is heated next winter, whatever the emergency. If he waits until Joe's other creditors have talked with him he will be too late.

There is no short cut to collecting money in what is euphemistically called an economic emergency. If a company cannot adjust its collection policy to meet the customers' problems on their own grounds, the company's days are numbered. The best hedge against emergency—a conservative credit policy—is hard to enforce and explain in prosperous times.

THE TELEGRAM AND THE TELEPHONE CALL IN COLLECTING

The *telegram* has its greatest usefulness near the end of a collection series, where the urgency that this form of communication always suggests is of special value. Obviously, it will be used for relatively large indebtednesses more often than for small ones. But we should remember that a short telegram may actually cost less than a long letter requiring the time of a dictator and a stenographer.

The *telephone* has become increasingly important in collections, not so much alone as when used as an aid to letters. Since it is fundamentally

---

Check Here:
☐ 3 Years (156 issues)
☐ 2 Years (104 issues)
☐ 1 Year (52 issues)

AN URGENT MESSAGE FROM

NEWSWEEK
NEW YORK

Wire Services:
1. United Press
2. N.B.C. and C.B.S.
Listening Posts
★ ★ ★ ★
Cable Address:
"Newsweek"—New York

TO:

NEW YORK 18, N. Y.

IMPORTANT! CURRENT ISSUE OF NEWSWEEK IS THE LAST ONE DUE ON YOUR PRESENT SUBSCRIPTION. TO CONTINUE SENDING YOU NEWSWEEK'S AUTHORITATIVE AND ESSENTIAL STORY OF NATIONAL AND INTERNATIONAL NEWS WE NEED YOUR RENEWAL INSTRUCTIONS AT ONCE. SIMPLY CHECK AND INITIAL THIS BLANK, AND MAIL IT BACK TO US TODAY. THANK YOU!

FRANK WARE
CIRCULATION DIRECTOR

PLEASE INITIAL HERE_____AND CHECK: ☐ REMITTANCE ENCLOSED   ☐ BILL ME LATER
(ALSO BE SURE TO CHECK BOX IN UPPER LEFT HAND CORNER)

Fig. 48. Telegram-style letter. This subscription-extension letter in telegram style implies urgency and simplifies renewal, not forgetting to include a selling point for the magazine. (Used by permission.)

important to get a response—any response—on an account that has become seriously overdue, the telephone naturally comes to mind, for if the person can be located at all, he will not be likely to hang up without giving some kind of response. For this reason it might seem that the telephone would almost completely displace the letter of discussion. This might have happened but for the fact that many persons resent having to discuss their accounts on the telephone. In some situations, of course, they are placed under direct embarrassment.

The telephone collector needs, if possible, even more tact than the letter writer. He must have a pleasing voice, and he should take the attitude that the only reason the account has not been paid is that it has not been properly brought to the debtor's attention (which may be true when addresses change or when one person contracts the debt and another is to pay it). The very annoyance value of the telephone call tends to make it effective for collecting certain obligations, but its indiscriminate use may violate the basic rule of good collection policy by antagonizing the customer. In any case, the telephone call should be regarded as an adjunct to the written forms rather than as a substitute for them.

CREDIT APPRECIATION USED IN BUSINESS PROMOTION

Although poor-pay customers usually receive most of the collection letters, within the last few years there has been an increase in letters of appreciation to those customers who regularly pay promptly.

Fred D. Nosal of the Mastic Corporation in South Bend, Indiana, wrote the company's discount customers thanking them for their business and proposing that they "use Mastic as a credit reference" any time they wished. The reaction to the gesture was shown in the 10 per cent response to Mr. Nosal's letter and in salesmen's reports that customers were pleased to be considered *good* customers. The president of the Franz Wholesale Supply Company, Chicago, wrote that Mr. Nosal's was "the first letter of this kind we have ever received from any of our suppliers." [5]

Following are samples of the letter of "credit congratulation" which can serve to build further sales:

Credit Clothing Store

Dear Mr. Field:

As President of the Quality Clothing Company, I would like to thank you personally for the splendid manner in which you have taken care of your charge account.

---

[5] "Don't Ignore Customers Who Pay Promptly," *Credit and Financial Management,* January, 1964, p. 18.

LILY - TULIP CUP CORPORATION

1100 North Glenstone Avenue, Springfield, Missouri

SPRINGFIELD 2-2744

GOLD MEDAL

Dallas Paper Company
1876 Water Street
Dallas, Texas

Gentlemen:

THANK YOU!

Yes, we most certainly owe you a special word of thanks. Normally we are so busy with our problems we seldom take time to express our appreciation to customers such as you who pay their accounts, month after month, year after year, quietly and regularly, with no effort on our part.

It has been said, and it is true, a credit man is so busy saying "Please remit" he overlooks the opportunity to say "Thank you". So we are forgetting the problems for the moment to express our gratitude to you and your entire organization for your acceptance of our product and the fine manner in which you have consistently maintained your account.

The success of our efforts depends entirely upon the cooperation of our accounts so it is to you we feel most indebted. Our appreciation is great — our thanks sincere.

Cordially yours,

LILY TULIP CUP CORPORATION

J. A. Patterson
Division Credit Manager

JAP:wh

Fig. 49. Such a letter reminds regular customers that they are more than mere account numbers. (Used by permission of the Dartnell Corporation.)

To show my appreciation, I am enclosing a lifetime Credit Courtesy Card which automatically establishes your credit in any one of our Chicago stores. This courtesy card will also serve as your permanent identification.

I hope that the satisfaction you get out of using this card will be equal to my pleasure in sending it to you.

Very truly yours,

Firm Selling Cash Registers by Direct Mail

Dear Mr. Jones:

A credit man spends so much time and effort in saying "please remit," that it's a real pleasure when he has the chance to say "thank you."

That's why I get a real kick out of thanking you for the fine
way you have handled your account.

If all customers were half as thoughtful and considerate as you
have been, a credit man could go home every night to his family
with a smile on his face and a song in his heart.

                                        Thankfully yours,

                                        Credit Department

The success of all these letters is a new exemplification of the old
axiom of financial success, "Business goes where it is invited and stays
where it is well treated."

DON'T'S AND DO'S FOR CREDIT AND COLLECTION LETTERS

Don't go after an account as if your only object were to get the money.

Do remember that good collection policy includes keeping the customer as well as collecting the account.

Don't scold the customer or lower his self-esteem by emphasizing his unbusiness-like behavior.

Do be positive and constructive in your approach; help the customer build self-esteem through becoming business-like in handling his obligations.

Don't be gloomy, lugubrious, in the tone of your letters, making the debtor feel worse than he did before.

Do be cheerful, optimistic, about the indebtedness—of course he can pay and intends to—just make the arrangements.

Don't "burst into tears in the first sentence and scream for the law in the second"—that is, don't be frantic or act as if you have been hoping for an excuse to go to law.

Do be dignified and considerate, keeping on polite, friendly relations with the debtor just as long as possible.

Don't use negative, indefinite language in your letters; the customer will be negative and desultory in return.

Do be definite, positive. What you want is action; so you must get the debtor to think in terms of specific, dated action. Always include amount due.

Don't forget the value of resale language in your letters; the customer will pay much more readily for something that has value to him.

Do remember that what made the customer purchase in the first place is more likely to make him pay cheerfully than anything else.

Don't think that a customer has more respect and affection for a store which has an easy credit policy. He will be quick to see that credit losses are bound to show up in prices.

Do seize the opportunity to educate customers on the relation between prompt payment and low prices and a square deal for all.

Don't fail to express appreciation for business-like and prompt payments.

Do use credit appreciation as a means of building good will and of increasing sales.

Don't forget the importance of good composition in credit and collection letters—positive action comes easier where there is respect.

Do remember that one correctly planned, well-written letter may do more work than a number of ordinary ones—and, with alterations, can be used again.

Do Your Collection Policies Protect Your Future Business? *

by Louis F. Thomann

A sizable amount of today's advertising money is wasted by advertisers' own credit departments because there is insufficient liaison between zealous collectors and advertising-public relations people within companies.

Need for a closer working relation between these departments is important to save customers and some sales in today's market. Bill payments are beginning to lag. A *Wall Street Journal* spot check in late October reported department store collections running 5% to 25% behind a year ago, and the latest boost in personal income taxes can be expected to aggravate the condition. On the other hand, looking forward to future sales volume, it seems imperative for credit managers to practice greater leniency. The little fellows struggling along now may grow into substantial buyers tomorrow. And the slow-pay customer is going to buy some place—and pay ultimately—as long as he has any credit rating.

Granting then that a need for closer liaison between credit and advertising-public relations exists, what can be done about it? Here are examples of what some companies are doing:

General Petroleum Corporation practices credit and collection pretty much the way a company with close liaison to its advertising-public relations people would do it, although this Los Angeles marketer does not have such a policy. It takes a realistic approach that 70% current is a good credit job. Out of the other 30%, two thirds will run 30 days slow, and this group is continually changing. The other 10% owe for more than 60 days, but these accounts can be 90 days past due and under $100 without causing consternation. When it creeps up over $100, this is considered the warning point.

The credit department pulls the card to see who the customer is and then takes the next step largely by instinct. Discreet inquiries are made with a

* Reprinted, by permission from *Printers' Ink*, January 11, 1952, at which time Mr. Thomann was Western Editor of that publication.

GENERAL PETROLEUM CORPORATION
A SOCONY-VACUUM COMPANY
612 South Flower Street, Los Angeles 54, Calif.

The condition of your retail charge

account requires attention without delay.

We ask for immediate payment to permit

continuance of your credit privileges.

Yours very truly,

CREDIT DEPARTMENT

Fig. 50. Brief collection note. (Used by permission of General Petroleum Corporation.)

GENERAL PETROLEUM CORPORATION
A SOCONY-VACUUM COMPANY
612 South Flower Street, Los Angeles 54, Calif.

Mobil Credit Check Books are furnished our
customers for convenience in purchasing
their automotive needs. To insure this
convenience, accounts must be paid when
due, or if extenuating circumstances arise,
a definite plan of settlement should be
arranged.

You appreciate the value of maintaining a
good credit rating and surely realize the
importance of paying accounts when due.

If you cannot pay the balance now due, and
to avoid further impairment of your credit
record, please return the unused portion of
your Credit Check Book in the enclosed
envelope.

                    Yours very truly,

                    CREDIT DEPARTMENT

     Encl.

Fig. 51. Reminder note. Longer and still polite, this reminder cites value of maintaining credit, suggests return of card. (Used by permission of General Petroleum Corporation.)

check on current charges. This usually results in no direct contact with the customer. A casual contact can be made for the purpose of bringing files up to date, and if the account is good, there will be no further trouble.

When letters become necessary, the General Petroleum policy is "Don't say too much." Lengthy letters are out. A series or cycle of letters is used leading up to the final demand before turning over to the attorney, which is very definite on results. But throughout the collection process, the credit department keeps in mind the desire to reopen the account in the future because "we want them to keep on buying from us." Marketing management approves the form letters used, but a company spokesman (in the credit department) thinks it might be a good idea for public relations to look them over too.

Clary Multiplier Corporation, adding machines, calculators, and cash registers, San Gabriel, California, has a policy which calls for maintaining good public relations along with good credit and collections. The advertising department is available for consultation any time the credit department wants it, but there is nothing in the company's rules forcing such consultations. Rather, it's a matter of teamwork within the organization that finds the advertising department preparing illustrated reminders and letters that will good humoredly jog delinquent creditors into paying up their accounts. A series of postal cards with cartoons has been developed as gentle reminders when accounts become past due so many days. And for inside office use, an elaborate *aging chart* for keeping track of delinquent accounts was created for the credit department by the company's advertising department.

Merwin Eberle, advertising and promotion director for Clary, says: "Experience has shown that a courteous personal business letter is the best means of collection by mail. We use the humorous cards generally on big accounts that might be offended if we needled them too hard."

Golden State Company, Ltd., dairy products, San Francisco, had its public relations department review and revise a form used in requesting information from prospective customers. Brief and pertinent, it now looks like a simple request from the home delivery driver-salesman as his friendly gesture toward wanting to know his customer better. Otherwise there is no working relation between credit and advertising-public relations in this company. It leaves most of the collection details up to 53 branch managers throughout California. These managers get help and coaching from credit manager Ralph Rowe, who has been with Golden State for 23 years.

This company has a reputation for being liberal in extending credit, yet its over-all credit losses are extremely small. In fact, if it were to retain the services of a retail credit association for information on applicants for credit, the costs of this service would run from 6 to 10 times the amount of bad debts written off, a company spokesman says. Leaving much credit collection to branch managers is an important phase of Golden State's success, for public relations is regarded as important throughout the organization.

Pacific Telephone & Telegraph Company's business offices handles the credit and collection operation, and there is no direct connection with advertising-public relations. But this company also emphasizes the importance of public relations throughout its highly personalized contact with subscribers. Reminder notices tactfully call attention to payment delinquency. Even when service must be discontinued for nonpayment, the company attempts to make the unpleasant job as pleasant as possible. Sometimes the telephone instrument is left in the house but is disconnected. After the bill is paid and service is restored, the company in some instances requires a deposit for guarantee on future bills.

In these four examples, only one has a continuing liaison between the departments. Another has called on public relations for one specific job. The other two in other ways practice good public relations in their credit operations.

Exercises and Problems in Communication

1. Rewrite the letter on page 329, inviting the customer to open a charge account. Shorten the letter without affecting its tone.

2. As a retail clothing merchant you have a customer, Gail Ketchum, who has a six-month-old unpaid account of $87.50. In answer to your letter telling him that you will submit his name to the credit bureau of your town, you receive an explanation for non-payment. The major detail of his letter is that one of his children has been in the hospital; no details of the hospitalization are given. You know that the family income is around $5,000 a year. Mr. Ketchum has always paid all accounts within two months in the year and a half that he has had an account with your store. Write him in response to his letter.

3. For vocabulary development, look up in a thesaurus or book of synonyms the entries or sections on money. (In *Roget's International Thesaurus* the topic is listed as "Monetary Relations.") Do assignments with the words as directed by your instructor. Study of the antonyms is good practice in developing a strong vocabulary of neutral and prepossessive words as discussed in Chapters 3 and 6.

4. Write a paper or prepare a talk describing your personal philosophy of money. If the assignment is to be written, do it in form of a letter to a business associate of long standing, assuming that some incident in your career has made such a letter suitable. Or as a sales manager, write a three- or four-sentence paragraph summarizing the thoughts in the letter just suggested. The paragraph would be an item in a monthly two-page letter (quips, jokes, and philosophical tidbits) you write to salesmen as an employee relations piece.

5. Prepare a light three-minute talk to your class on money. Keeping in mind the functions of language, your purpose will be affective, rather than informative or persuasive. One or two suggestions for development: "My philosophy on money is 'I like it; I want it' "; "Money may not be the best thing in the world, but it's way ahead of whatever is in second place"; "The famous evangelist always says before the offering, 'Brothers and sisters, we want to hear a rustle, not a rattle, as the plates go around.' "

6. On pages 20–22, 51–52, and 72 in Robert L. Heilbroner's *The Worldly Philosophers* (New York: Simon & Schuster, Inc., 1953), read the brief descriptions of the part capital played in early economic developments.

7. Assume the position of manager of the billing department of a utility company. For the past twenty years monthly bills have been sent as a two-part perforated card, one part to be returned with payment. Now you are going to send the card in an envelope, with a smaller envelope enclosed for returning the office half of the bill. For the customer relations department of your company to send with the first mailing under the new plan, write a letter explaining the advantages of the innovation. (One point to make might be the privacy of

personal matters, such as the bill.) Explanation would be called for because people like to know "why" when an established plan or system is changed.

8. In *Business Management* for February, 1964, pages 46–50, read the article "How 239 Companies Set Credit Policy." This compilation of survey material gives a broad view of attitudes toward credit practices.

9. As a local agent selling fuel oil to consumers in a city of 50,000, you have an unpaid account of $77.60 for Neil C. Cochran, a customer who opened a charge account with you a year ago. It is now April, and Mr. Cochran has not had an oil delivery since early in February. The heating season extends to mid-May. You have had no response to February, March, and April statements. Through a telephone call to his residence, your secretary learns Mr. Cochran has converted his heating system to gas. Write an appropriate letter for collection of the $77.60.

10. Read articles in several current issues of *Credit and Financial Management* to orient your thinking to current practices and policies in credit. Report, orally or in writing, those details new to you.

11. As a more sustained assignment, read some of the books listed below and report—as a talk to the class or in writing, as indicated by your instructor— on the part money plays in the books, either in the individual characters' lives or in the businesses the characters are associated with.

Louis Auchincloss, *The Great World and Timothy Colt* (Boston: Houghton Mifflin Co., 1956)

Cameron Hawley, *The Lincoln Lords* (Boston: Little Brown & Co., 1960)

William D. Howells, *The Rise of Silas Lapham* (There are many editions of this 1885 classic.)

John Keats, *The Crack in the Picture Window* (Boston: Houghton Mifflin Co., 1957)

John Keats, *The Insolent Chariots* (Philadelphia: J. B. Lippincott Co., 1958)

J. P. Marquand, *Sincerely, Willis Wayde* (Boston: Little Brown & Co., 1955)

Robert Ruark, *Poor No More* (New York: Holt, Rinehart & Winston, Inc., 1959)

Sloan Wilson, *The Man in the Gray Flannel Suit* (New York: Simon & Schuster, Inc., 1955)

12. Rewrite the following sentences from collection letters, to improve tone, clarity, and other aspects of the writing:

a. If your check is already in the mail, then may we take this opportunity to extend our holiday greetings.
b. You owe us $28.80.
c. This account must be paid.
d. We thought you were honest and dependable. Now we wonder!
e. You promised to pay.
f. Our store would not like to be the cause of a bad credit reputation for you.
g. Please let us keep thinking highly of you by settling your account today.
h. We have written you seven letters and you have ignored them.
i. You are delinquent.
j. We hope you haven't had any bad luck that has caused you not to pay your account of $21.00.

13. Criticize the following collection letter from a credit clothier. Identify the appeal, or appeals, used and comment on the psychology and tone of the letter. Would it make you *want* to pay?

Dear Sir:

In spite of our several reminders you have not made payment on your account. Neither have you extended us the courtesy of a reply.

Perhaps there is a good reason why you have not sent payment. If so, we should like to know it. Otherwise we must have your remittance at once as per the terms in the contract you signed.

It is our wish to settle this in a most friendly manner and we hope you will cooperate with us to that end.

Very truly yours,

14. As you know, magazine subscription renewal letters continue to come for some time after the expiration date. Assume you have written the publisher to cancel your subscription, and three weeks later you receive this form letter:

Dear Subscriber:

Have you heard the one about the boy who asked his father "Dad, what does P.S. at the end of a letter mean?"

The father replies, "Why, Son, that means 'Please Settle.'"

We've been sending you [name of magazine] beyond the expiration date as long as the postal regulations will allow— and we have good reason to believe that you want this indis- pensable household companion to keep coming.

Will you P.S. the enclosed statement at once?

Cordially,

Subscription Manager

Write the publisher again. Try your hand at the light approach used in the manager's letter. Can you work in the P.S.? One application could be "Please Stop!"

15. You are treasurer of a civic and social club in your city. Dues are $9.00 a year. Several of the members have been attending meetings even though they are several months late in paying their dues. Write a form letter that could be sent to all who have not paid.

16. Three months ago Mr. Francis Jones, 812 Dayton Avenue, Miami, Florida, purchased the etching "Quail" by Churchill Ettinger from Associated American Artists, 711 Fifth Avenue, New York 22, N.Y. He asked that it be charged and sent and has since ignored two statements. He owes $5.00 for the etching and $0.50 shipping charges. Write the collection letter.

17. Secure a series of collection letters (from a business firm, from the family files, or elsewhere—a series of magazine subscription renewal letters will

do). Write a report on the collection techniques employed, showing especially how the psychological appeals vary from letter to letter. Your instructor may prefer to have this report in the form of a letter.

18. Here is an exercise in adaptability. The name and address of the company is constant: Thompson Feed Company, University Park, Pennsylvania. The name and address of the customer is constant: Harold Williams, Paddock Road, University Park, Pennsylvania. The amount of the bill is the same in all the problems: $46.80.

Write as many of these letters as your instructor assigns:

a. Reminder after two statements; good credit but generally slow pay.

b. Reminder after two statements and one letter have not been answered. Your secretary says he called this morning to order 400 pounds of feed.

c. Through some kind of mixup, he has paid for the feed delivered last month and the month before, but he still owes $46.80 for feed delivered three months ago. He has always paid promptly before.

d. Reminder after first statement has not been answered; new account to which you had hesitated in giving credit in the first place because of an erratic credit record reported by the credit bureau.

e. Reminder after two statements—he has been a customer for fifteen years, but you read in today's paper that he has taken a job on the West Coast and will leave town next Tuesday.

f. Fourth letter (the last one you plan to write before turning the account over to your attorney). The account is six months overdue.

g. A letter, assuming that Mr. Williams has lost his job and that there is little chance of his finding another job soon.

19. Write a brief report comparing the collection methods used by the Western firms described in Mr. Thomann's reading.

20. Although forceful, the following "threat" letter from a department store can be improved in a number of details. Rewrite the letter as you would send it.

Dear Sir:

This is directed to your place of business in the belief that our notices to your home did not reach you. Further we do not want to take any steps that may embarrass you without first notifying you of same.

Your account is considerably in arrears and we cannot wait for payment any longer. Unless you send a substantial payment by return mail we will be compelled to institute legal action against you.

Very truly yours,

Credit Manager

PART III

OTHER BUSINESS WRITING

13

Business Reports

Report me and my cause aright.—William Shakespeare, *Hamlet*

In 1959 the Chamber of Commerce of Fort Smith, Arkansas, organized local "minutemen teams," whose function was to attract new industry to that city. The teams, made up of business and labor leaders, were alert to any inkling of a firm's interest in locating in the region. Borg-Warner's Norge division, the "minutemen" heard, wanted to locate a plant to manufacture home refrigerators and freezers. It would employ 2,000 to 3,000. The company had surveyed a great number of states and had settled on the Missouri-Arkansas area. The Fort Smith group went into action.

A profile of Fort Smith's available labor supply and the wage scale (it averaged out to $1.85 an hour) was prepared. The Frisco Railroad Company offered to find a suitable site. The president of the Arkansas-Louisiana Gas Company and Arkansas' governor went to Norge's president. A Fort Smith suburb of 600 quickly approved a $7,500,000 revenue bond issue to finance construction of a 25-acre plant. When construction began, after Borg-Warner had signed a 30-year lease at a yearly rental of $450,000, with an option to buy at any time, Fort Smith built new streets and laid out new sewers to the plant. Public improvements totaled $230,000. Even educational institutions became involved; a vocational-training program for new employees was set up in the local junior college.[1]

With industrial, business, governmental, and educational organizations entering into this effort, it is apparent that a great deal of information had to be gleaned from many sources and passed on to

[1] The activities described were reported in *Fortune,* April, 1964, p. 121.

others. In addition to the statistics presented in the brief review above, there had to be consideration of utilities, transportation, housing, taxes; teachers for the vocational-training program, teachers' salaries and students' fees, space for classes. The street and sewer improvements necessitated transfer of information among various agencies, including condemnations of properties for right of way, engineers' findings, and estimates and bids on supplies and labor. All of this information took usable form as a *business report.*

Although obviously important, the part reporting played in this one situation is minute compared with the role of the millions of reports made annually in business. They vary in length and elaboration from the simple one-page memorandum or letter-report to the printed volume with bibliography and index, which in turn may be based on hundreds of simpler reports.

Aware of the constant and varied uses of reports, we can see the significance of the thought in the epigraph: "Report me and my cause aright." Report writing is of prime importance to individuals, and reports have been known to make or break companies. Therefore, it is of real consequence that we be specific, accurate, clear, and timely in what we "bear or bring back," the meaning of the Latin *reportare,* from which the word "report" comes.

WHY STUDY REPORTS?

There are two basic reasons for studying business report writing: (1) practically every person in business is asked at some time to write a report; (2) familiarity with the techniques of report writing is an important factor in the promotion of employees. The assistant general freight manager of the Rock Island Lines once told me that he has known very few persons who could make good reports and that in his company the man who can be sent out for a report is the man that the management relies on—and promotes. At General Electric, part of each management employee's job is to keep his superior informed of all developments, "good or bad." The superior in turn can keep *his* boss informed, and so on up the line. The company calls this the "man-boss" communications relationship, and considers it vital. The quality and effectiveness of such communication is one of the indexes used to evaluate a man's over-all performance.[2] A secretarial school which has enjoyed unusual success requires its students to make reports from the field of actual business practice as an integral part of their courses. Frequently these reports establish contacts that result later in excellent jobs.

---

[2] *Dun's Review and Modern Industry,* December, 1963, p. 66. (For further discussion of this type of communications relationship, see "the manager's letter" on page 481.)

Nowhere in the entire field of business communication is proficiency surer to yield returns than in report writing.

DEFINITION OF A BUSINESS REPORT

It is evident that the word *report*, as used in the business world, is not subject to very rigid definition, since reports vary greatly in both purpose and form. But as we need a working definition, let us say that *a business report is the result of the assemblage and scrutiny of facts and data concerning a definite business situation or problem.* The report is presented either to inform the reader on a matter in which he has a special interest (often a cash investment) or to enable him to decide on a course of action. For instance, holders of life insurance policies expect to check periodically on the financial condition of the insurance company; a plant superintendent needs to know the acceptability of a new milling process.

The business report has two main parts, the collection of the factual material and the presentation of this material so standardized and organized that the contents are clearly expressed in a simple, usable form which can be quickly digested by the busy (and high-salaried) executive.

RELATION OF REPORTS TO OTHER KINDS OF WRITING

When a report is mentioned, a student is likely to think of book reports or term papers. The book report is so far from standarization in form that there would be no point in comparing the business report with it. The business report is like the term paper in that both embody the results of research, but they are distinctly different kinds of writing, for they differ somewhat in content and even more in purpose and form. The term paper is nearly always based on library books and articles, and its material is presented in a general expository manner, reserving the findings for the conclusion. In the business report, the conclusions usually are presented first, leaving detailed discussions and groupings of data for the body of the report and the appendixes. The long business report, however, is like the term paper or thesis in having a bibliography and in some other ways.[3]

To the student majoring in science or the worker in the field of technology or applied science, a report suggests the laboratory, the factory, or the workshop. Engineering and laboratory reports are both numerous and important. Although they resemble business reports more than they do term papers or articles in scholarly journals, they have their

[3] For an introductory discussion of the relations of the different kinds of investigative writing, with emphasis on the college term paper, see Cecil B. Williams, *A Research Manual* (New York: Harper & Row, 1963), especially chap. i, "The Nature and Uses of Research."

EARNINGS-DIVIDENDS-CAPITAL STRUCTURE

As stated earlier, increased activity in all departments, particularly in the Loan Department, resulted in the highest operating earnings ever recorded by the Bank. The comparative analysis of earnings and expenses immediately following reveals operating earnings after applicable taxes increased 14% as compared to the 19X2 figure.

During the year some bond losses were incurred to take advantage of certain tax benefits. Such action insures fuller income on these funds in the coming years as well as possible bond profits.

COMPARATIVE STATEMENT OF EARNINGS

	19X3	*19X2*
Operating Income	$2,147,203.11	$1,946,967.13
Operating Expenses	1,638,755.73	1,474,343.57
Net Operating Earnings Before Income Taxes	508,447.38	472,623.56
Less Income Taxes on Operating Earnings	64,000.00	84,000.00
Net Operating Earnings	$ 444,447.38	$ 388,623.56
Net Operating Earnings per share	7.11	6.22
Cash Dividends Paid per share	2.00	2.00

RECONCILEMENT OF CAPITAL ACCOUNTS

Balance—Beginning of Year	$3,344,290.28	$2,845,011.32
Additions:		
Net Operating Earnings as above	444,447.38	388,623.56
Profit on Sale of Securities Net After Taxes	none	335,971.68
Transfer from Reserves	none	30,391.45
Total Additions	444,447.38	754,986.69
Deductions:		
Cash Dividends Declared	125,000.00	125,000.00
Loss on Sale of Securities Net	85,984.91	none
Transfers to Reserves	208,319.43	101,207.73
Charge-offs on Real Estate over Normal Depreciation	4,000.00	29,500.00
Total Deductions	423,304.34	255,707.73
Balance End of Year	$3,365,433.32	$3,344,290.28

Fig. 52. A page from an annual report to shareholders, showing aspects of both periodic and progress reporting. (Courtesy of the Purdue National Bank.)

specialized techniques also, including much use of blueprints, diagrams, and formulas. They are of interest here partly because of their resemblance in form to business reports, partly because modern business more and more keeps close to the laboratory. New-product development is vital to a company in these competitive times; according to *Dun's Review and Modern Industry*, "Such companies as Proctor & Gamble, Du Pont and Minnesota Mining and Manufacturing rank as the research leaders of industry. Indeed, 75% of the P&G household products on supermarket shelves today are new since 1945, Du Pont keeps 1,300 scientists on its payroll, and 3M officials 'eat, drink, dream and sweat' new products." [4] But in a business communication book we shall confine ourselves to the business report.[5]

KINDS OF REPORTS

The different kinds of business report are commonly named according to the jobs they do. Some authorities distinguish as many as five classes, but for our purposes three will suffice:

1. The *periodic report,* ordinarily used to check the current state of affairs, the status quo, at regular intervals
2. The *progress report,* used to check progress or trends, in order to satisfy investors or to influence policies
3. The *examination report,* used to decide for or against a project or plan in the light of the evidence obtainable

Periodic Reports

In Lewis Carroll's *Through the Looking Glass,* the Red Queen tells Alice that in her country you have to run quite fast to keep in the same place. Whether or not Carroll was poking fun at the tempo of modern life in general, we know that this description fits a great deal of business activitity. Individuals and firms are in constant competition with business rivals, with other divisions within the firm, and with the record of last year or last quarter. Periodic reports show whether or not a business is "running fast enough to remain in place," that is, whether conditions remain satisfactory. This type of report is used especially by banks as quarterly statements, by life insurance companies as annual reports to policyholders, and by corporations generally. Accountants' and executives' reports are also usually periodic. In its simplest form, as in the bank statement, the periodic report is merely a factual table, but more involved reports follow substantially the form of organization which we shall study here.

Progress Reports

Without frequent checks on progress and trends, the business world would make many more mistakes than it does. Progress reports are not always mere business reports, since they often have engineering aspects. Examples are reports on the progress of the New York subway lines, which were under construction for forty years, or the Hoover Dam on the Colorado River, which was six years in building. Business maga-

---

[4] December, 1963, p. 70.

[5] Among a number of good books to consult on the business report are A. G. Saunders, C. R. Anderson, and F. W. Weeks, *Business Reports* (3d ed.; New York: McGraw-Hill Book Co., Inc., 1957); N. B. Sigband, *Effective Report Writing* (New York: Harper & Row, 1960); and Raymond V. Lesikar, *Report Writing for Business* (rev. ed.; Homewood, Ill.: Richard D. Irwin, Inc., 1965).

zines publish the results of many business progress reports. Sometimes periodic reports are used as the basis of progress reports. A good example of this is the published survey of reports on advertising lineage submitted weekly or monthly by representative newspapers or magazines. Since advertising expenditures constitute a sensitive business barometer, when advertising increases, the conclusion is that the trend is upward; when it decreases, the trend is downward. Progress reports on sales trends in department stores are indispensable to the buyers to enable them to know what to stock. Nothing is known about the future except that it will differ from the present and frequently repeat the past.

Examination Reports

The most creative or constructive kind of report, and the one that involves the most planning and writing, is the examination or recommendation report. It is employed constantly by advertising agencies, chain store operators, railway companies, and manufacturers and jobbers of every kind. The contents of the examination report will determine whether a new restaurant should be opened at a site available opposite a large department store, how far eastward a chain store organization should extend, whether an air line should appropriate more advertising funds for newspaper or for magazine advertising, whether the food stores will run their largest ads in afternoon or in morning papers, whether an auto assembly plant should be opened in Oklahoma City. Just as trade is said to follow the flag, so business follows the line of opportunity—the best available opportunity in a highly competitive field.[6]

[6] Another classification of reports, through satirical treatment, points up some of the weaknesses in the thousands of reports that go daily from person to person and company to company. The following are "Don't" categories:

"Grab-bag—a mixed-up potpourri of pertinent and impertinent information.

"Poker-faced—wherein the writer somehow manages to assign a monotonous sameness of interest to both important and unimportant matters.

"Smoke-screen, or camouflaged—the 'standard progress report form for people who have no progress to report.'

"Sherlock Holmes—in which the writer tantalizes the reader (less skillfully than A. Conan Doyle) and saves everything until the end.

"How-many-hairs-in-the-horse's-tail—a self-explanatory category in which the writer flagellates his reader with unimportant details. Just the opposite of such famous reports of the past, as 'Sighted sub—sank same' and 'I came; I saw; I conquered.'

"Call-a-spade-by-any-other-name—otherwise known as beating around the bush." (A version of this type of report, too long to reprint here, was read by the speaker. His summation was four simple Anglo-Saxon words: "Let there be light.")

(From an address to the Eighth Annual Conference of the American Society of Tool and Manufacturing Engineers, May 14, 1960. Used by permission of the speaker, Professor V. E. Gibbens, Assistant Head of the English Department, Purdue University.)

FORM OF THE REPORT

Reports differ not only in purpose but also in makeup. The simplest reports are mere office memoranda. A clerk checks the inventory of office supplies, typewriter ribbons, or paper towels for reordering, and scribbles his report on a pad. A college professor reports attendance for the week on a prepared form. Slightly more involved is the student's report to his instructor on his comparative study of several business letters, or the foreman's report to his superintendent on the labor situation in his department. Thousands of reports, however, are made in the form of a letter, often with the important data tabulated for the convenience and better understanding of the reader.

From the simple memorandum or letter, the report extends to such forms as the stapled folder or pamphlet and even to the bound volume, often complete with illustrations, bibliography, and index. The Report of the Citizens Committee on River Straightening, made in Chicago in 1926 on prospects for opening several dead-end streets by moving railroad tracks, cutting a new channel, and grading and filling, is a bound volume of 214 pages, and includes many maps, sketches, tables, and full-page illustrations. The Annual Report of the Superintendent of Chicago Schools for a single year is a volume of about six hundred pages, including a sizable index. Needless to say, these large reports incorporate the findings of dozens, if not hundreds, of smaller reports.

GATHERING THE DATA

We now come to the most important part of our study of the report—how to prepare it. Assuming that the purpose or problem of the report has been clearly determined, there are three important stages in its preparation: (1) gathering the data, (2) organizing the data, (3) actual writing, or composition.

A report that does not yield full, pertinent, and dependable information on its subject is simply not worth making. First of all, then, let us consider how to get the information.

In general, there are the *library* and the *field* methods. Sometimes both are used in the same report, sometimes only one. Library materials have relatively less utility for the business report writer than for the scholar or the literary student, but they do have the advantages of convenience and efficiency; there is no point in doing laboriously again what someone else has already done sufficiently well. If you are working for a large firm, let us say the Singer Sewing Machine Company or Swift & Company, both of which do a large export business, and your employer wants a report on United States exports of certain commodities to Argentina and Brazil for the past five years, you will rely on successive volumes of the *Statistical Abstract,* published by the U.S. Bureau of Foreign and Domestic Commerce, and on other similar sources for your information. But if you are working for Swift's or Wilson's and are asked for a report on the number of persons in South Bend who use All Sweet margarine or Certified bacon regularly, you will have to resort to such field methods as the interview or the questionnaire.

Materials from the Library

By the time you come to report writing, you will probably have some familiarity with library catalogues and indexes. Recall what you learned when writing term papers, collecting material for debates, and the like. We shall review here only the most indispensable tools. Books which have a direct usefulness include:

1. The standard encyclopedias: *Britannica, Americana, Collier's, Social Sciences, International*
2. The encyclopedia annuals: *Britannica Book of the Year* (from 1938), *Americana Annual* (from 1923), *New International Year Book* (from 1907)
3. Special annuals and yearbooks: *American Year Book, Statesman's Year-Book, Whitaker's Almanack, World Almanac and Book of Facts, Statistical Abstract of the United States, Canada Year Book, Commodity Year Book,* Moody's and Dun and Bradstreet's reports, and *Poor's Register of Corporations, Directors, and Executives.*[7]

Other materials in the reference and catalogue rooms are useful chiefly as indexes to books, pamphlets, and magazines kept in the stacks. First in usefulness comes the card catalogue, which indexes source materials in three ways: by author, title, and subject. Thus every book has at least three cards and may have more since it can be classified under more than one subject. The subject headings are especially important, for they constitute a bibliography of the subject and will frequently yield several references to valuable sources then and there, as well as cross references or leads to others.

Of the numerous indexes which are printed in volume form and are constantly brought up to date, the *Public Affairs Information Service* (*PAIS*) has been described as "probably the most useful and practical general index for the businessman." It indexes many books, pamphlets, government documents, and other published materials, including more than nine hundred periodicals in the fields of political science, economics, sociology, and finance.

[7] The standard guide to the use of reference works is Constance Winchell, *Guide to Reference Books,* based on Mudge's *Guide to Reference Books* (7th ed.; Chicago: American Library Association, 1963). Also helpful is Cecil B. Williams, *A Research Manual* (New York: Harper & Row, 1963), chap. iii.

Indexes to periodicals are of tremendous importance to the report writer. Many times a subject is so new that books are of little use, and what is recent enough to have value must be sought in the magazines and newspapers. But one could never find what he needs in periodicals without help from indexes. Next to *PAIS*, which includes periodicals, the most useful periodical indexes are the *Business Periodicals Index* and the *Applied Science & Technology Index*, which index a diversified group of business and industrial periodicals. In 1958 these two indexes replaced the *Industrial Arts Index*, which was begun in 1913. For general magazines, there is the *Readers' Guide to Periodical Literature* and, of increasing value to the business writer because of the expansion of foreign trade, the *International Index to Periodical Literature*, which includes articles from foreign magazines. For articles prior to 1900, one must depend on *Poole's Index*, which is less complete and is mainly a subject index.[8]

Specialized indexes useful for certain subjects include the *Accountant's Index*, the *Agricultural Index*, and the *Engineering Index*. For American newspapers, chief reliance must be placed on the *New York Times Index*, but since all major newspapers cover important subjects simultaneously, an index to one newspaper is to some extent an index to all. To ascertain what magazines and newspaper files are available in any particular library, consult *New Serial Titles*, published by the Library of Congress, and *Newspapers on Microfilm*, by George A. Schwegmann, Jr., Chief Editor (Library of Congress, 1963).

Many large city and university libraries are depositories for government publications which supply useful information for business reports. Instruction in the use of these publications is found in *Government Publications and Their Use*, by Laurence F. Schmeckebier and Roy B. Eastin (Washington, D.C.: Brookings Institution, 1961). The office of the U.S. Superintendent of Documents in Washington, D.C., publishes periodically a catalogue of all Government publications and also supplies frequent lists of documents for sale. The Library of Congress has published many useful bibliographies, now included in the *Bibliographic Index* (begun in 1938).

Advertising agencies and radio stations commonly maintain small but good reference libraries of their own, as do also many manufacturing establishments. Historical societies and newspapers offer some special facilities. Several libraries are sometimes more useful than one, however fine that one may be. Resourcefulness is at a premium in all library research work; one person often finds in a few minutes what another

---

[8] A much more complex index to periodicals for 1890–1899 was published by The H. W. Wilson Company; work on indexing periodicals for earlier decades is in process.

overlooks for hours. By the same token, those consulting source materials may save many hours of work. Published results of experiments and studies many times save duplication of effort when someone finds in the literature reports of earlier work such as that which he is contemplating or is involved in. This duplication of time and energy is the lament of businessmen and industrialists as it is of academicians.[9]

Although company libraries are being used advantageously by more and more employees, considerable orientation work will have to be done if company personnel is to make optimum use of available resources. Too many seem to shy away from reference work. A Western Electric engineer may have been explaining reluctance for library work when he said, "Going to look up something in the library is too much like school." A psychologist has attributed this reluctance to the individual's feeling that to do his work he does not need help from others. A manager in research and development at IBM said that one of the greatest services a consultant could perform for the company would be to cultivate the "library habit" among the personnel.

What you have learned about *note-taking* for other research writing also applies in doing research for business reports. Use cards or small slips of paper; copy accurately and clearly what you want to quote; summarize concisely without misrepresenting the sources; do not write too much on a card; and be sure to have exact page references for every note. You will not have so many footnotes in a report as in a term paper, but in any case you must be sure of the source.

Materials from the Field

In the field, as distinguished from the library, three chief pathways to information are open. You may gather usable material through observation, through interviews, and through the mails, chiefly by means of the questionnaire. Keep in mind, of course, the fact that you can always combine methods. For both school practice reports and business reports, you may draw part of your material from library and part from field sources. If you were commissioned by the J. C. Penney Company, for instance, to report on the advisability of opening a chain store in a midwestern town, you could find from library sources the population of the city and a great deal about its standing as a business center. You would need, however, to visit the town, observe what department stores were already there, and interview people to ascertain their buying habits and also their attitude toward chain department stores before your report would be complete enough to have much value.

[9] For the account of a costly ($250,000) duplication, see the section "Technical Writing" in Chapter 15.

An important source of facts and data is *observation;* in some simple reports, it may be the chief or only source. In making a comparison of two metropolitan newspapers as advertising media, you would examine the two papers closely, ruler in hand. By means of such direct observation, you could ascertain the total column inches of national and of local advertising, the number of lines of classified ads, the relation of advertising matter to news matter, the number of feature articles tied in with advertising, and the variations in advertising from day to day or from week to week. In short, you might from observation alone make a report that would enable your employer to decide which paper would be better for an advertising campaign. Although observation is by no means always the chief source of information, it is so often fruitful that you should not overlook its possibilities.

For many reports the favored means of access to the best material is the *interview.* To investigate the success of a housing project, you would necessarily interview persons both in the management and among the tenants. It is now generally recognized that a good interviewer can obtain information not available through any other approach, and that information so gained is normally the most dependable kind. But the interviewer needs a good technique. Decide in advance just what you are after; even draw up a set of questions. Be tactful in your approach, or the person will refuse to talk. Train your memory so that you can write the information later if the person is "pencil shy."

In so far as possible you must get the requisite information from every person interviewed. Probably you can offer him no reward other than the satisfaction derived from participation in a worth-while project. Let him know that his contribution will materialize in something that will make his world a better world to live in. So often our business procedures boil down to this: to be a good business person, be a good human being.

Finally, a great deal of business information must come through the mails. At this point we come back to the *letter of inquiry,* or variations of it. The chief device employed to collect information by mail is the *questionnaire.* This is a list of questions especially designed to secure certain definite information. Unfortunately for our purposes, the questionnaire has lost favor in recent years. It is such an obvious device that it has been greatly overused, frequently in most annoying ways. Many persons have come to regard all questionnaires as a nuisance and chuck them promptly into the wastebasket. We cannot hope for 100 per cent returns on questionnaires, but by using them properly we can obtain information from sources where observation or interviews would be out of the question.

Here we shall consider a few points which efficient users of the questionnaire should observe. Make up the mailing list carefully. We have learned that this is important in all direct-mail work; it is especially so here, both to insure getting returns and to insure that the returns will be suitable and usable. Supply a covering letter (letter of transmittal) to accompany each questionnaire. The person who answers has a right to know why you want the information and what you intend to do with it. Ask as few questions as will enable you to obtain the requisite information. Checking has shown that far more persons will answer a short questionnaire than a long one. Avoid leading questions, or your information will be valueless. "Is Camels your favorite cigarette?" will get more votes for Camels than "Which is your favorite cigarette?" followed by the names of four leading brands. Avoid ambiguity also, or the results will not be classifiable. "Why do you prefer Wheaties?" may get such answers as "Recommended by my best friends" or "I don't like cooked cereals" when what you want is something you can quote or cite on their nutritive or appetizing qualities. A final word: Make your questionnaire as easy to answer and as foolproof as possible—and don't forget to enclose a stamped envelope for its return.

ORGANIZING THE INFORMATION AND DATA

If the report has been well planned and the collection of material is systematic, analyzing and sifting should not be too difficult. Some questionnaire replies are duds. Here and there a prankster has a sense of humor which causes him to look on a questionnaire as an opportunity for him to exercise his facetious bent. A few will be so incomplete or badly filled out as to be unusable. You must be careful, however, not to discard any that are honestly answered, just because they disagree with the findings you want. An erroneous interpretation is bound to kick back sooner or later. If your notes from observation, interviews, and library work are in good order, you can begin at once to sort and arrange them. All the while you are preparing to write your conclusions, which will depend in part on statistical compilation and in part on the impressions you have gained during your work.

At this stage you will plot your graphs and make your tables, if the report is to include these, and it probably will. *Graphic representation,* that is, the use of lists, tables, diagrams, charts, maps, and graphs, is usual in business reports. If one picture is worth a chapter of writing, one chart or graph may make quantitative relationships more apparent than any amount of discussion. In practice, however, both graphic representation and supplementary discussion are used. Effective correlation of the two phases of a report is shown in the sample company reports at the end of this chapter.

WRITING THE REPORT

All that we have done up to this point is preliminary work. We still have before us the writing of the report, and that is where we use what we have learned. Good research work and good analysis will not in themselves guarantee a good report, although they are essential. Let us turn now to the report as an exercise in writing, a composition, and see what we can do about planning and composing it.

Like any other composition, a business report must have a *plan*, but its plan is different from that of other compositions. In a sense it is written backward; in that respect it is like the journalist's news story. Reports are usually prepared by subordinates for the use of busy executives and administrators. What the executive ordinarily wants is to determine a course of action, or to decide whether or not any action is indicated; hence he wants to get at the conclusions of the report first of all. He may skim over the supporting evidence, but if he has confidence in the person preparing the report, he will not even do that.

How a report is actually used, with the bearing that this has on its organization and composition, is indicated by how much of it is read by persons at the various levels of management. It is an accepted fact in business, industry, and education that the higher the person's position, the less he reads of the details in a report. It is the fellow farthest down the ladder who will read the minutiae.

The plan of organization for reports is not completely standardized. It is much simpler for short and informal reports than for long formal reports. We shall outline the long report first, and then we can decide on necessary modification for the simpler type.

1. Cover
2. Title page
3. Letter of authorization
4. Letter of transmittal
5. Preface or foreword, with acknowledgments if any
6. Table of contents
7. Table of charts and illustrations
8. Summary-synopsis, including recommendations
9. Detailed discussion and analysis
10. Appendixes
11. Bibliography
12. Index

This outline is adequate for all but the most elaborate reports, which may include also letters of acceptance and approval, a copyright notice, and a breakdown of the detailed discussion and analysis into several parts—since this is the body of the report, occupying more space than all the other parts together.

We shall comment briefly on the different parts. The *cover* varies from the standard-type book cover of the elaborate report to the plain manila filing folder into which a brief report can be stapled. On it will be written or printed at least the name of the writer and the title of the report; for student work, preferably also the name of the instructor, the name of the course, and the date. The *title page* duplicates in a neat arrangement the information just described. Figure 53 shows a sample title page. The *letter of authorization* is the request for the report from the executive or administrator, describing what is wanted. The *letter of transmittal* replies to the letter of authorization and explains the scope and limitations of the report, the methodology employed, special problems encountered, and points of unusual interest in the findings. Since the letter of transmittal may easily include prefatory material, a separate preface or foreword is hardly necessary except in the very long formal report. If included, it gives the reasons for the report, the methodology, and usually the acknowledgments of special help rendered and of permissions to use copyrighted or previously printed material or illustrations.

The *table of contents* lists the various parts of the report with the page number where each begins. The *tables of charts and illustrations* supply page numbers for the pictorial matter. In short reports, the two tables may be combined. The *summary-synopsis* is self-descriptive; in it the writer sums up the gist of his findings so that the reader can determine very quickly what conditions or trends the report shows. If the writer is expected to make recommendations, it is preferable to make them immediately after the summary of findings. Some authorities reserve them to follow the discussion, but this seems to violate the principle of efficiency that governs the making of reports; it would have advantage only if the writer and the reader are accustomed to that order. For a report going to personnel in various departments, some companies have different summaries prepared for one report. The summaries contain points of greatest impact or most interest to the individual departments. The rest of the report is prepared in duplicate. This practice is based on the story-line, or circular technique, which "starts a story at the most important point"; it is especially useful in *rewriting* technical reports for business purposes.[10]

The *detailed discussion and analysis* is the body of the report. It is the full explanation of the factual matter, interspersed with tables, graphs, and pictures, and supported where needed by quotations, identified in footnotes, where supplementary explanations may also be found. It

[10] Thomas L. Bonnitt, "Editing Technical Reports for the Businessman," *TWE Journal*, Spring, 1955, p. 27.

PROSPECTS FOR

THE SPRING MARKET

IN

LADIES READY-TO-WEAR

Prepared for

Cara-Lynn Company, Inc.

Purchasing Department

by

Harrison Cline Associates

New York City

September 2, 19--

Fig. 53. A sample formal-report title page. In business reports to employees, shareholders, and the public, a cover frequently serves as the title page.

should be written from a carefully prepared outline following a chrono-logical or analytical plan. Here the principles of unity, coherence, and emphasis apply as in any good composition. And you should not forget that use of concrete fact and specific detail lends both interest and conviction.

Material that is relevant to the purpose of the report, but which is needed for reference only, is included in the form of an *appendix*. Some reports have several appendixes, consisting, for example, of legal statutes bearing on the report, specimens or illustrations of points under discus-sion, or a large amount of statistical data. Only a minority of reports have a *bibliography*. If, however, the report is based chiefly on library materials, the full list of books, pamphlets, and articles used should be included, alphabetically arranged, with all entries correct and complete. Exceptionally long reports, especially those that may be consulted long after their writing, may have an *index*. This should be prepared with the same care that is devoted to book indexes. The guiding principle for what goes into the index is to include everything that will help the reader locate as easily and quickly as possible the pertinent facts which the report has divulged.

PLAN FOR SHORT REPORTS

For short reports, including practice reports in college, the following simpler plan is recommended:

1. Cover
2. Title page
3. Letter of transmittal
4. Table of contents and table of illustrations
5. Summary-synopsis, including recommendations
6. Detailed discussion and analysis
7. Appendixes (if any)
8. Bibliography (sometimes)

For the most part, the explanation of the parts of the long report applies also to the short form. For brief reports which are still too long for the letter or memorandum form, the cover may be omitted, but the pages of the report should be stapled at the left side. Also, the letter of transmittal may include the summary-synopsis; but if the letter must be long, indention and tabulation should be used to make important points stand out.

PROCEDURE IN WRITING THE REPORT

After we have sorted and organized our note cards, prepared our graphic material, and jotted down in rough outline form a plan appro-priate to the type of report we are writing, we are ready to start working on the discussion and analysis—the body of the report.

The first problem we must lick is the bugaboo of the first sentence. One of my friends in college always spent at least two hours on the first sentence of a letter, theme, or story; after that he finished the rest in about twenty minutes. But there is no point in wasting time composing that first sentence in deathless prose; we probably will change it later anyway. The best thing to do is to plunge right in, expanding and developing the material from our note cards until we have produced several "tentative" pages that we can always come back to and revise.

As we build our report, we soon encounter the problem of transition from one topic to another within the report. Such a phrase as "The next item to consider is the preferred stock" seems artificial; most modern reports instead use subheadings, just as this textbook does. We may begin the paragraph in this way:

Preferred stock. One hundred thousand shares of 7% preferred stock are outstanding.

Note that the first sentence of the paragraph should make sense without referring to the subheading; "One hundred thousand shares of this are outstanding" would be poor usage. First-sentence tie-in with subheadings is demonstrated on page 385.

Sometimes we find that some of the important material we would like to use seems out of place in the plan of the report. It may be corroborative material which we need to prove the point we are making; yet it seems to be like a long digression or interruption when we put it in the body of the report. The place for such material is the appendix. By judicious use of the appendix we can make the body of the report move steadily toward the conclusion without unnecessary delays for the reader.

After completing the first draft of the body of the report we are ready to revise. We read the first draft to ourselves, listening to the way it sounds as if we were reading it aloud, and keeping the question of meaning in mind: "Does this mean what I meant it to mean?" We correct all errors, shifting word order and changing sentence structure to improve clarity and coherence. If we sorted the note cards correctly in the first place, the order and organization should be logical; but we should check once more to be sure.

Next we are ready to write the summary-synopsis and the letter of transmittal, and to prepare the title page, table of contents, and list of illustrations. After typing the final draft of the report, we assemble it and bind it in the proper order.

REPORT WRITING AND HACK WRITING

This is probably a good place to point out the difference between report writing and hack writing. Let's face it: a great many high-school and college term papers are written by the hack-writing method—two or three books or magazine articles are spread out on a desk and more or less carefully combined, a sentence out of one, a paragraph out of the other, in jigsaw puzzle fashion. If penalties for plagiarism have been emphasized, the sentences and paragraphs are paraphrased in this manner before being fitted into the hack-work paper:

> Reinsurance is the term used to denote the transaction whereby a person who has insured a risk insures again a part or the whole of that risk with another person. The purpose of reinsurance is to relieve the original insurer from a liability which is too heavy for him to carry. [*Encyclopaedia Britannica*, 1947 ed., vol. 19, p. 81.]

The transaction in which someone who has insured a risk insures all of that risk or part of it with someone else is called reinsurance. Reinsurance has as its purpose relieving the original insurer from too great a liability. (Paraphrase which seems to the student to remove the danger of a plagiarism penalty.)

This hack-work method is not report writing; it is not research writing. In a way it is more dangerous to the student than outright plagiarism, because the student may think he is learning something or accomplishing something by hack writing when in reality he is not. Such hack writing is a worthless commodity: no firm will pay anyone to do it. A firm wants a real job of research, adapted to the firm's own special problems, using the educational background, the experience, and the special skills of the researcher, and written clearly and concisely in the researcher's own language.

STYLE IN REPORT WRITING

The style of report writing is relatively formal. Often a report is passed around at meetings of executives, or it may be used or reused years after it is written. What is wanted is objective information rather than personal communication; hence the material is generally presented in the third person consistently, in a clear straightforward manner. However, if the writer knows that only one person is to use the report, and writer and reader are personally acquainted, first-person style and informality are in order. Whether the situation calls for the formal or the informal style, clearness and conciseness are always essential. The best style for reports uses language as a perfectly transparent medium. Clear, clean glass, though not as beautiful as stained glass, lets in more light; in the same way a plain, clear style does not call attention to itself but does pass along the facts with maximum efficiency.

SOME FINAL WORDS ON REPORT WRITING

Now we are back where we started. The report writer's job is to secure—to "bring back"—information needed in the various types of businesses. The business world is a realm of uncertainty and change where conditions, trends, and tendencies must be constantly watched. The report writer cannot prevent these changes, but he can keep business geared to modern trends. By utilizing the facilities of the library and the field he can get at the necessary information and data. By practicing the principles of English composition with special reference to the purposes and needs of those who read his reports, he can perform useful business services and at the same time promote his own advancement, for the demand for good reports is always greater than the supply of good report writers.

In addition to these general admonitions, our final word should include a few more pointed suggestions:

1. Be as clear and as brief as you can through exactness and consistency.
2. Design the report material for your intended audience; write *to people* rather than *about things.*
3. After you have written the first draft, wait as long as possible to revise the report for the final draft; this procedure helps the writer to read from the standpoint of his intended audience.
4. Discuss results, insofar as possible, rather than methods or manner of gathering the information.
5. Save others' time (and your own, in the long run) by *planning* questionnaires and interview materials.
6. State conclusions and recommendations if your results warrant those opinions and if you have been authorized to.
7. Keep all graphic aids simple, key them to the text of the report, and label them meaningfully.
8. Avoid repetition, by combining the presentation and discussion of results wherever possible.
9. Provide a table of contents for any report of more than three pages, letting the entries serve as an outline to the report.
10. Test the importance of details by relegating them to an appendix; you can determine whether they (a) need to be in the body, (b) should be in the appendix, or (c) in many instances, eliminated altogether.

SPECIMEN REPORTS

The actual business reports on the following pages serve various purposes. The first is the memorandum report to branch-store managers. The second, selected pages from the annual report to shareholders of one of the country's leading home builders, illustrates how graphic aids can present a 20-year analysis without detailed text; too, the "Financial and Operating Review" illustrates that subheadings can, without abruptness, take the place of wordy transitions. The third entry is adapted from the first 24 pages of the 51-page annual report of the E. I. du Pont de

Nemours & Company. The later pages of the report include the various balance sheets, accountants' certification of the report, and the company directory of the Du Pont industrial departments, principal consolidated subsidiaries, and principal affiliated companies not consolidated.

THE BOSWORTH COMPANY

Central Office   Department 5

Date: October 1, 19__

To: Messrs. J. E. Block, E. B. George; Miss A. Leonard

From: L. T. Monroe, General Manager of Sales

Re: Summer Stocks

In preparation for the 19__ summer season, the following information is given from quarterly resumes of your various stores. The figures will serve as the basis of the meeting on October 15, in the Central Office conference room.

Purchases

Two lines—Briggs and Cantrall—were overbought.
Three lines—Cawlon, Street, and Phillips—could have been re-ordered, since stock moved by July 7.

Sales

Condition is reflected in the preceding and following statements.

Advertising and Display

Newspaper. Briggs and Cantrall were advertised more regularly and longer than the other three lines. Relative figures:

Briggs and Cantrall — 7 runs each; cost, $2500
Cawlon, Street, and Phillips — 4 runs each; cost, $2100

Window and department display. Briggs and Cantrall were displayed for a total of 12 days in full windows, and 3 days each on the department rotor-tables.
The other three lines were shown with other merchandise for 8 days total in windows and rotor-tables.

Profits

Briggs and Cantrall — 8% (considering 134 items left in stock)
Cawlon, Street, and Phillips — 19%

Questions for Consideration

Since you have been in your stores for 5 years or longer, we may need re-analysis of conditions (economic and buying habits) in your respective communities. The Briggs and Cantrall lines may be higher-priced than we can move profitably in your communities. Did combination displays, using the Cawlon, Street, and Phillips, help move those lines? Do combination displays help move merchandise in general?

Answers to these questions and any other analysis of these comparative figures that you can have ready on the 15th will expedite the meeting and help our 1965 sales.

FINANCIAL AND OPERATING REVIEW [11]

Production

During 1963, National Homes Corporation and its manufacturing subsidiaries produced 14,831 houses, including 13,306 single-family dwellings and the equivalent 1,525 houses in multi-family units. This compares with 17,289 single-family houses produced in 1962.

Revenues

Consolidated revenues in 1963 amounted to $68,921,958 compared with $79,159,023 in the previous year. The lower revenues in 1963 are attributable to the sharp decrease in single-family house sales, partially offset by sales of multi-family units, a field which the company entered in 1963. These sales resulted in revenues of approximately $5,350,000. The single-family housing market is discussed in detail in the "Letter to Shareholders."

Earnings

Our earnings before provision for federal income tax totaled $1,341,498 in 1963 compared with $3,528,750 in 1962. Net earnings were $704,498 in 1963 compared with $1,693,750 in 1962.

On the basis of 4,720,515 shares outstanding as of December 31, 1963, our earnings amounted to 15 cents per share compared with 36 cents in 1962.

Financial

The Company's working capital at December 31, 1963, totaled $20,068,122 compared with $20,568,664 for the previous year end. Cash balances at the end of the year were $2,032,929 compared with $3,800,481 at December 31, 1962. Our investment in trade receivables increased by $759,971 to $8,205,112 at December 31, 1963. Inventories aggregated $11,951,269 at the end of the year compared with $11,557,837 at December 31, 1962. The net worth of the parent company and its consolidated subsidiaries at the end of 1963 was $32,-407,568 compared with $31,461,939 at the end of the previous year.

Book value of the common stock, based on the number of shares outstanding on December 31, 1963, was $6.87 per share compared with $6.66 at December 31, 1962.

Listing of National Homes Common Stock and Warrants

National Homes Corporation common stock and warrants were listed on the Midwest Stock Exchange on September 23, 1963. This action was taken by the Company to provide a more orderly and broader market for its stock and warrants. The shareholders, at a special meeting on August 14, 1963, approved the elimination of the A and B classes of National Homes common stock in favor of one class of common stock.

[11] Reprinted by permission of the National Homes Corporation.

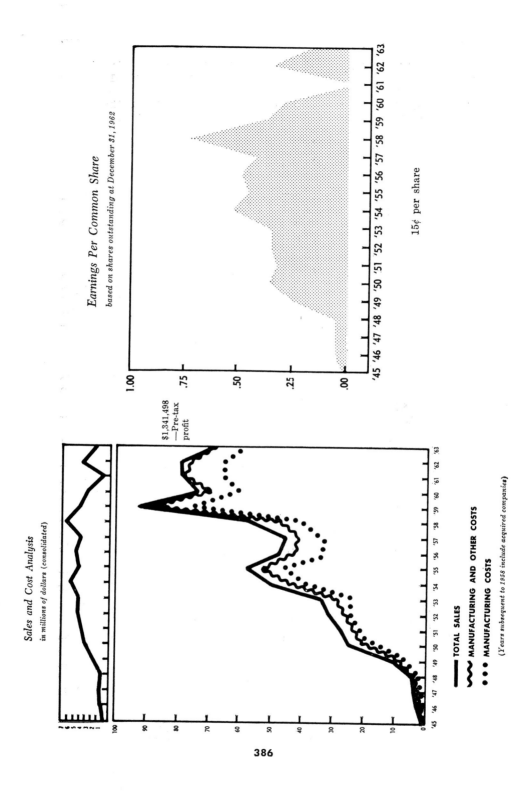

Sales and Cost Analysis
in millions of dollars (consolidated)

$1,341,498
—Pre-tax
profit

TOTAL SALES
MANUFACTURING AND OTHER COSTS
MANUFACTURING COSTS

(Years subsequent to 1958 include acquired companies)

Earnings Per Common Share
based on shares outstanding at December 31, 1962

15¢ per share

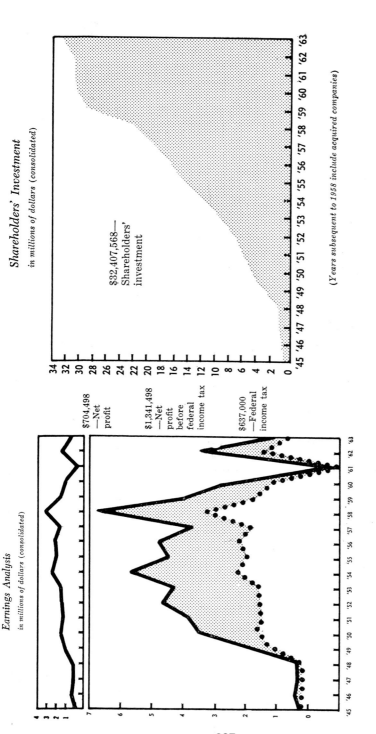

Shareholders' Investment

in millions of dollars (consolidated)

$32,407,568— Shareholders' investment

(*Years subsequent to 1958 include acquired companies*)

Earnings Analysis

in millions of dollars (consolidated)

$704,498 —Net profit

$1,341,498 —Net profit before federal income tax

$637,000 —Federal income tax

EARNINGS BEFORE TAXES

NET EARNINGS

● ● ● **FEDERAL INCOME TAX**

(*Years subsequent to 1958 include acquired companies*)

By permission of the National Homes Corporation.

387

250,000th National Home

A milestone of importance occurred when the 250,000th National home was produced on September 24, 1963. National is the first to produce this volume of homes—sufficient shelter for a million or more people. National Homes builders throughout the country participated in this historic event, each focusing attention on a 250,000th Celebration Home in a local ceremony.

Disposal of Assets

In compliance with the settlement of the government's anti-trust suit, we have sold plants in four locations, which represents all real estate to be sold except that in Collins, Mississippi, and Memphis, Tennessee. We have also disposed of the majority of the machinery and equipment at the closed plants. The sale of the closed plants and machinery and equipment resulted in a gain of $494,432. It was decided to defer this gain until the amount receivable on the sale of the largest plant is collected and the remaining plants and machinery and equipment are sold. In addition, expenses amounting to $149,941 incurred in connection with the closing of these plants have been offset against the deferred gain.

Builder Recruitment

As pointed out in the Letter to Shareholders, we are emphasizing our builder recruitment program. A major change in our sales organization was accomplished during the past year to insure a continuous, year-round recruiting program. The sales organization has been split into two divisions—one devoted exclusively to the servicing function and the other to full-time recruiting of new builders. This change in organization already has produced visible improvements as the number of new builders franchised is up substantially over the levels of a year ago. We believe this to be the surest way to increase our market penetration.

We are emphasizing to our builders not only the standardized quality and the economy of our product, but also the exclusive sales and management services we offer builders to insure their success. For example, we recently expanded these services to include a monthly mail-in accounting system that provides builders with a continuing control over costs as well as other necessary financial information.

Today's highly competitive market is making builders acutely aware of the need for such cost controls, in addition to other management services that reduce overhead charges. We feel that this and other special services National Homes offers will be increasingly attractive to builders, both large and small.

E. I. du Pont de Nemours & Company, Wilmington, Delaware, Annual Report for the Year 1963 *

HIGHLIGHTS

	1963	1962
EARNINGS	Per Share	
From Du Pont sources (after Preferred dividends)	$ 6.84	$ 6.73
From General Motors Corporation dividends	3.21	2.87
Total	10.05	9.60

* Courtesy of the Du Pont Company.

LESS—DIVIDENDS PAID	7.75	7.50
RETAINED IN THE BUSINESS	2.30	2.10
TOTAL TAXES (including all Federal and foreign taxes on income, property taxes, etc.)	8.89	8.42

EARNINGS	Millions of Dollars	
From Du Pont sources (before Preferred dividends)	$ 325	$ 320
From General Motors Corporation dividends	147	132
Total	472	452
SALES	2,555	2,407
OPERATING INVESTMENT	3,605	3,341
SPENT FOR NEW AND IMPROVED PLANTS	370	245

EMPLOYEES AT YEAR END (excluding those at Government-owned plants)	100,468	93,159
OPERATING INVESTMENT PER EMPLOYEE	$36,300	$37,200
STOCKHOLDERS AT YEAR END	233,985	230,610

From Lammot du Pont Copeland, *President*

To the Stockholders:

For the Du Pont Company, 1963 was a good year and one of intense activity and increasing competition. Profit margin decreased because of rising costs and lower selling prices. In spite of this, however, company sales, net income, and dividends paid to stockholders were at record highs. Increased dividends received from General Motors Corporation were a major factor in contributing to Du Pont's record net income and dividends paid.

The year 1963 also marked the 25th anniversary of the company's announcement of nylon, the first completely synthetic fiber. The growth and versatility of this fiber are discussed on pages 9 and 10.

Your attention is directed to the section of the report which discusses certain trends regarding both established and newer products and also to the article on research which mentions several products recently emerged from the company's laboratories.

The company's participation in the New York World's Fair during 1964 and 1965 is described on page 14 of the report.

It is particularly gratifying that for the second consecutive year the employees established a new company safety record with fewer injuries, and also that there were no fatalities in 1963. Improvement of our safety performance is a rewarding and continuing objective.

Financial Review

Higher Earnings from Du Pont Sources

Earnings from Du Pont sources before taxes applicable to the common stock were at a record high of $652 million as compared with $632 million in 1962. The increase was due chiefly to a higher physical volume of sales offset to a large extent by lower selling prices and increased costs.

Earnings after taxes from Du Pont sources were also at an all-time high of $315 million or $6.84 a share of common stock. Comparable earnings for 1962 were $310 million or $6.73 per share.

Earnings per share of common stock were as follows:

	1963	1962
From Du Pont sources	$ 6.84	$6.73
From GM dividends	3.21	2.87
Total	$10.05	$9.60

Higher earnings in 1963 from General Motors Corporation resulted from increased dividends paid by that corporation offset in part by the fact that, because of the July 1962 distribution of GM shares by Du Pont, a lesser number of GM shares was held throughout 1963.

Dividends $7.75 Per Share

Dividends paid on the common stock were $7.75 per share, exceeding the previous high of $7.50 paid in 1962 and in 1961. Interim and year-end dividends paid by Du Pont in 1963 and 1962 were:

	1963	1962
1st interim	$1.50	$1.50
2nd "	1.50	1.50
3rd "	1.50	1.50
Year-end	3.25	3.00
Total	$7.75	$7.50

The year-end dividend for 1963 was the 237th consecutive quarterly dividend paid on the common stock.

The usual quarterly dividends were paid on the $4.50 series and $3.50 series preferred stock. Earnings available for dividends were 47 times preferred stock dividend requirements.

Total dividends paid on both the preferred and common stocks were $366 million, or 78 per cent of earnings for 1963. This compares with 80 per cent for the ten-year period 1954 through 1963.

SALES AT A RECORD HIGH

For the fifth consecutive year sales established a new high, amounting to $2,555 million or 6 per cent above the $2,407 million for 1962. Practically all of the company's product lines enjoyed an increased volume over 1962.

Physical volume of sales was 7 per cent greater than in 1962. The company's index of selling prices averaged 1 per cent lower than in 1962 and 13 per cent lower than the peak in 1953.

Shown below is a comparison of 1963 sales by quarters with those for the corresponding quarters of 1962:

	1963	1962	% Increase over 1962
	(in millions)		
1st quarter	$ 607	$ 579	5%
2nd "	665	631	5
3rd "	637	599	6
4th "	646	598	8
Total	$2,555	$2,407	6

A chart on page 42 illustrates the wide diversification of the company's business and shows the percentage of company sales to principal industries.

OPERATING INVESTMENT UP 8 PER CENT

Average operating investment for 1963 was $3,605 million, an increase of 8 per cent over the average of $3,341 million for 1962. The average per employee was $36,300 in 1963 and $37,200 in 1962.

As the net earnings from operations increased only slightly over 1962 and the average operating investment increased 8 per cent, the ratio of net earnings to operating investment decreased from 9.1 per cent in 1962 to 8.6 per cent in 1963.

CASH POSITION

During the year the total of cash and marketable securities decreased from $358 million to $271 million. As will be noted from the statement shown below, the company's construction program was a major factor in contributing to the decrease.

	1963	1962
	(in millions)	
Cash and marketable securities— beginning of year	$358.4	$351.3
Source of Funds		
Net income	472.3	451.6
Depreciation and obsolescence	199.5	180.7
Miscellaneous—net	25.7	(1.9)
	697.5	630.4

Use of Funds

Dividends	366.5	354.9
Construction	370.0	245.0
Increase in net working capital— excluding cash and marketable securities	48.8	23.4
	785.3	623.3
Cash and marketable securities— end of year	$270.6	$358.4

On page 43 will be found a simplified statement of gross receipts from operations in 1963 and their disposition.

Operations Review

PRODUCT TRENDS

The important developments during the year concerning some of our new products, as well as older ones, are summarized as follows:

Fibers—Sales of Du Pont fibers in 1963 were at a record high. Gains were contributed by all fibers except "Super Cordura" rayon, production of which was discontinued at mid-year. Discontinuance of "Super Cordura" manufacture removed the company completely from the rayon business.

The year was a good one for the textile business in general, with man-made fibers showing particularly good growth. Competition for this growing market is expected to increase further as additional companies complete their announced plans to manufacture nylon and polyester fibers.

Twenty-five years ago Du Pont announced construction of a new plant at Seaford, Delaware, to produce nylon, the first completely synthetic fiber. The versatility of this product has been such that today its sales are still expanding for all end-use purposes. Continued Du Pont research and development has contributed importantly to the success of nylon by improving it for established applications and creating new varieties and modifications for new uses.

During 1963 nylon made noteworthy gains in outerwear apparel, in carpets, and in tires. In the last category, 51 per cent of all domestically produced tires were made with nylon cord as compared with 49 per cent in 1962. In the hosiery market, a principal source of nylon's initial peace-time impetus, we have been selling introductory quantities of a new variety designed to improve the comfort, fit, and appearance of women's full length hose. This yarn, called "Cantrece" nylon, will be available soon in commercial amounts. Additional capacity is being installed for all types of Du Pont nylon fibers, and our older manufacturing facilities are undergoing modernization.

"Dacron" polyester staple in blends with other fibers, particularly cotton, continued to find wider application because of the basic soundness of the ease-of-care concept pioneered by Du Pont. "Dacron" continuous filament yarn sales also increased in both industrial and apparel markets. A special high tenacity yarn for tires and other industrial uses was marketed in limited quantities. Additions to "Dacron" staple and yarn capacities will be ready for operation early in 1964.

A commercial plant for spunbonded polyester products is scheduled to begin production later this year. These cloth-like sheet structures, which can be varied in character from soft and supple to crisp and stiff, are being produced in a semiworks and are undergoing evaluation in a range of industrial and utility end-uses.

Sales of "Lycra" spandex yarns, first produced commercially in 1962, expanded rapidly in both domestic and export markets. "Lycra" provides good elastic support in swimwear, foundation garments, and support hose as well as sheerness where this is desirable. It is being used to impart controllable stretch and conformability to fabrics of other fibers. This new concept in stretch fabrics is expected to find broad application. Additional capacity for "Lycra" was completed in 1963.

Films—Sales of film products again increased. Customer acceptance of our "K" polymer-coated cellophane, particularly the high-coverage per pound types, and of polyethylene films for packaging, increased appreciably. Also, the growing interest in "Tedlar" polyvinyl fluoride film as a laminate on metal, wood, and plastic surfaces for outdoor exposure uses by the construction industry has been gratifying.

New facilities were completed during the year for the production of oriented polyolefin films at Clinton, Iowa, and "Teflon" fluorocarbon film at Circleville, Ohio.

Finishes—Sales of finishes increased in all major market areas. The use of "Lucite" interior wall paint continued to expand and the introduction of "Lucite" exterior house paint met with excellent acceptance. Cookware coated with "Teflon" anti-stick finish continues to gain in popularity with housewives due to its ease of cleaning.

"Nordel" Hydrocarbon Rubber—Our new ethylene-propylene terpolymer is being produced at Beaumont, Texas. This high-performance, general-purpose elastomer has excellent chemical and mechanical properties with especially good resistance to weathering. Initial uses include automobile and appliance components, industrial rubber goods, and high-voltage electrical equipment. Many other industrial and consumer uses are under development.

Pigments—Sales of pigment colors and titanium pigments improved over 1962. We are now producing "Ti-Pure" pigments by the superior chloride process in a new plant at Antioch, California; this plant has capacity to meet projected West Coast requirements.

Plastics—Shipments of plastics were generally higher than in 1962, but dollar volume improved only slightly because of price reductions in certain of our product lines. Our plastics business is facing increased competition in many areas as a result of new producers entering the field. To maintain and strengthen our position, we have intensified efforts to develop new types and forms of plastics that will expand existing markets and provide entirely new sales opportunities.

We commercialized a new nylon product, "Dymetrol" strapping, for use in packaging applicants where its combination of strength, elasticity, and ease of handling offers advantages over other types of strapping materials. Good progress was also made in developing a new market for "Zytel" nylon resin as a jacketing material for electrical wire used in the building industry.

"Teflon" fluorocarbon resins found growing acceptance in industrial applications. Typical of these are the increased use of "Teflon" as electrical insulation for heating cable and as a lining for overbraided hose for the process and transportation industries.

Production capacity for high-density "Alathon" polyethylene resins was expanded to supply increasing quantities of new, improved resins for such uses as blow-molded containers.

Sales of "Delrin" acetal resin were increased through development of new uses, particularly as a replacement for metal parts in mechanical applications.

Shoe-Upper Material—Our poromeric material, which has been under extensive development tests in cooperation with shoe manufacturers, has been given the trademark "Corfam". A commercial plant will be completed by mid-year so that men's and women's shoes should be available in retail stores early in 1965. Limited quantities of shoes are now available from material made in pilot plant facilities.

Tariff Negotiations

The United States Government has announced plans to participate in tariff negotiations in 1964 with other member nations of the General Agreement on Tariffs and Trade implementing the tariff reduction authority granted the President by the Trade Expansion Act of 1962. The preliminary list of products on which tariff reductions may be offered by the United States includes a wide range of company products. While we share the Government's announced objective of increasing exports and improving the balance of payments situation, we are quite concerned that concessions by the United States in these negotiations will merely result in a substantial increase in chemical imports without a compensating increase in chemical exports. Our views have been presented to the United States Tariff Commission and to the Trade Information Committee of the Office of the Special Representative for Trade Negotiations with respect to the tariff treatment of all company products which we believe will be importantly affected. We intend to follow closely the course of these negotiations and to take such further action as may seem appropriate.

Research and New Product Development

Approximately 1300 scientists and engineers were engaged in pioneering research in 1963, with an expenditure of $58 million, excluding the cost of laboratories and equipment. This research is of broad scope, covering many areas of chemistry, engineering, physics, and biology. It comprises the search for new scientific knowledge and the more applied but no less demanding work involved in turning new scientific discoveries into technological innovations. Our pioneering research program, the source of major Du Pont earnings in the past, is continuing to provide opportunities for new investment.

In keeping with today's increasing technological demands, a series of products capable of withstanding high temperatures are under development. The experimental nylon called "Nomex" (formerly HT-1) is being tested for high-temperature military and industrial uses in paper and fiber forms. A pilot plant to supply material for this program has gone into operation in Richmond,

Virginia. A new class of polymers, the polyimides, shows promise in a variety of high-temperature applications, including films (H-film), wire enamels and coated fabrics ("Pyre M.L."), and structural uses. In the field of metals, a new alloy, TD (thoria dispersed) nickel for use in service at temperatures up to 2400°F., has been introduced in sheet form.

Research discoveries in fluorine chemistry have resulted in the development of "Zepel" fabric fluoridizer which makes clothing and home furnishings water- and oil-repellent and stain-resistant.

A new type of film called "Cronapress" conversion film has been introduced to the printing trade. This is an opaque film that becomes transparent where pressure is applied. By suitable pressure against metal type, for example, a negative is produced which can be used in preparing lithographic or "Dycril" photo-polymer printing plates. The "Cronapress" system offers a new level of quality, increased speed, and operating economies.

From our biochemical program has come the highly effective "Hyvar" X bromacil weed killer which is being introduced for nonagricultural uses. This material is of low toxicity to animals. Its weed-killing action depends on inhibiting photosynthesis, a process vital only to plant life.

Du Pont Pavilion at New York World's Fair

Stockholders, with their families and friends, are cordially invited to visit the Du Pont Pavilion at the New York World's Fair. The Pavilion entertainment, titled "Wonderful World of Chemistry", will be performed in two theaters and a large display area.

In the theaters, actors, synchronized with motion pictures, will provide a lively musical-product revue. Exciting chemical demonstrations will follow in the display area.

The Fair opens April 22, 1964, and will run for two summer seasons.

Record $370 Million for Plant Construction

The company's heavy engineering work load continued through 1963; construction expenditures of $370 million exceeded by far the previous high of $245 million in 1962.

Activities included construction of new plants, modernization and increased capacities at existing locations, and a number of service facilities and laboratories.

In addition to the major nylon modernization and expansion program, substantial expenditures also were made on other projects at various locations. These included the following:

Products	*Locations*
"Dacron" polyester fiber	Kinston, North Carolina Old Hickory, Tennessee
Spunbonded polyester products	Old Hickory, Tennessee
"Lycra" spandex yarn	Dordrecht, Netherlands Waynesboro, Virginia

Products	*Locations*
"Hylene" organic isocyanates	Deepwater, New Jersey Londonderry, Northern Ireland
Neoprene synthetic rubber	Louisville, Kentucky Montague, Michigan
"Nordel" hydrocarbon rubber	Beaumont, Texas
"Mylar" polyester film	Luxembourg
Polyolefin films	Clinton, Iowa
"Teflon" fluorocarbon film	Circleville, Ohio
Photographic films	Brevard, North Carolina Parlin, New Jersey
Titanium pigments	Antioch, California New Johnsonville, Tennessee
"Corfam" poromeric material	Old Hickory, Tennessee
Hydrofluoric acid	Houston, Texas
"Freon" fluorocarbons	Montague, Michigan
"Alathon" polyethylene resins	Orange, Texas

Construction expenditures in 1964 are expected to be about $295 million.

BUSINESS ABROAD CONTINUES TO GROW

Business abroad again showed significant improvement as the Du Pont Company moved to strengthen its position with established products and continued expansion of subsidiary and affiliated companies in Europe, Canada, Japan, Mexico, and Argentina.

Total foreign business, including nonconsolidated foreign affiliated companies, amounted to $444 million, compared with $388 million in 1962. Europe accounted for 33 per cent, while 27 per cent was in Canada, 23 per cent in Latin America, and 17 per cent elsewhere in the world.

Operating investment of Du Pont's foreign subsidiaries and nonconsolidated affiliated companies at the end of 1963 was approximately $530 million; about $195 million was in Europe, $175 million in Canada, $120 million in Latin America, and $40 million in Japan.

In 1963, exports of products manufactured in United States plants were $206 million; this compares with the same amount in 1962 and $192 million in 1961. Substantial advance shipments were made in December, 1962, in anticipation of a scheduled longshoremen's strike, and probably reduced 1963 exports accordingly.

In Japan in 1963, Nitto Fluorochemicals Company, Ltd., a joint venture, was formed to manufacture fluorocarbon products. Of our other two joint ventures in Japan, Mitsui Polychemicals Company, Ltd. is expanding its polyethylene facilities, and Showa Neoprene K.K. began production of neoprene synthetic rubber.

In Europe, initial production by new plants included "Hylene" organic iso-cyanates by Du Pont Company (United Kingdom) Limited; finishes in Sweden by Du Pont de Nemours Nordiska A.B.; and fungicides by Desarrollo Quimico Industrial, S.A., an affiliate in Spain. In addition, Du Pont de Nemours (Neder-land) N.V. started operating a plant for finishing "Delrin" acetal resins. Du Pont de Nemours (Belgium), S.A. started construction of a plant for finish-ing "Corfam" poromeric material, and Du Pont de Nemours (Luxembourg) S.A. is constructing a plant to manufacture "Mylar" polyester film.

In Latin America, Du Pont de Colombia, S.A., a practically wholly owned subsidiary, was organized to manufacture fungicides in a plant now under construction in Colombia. Ducilo S.A.I.C. expanded its nylon yarn facilities in Argentina. Pigmentos y Productos Quimicos, S.A. de C.V. started enlarging its Mexican titanium dioxide plant. Compania Mexicana de Explosivos, S.A. was merged into Du Pont, S.A. de C.V. to simplify corporate structure.

In Canada, Du Pont of Canada Limited expanded its "Freon" fluorocarbon facilities during the year and is again increasing its nylon yarn capacity.

Activities for U. S. Government

The company has continued its work for the U. S. Atomic Energy Commis-sion. The contract, originally entered into in 1950, was extended for the third time on November 7, 1963. The new expiration date is June 30, 1969.

Work under the contract is centered at the Government-owned Savannah River Plant in South Carolina, which the company designed, built, and oper-ates. During 1963 operations remained at about the level of the past several years. Total expenditure for the year was approximately $100 million from funds made available by the AEC to the company as needed.

The coming year's operations are expected to be at a reduced level since the AEC has announced that, as a part of the national program of curtailment of production of special nuclear materials, one of the five Savannah River pro-duction reactors will be shut down about July 1, 1964. This shutdown will result in a reduction of about 500 in the present Savannah River operating force of about 6300.

The primary task of the plant and of the supporting research and develop-ment work at the Savannah River Laboratory is the production of nuclear materials for national defense. However, as in recent years, a part of the re-search and development effort is being devoted to civilian application of atomic energy.

During 1963 one of the plant's major production areas completed ten years of operation without a major injury. For the plant as a whole, since startup there has never been a lost-time injury as a result of exposure to radioactive materials.

The company continues to have supply, research, and development contracts with the Army, Navy, Air Force, and National Aeronautics and Space Admin-istration.

$1.9 Million for Aid to Education

The Du Pont Company has authorized nearly $1.9 million for grants to universities and colleges in 1964 under its 47th annual program of aid to education. The grants, which went to 168 institutions in all parts of the nation, are designed to advance education in science and engineering by strengthening instruction, assisting in the support of uncommitted basic research, and providing new facilities.

Through this program, the company not only extends direct support to academic fields that are of immediate concern to it but also helps meet the growing financial needs of the schools.

Divestiture of General Motors Stock

The company has made two distributions of General Motors common stock to holders of Du Pont common stock, in compliance with the final judgment, which became effective May 1, 1962, in the Du Pont-General Motors antitrust case. This final judgment requires divestiture of the 63 million shares of General Motors common stock then owned by the company by February 28, 1965.

Approximately 23 million shares of General Motors stock where distributed to Du Pont common stockholders in the initial distribution made on July 9, 1962, and a second distribution of nearly 17 million shares was made on January 6, 1964. The company sold 409,000 shares of General Motors stock in an underwritten public offering early in 1964.

It is contemplated that substantially all of the remaining 23 million shares of General Motors common stock will be distributed to holders of the company's common stock.

Under a complaint filed in June, 1962, in the United States District Court for the Southern District of New York, two holders of Du Pont preferred stock are asking that Du Pont be enjoined from distributing General Motors stock to Du Pont common stockholders. On June 26, 1963, the District Court entered judgment dismissing the plaintiffs' case on the merits. Plaintiffs' appeal from this judgment was heard in February, 1964, by the United States Court of Appeals for the Second Circuit, and it is expected that the Court will hand down its decision sometime during 1964.

Du Pont People . . . . .

Employee Relations

The year 1963 was the seventh consecutive year during which there were no production stoppages due to disputes between employees and management at any company-operated plant.

At the end of the year, there were 100,468 employees here and abroad, not including 6,930 at Government-owned plants. At December 31, 1962, there were 93,159 employees. Increased activity in both construction and manufacturing contributed to the higher level of employment.

Employment of Minority Groups—It has been the policy and practice of the company to employ qualified members of minority groups. In June, 1962, the company signed the "Plans for Progress" statement with the President's Committee on Equal Employment Opportunity. The latter is a voluntary agreement not to discriminate in matters of employment because of race, creed, color, or national origin. The company is giving close attention to the application of this agreement.

Employee Benefits—Salary and wage payments for 1963 to all employees, excluding those at Government-owned plants, were $757 million and included vacation, holiday, and disability payments of $75 million.

Other employee benefits such as pensions, life insurance, hospital and surgical policy, and contributions under the company's Thrift Plan amounted to $107 million. The total cost of employee benefits was $182 million, or the equivalent of 27 per cent of salaries and wages for time actually worked.

The company's Pension and Retirement Plan, one of the earliest employee benefit plans in American industry, was adopted in 1904. The company's contributions to the Pension Trust—$64 million in 1963—are deductible for Federal tax purposes, and the income of the Trust is exempt from such tax.

At the end of the year the total assets of the Trust, at cost, were $790 million. The assets held by the Trustee at December 31, 1963, were invested as follows:

	Assets at Cost	
	Amount	% of Total
	(in thousands)	
Cash	$ 111	—%
U. S. Government obligations	111,887	14
Corporate obligations	348,549	44
Preferred stocks	39,301	5
Common stocks	290,623	37
Total	$790,471	100%

The Trust holds no securities of the Du Pont Company or its affiliated companies.

Safety—The company's safety performance for 1963 established a new record for the second consecutive year. The frequency rate of disabling injuries was .28 per million man-hours worked compared with the previous record rate of .31 for 1962. This compares with the latest available frequency rates of 3.31 for the chemical industry and 6.19 for all industry. Particularly gratifying was the absence of any fatal accident in the company during 1963.

The National Safety Council presented its Award of Honor to the company for the twentieth time in recognition of our 1963 safety performance. Du Pont has won this top award for safety performance more times than any other company.

BONUS PLANS

For many years the company has awarded bonuses for outstanding contributions to the company's success. The incentives provided by the plans have been an important factor in the company's progress. Information concerning the company's three plans will be found on pages 40 and 41.

MANAGEMENT CHANGES

Henry B. du Pont, after 35 years of service with the company, retired voluntarily in May as vice-president and member of the Executive Committee and was elected a member of the Finance Committee. He continues as a member of the Board.

Pierre S. du Pont, a member of the Board, resigned as secretary of the company and as a member of the Finance Committee and was elected a vice-president and member of the Executive Committee, effective June 1.

Henry E. Ford, who was director of the Development Department, was elected secretary of the company.

The death on January 31, 1964, of T. Crawley Davis, a director, vice-president, and member of the Executive and Finance Committees, is reported on page 26.

R. Russell Pippin resigned as treasurer of the company and was elected a member of the Board of Directors, a vice-president, and a member of the Executive and Finance Committees on February 17, 1964, to succeed Mr. Davis.

H. Wallace Evans, formerly first assistant treasurer, was elected treasurer succeeding Mr. Pippin.

Robert L. Richards and Emile F. du Pont, directors of the company, were elected members of the Bonus and Salary Committee in April, 1963, and February, 1964, respectively.

In February, 1964, Jasper E. Crane resigned as chairman and a member of the Committee on Audit. Irénée du Pont, Jr., a director of the company, was elected a member of the Committee on Audit and Walter J. Beadle, a member of that committee, was designated chairman.

STOCKHOLDERS NUMBER 234 THOUSAND

At the end of 1963 owners of Du Pont common and preferred stock totaled 233,985, a small increase over the number at the end of 1962. The holders of common stock increased from 214,654 to 218,280; preferred stockholders numbered 20,676, a slight decrease during the year. There were 4,971 who held more than one class of stock.

About 50,000 employees of the company were shareholders at the year end. It is a source of pride to the management that nearly one-half of the employees are shareholders; this ownership provides an additional interest in the company.

Company shareholders reside in every state of the Union, the District of Columbia, several territorial possessions, and in 61 foreign countries.

Continuing widespread interest in the affairs of the company was evident at the annual meeting held in April, 1963, when 89 per cent of the shares eligible to vote were voted by 145,397 holders of common stock, about 68 per cent of those entitled to vote.

The management appreciates this display of interest and urges each holder of common stock to exercise his right to vote.

The loyalty and high standards of performance by company employees throughout the world were very much in evidence during 1963. It is these qualities which will assure the prosperity of the company in the years to come. It is fortunate indeed that the men and women who have chosen to make their careers in the Du Pont Company are such an outstanding group.

LAMMOT DU P. COPELAND, *President*

Approved by the Board of Directors,

CRAWFORD H. GREENEWALT, *Chairman*

March 13, 1964

Exercises and Problems in Communication

1. Assume that a person from another state has read in his local newspaper a wire release story of a $25 million industrial development in your community. He has written your company asking that you find a likely location for a motel in or near your town. Choose a site that might serve, collect all the information necessary, and write a report to your prospect. In addition to data on tourist traffic, existing competition, utilities, building costs, available labor supply, pertinent population information, and maintenance costs (which points were in the inquiry), you may get additional information on the cost and maintenance of a swimmig pool and of a dining room. Make your report without visual aids, including maps.

2. Write five questions to be asked employees for opinions on the company credit union, on the last company picnic, or on the recently announced lunch period change (from 45 minutes to 30 minutes, with a 15-minute earlier quitting time). The questions are to be asked of five people in each department of the company and will be published in the company magazine.

3. Write the article for Exercise 2.

4. Devise a questionnaire to be published in the company magazine, asking for reader reaction to the magazine.

5. Assume data derived from the questionnaire in Exercise 4 and write a report to the editor of company publications.

6. Devise a questionnaire pertaining to some issue current on your campus. Interview ten students, using the questionnaire, and report your results orally or in writing.

7. Interview a member of your college library staff for information on resource materials of interest to business communication students. Remember that library personnel are "specialized"; in other words, be sure always to go to the person best informed on the subject you are studying. Report your findings.

8. You are asked, as a member of a service group, to get information that will reflect the current opinion of some national or international organization such as the Peace Corps, the American National Red Cross, the Salvation Army, or a labor union. Construct a questionnaire for both *personal* and *telephone* interviews, including your introductory remarks to the interviewee (to establish rapport). Assume data from these two sources and write a report to the group in Washington, which asked your help. Give details of your sampling, that is, how you selected the persons interviewed, how many, etc.

9. Write a memorandum report to the advertising director of your company on the attention, appeals, conviction, and action steps in ten or more direct-mail advertisements.

10. Compare the treatment of report writing in two or more of the following texts:

Anderson, Saunders, and Weeks, *Business Reports* (New York: McGraw-Hill Book Co., 1957)

Brown, *Effective Business Report Writing* (Englewood Cliffs, N.J.: Prentice-Hall, Inc., 1955)

Dawe, *Writing Business and Economics Papers* (Totowa, N.J.: Littlefield, Adams & Co., 1965)

Department of the Air Force, *Guide for Air Force Writing* (Air Force Manual No. 10-4) (Washington, D.C.: Government Printing Office, 1960)

Hay, *Written Communications for Business Administrators* (New York: Holt, Rinehart & Winston, Inc., 1965)

Schutte and Steinberg, *Communication in Business and Industry* (New York: Holt, Rinehart & Winston, Inc., 1960)

Sigband, *Effective Report Writing* (New York: Harper & Row, 1960)

Ulman and Gould, *Technical Reporting* (New York: Holt, Rinehart & Winston, Inc., 1959)

Write an analysis for your instructor. Use the newest edition of each text. Compare such points as (1) qualifications of the author or authors for writing on the subject, (2) facts of publication, kind of publisher, etc., (3) purpose or objectives of the book as announced in its preface, (4) treatment of report writing in detail, (5) style and general characteristics of the book.

11. Write three pages of detailed discussion and analysis of a report on any subject you choose. Study the pages to reduce the length by one-sixth to one-third by transferring some of the data to an appendix.

12. Compare two or three periodicals listed in the front of the *Business Periodicals Index*, to ascertain their respective values for the student of business communications. Here are some suggested points for comparison:

a. Articles on particular kinds of business letters and direct-mail advertising
b. Articles on effective speech in business and industry
c. Articles on developing better reading skills
d. Articles on improving listening for more effective performance and cutting costs
e. Articles on advertising (magazine, newspaper, TV, billboard, etc.)
f. Departments in the various publications (such as "Which Ad Pulled Best" in *Printers' Ink*)
g. Statistical studies, graphs, and similar material of use to the business person
h. Articles on the importance of reporting in business and industry

You will find the above topics listed alphabetically under various headings, such as "Correspondence," "Communication," "Reports," etc.

13. Study the visual devices in five issues of *Fortune, Dun's Review and Modern Industry, Forbes, U.S. News & World Report,* and *Business Week.* Report your findings, using some of the visual aids (roughed out, if your instructor approves) that you found in the periodicals. Use a minimum of text.

14. Using the pages from the National Homes Corporation report as a guide, write subheadings and opening sentences for a page of summarized review of at least five aspects of a company's operations.

15. Write your reactions to the Du Pont report. Using subheadings in a

one-page memorandum, write to your instructor. Assume that your reader has not seen the report.

16. Do as directed in Exercise 15, assuming that your instructor *has seen* the Du Pont report.

17. At your own place of employment, determine a suitable project for study and analysis and prepare a report on it. Use both observation and interviews in getting your information.

18. Interview a number of businessmen, industrialists, or college professors (especially in your major field of study) on what they think should be taught in a college course in business communication. Write a report summarizing the results.

19. Choose a report topic suggested from the following list; prepare the report.

Treatment of reserves on the balance sheet
Financial analysis of _____ Corporation
The effect of U.S. tariff laws on the watch industry of Switzerland
The qualities accounting firms seek in new employees
A market research survey for _____ Company
The use of photoengraving in advertising
Capital gains and losses on the balance sheet
The municipal income tax of _____ (city)
A survey of the effectiveness of _____ (radio or television station) advertising
Testing advertising copy
The operation of radio station _____ (technical)
Film distribution in _____ (area)
Evaluation of salesmanship and personality of department store employees
Executive training program of _____ (store)
Factors influencing choice of a restaurant (questionnaire)
Greenhouse operation
Enrollment trends at _____ (college)
Suitability of _____ (city) for _____ (type of industry)
Report on the _____ department of _____ (plant, store, school)
Survey of current magazine advertising appeals
The prevention of marine boiler scale (technical, NROTC)
A wage incentive system
Promotion of personnel from the ranks
Analysis of daily use of library
Morale of employees and quality of work
Installing a cost-accounting system in a small store
Methods of training door-to-door salesmen
Standard job descriptions of all positions in a small business house
Prepare a section of an Office Manual on letters, reports, etc., for a small business
Prepare a complete report on a small business suitable for a Dun & Bradstreet credit rating
Use of a pay telephone in a busy spot for one day

20. Through the subject and title card catalog in your library, select a book on automation. Write a report comparing or contrasting the author's treatment of the subject with treatment in three or four magazine articles listed in each of the following: *Business Periodicals Index, Applied Science & Technology Index,* and *Readers' Guide to Periodical Literature.*

14

Direct-Mail Advertising

The public at large little suspects the extent to which adver-
tising has been made "respectable" in the last dozen years. There
is much wrong with it still, and always will be, so long as it
*remains a mirror of mankind. . . .—*E. S. TURNER, *The Shocking*
History of Advertising [1]

It is a truism that whenever any circumstance or condition exerts great
influence on a way of life, the people affected have a moot question to
debate, scrutinize, and—less consequentially—to bicker about. Advertising is such a phenomenon, along with weather, education, politics, and
the myriad other phases of life that lend themselves so easily to controversy. A further obvious statement is that advertising does affect the vast
majority of mankind, in some form or another.

Relatively few, to be sure, would be influenced by some of the efforts
to "get the public to buy." An athlete's swimming the English Channel
to laud a certain food product, by having the name of the manufacturer
emblazoned on his shirt, would reach only a handful. "Publicity releases" used daily to promote some ware, event, or person are seen by
more than would be affected by the swimmer's feat. One such release is
included in Bennett Cerf's *Try and Stop Me.* A guest, registered as T. R.
Zann, in a New York hotel requested that a crated "piano" be hoisted to
his room. Shortly, hotel room service had the guest's order for some
fifteen pounds of raw meat. The bellboy delivered the meat to the room,
to be greeted by a roaring, but ancient, lion. In his hasty retreat down
the stairs and through the lobby, the boy was pursued by the animal,

---

[1] This engaging book (London: Michael Joseph, 1952)—not so much an exposé as
the title may imply—gives a comprehensive view of advertising through the past three
centuries. Although the emphasis is on British practices, there is a good look at the development of promotional work in America.

causing other guests to faint, climb onto tables, and hurdle sofas. The metropolitan newspapers that carried the account of this bizarre incident also carried the advertisements for the first of the long series of Tarzan movies. Reader reaction to such promotion is likely to be amusement rather than an impulse to spend money.

Many readers of newspaper and magazine advertising may be affected adversely by what they see, but they can "escape" annoyance by turning the page. The television and radio commercial can be "tuned out" by auditory defense or turned off at will. Although these various ubiquitous attempts to sell may affect the "prospect" unfavorably, supplying substance for governmental investigation and social conversation, it is direct-mail advertising that seems to be under heaviest fire.

As we consider the two sides of this form of sales writing, we should be cognizant, if we are to take a reasonable stand, of Mr. Turner's opinion that advertising is the mirror of mankind. In other words, we are not on one side or the other; we are *in* the fray. "They" are not thrusting something on "us."

What is it about mail advertising that induces more personal reactions than those induced by other forms? The factors seem to be psychological and economic. First, when something is delivered to a person with his name imprinted on it, it "involves" him more than the magazine or newspaper ad; and although the radio and television commercial may "invade the individual's privacy," the words and picture, the recipient reasons, are reaching countless others at the same time. Even when the impersonal "Householder," "Resident," or "Occupant" is used on the envelope, the reaction still is more personal, because his address is his own. An economic detail frequently voiced regarding direct mail has to do with the reduced postal rate for third-class mail, under which the bulk of advertising is sent. "I am paying for this for the advertiser," is the complaint, "by paying more for my first-class mail, because 'they' are getting lower rates." These attitudes have resulted in open, concerted disparagement of advertising by mail; the label "junk mail"[2] is commonly used.

Our purpose here is to see whether conditions may be corrected, to eliminate some of the criticism. Is the problem quantitative or qualitative?

If, as noted in Chapter 8, 85 per cent of the 18.4 billion pieces of third-class mail and 10 per cent of the 35.8 billion first-class mailings are advertisements, perhaps some of the difficulty does lie in volume. If, as mentioned throughout this book, the quality of writing needs improvement, then that side of the question bears examination.

The question may be partially resolved when we realize that some mail advertisers have returns on a mailing as high as 80 and 90 per cent; and that these successful campaigns do not necessarily involve small,

---

[2] *The Wall Street Journal,* July 1, 1964, p. 1.

BACHRODT, NEWELL, O'KANE & GANO, INC.

Advertising

75 EAST WACKER DRIVE · CHICAGO 1 · FRanklin 2-4883

GOLD MEDAL

'50 PERCENT RETURN
ON POST CARD SURVEY
OF READER INTERESTS

"Results seem to indicate
that one can inject enough
warmth and appeal into
three short paragraphs to
induce one of every two
recipients to reply," comments Award Winner J. C.
Bachrodt, of Bachrodt,
Newell, O'Kane & Gano,
Inc. Purpose was to learn
readership preferences of
men who did buying of
client's products.

. . . .
. . . .
. . . .

Dear Mr. _____

Gaso Pump & Burner Mfg. Co., our clients for more than 25 years,
are naturally anxious to place their advertising where it is most
likely to be seen by men in positions like yours.

Would you, out of the kindness of your heart, help them by filling
in and returning the enclosed postal card?

It's a two-minute favor that will be warmly appreciated both by our
clients and ourselves. Thanks, sincerely, for your cooperation.

                    Cordially,

            BACHRODT, NEWELL, O'KANE & GANO, INC.

                    J. C. Bachrodt   (Signed)
                    President

Fig. 54. An example of an advertising agency's effort to get information for
a "right" medium for one of its clients. As implied in the explanatory note
(upper right-hand corner), a brief letter can be warm. (By permission of the
Dartnell Corporation.)

select mailing lists. Hazarding an easy out here, then, we can say that it
is not *getting* the third-class mail that creates antipathy; it is the quality
of the contents. Let's explore the possibilities of improvement.

WHAT IS DIRECT-MAIL ADVERTISING?

Through personal experience, most persons think of direct mail as
being an envelope containing a printed sales letter, a folder or circular,
a return card, and a return envelope. This is one kind of mailing and
the one we shall discuss first; however, as described later in the chapter,
mail advertising is sometimes issued in more elaborate, artistic form.

We do distinguish between the sales letter, discussed in Chapter 8,
and this type of sales writing. A mail advertisement will commonly have

a mass-produced letter and the pieces mentioned in the preceding paragraph.

To be successful, either medium will meet the requirements of a persuasive sales presentation: attention, appeals, conviction, and action. The sales letter will embody these four steps; the mail advertisement will also, but they may also be found among the pieces included with the covering letter. Other, more extensive, campaigns may, as we shall see, apply the various steps in different mailings during the campaign.

OTHER FEATURES OF DIRECT-MAIL ADVERTISING

In addition to the fundamental parts of sales writing, there are other factors to be heeded to maintain standards of advertising, as established by the American Association of Advertising Agencies.

The writing must be in good taste. Because of varying principles and tastes among individuals, a writer must be wary of offending readers' sensitivities. Caution must be exercised in any area of a personal nature. Moral, social, ethnic, religious, and political insinuations can be hazardous. Violation of good taste is illustrated in a letter sent out by a heating contractor. To be delivered just before Veterans Day, the envelope contained a four-page folder with pictures and specifications of heating units. In the upper left-hand corner of the letter was a picture of a grave with a cross. The opening sentence, "It's time to reflect on his sacrifice," replaced the salutation. The first paragraph of three or four sentences dealt with the futility of war. The second paragraph began: "And it's time to think ahead to keeping warm this winter."

Danger of offending is the bane of an organization's existence, especially of firms selling to the public. Great care is taken, not only in advertising, but also in texts of radio and television programs sponsored by companies not to suggest aspersion or criticism of groups or persons.

The writing should be logical. Exaggerated claims and unsubstantiated or incredible conviction steps enfeeble much sales writing. A lack of logic results from not considering readers' sensibilities. Or a writer may follow the line of least resistance and resort to stereotypes, overusing superlatives. On this point, David Ogilvy advises that a writer never write an advertisement that he wouldn't want his own family to read. He elaborates:

You wouldn't tell lies to your wife. Don't tell them to mine. Do as you would be done by.

If you tell lies about a product, you will be found out—either by the Government, which will prosecute you, or by the consumer, who will punish you by not buying your product a second time.

Dear Fellow Alumnus:

The well-known painter, Ivan Albright, once told about the difficulties he encountered with English composition at the university he attended. Paper after paper that he submitted came back with the grade of 60. Annoyed, he "borrowed" an essay by Stevenson, submitted it, and was transfixed when Stevenson came off with the same grade. So he entered Poe, Conrad, and Bret Harte. When they all were returned with a grade of 60, Albright decided that literature was hopeless and took up the brush.

My problem is that in the last few years during which I have been writing you, I haven't drawn a single response. My score is zero. Even 60 would look good to Ludgin, who by the way hasn't Albright's choice, because he can't paint.

Last year, 1,700 additional alumni contributed to the Alumni Fund. If I had presented the University's case adequately, I am sure you would have been among them.

"Time" Magazine took a look at the general situation and in the January 18 issue reported:

"The U.S. private educational plant is in trouble. An estimated 50% of the private colleges operate in the red.

"Furthermore, too many contributions are donated for specific scientific projects which tend to unbalance the college as a whole by building up one department at the expense of the others. Universities need unrestricted funds."

At the University of Chicago, which has always been noted as a superlative graduate school, we have many alumni who took only their graduate work at the University. They may find it hard to contribute both to their undergraduate college and to the University. If you are one of these, let me hasten to say that a dollar ($1) would go a great way toward indicating interest, gratitude, nostalgia, or here-it-is-now-leave-me-alone.

The University does need your help. Chancellor Kimpton announced recently that for the first time in years the budget is in balance. But precariously. And the Alumni Fund is an important part of the base. When you send your dollar (or $5 or $10) your University will indeed be grateful, and you will spare yourself from reading compositions by Poe, Conrad, or Bret Harte, to which I must have recourse if my own efforts fail.

Very sincerely,

[signed—Earle Ludgin]

Chairman

Good products can be sold by *honest* advertising. If you don't think the product is good, you have no business advertising it. If you tell lies or weasel, you do your client a disservice, you increase your load of guilt, and you fan the flames of public resentment against the whole business of advertising.[3]

Or, trying to be original, the writer may become fascinated with his own composing, forgetting that he is writing to *people* and that his purpose is to persuade, not to affect. Of this failing, Mr. Ogilvy says that the copywriter insults the prospect's intelligence, in assuming that a mere slogan and a few vapid adjectives will persuade him to buy anything. What with competing brands becoming more and more alike, there is a tendency away from facts in advertising because the copywriter concludes that there is little point in describing what is common to all brands. Salesmen find that customers want facts; the sales writer will do well to use them too.

The writing should be straightforward. Although buyers want to have confidence in a seller and look to him for knowledge, they resent a patronizing tone. The average person wants an attitude of equality in understanding, if not in knowledge.

Often, a writer injects a tone of condescension through wording, merely through a lapse in the "you" attitude. An example is in a June letter on Christmas merchandise from a novelty manufacturer to suppliers. The writer *told* his readers that Christmas was six months off. "If you visited our warehouses today, you would check your calendar thinking it was Christmas," he wrote. "But the Yuletide season is about six months away." Not only would suppliers know the months of the year, but more damaging is the suggestion that they would not know that holiday merchandise is advertised to them in summer. If the writer wanted to "justify" his letter, he could have *alluded to* the time span with some such comment as "You'd never think Christmas is still six months away if you could see our packed warehouses."

Sales writing "pull" should be tested. A few years ago, a Midwestern lamp manufacturer sent me four letters he had composed, asking that I rate the selling power of the individual letters. I declined to "rate" his compositions. I explained my refusal by instructing my acquaintance to make four sample matched mailing lists and to use one of his letters for

[3] *Confessions of an Advertising Man* (New York: Atheneum, 1963), p. 99.

Fig. 55. The attractiveness of this solicitation letter is evidenced by its being used in modified form by other college alumni associations since Mr. Ludgin wrote it over a decade ago. (Used by permission of Mr. Harry Sholl, Director of the University of Chicago Alumni Fund.)

each of the lists. If he followed that advice (I haven't heard from him since my letter), he got the only meaningful rating possible: the number of orders or inquiries received in answer to a mailing. The effectiveness of sales writing is gauged by present sales and future contacts stemming from the writing, not by the writer's or an "expert's" *opinion* of it. Before a company spends thousands of dollars on a direct mail campaign, the mailings can and should be tested by sample mailing.

Only newspaper advertising, among the various media, can be tested more readily than direct mail. An ad appears in an issue and the merchant knows by the next day whether the copy has been effective. Radio, television, and magazine advertising are slower in showing returns. An advertiser sends out his mail and within days he can know whether it is profitable.

For the mail advertiser, some of this advantage in testing is in the direct line between the seller and the buyer. To quote Mr. Ogilvy again: "The mail-order advertiser has no retailers to shrink and expand their inventories, to push his product or to hide it under the counter. He must rely on his advertisements to do the entire selling job. Either the reader clips the coupon, or he doesn't." [4] Whichever action the recipient takes tells the advertiser how effective his campaign is.

If the ad is successful, authorities say to continue using it until it wears out. This general principle needs some modification. Often a strong letter loses its vitality because the basic quality that has made it successful is copied and used by other advertisers. An ad may be directed at a limited market, making it short-lived. New markets are necessary for some products. Too, it is found that mail advertising successful in one section of the country may not pull in another. Time, Inc., has had this experience with subscription letters.

THE PARTS OF A MAILING

A mailing is what you hold in your hand when you take a letter from your mailbox. It includes the envelope and everything inside the envelope. The letter is part of the mailing, but only part—you would not expect to sell an automatic stoker, oil furnace, or automobile by letter alone. Your prospective buyer must see what these things look like and how they work. Some enclosures show the reader the product and explain how it works; other enclosures make it easier for the reader to order; all the enclosures work right along with the letter to do the selling job. The most frequently encountered elements in a mailing are these:

1. *The outside envelope.* The envelope may determine whether the sales message will be read or thrown into the wastebasket unopened.

[4] *Ibid.,* p. 91.

It is therefore not a factor to be underestimated. There are two opposing theories about the envelope: some say it should conceal its advertising content, and others say it should proudly show pictures, cartoons, or slogans related to the product to be sold. The envelopes which attempt to conceal the nature of their contents look as much as possible like first-class business letters, with modest printed return addresses and typed inside addresses; the frankly sales-directed envelopes are colorful and clever, appealing to the curiosity or probable "weaknesses" of the reader (one of my weaknesses is seed catalogues, and I can always recognize the pictorial envelopes they come in). Special tricks include brown manila envelopes similar to those checks are mailed in (return address, "Treasurer's Office"; contents, finance company advertising) and strips of stamps used to pay the third-class mail rate while looking like extra postage for special delivery (an illusion aided by a rubber-stamp marking "URGENT"). Color studies show that yellow, pink, or green outside envelopes consistently produce more orders than white.

Competing for readers' attention, many advertisers announce the contents on the envelope. "Free Gift Offer Inside," "Valuable Coupons Enclosed," "U.S. Coins Enclosed," or "Air Mail Reply Requested" entice the reader to open the envelope. Although critics of these envelope attention devices are aware of the economy in using third-class mailings containing air-mail reply cards and envelopes, they express resentment at what they term the inconsistency of sending "urgent" mail other than first class. The D. E. Robinson Company, Cleveland, reports that mail-order statistics have proved time and again that "teaser copy" on the envelope helps increase replies.

There are other "envelope features" for attention getting. The *Reader's Digest* has used the anecdotal opening, giving some fifty to one hundred words of a quickly developed narrative on the left front side of the envelope. The climax is reached in the last lines on the envelope, and the story is continued in the first lines of the letter. Cartoons have helped get the reader inside. Advertisers also "start the sale" by picturing their products on the reverse side of the envelope.

2. *The letter.* An important point to remember is that no reader likes a letter to attempt to "lead him by the hand" through a folder or booklet. The letter should be planned to correlate with the enclosures, but it should not be considered a guided tour through them.

3. *Folders, booklets, catalogs.* The biggest disadvantage of sales letters has always been their lack of pictures. A sales letter to be effective must be reasonably short; it seldom has room or appropriate place for charts, graphs, photographs, diagrams, cartoons, testimonials, and other material to illustrate or explain the main selling points. The ideal

place for such corroborative material is a colorful pamphlet, booklet, or folder to be included in the mailing. An 8½ × 11 sheet folded twice to make a 3⅔ × 8½ folder is the least expensive; it can be printed in one color for as little as $15 a thousand. At the other extreme in price are booklets printed in full color at a cost of $900 or more a thousand.

4. *Samples.* Direct mail has used many unusual samples: swatches of car upholstery, miniature mimeo stencils, tiny vials of lubricating oil, perfume-saturated cutouts of tigers and straw hats, cellophane envelopes of aluminum nails, plastic countertop material in the shape of checkers, and pages out of the middle of new books being offered for sale. It is possible to build the sales message of the letter around the sample. For example, a home insulation company attached a small piece of rock wool insulation to the top of the page, and in the text invited the reader to try to light it and to try to get it to absorb water; the reader could thus prove for himself that it was fireproof and water-resistant.

A custom tailor in Hong Kong sends American customers four or five sheets (each sheet containing 24 swatches, 1 by ¾ inches) of samples of fabrics, available for garments. The expense of this display, more elaborate than printed pages, is reportedly more than offset by increased orders.

5. *Customer service reminder.* A customer service reminder is a gift from the company that is so useful or valuable that the recipient will not throw it away. Generally the reminder has the company name imprinted to keep it before the customer. The most common examples are blotters, calendars, desk pads, pocket reminders, pencils, wallets, and key cases. Firms selling to specialists sometimes develop extremely clever customer service reminders to fit the needs of the specialists they serve. A drug company, for example, wishing to give an inexpensive but useful gift to physicians, prepared a plastic X-ray exposure calculating wheel which saves valuable time for its users.

6. *Order blank.* Although the order blank is still sent out by nearly all wholesaling firms, it has been largely replaced in retailing by the reply card and the special offer coupon. The special offer coupon is really a kind of small order blank made to look more like a stock certificate in order to emphasize its "value" to the customer when he fills it out and sends it in.

7. *Reply card.* The prepaid business reply card has become a direct-mail trademark; some customers feel a bit abused nowadays if they do not receive it. There has been little change in the reply card since its introduction, although the typography has become more interesting, the colors are brighter, and the size tends to vary more.

8. *Reply envelope.* The envelope has one great advantage over the card: you can put a check into it. The card is easier to fill out and mail, however, and it permits the customer to defer payment for his purchase. Some companies cover all bets by sending both reply card and reply envelope.

9. *Apology for possible mailing list duplication.* Since it is often impossible or impractical to check a new mailing list against old ones, the kind of enclosure reproduced as Figure 56 is rather common.

Obviously no mailing should ever contain all the items mentioned above; if one did it would have to be sent by freight! Most mailings use three or four of them. Sometimes the parts of the mailing are combined; I have in my collection examples of combination letter-folders, customer-service-reminder-samples, letter-samples, outside envelope-folders, outside envelope-letter-folder-reply cards (all in one piece), and reply envelope-letters.

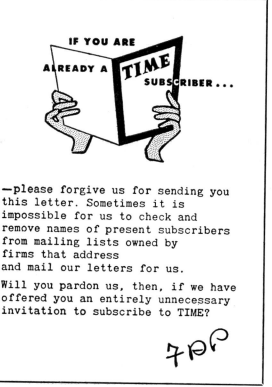

Fig. 56. Apology for duplicate mailing. (Used by permission.)

CALDWELL-CLEMENTS, INC. • 480 LEXINGTON AVENUE, NEW YORK 17, N.Y. • Plaza 9-7880

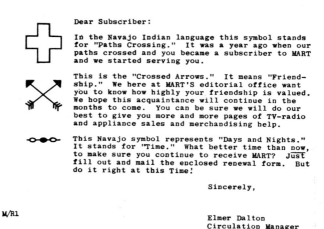

Dear Subscriber:

In the Navajo Indian language this symbol stands for "Paths Crossing." It was a year ago when our paths crossed and you became a subscriber to MART and we started serving you.

This is the "Crossed Arrows." It means "Friendship." We here at MART'S editorial office want you to know how highly your friendship is valued. We hope this acquaintance will continue in the months to come. You can be sure we will do our best to give you more and more pages of TV-radio and appliance sales and merchandising help.

This Navajo symbol represents "Days and Nights." It stands for "Time." What better time than now, to make sure you continue to receive MART? Just fill out and mail the enclosed renewal form. But do it right at this Time!

Sincerely,

M/R1

Elmer Dalton
Circulation Manager

P.S. I'm sure you agree MART'S PRICE-FAX repays you the modest subscription fee many times over. There you receive more data on new models and prices than any other source or sources – and at no extra charge.

Fig. 57. A periodical-renewal letter using artwork for attention. (Used by permission of the Dartnell Corporation.)

The letter-folder is generally a four-page combination. The first page contains the sales letter; pages two and three open as a circular or spread, usually with one or more illustrations of what is for sale; and page four may have more illustrations and an order form. Thus a company selling cash registers uses the first page for a letter directed to the attention of the manager, auditor, or treasurer of a firm; the center spread for illustrations in color and full descriptive information; and the back for a clever illustration and the local dealer's name and address. A stationery company employs a similar four-page combination, with illustrations of its stationery and an order blank at the end. For a book the center spread might show the table of contents.

The reply-o-letter, a relatively new invention, allows a reply card or envelope to be slipped into a pocket in the letter sheet so that the name and address of the addressee (printed on the back of the card or inside flap of the envelope) can show through a window above the salutation. The letter can be folded in such a way that the same name and address will show through a window in the outside envelope and serve as the outside address. Figure 58 shows this device.

GOLD MEDAL

A FREE GIFT
For Your Baby

From
WASHINGTON NATIONAL INSURANCE COMPANY

This beautiful
SOLID GOLD RING

16 PERCENT RETURN ON LARGE MAILINGS WITH PROCESSED LETTER AND REPLY CARD

Do sales letters have to be personalized? No! says Award Winner Frank Elston, of the Washington National, who got a consistent 16 percent reply from several mailings of this letter and the window-pocket card which accompanies it.

I want you to accept, with our compliments, this beautiful solid gold ring for your baby.

It's just our way of saying "Welcome" to the new arrival and "Congratulations" to the proud parents! Simply return the card in the window above to me and I'll send the ring to you right away.

This lovely ring is pictured above. Notice the dainty engraving -- you'll be proud to have baby wear it. And it will fit right now, for it was specially designed to twinkle on a tiny finger.

With the gold ring come our wishes for a lifetime of good things for your new baby.

You probably want your child to enjoy the benefit of a college education, and the greater earning advantages this training can provide. You may now save for your child's college education gradually . . . through the Washington National Education Plan, which assures your child the advantages of college no matter what the future may bring.

To receive your baby's precious gold ring and additional information on this excellent Education Plan, just pull out the card and drop it in the nearest mail box. As you see, it needs no postage or signature.

Cordially yours,

KM:EP   Vice President

Fig. 58. An illustration of the reply-o-card for easy response. Names for the mailings were obtained from birth announcements in newspapers and from county clerks' files. (By permission of the Dartnell Corporation.)

DISTINCTIVE DIRECT-MAIL CAMPAIGNS

Selling by mail, as mentioned earlier, is not restricted to consumer goods. Suppliers and manufacturers use the medium too. A feature of the Direct Mail Advertising Association annual convention is the competition among direct-mail entries. Description of one award-winning entry will emphasize the contrast between the "four-piece" mailing just discussed and a DMAA award-winner.

The Union Bag and Paper Company, makers of mailing and shipping cartons and bags, sent out over a year's time, a nineteen-piece series, to a mailing list of purchasing agents of prospective companies. The first three mailings, at three-day intervals, did not identify the sender of the attractively simple brochures. The third mailing contained the Chinese ring puzzle (with instructions for solving it), suggestive of the joined rings, which are a part of the company's trademark. These mailings were postmarked from China, Maine, in keeping with the fictitious Chinese character Yoon Yun, who personified the company throughout the campaign. The remaining sixteen pieces were sent from the home office at three-week intervals.

Much of the copy was in narrative, with Yoon Yun telling the story. The copy, the artwork, the printing all followed the Oriental motif. About every fourth mailing included a game (an attractive set of magnetized pick-up sticks), a puzzle, an edible fruit (litchi nuts). Each of these, a conversation piece, was correlated with the company products. Even those mailings that contained no novelties were six- and eight-page brochures and booklets produced in four and five colors.

Colorful accounts of the history and a full description of the manufacture of cardboard products served as appeals. Conviction consisted of reference to present big-name customers, photographs of product testing, and actual use of the product, Union Bag containers being used for the mailings.

Although action was invited intermittently throughout the campaign, the full action step was in the nineteenth piece. A 3-by-5-inch card asked that the recipient of the series receive the company representative when he called. The card (the message on which is given here to show the tone of the campaign) was printed in "Chinese script" and accompanied a trick-box with secret panels, and instructions for working it. The box contained two decks of playing cards, with Yoon Yun's picture on the back.

Honored One:
It has been truly said that man does not plant a tree for himself.
This humble one would feel richly rewarded if, as in previous visits, he has been successful in conveying seeds of good packaging.

As time for Yoon Yun's leave-taking draws near, please accept this modest remembrance.

Box not altogether ordinary. One may open and see nothing. With second look, same container yields hidden treasure. Small memento may remind of many unseen virtues of dependable Union corrugated shipping container.

Attached business card bears name of illustrious associate who soon will call on you. A brief audience will be most sincerely appreciated by him, and by your faithful

Yoon Yun

P.S. Secret panel for box shown under flap.

Favorable reactions to such series make them worthwhile for the advertiser, because he has departed from commonplace practices.

THE MAILING LIST

The key to success in mail advertising is *circulation*. Even the best-planned letters and brochures must go to the right persons to be successful. A good mailing list enables the letter to achieve the circulation it needs in order to realize its advantage of being a fuller and more personal selling message than the periodical advertisement or the radio or television commercial can possibly be.

You have probably wondered why you continue to receive duplicate advertising over a period of time. The experience is likely the result of your name's appearing on different mailing lists used by the sender. And your name has not been deleted from the lists because of the notion that to screen names is more costly than to send duplicate mailings. Using an unscreened list can be a false economy. Homer J. Buckley, of Buckley, Dement and Company, advertising consultants in Chicago, expresses his willingness to spend one-fourth of a mail-campaign budget for a qualified prospect list. To support his stand, Mr. Buckley describes mail advertising as a *class* medium, not a *mass* medium.

William Baring-Gould, formerly Time, Inc., circulation promotion manager, restricts the function of selling by mail even more than Mr. Buckley does:

. . . when you are advertising to register how big you are, how good you are, how strong you are, you had better not try to do it with direct mail advertising. But when you want an important prospect to realize what your product or service or cause can mean to him *personally*, then it is time for you to begin thinking about direct mail *too*, by way of reinforced coverage to carry your message quite literally home to the people you are most interested in reaching.[5]

The course of prospect lists is illustrated in a seven-year-old's experience. To relieve the youngster's disappointment because he was not

[5] From an unpublished paper "Direct Mail Advertising—How *Time, Life,* and *Fortune* Use It."

receiving mail as his sister, twelve, was, he was allowed to clip a "free booklet" coupon from a magazine advertisement for a Canadian resort. For over two years he received advertising on travel, hotel accommodations, resort facilities, and real estate investments from Florida, Wisconsin, and the New England states. All these were addressed to Miss Rose Gregg. In his indistinct printing, his name, Ross, had apparently been misread as "Rose" on the original coupon to the Canadian resort.

An unscreened mailing list is the proverbial blind target. After a company's identity has been established (oftentimes before the envelope is opened), a letter to an "unlikely prospect" is likely a waste of money. The president of an Iowa company (in his late fifties) was hardly convinced by the opening statement, "There's a bright future for you in Television," in a letter from a Chicago firm, training television technicians. To add to the inappropriateness, the letter was sent to the man at his company address.

HOW TO COMPILE A MAILING LIST

Since the quality of the mailing list is so important, it will be worthwhile to learn how to build it. Compiling a mailing list should be approached with the attitude of the sales manager. As has been said, a prospect list is good or bad directly in proportion to the business obtained by its use. In general, there are four sources of lists: (1) free lists (those available for the taking, for example, from directories); (2) created lists (those made up by the user himself); (3) purchased lists; and (4) traded lists.

Directories are the commonest source of *free* lists. The basic telephone book is not a good source of lists except for such a purpose as a community fund, but the classified directory frequently is, since it is selective to the extent of grouping names according to occupation or trade. Some clubs and associations print their memberships, thus supplying somewhat specialized lists, usually with up-to-date addresses. Government records are a fruitful source of mailing lists for certain advertisers. An enterprising bank secured a very large number of savings deposit customers through a mailing piece addressed to newborn children, the names obtainable, of course, from the city clerk's records of birth certificates. Names of newly-weds, automobile owners, and other lists from public records are obtainable if the officials are obliging enough to permit copying them, and many are.

There are almost countless ways of *creating* mailing lists, limited only by the resourcefulness of the seller. The familiar department store Santa Clauses at Christmas time commonly secure names and addresses from the children. Tire dealers may pay filling station operators for license numbers of autos whose tires are badly worn, then secure from the auto registration lists the names and addresses of the owners. Free offers of merchandise in department stores or offers with coupons in magazine or newspaper advertising will bring in names. Customers who are actually in a department store are better advertising prospects than those who are not; individuals who fill out coupons may be presumed to be at least somewhat interested in the article being advertised. Salesmen on the road can readily secure names of likely prospects, and customers respond readily to requests for names of their friends. Also, employees of large firms may be an excellent source of a mailing list for articles being manufactured, since every employee may know several persons in need of the product.

Dealers in building materials and paints use "scouts" or "canvassers" to get names of prospects. A need for such commodities as roofing, paint or siding, screens, or awnings is easily discovered; merchants employ persons such as members of teen-age clubs to cover sections of town and report addresses (and names, if known) for the compilation of names for mail advertising. There are few consumer products that do not lend themselves to selling from a list made from a telephone canvass. Under this approach, the canvasser works from the telephone directory, calling to describe the product or products the merchant is selling. In many of these programs, if the person called shows any interest at all, a letter telling more about the product is sent to him. To be effective a letter used in follow-up should refer to the phone call. One dealer opened his letter with "It was good to learn of your interest in [name of product] when we phoned you the other day."

These are only a few suggestions for plans that may be used in developing mailing lists. Creating excellent lists is limited only by the individual seller's imagination and resourcefulness.

Many advertisers find it advisable to *buy* good mailing lists prepared by individuals or firms specializing in such work. The classified section of any metropolitan telephone directory shows scores of sources for lists. Even relatively small cities will have one or two commercial listings for this service. Look in the classified section of your telephone directory under "Mailing Lists" and "Addressing Service" to see how many names are listed. Call one of the names under the second category and you will likely learn that the company (or individual) has lists for sale, also.

The diverse coverage of available lists is shown in referring to a mailing-list company catalog. One company catalog devotes 79 pages to categories by interest, age, and occupation; these entries range from AAA Branch Offices (720 names; price for the list, $24.00) to Zwieback Manufacturers (24 names; price, $9.00). The company can supply names of 7,002,000 women wage-earners (at $27.50 per thousand) or one Household-Cleaning-Utensils Museum ($4.50). This company advertises that one additional name in a group may prove invaluable. Years ago, the company added George Bernard Shaw to its list of publishers, mailed him a company catalog, and he became a regular client.

Trading mailing lists is ordinarily carried on between non-competitors selling to the same general classes of people; associations are sometimes formed for the purpose of such exchanges. It is quite possible that the incident related about the seven-year-old's direct-mail experience hinged on such an exchange of names among companies in various regions.

The following sources are listed as starting points from which refined, specific lists may be made:

1. Customers (active and inactive accounts, service tickets, C.O.D. orders, etc.)
2. Federal government records
3. County and state records
4. Municipal records
5. Business organizations
6. Professional organizations
7. Social organizations
8. Civic and service clubs
9. Schools and colleges
10. Churches and affiliated groups
11. Directories (city, telephone, manufacturers, etc.)
12. Voter registration lists
13. Names obtained through various advertising media (newspaper, magazine, television, radio, and telephone)
14. Newspaper clippings
15. Purchased and rented lists
16. Traded lists
17. Convention and conference rosters
18. Directories of names in various fields of endeavor (education, medicine, law, engineering, theatre, etc.)
19. Credit agency reports
20. Publishers' and manufacturers' listings and reports

Although it may seem an obviously necessary step, many advertisers do not apply the "you" attitude in considering their mailing lists. For a campaign to be successful, certain specifications about the typical prospect should be established. Who is he? Is his income a factor in the item you are selling? Does his age play a part in the commodity or service you are offering him? Is his occupation a factor? If you are advertising to a firm, is size a factor?

SELECTIVITY AND CURRENCY AS FACTORS IN MAILING LISTS

Just as a discerning salesman will not call on an unlikely prospect, so the perceptive merchandiser will use judgment in *pruning* and *sub-*

classifying lists. When the mailing piece is relatively expensive (for instance, a large profusely illustrated catalog), or when the object is to line up prospects for salesmen's calls, it is advisable to make the list quite selective. This may be done by mailing out a letter calling for the return of a card or other evidence of special interest in the article or service for sale.

The fact that a mailing list was good once does not mean that it will be good indefinitely. Millions of first-class letters with advertising are received every year in the Division of Dead Letters and Dead Parcel Post. The number of circular letters and third-class material is astronomical. Some of this lost effort for the advertiser is due, of course, to the mobility of the American public. Residents and dwellers are moving constantly; even business addresses change around 20 per cent each year.

In addition to the waste of materials and postage in these missent mailings, they are a source of antagonism. Old customers do not like to be treated as prospects, nor do new residents like having their mail boxes filled with advertising addressed to their predecessors. Resentment toward mail-advertising growing out of unscreened and undiscriminating prospect lists results in other costs to advertisers.

One cost increase comes from the advertisers' paying postage on lead washers, metal slugs, and other pieces returned in the addressed envelope, which designates that return postage on the mailing will be paid by the advertiser. These mailings frequently include derogatory notes telling the advertiser to "quit sending me this trash advertising," to "lay off with this junk in my mailbox," or that the advertiser will receive "a much heavier package to pay postage on the next time."

Another action taken by disgruntled addressees is filling in the order card with another person's name and address. This antic creates a bigger problem for the advertiser in customer relations; he must appease the person who receives the unwanted order and the attendant collection letters. Robert Clarke, former vice-president of Grolier Enterprises (encyclopedias and other reference books), reports incidents of order cards returned to advertisers for merchandise to be sent to 1600 Pennsylvania Avenue, Washington, D.C. The usual follow-up mailings, including letters for payment, go subsequently to the President of the United States, his family, or members of the White House staff. It is quite often found that the order has been sent by some "joker," who had been harassed by receiving advertising he had no interest in.[6]

To some, these isolated cases (they are becoming more numerous) might argue against the expediency of direct-mail advertising as a medium. This reaction is unwarranted; as a concept, direct mail is still sound. As in any phase of activity, indiscriminate applications can play havoc with a system or plan.

[6] *The Wall Street Journal,* July 1, 1964, p. 1.

Since for purposes of economy in large mailings, form letters are used, the most important general method of *personalizing* the direct-mail message is careful selection of the mailing list. As we have already seen, it must be planned so that one type of purchasing group will receive a letter written to appeal especially to that group. Such care can avert some of the antipathy just discussed; it can go a long way toward keeping the person receiving the form letter from thinking he is only one among many. He knows his wants, and if he needs what is offered in a form letter, he will consider the transaction as between only himself and the seller.

CONTINUOUS, CAMPAIGN, AND WEAR-OUT SERIES

The simplest type of the follow-up series is the *continuous*. It is used by a firm that wishes to increase its sales to the customers it already has; its mailing list is merely the store's customer list. Each customer will stay on the list until he dies or moves away; over a period of years he may receive as many as a hundred mailings from the store's continuous series. The continuous series differs from the two types which follow in that the letters in the series may sell different products. One letter from a department store may emphasize new fall clothing; the next may announce a back-to-school sale; the next might be a reminder to do Christmas shopping early. The seasonal nature of this series is common to most continuous follow-up plans; as winter follows fall and spring follows winter, letters appropriate to the coming season are prepared and mailed. Thus a flower shop or a candy store would send letters before Christmas, Valentine's Day, Easter, Mother's Day, and perhaps graduation. A service station would mail suggestions to change grease and oil or to check the antifreeze. There is a tendency to use the continuous series to build business in a weak season by creating demand where none existed; if the customers would ordinarily stay away in January perhaps a special sale would bring them in.

The *campaign* series is theoretically the most effective but actually the riskiest of the follow-up types. Traditionally the campaign series has been used to introduce a new product or to produce the maximum cumulative sales effort for a comparatively expensive product. The theory seems logical: if you are going to send several letters selling the same thing it would be more effective to concentrate all the conviction material in one letter, all the action in another, than to divide the conviction into dribbles of three or four lines in each letter. To put this theory into practice a conference is generally called to plan the campaign. A direct-mail specialist with the aid of the company's advertising department prepares what might be called one long letter containing all the selling points and all the appeals that will be used in the campaign. If this long letter were typed on a continuous sheet of letterhead stationery it might be three or four feet long. Next the letter is divided into lengths of logical letter size, and after certain modifications it is sent out in installments, much as if you were to cut the three-foot length of letter into smaller pieces with scissors and send the pieces out one at a time. If the original letter were cut in four parts, the reader would probably find that the first part would contain only the attention and interest steps of the sales process; the second part, the appeals; the third, conviction; and the last, action. If more than four letters are sent, there will be two or even more appeals letters and conviction letters, and perhaps separate letters for attention and interest.

Of course the preparation of any campaign series is not as simple as writing a long letter and then cutting it apart. For one thing, there is the possibility that the customer will become interested enough to buy the product before the company gets around to mailing him the action letter. Rather than make the customer wait until the last letter before making it possible for him to buy, most firms which use the campaign plan include an action postscript or enclose an action reply card with all letters in the series. Also, the cumulative effect for which the campaign series strives is aided by some kind of unifying keynote appearing in each letter and binding the series together. This keynote may be a brief reference to the attention-interest letter, or a cartoon, design, or color that all the letters have in common.

Figures 59A through 59D, like the Yoon Yun campaign, pave the way for a salesman's call. Observe the use of nautical jargon, variation of length, and the repetition of selling points in the series.

In the *wear-out* series what is worn out is not the customer, nor the customer's sales resistance, but the list. The wear-out series has been used in the past mostly when the authenticity or currency of the list is doubtful or when the product to be sold is comparatively inexpensive. This type of series keeps loss from any cause strictly under control and actually may earn more income from a good list than would a campaign series.

The required return for the first mailing of a wear-out series is determined by simple mathematics. For example, if the unit cost for the mass-produced mailing is 20¢ (including printing, postage, dictator's and secretaries' time, office upkeep) and the number of names on the list is 10,000, the net cost of the mailing will be $2,000. If the net profit on each item sold is $5, 400 items would have to be sold for the first mailing to break even. Every unit sold over 400 is clear profit; every unit under 400 is net loss. If we assume that the first mailing of 10,000 letters brought back 600 orders, that mailing would show a profit of $1,000. Encouraged by this profit, the firm might decide to send a second mail-

Chicago   *Los Angeles*

ORegon 9-7200

WORLD'S LARGEST SELLING BOATING MAGAZINE

ONE PARK AVENUE — NEW YORK 16, NEW YORK

XXXXXXX XX XXXX

XXXXXXXXXXXX
XXXXXXXXXXXX
XXXXXXXXXXXX
XXXXXXXXXXXX

Dear xxxxxxxxxx:

<u>Big boats don't come in small packages</u> . . .

and real ones are expensive . . . so we have sent you a model of a type we think suitable for treasure hunting in the Mer des Antilles.

In case you're curious, a real boat like this could cost upwards of $300,000. We know -- some of our POPULAR BOATING readers own similar vessels.

If this kind of investment makes you hesitate in your search for Spanish gold, you might use this boat in a bottle as a reminder of the far greater sea treasure that is waiting to be shared by you.

The real treasure of the sea is to be found in the 644,000 readers who comprise the POPULAR BOATING luxury market. Not only do these people hold better jobs and have higher annual incomes than readers of most other magazines, but they <u>spend</u> their money too. Last year, for example, POPULAR BOATING readers spent <u>$31,000,000 on entertainment while afloat.</u> They are a luxury-conscious group and a wonderful market for any premium product.

I'll be at the POPULAR BOATING booth at the New York Motor Boat Show all week. If you stop by, you will see how rich the Boating market is, and learn how you can share in its wealth.

But if you should decide to buy a boat instead . . .

I know someone who would like to crew.

                             Cordially,

                             Dick Manning
                             Advertising Director

Fig. 59A. The mailing list for this series comprised the names of 50 company presidents and 50 account executives of companies who were considered prospects for buying advertising space in *Popular Boating.*

ORegon 9-7200

WORLD'S LARGEST SELLING BOATING MAGAZINE

ONE PARK AVENUE — NEW YORK 16, NEW YORK

XXXXXXXXXXX XX XXXX

XXXXXXXXXXXXX
XXXXXXXXXXXXX
XXXXXXXXXXXXX
XXXXXXXXXXXXX

Dear xxxxxxxxxxxxx:

<u>Mal de mer</u> . . .

is one of the hazards we neglected to mention in the letter we sent with your treasure map. Not that we wish to deter you from sailing to warmer seas in search of Spanish gold -- we just thought you should know.

As we haven't heard from you it has occurred to us that you might be seriously contemplating the voyage and so we thought you should be equipped with a proper telescope. With it you can spend many hours in the broiling sun, standing on the quarter-deck scanning the bounding main.

While you are doing that, you might keep in mind that scanning POPULAR BOATING's rich market is a far easier way of finding treasure in the sea. As any of our Sales Representatives can tell you, 48% of POPULAR BOATING's 644,000 readers are in professional, management, and proprietary categories. They represent a high income and quality-minded market for Diners' Club cards.

If you will invite me to send a member of our crew to see you, he will help you chart your course to the greatest sea treasure of all . . . and avoid the need

for Dramamine!

Cordially,

Dick Manning
Advertising Director

Fig. 59B. These letters accompanied the attractive gifts mentioned in the individual letters.

ORegon 9-7200

WORLD'S LARGEST SELLING BOATING MAGAZINE

ONE PARK AVENUE — NEW YORK 16, NEW YORK

XXXXXXXXX   XX   XXXX

XXXXXXXXXXXXXXXX
XXXXXXXXXXXXXXXX
XXXXXXXXXXXXXXXX
XXXXXXXXXXXXXXXX

Dear xxxxxxxxxxxxxxxx:

Stories of treasure are hard to believe . . .

which is probably why you haven't invited us to call. However, we won't give
up trying. We feel the POPULAR BOATING treasure story is a convincing
one . . . one that you ought to hear.

Whether or not you ask us to call, we hope you will accept this last symbol
of treasure that comes from the sea. The chest contains:

> (1) a pearl
>
> (2) a clue to the rich treasure we have to offer

I hope you find use for both of them.

Cordially,

Dick Manning
Advertising Director

P.S.   Call me if you have trouble opening the chest. My salesmen
all have keys.

Fig. 59C. The "clue" in the chest was appeals and conviction in *Popular
Boating*'s sales message. Note the effective use of the postscript, even in a short
letter.

POPULAR
BOATING

WORLD'S LARGEST SELLING BOATING MAGAZINE

ONE PARK AVENUE — NEW YORK 16, NEW YORK

XXXXXXX XX   XXXX

XXXXXXXXXXXX
XXXXXXXXXXXX
XXXXXXXXXXXX
XXXXXXXXXXXX

Dear xxxxxxxxxxx:

Just so you'll know what to look for . . .

we've enclosed a real piece-of-eight. Since we haven't heard from you, we
thought you might have decided to hunt for Spanish treasure after all; and
we wanted to be sure you had a sample of the treasure and knew something
of its value.

This piece-of-eight came from another sunken galleon. It is worth from
$3 to $6 . . . but the market is unstable. The price will go down as more
pieces become available . . . so watch how you pick up the pieces!

However, as we have been saying all along, the value of POPULAR
BOATING's 644,000 readers is highly predictable. They represent a
rich treasure whose real (and increasing) value can be readily determined
by studying "Navigation Aids for Marine Advertisers", a survey of the
Boating market and the magazines that serve it.

All of the information is at our fingertips. If you will contact me, I'll
have one of our sales crew show you where to find the real treasure of
the sea and tell you how you can . . .

pick up all the pieces.

Cordially,

Dick Manning
Advertising Director

Fig. 59D. The series brought 36 invitations for salesmen's calls, or a 36 per
cent return. This figure is well above the 4 to 5 per cent, the objective of the
average direct-mail campaign. (The series is used by permission of the Dartnell
Corporation.)

ing to the 9,400 persons who did not reply the first time. Assuming an inexpensive method of deleting the 600 names, the mailing cost will be less: $1,880 this time. If 376 items are sold, the second mailing will pay for itself. If we assume that only 350 orders are received, the loss would be $130, and the series would be terminated. The 9,050 names from which there was no response represent the worn-out list; the 950 names of active customers would be worth keeping to begin a continuous series or to use as a nucleus list for mailings selling a related product. The net profit on the two wear-out mailings is $870.

The value of the wear-out series is shown dramatically by a comparison with what would have happened in a four-letter campaign series with the same unit mailing cost, the same profit margin per item sold, and the same mailing list. If only 950 sales had resulted, the net loss would have been $3,250.

The wear-out series makes no effort to build to a cumulative effect. Each letter progresses through all four steps of the sales process; each aims at making the sale. The letters in a wear-out series could be sent in any order without changing their effectiveness. An unwritten law of the wear-out series is that no letter makes reference to any previous letter.

A feature of the wear-out series that is making it rise in popularity is the variety of selling approaches that it makes possible. The first letter, for example, may appeal to pride; that failing, the second may appeal to duty, or curiosity, or ambition. The third may strike the right note by appealing to economy: the can't-resist-a-bargain psychology. There is a good chance that in a series of several letters the writer may hit on the right approach or the right combination of approach and reader's bank balance. In the campaign series, on the other hand, the writer is committed to stick to one basic approach for the whole series.

The newest tendency is toward the use of a combination of the features of the campaign and the wear-out series. The letters are planned ahead of time, built around a keynote, and aimed at cumulative effect; however, each follows through all steps of the sales process, and each takes a different approach to the sale. Since they do not test the list as the wear-out series does, they should be used only with a good list.

A FINAL WORD TO THE SALES WRITER

From the foregoing it is evident that direct mail is a highly important part of business writing. Even if selling by mail involves enormous waste and, through misapplication, sometimes alienates the public, it achieves for its best practitioners such success that it will continue to be a major factor in bringing goods and services to the attention of the buying public. Mail advertising cannot work miracles, but, judiciously used, it can prove to be among the best business investments.

Some Don't's and Do's in Sales Writing

Don't use carelessly prepared, unsuitable, or worn-out mailing lists.

Do spend at least as much care on your mailing list as on your letter.

Don't try to sell a class product to a mass group.

Do adapt the letter to the product as well as to the reader.

Don't use sales messages unworthy of the products they advertise.

Do be sure your letter or series embodies the psychological steps to the sale.

Don't think the appearance of the form sales letter doesn't matter.

Do be sure to select the right form of letter reproduction to insure a suitably attractive letter.

Don't send large bulk mailings without first sending small test mailings.

Do select the letter which does best in tests, whether or not you like it best.

Don't send out expensive catalogs and booklets without accompanying letters.

Do put vitality into your letters, remembering that the customer makes purchases in a mood of cheerful buoyancy.

Don't forget that up and coming firms are constantly alert to opportunities for sales promotion.

Do be observant constantly of your customers, of your competitors, of your product—thus you can serve better, and sales will grow.

The Sins of Omission and Commission in Direct-Mail Advertising *

by Homer J. Buckley

"Half of the direct-mail matter I get goes into the wastebasket unread," said a friend of mine recently. "A vast amount of it is money wasted." He looked at me apologetically, half challengingly. He expected me to be crushed, or at least show signs of anger.

"Your estimate is too low," I responded. "My own figure is that 75 per cent of all direct-mail advertising material that is produced and distributed is wasteful."

* Mr. Buckley's significant contribution to the field of direct-mail advertising and the pertinence of his advice to today's practices warrant continued publication of this address. As president of Buckley, Dement & Company, Advertising Counselors, Mr. Buckley gave the talk before the Fourth Annual Convention of the American Business Writing Association, December 29, 1941. It is reprinted from the *ABWA Bulletin* May, 1942, by permission of Mr. Buckley.

This statement may surprise most of you in this gathering today, and cause you to say . . . "Why is this situation tolerated?" "Why does not someone do something about it?" "What is the remedy?"

Well, let's first get this thought clearly registered in our minds. Direct Mail is the only medium of advertising which is wide open, with no restrictions of authorized or official recognition, in which the amateur is permitted to engage. He can write, print, and mail—to his heart's content—or to the extent of his available funds. These amateurs—with some knowledge of the graphic arts, typography, layout, and copy—contribute in a large measure to this waste.

Another group comprising experienced advertising agency men who employ direct mail, often as an adjunct to a major national advertising campaign, also contribute a substantial share to the waste.

In both of these groups, the waste occurs through sins of omission and commission that are chargeable to ignorance, indifference to the functions of direct mail, or carelessness. The result is—we see the wrong thing done or the failure of the right thing or number of right things to be done. In other words, a lack of understanding of important and very essential details that make or break a direct-mail campaign.

Briefly, let me at this point summarize a few of the common sins of omission and commission in direct mail.

1. Failure to fully understand and appreciate that direct mail is a class medium and not a mass selling and advertising medium.

2. Selectivity being a prime essential in direct mail, refinement of mailing lists by classes, ratings, urban or rural markets should be a determining factor in copy appeal. This factor is shockingly lacking in many direct-mail campaigns.

3. Timing. Improper timing has killed many an otherwise well-prepared direct-mail campaign. This important factor seems to be in the category of the forgotten man. It gets little or no consideration, and if given any thought, it is usually guesses or hunches.

4. Failure to recognize the importance of the letter, and its effective use in staging the catalogue, booklet, or brochure.

5. Testing. Altogether too many campaigns are launched without sufficient testing and preliminary survey of lists and copy to determine the proper approach in economically obtaining results.

As I stated before, direct-by-mail is a class medium. It permits concentration of sales effort on one specific type of prospect. It is distinctly designed for class purposes, and when used for mass selling, it is wasteful and the reason it is wasteful is because you cannot do a direct-mail job on a mass list. It is wasteful to send the same sales letter to 45,000 druggists without regard to the selling conditions that may exist on Main Street in Tuscaloosa as compared with Broadway in New York. The reason we have a tremendous amount of waste is because altogether too many advertisers do not confine their program to class appeals, for very definitely direct-by-mail calls for refinement of a class appeal.

And the amateur advertiser isn't always the one, either, who makes this mistake. Often the experienced advertiser will send out a piece of literature to a mass list without regard to the particular living conditions, the buying power, or to one of the thousand other conditions that should be considered.

Anyone in sales promotion and advertising work, if he will give some study to the refinement of his appeals in direct-mail advertising, can enhance his returns tremendously. If direct-by-mail advertising is not getting results, probably the advertiser is using it wastefully on mass selling when it should be applied as class selling.

You don't have to go far in any business to find a good line of prospects. I can go into any business and find a gold mine there to work on.

For instance, I happened to go to Cleveland a few months ago and in talking with the merchandising manager of one of the leading department stores, I asked the question, "When is a customer a customer in your business?"

"When he buys regularly from us," the manager replied.

"No, that is not a customer," I said.

"What is your definition of a customer?" I was asked.

I answered: "A customer in a business can only be classified as a customer when he is buying from you substantially all his requirements that you are in a position to furnish. That is a customer. The other is only a part customer."

The merchandising manager said, "Define your statement a little further for me."

"Well," I replied, "in your business you have 108 departments in your store. I will venture the statement without knowing the facts in your business, but I know this to be typical of nearly every business that I come in contact with—that more than 50 per cent of the best customers you have on your books do not patronize more than 40 per cent of your departments."

"You must be mistaken!" he exclaimed. "Let's make the examination and find out." So he took 1,000 of the very best customers they had on their books and checked back their accounts for a year. Here is what he found:

Out of the 1,000 customers, 485 purchased hosiery. The balance did not. We are living in a hosiery age and the hosiery counter is on the main aisle of the center door. Five hundred and fifteen who regularly month after month entered that store never purchased hosiery. Two hundred thirty-four out of the 1,000 purchased ready-to-wear suits, dresses, frocks, and gowns. The balance did not. Eighty-eight out of 1,000 purchased carpets and household appliances, and so on down the list. And yet, all of them made purchases in the store.

He said to me: "From this day on I am going to give more attention in our business to developing more trade from our present customers. We have been spending all our money shouting from the housetops, telling about our store, doing mass selling, inserting double spreads in every Friday issue of the newspapers and a full page almost every other day in the week to the great multitude of the city of Cleveland. And here we have 1,000 of our very best customers whose credit is wonderful, who represent the very best purchasing power in our town, that are not patronizing all our departments."

Many firms have tried direct-mail advertising and have given it up as

unprofitable. The trouble generally is they turn the work over to some indifferent clerk, who sends out letters automatically and pays little or no attention to
the work he is doing. Often people who are dead or have moved are continually circularized.

It is essential to keep your lists up-to-date and accurate, because the very
force of direct mail depends upon the sureness with which it reaches the class
of customer it is intended for.

The term "mailing list" often is misleading, since it suggests only a list of
names used for mailing purposes. Perhaps the better name to use is "prospect
inventory" since any good list should represent a complete inventory of all
prospects in a given territory or in a specific buying class.

A prospect inventory is as important and as necessary in every business as
the usual stock inventory or an audit of the books. Such an inventory will show
you not only the possibilities of the market you are now reaching, but it will
open your eyes also to the potential market which may be awaiting your products or services.

A prospect inventory will show also where your biggest and best sales opportunities lie—where your richest territories are—where it will pay you to
concentrate sales effort. Without this definite inventory of prospects, it is impossible to develop sales or to plan expansion programs intelligently.

Once you have taken your prospect inventory, you are in a position to proceed along a definite course to the sales objective you seek. To attempt to
proceed without it would be like trying to sell without a chart. The trouble is
that many business houses do not know to whom they are selling—whether they
are selling what they should—why they don't sell more and how they can increase per-customer sales.

It is possible to buy lists of prospects under most any classification. The
members of golf clubs throughout the country—the directors of banks—graduates of colleges—automobile owners—everyone is on some list or other. And
all of us buy when the right merchandise is presented to us.

Some firms make a mistake in ordering quality printed matter and then
employing a cheap or poorly selected or defective mailing list. This is false
economy.

Many firms go through the motions of direct-mail advertising, but fail to get
results because of their half-hearted efforts. Success is not automatic. The
prospect may be ready and waiting to buy, but he can be lost or discouraged
through inefficient handling.

An inquiry from an interested party may cost anywhere from 50 cents to
$100. If I were advertising for inquiries about stoker equipment for an indus-
trial establishment, I would be willing to pay as high as $100 for an inquiry.
Inquiries cost money. But you wouldn't think so, the way they are treated in
business. Indifferent follow-up loses many sales and hence raises the costs of
the sales that are made. Perhaps an advertiser finds it costs $25 to close sales
resulting from advertising placed in a certain magazine. He blames the magazine because he cannot make the inquiries pay. The trouble probably lies in
the way he handles those inquiries: for example, sending a 32-page catalogue

and a form letter when the customer wants definite data about maintenance costs in his special business.

So much for following up present customers, or getting business from people who already know your merchandise and your service. Now for some rules on the art of selling by mail.

Selling by mail is neither a mystery nor a miracle. It is a plain business proposition. Do not think that it will, by its own power, pull itself through and yield big profits. Count the cost—just as you would if you were building a factory—and know just how much you are going to spend, why, and how you are going to spend it, and what reasonable results may be expected. That is the safe way.

No matter whether you are selling leather belting, a patented motor device, or wheeled scrapers, you are handling a product that appeals to a certain list of users, dealers, or agents. Perhaps you cannot afford to cover your field with salesmen because of the cost. Yet rich sales possibilities are there—people are buying or handling products similar to yours—they want the best. If your product has advantages that mean more money or better satisfaction to them, they would want to handle or buy your product.

It is up to you to put your facts before them—to plant the seed that will grow into new channels of output—to tempt your prospects with the strong points of your proposition.

This should be done in a manner that will command their interest—that will grip their attention—that will cause them to act. You can blanket your field with trade papers—you can use space in magazines—you can advertise in technical journals and newspapers and theater programs; but don't overlook the great opportunities in selling by mail.

Successful direct-mail advertising is a highly specialized business, calling for the best brains in the preparation of copy, classifications, study of lists, and selection of the type of mailing pieces that will prove most effective to the various lists that are to be covered. Careful thought should be given to the number of times the prospect should be covered and during what length of time, so as to tie in most successfully with the general advertising and merchandising program. The omission of any of these points, or an error in judgment—which is often based on guesswork instead of experience—very frequently results in failure and waste.

Third-class mailings are often employed when they are a criminal waste of the advertiser's money. Some advertisers depreciate the value of letters and will not use them in a campaign; yet the letter is the ace in the deck of a series of direct mailings, if judiciously employed. I say "if judiciously employed" advisedly, for the letter is more often abused than otherwise.

Direct-mail copy, be it for a mail-order piece or designed to parallel personal selling to get an inquiry, is the most difficult kind of advertising to write. Men who are versatile copy space fillers for general publicity are not as a rule successful direct-mail copy men. The whole approach is different. A man of this type is invariably skilled in writing to the mass reader mind, but when it comes to the direct-specific appeals, he falls flat.

I know men who are positive geniuses in writing newspaper or magazine copy, but who are miserable failures at writing a sales letter, folder, or other mailing piece, and the exception to this is rare. Of course there are men who can and do write mass appeal copy for direct mail, and this literature I class without hesitation as waste. Unfortunately, there is much of it going out all the time.

Thus you can see that direct mail is not regarded as perfect, and that if 75 per cent of it is being wasted, the fault is due to carelessly selected lists, poorly written letters, cheaply printed material, and ignorant or indifferent handling of many of the details. This is not an indictment, but rather an outlining of the way that wastefulness in direct mail can be avoided.

Let us now summarize the benefits which direct mail can be expected to accomplish. There are ten of them.

First: To keep your product or service before all customers at regular intervals, aiming to make each customer order each year, and to retain the good will of all. I don't care what kind of business a man may be in, he should maintain in his business a complete record of customers and apply intelligently and systematically a follow-up plan to build more business. He should work to bring back to the fold those customers who may have wandered away for one reason or another, and to make a division of customers according to their purchasing possibilities.

Second: To reach prospects systematically by mail and at regular intervals, seeking to bring in inquiries or orders or build good will. In that way a concern can get leads for salesmen and put new names on the ledger.

Third: To support the salesmen in territory covered by them. Nothing is more tragic to me than to witness sales managers sending men out without proper support. More good salesmen die a death of despair and distress and disappointment making "cold canvasses" on people that know little about the company or the product, when all that preliminary work should be done direct-by-mail, paving the way for the salesmen's calls. I know businessmen who spend thousands of dollars on salesmen, but who will hesitate about spending ten dollars in good advertising to pave the way for them.

Fourth: To get orders from towns not covered by salesmen. It is far better to have the men concentrate on prospects who can give you an increased volume rather than to have them calling on ten or twelve types of prospects whose business does not justify the expense.

I have found frequent cases in my investigation of salesmen who have spent more than 60 per cent of their time calling on prospects where the only possible business they could get never would justify the calls. Their expenses would be as high as $150, just making calls on one prospect over a period of years, and our analysis showed that they could get no more than $100 worth of business out of that prospect. All of this should have been handled direct-by-mail, on a sales letter basis.

Fifth: To encourage reordering by mail.

Sixth: To circulate enclosures with buying suggestions in outgoing envelopes, packages, etc. A number of concerns have great sales possibilities with the printed circular and should use it to introduce new items of merchandise and to build up additional sales from that customer who already has made a purchase.

Seventh: To arrange dealer aid plans that will help bring people to dealers' stores and thus help dealers sell more goods.

Eighth: To support national and trade paper advertising with hookups to dealers, merchandising, and general advertising efforts.

Ninth: To efficiently follow up inquiries and arrange plans so that worthwhile local dealer follow-ups can be secured.

Tenth: To harmonize the departments of a business in support of sales promotion by mail and to develop the efficiency of salesmen by correspondence.

Millions are spent for circulars and follow-up letters—much of it wastefully. Yet with all its faults, direct-by-mail wins friends because it supplements the work of magazine and newspaper advertisements, and adds to the effectiveness of the salesman's call.

How to correct its shortcomings and strengthen its advantages is a study deserving of real thought. It is a problem to which every businessman hopes for an answer, and to which members of the American Business Writing Association can contribute much valuable help.

Exercises and Problems in Communication

1. Referring to the suggested list sources on page 420, build mailing lists for the following:

   a. To sell parts, metal restoratives (paint, etc.), and upholstery materials to antique-automobile owners
   b. To invite support for a political cause on a statewide basis
   c. To advertise an Independence Day celebration at a local park
   d. To sell air-conditioning units to home-owners
   e. To sell a business-communication textbook for use in universities in the United States

2. Write a list of "specifications" for the typical prospect in each of the lists in Exercise 1.

3. Write the covering letter and rough out the accompanying pieces that you will include in the mailings in Exercise 1.

4. Report, according to your instructor's assignment, on "How to Profit from Direct Mail Testing," in *Successful Direct Mail Advertising and Selling,* by Robert Stone (New York: Prentice-Hall, Inc., 1955).

5. Consult the *Business Periodicals Index* for current discussion of the merits and practices in newspaper, magazine, and direct-mail advertising. What factors in each medium do you find most effective, according to the authors of the articles? Report orally or in writing.

6. Write the public relations department of a magazine-publishing firm and ask for a series of the company's subscription letters. Analyze the letters for attention, appeals, conviction, and action. In your request, you might also ask for information on the "pulling power" of the various mailings; some publishers test their mailings.

7. Although the letters in Exercise 6 are written by professionals, try your hand at redoing some of the steps, e.g., the conviction.

8. From a department store or a mail-order retail outlet (either store or catalog service) get a collection of the advertising pieces used by the company in mail advertising. Set up a program for using the pieces.

9. Using Mr. Buckley's talk as your source, prepare an outline for your portion of a panel discussion at a direct-mail advertising convention.

10. Collect as many complete mailings as possible. Which of them strike you as violating principles of effective direct-mail advertising, as discussed by Mr. Buckley?

11. Read a chapter (or more) in *The Shocking History of Advertising* (quoted in the opening of this chapter). Report orally to the class, remaining as objective as possible. Your purpose here is not to "take sides"; in other words, you will be *informing* your audience.

12. Read as you choose in David Ogilvy's *Confessions of an Advertising Man*. Report orally to the class, persuading your listeners that when they are in a position to advertise, they should by all means use the services of an advertising agency, rather than develop their own advertising campaigns.

13. Read in *Advertising, Its Principles and Practice*, by Harry Tipper *et al.* (New York: The Ronald Press Company, 1915). A passage lending itself well to this assignment is Chapter 6, "The Chief Human Instincts, Needs and Emotions." Report on your reading to the class, comparing or contrasting "the instincts and their corresponding emotions" as discussed, with a more current list of "appeals" (see Chapter 8 of Vance Packard's *The Hidden Persuaders*). Although your presentation will be informational, the purpose of your talk is to be *affective*. You can use the advantage of nostalgic reporting for the pleasure of your listeners.

14. As in the preceding exercises, read in *The Story of Advertising* by James P. Wood (New York: The Ronald Press Company, 1958). Write a report with a title such as "Advertising Grows Up," basing your writing on Chapter 4, "Benjamin Franklin, Advertising Man—Early American Advertising"; Chapter 9, "Phineas Taylor Barnum: 'I Thoroughly Understand the Art of Advertising' "; Chapter 11, "John Wanamaker: 'Advertising Exerts . . . an Irresistible Power' "; and Chapter 29, "The Newer Advertising."

15. According to your instructor's assignment, plan and write continuous, campaign, or wear-out series for advertising by mail a product or service of your choosing.

15

The Larger Field of Business Writing

The village all declar'd how much he knew,
'T was certain he could write and cipher too.—
Oliver Goldsmith, *The Deserted Village*

In professorial circles, there is a saying—in fact, in some departments of some universities it is said to be policy—"Publish or perish." In other words, department members must publish articles, books, monographs, etc., or be discharged. Whether the policy is generally followed, few, if any, can say.

In business and industry, writing for publication, other than for those employed in writing positions, is hardly a requisite for continued employment. However, even a cursory glance through business or general publications will reveal that many persons in business and industrial positions are writing, sharing their experiences for improvement of work in their respective fields or putting down their thoughts for possible general betterment. Throughout this book are references to the first type of article: William Gruver of Hal Marlowe Associates writes about improving public relations activities; Robert E. Johnson, United Air Lines, brings word of his company's working with the dissatisfied customer; Fred D. Nosal writes about Mastic Corporation's credit practices. These men's ideas will be adopted by some and adapted by others in their particular lines of endeavor, bringing improvement in the operations of readers' companies.

Articles expressing the writer's personal attitudes on more general subjects than mercantile operations are to be found in all types of pub-

437

lications. Clarence B. Randall, former chairman of the board of Inland Steel, writes in *Dun's Review and Modern Management* and in *Think* on effective writing in business and on the values of liberal arts education for the person going into management; Crawford Greenewalt, chairman of Du Pont's board, writes in *Saturday Review* of the cultural interests of top-flight executives, his point being that culture is "not a monopoly of the academic world"; Henning Prentiss, Jr., formerly an executive of Armstrong Cork, writes philosophically (also in *Saturday Review*) of the individual's place in society—Mr. Prentiss suggests that man reaching "mid-stream" asks himself what he has contributed to his fellow man, what is his purpose in existence.

Businessmen and industrialists leave their jobs to spend their time writing. One well-known author who made this change is Cameron Hawley, who, as a vice president of the Armstrong Cork Company, wrote the highly popular *Executive Suite*. Mr. Hawley followed this success with the even more widely read and controversial *Cash McCall* and *The Lincoln Lords*. Robert Graham, author of *The Annals of Logan*, a book of monologues in verse dealing with the tenor of management, left an engineering position for writing.

Creative composition does not require that a person leave his career; it is a constructive diversion for many still very much involved in making a living. Such a person is Dan Helsdingen, assistant advertising manager of the Inland Steel Company, whose choice of subject matter supports the opinion that "poetry is all around us." The lines below are a sample of Mr. Helsdingen's lyrics, from a poem, "The Age of Steel," published with others in *Inland News:*

> Steel is man's tool,
> For hewing rock and tree,
> For tilling soil and planting grain.
> Steel is the weapon of the hunter,
> The shield of the soldier.
> Steel is the carrier of messages
> And electricity,
> The towers rising in the noon sun.

If these examples of published writers are tinged with the glamor frequently associated with successful authorship, that glorification has not been the intent here. The discussion has been merely for a little seed-planting for that business communication student who might be interested in business writing as a vocation. And there are innumerable opportunities for that person because of the extensive part writing plays in mercantile pursuits.

Business Journalism

Newspapers always excite curiosity.—CHARLES LAMB

Business journalism is not a completely satisfactory term for what we want to discuss. Strictly speaking, journalism is itself a part of business activity; magazines and newspapers are published for profit as truly as automobile factories and textile mills are run for profit. "Business activity as it is represented in journalism" might be better, since what we mean is the role that business activity plays in journalism, or the space in periodicals which is filled with material that deals directly with business. But this would be too unwieldy a term; so we shall stick to *business journalism.*

What does business journalism include? A very large volume of material indeed. We may classify it under two main headings: (1) business material in general periodicals, and (2) publications devoted primarily to business.

BUSINESS MATERIAL IN GENERAL PERIODICALS

Magazines and newspapers of general circulation devote considerable space to news of business activity. *Time* and *Newsweek* include business departments, and among the articles in a weekly issue of the *Saturday Evening Post* is ordinarily one or more of basically business interest, such as "Why Didn't You Get That Raise?" (functions of the personnel office), or "I Want My Money Back" (details of adjustments at Macy's).[1] The *Saturday Review* periodically devotes an issue to the business and industrial scene. All metropolitan newspapers have financial sections, as well as news stories and features of business interest.

PUBLICATIONS DEVOTED PRIMARILY TO BUSINESS

Business has long figured so centrally in American life that many publications, even many classes of publications, have been developed primarily to carry various aspects of business news; the chief ones are:

1. Business magazines
2. Industrial and trade journals
3. Professional journals, class publications
4. Publications of clubs and other organizations
5. Company newspapers and magazines

Certain business magazines cater to the field as a whole, such as *Business Week, Business Digest,* and *Dun's Review and Modern Manage-*

[1] This article is pleasant and informative reading—*Saturday Evening Post,* March 8, 1958, pp. 100–102.

ment, which dispense much information of interest to enterprising businessmen, especially executives. Industrial periodicals are planned to interest designers and manufacturers who are consumers of raw materials, not of finished products, that is, buyers of iron, steel, lumber, or other goods for processing. Trade journals appeal to jobbers, dealers, and retailers in specific merchandising fields, such as hardware, jewelry, drugs, and electrical appliances. Professional journals and class publications cater to selected groups of ultimate consumers, e.g., doctors, dentists, teachers, architects.

Much business information is also found in publications of clubs and organizations, e.g., traffic clubs, associations of teachers, and associations of business and industrial communications directors (especially the American Business Writing Association, with its *ABWA Bulletin* and *Journal of Business Communication;* the International Reading Association, with the *Journal of Reading* as its official publication; and the National Society for the Study of Communication and its *Journal of Communication*). Civic and service clubs, such as Rotary, Kiwanis, and Lions, have official periodicals.

Company magazines are published by large and small business and industrial firms. The Du Pont publications program alone includes 40 employee newspapers and magazines. In the United States and Canada, company editorial staffs employing some 15,000 persons prepare publications numbering 300 million copies per issue, or double the total circulation of the top 120 magazines in the two countries. Firms sponsoring these publications budget around $500,000,000 a year for their issuance. According to the Industrial Council of Industrial Editors, the amount is well spent in the cause of employee relations.

The periodicals range from the four-page mimeographed human interest and news sheet of employee "personals" to expensive publications containing business articles and significant addresses by company officials and other leaders in the business world. Whatever the size or format, there are, according to a survey conducted by The Metropolitan Life Insurance Company, four underlying purposes of company publications: (1) to give information on company operations, policies, and problems; (2) to draw individual employees into closer contact with the company; (3) to make employees feel they are members of a single organization; and (4) to help employees understand each other.[2]

---

[2] Eighty-eight industrial editors listed these points, as reported in *Employee Publications* (New York: The Metropolitan Life Insurance Company, 1951).

The scope and objectives of industrial and business journalism are comprehensively covered in William C. Halley, *Employee Publications* (Philadelphia: Chilton Company–Book Division, 1959), and James McCloskey, *Industrial Journalism Today* (New York: Harper & Row, 1959).

WRITING FOR BUSINESS PUBLICATIONS

The writer for business publications is the interpreter, the go-between, who endeavors always to contribute to the interest that potential buyers have in whatever is for sale and to preserve a favorable image of the business scene. Always he must be interesting, and interest is largely a matter of the concrete fact and the specific word. But, whatever the basis for business writing or the requirement of the business writer, business journalism may take many forms.

BUSINESS ARTICLES

In general magazines, the business article does not differ materially from any other informative article except in its slant. Like other types of articles, it requires: (1) the choice of a timely and sufficiently important subject; (2) the collection, through extended research procedures if necessary, of relevant facts, figures, and illustrative incidents; (3) the logical organization of material according to a clear plan; and (4) careful writing, with emphasis on clear, concrete, and effective presentation (which sometimes includes the use of charts or graphs), keeping constantly in mind the readers to whom the article must appeal. It is apparent that in content, though not in form or purpose, the business article may closely resemble the business report.

Who writes business articles? All sorts of people, as mentioned in the opening of this chapter: advertising men, executives of manufacturing firms, public utilities executives, sales managers, department heads—anyone from any level, within reason, writes them. And many of those who are writing are advancing. They attract attention. I know one man who changed jobs, much to his advantage, as a result of a rather short article published in a professional journal. Within two years, he had made another advantageous change, thanks to the same piece of writing. Cases are known of students who have reworked the material of an assigned business report into a salable article which brought them favorable publicity and a job, in addition to the cash payment. Although the majority of business articles in established journals are by staff writers, a good writer who is willing to learn the business slant should be able to produce successful business articles.

OTHER KINDS OF WRITING FOR BUSINESS PUBLICATIONS

In addition to the business article, which is the lengthiest and most ambitious form of writing in business journalism, there are other shorter forms, including:

1. News items
2. Business personals and biographical sketches

3. Interviews
4. Public letters
5. Publicity releases
6. Public relations stories
7. Editorials

Business *news items* may tell of the opening of a new branch store of a mail-order company, of the retirement of a certain stock by a railroad or chain drug company, of the installation of modern-type escalators in a department store.

Business personals describe interesting activities of individuals and groups, and announce promotions, marriages, and births. Some business journals have a special department for personals; others distribute such items throughout the publication. Biographical sketches are lengthier and are commonly written for city and neighborhood papers when a citizen becomes an executive or a member of the board of directors of a bank or other business organization, or receives similar distinction.

Interviews are written as the result of a call by a news reporter or staff writer on a government or company official to secure information on a subject of current interest. The official's viewpoint is the part of the interview which interests the public and which receives the most space in the article, but a skillful interviewer learns interesting facts while talking with the official, and these are used to add personal interest.

The *public letter* also expresses the opinion of an individual, but here the initiative is with the official, who chooses this means of securing publicity for a policy which he is determined to follow. The letter is addressed, for example, by an employer to a government official or even to his own employees; by an editor to the Postmaster General on matters of censorship; or by a representative of a labor union to an employer. Publicity comes through the publishing of the letter in one or more magazines and newspapers, often as paid advertising. You may have seen open letters by International Harvester Company, Montgomery Ward & Company, and the *Saturday Review*, to name only a few examples.

The *publicity release* is a story of general interest that is directly tied in with an event such as the opening of the opera season or the première of a movie. It may relate closely to the business personal or biographical sketch in that it is frequently centered around one or more of the most colorful personalities involved.

A vivid example of the uses of publicity is in the opening of a World's Fair. Items are released periodically for magazines, newspapers, television, and radio. These include statistics of the physical features of the exhibition, such as the amount of electricity that will be used in one day, the time required for one person to visit all the exhibits, personality sketches of the administrators or the entertainers, and even such familiar subjects as recipes from certain of the restaurants. The opening of a new branch of a bank or a new plant of a company may be publicized in somewhat the same manner, telling the public, prospective customers, and the employees what to expect.

Public relations is used increasingly as the generic term for opinion management, as discussed in Chapter 10. In this sense, it includes many kinds of writing and speaking, but no satisfactory substitute has been found for the term *public relations story.* This applies to stories and articles published by utility companies, investment houses, meat packers, insurance companies, and similar large business organizations, to induce favorable opinion or to counteract unfavorable publicity. They are often written especially for anniversaries of inventors and inventions connected with the product or service sold by the company, for example, facts in the history of electric lighting and the telegraph. They may relate the aims of business to the public interest; they may attempt to tell the point of view of management directly to explain a misunderstood point on labor relations or governmental control.

The *editorial* in business publications, and to a degree in general magazines and newspapers, discharges business functions. It is especially useful in giving pioneer advertising to discoveries of new products and processes, in lobbying for or against legislation affecting business, and in interpreting business trends and tendencies. Typical examples are "Crediting the Creators," a commentary on the anonymity of ad writers and art directors, in *Advertising Age* (August 17, 1964, p. 20) and "How to Forestall the Feds," a discussion of the federal government's role in water pollution, in *Chemical Week* (March 14, 1964, p. 5). The editor's chair is an especially good post for observing the effects of legislation, fashions, educational trends, and other factors on the business procession.

Advertising Copy

If all the advertising ever printed were wadded into a ball, there would not be room for it. If all the advertising spoken since the beginning were likewise compressed, it would form a gaseous envelope about as large as that provided for the circling of all the planets around the sun. If all the emotions advertising has stirred, all the actions it has provoked, all the hypnotism it has exerted, and all the gullibility it has evoked could be added up, the sum would approximate the dimensions of total human nature.[3]

[3] James Playsted Wood, *The Story of Advertising* (New York: The Ronald Press Co., 1958). Mr. Wood's book, in its comprehensive account of advertising, reflects the thought in this quotation from the Preface. His treatment is the readable, human side of this phase of business, not the statistical.

Up to this point we have been considering the news, that part of a publication which is paid for by the management, in contrast to the advertising paid for by the advertisers. It is commonplace knowledge that, with few exceptions, publications do not derive all or even the greater part of their revenue from their subscribers. The revenue from paid advertising is usually much greater, and frequently the paid advertising space is more than half of the total, occasionally reaching as much as 80 per cent in metropolitan daily newspapers and 60 per cent in the leading news magazines. Early in 1964, revenue from newspaper advertising for the year was estimated to hit $810,788,000.[4]

Perhaps, as has been conjectured, the cave dwellers wrote the first advertising copy to dispose of a surplus of fresh meat or fish from a lucky kill or catch. Certainly compositions intended to sell services and merchandise through public display of the message have been known for a very long time. But *advertising copy* as we know it today is a highly developed form of composition with its own special techniques. It is the writing which we see displayed on posters and billboards and especially in magazines and newspaper advertisements. Frequently, the text is subordinated to the pictorial material, especially when the latter is in color. But the text must be chosen carefully and arranged skillfully so that the words used will induce good will or increase sales to an extent which will justify or repay the high cost of advertising space in important magazines and newspapers.

ADVERTISING COPY COMPARED WITH DIRECT MAIL

Although display advertising has been preferred to direct mail, both media have their advantages.

Advertising Copy	Direct Mail
Better display facilities for illustrations.	Good mailing lists are more selective than the subscription lists of periodicals.
Wider circulation for the same cost.	Message can have personal appeal to selected groups.
Prestige of the medium adds value to the advertising, as the public is inclined to believe what it "sees in the papers."	Descriptions can be more detailed—not possible in periodicals as readers scan the advertisements hurriedly.
Possibilities for tie-ins with current news.	Enclosures, usually highly effective, add to the sales appeal of letters.
Not so likely to be completely ignored as are the sales letters that go into the wastebasket unread.	Cumulative momentum of campaign series of letters tends to retain the attention of the individual.

[4] *Advertising Age*, April 27, 1964, p. 3.

It is apparent that theoretically the two media are evenly balanced; the shrewdest merchandisers take advantage of both.

THE WRITER'S PART IN AD WRITING

At this juncture, it would be well, to save repetition here, if you would turn to Chapters 8 and 14 and review the principles of effective sales writing. The ad writer will apply much of what was said there. He must get the "prospect's" attention, he will use appeals, he should inject some conviction as proof, and he will suggest or ask for an action.

The writer's work in an advertisement consists of (1) the headline and (2) the copy.

The Headline

With any accompanying pictorial devices, the headline is the attention factor of the ad. According to David Ogilvy in *Confessions of an Advertising Man,*[5] a headline should have the following qualities: (1) it should flag down the readers who are prospects for the kind of product being advertised; (2) it should promise the reader a benefit; (3) if possible, it should carry news, news suggested by "the two most powerful words" in a headline: *free* and *new;* (4) the headline should use other words which "work wonders," among which are *how to, now, the truth about, advice to;* (5) it should contain the brand name, since five times as many people read the headline as read the body copy; (6) it should contain a selling promise; (7) it should lure the reader into the copy (most people do not read copy following a "blind," self-contained headline); (8) it should be free of "puns, literary allusions, and other obscurities"; [6] (9) it should be free of negatives.

The importance of the headline is shown in the statistic that a change in headline can make a difference of ten to one in sales.

Importance of Copy

In reading the advertisements in publications where space is obviously costly, you may have marveled at the apparently extravagant use of color and at the large amount of white space and the few words of copy. In fact, the copy may have seemed unimportant, and the pleasing effect of the ads due only to the pictures. New color processes have tended to increase the use of glamorous displays and to minimize the copy, but with few exceptions, the message must be put in words. Without good copy, the most expensive ad is more likely to fail than to

---

[5] (New York: Atheneum, 1963), pp. 104–7.

[6] Articles in *Printers' Ink, Advertising and Selling,* and other leading sales and merchandising magazines indicate that this is a controversial point.

succeed. Two advertising executives make the point in the light of credibility:

> The dual objectives of your body copy are conviction and action. Conviction stems from belief, belief from truth.
>
> One good technique to inspire belief is to begin with a statement the reader knows is true. This quickly helps establish an area of belief and confidence.
>
> Second—consider your copy as your personal sales talk. If the reader were in front of you, you wouldn't risk the embarrassment of being caught in a lie. In print or on the air, a lie or over-exaggeration earns quick contempt and a fast dismissal of your product. The truth is not only a more effective sales tool, but a more gratifying area in which to work.[7]

Principles of Effective Copy

If the copy in an advertisement consists of twenty words or more, it may be treated as a composition, and the rules of unity, coherence, and emphasis apply. Like the sales letter, it must have a dominant keynote or core thought selected with the "you" attitude—the service value of the article to the consumer—in mind. One advertising man puts this point well in contrasting "showmanship" with "show-off-manship" in copy writing. Good salesmanship, Zenn Kaufman writes, lies in making the buyer the "hero" of the sale: "There's only one hero in any sale— the customer. The minute we take the spotlight off him, or her, our show is over and we may as well go home."[8] The copy writer, like all sales writers, must stay behind the scenes; he must express not his own individuality but that of the product described in his copy. The much-quoted James Webb Young puts it this way:

> It is said that Roy Howard once instructed Scripps-Howard editors somewhat as follows: "When you want to attack a man don't call him libelous names. Just tell what he did in such a way that the reader will say: 'Why the dirty so-and-so!'" The suggestion holds good for ad writers. Don't praise the product. Just tell what it does, and how it does it, so that the reader will say: "I must try that." In short, go light on the adjectives and heavy on the verbs.[9]

Possibly more than any other kind of writing, advertising copy must be dynamic, not static. A rather general reaction to much current advertising is expressed by Whitman Hobs, vice president of Batten, Barton, Durstine, and Osborn (a leading advertising agency, popularly known as "BBDO"):

Advertising has gone stale; everybody is moving in toward center. We look alike and sound alike. We're playing ring-around-a-rosie . . . and rosie is

[7] Martin Solow and Ed Handman, *Effective Advertising* (New York: Grosset & Dunlap, 1964), p. 28. This concise book is a good starting point for the person considering advertising as a career.

[8] *Printers' Ink*, June 20, 1958, p. 11.

[9] *The Diary of an Ad Man* (Chicago: Advertising Publications, 1944), pp. 213–14.

singularly unimpressed. In fact, she's bored. She has plenty of money in the bank—and in the cookie jar and under the mattress—but it looks more attractive to her than the things she can buy with it: the things we have to sell, the things that advertising isn't selling, the things that compelling advertising could sell.[10]

As mentioned of the public relations writer in Chapter 10, the advertising writer will be ever alert to everything about him to get material that sooner or later may go into his copy. The socio-economic, the fads, the political—no facet of life should escape the ad writer's attention. One writer availed himself of a fad to turn out an effective piece of copy. When the Davy Crockett craze was rampant with the pre-teen and teen sets, and merchandise—from trinkets to full wardrobes—was being sold faster than it could be manufactured, Steuben Glass advertised its Tennessee Bowl. With a picture of the bowl, showing the exquisite lines and masterful workmanship that characterize Steuben creations, the copy explained that the company had had no intention of releasing the bowl at that time. "But the Davy Crockett movement is too strong," the ad pointed out. "Probably the most expensive Crockett item in existence. $1500."

Examine the ads of prominent companies in the important magazines in various fields—news, fiction, trade, and household. You can be sure that the ads that represent a heavy investment [11] will for the most part pass the practical test of returning to the advertiser at least as much in business profits as the cost of preparation and presentation. The growth of advertising in America has been phenomenal; as you examine the ads in magazines and newspapers you will find yourself catching the spirit of this exciting and highly competitive game.

Radio and Television Writing

Around the world by radio.—ARTHUR GUITERMAN
Television is, for the arts, the greatest invention since the printing press.—GILBERT SELDES

Among twentieth-century technological developments, only the automobile has equaled radio and television as an influence on American life. During the 1920's and 1930's the radio knit the nation's people more closely politically, economically, and educationally. They were invited to buy the same products, hear the same music, laugh at the same jokes, and develop the same attitudes.

In the late 1940's television took over a large part of radio's audience and influence. Mushrooming so rapidly that suppliers could not keep

[10] *Printers' Ink*, June 20, 1958, p. 11.
[11] Check the *Standard Rate and Data Service* in your library for current advertising rates for all magazines and newspapers.

up with the demand for sets, the new industry developed new stars and new techniques, changed the entertainment habits and furniture arrangement of the nation, and seriously threatened the motion picture industry. At times the combined radio and television audience may number nearly half the nation; the electric companies know they will have to supply extra current for significant nation-wide programs.[12] No other advertising media can match the range, coverage, and dramatic qualities offered by radio and television.

Although radio and TV programs are not read by their audiences, in no other field of communications is greater emphasis laid on writing, and very exact writing at that. Since the majority of programs must be run off in fifteen or thirty minutes, and commercials are ordinarily limited to 10 per cent of program time, the whole must be planned with the greatest precision. The listener can flip a knob even more easily than he could lay down a magazine or book to choose another; what is written must be interesting to see and hear. Is it surprising, then, that the highest paid script writers get several thousand dollars a week? And since commercial television time costs a client $500 per second,[13] the commercial writer must be highly qualified to make the most of the fifty-eight seconds he has to "make the sale" for his client.

KINDS OF RADIO AND TV PROGRAMS

From the audience point of view, there are only two kinds of programs: good ones and bad ones—those they like and those they do not. From the viewpoint of radio and TV management also, there are only two kinds of programs, but the classification is different: commercial or *sponsored* programs, and noncommercial or *sustaining*. Large advertisers have discovered that it is worth while to sponsor programs of music, drama, variety, or even educational material for the privilege of having the names of their products associated with such programs, plus the opportunity to include a small amount of strictly advertising material. The situation here, you will note, does not differ essentially from magazine advertising, since usually the advertisers provide more of the income of a publication than do its subscribers.

In addition to being grouped as above, programs are also classified according to the type of material presented: music, variety, drama, western, quiz, mystery, talks, forums, church services, children's programs, news analysis, and various others. These many different kinds of

---

[12] Through the *Reader's Guide to Periodical Literature*, the *Business Periodicals Index*, and the *Applied Science and Technology Index* for 1960, find some articles pertaining to the technical details of televising the "Great Debates" between presidential candidates John Kennedy and Richard Nixon, during the 1960 campaign.

[13] *Confessions of an Advertising Man*, p. 131.

NATHANIEL: Well, we shall see. Other persons have bought large estates and built splendid mansions with such little books as I mean to write; it is perhaps not unreasonable to hope that mine may enable me at least to build a small cottage. How much depends on these little books!

(MUSIC: BRIEFLY AND FADE OUT)

NARRATOR: The little books did not soon bring much gold. But Nathaniel and Sophia were married, and lived in idyllic happiness in the Old Manse at Concord. Children were born, Una and Julian and Rose. To make more money, Hawthorne moved his family to Salem, where he worked in the Custom House. But here he could not write, and both he and Sophia knew that his greatest books were yet unwritten. Then an election cost him his place in the Custom House in 1849. He sought for words to break the news gently to Sophia, but none came until he reached his own doorstep.
(FADE)

SOPHIA: What is it, Dearest? Surely you are not well!

NATHANIEL: I'm afraid I am as well as a man can be who has left his head behind him. They won't want me any more at the Custom House.

SOPHIA: Why--why that's splendid, Dear--now you can write your book!

NATHANIEL: You know how I wish I could, but where will our bread and rice come from while the story is writing?

SOPHIA: That's my choicest secret. Just a minute.

           (SOUND OF QUICK MOVEMENTS AND GOLD
           COINS BEING POURED ON TABLE)

           There's a hundred and fifty dollars--I've been saving for just this. I'll have the study all ready for you to start tomorrow morning.

(MUSIC: SOFTLY AND FADE BEHIND)

NARRATOR: And so Hawthorne set to work on THE SCARLET LETTER, still called by many the greatest American novel. For a dozen years the story had been taking shape in his mind. Soon, as Sophia said, he was "writing immensely."

Fig. 60. Specimen page from radio script. From Fame Was Born," a radio dramatization of the life and writings of Nathaniel Hawthorne, by Cecil B. Williams. Note that sound effects, music, and speech are all indicated differently.

programs have their special writing requirements, but like all business writing, they must interest the audience at which they are aimed. Since the radio or TV program comes to people when they are at home, relaxed and receptive, its cultural, educational, and commercial possibilities are almost infinite.

THE RADIO SCRIPT

Writing for radio is a very specialized kind of writing, and the form of the script is now well established. On page 449 you may observe the treatment of the three tools of radio: sound effects, music, and speech. *Sound effects*, particularly, give radio a great advantage over communication by words alone. Sounds of waterfalls and rustling pines suggest a mountain scene with practically no aid from words. Galloping hoofbeats, steps on stairs, or the closing of a door—all help the listener to visualize a scene and the progress of events.

Important also is the *flashback* technique, which provides economy of time. In a biographical drama of Benjamin Franklin, for instance, a good presentation can be given in thirty minutes because at any point in the narrative there can be a flashback, let us say, to the Continental Congress or the court at Paris, where a significant action in Franklin's life can be quickly depicted in the script. A script can focus interest on a person or on an event: Washington can seem to be at Valley Forge and at Mt. Vernon within a few minutes, Edison in his laboratory, Luther Burbank in his gardens; or the great moment in the discovery of penicillin can be instantly visualized for the listening public.

Music, too, has many radio uses and possibilities. It may be the entire program or its principal part, or it may be subsidiary—to bridge from one locality or time to another, to fade speakers in or out, to tone climactic moments in the program, or to serve as a softening background for speech itself. *Speech*, of course, has tremendous radio possibilities, as we know from the public following of favorite newscasters, from the demand for certain announcers, and from the fact that a program can call for almost any number of voices. In writing his script, the writer must never forget the possibilities of all three of his tools: sound effects, music, and speech (which will be discussed more fully in Chapter 17).

THE TV SCRIPT

Television writing is more closely related to playwriting than it is to radio writing; the newcomer to the field should prepare himself by studying the theater, by reading and watching stage plays, and by watching movies and television plays. Television is far more intimate than the theater, however; the television actor does not project his lines to the back of a hall, but into a quiet family group not more than a dozen

A MACHINE TO ANSWER THE QUESTION

-19-

REPORTER: It's in here . . . some place.

DETECTIVE: The machine? I don't know. I think the whole thing is wacky. Doctor Bukoff dead from a blow on the skull. And Chesney--a suicide. And the only witness-- a machine . . . that keeps saying--the answer is tonight!

(THE REPORTER FLICKS THE MACHINE ON)

MACHINE: The answer is--tonight. The answer is--tonight.
(CONTINUES UNDER)

DETECTIVE: I think I'll go home and take a bromo. (LOOKS OUT THE WINDOW) Pretty night. Clear as a bell. Well . . . at least you've got a story that'll take those crazy flying saucers off the front page. See yuh around, buddy. (HE EXITS)

(THE REPORTER WALKS SLOWLY TO THE MACHINE. HE TOUCHES IT)

REPORTER: I hope so. But I wonder. . . . (LOOKS AT MACHINE) What question did they ask you--that made Chesney put a bullet in his head? (PAUSE) You can't answer that, can you?

MACHINE (GROWING LOUDER): The answer is-- tonight. The answer is tonight. (CON- TINUES . . . GROWING WEAKER . . . FINALLY FADING OFF)

Pan slowly to window.
Dolly in to it for
shot of starry sky
. . . then through it
for shot of sky as
in the beginning.

MUSIC: SNEAK IN . . . . A DIRGE. . . . SUSTAIN BEHIND

VOICE: This is the universe. A sky crowded with billions of tiny

(MORE)

Fig. 61. Specimen page from television script. From a television play by Rod Serling, "A Machine to Answer the Question." (Used by permission.)

feet from the screen on which he appears. And of course TV has far more fluidity than the theater: the actors may move from one set to another without delay, and filmed inserts may take them outdoors, let them drive in a car, fly in a plane, or walk down Fifth Avenue.

The main difference between radio writing and TV writing is pointed out by Larry Menkin, former associate director of programs for the Dumont Television Network:

> Characterization in radio writing is accomplished by a combination of that which is written by the author—*and that which the listener imagines.* The radio listener creates his own illusions as to locale, time, and the personality and looks of the characters in the story. But in television the viewer actually sees before him the characters created by the author. The viewer loses his freedom of imagination: the characters must be written in the script. And the characters cannot be purely one-dimensional—all voice.[14]

The television writer thus adds another tool to the list used by the radio writer, the most important tool of all, and one which occupies a separate column in the script: *visual.* Before the writer can introduce a situation he must think of how it will look on the screen; the secret of holding his audience is action and visual interest. In the visual column of the script lie the challenges and the opportunities of the new medium.

Aside from a real feeling for dramatic effect and the willingness to learn from experience in developing the visual possibilities of television, the TV writer needs the same qualities that make good radio or short story writers: the ability to produce sound dialogue, convincing characters, and well-knit plots.

WRITING FOR RADIO AND TELEVISION

Radio and TV writing is done (1) under contract, (2) on staff, or (3) on the open market. "Big name" writers are in demand to write special programs so that the prestige value of their names can further enhance the pulling power of the script. Thus, Robert E. Sherwood as the author of the play, *Abe Lincoln in Illinois,* is a natural selection to write a TV drama for Lincoln's Birthday *under contract.*

All in all, the most important part of radio and TV writing is done *on staff.* That is, the studios and the advertising agencies employ skilled writers and keep them busy producing scripts. Large studios must have writers to prepare announcements and continuities of various kinds, as well as some of their regular shows.

Many studios, however, and some advertising agencies still welcome scripts on the *open market;* that is, anyone interested in writing for

---

[14] In Jo Ranson and Richard Pack, *Opportunities in Television* (New York: Vocational Guidance Manuals, 1950), pp. 30–31.

radio or TV may incorporate his ideas into salable scripts, either for new programs or to fit into series that are already running.

The person who wants to break into radio or TV, then, unless he is already a well-established writer, has his choice of submitting scripts on the open market or seeking employment with a studio or advertising agency. If he follows the latter course, he may find that he will not get a chance at script writing immediately but must start as a studio assistant or stenographer while getting the atmosphere of the field. However and whenever his chance comes, the radio and TV writer should remember that successful writing is the result of industrious and conscientious application of the special techniques required. The writing must produce the desired effects, and in the case of scripts, this is judged by listeners and viewers instead of readers.

Business Writing as a Vocation

Of all those arts in which the wise excel,
Nature's chief masterpiece is writing well.
JOHN SHEFFIELD

Up to the present chapter, we have considered writing as an adjunct to a business career, not as a career in itself. More and more, everyone in the business world must do some business writing, hence the necessity of becoming familiar with the basic communication forms and learning the principles of effective composition. It may be, however, that you will want to make your living directly and exclusively by means of business writing.

This can be done. It is being done increasingly every year. Many employees are needed on business journals; newspapers need financial editors and writers of business features; a man who can edit a good company magazine may be one of the most valuable members of a company; and, as we have just indicated, commercial writing for radio and television is the newest writing profession. The alert—and exceptionally good—business writer will find that he has a considerable range of opportunity in this field. For direction of markets, he need only look to *Stet, the House Magazine for House Magazine Editors, The Editor's Notebook,* by the American Association of Industrial Editors, or *Reporting for People in Industrial Communications,*[15] published by the International Council of Industrial Editors; and writers' catalogs and directories list several thousand publications that buy the work of free-lance writers.

[15] For a penetrating, provocative article on industrial journalism, read "Who Would Miss Our Magazines If They Never Appeared Again?" by Herbert R. Mayes in *Reporting,* July, 1964.

And for the mail clerk, department head, or board chairman who would create novels, plays, or poetry, there is always the possibility of graduating into the creative writing field as have Cameron Hawley and others mentioned earlier in this chapter.

HOW TO BECOME A PROFESSIONAL

Professional writers are like farmers in that they are either on their own or are under contract to someone else. They may be *free-lance writers,* living where they choose and writing about whatever interests them or what they think they can sell; or they may be *staff writers,* working for the most part in studios and offices, and producing what someone else wants written, though they often retain considerable voice in the matter. Of free-lance writers, we need say little, as most of them are not chiefly business writers: although they may produce and sell a number of business articles, business biographies, and human interest stories, they are more likely to be established novelists, poets, biographers, or short-story writers. Of staff writers, we are chiefly interested in three classes: those employed by (1) magazines, newspapers, and journals; (2) manufacturers, wholesalers, and jobbers; and (3) advertising agencies. Radio and television stations and systems might be named as a fourth class, but there is much duplication here, especially of the advertising agency, so that it does not seem necessary to recognize this field separately, although radio and television do employ directly a number of writers.

BUSINESS WRITING FOR PERIODICALS

We discussed writing for periodicals at the beginning of this chapter; here we are interested in this field with *employment* in mind. What kinds of jobs on periodicals are open to the beginner in business writing? Here, as elsewhere, nothing can be promised him. He will have to work his way up. He must be willing to do "leg work" and frequently be something of a research worker. He will also need to acquire specialized information.

Eventually, however, the beginner may become business editor for a news-magazine, financial editor for a large newspaper, or a staff writer for one of the many business and trade journals or professional and class publications. The argument still goes on as to whether it is easier to train persons with technical knowledge to write or to get the writer to secure the requisite technical knowledge for the desired articles. The present preference is to send the writer for the technical information rather than to train the technical man to write.

BUSINESS WRITING FOR MANUFACTURERS, WHOLESALERS, AND JOBBERS

In this field, the opportunities are chiefly in writing for house magazines, news letters, bulletins, instruction sheets and pamphlets, training films, and the like. As we have observed above, firms like Chrysler Corporation, Aluminum Company of America, and United Air Lines do a great deal of publishing on their own. They find that the house magazine is useful in maintaining *esprit de corps,* and is a ready means for passing along changes in company policy, announcements of new government regulations, and countless other matters. Not always is there an employee already on the pay roll who has been trained for this particular work. If you are hired in another capacity by such a firm, seek the opportunity to use your training by applying for such an opening. The supply of available writers who can initiate and develop house publications for business organizations is never very large, and the use of the various types of these publications is increasing.

WRITING FOR AN ADVERTISING AGENCY

In *The Story of Advertising,* James P. Wood, quoted before, writes, "Over the centuries, advertising has experienced changes in the proportioning of its ingredients, in direction, in application, but something of the first advertisement survives in the latest, and there will be traces of it in the last." [16] That trace will, in all probability, reflect the effort of someone in an advertising agency, of which there are several thousand in the United States, ranging from the one-man agency or counselor to the huge enterprise which handles single accounts reaching into eight figures.[17]

What is an advertising agency? Basically, it is an organization which handles advertising on a commission basis. It buys newspaper or periodical space; it plans, writes, and illustrates the complete advertisements. It contracts for radio or television time; it often hires the talent and sees to the actual presentation. A realistic view of the advertising field is given by Solow and Handman in *Effective Advertising,* which was cited earlier in this chapter.

The reputed glamor of the advertising business as represented in sundry novels, movies and plays draws many people to it. Dismiss 99% of what you've seen or read. It's nonsense.

[16] *The Story of Advertising,* p. 502.
[17] Ogilvy, Benson & Mather has billings of $55,000,000 a year and a pay roll of $5,000,000.

The advertising business is tough; the glamor rubs off once you get in it. Yes, the rewards are high—for those few with the talent to get to the top. But that's true of almost any field. In the general run of jobs, the pay is about what it is in many other fields. Nevertheless, each year many youngsters do descend on the business determined to break in.

Keep this in mind: there are not too many jobs in advertising. Agencies employ about 60 to 70 thousand people; altogether, there may be 150,000 jobs available which require some knowledge of advertising. . . .

. . . .

If you want to work as a writer, swallow your pride and take the money offered to you, no matter how little, to get the experience. But learn while you write and when you've absorbed enough in one job, move on to a better job if possible. . . .

Check your local library and read textbooks on advertising, on marketing and merchandising, on writing. True, no book can teach you any of these subjects, but they can tell you what they're all about. If you're *not* a writer— you're not going to be one. But if you have *ideas*, there's a place for you. Don't be afraid to let go of one good idea. If you're bright—there will be more. If the executive over you swipes your idea—and that can and does happen—be more careful next time. Put it in a memo. Let other people know about it. But don't be offensive. If you're good—you'll get a job and advancement eventually.[18]

Technical Writing

Scientific men too often look upon writing reports or making talks as an irksome part of their job and do as little of it as possible. Engineering work is not finished until the results are clearly recorded and presented to others.—CHARLES F. KETTER-ING, *"The Importance of English to the Engineer"* [19]

This section would probably be better titled "Writing About the Sciences," because *technical* is too limited in connotation and the activities of the writers are too diverse to be circumscribed by the term. As you will notice in the quotations cited in this section, various designations are used for those engaged in the field.[20] Too, you will see that if you have had only a vague notion of what technical writing entails, you are not alone. Those closely related to the work look for delineation. But these uncertainties do not diminish the importance of the work being done or the demand for competent people to do it.

In a report published by the National Association of Science Writers, Dr. Hillier Krieghbaum of New York University, states objectively the

[18] *Op. cit.*, pp. 93–95.

[19] From the *Journal of Engineering Education*, January, 1937, p. 442. Mr. Kettering, the famed inventor, was for many years the Director of the General Motors Research Laboratories.

[20] In addition to "science writer," "technical writer," "engineering writer," "publications engineer," etc., seen here, literature in the field contains such labels as "scientific communicator" and "company writer." Many newspapers have "science editors."

case for science writing and the case against the quality of much of the scientific and technological information disseminated today. Among other highlights, the report, entitled "Science, the News, and the Public," included the following:

With more and more students going through high school and going to college, and with many of them studying science, the market for science coverage in the popular communications channels will certainly expand in the years ahead.

. . . As some scientists are seldom hesitant to proclaim, there is room for improvement in the popular reporting of scientific developments.

. . . Reporters and script writers, given more training and more time in their assignments, would be able to provide more details, greater background, better interpretation, and, it is hoped, higher accuracy. Such changes might help correct present distortions in the public image of science and scientists and promote the idea that they are part of, not divorced from, contemporary living.[21]

The prediction that science coverage will expand is borne out daily. The attendant demand for science and technical writers is proclaimed from the "Help Wanted" pages of any city newspaper, in the daily advertisements by manufacturers, advertising agencies, consulting firms, and government agencies. Cursory examination of other sections of the newspaper indicates the part that science writing plays in the average American's life.

WHAT DOES A TECHNICAL WRITER WRITE?

Very likely, the banner article of the newspaper referred to reflects the work of a writer in some phase of the space program, a medical advancement, or other scientific progress, who is interpreting technological advances for the public. The editorial page with its many featured columnists carries opinion on scientific developments in the space program, gerontology, or new consumer products. There is no end to these topics treated in the news and features, since science affects our everyday lives so completely. The ads throughout the newspaper are also influenced by the technical writer because, just as journalists use his words translating the technology of engineers, physicists, chemists, etc., so do ad writers draw upon the technical writer's interpretations. Even the comics page has two or three strips dealing satirically or romantically with man's dependence on science. "Sunday supplements" are apparently incomplete unless they have a "science fiction" story.

The intermediary role of the company-affiliated writer is succinctly described by John B. Bennet, manager of the Publications Section of

---

[21] As reported by Leon E. Trachtman in "Writing about Writing," *PRF Horizon* (Purdue Research Foundation), June, 1962, pp. 1–2. *PRF Horizon* is exemplary as science writing itself.

the Hazeltine Electronics Corporation, Little Neck, New York. The quotation is from Mr. Bennet's description of a company program and shows the important part the writer plays.

> The publications engineer is trained and experienced in the preparation of publications to provide technical information to engineers, technicians, and administrators. He knows how to explain technical facts. He has a good understanding of the company's products and, *even more important*, he has a feeling for the company's spirit and way of doing business. He can therefore present technical achievements made by the company in the best possible light to the general public and to specific customers.[22]

Whatever aegis the science writer works under—government, commercial, or free lance—he has a larger responsibility than just to enlighten the public for more rational consumer choices or for a better image of science or for sounder political attitudes. Technological growth involves social and emotional issues on an international scale, such involvements having been clearly seen in the space race between the USSR and the United States. On the domestic scene, a striking example of the impact of science writing was the 1962 best-selling book *Silent Spring* by Rachel Carson. Miss Carson, a scientist turned writer, deplored the indiscriminate use of insecticides and weed killers, which practices she pointed out, through documentation, endanger wild life and man himself. Despite considerable critical reaction accusing the author of scare tactics and gross distortion, the book prompted federal legislation to avert further damage to wild life and to curtail ensuing hazards to humans.

We can sum up the technical writer's job realistically with the comment that he writes just about as his counterpart the "business writer" does, depending on the level of his position. In the aerospace industry, for example, among thirty different types of writing "assignments" at the corporate level, there are research and development statements, technical and professional personnel resources statements, speeches to technological groups. At the division level, with even a larger number of categories, there are manuals, proposals, specifications, and research reports. Of course, letters and memos at both levels comprise a sizable share of the company's writing.

QUALIFICATIONS OF THE TECHNICAL WRITER

In a career-oriented society such as ours, no few people think that special curriculums should be devised for every job. Many educators look on such specialized instruction as *training* rather than *education*. Despite these differing opinions, demand has resulted in the establish-

---

[22] From a talk, "The Technical Writer's Role in Advertising and Public Relations," before the Association of Technical Writers and Editors, May 12, 1955.

ment of curriculums in technical writing, editing, and journalism in a number of colleges and universities. Among those that offer undergraduate degrees in these areas are Carnegie Institute of Technology, Colorado State, Oklahoma State, Pennsylvania State, Purdue, and Simmons. Rensselaer Polytechnic Institute offers a master's degree to candidates who have completed undergraduate engineering degrees or B.S. degrees in the natural or biological sciences.

Although such specialized study would be helpful, if you have a desire to go into this field with its many opportunities, you should not let the lack of study in particular subjects deter you from looking into and considering it. The opinion stated and supported throughout this book that the type of education is secondary to the individual's bent and predilections is borne out by the employment record in technical writing.

An advertisement for technical writers in an electromechanical engineering firm supports this stand. The ad, which appeared in a professional magazine, begins:

> Little boys are made
> of frogs and snails
> and puppy-dog tails.
>
> Little girls are made
> of sugar and spice
> and all that's nice.

Then it continues,

but what are TECHNICAL WRITERS made of?
We're not so sure that we know or that anyone knows. . . . We do know that it takes a lot of people with different skills to put one of our publications together, and these people must work as a team.
Our technical writers have not all been cast in the same mold. Some have degrees in the sciences, some in English and Journalism, some have no degrees. They have worked as physicists, mathematicians, engineers, technicians, teachers, film writers, public relations men, and so on. . . .
We can, however, tell you what our technical writers are jointly required to do. They must write easily, clearly, and logically. They must know their subject matter, their readers, and their publication requirements. They must be able to think independently, analyze, plan, and organize their work.[23]

The ad concludes with an invitation to prospects to write the company.

The range in educational background among technical writers, mentioned in the ad was shown further in a panel discussion at the 1960 annual seminar of the Southeastern Michigan Chapter of the Society of Technical Writers and Editors, at Wayne State University. The five panelists, two women and three men, described their education and the application to their work. One woman had a master's degree in library

[23] From a full-page ad in the *STWE Review*, April, 1960, p. 33.

science; the other had a B.A. in the humanities; the three men had degrees in civil engineering, mechanical engineering, and biology respectively. All five were engaged in technical writing for industrial firms in Detroit, the first three being in one of the country's largest missile programs.

Three personal qualifications closely related to the education of the technical writer—curiosity, observation, and exactitude—are mentioned repeatedly in the literature of the field. The first is thought of in its most practical, everyday sense and leads directly to the second. A writer, for example, questioning a certain minute detail of a scientist's drawing or a mathematician's illustration may be observing and checking, for correction, a costly error of commission or omission in the work of another member of his group. Exactness is a necessity in technical writing, in specifics of description of processes and materials, as to time, numbers, amounts, sizes, etc. Equally important, especially in contractual writing is precision of words. Not only is clear, concise, and simple writing necessary, as we have discussed throughout the course, but the technical aspects of language must be observed. For example, if in the contractual part of a specification, the word "shall" is used implying the imperative, the point is a command and must be observed; if, however, "will" implies the indicative, there is the inference of choice or discretion. Just another instance of the significance of the knowledge of our language in communication.

WHY GO INTO TECHNICAL WRITING?

Although we have looked briefly at advantages and disadvantages of the "life of the writer," whatever aspect of business or industry he may choose, to leave this section on the note of indecision about the various phases of technical writing would be a distortion. The gratifications in the work are many. Not the least of these is revealed in the faces of the large teams of individuals—scientists, writers, technicians, administrators —shown in news pictures, at the culmination of a successful project such as the moon shot of Ranger VII or the development of a life-saving vaccine. Because of the mutual dependence of members upon each other in groups involving the technical writer, a strong rapport exists, even in the absence of success. To the more money-minded prospect, it can be pointed out that supply and demand operates, with salaries running high. " 'Publications Engineers,' as one company calls them, usually get equal if not higher pay than technical men in more conventional fields. Top salary for an experienced writer ranges from $8,000 to $12,000, with editors receiving more." [24]

[24] *The Wall Street Journal*, December 4, 1956.

The growth of the technical communications field involving hundreds of thousands of individuals speaking scores of languages, from English to Tagalog and from Russian to Chinese, makes it a fascinating spot for the individual who would not "wither on the vine." Its diversity of subject matter from interplanetary travel to hair coloring, from insecticides and polio vaccine to alcoholism and juvenile delinquency add to the excitement. Its active participants work in industries, research organizations, university laboratories, institutes, and foundations.

Over and above the monetary and the social rewards in technical writing, there is yet another one, more momentous and, to some, even more gratifying. It is well articulated by Eli Arlock, Chief of the Foreign Languages Publications Branch of LaDriere, Inc., Detroit.

Cumbersome as it may sometimes seem, with all its inconvenient safeguards, checks and balances, democracy is our way of life. It may well be, as its detractors claim, the most inefficient, expensive and difficult way of living that there is, but it is the only free way. To maintain it, and preserve it, in our space century, we must be well informed; we must keep abreast of progress, not only our own, but everybody's. The free transmission of scientific knowledge is today, more than ever, essential to the maintenance of every other kind of freedom; and the preservation of those other kinds of freedom is the responsibility not of one individual to another, nor even of one government to another; it is the responsibility of all free men to all men who would become or remain free.[25]

A FINAL WORD TO THE WRITER

In this chapter, we have viewed a wide field of writing. If well equipped, a person should feel at home in this field, whether or not he finds his vocation in it. That vitality so characteristic of American business and industry is nowhere more apparent than in its writing—its business and technical articles, advertising copy, radio and television programs, and commercials. If you can contribute sparkle, or even clarity and common sense, to the communications that are an indispensable part of the lively game of producing goods and supplying them to consumers, you may very well seek your vocation in the field of commercial writing.

An incident involving the late Sinclair Lewis, Nobel Prize winner and incomparable American satirist, serves well as the last word of advice to the would-be writer. The account has it that Mr. Lewis, as author-in-residence at the University of Wisconsin, was to talk informally with a select group of writing students one evening in the home of his host, a professor. The students, comfortably situated about the room, on chairs,

[25] From Mr. Arlock's paper "Russian and American Technical Communications," before the Society of Technical Writers and Editors, Southeastern Michigan Chapter, at Wayne State University, January 30, 1960.

sofas, and the floor, anxiously awaited the advice of the renowned author. Mr. Lewis scanned the group, asked perfunctorily as his opening remark "How many of you here are interested in writing?" Everyone raised a hand of course. "Then," Mr. Lewis rasped, scowling, "why in hell aren't you at home writing?"

If you would write (rather than dream of becoming a writer), assimilate the steps outlined in this chapter and elsewhere in the book and start writing. Somewhere, there's a market for your "stuff." Write it, study your market—or reverse those steps—and send it off. Have an envelope addressed to another publisher, ready to send the manuscript off again when it comes back from the first one. Remember the returns expected in direct-mail advertising. Acceptances of unsolicited manuscripts are comparable—but thrilling when they come.

Let's Put Words to Work *

Words may be fragile verbal tools, dulled by wrong usage and often not readily at hand, but they are the only medium by which we may make ourselves understood by other people.

They came to us from a slow-moving past, and our faulty use of them in this faster-than-sound age has much to do with our personal confusion and the disorder in human affairs. To discuss putting words to work is not to talk about a bookish frill, but about something needed for rational contact with the world around us.

Some business letters are sadly down at heel. Some seem to say things that do not need saying, in a way that shows the writer to have had no interest in saying them. Others look all right on the outside, being carefully typed on good paper with the proper margins, but they are as indigestible as a gaudily iced cake filled with concrete.

These things don't matter much to a writer whose loftiest notion about his job is to keep the paper flowing. Such a man is depriving himself of a great deal. His limp words rob him of the pleasure of communicating his thoughts and emotions, of attracting admiring attention, of moving people to do what he wants them to do.

One of the graces of a rich language like English or French is that its words may be put together so as to say the same thing in many different ways. There are earthy words, carrying weight; airy words as light as soap bubbles; missile-like words, speedy and explosive. All of these have magic in them, the magic of carrying your meaning weightily, lightly, or cracklingly into your reader's mind.

* *The Royal Bank of Canada Monthly Letter,* May, 1963. (Used by permission.)
Nearing the end of the course seems a fitting time for review of the principles and uses of words, the writer's stock in trade. Although there are frequent references in the reading to letters, the primary concern of this book, the precepts apply just well to other forms of business communication.

Language did not start in a grammar book: it started because people wanted to talk with one another. To build it up over the centuries has been a grand adventure in which we can still join.

We read with delight letters written hundreds of years ago. The writers' painfully labouring goose quills wrote words with meaning and feeling.

Consider the reader

Everything we write—except the occasional pieces we scribble just for the joy we find in putting words together—should take account of the reader's comfort, interest, and capacity to understand. His personality is more important than ours in dictating what words we shall use, but our own character, mood and purpose must show through. Apply that specification to sales letters, answers to complaints, welcomes to new customers and shareholders, and even to greetings and compliments, and you will find that it is a vital part of good communication.

The words you use will be different if you are writing a letter of exactly the same meaning to two persons of widely different position and interests: for example, a stockholder who has investments in a dozen concerns and a mother who spends ten minutes judging the relative value of two pairs of children's shoes with a price spread of a quarter. But this is a truth often obscured by our present passion for form letters and the low standard allowed to prevail in business correspondence.

Writing has no purpose save to meet the needs of the reader. Before the days of the pony express and airmail, communication on this continent was by smoke signal. When the Indian was making signals it was he and not the friend with whom he was communicating who got smoke in his eyes. Let's absorb the smog at the point of origin, so that our communications arrive crisp and clear.

We must choose our words so that the reader will be sure to understand them without waste of time and thought. They must tell the necessary facts on the vocabulary level of the reader. They must convey to the reader something of the way we feel toward him.

Give your letter some immediacy of impact. Get the recipient involved. If you talk too much about yourself, your firm or your product, you will find yourself talking to yourself. Try the dialogue form of composition, which invites the reader, whom you assume to be a person of intelligence and breeding, to join in the conversation. Don't start out by telling him what he told you in his last letter: he already knows, or he can look up the carbon copy. Begin by telling him something new.

Good manners enter into the choice of words, partly because they are due in propriety toward the reader and partly because his own dignity demands them of the writer.

When a man receives a letter with specific words aimed directly at his situation, he knows that some real, live human being has taken the trouble to invent sentences to convey a message specially to him.

Are the time and trouble involved in this carefulness justified in the writer's busy day? Look at it this way before answering: the only justification of a letter is the crucial five minutes when it stands, naked and alone, fighting the busyness and clamouring for the attention of the person to whom you addressed it.

Your choice of words is of vital value in this confrontation. The words need to convey a feeling of interest, a glow of friendliness, the assurance of sincerity, and the impression that you believe the message to be of sufficient importance to warrant the reader's attention.

Don't be foggy

No one can draft an effective circular, write a memorandum, frame rules, or dictate a letter unless he has a good sense of the fitness of words. You may not be blithe by nature, but you cannot be stolid and dull in your writing if you are to thrive in this competitive arena.

A fitting word is one that has meaning. It must represent the same thing to the reader as to the writer. A private meaning has no meaning at all. We recall the airman on a life raft in the Pacific who could feel sharks nuzzling his frail craft. He read aloud to them from a survival booklet describing how seldom sharks attack men. It wasn't their language and, in fact, it seemed to enrage them.

Words need to be meaningful. We must not think of language to the exclusion of ideas. The environment is important—the environment of the reader and the environment of your proposition—because it affects the sense of your words.

The secret is to let the meaning choose the word, and not the other way about. If you are going to soar into the freedom of using a word apart from its customary meaning, at least know what that meaning is and estimate the likelihood of your reader's understanding your modification of it. What do you gain, except perhaps a sort of childish amusement, by writing in an involved, pompous and tiresome manner?

Words need to be clear. Even if people do not agree with you, write so that there may be no doubt about what you are saying. To put a thing into appropriate words so that the message comes through clearly has the virtue of making it seem more real and possible and believable than if you say it muddily or smother it under ornament.

Even if you are dealing with an obscure subject, or if you are being stormily angry about a fault, or if you are being wide-eyed about a pet project: perhaps then more than at other times, use language that is not ambiguous.

Words need to be sharp. They must cut through superfluous matter to reveal what you wish to convey. Sometimes we feel frustrated by our inability to bend a word to express our exact thought. It isn't enough merely to scowl in vexation: find another word or use a phrase.

Every executive knows how annoying indeterminate words can be. Business and technical writing is dominated by the fact that specific meanings cannot be tampered with. The price is so many dollars, the replacement part is number such and such, the tolerance allowed is blank thousandths of a millimetre. To convey facts like these we must be specific. Generalities are acceptable only when they are appropriate.

Keep the reader awake

Words need to be vigorous. There is no excuse for having a letter come on to the stage with no more liveliness than a wet sponge and then slither out listlessly as the "Yours truly" curtain drops. Use of a virile word occasionally in a letter will impart a feeling of your aliveness. Use of active sentences will keep your audience awake.

Words need to be strong. Don't choose a word for its costume. It has to do something, so choose it for its muscle. Bleached-out, worn-out words do not make an impression on the mind.

Use strong words like urgent, crisis, fatal, grave, essential, and the like, for strong occasions. The inappropriate use of strong and long words debases them to the point where they no longer serve their purpose. When used on a thin topic, heavy words break through. They are as out of place as a driver on the green with the golf ball six inches from the hole.

Words should be simple. This is not to say that they should be in the primer class. People who demand immediate intelligibility without giving thought to what they read cannot hope to go far beyond comic strip or cartoon grade.

Writing simple words means expressing meaning as purely, clearly, definitely and shortly as possible. Churchill's famed "Blood, Sweat and Tears" would not have sparked the nation if "sweat" had been dressed up as "perspiration."

If there is a whiff of old-fashioned simplicity about your writing, that is perhaps a good thing. Consider William Harvey's *Motion of the Heart and Blood in Animals,* published in 1628, just eight years after a few of his fellow-Englishmen landed on Plymouth Rock. It was a significant book, defying the prejudices of several centuries, giving a new direction to the study of physiology. The magnitude of the subject might have justified the use of big words and bulging phrases. But here is how Harvey told his story: "I began to think whether there might not be a motion, as it were, in a circle. Now this I afterwards found to be true."

Words need to have rhythm. Whether you look at a landscape or at a painting, or listen to a brook or to an orchestra, you sense rhythm. There is harmonious flow. There should be rhythm in your use of words, too.

Many letters and other pieces of writing are made up of what used to be called in newspaper city rooms "ding dong" sentences. They have a constant chiming of the same structure in sentence after sentence, in which object follows predicate as surely as the clanging of a bell follows each stroke of its clapper.

Rhythm is not poetry but the pleasing movement and variation of syllables and phrases. It can be seen in the works of good authors of the past and present, and it can be learned from them.

Paint a word picture

There are three main sources of colour in language, and all of them involve words: vividness, activeness and pleasantness. The first makes the picture clear, the second makes it lively, and the third makes it easy to look at.

Colour words are not words in dress suits, nor tall opaque words, nor ornamental words, but words which tell better than any others the things the writer wishes to convey. Some good words appeal to more senses than that of sight, thereby adding to their force or understandability. If you say "he closed the door" that appeals only to sight; try "he slammed the door", which brings hearing into play. To "weep" is a visual verb; to "sob" has sight, hearing and movement.

Aesop Glim, a master copy writer, is quoted as having said that the reason for the Chinese slogan "one picture is worth a thousand words" is that it is so difficult to write a thousand words in Chinese. Your words, easier to write than Chinese, can become pictures when they are put together so as to call forth in the mind of your reader the scene, article or person you are writing about. Many a business letter would be improved if the writer took care to write about his product, factory or purpose as if he had seen and examined them, not merely read about them in catalogues or heard about them from fellow workers.

Bring down your thoughts from the abstract to the concrete. Note how much easier writing is to read when it turns its general ideas into physical form.

The Biblical Job does not say that he avoided destruction by the narrowest of margins: he says: "I am escaped with the skin of my teeth." When Solomon discoursed on the folly of excessive rest and relaxation, he put his warning into physical form with a reference to "folding of the hands to sleep." Horace does not speak of love, but of a particular girl; not of the austere life of old Italy but of sons carrying faggots in obedience to a stern mother. Shakespeare, in play after play, forces you to touch and see, because he chooses concrete words. When he has to use an abstract noun, for example "concealment", he immediately turns it into a visible worm "feeding" on the visible bud.

Use your imagination

Words can be put together so as to make metaphors, which are figures of speech in which the characteristics of one person or thing are ascribed to another. Metaphors are used to sharpen and extend the reader's understanding of a complex idea by presenting him with an image drawn from the world of sensory experience. Some examples are: the ship plowed the sea; the sands of his values are already shifting; he attempts to lash himself into the fury he thinks he should feel.

By using metaphor, our words can be made to appeal to all the senses. They play on colour, form, hearing, smell, touch and movement. In adjectives, for example, we can say: a blue outlook, a square deal, a ringing challenge, a rosy hope, headlong eagerness.

Metaphor should not be made obvious, nor should it consist of something incongruous. Consider these examples: a teen-age girl describes a school dance as a "disaster", while the bomber pilot limping home with a battered plane describes his mission as "quite a ball." Avoid, too, the absurdity caused by mixed pictures: "The target was handsomely beaten." (One strikes a target, beats a carpet.) A large heading in a newspaper said that Quebec had approved a bill "to increase the farm loan ceiling." (One raises the ceiling, increases benefits.)

Audacity is not the principal feature in good use of words; one requires imagination to use them in the right way to get the effect desired. Imagination detects the possibility of using some word, phrase or metaphor in such a way as to heighten interest in what is being said or to make clear something that may be obscure. It raises the ordinary events and communications of everyday life to a level where they are no longer commonplace.

Use of imagination does not mean that we become freakish. The tendency of business is away from all sorts of writing capers. A letter that seeks to snare attention by some peculiar and unusual layout, or by novel words used for the sake of novelty, labels itself the product of a childish mind.

Use active words

The most important characteristic of life is movement, and we show this in our writing by using active words. Our verbs should not be passive, but in vigorous action doing verb work.

Instead of writing "It was understood from you that shipment would be made by March 6th", write "You said you would ship by March 6th." George Washington didn't say about chopping down the cherry tree: "It was performed with a sharp edged instrument": he said: "I did it with my little hatchet."

Some people suggest that the desired sense of activity can be attained if you will just "write as you speak," but there are some differences you need to keep in mind.

It is easier to get an idea across in speech than in writing. One reason is that in speech we can stress the right words and pause at the right places. In writing, all the words of a sentence are printed in ink of equal blackness, separated by the same amount of space. If we try to overcome this disadvantage by underlining words, capitalizing them, or putting them in Italics, we indulge in a lazy device that makes a page look ugly and makes reading difficult. The right solution is to put the rhythm and emphasis into the words and into sentence structure.

We have to be more careful in writing than in speaking because our slips show more. There is not a distinctive language for speaking and writing, yet words which are in daily conversational use are not always suited to writing.

This does not mean that we must construct our letters as meticulously as a Swiss watchmaker putting the works together. It is possible so to measure and arrange syllables as to construct grammatical sentences which nevertheless do not convey our meaning. There are no grammatical laws by which we can compose Iliads or write effective selling letters.

The practised writer may allow himself a certain old-shoe casualness with grammar, so long as his meaning is clear and the effect is what he desires. But he should at least know the rules, so that he can discriminate between good and bad and so that he knows how far it is safe to go from the base. Before trying to steal home he will have achieved competence in reaching third.

The minimum objective in any writing is to convey meaning, but beyond that are the really interesting objectives: precision, grace, logic and clearness.

Alliterate with care

A device like alliteration must be used cautiously. In abundance, it becomes tiresome. Overdone, it interferes with understanding.

Alliteration is a tool which can be used effectively only when the reader doesn't notice it. It will make effective use of alliteration easier to understand if we consider it not so much as the repetition of a letter as the echo of a sound. Subtle alliteration uses half steps, as in music. The alphabet used in shorthand is a good guide to these half steps: T and D, L and R, K and hard G, F and V, P and B, M and N.

Repetition of noticeable words is as irritating to a reader as is obvious repetition of sound. You can avoid it by enlarging your vocabulary, not only in the number of words you have at the tip of your pen, but in the diameter of the words so that you know the many meanings they have.

The first word that occurs to you may not be the best word. It may be very good, but a better may present itself when you invite it. Don't, however, allow the desire for a perfect word to become a passion which interrupts your flow of thought. Get your ideas on paper, and then polish up what you have written.

Keep a couple of reference books handy for this burnishing. One of the most useful, because it is so complete and so easy to handle, is *A Dictionary of English Synonyms* by Richard Soule, now available in paper covers. A second might be *A Dictionary of Modern English Usage* by H. W. Fowler. The first gives you a wide selection of words for what you wish to say, and the latter, written with gusto for the correct and severity for the incorrect, will help you to keep on the track of right usage.

It is better, even in a business letter, to have a slight odour of the study lamp than to have thoughts presented in shabby terms. A letter that is well written flatters the receiver.

Read what you write

Even after following all the best precepts in writing your piece, there is more to be done. You must read your script to ascertain whether the words are the right words, saying what you wish to convey, and whether the sentences are equal to bearing the strain you ask them to carry.

Ovid, the Roman poet who wrote at the turn of the Christian era, was not ashamed to admit this need. He said: "When I re-read I blush, for even I perceive enough that ought to be erased, though it was I who wrote the stuff." Thomas Jefferson spent eighteen days writing and rewriting the Declaration of Independence; Victor Hugo made eleven revisions of one novel; Voltaire was known to spend a whole night toiling over one sentence. Artists, too, make revisions. Leonardo was one of the first to welcome painting in oils instead of in water colour: he said it allowed of so many afterthoughts, so refined a working out of perfection.

There is a happy mean between being content with the first thing that comes into your head and the craving for perfection. The letter you write need not be excessively polished, but it must be workmanlike. Do your writing painstakingly, but don't let it show.

When a thing is thoroughly well done it often has the air of being a miracle. There is no miracle about successful use of words: just hard work gathering facts, hard work recalling precedent pictures; hard work fitting them into the present setting; hard work writing carefully and brightly. In short, most successes in writing can be explained by diligent work, seasoned by lively imagination and warmed by sincerity.

You should take for granted that everyone who reads what you write will look for the best he is capable of appreciating. That sets your goal: you cannot rest content with mediocrity when excellence is within your reach.

Exercises and Problems in Communication

1. Assume you are to be on a four-member panel for a convention program of a company correspondents' national organization. Prepare a five-minute résumé of "Let's Put Words to Work" as your part of the session.

2. Write a magazine article (length and type at the discretion of your instructor) about a successful person *you know*. Interview the person for the details of his life, if you don't have enough information from acquaintance. Put the emphasis on those characteristics that led to his success, rather than on the events of his career. Name the publication to which you would submit your manuscript. This requires your studying the publication for style. (This assignment does not involve library research, in which you read about famous tycoons.)

3. Write a magazine article describing a job you would like to create, stressing your qualifications for the job. You may want to write the piece in the third person and cast it into the future, as if you were already in the position. A *new* type of work would of course include some aspects of existing jobs. This exercise can test your ingenuity, a characteristic employers are looking for in their employees.

4. In one of the versions of *Who's Who* or other biographical directories of persons well known in their fields, read the details about one of the entries. Write a sketch (some 300 words) about the person. Assume that he is a newcomer to your company or your town.

5. As public relations director of a company, plan all phases of a publicity campaign for the opening of a new company installation—a branch office or a manufacturing plant. Use all available media—local newspaper and appropriate radio and television facilities available in the community.

6. In connection with Exercise 5, write a newspaper release about the new installation. Keep in mind that many newspapers will use prepared copy, but, because of limited staff and time, will not assign someone to get the story. Remember, too, that an editor will cut copy to fit space; so use discretion in writing to interest the subscriber rather than to extol the company.

7. Write the lead questions for a five-minute radio or television interview between media personnel and the top executive of the new installation.

8. To get coverage of such an event as company expansion, it is helpful in some instances to buy newspaper space to publicize the happening. Write an open letter to occupy a half page (600 to 700 words) of the local paper, stating why your company chose the town for its new quarters, something of what the company hopes to contribute to the community, etc. Your company will pay for the space.

9. If there are no company magazines in your college library, such as *The Waggin' Tongue* (National Lead Company, St. Louis), *U.S. Bank Notes* (U. S. National Bank, Portland, Oregon), *Sealtest Eastern News* (Sealtest Foods Division, National Dairy Products Corporation, Philadelphia), *Pioneer* (U.S.

Borax and Chemical Corporation, Los Angeles), write the public relations department of a company you are interested in, asking for a few issues of its publication. Analyze the magazines for editorial objectives. How much stress is there on the employee, showing him the part he plays in the operations of the company? Is there indication that the magazine is used to help the employee be proud of the company; to let him know something of company policies; to help him to see he is not merely a man doing a job of work, but an employee of a company engaged in work? Make a report, according to your instructor's direction as to form, on your reaction to the magazines.

10. Write the Associated Press, New York, and request a copy of the leaflet "What Makes a Good Newspaper?" In the light of the criteria discussed in the leaflet, study a daily paper of your choice. Does the newspaper meet the standards of accuracy, responsibility, integrity, and leadership as set down by the Associated Press? Prepare an oral report.

11. Read several current issues of *Editor & Publisher* for principles and practices of today's journalism. Write an article for *Editor & Publisher*, commenting on the newspaper you studied for Exercise 10.

12. Interview someone you know on the timely subject of retirement. Someone already retired or some person who is planning systematically for retirement (such planning involves more than just financial arrangements) makes a likely candidate. The purpose of the interview is getting material for an article for a newspaper, a company magazine, or a professional magazine. The theme of your piece would be the aspects of a reasonable retirement program for the readers of the magazine you're writing for. Write the article.

13. Talk with a professor on your college faculty who has been away on leave, preferably on an assignment abroad. Write an article describing his experiences, for a professional magazine.

14. From a comparable interview, write a human interest story, telling how the professor of Exercise 13 (and his family) spent their time away. If the professor's leave included foreign travel, you could write on the country's customs, living conditions, political climate, or educational system.

15. Write an "editorial" on a company problem, such as absenteeism, safety violations, or indifference to employee-club activities, for a company publication. Keep in mind that persuasion is not nagging. This type of article frequently fails because the writer injects a domineering or a patronizing tone. Write to develop the employee's interest in the company, appealing to a personal desire, such as pride in association with the company or with the employee organization.

16. Choose three ads for the same product—not necessarily the same brand. Rate the ads "good," "mediocre," and "poor" according to attention, appeals, conviction, and action. Label the appeals and conviction steps according to the categories discussed in Chapter 8. Write a report on how the ads might be improved.

17. Unless you are apt as an artist and can prepare your own illustrations, select three pictures from current magazine advertisements and write headlines and copy to accompany the pictures advertising products other than those in the original ads.

18. Read in business and general magazines and in business sections of a newspaper discussions of the status of advertising. In a form suggested by your intructor, write your reactions to the ideas you have read. Take a stand on the attitudes toward or the condition of advertising—pro or con—and support

your opinion from your reading. (As a start for your reading, see "Advertising Ethics" in the *Business Periodicals Index.*)

19. Write three television commercials for three different commodities. You are responsible for the entire "scripts," including lines and visuals. Keep in mind that you have 58 seconds for each presentation.

20. Read various articles in *Scientific American* and *Science Digest* for comparison of style and level of writing. From those and articles in other scientific and technical journals choose one on a subject of interest to you. Rewrite the article for a less sophisticated audience than the original was presumably written for.

16

Dictation, Advancement, and Supervision

Let your speech be alway with grace, seasoned with salt, . . .—
COLOSSIANS IV: 6

Perhaps this might be a good time to turn back and reread "Effective Letters Are Attractive, Too," at the end of Chapter 2. Much of what Mrs. Woods says in her introductory remarks to the dictators and secretaries is echoed here. The following suggestions for dictation might well be part of her instruction in the individual class sessions she spoke of. As pointed out in her talk, dictation is an efficiency step in business. To be effective, the process is a cooperative effort between dictator and transcriber; and it requires just as much concentration and precision of thought as writing does. In fact, dictation has been called "voice writing."

SOME CONSIDERATIONS OF DICTATION

Although dictation is generally accepted as an efficiency process in business, it is not as efficient as it should be. There are many who have great difficulty in developing proficiency in the procedure; there are also many who shun dictation whenever possible, despite their years of composing letters, reports, memos, and other company writing. Much of the difficulty is laid to the mental block that dictation instructors call "mike fright."

To start well in this process, the person must dispel mike fright, and the only way to do this is to start dictating. If you should find yourself hesitant in dictation, you can dictate and "play back" to check your strengths and weaknesses; if you are to dictate to another person, you will accept the fact that dictation is a part of your job that you must improve, and call in the stenographer. Remember that your time is more valuable to the company than hers. If you are to make the most of your position, become proficient in all aspects of it. In either procedure of dictation, you can improve by studying carbon copies of your transcriptions. Having two carbons made of your dictation—one for your perusal and one for your file—is an expedient used by quite a few beginners. Many companies have multiple carbons made for circulation among staffs, to inform a department or officers of transactions.

Even without a knowledge of the technicalities of the physical factors, structure, and purpose of speech, managers have improved their dictation through attention to sounds in speech. Labeled "audio-scriptics" ("of or for hearing" plus "writing"), these techniques assist the writer (or dictator) in making language "more effective with patterns of the tone, timbre, time, and power in the sounds of speech." [1]

For those who would pursue this technique, a brief excerpt from Mr. Robson's explanation will serve as a starting point.

An early stage in developing audio-scriptic intelligence is the perception of the time value of the syllables, words, phrases, pauses, and paragraphs. A late stage is to see the rises and the falls in the tones of words and the powers of words that move with the passage of time. The final stage of phonetic control is to create or analyze language from the point of view of a word composer, a point of view not too different from that of a musical composer. This is the stage where leadership can arise. The patterns of speech may organize tone to make writing sing. They can use timbre to make statements decisive. They can feature time and power values to make the writer's ideas and thoughts rhythmic and clear. The full orchestration of our voice in written language, as the full instrumental score of a musical orchestra, offers this creative opportunity. [2]

A third point that arises in connection with dictation is the question of added length when a correspondent changes from "composing by hand" to dictation to either stenographer or machine. The director of correspondence in a Chicago company was disturbed to learn, after dictating equipment was put into use, that letter length increased by about 25 per cent. He found, however, that the increase was actually an improvement, because the dictated correspondence was freer of clichés and terseness. This is not to say that dictating insures improvement in writing or that length, in and of itself, is desirable. If, as was mentioned in Chapter 4, length contributes to tone, it is not to be avoided. No matter

---

[1] Ernest M. Robson, *The Orchestra of Language* (New York: Thomas Yoseloff, 1959), p. 21.
[2] *Ibid.*, p. 21.

the method by which his thoughts get onto the page, a correspondent must apply the principles of effective writing.

Keep in mind that you have not done the full job as far as the letter, memo, or report is concerned until you have proofread it.

ORGANIZING FOR EFFECTIVE DICTATION

Whether you are a newcomer or a veteran at "speaking your correspondence," you will start the actual dictation only after you have organized your materials. You will check prices and figures personally or through subordinates, glance through previous correspondence on continuing matters, and decide the proper disposition of the problem presented by the letter. In other words, you will plan before dictating. Many persons pencil on the letters to be answered rough working outlines to direct their thinking as they dictate. This planning allows for uninterrupted work—no breaking off to send someone to the files, no keeping the stenographer with pencil poised while a phone call is made, no pacing the room while trying to arrive at a decision. Good dictation is *planned* dictation.

The following four-step plan serves well in effective dictation:

1. Read the letter to be answered. While reading, make very brief notes on a 4 x 6 sheet of paper, outlining points requiring reply. (Making notes on the sheet rather than on the letter being answered saves having untidy penciled materials in the files.)
2. Get any additional information necessary for the reply, adding further notes to the 4 x 6 sheet.
3. Quickly review the 4 x 6 sheet, establishing the order of ideas for the letter. Mentally phrase the opening for the letter and turn on the machine.
4. Dictate the letter without a break, from beginning to end, referring to the notes for continuity of ideas.

CLEAR ARTICULATION OF SOUND AND THOUGHT

The dictator has gone far toward making his dictation effective when he has organized and planned his correspondence. Before the stenographer can prepare the neat letters which are to carry the dictator's messages to his clients, however, there remains the actual enunciation of the words, and all but a fortunate few among stenos experience some bad enunciation. The voiced pause—the "ah" and "er" of the fumbling dictator—annoys the stenographer and wastes valuable business time. Extreme change of pace from very rapid to very slow, or vice versa, makes dictation difficult to take down. Natural speech rhythms must be observed; that is, pauses should not break up the material artificially, but should come at the ends of thought units, usually phrases or clauses.

Monotony of tone tends to induce mental sluggishness if not actual sleepiness on the part of the stenographer. Swallowing the ends of words or other failure to enunciate clearly and fully makes the fault the dictator's rather than the stenographer's when letters are transcribed incorrectly.

Some men are naturally more fluent than others, but it is certain that, even without more ability or knowledge, the average dictator could exert himself to enunciate better than he habitually does. Moreover, if he will take some lessons in voice production from a competent teacher, or even study a good book on the subject, he can improve his speech. The laws of voice production, largely matters of correct breathing and adequate jaw and lip movement, are after all so simple that practically anyone can learn to speak clearly and effectively if he will bestir himself. Few kinds of effort pay bigger dividends in the business world.

DICTATING MACHINES

One of the most useful business devices is the dictating machine, offspring of the telephone and the phonograph, in which a wax cylinder or composition disk or tape is substituted for the stenographer's shorthand pad. Some of the earliest experiments of Thomas A. Edison and Alexander Graham Bell and his associates were devoted to developing devices for recording and reproducing human speech, but it was not until the twentieth century that satisfactory machines were perfected. The dictating machine of today is a mechanical wonder, but its possibilities have not yet been fully utilized.

This method of dictating correspondence has become an integral and ever-increasing part of modern business. The executive dictates to the machine, and the transcriber later types the dictation directly on letter sheets. By using a dictating machine, the executive can dictate at his convenience. He need not schedule all his correspondence for a certain time of the day, but can dictate a letter as it fits into his program, and he can, if necessary, dictate out of office hours or even on a plane or train. Despite implications of auto-traffic safety, considerable machine dictation is done in cars by salesmen, field representatives, and executives who commute distances by auto. One transcriptionist can handle the correspondence of a number of executives. In a large organization, the disks, belts, tapes, or memo-belts are collected at intervals throughout the day and relayed to a central transcription department.

A refinement of the individual dictating machine is a plant- or office-system in which the dictator dictates into a phone. The dictation is recorded in a central department, where transcription is completed and the copy is returned by interoffice mail to the dictator for proofreading and signature. Another refinement makes possible the two-way recording of telephone conversations and also across-the-desk conversations. The advantage of having a permanent record of both ends of an important business telephone conversation or conference is obvious.

To assure efficient use of the dictating machine, both dictator and transcriptionist must become well acquainted with it. Devices are provided for giving the transcriptionist any necessary instructions concerning the letters, such as the number of copies required, the length of the letter so that she can provide for proper margins, and identification of any errors in dictation.

ALPHABETICAL CODE FOR TELEPHONE OR DICTAPHONE USE

It is important to make sure of the spelling of names in oral communication. This is not difficult if identifying words are used for letters wherever there is likelihood of misunderstanding, especially in telephoning telegraph messages or dictating to a machine. The following code list is recommended by the Western Union Telegraph Company and is much used in general business. Most persons can readily memorize this list.

A—Arthur	J—John	S—Sugar
B—Boston	K—King	T—Thomas
C—Chicago	L—Lincoln	U—Union
D—Denver	M—Mary	V—Victor
E—Edward	N—New York	W—William
F—Frank	O—Ocean	X—X ray
G—George	P—Peter	Y—Young
H—Henry	Q—Queen	Z—Zero
I—Ida	R—Robert	

Advancement

You can't get your name on the door until you get it on the payroll.—J. P. McEvoy, "Youth, Get Your Toe in the Door"

Getting your name on the payroll does not guarantee getting it on the door, to be sure; needless to say, however, having it on the payroll is one big step.

In Chapter 9, we discussed essentials of correspondence necessary in most job-getting. Let's go one step further and look at the part communication plays after your name is on the payroll.

You are likely a little jaded from teachers' admonitions that because of today's organizational structure, you can best make yourself known in your job through your writing ability. This *is* true, to an extent; but in even the largest organization, personal contact among employees—peer, superior, subordinate—plays a major role in business operations and, in turn, in promotion. In either situation, in writing or in person-to-person dealings, the individual's success will come largely through his communicative ability.

It has been made clear throughout the course, I trust, that we have not been dealing with merely the physical and typographical aspects of speaking and writing. Communication implies more than an ability in expression of thoughts. It involves the speaker's or writer's traits, qualities—his personal being.

WHY IS THE COLLEGE GRADUATE HIRED?

A college graduate may be hired ostensibly for a specific position, but, as a matter of fact, an applicant's potential for advancement is a major consideration in much of today's hiring. Certain latent qualities, *acquired* and *personal,* promise effective performance and continued employment to reduce the costly turnover experienced in business and industry today, especially in the early period of a person's tenure. Since wise selection and judicious promotion of managerial personnel are among management's biggest problems, they are the subject of much writing and conference discussion. Long lists of qualities looked for in employees are found in the professional literature and are used, to greater or lesser degrees, by companies. Digested from statements of executives, principally from personal correspondence of John Mills, former personnel director, Bell Telephone Laboratories, Inc., seven such qualities seem pertinent to our discussion of promotion: (1) intellectual curiosity, (2) the ability to study, (3) the habit of study, (4) the ability to learn from men, (5) the ability to cooperate with men, (6) the promise of ability to lead and influence men, and (7) the "courage to fail." [3]

The first three of these, as you can see at once, relate closely to, but are not necessarily proved by, attaining a college degree. Numbers 4 through 7 may be surmised from a record of extra-curricular activities and a past employment record, if there is one.

Intellectual curiosity does not connote a casual or idle frame of mind. The attribute may be reflected in the person's interest in what goes on about him, in how his position fits into the whole operation of a department or the company, in why certain policies or procedures are followed, etc. But real curiosity is more than inquisitiveness; it is an orderly and continuing effort to determine the why of social and physical phenomena of the world about the individual. The trait becomes a motive or urge within the person.

---

[3] John W. Gardner, *Self-Renewal: The Individual and the Innovative Society* (New York: Harper & Row, 1964), p. 14. The author of this estimable book on personal development was president of The Carnegie Foundation for the Advancement of Teaching at the time of its writing. Mr. Gardner was named Secretary of the Department of Health, Education, and Welfare in 1965.

The second factor, the ability to study, is misconstrued by many. Although, as just mentioned, study is implied in a college career, the ability to study is not necessarily shown merely by class attendance or by reading an assigned book. Those activities as usually practiced are more akin to learning—gaining knowledge, an understanding, or a skill; whereas study represents applying the mind and acquiring knowledge *by one's own efforts*. There are notably fewer persons with this ability than there are with academic degrees.

The *habit* of study is acquired over a period of time, and the years an individual is in school have frequently proved insufficient time for its development. It is the habit of study growing out of intellectual curiosity that will be a young employee's source of growth during his early period of employment. Too, it can help him bridge a gap attendant upon the change in intellectual activity in going from school to a job, a void that many executives recognize as the reason for unrest in the new employee. The college graduate has spent a number of years, especially the junior and senior college years, in rather intensive study in economics, psychology, philosophy, sciences, literature, and mathematics. He has been working on a rather high intellectual level. In business and industry, he finds that his first work often consists of routine matters, such as becoming familiar with merchandise, lists of customers, or detailed technical or operational procedures—"chores" that he must know in learning the company, but activities that can be handled, in large part, by someone with much less education than he has. Because of this change in intellectual pace, there is a tendency toward impatience; the new employee feels that he is engaged in work below his mental abilities.

To offset the detrimental reactions to this change of pace, firms have instituted management-training programs. In these programs for developing employees for management positions, the "trainees" attend organized classes like those they have recently come from in college and they have on-the-job experience in various departments. In many instances, these programs have helped to sustain the newly employed college graduate between the time of newness and mental inactivity and the time of acquiring the company experience and the information that equip him for responsibility.

Maintaining the habit of study will further help him when in the course of advancement, because of his business acumen, human adaptability, and experience, he arrives finally at a position that requires intensive study on a high intellectual level. If the person is habituated to study, he can more readily attack the tasks of his more demanding job with a semblance of scientific thought, rather than be guided by hunches or conscious or unconscious emulation of the practices and methods of others.

TRAITS FOR WORKING WITH PEOPLE

The next three specifications in the seven named have to do with attitudes and abilities in human relationships, and from both individual reports and extensive surveys, it is clear that there is a shortage of employees with these abilities. This dearth is regularly the subject of many articles in management journals.

The need for talent in working with others is manifest in the attitudes of many in their first employment just after college. The sixteen years of theoretical exposure sometimes throw a person off balance, to the extent that he either "knows all the answers" or he believes that the only way to learn is in organized educational programs. The complaint is frequently heard that the newly graduated employee resists too strongly the proffered teaching of an experienced person on the job. Such resistance many times stymies the new person, the effort to teach him often being an attempt to groom him for the next step up. The converse of this situation also reflects an inability in human relationships. The new employee is willing to learn, but the older one is reluctant to teach him. This condition has kept the older one from progressing. He cannot be promoted because he has not made provisions for someone to take his present place. Very much a matter of communication in the sense discussed here, an employee's hesitation to teach another frequently results from a fear that his position will be jeopardized by the younger employee.

The absence of salutary relationships among employees is shown on a larger scale in surveys of causes for dismissing employees in business and industry. These studies, involving large and small firms, show that as high as 90 per cent of dismissals are due to inability to get along with others, as contrasted to 10 per cent for lack of job knowledge.

Many persons find it difficult to reconcile differing philosophies about the seventh trait, the courage to fail. Part of the difficulty is due to the repeatedly voiced notion that a person progresses only through conformity, that he must become a "company man." Also, as John Gardner points out in *Self-Renewal*, society—chiefly parents, teachers, and managerial personnel—curb trial and venture by instilling fear, punishing failure, or by making success seem too precious. In much of the literature on business, both fiction and non-fiction, conformity and the disapproval of failure have been emphasized.

Quite the opposite attitude is generously expressed by many in the upper echelons of management. Consider the following opinions on the apparent demand for individualists in management. Donald E. McKee, a vice-president of IBM, says that "a man flattened by an opponent can get up again; a man flattened by conformity stays down for good." The president of Litton Industries, Roy L. Ash, states that his company looks for the person who "doesn't wait for opportunity . . . he creates opportunity . . . he creates change and thrives on change, rather than expending his energies to resist it." Addressing himself to teachers and managers, Edward G. Uhl, president of the Fairchild Hiller Corporation, suggests: "Let us not teach them to fear insecurity and risk. . . . Teach them it isn't a crime to make a mistake or a wrong start." [4]

Whatever stand you take on the question of individuality versus conformity, it is well to be mindful of the price we pay for our fear of failure. It narrows the personality and prevents exploration. In keeping with the continued habit of study, it can be repeated that there is no learning without some fumbling and reversals. To keep on learning, we must keep on risking failure. As Goethe said, men will always be making mistakes as long as they are striving after something.

METHODS OF EVALUATION FOR PROMOTION

In promotions, as in dismissals, although to a lesser extent, personal qualifications carry more weight than job knowledge.[5] How are an individual's personal traits measured and evaluated? Practices among companies range from the all but superficial interview between a superior and the employee to the elaborate testing program. Tests contribute to objectivity, according to those who use them; to the other camp, those who depend on daily experiences with employees and observation, measurement of human traits cannot be reduced to a piece of management science.[6] As in all activity, the subject of testing has had some lampooning. A diverting treatment of this phase of management is "How To Cheat on Psychological Tests," a section of William H. Whyte's much discussed *The Organization Man.*

Another projective technique for evaluation is the structured interview. This involves a system of lead questions, answers to which tell something of the individual's personality, and where he might best fit into the company. One such plan includes discussion of the employee's interests. Is he impelled by a concern for ideas? for people? for things? for economic symbols?

The order into which these interests fall is interpreted by the psychologist, indicating the nature of work the employee is suited for, in the light of his potential for permanence with the company. Examples of the interpretations of these traits would be to consider the person for cost or accounting work if the order of his interests were ideas, economic symbols, men, things; or the salesman or business manager type would express a preference in the order of men, economic symbols, things, and

[4] Excerpts from addresses at the dedication of the Krannert Graduate School of Industrial Administration, Purdue University, April, 1965.

[5] "Who Do You Promote?" *Dun's Review and Modern Industry,* May, 1964, p. 51.

[6] *Ibid.,* p. 52.

ideas. These interpretations are not fixed, of course, there being combinations among the four, with primary and secondary interests.

THE "MANAGER'S LETTER"

Although one other plan used by some companies is primarily for exchange of ideas among managers about company objectives, it often has direct bearing on appraisal of subordinates' performances—for promotions. The involvement of written communication in the plan, described in *The Practice of Management*, is clear.

> Some of the most effective managers I know . . . have each of their subordinates write a "manager's letter" twice a year. In this letter to his superior, each manager first defines the objectives of his superior's job and of his own job as he sees them. He then sets down the performance standards which he believes are being applied to him. Next, he lists the things he must do himself to attain these goals—and the things within his own unit he considers the major obstacles. He lists the things his superior and the company do that help him and the things that hamper him. Finally, he outlines what he proposes to do during the next year to reach his goals. If his superior accepts this statement, the "manager's letter" becomes the charter under which the manager operates.[7]

Some firms using the technique as an appraisal measurement—and for correction of conditions needing attention, as revealed in the letters—include all managerial levels from foreman to president.[8] As Mr. Drucker points out, such letters among managers can bring problems and misunderstandings out into the open. The letter program has been less than successful because of the conventional management pattern of power and submission. Advantages and disadvantages of the system, however, do not alter the apparent necessity of writing ability.

Supervision

> *I never saw his like; there lives*
> *No greater leader.*
> —ALFRED TENNYSON, *Idylls of the King*

As a person moves up the managerial ladder, communication is more important with each step, because with each step he is moving farther away from "doing the work" himself. As one executive put it, the higher you rise, the lower the ratio in work with people and with things and the higher with abstractions. He says that the newly appointed supervisor, or manager, finds himself in a peopled landscape of human traits, work rules, and pressures from above, factors that he must understand, ration-

[7] Peter F. Drucker, *The Practice of Management* (New York: Harper & Row, 1954), p. 129.
[8] Francis B. Torbert, "Experiments with a Manager's Letter Program," *Personnel,* January–February, 1964, p. 30.

alize, and subordinate, according to the circumstances of a given situation.

ATTRIBUTES OF A SUCCESSFUL MANAGER

What kind of person can adapt to this change when he is expected to lead people, through their cooperation? Of the many components considered as contributing to successful management, there are four recurring ones that warrant a close look. To do well in his job, a manager (1) reflects confidence, (2) is sympathetic, (3) is sincere, and (4) understands social dynamics; for he must be prepared to encounter resistance before he wins acceptance.

Confidence is not the blind hope that many think of when they hear the word. It is a condition made up of two distinct, constructive parts: knowledge and positiveness. A manager's knowledge consists of those factors of his job that he has learned on his way up and those details gleaned as a result of his intellectual curiosity mentioned earlier. Positiveness is more than optimism; it is a belief in others that comes from understanding, through learning, of human behavior. Positiveness is also more than the opposite of negation, a characteristic of too many managers. As one first-line supervisor said of his superior, "He can speak four different languages, but he can't say 'yes' in any of them." Peter Drucker, just quoted, in writing of this phase of management, says that

A man should never be appointed to a managerial position if his vision focuses on people's weaknesses rather than on their strengths. The man who always knows exactly what people cannot do, but never sees anything they can do, will undermine the spirit of his organization. Of course, a manager should have a clear grasp of the limitations of his people, but he should see these as limitations on what they can do, and as challenges to them to do better. He should be a realist; and no one is less realistic than a cynic.[9]

Because of loose common usage, a definition of *sympathy,* the second trait, will help here. The word is often confused with *pity,* which is defined as "a sympathetic or kindly sorrow excited by the suffering or misfortune of another, often leading one to give relief or aid or to show mercy." Sympathy, on the other hand, is the "community or agreement in feeling, as between persons or on the part of one person with respect to another." Sympathy, then, is not a gullibility for a hard-luck story, nor acceptance of someone's deficiencies or shortcomings. It is basically the "you" attitude, a willingness to see and the ability to understand another's position.

If a person would lead others in their work for the profit and growth of a company, he must have sympathy; but in his agreement of feeling,

[9] *Op. cit.,* p. 157.

he must be cognizant of that factor in communication, spoken of in Chapter 1: the basic fact of difference. In a business situation, this is the condition that separates the manager from the very persons whose cooperation he seeks. In the passage previously quoted from William Whyte's *Is Anybody Listening?*, there is the sentence "All the communication in the world is not going to make a coal miner think like a coal operator." To paraphrase the thought, you as a manager are not going to think like your subordinates or your superiors, nor are they going to think as you do. Differences in your backgrounds, experiences, and motivations separate you.

The part that difference plays in communication becomes conspicuous at promotion time. Assume that two individuals have worked closely together at a management level for a considerable length of time, when one of them is promoted. If they are to continue to cooperate, both will do well to accept the differences created by the promotion of one of them. They are no longer the same persons to each other. But a genuine sympathy, a community of feeling, will help them to cooperate. A terse, but intelligent, reaction in such a situation was shown by the comment of a person in business—the one who was not promoted. On reading in the daily office letter that one of his peers had been promoted to a next-level position, the young man went to his friend's desk, extended his hand, and said, "Good morning, George; good luck; and good-by."

On the third point of leadership in management—sincerity—there is far more to be said than our space allows or our purpose requires. Of personal traits demanded for good management, it is the one most looked for in others. In the clamor of making a living, we develop cynicisms; we suspect others' motives. Almost any move on the part of an individual or an organization can provoke the questions: "What's he up to?" "What are they after?" An example of this was in a labor union's giving the Boy Scouts of America $350,000 for a headquarters building in Washington, D.C. At the time, one of the union officials was getting adverse publicity. There was general suspicion of the news of the contribution.

A man in a high position in a family-owned company majored in business administration in college. He has helped employees' families and others anonymously; although he is mild-mannered, he has definite goals and strong convictions. Yet, common comments from those who work close to him reflect doubt as to his integrity. One of his co-workers voices the attitude in his appraisal that "When Ken says something in meetings, or anytime he asks somebody to do something, I always feel that he's doing what it said to do on page 43 in one of his management books."

As intimated in the chapters on sales writing and public relations, motives in those two fields are questioned regularly and generally.

But these notions of mistrust and questioning do not preclude a sincerity among individuals, despite the egoistic nature of man. As mentioned earlier, each man can be seen as the center of his own universe. He is his own individual. But it is not blind folly to believe in the basic goodness of man. And as you look to your superiors for guidance, you seek that reassuring condition of sincerity, just as your subordinates will expect the truth from you.

It is not uncommon to hear the comment that a combination of sympathy and sincerity robs a person of his individuality. He becomes a chameleon, it is said, changing his personality to blend or conform with those around him at the time—anyone so unstable will never be a leader. Sincerity in no way precludes steadfastness of belief or firmness of convictions. The severest taskmaster can be depended upon for consistency in fairness.

If we were to categorize the three traits discussed, they might fall under one label of personal attributes, although confidence depends upon the acquisition of knowledge, a factor that can be measured. The fourth requirement for managerial leadership is based unqualifiedly in a person's understanding of behavior, or communication. It is the normal fact of resistance before acceptance. The new boy in school who must prove himself, the pledge in a fraternity who wants so much for the brothers to like him, the new employee who is sure he is resented by the older employees—all these persons are threats to the status quo. They are aggressors; they are invading the domain of the present group. They are, in general, resisted. The person with leadership qualities will accept this fact of social dynamics. He will not let his eagerness for immediate reception become an anxiety; he will bide his time.

There will always be those who exude enthusiasm of welcome to the new person. In general, they are not the stalwarts, the standbys, the ones from whom genuine cooperation can be expected.

To bring the point into your frame of reference, let's sum it up with the admonition that as the new employee, you, through understanding, accept any apparent antagonism from those who are "in," and that later as the manager, you expect resistance from those you are newly appointed to supervise. If you season this insight into the causes of behavior and the nature of motivation with confidence based on knowledge and the personal traits of sympathy and sincerity, your writing and your spoken directives—up, down, or across—will pay dividends to your company through the cooperation of those for whom, as a manager, you provide leadership.

As a specialist in personnel administration, the president of the McMurry Company of Chicago, sums it up, in describing factors contributing to an executive's success: "Other vital qualities are: skill in communication, both oral and written, to the extent that he can convey a message in such a manner that it is understood, believed, and accepted, and the ability to adapt his leadership techniques to the needs of the group he is guiding." [10]

Work and Management

by LILLIAN M. GILBRETH [*]

Management is as old as time. It has been defined as getting work done through your own effort or that of others. Some persons are inclined to think that management means getting some one else to do your work for you, that the work can be delegated and then you can go on your way rejoicing. Of course, this definition is completely inappropriate.

The people who started the scientific management movement did not have the advantage of an arts and letters background, or training in philosophy, and they did not read or speak other languages fluently or travel a great deal. They were mechanical engineers, trained in the fashion of their time. They went into industry and devoted their lives to making the best use of their own and other people's time, energy, and money. They did not realize that management was something that had come down through the ages and was being practiced in some form or other in every country in the world.

As it turned out, many things which were done quite independently in the United States proved to have been done previously in other countries. For example, my husband found, after he had spent a long time developing the cyclograph method, that Marey had done it in France years before. References in the "Golden Book of Management" to Boulton, Owen, and Babbage of Great Britain, Solvay of Belgium, and Fayol of France furnish other instances.

Lacked Some of the Ready-Made Aids

In the beginning, management lacked some of the ready-made aids available to us today. The term *interdisciplinary cooperation* and today's fine classification and labeling of those who cooperate—physiologists, psychologists, psychiatrists, sociologists, etc.—were not part of their everyday vocabulary. But even in the early days, forward-looking people gave thought not only to the handling of materials but to the handling of people.

In those days, economics was a comparatively narrow field, although the first real paper in our management history was Henry R. Towne's "The Engi-

[10] Robert N. McMurry as quoted in *Dun's Review and Modern Industry*, October, 1963, p. 58.

[*] Dr. Gilbreth, known as the "world's greatest woman engineer," is President of Gilbreth, Inc., a management consultant company that she and her husband, the late Frank B. Gilbreth, organized before World War I. Two of the twelve Gilbreth children wrote the bestseller of a decade ago, *Cheaper by the Dozen*, a gay, heart-warming story of life in a large family.

"Work and Management" appeared originally in *Advanced Management—Office Executive*, September, 1962. It is reprinted here from *Advanced Management Journal*, September, 1963, pp. 119–23, by permission of the Society for Advancement of Management.

neer as Economist." In this paper, Towne shows that he, a forthright engineering thinker, realized that the typical training of the engineer must be broadened by an understanding of economics. He said we ought to know, in addition to production, something of marketing, sales, and the problems of the consumer. Psychology, which in Towne's era was just beginning as experimental educational psychology, and sociology, which had no such label at that time, and all the social sciences need to be included.

One can review the whole field of management through these years. Research and the technical side of engineering have implemented the management fields, but the engineer has come to realize that his abilities to handle materials must be supplemented by skill in handling human relations and that a fine friendly feeling and the wish to develop and help other people is essential.

The objective of work and of management remains one and the same. It has been simply stated in the engineers' code: "To utilize the resources of nature and of human nature for the benefit of mankind"; and we must not only use the resources we have today but must press on to develop new ones through new discoveries, new technics.

The difficulty with trying to define "for the benefit of mankind" is that of determining *who* decides *what* the benefit of mankind is, both in the short run and in the long run. Part of this question, of course, involves delayed returns. Too often we calculate quick and useful returns from a short-term view, whereas if we were patient enough to take the long-term view we might find the delayed returns far better.

The question on returns points up the value of historians, not only historians of the past but also historians who recognize that the present is going to be part of the past—of history. Historians keep the records from which correct conclusions can be drawn later.

I spend more time than most in reading the history of management from the works of individuals I knew in this field. One person, whom almost nobody in this country knew, was Mary Follett. She was the only woman who ranked as one of the pioneers. She was not a part of the group who lived in New York, and she was not an engineer. She was a sociologist and spent much of her time in England, but she did more to show the interrelationships of people, and how these developed, than almost anyone we have had.

Delayed Returns Must Be Part of the Picture

Mary Follett died too soon to know the results of her activities, but her papers were collected and one finds more and more people reading and quoting from them. Hers were delayed returns. She is an apt illustration of my point that one should do the best he knows and put it on the record, then proceed to do the best he knows the next day. It does not pay to look back and wonder if it was worthwhile; delayed returns must be a part of the picture.

And now to the application of management. Wherever there are two or more people there is a management problem. Is the answer to share the management, or to have one manage the other, or what? I feel we have omitted in our management theories one of the most important concepts—managing oneself.

Most people assume this comes with experience and practice, but practically it is a difficult thing to accomplish. When you start to examine the problem of managing yourself you may be appalled at the size and complexity of the undertaking. The pioneers based their work upon the engineers' code, and they took more than a hint from Kipling's little verse: "I keep six honest serving men; they taught me all I knew. Their names are what and why and when and how and where and who."

The pioneers added these six questions to the code and applied them to the whole scope of work activity. But until the social sciences came more completely into the picture, we did not fully realize that managing ourselves was our first responsibility.

How can you learn to manage yourself? Go over your assets, neither overestimating nor underestimating them. Go over your liabilities, neither overestimating nor underestimating them.

Try to plan your formal education and your reading in such a way that you can gain a better understanding of your personal drives and learn to develop your assets while you gain control over your liabilities. Then, realizing that everybody in the world is faced with the same problem, try to develop skill in productive cooperation with other people.

Offers Your Greatest Opportunities to Master the Art

The second area in which good management is vital is that of the home and family life. This area probably offers your greatest opportunities to master and practice the art of self-management and cooperation with other people. It is impossible to overestimate the importance of a well-managed home, where the human relations are good and the housekeeping adequate, for each morning an orderly home sends forth the family members into industry, business and school, prepared to meet whatever challenge the day may bring; and welcomes them home again at night for relaxation, refreshment and understanding.

Life is full of tensions, and sometimes the home needs to act as a safety valve to counteract the pressures of the outside world. I remember so well one of my boys, who was no problem in school, but really a problem in the home. I don't know whether his father and I were more pleased and proud when the good school reports came in or were most annoyed when we could not turn out a similar report in the home situation.

One day I said to this son: "These are wonderful reports and I am proud of you, but why under the sun can't you act this way at home?"

My son replied he could not act that way all the time—"If I were good at home I would have to be bad at school, and if I am good at school, it is all I can do to wait until I get home."

"If this is true," I replied, "then we'll have to grin and bear it at home, because it is very necessary that your school record be good."

If the home has an atmosphere of warmth and understanding, it is possible for us to express ourselves completely while there. But, on the other hand, this same atmosphere demands of us corresponding consideration for the other members of the family group. It is natural, perhaps, when we think of family life, the human relations aspect is the first to come to mind, but we must not lose sight of the fact that a serene, well-ordered family life is in part the product of a well-managed job of homemaking, technically and otherwise.

For decades the accepted industrial technics of job analysis and improvement have been applied to the many and varied tasks of housekeeping. Extensive research in our schools and colleges has developed new work technics, new storage patterns, and made it possible for today's homemaker to handle an incredibly complicated job. Incidentally, this research has led to better design of equipment and greater efficiency in operation.

Have Benefited Homemakers, Sick or Well

One group of homemakers with special problems has been given a great deal of thought. Women who are physically handicapped as a result of illnesses such as heart disease or polio obviously need a great deal of help in surmounting these difficulties, and industrial engineers have joined with the medical profession, home economists and teachers to provide individual help and general instruction on a nationwide basis. Interestingly, the technics developed and equipment designed to fit the special needs of the handicapped have benefited all homeworkers, sick or well.

The third field is the citizen's job. We are all proud of our management people in the various organizations devoted to community projects. They are not confined of course, to industrial engineers, engineers, or management people—they are a part of everybody's responsibility. But the man with management training can and should carry on effectively in this role.

If you will review the history of the pioneers, you will note how many of them, willingly and without any special type of appreciation, did give a great deal of time and energy. For example, consider Mr. Herbert Hoover. After a boyhood struggle to obtain an education, he made quickly and easily all the financial return he felt necessary, then proceeded to devote the rest of his life to the service of his country, without any compensation whatever.

Everyone knows people who have definitely considered citizenship activities as a part of their contribution to society, especially those who have had long-term management experience. Members of a chapter of one of our societies in New England, for example, went to the city officials and offered to make a survey of the work performed by the city government. Members from another group went to the librarian in their town and offered to read all the books on engineering to bring the collection up to date. They suggested which books should be removed and what new ones should be ordered.

The fourth field is the volunteer job. I have a little difficulty defining this term because a volunteer may appear in any group. Anyone who gives more than is expected and who wants to give generously is a volunteer.

Volunteer activities, such as boy scouting and girl scouting, take much giving. We give to them time we might be happy to devote to our families, our friends, our work—were it not that we recognize volunteer activity as an important part of our lives. We have difficulty if we begin to separate the part of our work which is prescribed activity from that which is volunteer activity, but that doesn't matter. Volunteer work provides a certain definite kind of satisfaction.

I am not going in any great detail into business and industrial activities because that is the way you spend your time. It is a different area, and we should expect this. I feel that differences are important, especially individual differences in our beliefs in the importance of the human element and in dignity in the life of man, but there are likenesses between people which are interesting, too, and tremendously important to us all.

I want at this point to discuss briefly the management concepts in other countries, to consider this area as it was in the days of the pioneers, look at it as it is today, and consider what it may mean tomorrow.

The first International Management Congress was held in 1924 in Czechoslovakia. I am especially interested in the 1924 Congress for several reasons. You will remember that at that time Czechoslovakia was a republic with a government modeled after that of our own country, which the people felt could work successfully. In February of that year my husband was invited to help plan a management congress to be held in Prague in the summer. He helped with the plans but he passed on just as the Congress was started.

If We Could Have Kept Close Together . . .

Representatives to that first Congress came from both sides of what was to become known as the Iron Curtain. At that meeting we had an opportunity, management-wise, if we could have kept close together in our thinking, to do a very constructive job. But we were not close knit enough and we were not able, in spite of all our common aims and attempts to speak the same management language, to prevent the series of wars, and naturally, we show the marks of it.

There are 30 nations in the international movement now. Our last meeting was in Australia. Our next, in 1963, is to be in New York. People may feel that Australia is far away and different from us. It is not so far by jet, and it never was far when it came to thinking. The Australians have the same goals and ideals as we have. In fact, the English-speaking group everywhere is far more alike than we sometimes realize.

The International Committee for Scientific Management, which is called CIOS (from the initials of the French version of the title), is made up of 30 nations, each with something to teach to all the others, for we must recognize the importance of the human side of life in every country, the social science, technical, religious, philosophical, scientific art and medicine, as each knows it. Can you imagine coming to this country from a country which has been rated underdeveloped, only to realize that here no one realizes that your own country has had anything to contribute until, and unless, we have rescued its people with money, opportunity, and education?

At the fine management center which the late Mrs. Wallace Clark gave to New York University in memory of her husband, I have met men from these so-called underdeveloped countries. All around the room there were bookcases, books, and manuscripts, diplomas from other countries—treasures which had been given to the center. Mrs. Clark would often say, "See that picture from your country? We were there such-and-such a time," or "Someone brought it to us from your country." I have seen the entire morale of the visiting group go up because reference was made to their country, what it had done and what it could do.

I frequently ask men from other countries, who are here, either alone or working in teams, "How much have you told of the work in your country?" And they are apt to reply: "Well, nobody asked me about the work in my country. I don't really think anyone thinks there has been anything accomplished in my country."

That Is the Feeling People Take Back Home

And yet there are countries where people are far more articulate than we are about religion and spiritual values. I don't believe that we in this country care only for money or production, but that is the impression we give, that is the feeling people take back home with them and remember. How many management people could get on their feet and talk about spiritual values, quite at ease and quote fluently? The two I know best, and have heard most frequently, happen to be an American and a Canadian, and both of them, I am pleased to say, have gone from busy lives into teaching. But by and large, others do not have the gift.

On the other hand, I could name in country after country people who not only know and appreciate spiritual values, but can write and talk about them. They can make themselves felt.

Surely they don't need to come here feeling they have nothing to give— philosophy, logic, ethics, aesthetics, psychology. They have a great deal to give. Their countries are beautiful, and the beauty is fully realized and appreciated. And think of a country where age is respected, where no older person is made to feel he is not needed or wanted, where there is still a use for wisdom that may be correlated with age increasing, instead of diminishing. Every country has something to give.

The application of management to work in business and industry is meaningless without some judgment about what it will do for the other areas of our living. We must question our decisions: Will they make it better or easier for the individual to manage his own life? Will they affect the home and the family habits? What will they do to our citizenship job and our volunteer job?

With this view you may think we have to spread ourselves so wide, thin, deep, and high we won't be able to focus on immediate decisions. Somehow, I don't think that is true.

If we are willing to expend the time and energy, we may not come up with answers to all our problems, but usually we can at least discover what the problem really is. And this is important, for it is all too easy to spend time on an elaborate solution, only to find that the problem we have solved was not the basic one at all.

There is an increasing need for varied types of education to fit the capacity of individuals. I somehow feel we are not putting the proper emphasis on the educated hand. Creative activity through the use of the hand gives such a sense of satisfaction to people who have skill. Look at the work from Denmark, for example, and the part the educated hand has played in design and production. Perhaps most important of all is the educated heart—a recognition of the dignity of the human spirit, the importance of spiritual values, the complete life, which are necessary to build concept of service we hold.

The 100th Anniversary of the birth of Henry Lawrence Gantt reminds us he was the pioneer who put into words this feeling that unless you have service for your motive you cannot have truly constructive action.

Our problems are complex and difficult, but what kind of life would it be if we had no problems, if we had no urge to make any decisions or to work for any solutions? It wouldn't be life.

Actually, life and our code both pose a great challenge: "to utilize the resources of nature and of human nature for the benefit of mankind." Through management we attempt to meet this challenge and do a satisfactory and, let us hope, a satisfying job.

Exercises and Problems in Communication

1. As intimated in the sections of this chapter on philosophies of management, practices vary considerably from company to company, and from department to department. To learn of current practices and policies, read widely in the professional publications, such as *Personnel Administration, Personnel Journal, Personnel, Advanced Management Journal,* and *Personnel Management.* Report your reactions to the readings in written or oral form, as your instructor assigns.

2. Consult earlier editions of the various periodical indexes (say, for ten or twenty years ago) for direction to journal articles on management. Read widely enough so that you can get an idea of the practices of firms at the time. Compare or contrast the descriptions of earlier opinions with those of today. You might report orally to the class on the articles from other years, without identifying the eras, and, from their experiences in summer employment, part-time jobs, etc., have your audience determine whether you are relating current thinking. This exercise hinges on an executive's comment that "the literature describes one set of criteria for successful management, but we work under another set."

3. For further consideration of appraisal of workers, read the chapter "Measures of Performance" in *Principles of Industrial Management,* by L. P. Alford and H. Russell Beatty (New York: The Ronald Press Co., 1951).

4. If you have access to dictating equipment (there are inexpensive tape recorders on the market), try dictating your outside assignments. Write or type your final drafts from the playback. If the second step is awkward or too time-consuming, at least dictate to analyze the playback for your strong points and deficiencies. Effectiveness of this exercise will be measured to a considerable extent by your visualizing letter parts, paragraphs, etc., as they will appear on the typed page. Experiences with letter appearance throughout the course will guide you in this effort.

5. Although time-consuming, an exercise used in some letter writing courses involves students dictating to each other, with the "stenographer" taking the dictation in as abbreviated form as possible. Such practice can be profitable to both individuals, in developing a sense of organization of dictated material. If your instructor has no objection, try this mutually beneficial exercise.

6. Some teachers of business communication courses borrow dictating equipment from department offices for students to use in dictation practice.

In some such units of instruction, the instructor is able to have a departmental typist transcribe the students' work. The transcribed letters are returned through the teacher to the student for his signature or corrections. Then the assignment is submitted to the teacher for grading. If your class has services available for actual dictation, be sure that you proofread the typist's finished copy for any grammatical or letter-form corrections.

7. Dictating equipment companies issue booklets (some quite comprehensive) giving instructions for efficient dictation. From the library or the business offices of your school, borrow a copy of one of these manuals. Study it and prepare a report on this time-saving phase of business operations.

8. In publications advertising office equipment, read ads for dictating machines, and write a company requesting such instructional material described in Exercise 7. Make your letter complete enough that further correspondence will not be necessary; for example, let the company know whether you are willing to pay for any materials if there is a charge. If you get a favorable response from the company, of course a note of appreciation would be in order.

9. In the spirit of a "manager's letter," write your instructor. Rather than discussing objectives and standards as Mr. Drucker describes in the quotation on page 481, you will discuss with your instructor suggestions for improving the course you are enrolled in. The relationship between you and your instructor is comparable to the connection between the two persons in a firm using the manager's letter, your instructor and the superior being in the "driver's seat." Since you are preparing for a career in which you will be expected to furnish ideas, you should have *at least* one suggestion for improvement. Your letter of course must have a tone of suggestion rather than of complaint. The objective of this assignment is exercise in upward communication, to persuade or affect, rather than to inform, which is the function of most of your communication with persons above you.

10. Assume that as a manager (after four or five years employment with the company) you are called into your immediate superior's office. After the usual exchange of "small talk," your boss's comments indicate that the present conference is for discussion of "your plans as far as the company is concerned." After you express your interest in staying, he asks, "What job, then, in the firm would you want to have?" Following a few seconds' thought, you say, as did the young man in a large Midwestern utility company, "Yours." Write a letter to your superior, outlining the steps you plan to take to reach the goal you have set for yourself. For the assignment of writing the letter, you may assume further that your boss said, as did the superior in this conference, "Well, if that's where you are going, we'd better start getting you ready for the job." Disregard the type of company mentioned and write the letter imagining yourself in a firm or school (if you are going ino teaching), whose levels of management you are acquainted with.

11. For class discussion or for your contribution, either pro or con, in a debate before the class, read in general and business publications on the subject of the advantages and disadvantages of liberal arts education for persons preparing for management positions.

12. For subordinates' reading, write a brief editorial, letter, or memo on the opinion that "the engineer has come to realize that his abilities to handle materials must be supplemented by skill in handling human relations and that a fine friendly feeling and the wish to develop and help other people is essential." You may substitute for "engineer" a term fitting your field of endeavor.

13. Read generally, to prepare for discussion, according to your instructor's assignment, on Mrs. Gilbreth's statement: "The difficulty with trying to define 'for the benefit of mankind' is that of determining *who* decides *what* the benefit of mankind is, both in the short run and in the long run."

14. As in Exercise 13, prepare for a discussion on self-management. In addition to rereading Mrs. Gilbreth's brief direction for such self-understanding, read in other books on the subject. You will find provocative points in Dalbir Bindra's *Motivation: A Systematic Reinterpretation* (New York: The Ronald Press Co., 1959). The sections "Motivational Phenomena" and "Human Motivation" will give you direction for your discussion. Also read Ralph Waldo Emerson's essays "Self-Reliance" and "Compensation." Look into the books of quotations you have consulted throughout the course; under the headings of "self-reliance," "self-discipline," "determination," etc., get references to poetic and philosophic writings for points to support your discussion. One bit of advice you might draw from is Polonius's words to Laertes in *Hamlet:*

> This above all: to thine own self be true,
> And it must follow, as the night the day,
> Thou canst not then be false to any man.

15. Write an article on a successful person you know, who meets Mrs. Gilbreth's criteria of the individual's home life, community activities, and career.

17

General Communication
in Business

*The only message that counts in terms of what the receiver
does is the message received—not the message sent.*—W. Charles
Redding, *Business and Industrial Communication* [1]

Although the stress on writing and to a lesser degree on speaking in
Effective Business Communication has been directed toward the *sender*
of a message, it has been made clear that an understanding of the *receiver*
is imperative in successful communication. In dealing with writing to
customers and the public, with the function of our messages to persuade,
we looked comprehensively at human needs or drives. In the briefer
treatment of intracompany communication through company journalism
and managerial correspondence, we discussed the importance of considering the individuality of the reader. In other words, throughout the
course we have said to write to *somebody*, somebody whose individuality
we recognize and respect, somebody whom we want to reach with
information to the end of getting a job done through persuasion, or, in
the case of affective writing, somebody with whom we would share
our feeling of well-being and pleasure.

As we look more particularly to speaking (the second form of the
sender's function) and to reading and listening (the receiver's), we are
not shifting emphasis at all. An effective communicator is by turns the
sender and the receiver in a given situation. We are only accentuating
the principle that, as stated in the chapter-opening quotation, the end

[1] W. Charles Redding and George A. Sanborn, *Business and Industrial Communication* (New York: Harper & Row, 1964), p. 31.

result of communication of any kind is response and, in turn, action on the part of the reader or listener.

The purpose in this final chapter, then, is to consider phases of communication other than writing, to develop them for their possible contribution to fuller effectiveness of the complete communication process.

A research study [2] has shown that 70 per cent of the *average* American's waking day is spent in verbal communication and that 45 per cent of word usage is in listening, 30 per cent in speaking, 16 per cent in reading, and 9 per cent in writing. (See page 503 for another figure on reading.) In addition to the many leaders cited throughout this book who attest to the need for verbal competence, we quote one more. A. A. Potter, Dean Emeritus of Engineering, Purdue University, and consultant to various industries, speaks forcibly on the issue:

> My career in engineering education and in industry, which has extended over a period of 59 years, has convinced me that the individual's success in his calling, irrespective of his competency in his field of specialization, depends upon his power of expression.
>
> In speaking to the thousands of engineering students with whom I came in contact, I tried to impress upon them the fact that a sound knowledge of their mother tongue is expected of professional people, and that the most important subjects for them are those which enable them to gain mastery of written and oral English.
>
> I have pointed out to them that if . . . thought is to be conveyed without loss, the medium must be substantially perfect. The character of one's expression exhibits his breeding and education, and may affect his professional and social standing.
>
> In my talks before engineers and scientists who have completed their formal education, I have tried to bring out the following:
>
> A scientist or an engineer becomes known by his writings and speeches, and must be able to present his findings in a manner so that he is easily understood by people in other callings. I have called their attention by names to the leaders in our profession who are examples of excellence in communication. Among these I have included Steinmetz and Pupin, the electric wizards of the early days in my career, and Sarnoff of RCA, Sporn of American Electric Power and the physicists, Millikan and the Compton Brothers, of the present time. These engineers and scientists not only showed a fine mastery of English but spoke audibly so that they were heard and their enunciation was such that they were easily understood. The popular idea that scientists and engineers can only be understood by their peers in their specialties is untrue; this attitude is also detrimental to the appreciation of science and technology on the part of the general public.

[2] Paul T. Rankin, "The Importance of Listening Ability," *English Journal* (College Edition), October, 1928, pp. 623–630. More recent research has not shown any appreciable change in the proportions of these activities, despite the increase in business and industrial writing in the past two decades. It is this increase that has prompted the fuller instruction in writing, as shown in *Effective Business Communication* and in the establishment of more courses for writing improvement in business and industry.

In applied research the creations of the laboratory must be put to work, that is they must be translated into processes, machines, structures and the articles or devices which can be sold competitively at a profit; as profits, progress and individual freedom are interdependent partners in the American way of life.[3]

Speaking

He ceas'd; but left so pleasing on their ear
His voice, that list'ning still they seem'd to hear.
    —ALEXANDER POPE, *The Odyssey of Homer*

THE IMPORTANCE OF EFFECTIVE SPEAKING

In connection with employment writing, we spoke of the part that oral communication, when it reveals advance planning and composure through self-confidence, plays in getting a job. Also, we have looked at competent dictation to cut costs and get a job done. And there has been consideration of the value of good speech in moving up the managerial ladder. Applications of oral communication in the 30 per cent of the day we spend in speaking are practically without number.

Telephone

After face-to-face contacts, the most important of these applications at any level of business involves the telephone. Business offers are made and accepted by telephone; critical problems are adjusted, and refractory accounts are collected. As a means of business communication, the telephone has three advantages over the letter: (1) two-way communication, making possible immediate settlement of the business under discussion; (2) the exercise of personality, the human factor, through use of the voice; and (3) speed in disposing of business matters—in the case of calls, at less cost than by letter.

In addition to observing the principles of good speaking, the user of the telephone should employ certain special techniques that have been developed. The receptionist learns to answer calls for her employer with "Jones and Company, general offices," or "Smith's, service department—with whom do you wish to speak?" instead of the conventional "hello" of social usage. When calls for an executive are passed on to him, he answers his phone with "Johnson," "Charles Johnson speaking," or something like "This is C. R. Johnson of the credit department. May I help you?"

The important point in opening telephone conversations is to cut through time-wasting verbiage and get to business at once—just as in

---

[3] A. A. Potter, "Communication Problems in Industry," American Business Writing Association *Bulletin*, October, 1962, pp. 4–5. (From an address to the Midwest Regional Conference of the ABWA, April 28, 1962.)

business writing we have learned to avoid meaningless rubber-stamp phrases. Once the conversation is begun, the caller states his business clearly and courteously; the person called replies in similar tone with what he can or cannot do. Although persons talking on the telephone are safe from immediate fisticuffs, this does not excuse rudeness of any sort. A good telephone voice and manner is indispensable to the person who collects accounts by this means, or to the interviewer for the Gallup, Roper, or Harris opinion poll, but it is a valuable asset to anyone. And the "you" attitude applies here the same as in letter writing; visualize the other person's reactions and work from this point of view.

Conferences

Business procedure involves numerous conferences: branch manager and salesmen, personnel of a bank or division of a department store, directors' meetings, negotiations between representatives of management and labor, the engineer or technician and the company publications editor. More and more, an especially important type of conference is the one between company personnel and reporters or other writers who will interpret fiscal operations and scientific or technical developments to the public.

The crucial part that communication plays in intracompany proceedings is revealed by examination of some of the leading firms of our time. Among the six features common to the ten "best-managed" companies listed by Dun & Bradstreet,[4] decentralization is described as a highlight. Subsidiaries of these companies operate with complete autonomy; divisions compete against each other; and even brand managers within a company such as Procter and Gamble have been criticized for having too much power. With decentralization comes a stress on communication, the term meaning here more than simply "getting the word around." In some of the companies, the broader context of communication is "getting personnel around" by moving people back and forth across departmental and divisional lines for broader experience and a continual exchange of information and ideas. Thomas J. Watson, Jr., of IBM says a corporation's communication must increase out of proportion to its growth rate if it is to overcome the very real problems created by change. Executives of the other leading companies agree that information among personnel is imperative for continued growth. Even the committee, however criticized and satirized,[5] is an integral part of communication in these companies. At General Electric, meetings are considered equal in

[4] Jack B. Weiner, "What Makes a 'Best-Managed' Company?" *Dun's Review and Modern Industry*, December, 1963, p. 40 ff.

[5] Perhaps the "most unkindest cut of all" about committee efficiency is this definition: "A camel looks like something put together by a committee."

importance to internal correspondence, telephone contact, and company publications.

With such emphasis on oral communication, especially when the exchange is three-directional—vertical, horizontal, and diagonal (or functional)—it is easy to see that your capabilities in expressing yourself in your job will soon be tested, since, as has been mentioned, in employment, the college graduate is hired in general as a potential manager.

In such a position at any level, you will be dealing with four levels of information as far as subordinates are concerned: (1) what the employee has to know to do his job properly, such as details of new equipment, new procedures, or changed policies; (2) what he should know such as reorganization at higher levels, new contracts; (3) what might be helpful to him, such as the company's financial statement or recent inventions in the industry; and (4) the information that is not ready to be passed on, because (a) disclosure might be harmful to the company, as with new models, (b) the data may be covered by security regulations, (c) the plans may involve other companies, as in mergers, or (d) the information must pass through channels, possibly to avoid interference with publicity or promotion.

The first three types of information will be given without hesitation, or they should be. In cases of the fourth type, the person who cannot divulge present conditions will do well to follow four admonitions, whomever he is dealing with (another employee, the customer, the public, representatives of the press): (1) explain that there is a reason that disclosure cannot be made; (2) emphasize the time element, that the news will be released as soon as feasible; (3) acknowledge the person's right to inquire about what he has heard; and (4) be honest.[6]

And whoever the audience, or "receiver," among the individuals or groups just mentioned, a speaker can do a better job of persuasion and save time in the process if he is cognizant of how people learn. To help a listener remember, a speaker should itemize his message; itemizing furnishes helpful "pegs" for the listener. Just as rehearsal improves public performances, so rehearsal of arguments for persuasion can give order to what is to be said. As pointed out earlier, an advantage in personal contacts over written communication is the interpretation of a listener's reactions to the message as it is being given; if information is to be given to several persons or groups individually, the speaker should correct possible weak spots for subsequent deliveries. The effective speaker will vary his pitch, whomever he is talking to, to keep his presentation fresh. And, in management, the discerning person will evaluate and use reports from his associates—commonly termed "feed-

---

[6] "When You Can't Tell Them Everything," *Supervisory Management,* May, 1964, pp. 16–20.

back"—to improve his powers of persuasion for more effective management. Good rapport with associates serves a person well.[7]

The importance of ability in speaking and listening is indicated by the extent to which companies rely on conferences. At least 70 per cent of the major companies in the United States use conferences to keep people informed, to solve problems and draw on resources of the group, to train and instruct, and to afford a participation medium for the individual.[8]

Addresses, Informal Talks, and Other Program Participation

In Chapter 15, we discussed the various avenues open to you to let your work and, in turn, you as a person be known through writing for professional journals, trade publications, and general magazines. Just as widespread opportunities in speaking are open to the businessman and the industrialist. The hundreds of gatherings of professional, trade, social, and civic organizations held daily throughout the world draw heavily on business and industry for participants. The participation includes commencement addresses, dinner speeches, convention keynote addresses, and panel talks.

When your name is high enough on the organization chart, you may assign someone in your organization to the task of writing your presentation for you, as mentioned in connection with "The Larger Field of Business Writing." Until that time, when you are to be a program speaker you will turn to the references mentioned throughout this book as source material for background and current happenings in the particular field of interest. Or you will develop from your own experience and observation on your job the details of your presentation.

From whatever sources your information is derived, after you have conscientiously mastered the material your next problem is communication in the twofold sense of *selling both personality and message.* An audience likes speakers to be straightforward, neither obsequious nor domineering, usually a bit humorous, especially in their introduction, and easy to listen to because of clear enunciation and well-modulated tone. Avoidance of monotone and general monotony is most important, especially in the case of after-dinner speeches, during which the audience is likely to be a bit sleepy anyway. The use of concrete homely

---

[7] John S. Morgan, "The Supervisor's 3 Toughest Communication Problems," *Supervisory Management,* March, 1964, pp. 4–8. Mr. Morgan's advice here is on persuasion. Equally good articles on "Training" and "Appraisal," the other two difficult problems, are in the April and May, 1964, issues of this same magazine. In addition to giving sound advice, the articles provide interesting analysis of their subject matter. They relate directly to the persuasive, informative, and affective.

[8] Harold P. Zelko, *Successful Conference and Discussion Techniques* (New York: McGraw-Hill Book Co., 1957), p. 9.

illustration has greatly increased the effectiveness of countless speeches, especially those dealing with technical or statistical material. Mere utterance of words will not make you a speaker in the practical sense. To succeed as a speaker, you must communicate your thoughts so well that your listeners will be interested and will have no difficulty in understanding what you wish to convey to them.

To improve as a speaker, a person may be attentive to the more specific details included in the following rating chart:

Language: Is the speech above average, average, or below average in *sentence structure, vocabulary*, and *fluency of delivery?*

Physical Manner: Is the speaker above average, average, or below average in *neatness, posture, facial expression, gestures, eye-contact?*

Voice and Voice Usage: Is the speaker *conversational* or unconversational? Does he vary his *pitch, rate*, and *loudness*, or is he monotonous in these respects? Is his voice *quality* nasal, breathy, or harsh?

Pronunciation and Articulation: Are his *pronunciation, articulation*, and *general oral accuracy* good, average, or poor? [9]

SOME GENERAL CONSIDERATIONS IN ORAL COMMUNICATION

All too many persons who would communicate seem to agree with the professor who said that there are only two means of teaching: textbooks and lectures. However, more of the media available to help the communicator "get his story across" are being used. The seller has learned the value of the manifold approach in getting to the buyer: Direct mail, newspaper and magazine advertising, demonstrations and displays, radio and television commercials have all proved effective. The credit and collection departments use the telephone as well as writing. Civic organizations and business firms use exhibits to advantage in public relations endeavors. But, in intracompany communication, many resort to words, written or spoken, as the only method of letting themselves be heard. A superintendent of safety, concerned about the high rate of injuries directly attributable to defective machine parts, realized that regular memos, "safety meetings," lecturing, and bulletin board displays were not reducing the accident rate. From the National Safety Council, police headquarters, and local newspapers, he gathered pictures showing the effects of injuries due to defective equipment. As he talked with personnel in his department, he casually showed the excerpts and clippings. The resulting drop in injuries does not prove that the superintendent's earlier efforts had no effect; but, since the drop followed the device of "visuals" coupled with conversation, the advantage of using different media is apparent.

[9] Adapted from Ralph G. Nichols and Thomas R. Lewis, *Listening and Speaking* (Dubuque, Iowa: Wm. C. Brown Co., 1954), p. 161.

Timing in communication, as emphasized in Figure 62, can mean the difference between success and failure. Someone is to be persuaded to act, but the time is not right. The communicator may have to plan a campaign, his first communication giving information that will make the desired action more likely at a subsequent time. The more complex the matter to be resolved, the more drastic the action to be taken, and the larger the group involved, the more cautious the person must be in mapping his campaign. There is marked danger of accepting short-sighted programs when our over-all objective is not clear.

As mentioned earlier, most of what we learn is the result of questions, either voiced or unspoken. The person who gets his reader or listener to become involved in the message to the point of asking a question will have gone far in getting his message across. A writer or speaker, how-ever, cannot hope for a receiver's participation if the receiver is viewed only as a *target*. Although in some instances, because of the circum-stances surrounding the message and the pressure of time, information needs to be given without time for questioning, planned communications can result in a climate for exchange of ideas. Few, if any, enjoy being talked at.

For various reasons, one of the most important steps in communica-tion is not taken by many who depend on others to act according to information given them. The step is the follow-up. Among the reasons for this oversight are the sender's reluctance to seem to nag or show mistrust, the fear of nurturing the habit of inattention in others, and the danger of losing status through having to repeat instructions. The effective communicator uses the follow-up in the best ways—to reinforce a message when necessary and to check on results of prior messages. When reinforcement is not needed, two persons are gratified, thereby enhancing rapport. When repetition is necessary, the astute person takes a new approach to the situation, probably using a different medium, to get his message across.

SO TO SPEAK

The several pointers and the quasi-rationale given in this section and the exercises throughout the book calling for your practice in speaking have, it is hoped, given you a feeling for the real part that oral com-munication can play in your life. Although your making a convention keynote address may seem an occurrence of the remote future, other less auspicious occasions may not be so remote. Take advantage of any opportunity to participate, whatever its magnitude; in fact, *look for* opportunities. The person who does use such occasions develops the fiber of confidence and ability, those attributes that characterize the effective speaker in his communication with individuals as well as from the platform.

Another expression on the speaker-listener relationship, the following miniature essay is from Norman G. Shidle, *Instincts in Action* (New York: Publishers Printing Co., 1961). It appeared originally in "For the Sake of Argument," in the *SAE Journal*, and is used here by permission of Mr. Shidle and the Society of Automotive Engineers.

Variable Rate Listeners

IDEAS ARE ACCEPTED by the emotions as well as by the mind. Some quick-minded people are slow emotionally—and vice-versa. . . . So, an idea or a program trying to get across to a man or group has to run on this double track road. Monorailing it may wreck it.

The man who is quick emotionally as well as mentally is in particular danger of cockeyed performance. . . . Working with people of equal or better mental equipment, he may figure that his listeners also have equal speed of emotional adjustment . . . emotional decisiveness.

The ideas he shoots out may go into other minds at a quick tempo—like the pace of a chorus singing Yankee Doodle in march time . . . but the emotional acceptance may be proceeding much more slowly—like the other half of the same chorus simultaneously singing My Country 'Tis of Thee. . . . The two absorption paces have to get synchronized before harmony prevails in the listener. . . . The two tunes sung simultaneously can give a fine, harmonious effect. . . . But the discord is terrible until the synchronization takes place.

A skilled "presenter" will keep his awareness sufficiently objectified to be conscious of what is happening to his listeners. . . . He will realize that others need time for emotional readjustment. . . . He may even slow up his presentation, "overtalk" on points which—mentally—need no amplification, to give time for emotions to catch up. . . . He even may purposely get final decisions delayed until a later date.

Reading

A man ought to read just as inclination leads him; for what
he reads as a task will do him little good.
—JAMES BOSWELL, *The Life of Samuel Johnson, LL.D.*

The age-old controversies about reading continue without abatement. What is the best method for teaching reading? What is the reading rate of the average American? Which one of the myriad lists of titles recommended for every citizen should a person read? Whatever turn the discussions take—there are no conclusions in these arguments—in any conversation about reading, a few immutable facts remain. An individual's reading skills are developed through the "look and see" or the phonics method; or, if his teacher is intelligent, through the best features of the two methods, according to the pupil's needs. Also, the individual reader is probably spending more time than is necessary, and, Mr.

Johnson's opinion notwithstanding, businessmen can hardly read "as inclination leads" them. The fact that many businessmen spend one-fourth to one-half of their working hours in reading [10] precludes that happy state of affairs. If, as described repeatedly in business and industrial journals, the businessman's opinion on his reading is to be taken literally, he does agree that that part of his work is a task.

SOME OBSTACLES IN READING

Discussion of ineffective writing in earlier chapters of this book leaves little more to be said on that subject as a negative factor in reading. We can remind ourselves that clear, brief, pertinent writing brings results by helping the reader. Although poor writing does create problems for readers, inadequate reading skills are a greater deterrent to effectiveness in this phase of communication. Well-composed reports, challenging professional articles, and excellent literature go unread because of antipathy to reading, an attitude due largely to time-consuming inefficiency.

Perhaps a young professional engineer pinpointed this major obstacle to reading when he said that the only benefit he had had from a developmental reading course his company had sponsored was that he was "not afraid to pick up a book any more." The aversion to spending time in getting through a piece of writing prevents many persons from picking up a book, magazine, or report, whether it be for leisure or for reading on the job. The procrastinating "I'll get to that tomorrow" causes desks and files to be piled up with journals, abstracts, reports, and prospectuses.

A third factor that militates against reading has social implications. As a vice-president of an Indianapolis manufacturing firm said: "At the office we talk about our golf scores of yesterday afternoon or how the new house we're building is coming along. We don't talk about what we've been reading." It is known from surveys that individuals' current reading is not a much-discussed office topic. Despite a general admiration for the well-read individual, there is still an aura of excessive erudition about the person who talks about his reading. A causative factor in this attitude is manifest early in the reader's formative years. Generally, parents show pride in their children's reading interests, that is, until reading exceeds that point considered "healthy," especially in the case of boys. Then there arise the parental misgivings of "Doesn't it seem to you a little abnormal for a child to spend so much time with

[10] *Reading Improvement and Executive Development* (Chicago: Psychotechnics, Inc., 1958). This manual, prepared with the help of E. Glenn Griffin and Bernard Schmidt of the developmental reading program at Purdue University, is a complete, concise guide for industrial training in reading.

books, and not be out playing with other kids?" Surveys of reading habits of children and parents reveal that few families discuss books, largely because of the disparity in reading interests among the members. Also, there is evidence that requiring the child to attend to his homework while the rest of the family is occupied with non-reading activities creates a feeling of isolation that alienates the child against books and reading.

To mention one more barrier to effective reading, we look at the curriculum of American schools. Until recently, a mere handful of schools taught reading as a skill after the sixth grade. It was assumed that by that stage in his education the student had learned all he needed to know *about reading*. The past decade or two have seen a change in this mistaken notion, with the result that instruction in developmental reading has been introduced at all educational levels. Secondary school and university curriculums and company training programs throughout the country include courses in reading improvement. Developmental reading is concerned with perceptual skills, those physical actions of the eye involved in the transmission of symbols from the printed page to the brain, and with the various factors of comprehension. The instruction is not to be confused with that in remedial reading, which, as the title implies, is for those readers who, for physiological or psychological reasons, are deficient in basic word-recognition skills. Developmental reading is for the average or above-average reader who has the basic skills and, through improvement of perception and comprehension, can make his reading a pleasurable, profitable, less wearing endeavor.

Success in developmental reading courses in educational, professional, business, and industrial groups is shown by results on validated tests. Adults whose reading patterns are well established repeatedly show 100 per cent gains in speed after instruction in 20- to 30-hour programs. Comprehension goes up 5 to 10 per cent. Studies at Purdue University and at the Pentagon show that a year after instruction, 65 per cent of the gains are retained. From course to course, results are consistent whether or not instruction includes reading pacers, films, and other "mechanical" devices. Some courses are based entirely on workbook exercises and discussion of the reading process.

CONFIDENCE AS A FACTOR IN READING

Repeatedly, in post-course evaluation of reading programs, students and trainees report increased confidence as their most marked benefit from the course. Despite the fact that the attitude is unmeasurable, the reaction is a most desirable one, for, if the reader is conscious of the physical aspects of the process, to the point of articulating them, he is not reading. That is, when concerned with what his eyes are doing or whether he is vocalizing, he is not assimilating ideas from the printed page. In reading, as in any activity, confidence is a by-product stemming from knowledge or improvement of other details of the process. We can look at those more concrete details, which through consistent and conscientious practice lead to confidence.

THE PHYSICAL FACTORS OF READING

It is not uncommon to find people incredulous, or even disturbed, when they are told that their eyes do not "just sweep across the page" as they read. However, the eyes do stop, or *fix*, at intervals during reading, and, as they stop, they take in a certain number of characters—letters, numbers, spaces. The scope of the material seen is called the *span*. Even as a reader *regresses*—going back to locate the last spot where he was concentrating in his reading—his eyes fix. Another physical aspect of reading—of ineffective reading, that is—is *vocalization*.

The Fixation and the Span

The named aspects of reading can be quickly observed and reckoned. Sit across from a person, and watch his eyes as he reads a line of print. You can see the eye action. The number of fixations can be counted with considerable accuracy, and dividing the number of words he covers by the number of stops gives an approximation of the span. The fewer fixations per line and the shorter the duration of the fixation, the more efficient the reading. By photographing eye movements, the American Optical Company found that the average reader reads ten to twelve characters in 1/25 second and that the average reader *can* read twenty to twenty-four characters in 1/100 second after practice in reading. These figures show the possibility of improvement; a quick calculation of seeing twice as much in one-fourth the time in a piece of reading such as a 60,000-word book points up what efficient eye movement can mean in saving time. Such facility means that a reader takes bigger "bites" and thereby makes assimilation of the author's ideas easier than if he "nibbles" the material word by word.

Regression

Regression, which is due largely to poor concentration, is merely jumping back over words, lines, or even pages to pick up the thought where the reader realizes he was last *reading*. It has been said that, because of regressions, the average reader takes ten times longer than necessary for a given piece of reading. This fault may be remedied rather easily in two ways: One depends on the physical; the other, on the psychological. Reducing the duration and the number of stops,

widening the span, and developing a rhythmic pattern of eye movements improve concentration, thereby curtailing regression. The other
method for correcting "going back" is a matter of self-discipline. Many
readers being made aware of this costly habit have corrected it by
sheer resistance to it. You may say that you will never know what you
missed if you don't go back. Fortunately, what a reader dreams through
is often clarified through subsequent points in the material. The
salutary aspect of this disciplinary step, however, is in the psychological
effect of deprivation; not knowing what is missed helps a reader wean
himself from regressing.

Vocalization

This handicap, the reader's saying words that he reads, is manifest in
three ways. Two of them are easily spotted and corrected. The reader
who more or less whispers the word, moving his lips, can break his habit
by placing his finger across his lips. In any large group of readers of
any age, it is easy to spot a few such readers. Working hard at a difficult subject, they are resorting to the next step to reading aloud, the
hope of being able to grasp the material more readily.

A second level of vocalization is in the larynx, the formation of words
being a physical response in reading. The reader thinks the words, with
the voice apparatus working accordingly. The person who hinders himself with this slowing act can feel the vibrations by placing his thumb
and forefinger on his throat. Continued application as they read has
helped many persons counteract this fault.

The third fault, called "subvocalization" by some authorities, cannot
be observed by another person or actually felt by the reader himself as
can the other two. This one is a sort of internal hearing, a word-consciousness. Despite the controversy in the reading field as to the nature
and possible elimination of subvocalization, a person can know whether
he is "hearing the words" as he reads. To test this, contrast your own
experiences in two reading situations. Consider your awareness of words
as you have read in a difficult subject; then recall some of your more
pleasurable reading. Suppose, for example, you had the common childhood experience of being told to put away your book and go to bed
because "tomorrow's a schoolday." You went to bed, but with the book,
and, either with your door closed to conceal the light or under the
covers with a flashlight beamed on the pages, you continued the excitement of pursuit to learn how the hero would subdue the villain. It is
highly improbable that any word reading was taking place; the visual,
or mental pictures, took precedence over the auditory, or internal hearing. In such rapport between author and reader, communication is at
its highest level, bordering on communion.

Vocalization is seen as a deterrent in reading by harking back to the average speaking rate of 125 to 150 words per minute. If words are forming on a reader's lips, in his larynx, or in his ears, he can hardly exceed the rate of speech in his reading. As he corrects deficiencies in fixation and span, thus increasing his speed, vocalization will diminish, and a barrier that had limited reading will be surmounted.

Flexibility

Based on *purpose* in reading, flexibility is merely controlled reading speed, or the reader's adapting his rate to his purpose in reading and to the difficulty of the material. One of the surest marks of a proficient reader is flexibility; he reads at a number of different rates. In a course in which he is acquainted with the subject, a student should read considerably faster than in one whose subject matter is unfamiliar. An executive should read memos and reports at variable speeds, those from departments familiar to him being covered at a faster rate than those from departments whose operations and terminology he does not know so well. Tests show that the majority of adult readers have one rate for all reading—and that one is generally slow.

To adapt rate to purpose, the following suggested rates may be used, depending upon what is to be understood and retained from the material:

1. Skimming. Very fast rate in looking over material is useful if you want merely to size up general content, to see what relevant ideas the reading contains, to make sure that you can find the information you seek. Skimming makes use of all possible guides like headings, listings, and titles. Trained readers can skim at 700 to 1000 wpm [words per minute]; some go even faster.
2. Fast reading. If you are reading informative prose *for general information,* such as collateral reading in a social science, you can well choose your fastest pace, the rate that enables you to read the material in its entirety without dwelling on style or re-reading provocative paragraphs or pages. Similarly an efficient reader first skims a newspaper page to see what he wants to read; then he settles on a story or two for fast reading. Well-trained readers can use a fast rate on rather mature writing if the purpose is basic comprehension—an understanding of just what the author says. An efficient fast rate varies with each individual of course; but speeds of 400 to 600 wpm are attainable by most people.
3. Moderate reading. Often you will want to understand rather fully, to re-read occasional sentences or paragraphs, to reflect on what you read. A moderate rate is a good choice here. Well-written fiction, good magazines, non-technical prose should in many cases be read at less than your fastest rate. With moderate speed, you can do most of your studying efficiently. (Again, an appropriate moderate speed is hard to make precise.) For most trained readers, a comfortable moderate rate will range from 200 to 400 wpm.

4. Reflective reading. The slowest rate should be reserved for the most difficult reading: artistic writing like that in poetry and in many essays and novels; scientific writing like that that we encounter in physics and chemistry; technical writing that describes physical processes or reports experiments. If the material is very difficult, your rate may be only a phrase or a sentence a minute; or in more cursive writing you might read as fast as 150 to 200 wpm.[11]

It is well to keep in mind that speed will vary within a piece of writing, the variation being determined by changes in style or layout and by the reader's knowledge of the various parts of the material.

Another "rate" has been evolved to help the businessman compensate for a writer's inadequacies. Called "skip-reading," the procedure is as follows:

"In reading business letters a three-step technique will visually tell you if a thorough reading is necessary. The letterhead will tell you where it is from; the signature will tell you whom it is from; and the first sentence will tell whether the writer is getting right down to business. If he isn't, drop two-thirds of the way through the letter for the central point." [12]

A comparable approach can be worked out for any reading task. The good reader surveys any writing—by going over headings and subheadings, first sentences of paragraphs, italicized words, summaries, etc.—before he turns to more thorough reading.

COMPREHENSION

In addition to efficient perceptual skills, which aid comprehension, effective reading depends upon language skills and reasoning skills. The first of these include familiarity with meanings of individual words and the ability to recognize meaningful groups of words such as phrases, clauses, and sentences; reasoning skill is the ability to understand the author's thoughts and to evaluate them or react to them by relating them to the reader's own experience.

It is these facets of reading that make *comprehension* the broadest term among those dealing with reading. For example, the sentence "I see the house" is relatively simple. The essential facts concerning the sense of sight and a structure are the same to a child of six and an adult of sixty. But the sentence "A market in which commission business is generally unprofitable always has some tendency toward speculation" is another matter. Comprehending the thought depends upon a complex group of circumstances surrounding the reader: his background, his predispositions, his very purpose in reading the sentence, his judgment, and his intelligence. To one reader, the terms could be meaningless, but

[11] Russell Cosper and E. Glenn Griffin, *Toward Better Reading Skill* (2d ed., New York: Appleton-Century-Crofts, Inc., 1959), pp. 185–86.
[12] "Five Steps to Faster Reading, Lesson III," *Product Engineering*, January 19, 1959, p. 21.

they would not be to a reader who has had a career in the stockbrokerage business. Comprehension will depend also on whether one of the terms —*speculation,* for example—or the entire thought antagonizes him, or whether or not he has just made a handsome sum from lending to margin customers at 6 per cent.

These sentences exemplify the fact that comprehension is not an absolute. There are *levels of comprehension,* which relate to the complexity of material (or the writing), and *degrees of comprehension,* related to the understanding of any piece of material (or the reading). The reader can facilitate his work considerably by contemplating what he is looking for as he starts to read, thus establishing both level and degree of comprehension. Awareness of purpose in reading any given material will alert a person to a better reading pattern. What is he looking for, or what kind of comprehension is he concerned with? As can be seen in the following partial list of kinds of comprehension, a reader may be concerned with only one of them, or he may be concerned with several in any given reading assignment or task. To see their consequences in reading, note the implications of the informative, persuasive, and affective functions of language, discussed in connection with writing. Some of the general purposes in reading are

1. To get a simple fact or facts
2. To get general information
3. To get a main idea
4. To follow directions
5. To form opinion
6. To verify opinion
7. To solve a specific problem
8. To be gratified, through beauty, pleasure, aesthetic appreciation
9. To escape reality

To help in achieving these comprehension goals, aids that a reader may cultivate and use include

1. Recognizing guides in writing: paragraphing, punctuation, topic sentences, charts and tables, headings and subheadings
2. Grasping key words and phrases
3. Being aware of his own emotional preoccupations
4. Asking questions (mentally in short reading tasks, writing them in longer ones) to involve himself with the writer
5. Increasing his word knowledge
6. Reading widely outside his own field
7. Developing his concentration

While comprehension improves with better concentration, concentration, it is found, increases as the person's comprehension improves through the various aids the individual reader uses.

CONCENTRATION

Like confidence, concentration is a "personal matter." It comes from within. Although abstract in definition and elusive in application, this most desired of all the components of reading and listening can be bettered by an awareness of certain conditions of learning and by following certain practices whose efficiency has been proved.

You may still remember a schoolteacher's warnings against studying with the radio on, reading with improper lighting, and not having an orderly regular place to study. Paradoxically, many students who disparage all or parts of that advice avoid studying in a library because activity around them is distracting. Without entering into the argument, I can point out cases of straight-A students who study surrounded by noise and clutter. Jane Austen, it is said, did much of her writing in the parlor of her home, in the midst of conversation between her family and guests. However, since most of us are not pre-eminent students or Jane Austens, to aid concentration it is advisable that we accept the fact that *physical surroundings* do affect concentration and that we should, therefore, find a favorable place for study and use it.

In business and industry, on-the-job reading is done under all sorts of conditions—telephones ringing, machines whirring and grinding, other personnel conferring and dictating. In these circumstances, the reading gets done, just as it does in the utopian private soundproofed office. From either quarter, however, there is the common complaint of "I can't concentrate."

Perhaps a student in the environment of study can more easily find suitable surroundings for reading than can the person on the job, who hasn't the leeway to move about among study rooms, lounges, libraries, and spare classrooms. But precious time is taken in the student's shifting about and in the businessman's taking home his attaché case filled with work reading. So other factors in concentration need to be considered.

As implied in connection with comprehension and rates, *emotional attitudes* play a prominent part in concentrated reading. If you have just had a test paper returned with a lower grade than you had expected, it is probably difficult for you to settle down to study until the effects of disappointment, anger, or defeat have worn off. The salesman who has just missed a sizable sale will be hard put to concentrate on letters, memos, or reports that come to his desk. This is not to say that success necessarily increases reading rate and comprehension. Elation can affect concentration adversely just as dejection can.

Whether student or employee and whatever the distractions, a person can help his concentration by observing a few simple procedures. When his mind "starts to wander," the reader will save time and energy by turning to something else for a brief time, because, as mental fatigue increases, powers of attention decrease. He can make a phone call, go to the coke dispenser, or dictate a letter, that is, engage in an activity dissimilar from the reading. From such a respite, he will probably come back to his reading better able to concentrate.

Underlining *important points* in reading helps concentration and retention; better yet, the reader can jot words or phrases *in his own words* in the margin or on a separate sheet if he can't mark the letter, report, or book he is reading. This step, using the kinesthetic calling into play another one of the senses, helps concentration. At intervals in a longer reading assignment, the person can go over his underlinings and notes to bring the author's message into focus. As he ties together ideas, he is contributing further to concentration. Most importantly, the reader must accept the basic concept that concentration is reader involvement. To rephrase a point made in connection with speaking, the reader cannot consider himself merely a *target* of the writer. And, to repeat another point, formulating questions, or "talking back" to the writer, is one quick way for a person to become an *active* reader. Active readers concentrate.

THE END RESULT

With the improvement of reading skills, achieved by reducing the time and number of fixations and by widening the span, to help in reducing regression and vocalization, a reader can curtail the time required for reading in pleasure, study, or work. He will find comprehension easier through more sustained concentration. Because most of us read at varying levels of comprehension, we can apply rates to our different ways of reading to fit the degree of comprehension necessary. In short, as efficient readers, we can get the optimum from reading that, to paraphrase Sir Francis Bacon's well-known comment, is variously to be tasted, swallowed, or chewed and digested.

Listening

> *For the real master of communication . . . listening and talking are interwoven . . . like the warp and the woof of a piece of cloth. When he is listening, he is standing at the threshold of his companion's mind; and when he is talking, he invites his auditor to stand at the doorway of his own thought.*—ROBERT T. OLIVER, "One Man's Opinion" [13]

In written communication, the reader has only the author's words to react to, unless correspondence is between acquaintances, in which

[13] From *Today's Speech,* November, 1957, p. 28.

case recollection of earlier contacts might introduce other factors into the message. In listening, the counterpart of reading in communication, many factors other than the speaker's words affect the message. In addition to those bodily and vocal attributes of speakers and speaking mentioned in the earlier section of this chapter as affecting listening, there are, as in reading, emotional reactions, attitudes, and feelings—called "untalk" by one communication consultant.[14] In oral communication, however, the emotions of both speaker and listener affect the exchange. Although, as implied in the quotation, a person is sender and receiver concurrently, certain features on the listener's side of the coin bear looking at to see what can help to make good listeners. In this quick survey of that part of verbal communication in which we spend 45 per cent of our time, two aspects of the process will be discussed: the student's role in listening and listening in business and industry.

The Student as Listener

At the mention of listening in college, most persons' minds go to lectures because of the preponderance of instruction given by that method. However, if we consider the time spent in recitation sections, in conferences with instructors, and in study sessions, it is clear that there are sources of information other than the professor at the lectern. To look at these other sources, consider a quite common reaction when another student is speaking in class. There is a tendency on the part of many to consider others' recitation as an exchange between the instructor and the individual, who is reciting for a grade, or to believe that the class is not to be held responsible for what emanates from the students' side of the teacher's desk. More personal reactions hinder listening at such times also, two of them being deprecation of what the student is saying and, the opposite, that belittling thought of "Everybody in the class is smarter than I am." In either of these situations, attention to ideas is low. In connection with teacher-student conferences it has been said that there is much more teaching done across the corner of a desk than there is across the width of the desk in the classroom. This is to be expected, since the exchange is a give-and-take between two persons, with questions very likely motivating the discussion. Although the study session frequently involves more than two persons, there is ordinarily a homogeneity in the group which raises the level of listening among the members. In any of these situations most individuals can improve their listening. The improvement is effected, as it is in the lecture room, principally through changing certain long-held notions and through some self-discipline.

[14] A. W. Lindh, "Plain Talk About Communicating in Business," *Business Management,* April, 1964, p. 93.

Three Speeds: Speech, Thought, and Writing

Much of what one learns in listening is embodied in notes. A student may complain that he is at a disadvantage in taking notes because he cannot write as fast as the lecturer can talk. Such a student does not understand the basic purposes in lectures and note-taking. Effective note-taking does not consist of "getting everything the lecturer says"; it is a matter of writing central ideas as concisely and as expeditiously as possible for study and expansion as soon as possible after the lecture. The thinking student doesn't expect a high correlation between how much is said and how much he writes; his emphasis is on what is said.

In the process of note-taking, the truth of the matter is that the student has an advantage over the lecturer in the ratio of speech speed to thought speed. The average rate in speaking is around 125 to 150 words per minute, and thought speed, determined roughly from rates in silent reading, is around 400 words a minute. The listener, then, can "run ahead" of the speaker's thought and be taking notes as the lecturer catches up to him.

Central Ideas

The reasoning skills in reading comprehension come into use also in listening. The listener must determine the speaker's purpose—informing, persuasion, entertainment. Whatever the purpose, listening entails following the speaker's thought. If the message is to inform or to persuade, the listener must relate the speaker's words to his own experience for understanding, and then he must evaluate the ideas for acceptance or rejection.

Getting central ideas is often a matter of attending to signposts in the speaker's delivery. The following are some of the clues to important points that many speakers use: (1) *Repetition* is exemplified in such statements as "Once again we see that effective communication is . . ."; giving another example indicates that the point is important. (2) A statement reflecting *consensus* is probably worth noting, as in "All authorities now agree that. . . ." (3) *Issues,* the opposite of consensus, also point up major ideas; the lecturer says "Some managers consider automation a boon . . . ," and the attentive listener immediately formulates a question: "What do others say?" (4) When a speaker, showing a *general-to-specific relationship,* says something like "The well-operated credit department depends on its various levels of personnel," it is well for the student to gear himself for a listing or discussions of the levels. (5) Speakers signal their intentions to present a number of points by *foreshadowing* with such remarks as "From all this, we see emerging three reactions." (6) A speaker's taking time for *examples* with such introductory remarks as "To illustrate, . . ." can signify that the ensuing information is worth noting.

A student may help himself a great deal in lectures if he accepts one of the basic differences between lectures and textbooks, as far as clues are concerned. A book is replete with indicators. Headings and sub-headings, italicized words—even paragraphing, as mentioned in connection with reading—indicates shifts of thought, which are not so readily apparent in the speech. The lecturer probably presents only a few major points in each lecture, most of the class time being taken to expand, exemplify, and support those points. Despite the admiration for the lecturer "who packs a lot of ideas into 50 minutes," quantity is hardly a measure of excellence. As has been said, a poor speaker covers twenty points; a good speaker uncovers one.

In recognizing central ideas, it is well to avoid that alibi of the poor listener: "I listen for the facts." His notebook is probably filled with minutiae such as dates, names, and figures, and, just as likely, he has no notion of their significance.

Emotions as Deterrents to Listening

Although communication requires active participation on the receiver's part, there is *involvement* that can hurt listening. This point is reached when a person allows himself to quit listening by becoming upset by words or opinions in the lecture. References to nationality, denomination, class, occupation, politics, etc., can set a listener off so that he spends his time mentally putting the speaker in his place. Let the disagreement or affront rest; get the remainder of the speaker's ideas, and then discuss it with him or with other students.

Certain personal problems may have enough emotional impact to make the subject matter of a lecture or recitation period of little importance. Because listening demands alertness, a person will help himself by resolving these problems, or putting them into perspective, through talking them over with someone—his adviser, a clergyman, a friend. Sometimes even the instructor himself may be a logical source for cathar-sis. If the emotional preoccupation is due to difficulty in the course, prior preparation can help the attention span. By going over material in a textbook to outline lecture material ahead of time, many students are able to sustain their interest for comprehension.

The Speaker's Habits and the Listener

Unfortunately, not all speakers have or use the qualities of effective presentation discussed in the section on speaking, but for the listener to disparage the speaker is no remedy. Instead of being disturbed by poor eye contact and distracting gestures and body movements, a listener can maintain a level of attention, as many do, by turning his eyes to another part of the room, thereby making the communication entirely auditory. As one student said figuratively in commenting on a lecturer, "I turn off the picture and just keep the sound." In cases of lecturers with foreign accents, students have made listening easier by talking with the lecturer a few times in conference, to adjust to his speech. A droning voice may require a change of seat, if possible. Contrary to the advice that "the lecturer can't be heard beyond the fifth row, never sit closer than the sixth," a seat nearer the speaker may help in that a better view of charts, maps, blackboards, and other visuals can diminish the vocal monotony.

In optional seating, a poor listener frequently adds to his difficulty by sitting near the back of the room, near windows, or next to his "buddies." The very presence of those seated between him and the podium adds to his distractions, as do the activities seen through the windows and the inattention of his cohorts. Sitting near the speaker contributes to a psychological attitude of "acting like a listener," a sort of autosuggestion to help attentiveness.

Lack of Interest in the Subject

A preset conviction that the information in a course is never going to be applied makes not listening easy. But we can remind ourselves that education is not a process of gathering facts, principles, or concepts to be applied in specific careers. The attitude of indifference can be changed by appreciation of the very basis of education—those experiences of learning along the way that make possible a fuller understanding of subsequent experiences.

Also, a student may keep in mind that listening is one of the easiest ways of getting information, a quick way to grow culturally, and a mark of social maturity. There is a high correlation between ability in listening and other phases of communication. One of these relationships is illustrated by a class's best speakers' continuing their improvement by listening attentively to their classmates.[15]

A discussion of listening in the school situation would be incomplete if there were no mention of the student's availing himself of the varied non-classroom listening opportunities available to him. Out-of-class lectures, concerts, theatricals, professional meetings and conventions sponsored by university conference departments—all these are opportunities for a person to add to his knowledge and to his ability as a listener.

[15] Ralph G. Nichols and Thomas R. Lewis, *Listening and Speaking* (Dubuque, Iowa: Wm. C. Brown Co., 1954), p. 6.

Listening Skills in Business and Industry

Student experiences in appreciative, critical, and discriminative listening have their counterparts in dealings with the public, with customers and fellow workers, and with associates in general. The workday consists of interviews, conferences, informal conversation, and meetings, constituting the 75 per cent of verbal communication time spent in speaking and listening.

AGAIN, THE "YOU" ATTITUDE

In that 75 per cent—45 per cent listening and 30 per cent speaking —a person is alternately speaker and listener, as implied in the quotation at the beginning of this section. In other words, the situation involves the "you" attitude, discussed at length in earlier chapters about writing. The principle is most applicable in listening, as we consider abolishing prejudices, developing open-mindedness, and being alert—in short, *hearing* a speaker out, so his ideas may be evaluated. As one writer put it, "resolving most of the barriers of communication is a matter of speaking and listening as much as possible with the other person's position and interests in mind." [16] Because of the rapid interchange in business and industry, this alternating condition in speaking and listening has ready application in employment.

ORAL COMMUNICATION WITH CUSTOMERS

Contrary to a favorite notion that a good talker makes a good salesman, it has been said that the good salesman is likely to be a better listener than talker. Many salesmen, as mentioned in connection with sales letters, know that, until the customer starts asking questions, making a sale is unlikely. Through listening, a salesman determines sales resistance he must overcome and strong points of his sales talk to emphasize. In collecting accounts by phone and personal contact, a company representative, through listening, can often learn of conditions in the customer's circumstances that open the way for suggesting budgets, partial payments, and other means to help the customer meet his obligation. In adjustments, especially those in which the customer's demands cannot be met, listening can be difficult. Chances are that emotions will run high in these situations; the customer is frequently angry or irritated; the adjuster is fearful of losing status in the customer's eyes or impatient because of what is to him the customer's unreasonableness. In such cases, the adjuster will do well to heed the advice given in the reading

[16] Harold P. Zelko, *Successful Conference and Discussion Techniques* (New York: McGraw-Hill Book Co., 1957), p. 127.

in Chapter 11, to "listen. Look interested. Display concern. Get all the facts. Don't speak until you're certain that he has nothing more to say. A talked-out customer is the easiest one with which to deal." [17] To listen patiently in such situations is extremely difficult, but restoration of customer good will is worth the effort.

INTRACOMPANY ORAL COMMUNICATION

In business, as in the student's listening situation, one of the chief objectives of interchange is to inform and instruct. Closely related to this aim is investigating or finding facts in interviews and conferences. At all company levels, as pointed out in the discussion on speaking, personnel depends on meetings for solving problems, determining policy, and counseling. Whatever the size or nature of the meeting, listening is affected by those conditions discussed in connection with students. The listener has an advantage over the speaker in the difference of speech speed and thought speed; he must be cognizant of central ideas and use the speaker's clues for those ideas; emotions and differences definitely affect listening in company communication; and the speaker's habits, whether in large or small groups, and the physical surroundings play a part in the climate for listening. Even the lack of interest in the subject, that hateful state of indifference in a student, has its counterpart in the uninterested employee, who shuts out the conversation when he does not see specific relevance of the subject to his own particular job. The myopia that precludes a student's investing time in subject matter for possible future use is an affliction of many an employee who does not see that wide knowledge of company operations might help prepare him for advancement.

As the individual alternates between being speaker and listener, a manager, no matter where he is on the organization chart, changes roles as leader and participant in meetings and conferences. In either position, he has responsibilities as a listener. The leader must be alert to follow discussion so that he can direct the meeting toward objectives and maintain time limits. Through listening, the effective leader serves another function, that of drawing out members of the group for maximum participation.

Just as the student should analyze what is said in class discussion, so the participant will evaluate discussion in a meeting with regard to its furthering the group interest, his own interest, or the self-interest of the leader. The participant will be an alert listener, hearing everyone with equal interest. Although, to some, note taking in meetings is academic, the alert participant will usually take notes, reflecting an understanding that, in the learning process, we retain more of what is heard if we

[17] See "How To Turn Complaints into Extra Sales," p. 307.

repeat it; notes reviewed shortly after a session serve that purpose.[18] The alert listener, whether leader or participant, continually assesses the discussion, relating it to the group goal. In other words, he applies the whole-part-whole approach to learning; knowing the objectives of the meeting, he relates the parts, or the comments—his own and others—to those objectives.

AN OVER-ALL VIEW OF WRITTEN AND ORAL COMMUNICATION

Although the greatest emphasis in this book has been on the written phase of communication in business and industry, it should not be inferred that writing is considered more important than the other aspects of communication—speaking, reading, and listening. Excellence in all four is to be desired. Despite studies and surveys that report preferences among employee groups for either written or spoken communication, you will do well to be broadminded and employ all the devices for reading and listening that promise to do the job fully and economically of time and money. To do the job of communicating to the varied personalities among individuals or in groups, the effective communicator will rely on many, if not all, of the following means to get his message across:

Audial:
Face-to-face—conversations, interviews, meetings, conferences
Intermediate contact—telephone, radio, intercom, public address system
Symbolic—buzzers, bells, other signals
Audio-visual: sound films and film strips, television, demonstrations
Visual:
Written—individual messages, circulars, manuals, handbooks, bulletin-board notices and announcements, signs, newsletters, pamphlets, employee publications, standard forms
Pictorial—pictures, photographs, diagrams, pictographs, maps
Written-Pictorial—posters, silent films, film strips, charts, cartoons
Symbolic—insignia, flags, lights, other signals [19]

THE VITALITY OF COMMUNICATION

As indicated in the list of media, form can be important in communication, and, throughout the course, the importance of content of the

[18] A strong case for note taking as an aid to memory is found in Donald A. Laird and Eleanor C. Laird, *Techniques for Efficient Remembering* (New York: McGraw-Hill Book Co., 1960), pp. 11–12. As a foundation for four general memory techniques, the authors list "*Write it down*" as "The Fifth Commonsense Rule," which they say "is especially needed as one advances in responsibility and has more irons in the fire. It is the only way to get around the ceilings on the memory span, or on how much one can keep in mind at one time. These ceilings are rather low, and most high-level jobs require remembering more than the memory span can hold on to unaided."

[19] Adapted from Charles E. Redfield, *Communication in Management* (The University of Chicago Press, 1958), pp. 71–72.

message has been emphasized. But those significant aspects of relationships are secondary to others because of the person-centered nature of communication. In the peopled landscape of business and industry, success in communicating still depends most upon certain personal qualities, despite the stereotyped image of ulcers and a mad race for money. Those qualities were well stated by a New York management consultant after looking at communication in a large number of companies in a two-year study:

> The old values of honesty, sincerity, and trust, sometimes dismissed as Sunday school sentimentality, are actually Monday morning business realism in the quest for better communications. They create the climate in which communications grows. Where they do not exist, communications will be faulty, no matter how they are fertilized with methods and techniques. A man's character seems to have more influence than his personality in improving communications.[20]

Those admirable attributes are what the other fellow looks for in people he deals with, and they are what he should find. But what is the basic nature of the effective communicator? Two characteristics that mark him were illustrated in a talk by Dr. Lillian Gilbreth, the author of the reading in Chapter 16. In a lecture to Purdue University industrial-engineering students, Mrs. Gilbreth told her audience that "Managing yourself is the first requisite for success." Such control stems principally from the person's confidence, which, as mentioned in Chapter 16, consists of optimism *and* knowledge. By acquiring knowledge throughout your schooling, you have developed confidence, and wisely you will continue to learn, to sustain it. Mrs. Gilbreth also told the students what to do "when the boss throws a temper tantrum." Her advice: "Just sit there 'til it's over. When it's over, the serenity is wonderful. It's really a blessing. It's simple to move in quickly to get what you want from him." [21] Implications of Mrs. Gilbreth's advice are strong for effective listening. However, it involves more than just that part of communication. The person who can so react to a superior demonstrates a consummate trait: He will not be put on the defensive. Maintaining an offensive position in any human relationship means being in command. The effective communicator is in command at all times.

In the final analysis, success rests in the very subject of this book: communication in its broadest sense. An individual "sends" information, directives, and affections through writing or speaking, with the personal qualities of honesty, sincerity, trust, of resoluteness, and optimism serving as catalysts for the words themselves. If these conditions are present, the

---

[20] A. W. Lindh, "Plain Talk About Communicating in Business," *Business Management*, April, 1964, p. 94.

[21] As quoted in the Lafayette (Ind.) *Journal and Courier*, May 23, 1964, p. 2.

receiver "gets the message" in the best possible climate for communication, that of mutual respect. The sender recognizes the individuality of the receiver, and the receiver responds to that respect, with the ensuing understanding, so well summarized in Addison's *Cato:*

> 'Tis not in mortals to command success,
> But we'll do more, Sempronius,—we'll deserve it.

Such understanding admittedly presupposes a utopia, which, we are continually reminded, will never be attained, but remoteness of a goal does not lessen our responsibility to work toward it. Through your *deserved* success, may each of you take many a step nearer that goal.

Communications Clinic *

by ROBERT NEWCOMB and MARG SAMMONS

Communications Roadblocks—And Ways to Remove Them

Realistic employee relations officers recognize that the roadblocks to successful communication can be both high and hazardous. Sometimes these barriers are erected by habitual complainers, but often they are created by management itself. Perhaps little can be done about the first, but what about the hurdles that management itself puts in the way of communication?

The Clinic receives a constant flow of mail about communications roadblocks and ways to remove them. Here are a few of the communications problems we have come across in recent weeks, along with solutions we suggested.

The problem. An industrial relations manager reports that "our supervisory newsletter, which we introduced a few months ago, doesn't seem to be developing a readership. The informal reaction we get is that the men just aren't reading it, and we are seriously thinking of giving it up. What else might we do?"

Possible solution. To answer this question, it might be a good idea first to ask yourself some others. Why was the newsletter launched in the first place—in response to a widespread demand by supervisors, or because management thought it was a good idea? How much, if any, advisory participation is there on the part of the supervisors? Is there any really dependable feedback? Does the newsletter carry actual news, or does the grapevine have it before it's published?

As for procedures, we wouldn't trust "informal reaction" but would take the problem directly to the supervisors and invite their criticisms. A written poll—signed or unsigned—might also be valuable, if you pay attention to what it reveals about your readership. Before deciding to give the newsletter up as a bad job, see what it can accomplish with some guidance from its readers.

° From *Personnel*, March–April, 1964, pp. 70–75. "Communications Clinic" is a regular feature of *Personnel*, directed to those in supervision and citing actual company programs, problems, and successes. Used by permission of the American Management Association.

The problem. In another company, top management is reported to be "overenthusiastic" about communications. "Management wants frequent employee meetings, frequent employee bulletins, frequent employee everything. We think this is too much of a good thing."

Possible solution. This problem suggests a return to the drawing board—otherwise, the company's effort to communicate effectively, however sincere, will end up in chaos. It would be wise to go back and readjust the framework of the whole communications program—the devices you use, the subject areas you cover, the policies you observe, and tentative scheduling dates. We feel that it is confusing to introduce too many printed media, since we have found that employees tend to wilt under the bombardment and soon ignore everything but the pay check. In short, determine where you are going, when, and with what. Then take it one step at a time—the best communications programs are built that way.

The problem. "Management has introduced a program of economic education for supervisors, and on the whole is pleased with it. Some, however, are kicking about the loss of time resulting from these meetings, which are held on company time. Management now wants to suggest dinner meetings after working hours, with management picking up the tab. How can we make the switch?"

Possible solution. Why not state the case frankly to the group of supervisors and put it to a vote? First, however, be sure you're giving them an interesting program as a whole, and invite suggestions to improve it. Generally, by the way, it's a good idea to survey a program of this type from time to time to make sure it isn't running out of steam.

The problem. "We have 1,500 employees. We know that we should be closer to them, and that we could benefit from their views and questions. How can we do this without being too obvious about it?"

Possible solution. You might try the technique used by a printing firm (Kable Printing Co., Mount Morris, Ill.) that has done remarkably well with a social program of its own design: The company sets aside one evening a month for a dinner meeting, at which employees marking their first, fifth, tenth, fifteenth, and twentieth service anniversaries are guests. (The Quarter Century Club assumes responsibility after that.) Members of management mingle informally with the employees, encouraging their questions and expression of opinions. Groups are never overlarge, and the whole procedure, while establishing a congenial atmosphere, lets management in on employees' thinking.

Employee Attitude Study Sparks Improvements

When the Schlumberger Well Surveying Corp., Houston, conducted an opinion survey among its employees in 1962, it found that a large percentage of the employees felt that nothing would result from their suggestions, and this disquieting reaction triggered the introduction of an "Action Plan." [1] Under the plan, each location, division, and area manager was expected to analyze care-

[1] "Schlumberger's Action Plan," *Personnel,* July–August, 1963, p. 69.

fully the survey results that involved his particular group. He was then expected to list the steps he proposed to take to improve the situation under criticism; to make progress reports to his superior; and finally, to report in detail the steps that had actually been taken to solve the problems. (Of particular interest to the Schlumberger communications staff is the fact that the Action Plan called for, and resulted in, more face-to-face communication throughout the entire company.)

Last May the company's president, W. J. Gillingham, explained the details of the Action Plan in the employee magazine, and followed up in November with a progress report, quoting from many of the managers' reports.

Under the heading "Work Load," for example, one manager reported that regular discussions were being held with each employee to explain "why management must know how much time is required to complete specific jobs"; that job assignments had been rotated, where skills permitted, to lessen the monotony of routine work; that job outlines were being written for each work area to bring about better employee understanding of the job.

Another manager reported that employees were being encouraged to improve their educational levels to fit themselves for better jobs and better pay when "merit increases could not conscientiously be recommended."

Other progressive changes that resulted directly from suggestions or comments of employees in the survey included: a training program to improve the supervisory abilities of engineers; the introduction of weekly meetings between managers and employees; an organization chart distributed to employees; the reactivation of annual interviews; the revival of a divisional monthly newsletter; the scheduling of frequent, periodic meetings of employees; more company policy postings on bulletin boards; improved job descriptions where needed; the introduction in one location of a program of management "schools"; and more frequent visits to field locations by division and area representatives.

As Schlumberger's survey disclosed the need for change, so did its Action Plan reveal the concrete benefits of change. Take, for example, one of the managers' summing up:

Supervisors have improved communications with their people; have taken more time to be certain that job assignments and instructions are understood. We are doing a better job of advance planning to provide tooling ahead of job needs. Foremen have taken a stronger stand as members of first-line management. There is now better cooperation between shifts.

In April the managers are to make a final report covering the past year of follow-up action. The company management could ask for nothing better than more of the same.

Planning the Multiplant Program

Toward the end of each year, the public relations department of Falstaff Brewing Corp., St. Louis, calls in its field force of communicators. These are the men who, in the various plant cities, handle the important dual assignment of community relations and employee communications.

The purpose of these two-day confabs is fourfold:

1. To present the corporate public relations program for the coming year to the field communications personnel, and to discuss with them ways to localize the material by using plant facts and figures.
2. To analyze the corporate achievements of the past year, and determine in what ways the public relations people can aid in "intensifying Falstaff achievement motivation" in the various plant communities.
3. To examine, discuss, and appraise new or untried communications techniques that might make employees more aware of the need for healthy corporate profits.
4. To make it possible for all company communicators, as both headquarters and plants, to share their communications knowledge and experiences.

More and more multiplant companies are working these days toward an integrated, coordinated program of communications like Falstaff's. Programs issued from headquarters without the support of local programs have been far from satisfactory; neither has the autonomous local plant program been the answer. Local plant people want to know what is going on locally, but they also have an interest in the company's national picture, because they identify their own security with it.

The Falstaff communications program is blocked out in advance to cover a 12-month period. Each field PR representative is handed a printed schedule for the coming year, which includes oral as well as written communication and calls for specific subjects to be covered at specific times. Objectives are clearly defined.

The main printed device used by the PR people is a modest bimonthly magazine, distributed to all employees; it is edited by the headquarters staff, but is supplemented by bulletin boards and by newspapers or newsletters edited by the field public relations officers. Falstaff's communications kit also includes an unusual and effective tool—an internal wire service. The headquarters staff holds a loose rein on the local men. Since the schedule given each field representative identifies the theme, method, and timing of various projects, he is able to plan his local interpretations well in advance.

In the Falstaff philosophy, the economic story is only half told when it is told only in headquarters terms—it must be localized for the man and woman in the plant in order for it to be fully appreciated. The local communications products expose employees to the company's national economic problems, of course, but also to local problems. Samples from an "inquiring photographer" feature, for example, include such direct questions as: "Why did you choose Falstaff as a place to work?" "What does your job contribute to the assurance of Falstaff's premium quality?" and "What do you think we can do to further improve our position in the industry?"

It is this kind of employee involvement that the company is working toward through its plant communications representatives.

Miscellaneous Milestones in Employee Communications

The need for speed: After experimenting with a daily newsletter in certain plants, General Electric Corp. decided to combine it with the weekly plant newspaper as a daily "Newscaster." This changeover, initiated in January, means that one of the country's largest employers has streamlined its communications to produce a paper that is "business-oriented, containing both internal and external news that affects us as plant people and as GE people."

According to a GE spokesman, the success of the experimental daily newsletter as a means of more immediate communication with plant people indicated the "great value of the immediate availability of a daily publication. It was only one more step to decide that a greater emphasis on the daily news was the logical move to make" to keep up with the quickening tempo of business. Other companies may be expected to join the parade, since a daily plant publication need be neither onerous to handle nor costly to produce.

❖　　❖　　❖

Caution light of pollsters: A company that recently conducted a survey in order to determine reader reactions to its management newsletter got a bad jolt—for a few days at least.

The returns showed that certain topics dear to management's heart (i.e., company policies and plans, public affairs, and so on) were among the least popular and rated the lowest readership. This finding completely baffled management until someone thought to probe for the reason. It was simple enough: Readers were getting the same information from other management sources, and saw no value in reading the duplicate material. Moreover, there was a complaint of "overload." As soon as the saturation level was lowered and the subject matter of information better controlled, readership interest started inching up. Here, then, was a case of positive results from a negative survey.

Exercises and Problems in Communication

1. Consult the *Business Periodicals Index,* looking under "Communication," for those articles describing company programs for training in oral communication. Report your findings, according to your instructor's assignment.

2. Read articles, toward the same end as in Exercise 1, on companies' speaker "bureaus."

3. Read the latest editions of Dale Carnegie's books on improving relations through effective communication. Your library may also have issues of the Dale Carnegie courses. Compare or contrast the principles and methods discussed with those found in public-speaking textbooks in the library.

4. For a pertinent, readable discussion on "fallacies of words," read Chapter 4 in William V. Haney's *Communication Patterns and Incidents* (Homewood, Ill.: Richard D. Irwin, Inc., 1960). Prepare a three- to five-minute talk to the class on personal experiences demonstrating the points the author makes.

5. Write a report on the discussion of the nature of organizations in Chapter 4 of Lee O. Thayer's *Administrative Communication* (Homewood, Ill.: Richard D. Irwin, Inc., 1961). In your report, show the parts that written communication and oral communication play in the various levels of administration.

6. Devise a rating chart, using the factors of speakers and speeches on page 500. Use the chart to rate talks given by your classmates.

7. For a start in improving your reading skills, you may try the following exercises. These are obviously not going to correct your lifetime patterns,

because, as has been pointed out, sustained, conscientious practice is necessary. But any *continued*, meaningful effort will pay dividends. These few drills are given as encouragement to turn to some of the books listed after the exercises, which, with intensive practice, will help you, as they have helped others, to increase proficiency for maximum results with minimum time and energy.

A. Determine your perceptual skill by checking the word in the second column of five words that matches the key word in the left column.

1. sort	sought	fort	sort	fought	port
2. tell	tall	till	tale	toll	tell
3. happy	joy	happy	hoppy	hippy	huffy
4. five	live	love	four	five	fever
5. detail	resale	detail	retail	dovetail	entail
6. cape	coat	tape	tail	cape	cate
7. I've	Iva	I'll	I'd	Ives	I've
8. melon	mellow	mallow	million	melon	mildew
9. cart	coat	cast	cost	carp	cart
10. laugh	last	cough	rough	caught	laugh
11. catch	cache	latch	catch	watch	cough
12. haste	hast	paste	laced	haste	taste
13. deliver	liver	decipher	giver	believer	deliver
14. moron	more	more on	morn	moron	morgen
15. believer	deliver	reliever	deceiver	believer	belief

B. Try your vocabulary power by checking the word among the five choices that most nearly means the same as the word in the left column:

1. dress	fit	habit	outfit	garment	suit
2. light	land	heavy	right	sleight	soar
3. carry	harry	harass	convey	marry	merry
4. stain	hint	taint	plaint	tint	cover
5. lower	elevator	lover	descend	floor	remain
6. wild	flower	willed	untrammeled	wily	child
7. wicket	wicked	croquet	door	crime	mallet
8. mean	base	lean	equal	long	distant
9. peace	battle	theater	harmony	agreement	freedom
10. starve	start	stop	surrender	subdue	yearn
11. lure	lore	lurid	bait	pure	long
12. crib	corn	horse	crisp	bed	cribbage
13. thorn	shrub	shorn	thrown	spine	spin
14. incisive	incisor	incisure	trenchant	tooth	bite
15. showy	flowers	theater	staging	ostentatious	display

Answers: garment, land, convey, tint, descend, untrammeled, door, base, harmony, subdue, bait, bed, spine, trenchant, ostentatious

C. This exercise will serve as a brief estimate of your language skill with phrases. Select the phrase in the right column that means most nearly the same as the one in the left:

1. just now	a while ago	going ahead	serving everyone
	in the near future	at once	
2. at its best	fresh fruit	a superlative degree	not so good
	thrive upon	security for all	

3. phonics method   auditory ability   stereophonic machine
for teaching reading   eye movements   eye action

4. vice-president   up the ladder   inadequate training   front office
leader in crime   second in command

5. to vocalize   poor reading   opera star   in high voice   say words   folk music

6. basic word skills   secondary schools   tautology   primary grades word recognition   dictionary usage

7. under advisement   legal training   being considered   up to now to his attention   well done

8. negative factors   opposed to   away from   positive pole   not praiseworthy   deterring elements

9. to concentrate   a personal matter   improve reading skill exclusive attention to   forget all else   more and more

10. in charge   having supervision   owed to   shooting iron responsible to   for payment of

11. in the absence of   wanting   attendance report   absenteeism rarely seen   not in sight

12. to get directions   listen closely   to be guided   be lost   to go forth   turn to the right

13. run wild   juvenile delinquency   be on a rampage   fire on show indifference   uncontrolled anger

14. get out the vote   two-party system   voter registration   the spoils system   bring force to bear   motivate to exercise franchise

15. best regards   complimentary close   greeting card   felicitation   appreciation   *sayonara*

Answers: a while ago, a superlative degree, for teaching reading, second in command, say words, word recognition, being considered, deterring elements, exclusive attention to, having supervision of, wanting, to be guided, be on a rampage, motivate to exercise franchise, felicitation

D. The first paragraph of the section on reading is reproduced here in groups of words for practice in developing a wider span and a rhythmic pattern. The groupings are arbitrary; the particular arrangement will not be right for every reader. Those who read the material at the skimming rate will find the phrasing restrictive; those who read in smaller groupings can use the exercise to advantage.

     The age-old controversies   about reading   continue without abatement. What is   the best method   for teaching reading? What is the reading   rate of the   average American? Which of the myriad   lists of titles   recommended for   every citizen should a person read?   Whatever turn   the discussion takes— there are no conclusions   in these arguments—   in any conversation about reading,   a few immutable   facts remain. An individual's reading   skills are developed   through the "look and see"   or the phonics method;   or, if his teacher is intelligent,   through the best features   of the two meth-

ods, according to   the pupil's needs. Also, the individual
reader is probably   spending more time   than is necessary;
and, Mr. Johnson's   opinion notwithstanding,   businessmen
can hardly read   "as inclination leads them."   The fact that
many businessmen spend   one-fourth to   one-half of their
working hours   in reading   precludes that   happy state of
affairs. If, as   described repeatedly   in business and
industrial journals,   the businessman's   opinion on his
reading is to   be taken literally,   he does agree that
that part of   his work is   a task.

Now reread the paragraph, fixing your eyes at the center of each grouping. Observe that this movement will prevent your eyes from backsweeping to the left margin, thus assisting in developing a wider span.

8. Survey three or four of the following books to analyze the methods of improving reading skills. Assume that you are to recommend a book for use in a college class or an industrial training program. Write a brief report to the chairman of the reading program or to the director of training.

Russell Cosper and E. Glenn Griffin, *Toward Better Reading Skill* (New York: Appleton-Century-Crofts, Inc., 1959)

Doris W. Gilbert, *Power and Speed in Reading* (Englewood Cliffs, N.J.: Prentice-Hall, Inc., 1956)

Paul D. Leedy, *Reading Improvement for Adults* (New York: McGraw-Hill Book Co., 1956)

Norman Lewis, *How To Read Better and Faster* (New York: Thomas Y. Crowell Co., 1958)

Arthur S. MacDonald and George H. Zimny, *The Art of Good Reading* (Indianapolis: The Bobbs-Merrill Co., Inc., 1963)

Lyle L. Miller, *Increasing Reading Efficiency* (New York: Holt, Rinehart & Winston, Inc., 1956)

Nila B. Smith, *Read Faster* (Englewood Cliffs, N.J.: Prentice-Hall, Inc., 1958)

9. For a pleasant sojourn with an engaging writer, read I. A. Richards' *How To Read a Page* (Boston: Beacon Press, Inc., 1959). (Now a classic, the book was first published in 1942 by W. W. Norton & Co., Inc.) You can savor the author's facility with words in his discussion of what he calls "100 great words." If you meet the author halfway, you will read for sheer enjoyment; no written or speaking assignment is called for.

10. Read Chapter 4, "Making Reading Suit Your Purpose," in W. W. Farquhar, J. D. Krumboltz, and C. G. Wrenn, *Learning To Study* (New York: The Ronald Press Co., 1960). Prepare a report to the class on suggestions for lightening the college reading load. Use clues for your audience, as discussed in the section on listening.

11. Read "The Disease of Not Listening," in *The Art of Listening*, by D. A. Barbara (Springfield, Ill.: Charles C Thomas, Publishers, 1958), and write for a company magazine a 200-word article on faulty listening.

12. After reading Chapter 2, "Selective Listening to Speech," in D. E. Broadbent's *Perception and Communication* (Oxford, England: Pergamon Press, Ltd., 1958), write an article, adapting for lay readers the technical treatment of the subject.

13. Using at least three of the media in the list on page 518, plan a campaign for publicizing a change in your company (a new policy, a training program to be conducted at a local high school, a celebration to observe the company's thirty-fifth year in business, a new college-scholarship program for employees' children, etc.). Write the necessary letters, scripts, or article outlines (for speeches and individual conversations) according to the media you select.

14. Almost any discussion of human relationships includes something on the part silence plays in communication. In groups of three or four class members, discuss this concept for five or ten minutes, compiling lists of classroom situations in which a person's not talking is tantamount to communicating. After making a master list from the oral reports of all the groups, analyze the situations for their psychological and social implications. What applications are there for these situations in business and industry—in interviews, conferences, and meetings with customers and company personnel. For best use of group-discussion time, be sure that a leader and a recorder are appointed in your group and that the leader observes the techniques of effective leadership discussed in this chapter.

15. Consider the questions in the chapter reading, "Communications Clinic," about the supervisory newsletter—the first problem presented. As an exercise in getting employee opinion, set up a program for "dependable feedback." Contrast your methods with what you consider to be meant by the "informal reaction" mentioned.

PART IV

APPENDIXES

A

Postal Information

To achieve greater accuracy and speed in dispatching and delivering mail, the Post Office Department inaugurated the ZIP-code system, in 1963. As sorting and distribution of mail are increasingly mechanized, the system becomes more significant. The first of the five digits in the number indicates a geographical area; the second and third plus the first, a major city or sectional center; and the fourth and fifth, a post office or other delivery unit. The postal zone numbers in cities, introduced during World War II to expedite mail delivery, are incorporated in the ZIP code. For example, in Appendix Section B, the "20" (fourth and fifth digits of the number "10020") in the address of Time Inc. is the old postal zone number, entered then as part of "New York 20, New York."

If space on the envelope allows, the ZIP number should be entered on the same line as the city and state, with no punctuation after the state name except a period if the state name is abbreviated. There should be at least $\frac{1}{5}$ inch between the state name and the ZIP number. To avoid crowding or unbalancing the appearance of the address on the envelope, the ZIP number may be placed immediately below the last line of the address. The sender's ZIP number should appear in a similar position as part of his return address. For information on specific ZIP numbers, consult your local postmaster.

B

Forms of Introductory Address, Salutation, and Complimentary Close

(See Appendix Section A on ZIP number in address.)

Mr. Harold C. Hinman 889 East Erie Avenue Binghamton, New York	Dear Mr. Hinman: Dear Sir:	Sincerely yours, Very truly yours,
Mrs. Harold C. Hinman 889 East Erie Avenue Binghamton, New York	Dear Mrs. Hinman:	Sincerely yours, Very truly yours,
Mrs. Gladys I. Thorpe 3328 Third Street Los Angeles, California	Dear Mrs. Thorpe:	Sincerely yours, Very truly yours,
Miss Carolyn Edwards 38 Thuse Court Boise, Idaho	Dear Miss Edwards:	Sincerely yours, Very truly yours,
Mr. Jack C. Carr Public Relations Superintendent State Farm Insurance Companies Bloomington, Illinois	Dear Mr. Carr: Dear Sir:	Sincerely yours, Very truly yours,
Time Inc. Time & Life Building Rockefeller Center New York, New York 10020	Gentlemen: Dear Sirs:	Sincerely yours, Very truly yours,

The Nell Harden Study Club McVeigh, Kentucky	Ladies:	Sincerely yours, Very truly yours,

GOVERNMENT OFFICIALS

The President or The President of the United States The White House Washington, D.C.	Sir: Mr. President: Dear Mr. President: My dear Mr. President:	Respectfully submitted, Respectfully, Sincerely yours,
The President and Mrs. Smith	Dear Mr. President and Mrs. Smith	Respectfully, Sincerely yours,
The Vice President The United States Senate Washington, D.C.	Dear Sir: Dear Mr. Vice President: My dear Mr. Vice President:	Respectfully yours, Sincerely yours, Very truly yours,
Mr. Paul Jones: or The Honorable Paul Jones Secretary of State Washington, D.C.	Sir: Dear Mr. Secretary: Dear Mr. Jones:	Very truly yours, Sincerely yours,

(All Cabinet members are addressed and greeted similarly.)

Hon. Birch E. Brown United States Senate Washington, D.C.	Sir: My dear Mr. Senator: My dear Senator Brown:	Very truly yours,
Hon. Roy M. Kurt House of Representatives Washington, D.C.	Sir: My dear Mr. Kurt:	Very truly yours, Sincerely yours,
Hon. Carl J. Thomason Director, Federal Bureau of Investigation Washington, D.C.	Sir: My dear Mr. Thomason:	Very truly yours, Sincerely yours,
The Honorable James E. Bayes or The Chief Justice United States Supreme Court Washington, D.C.	Dear Sir: Sir: Dear Mr. Chief Justice:	Very truly yours, Sincerely yours,
(*Associate Justice*) Hon. Albert K. Coyne United States Supreme Court	Dear Mr. Justice: Dear Judge Coyne: My dear Justice Coyne:	Very truly yours, Sincerely yours,
(*Judge of State Court*) The Honorable Loren Slater Judge of the Supreme Court Salem, Oregon	My dear Mr. Justice: My dear Justice Slater: Dear Judge Slater:	Very truly yours, Sincerely yours,

The Honorable John C. Doyle
Governor of Texas
Austin, Texas
	Sir:
	My dear Governor
	  Doyle:
		Very truly yours,
		Sincerely yours,
		Respectfully
		  yours,

The Honorable Charles B.
  Carroll
State Senator
The State Senate
Indianapolis, Indiana
	Sir:
	My dear Mr. Senator:
	My dear Senator
	  Carroll:
		Very truly yours,
		Sincerely yours,

The Honorable L. Ray Burns State Representative House of Representatives Indianapolis, Indiana	Sir: My dear Mr. Burns:	Very truly yours, Sincerely yours,
Hon. Thomas Sweeney Mayor of the City of Taylorville Taylorville, Illinois	Sir: Dear Mr. Mayor: Dear Mayor Sweeney:	Respectfully yours, Sincerely yours, Very truly yours,

The Honorable David K. E.
  Bruce
Ambassador to Great Britain
London, England
  or
The Department of State
Washington, D.C.
	Sir:
	My dear Mr.
	  Ambassador:
	My dear Mr. Bruce:
		Respectfully
		  yours,
		Very truly yours,

His Excellency, Sir David
  Ormsby-Gore
The Ambassador of Great
  Britain
The British Embassy
Washington, D.C.
	Sir:
	Excellency:
	Your Excellency:
	My dear Mr.
	  Ambassador:
		Respectfully
		  yours,
		Yours very truly,

ECCLESIASTICS

To His Holiness, Pope Leo XIV
  or
His Holiness, the Pope
State of Vatican City
Italy
	Your Holiness:
	Most Holy Father:
		Respectfully
		  yours,
		Your dutiful son
		  (or daughter),

His Eminence, Peter Cardinal
  Ritter
Archbishop of New York
New York, New York
	Your Eminence:
	My Lord Cardinal:
		Respectfully
		  yours,

(*Archbishop*)
The Most Reverend John J.
  Lorenz, D.D.
His Excellency, the Archbishop
  of Cincinnati
	Your Excellency:
	Your Grace:
		Respectfully
		  yours,

(Bishop) The Most Reverend James Bryan	Your Excellency:	Respectfully yours,
(Monsignor–Papal Chamberlain) The Very Reverend Monsignor Paul Lakon	Very Reverend and Dear Monsignor:	Respectfully yours,
(Monsignor–Domestic Prelate) The Right Reverend Monsignor Leo H. Sanberry	Right Reverend Monsignor:	Respectfully yours,
(Priest) Reverend Comerford J. O'Malley, C.M.	Reverend and Dear Father: Dear Father O'Malley:	Respectfully yours, Sincerely yours,
(Brother) Brother Bernard Tolle	Dear Brother Bernard:	Sincerely yours,
(Mother of a Sisterhood) Mother Cecilia Patrick O.S.U. or Sr. L. Josephine, Superior	Dear Mother Superior: Dear Sister Superior:	Respectfully yours, Sincerely yours,
(Sister) Sister Rutafine,O.S.F.	Dear Sister Rutafine:	Sincerely yours,
(Protestant Episcopal Bishop) The Right Reverend Howard R. Brinker Bishop of Nebraska	Right Reverend Sir: Dear Bishop Brinker:	Respectfully yours, Sincerely yours,
(Methodist Bishop) The Reverend Bishop Gerald P. Williams	Dear Sir: Dear Bishop Williams:	Respectfully yours, Sincerely yours,
(Protestant Minister) Rev. Ira G. McCormack, D.D. or The Reverend Lawrence Nuir	Dear Sir: Dear Dr. McCormack: Dear Sir:	Sincerely yours,
(Jewish Rabbi) Rabbi Stephen Engel Reverend Stephen Engel	Dear Sir: My dear Mr. Engel:	Respectfully yours, Sincerely yours,

University Officers and Faculty

Dr. Lewis K. Foran President of Indiana University Bloomington, Indiana	Dear Sir: Dear President Foran: Dear Mr. Foran:	Sincerely yours,

Dr. Roy B. Burton   Dear Sir: Sincerely yours,
     or   Dear Dean Burton: Very truly yours,
Dean Roy B. Burton   Dear Dr. Burton:
Dean of the Evening Divisions   Dear Mr. Burton:
Northwestern University
339 East Chicago Avenue
Chicago, Illinois

Professor Beatrice L. Vail   Dear Professor Vail: Sincerely yours,
Chambers Building   Dear Miss Vail: Very truly yours,
Pennsylvania State University
University Park, Pennsylvania

OFFICERS OF THE ARMED FORCES

General Earle G. Wheeler   Sir: Respectfully
Chief of Staff   Dear Sir: yours,
United States Army   Dear General Wheeler: Sincerely yours,
Washington, D.C.   Very truly yours,

Admiral David L. McDonald,   Sir: Respectfully
     USN   Dear Sir: yours,
Chief of Naval Operations   Dear Admiral   Very truly yours,
United States Navy   McDonald   Sincerely yours,
Washington, D.C.

General Curtis E. Le May   Sir: Respectfully
Chief of Staff   Dear Sir: yours,
United States Air Force   Dear General Le May: Very truly yours,
Washington, D.C.   Sincerely yours,

Captain Clyde S. Lewis, USAF   Dear Sir: Sincerely yours,
AFROTC Unit   Dear Captain Lewis: Very truly yours,
University of Illinois
Urbana, Illinois

First Lieutenant B. C. White   Dear Sir: Sincerely yours,
U.S. Army, ROTC Unit   Dear Lieutenant   Very truly yours,
University of Oregon   White:
Eugene, Oregon

Chaplains are addressed *Chaplain;* Catholic chaplains may be addressed *Father.*

Cadets at the United States Military Academy and aviation and other cadets of the Army and the Air Force are addressed *Cadet.*

C

Special Letter Forms

Most of the illustrative letters used in this book were written in the United States. They represent the prevalent forms and trends in our own business writing. It is well to recognize, however, that other nations may have other preferences. Increased foreign trade and expansion of companies of the United States into foreign countries make it worthwhile to be acquainted with some of the practices and styles in commercial writing of other nations.

The indented address, closed punctuation, and some double spacing are still seen in British correspondence, especially from countries formerly of the British Commonwealth, showing the influence of the centuries of commerce with England. As shown in Figures 62 and 63, English letters are much like those that go through United States mail, especially in sales writing. It is the tone of the writing, however, that continues to distinguish foreign correspondence from ours. Deference or humility characterizes much of the writing from other countries; to many persons accustomed to the *businessese* of our domestic writing, the tone is almost obsequious.

Like Oriental correspondence (in Figures 64 and 65), Latin American writing has become simpler in recent years, but the Spanish correspondent is still more elaborately polite than we are. Business-like in spirit, however, his letters are much the same as ours. Formerly, the Spanish writer used *Sr.* (*Señor*) with a title such as *Doctor* or *Professor*, but the professional title is generally used alone now. (See Figures 66A and 66B.) (In German correspondence, *Herr* (Mr.) or *Herren* (Messrs.) still appears with professional titles, as shown in Figure 67A.) In strict usage, Spanish names are a compound of the names of the father and the mother, for example, Sr. Diego Lopez y Nogales (or Lopez-Nogales). Other differences between the manners of United States and Latin American commercial writing are discussed in C. R. Anderson's "Anyone Can Write Letters," in Chapter 7 of this book.

Despite differences that still exist, one sees in foreign correspondence the influence of our practices and style. This is not surprising when we know of such organizations as the Japanese Business English Association. Its publication *Business English*, capably edited by Shigeru Ozaki, a Harvard graduate, reflects the principles of modern correspondence, fostered by the American Business Writing Association in its *Bulletin* and *Journal of Business Communi-*

KIRKLAND BRIDGE CHURCH RESTORATIONS LIMITED

61, HEATH STREET, LONDON, N.W.3

GOLD MEDAL

Dear Father Costello,

On this first morning in 19--, I am in a fighting mood and proud of it -- but let me explain.

Everybody is saying "Prices MUST come down"; everybody is grumbling, grousing, growling "Prices MUST come down"; and I am so sick to death of TALK, that we are going to do something about it -- and NOW.

We are cutting down our "overhead" with a sharp knife, while reducing our "margin" at the same time. Our craftsmen have been firmly told that we require more work per hour from each man if we are to meet the economic challenge of 19--.

So, your Church can be cleaned, "touched up," distempered, painted or transformed to sheer loveliness; and, we are cutting all our estimates by a flat FIFTEEN PER CENT.

As some evidence of our integrity: any unaccepted Estimates dated 19-- or 19-- will be cut by 15%-- without argument -- if accepted during this present month.

Please read the enclosed brochure; every word of it is true.

Then call me at Hampstead 4606 or 6062 or 6063.

Yours very truly,

Kirkland Bridge.

Fig. 62. A London "sales" letter using economy and satisfactory service as appeals. The enclosed brochure listed comments of the firm's satisfied customers. (Used by permission of the Dartnell Corporation.)

cation, and through membership in foreign countries including Australia, Canada, Finland, Japan, and South Africa.

Our influence and direction in the business communication of the world are implemented through the work of other communication organizations and their publications. Among these are the National Society for the Study of Communication, which publishes the internationally known *Journal of Communica-*

KLEEN-STIK

SHOULDHAM HOUSE,
SHOULDHAM STREET,
LONDON, W.1

GOLD MEDAL

GO ON - PEEL IT OFF . . .

(There is a unique, "easy-to-lift" free edge.)

See that strip of clear adhesive left on the letter? Turn the letter
over and put it face down on your desk - see how it grips.

This is Kleen-Stik and it replaces spot or strip gumming, sticky
tape, etc., for window bills, posters, and many other point-of-purchase
displays. It also opens up new fields and ideas in design for your Art
Department, including transparencies, and low-cost dimensional displays.

Your clients will want this latest technique for their sales promotional material because it is the surest and most economical way to get
maximum co-operation from the retailer or shop manager.

We are now introducing Kleen-Stik in its many forms to this
country and it is available to all printers, silk screeners, and display
manufacturers. To learn more about Kleen-Stik and how it can help you
and your clients to get the most attractive displays shown at the retail
outlet, just sign the reply card and post it to us.

Yours sincerely,

I. A. Hayton.
Sales Manager.

Fig. 63. The advantage of a screened mailing list is felt anywhere in the
world. This letter, from another London firm, also demonstrates the value of
enclosing samples, as part of the conviction step in selling. (By permission of the
Dartnell Corporation.)

tion, and the International Reading Association, with its worldwide subscription
list of the *Journal of Reading*.

The letters in this section are presented, as others throughout the book have
been, for your objective analysis. You might view them subjectively as well;
with the spread of English as the international language of commerce and the
speed of transportation and communications facilities such as Telstar, Early
Bird, and Syncom, it is probable that many of you who use this book will find
yourselves not only observers of foreign correspondence but participants in
producing it. The world is quickly becoming little more than a vicinity in which
we are within earshot of, and but a step from, our colleagues and our competitors. In the foreseeable future, the term *foreign correspondence* may well
no longer designate the Italian, Scandinavian, Oriental, etc.; it may be applied
to the Lunar and the Martian.

STRAIGHTFORWARD RELATING
OF FACTS BRINGS 50% RETURN
ON SAMPLE LETTER
Written by Masao Hasegawa,
Gold Medal Winner in Kobe,
Japan, this clear, simple,
factual presentation has consistently brought up to 50
percent return requests for
samples each year—a tribute
not only to careful selection
of sales facts but also to
the principle of adaptability.

ESTABLISHED 1931

The Genryu Trading Co., Ltd.

P. O. BOX NO. 126
3, SAN-CHOME, KITANAGASA

KOBE, JAPAN

GOLD MEDAL

Barton Import Company, Inc.
201 Fifth Avenue
New York 16, N.Y.

Gentlemen:

You will be interested to know that some of the biggest department
stores in the U.S. are now buying Toyo feather flowers for decorating
handbags.

Before making Toyo flowers, our workers collect pure-white, flawless
feathers and, after coloring, form them into a wide variety of flowers.
The trimmings look so nice that we believe Toyo handbags, if adorned
with such flowers, will be a best seller in the coming season.

The large department stores intend to flower-trim handbags themselves,
but we feel that if you buy the already decorated handbags from us, you
will be money ahead.

For your reference, we are sending you samples of the feather flowers
only. Upon hearing from you, we shall gladly send you samples of
Toyo handbags complete with flowers. More samples of flowers will
be also forwarded for your selection.

If you act early enough, we feel sure you can forestall other firms.
So we would strongly recommend you to take up this business right away.

We are very eager to serve you, and shall be grateful for your early
reply.

Yours very truly,
THE GENRYU TRADING CO., LTD.

P. H. Chu
Export Manager

MH

Fig. 64. In contrast to domestic direct-mail writing, this letter has the "soft
sell" tone. The 50 per cent return requests for samples could raise the question
of whether a bombastic style is necessary in sales writing. (Used by permission
of the Dartnell Corporation.)

Fig. 65. "Broken English" and irregular grammatical constructions seem to
contribute to the sincerity in this follow-up letter from a custom tailor. The
material samples were four sheets with 24 swatches each, including fabrics
ranging from heavy woolens to fine seersuckers.

JAMES L. SEE & CO. CLOTHING MILL (H. K.) LTD.
HONGKONG, B.C.C.

April 22, 19--

Mr. & Mrs. L. T. Hine
5345 Montrose Ave.,
Indianapolis "9" IND.
U.S.A.

Dear Sir/Madame,

We thank you very much for your kind enquiry of recent date, and in reply, as per your requirements, are sending to you herewith some selected patterns of material for your good perusal. Hope you could find among them those you like. If not, further instructions from you would be welcomed.

It is explained that prices quoted are per yard ex our godown. Other expenses including packing and parcel postage etc. is US $1.00 for the first item and US $0.50 for each additional items of an order. Yardage of material necessary for various kinds of clothing is respectively stated at the bottom of the sample form,whereabout corresponding tailoring costs are also indicated. Whole expense for each garment can be figured out by adding the tailoring cost to the charges for the material to be needed therefor.

SIZE We could have sufficient information of your measurements would you complete one of the enclosed order blanks and return same to us.

METHOD of DELIVERY By parcel post through the local Post Office and by Air. If by Air, Air Freight from H.K. to U.S. $3.00 per lb., time required 1-1/2 weeks, to Japan $2.25 per Kilo., time required 1 week.

STYLE A picture of your description in details, or a diagram, to show the style you would choose for your order, would be available.

PAYMENT By personal check to be drawn on U.S. banks or by cash or by travellers checks, effectey on our advice of the delievery of your order(s). You may also deposit your money, by whatever means available, into the account of Mr. James L. See with the National City Bank of New York, Wall Street, New York City and advise us. As our bankers used to airmail this Credit information to us, we can know about this very quickly.

We are proud that there are thousands of our overseas clients who placed us their mail orders in as far from the United States to the area of Far East, giving us their recommendations for our services. We assure you that you shall be given every satisfaction by our overseas services as thousands of our other customers were.

Out thanks for your interest.
Encl: Order Blanks & Material Samples.

Faithfully yours,

JAMES L. SEE CO, (H.K.) LTD.

_____
Manager, Overseas Division

RODRIGO DE LLANO   GILBERTO FIGUEROA   APARTADO 120 BIS
DIRECTOR GENERAL   GERENTE GENERAL   MEXICO, D F

Oficinas y Redacciones: 30 de septiembre de 19   Talleres:
REFORMA 18   BUCARELI 17

Sírvase citar el departamento de:
SUBSCRIPCIONES

                    Dr. John Ball.
                    114 East Church Street.
                    OXFORD. OHIO.- U.S.A.

                    Muy señor nuestro:-

                            Atendiendo a sus deseos expresados en su atenta -
                    fechada el 26 del actual, nos permitimos manifestarle, que
                    al pié de la presente le damos a conocer los precios de sus
                    cripción de nuestro periódico "DOMINICAL", rogándole que --
                    si desea figurar en la lista de nuestros amables suscripto-
                    res, nos remita su importe por adelantado, ya sea en giro -
                    internacional sobre New York, cheque o en documento de fácil
                    cobro para nosotros. Si nos sitúa dicho importe, sírvase de
                    cirnos nuevamente su nombre y dirección.

                            En espera de vernos favorecidos con sus aprecia---
                    bles ordenes, nos repetimos de usted afectísimos atentos y -
                    seguros servidores.

                                        EXCELSIOR
                                        CIA. EDITORIAL, S. C L.

                                        R A Bauch

                                        LUIS G. BARRENECHEA
                                        JEFE DEPTO. SUBSCRIPCIONES

                    "EXCELSIOR" DOMINICAL
                    un año   Dls. 7.00
                    6 meses   "   3.50

                    LGB/cd

Fig. 66A. Latin American correspondence, in Spanish. (See Figure 66B for a translation.)

Our very [dear] sir:-

Attending to your desires expressed in your attentive [letter] dated the 26th of the present month, we allow ourselves to state to you that at the foot of this present letter we give you to know the prices of subscription of our Sunday newspaper, requesting you that if you figure to be on the list of our amiable subscribers, send us the amount in advance, be it in international draft on New York, check, or document of easy collection for us. If you remit us said amount, please tell us again your name and address.

In hope of seeing ourselves favored with your valuable orders we repeat ourselves your affectionate attentive and unfailing servants.

EXCELSIOR

Luis G. Barrenechea
Chief, Subscription Dept.

Fig. 66B. A literal translation of the subscription letter in Figure 66A.

Spezial-Foto-Handlung.
Gegr. 1895
Lieferant für Behörden, Röntgen-Institute, Krankenhäuser und graph. Anstalten

Abt. Herrn

    W i l l i a m s

    Hamburg 13

    Böttgerstr.15

Hamburg 36, den   4. März
Stephansplatz 2 Dammtorstraße
bei der Staatsoper   Li.// Kr.

Sehr geehrter Herr Williams !

Wir danken nochmal für Ihren Besuch in unserem Geschäft und freuen uns mit
Ihnen, daß Sie jetzt im Besitz einer so schönen Kamera sind.
Die von Ihnen noch gewünschte englische Gebrauchsanweisung legen wir mit.
bei und wünschen Ihnen noch viel Freude mit Ihrer neuen Kamera.
Sollten Sie noch weitere Wünsche haben, so stehen wir Ihnen gern zur Ver-
fügung.

                        Mit freundlichen Grüßen

Postscheck-Konto: Hamburg 361 — Bank-Konto: Haspa von 1827 Nr. 80/1001 und 41/77 — Fernruf: 35 25 05

Fig. 67A. A sample of German business correspondence received by one of
the authors of this book shortly after purchasing a camera in a large photo-
equipment store.

Very Honorable Mr. Williams!

We thank you again for your visit to our place of business and
rejoice with you that you are now in possession of such a fine
camera.

The English directions wished by you for using it we are enclosing and wish for you yet much satisfaction with your new
camera.

Should you have still another wish, we are eagerly at your
disposal.

                        With friendly greetings

Fig. 67B. A nearly literal translation of the German letter in Figure 67A.

D
Glossary

Certain words and terms cause difficulty in business writing. Some are so much alike, and yet so different in various respects—spelling, pronunciation, or meaning—that there is much confusion regarding their use. Others are outdated stock phrases which should be replaced by simpler and more exact language. Still others offer problems in idiom or grammar. Space does not permit an exhaustive list. The aim has been to make a helpful and instructive short list and not to compete with the dictionary, which is the court of final resort for most problems of diction.

Some words and terms have many uses, but only the most important or the most troublesome sense is shown here. Words labeled as colloquial are acceptable in general, but not in the most formal business use. Words labeled as slang may occasionally be employed. They are sometimes enclosed in quotation marks, especially in formal writing or when they have the effect of technical terms. Rulings here are more liberal than in most texts, for language is progressive, not static, and tendencies may as well be recognized.

A, An. Use *a* before words beginning with consonant sounds. Use *an* before initial vowels except in words beginning with a *y* or *w* sound, like *ewe* or *one-piece*. Sound, not spelling, governs. Words beginning with *h* are troublesome when the *h* is only semisilent, as in historical. Say *a history* but either *a* or *an historical novel, a* preferred.

Ability, Capacity. *Ability* is the power to use physical or mental energy; *capacity* is the power to receive and hold. He has great capacity to receive ideas but little ability to use them.

Above, Above-mentioned. Usually trite or vague. Prefer *preceding, foregoing,* or second mention of what is referred to.

Accept, Except. *Accept* means take, receive; *except,* bar, omit, exclude. I accept the new specifications, but the shipment now on the way must be excepted.

According to Our Records. Vague. Say "We find" or "Our copy of your order (letter) shows."

Ad. Colloquial form of *advertisement*. Acceptable for all but the most formal business use. Compounds *ad writer, ad man,* and *want ad* also acceptable.

Advise. Much overused. *Admonish, caution,* and *counsel* are synonyms. Say *tell* or *inform*.

Affect, Effect. *Affect* means to influence, to change, and is nearly always a verb; *effect* as a verb means to bring about, accomplish. If the companies effect a merger, the policies of both will be affected. *Effect* as a noun means result; synonyms are *consequence, issue, outcome*.

Aggravate. To increase in severity, to make worse. Applies to a condition or a situation. Often misused for *annoy* or *irritate*. The many annoyances and irritations of the morning had aggravated his natural gruffness.

Ain't. Slang. Incorrect contraction. *Isn't* is the contraction for *is not; aren't* for *are not. Am not* has no recognized contraction.

Alibi. Plea of having been elsewhere when act or crime was committed. Colloquially it is a synonym for *excuse,* especially a plausible but insincere excuse. His alibi for missing the board meeting was that he had to write some important letters.

All of. Colloquially prevalent where *all* would suffice. Use *all of* with pronouns. All the items had been checked off properly. All of them were included.

All right. The only allowable spelling; *alright* is never correct. *All right,* or its equivalent *O.K.,* is much used in business to signify acquiescence or approval.

Allusion, Illusion, Delusion, Elusion. An *allusion* is an indirect reference; an *illusion,* a deceptive, or fanciful, impression; a *delusion,* a false, often harmful, impression or belief. He recognized your allusion to the Chrysler Corporation. While I was seeing that movie, I had the illusion that I was living in the days of King Arthur. His delusion that his absurd plan would benefit the company proved ruinous. *Elusion,* sometimes confused with *allusion* and *illusion,* means evasion or adroit escape.

Almost, Most. *Almost* is an adverb; *most* may be adverb, adjective, or noun. *Almost* means nearly; *most* (adv.), greatest in degree. His action almost convinced us that he was our most unscrupulous competitor.

Along these lines. Vague, often meaningless. Use specific references or omit entirely.

Already, All ready. *Already* means previously; *all ready,* everyone or everything prepared. He had already checked the list to make sure that they were all ready to go.

Altogether, All together. *Altogether* means wholly or completely; *all together*, everybody, or all things, in a group. Are you altogether certain that they were all together when you saw them?

Among, Between. *Between* usually refers to two objects only; *among*, to more than two. I can choose between two presents, but if the choice lies among several, I am lost.

Amount, Number. *Amount* refers to bulk or mass; *number*, to units or individuals. A small amount of food and a large number of persons mean that someone will go hungry.

And/or. Accepted in business use to express cumulative or alternative possibilities. Can mean either *and* or *or*. The modern drugstore often resembles a department store and/or a community center.

Angry, Mad. One who is *angry* shows vexation or resentment; one who is *mad* is temporarily or permanently out of his mind.

Anon. Abbreviation of *anonymous*—of unknown authorship. Also at once, presently.

Anticipate, Expect. *Anticipate* means to foresee, forestall; *expect*, to look forward to or count on. He did not expect that I would anticipate his next move.

Anxious, Eager. *Eager* means keenly desirous; *anxious*, desirous but dubious about a successful outcome. Colloquially they are synonyms. He was eager to go to the game. The merchant was anxious for the arrival of the shipment.

Any place, Some place. Do not use as substitutes for anywhere and somewhere.

Apropos. Relevant, opportune, suitable. His remarks were very apropos.

Apt, Likely, Liable. *Apt* means inclined or disposed; *likely*, probable; *liable*, subject to risk or disadvantage. He is apt to make mistakes. She is likely to arrive tomorrow. You are liable to lose on that investment.

As . . . As, So . . . As. Use the former in affirmative statements; prefer the latter in negatives. He was as cool as could be. Your manner was not so confident as it might have been.

As to your proposition. Old-fashioned, round-about. Get to the point.

Avocation, Vocation. *Avocation* means hobby or pastime; *vocation*, main business. His vocation is banking, his avocation collecting golf trophies.

Bad, Badly. *Bad* is the adjective, *badly* the adverb. *Bad* is used with see, hear, feel, taste and other intransitive verbs.

Balance, Remainder. *Balance* means equality in weight or between the two sides of an account; or a portion of an account unpaid; *remainder*, the rest or the residue. I am sending $15.00 to be applied on my balance of $37.50. You can expect the remainder by June 1.

Beg, Beg to advise, Beg to remain. Old-fashioned business terms not found in good modern letters.

Beside, Besides. *Beside* means by the side of; *besides*, moreover, additional.

Between, Among. *Between* two persons or things; *among* more than two.

Between you and I. Common error for *between you and me.* Pronouns follow-ing the preposition take the objective case unless they are the subject of a noun clause that is the object of the preposition; *e.g.,* "Deliver the package to whoever answers the door." Watch *for* and *with* also, and be especially care-ful when the pronoun is the second part of a compound object.

Boss. Colloquial for foreman, manager, head, or superintendent.

Bug. Slang for a flaw or fault in a mechanism, organization, or plan. His scheme for reorganization had too many "bugs" to be feasible.

Bunch. Colloquial for class or groups. Means a collection of like things, as a *bunch* of grapes or bananas.

But that, But what. *But* is superfluous. Say "There is no doubt that. . . ."

Calculate. To compute, reckon, estimate. Do not use for expect, suppose, intend.

Can, May. Both originally meant to be able; colloquially, both now signify permission. Formal usage requires *can* for ability, *may* for permission or possibility. If I can get the car, I may go, and we may get home by midnight.

Carriage trade. The wealthier, more exclusive type of customers, who in former times were the only ones who could afford carriages.

Case, Instance, Instants. *Instance* is the general term for illustration or exam-ple; *case* means a particular situation or special instance. In every instance where this occurs, we find a case of neglect. *Instants,* sometimes confused with *instance,* is the plural of *instant.*

Censor, Censure. *Censor* means to pass judgment on and forbid when objection-able; *censure,* to find fault with or condemn. That book will be censored in Boston. The manager always censures anyone who receives social calls when at work.

Chisel, Chiseler. To *chisel* in business is to cheat through violating established business practices. Formerly slang, but coming increasingly into general business use.

Claim. As a verb, to ask for what is one's due—not a synonym for *say* or *repre-sent.* To be used cautiously as a verb because misuse has brought unfavorable connotation. As a noun, to enter a *claim* for a refund or replacement of damaged goods.

Clench, Clinch. One *clenches* his hands or his teeth, but *clinches* nails, an argument, or a deal.

Client, Customer, Prospect. Lawyers and advertising account executives have *clients;* otherwise *customer* is the preferable term. A *prospect* might become either a client or a customer if suitably approached.

C.O.D. Abbreviation for *collect on delivery.* The seller or his agent collects the amount due on goods when he delivers them.

Collaboration, Collusion. *Collaboration* is legitimate working together on the same thing or to a common end; *collusion,* secret cooperation for fraudulent purposes. Through collusion of the railroads and the trucking companies, excessive freight rates were maintained in that area.

Colloquial. Oral, conversational; not formal, technical. Colloquial language is permissible in all but the most formal business letters. Not to be confused with *provincial, sectional,* or *illiterate.*

Combine. Colloquial for amalgamation or combination of persons or organizations, especially for commercial or political advantage. Technical (agriculture) for combined reaper and threshing machine.

Complaint. A "red flag" word. Avoid it in business writing.

Compliment, Complement. *Compliment* is a tribute; *complement,* something that completes. My compliment on your performance was sincere. Your ability will so complement his that the partnership will be ideal.

Compose, Comprise. *Compose* means to put together, constitute; *comprise,* to include, make up. He composed a report which comprised seven parts.

Consul, Council, Counsel. A *consul* is an agent of one state who lives in a foreign state where he performs certain administrative duties. *Council* means a governing body. *Counsel* means advice, or one who gives advice, such as a lawyer. "The consul met with the council to give counsel on the new treaty." *Counsel* is also a verb.

Contact. Formerly noun or adjective only. Its technical and business use as a verb is still avoided in formal writing. It is a useful word, as in "The salesman was unable to contact three of his customers" (meaning he was unable to reach them by mail, by telephone, or in person), but it has become a catchall term. Rather than "I will contact you when I get into town," say, "I will come to your office . . . ," "I will telephone you . . . ," or "I will get in touch with you . . . ," thus avoiding the *businessese.*

Contents carefully (duly) noted. Old-fashioned. Modern business assumes that every letter has been carefully read before the reply is begun.

Continual, Continuous. *Continual* means occurring again and again; *continuous,* proceeding without interruption. The continual rains interfered with their planning. There was a continuous stream of customers.

Could of. Error for *could have.*

Creditable, Credible, Credulous. *Creditable* means estimable, worthy of credit; *credible*, believable, worthy of belief; *credulous*, gullible, believing too easily.

Data. Plural form of Latin *datum*. The data are accurate. However, *data* may be used with a singular verb if it is singular in sense, as in "This [collection of] data is just what I need to complete my report."

Date. Colloquial for business appointment or social engagement.

Deal. Colloquial for transaction or bargain.

Deprecate, Depreciate. *Deprecate* means to regret or disapprove; *depreciate*, to disparage or belittle. His friends deprecated the fact that he always depreciated the accomplishments of others.

Different. Used preferably with *from*, although the colloquial *different than* is becoming more common in writing. Avoid such usage as "Rich people have a very different outlook than poor people."

Direct, Directly. As an adverb, *direct* means by a straight route. *Directly* in modern usage has acquired the sense of soon, before long. He went direct to France. We are going directly.

Disinterested. See *uninterested.*

Dominant, Dominate. *Dominant,* an adjective, means controlling, most influential. *Dominate* is a verb meaning to rule, govern, control. Cf. *Predominant.*

Don't, Doesn't. Don't = do not; doesn't = does not. Be sure your verb agrees in number with your subject. Test contractions by expanding them; *e.g.* "He do not," "He does not," "They do not," etc.

Double Negative. As in "they don't do nothing." Double negatives are not acceptable in modern English.

Due to, Owing to. Adjectival, not yet established in prepositional use, but such forms as "Due to an unexpectedly heavy demand, our supply is temporarily exhausted" have the sanction of usage by some prominent writers.

Each, Every. Always singular; use with singular verbs only. "*Each* man is trained; *every* person knows his job."

Each other, One another. *Each other* is used with two persons; *one another,* with more than two persons.

Either, Neither. Use with two persons or things only. Singular verb follows. Either Mr. Jones or Mr. Brown was responsible.

Elicit, Illicit. *Elicit* means to draw out; *illicit,* illegal, unauthorized. Skillful questioning will elicit the information. The illicit traffic in narcotics was stopped.

Eminent, Immanent, Imminent, Prominent. *Eminent* means high in rank or repute, distinguished. *Immanent,* indwelling or inherent. *Imminent,* impending, or likely to occur at any moment. *Prominent*, important, leading, well known. "He was one of the eminent economists of the last century." "The personnel director's fear of a strike was immanent." "A strike was imminent." "The vice-president is a prominent civic worker."

Enclosed herewith. Omit *herewith* in letters.

Enthuse. A coinage which has come into considerable use as a verb because it is a short cut, but it is still disliked and should be avoided.

Etc. Means *and others.* Overused. Be definite. Do not use with *and.*

Even date. Referring to a letter, means today, this same date. Artificial; name the month and day, June 15.

Expect, Suspect. *Expect* means to regard as likely to happen, to look forward to; *suspect,* to distrust or be suspicious of. I expect the shipment by August 20. I suspect that collusion caused the delay.

Fake. Colloquial for fraud or fraudulent person. Also colloquial as a verb meaning to imitate with the purpose of deceiving.

Feasible, Practical, Practicable. *Feasible* means readily carried out; it is a close synonym of *practicable.* Both words refer to things only. *Practical* means sensible; it is applied to persons or things.

Fewer, Less. *Fewer* means not so numerous; *less,* smaller in quantity. When fewer persons attend, less food is needed.

Fix. Colloquial for repair, remedy, or take care of, as a verb; or predicament, as a noun.

Flair, Flare. *Flair* means bent, tendency, or preference combined with aptitude or ability; *flare* a flash of light or a burst of flame. She had a flair for neat and accurate typing.

F.O.B. Abbreviation for *free on board.* Seller pays charges of putting goods into custody of the carrier but not freight or delivery charges.

Former, Latter. *Former* means first of two; *latter,* last of two.

Forte. Pronounced like fort, *forte* means something in which one excels. Pronounced for′tā, it means loud or loudly. In baseball, his forte was stealing second base. The pianist played the forte passages with vigor.

Further, Farther. Not always differentiated, but *further* is preferred for reference to time, quantity, or degree; *farther,* for spatial distance. We shall investigate further. Kansas City is farther than St. Louis.

Get. The past participle *got* is preferred to *gotten.* Usage depends on rhythm and emphasis of the particular sentence. (A salesman, going to a college town on business, and his wife planned that he would get tickets for the next week's football game for them and three other couples, the wife and their friends to join him the following Saturday. During the week, the salesman wired his wife, "Have gotten tickets. Come ahead." The wife and four couples arrived in the college town; the telegram had read "Have got ten tickets. Come ahead." Had he used the preferred form—better yet, had he omitted the past participle—he would have been correct. Also, he and his wife could have seen the game rather than listened to it on their car radio as they drove home on Saturday afternoon.)

Good deal. Use "great deal" instead in such expressions as "a *good deal* of the time."

Had of. Do not insert *of* in the past perfect tense, subjunctive mood, as in "If I had of gone earlier."

Hadn't ought. A regional usage. Say, "ought not."

Has come to hand. An antique way of saying "We received . . ."

Hand you herewith. Obsolete rubber-stamp expression.

Hanged, Hung. Use *hanged* in reference to an execution of a criminal, otherwise *hung*.

Healthy, Healthful. Colloquially interchangeable, but formal use restricts *healthy* to possessing health, *healthful* to conducive to health. Persons are healthy; climates are healthful.

Homonyms. Words pronounced alike but different in meaning. This glossary provides many examples; for instance, *flair* and *flare; there, their, they're; companies, company's.*

Ibid. Short for Latin *ibidem,* meaning in the same place. Used in footnotes to mean the same reference as the one just cited. If the page is different, this should be specified.

If, Whether. "I don't know *if I should*"—use *whether.*

Image. Widely used in public relations and advertising circles, indicating reaction of a group or groups to the actions or activities of an organization (commercial, political, educational, etc.). "What will this promotion campaign do to the image of the party at election time?"

Imply, Infer. *Imply* means to hint, suggest; *infer,* to deduce from or conclude from. Do you imply that I did it? I infer that you think I did it.

Incidence, Incidents. *Incidence* means act or fact of falling upon or affecting; *incidents* are events or episodes. Whoever pays it initially, the incidence of increased unit cost will ultimately be on the consumer.

Indict, Indite. Pronounced the same. *Indict* means to charge with a crime; *indite,* to compose or write.

Individual, Party, Person. An *individual* is one human being; a *party* is normally a group of *persons.* In law or in a business transaction, *party* may mean one *person,* but do not use *party* as a loose synonym for *person.*

Ingenious, Ingenuous. *Ingenious* means inventive, clever, or skillful; *ingenuous,* frank, innocent, or naïve.

In re, or Re. Latin, *in the matter.* Prefer *concerning, regarding,* or *supplementing.*

In the amount of. A wordy but prevalent expression in business communication, meaning *for.* Instead of "Your check in the amount of . . . ," say or write, "Your check for . . . ."

Inst., Instant. Latin, *this, this month.* Avoid. Instead of 20th instant, give the exact date, June 20.

Irregardless. Colloquial for *regardless,* for which standard usage does nicely. *Irregardless* is not generally considered good usage.

Is when, Is where. Ungrammatical in such constructions as "A transaction *is when* the buyer and seller agree," "A convention *is where* representatives of organizations meet." Say "A transaction occurs when . . ." or "A transaction is an agreement between . . ."; "A convention is a meeting of . . ."

Its, It's. *Its* is the possessive; *it's,* the contraction of *it is.*

-ize. A proper suffix, overused in neologisms, giving an air of affectation: *summerize, winterize, posturize, channelize, finalize.* (One executive expressed the lament of many when he asked, "Why are people verbizing so many words nowadays?")

Kibitzer. Colloquially a meddler, a person not in a game who offers unasked-for and unwanted advice. Also used for an individual who is wise after the fact.

Kind of, Sort of. Do not use the article *a* after these expressions.

Lady. Feminine equivalent of *gentleman.* Formerly denoted aristocracy or nobility. Now little more than a polite synonym for *woman.* In most contexts *woman* is preferable.

Last, Latter. *Last* is used with a series of more than two, *latter* to indicate the second of two.

Lean, Lien. Often pronounced the same, though preferred pronunciation of *lien* is as two syllables. *Lean* means the opposite of fat or stout; *lien,* a property right similar to a mortgage.

Learn, Teach. An instructor can't *learn* a student anything; he can *teach* him. The student must learn.

Leave, Let. *Leave* means to allow or cause to remain; *let* means to permit. To *leave* a person alone is to allow him to remain in solitude; to *let* him alone is to refrain from bothering or molesting him.

Leery, Leary. Variant spellings of a slang term meaning wary, knowing, on guard. He was leery about stocking up heavily at such a time.

Lend, Loan. Either verb means to allow another to borrow. *Lend* is preferred in general use; *loan* is frequently used for a bank's putting out money at interest. *Loan* is also a noun.

Lengthwise, Endwise, Sidewise. Generally preferred over lengthways, endways, sideways.

Lesser, Lessor. *Lesser* means smaller; *lessor*, one who leases.

Liable. See *apt, likely.* Also means legally bound, obligated.

Lie, Lay. Do not confuse *lie, lay, lain, lying* with *lay, laid, laid,* and *laying. Lie* is intransitive (does not take an object); *lay* is transitive (takes an object). *Lie* means to recline or remain; *lay,* to place. Please lay the letter on my desk. It can lie there until I am ready for it. He lay on the couch where he had been lying for an hour.

Like. Considered an adjective or preposition only, but has reached the colloquial level as a conjunction in such sentences as "The Cardinals will win again like they did last year." Avoid conjunctive use in business letters.

Likely. See *apt.*

Loc. cit. Latin abbreviation meaning the place cited. Found in footnotes, but present tendency is to prefer a shortened form of the reference instead.

Lose, Loose. *To lose* is to fail to keep; *to loose,* to unfasten, set free. *Lose out* is colloquial for *lose* in such sentences as "The company lost out in its fight to prevent a wage increase."

Lot, Large number. Use *a large number* instead of *a lot.*

Luxuriant, Luxurious. *Luxuriant* means abundant in growth, as vegetation; *luxurious,* characterized by luxury. "One of the attractions of the luxurious motel was the luxuriant floral plantings."

Majority, Plurality. *Majority* means more than half; *plurality* (in elections), more votes than received by any other candidate. Do not use *majority* in expressions of quantity, such as "The majority of the wheat was of first quality."

May. See *can.*

Me working, My working. Use a possessive pronoun before a noun ending in "ing." "They knew of *my working* overtime."

Mutual, Common. *Mutual* means reciprocally given and received, having the same relation to each other; *common,* shared similarly by more than one. A mutual agreement; common effort or property.

Myself, Himself. Use a simple pronoun when there is no reflexive effect—"he and I" rather than "he and myself."

Nice. Overused to show approval or bestow compliments.

Number, Quantity. *Number* applies to separate objects; *quantity* to amounts. It will take a number of cars to haul such a quantity of grain.

Oblige. Means to constrain or bind by some favor rendered. Such usage as "Please reply by return mail and oblige" is now obsolete in business letters.

Of. Do not misuse for *have* as in will have, might have.

Off of. *Of* is superfluous after *off*. "Take the folder off the desk."

Oneself. Prefer this spelling to *one's self*.

Op. cit. Latin abbreviation meaning the work cited. Used in footnotes to refer to a work previously cited but not the last cited. Prefer a shortened form of the reference.

Our Mr. Brown. Prefer *our representative, Mr. Brown,* or *our representative, Mr. Henry Brown.*

Party. See *individual*.

Per, As per. *Per* is Latin; do not combine it with the English words. Use *a day, a year, a head, per diem, per annum,* and *per capita.* Do not use *as per* instead of *according to*.

Per cent, Percentage. *Per cent* means by the hundred, and is used of proportions or rate of interest. *Percentage* means a proportion or part of the whole. A large percentage of the loans were renewed at 5 per cent.

Phone. Colloquial for telephone.

Practicable, Practical. See *Feasible*.

Precede, Proceed. *Precede* means to come or go before; *proceed,* to continue, go on, or follow.

Precedence, Precedents. *Prece'dence* means right of priority; *pre'cedents,* cases cited to serve as examples for later cases.

Predominant, Predominate. *Predominant,* an adjective, means having power, authority, or influence over others; *predominate,* a verb, means to be the stronger or leading element, or to prevail. *Predominant* and *dominant* are synonymous; the distinction is shown in the following two sentences: "The dominant features of this set are economy, design, and utility." "Economy is the predominant feature of this set." (*Predominant* describes what is dominant over all others, or is more widely prevalent.)

Preferable. Means more desirable. Do not say *more preferable*.

Principal, Principle. As a noun, *principal* means a capital sum invested or used as a fund, distinguished from interest or profit; or the main body of an estate, distinguished from income; or the head of a school, a chief; *principle,* a general rule, law, or doctrine. *Principal* is also an adjective, meaning chief.

Pro, Con. *Pro* means for; *con,* against.

Prophecy, Prophesy. *Prophecy* is a noun; *prophesy,* a verb. "His prophecies are actually little more than guesswork." "He prophesies that success is inevitable if we follow his plan."

Proposition. The subject of an argument, the question, the proposal. Colloquial for offer or enterprise.

Prove. The preferred past participle is *proved,* not *proven.*

Providing, Provided. *Provided* is a conjunction; *providing* is not. Say "*provided* he agrees."

Pull. Slang for secret influence, special favor; *pull off* is colloquial for achieving something difficult or dangerous. Also, *pull through* is colloquial, meaning to survive, save.

Raise, Rise. Do not confuse the transitive *raise, raised, raised,* with the intransitive *rise, rose, risen.* The use of *raise* for rear, to bring up, is colloquial. His salary has been raised three times. He has risen rapidly in the company.

Rather, Quite. Colloquially as adverbs they are almost synonymous. *Rather* means somewhat; *quite,* noticeably, to a great extent or degree. It was a rather doubtful course to pursue. They were quite eager to have it over with. *Quite* also means entirely.

Re. A Latin foreigner, not at home in modern communication.

Real. Preferably an adjective. Colloquial adverb in "It's a *real* (prefer *very*) attractive offer."

Reason is because. The grammatical construction is "The reason . . . is that," but colloquially "The reason . . . is because" is gaining in use. Avoid in letters.

Receipt. A *receipt* is a written acknowledgment of money paid. Do not confuse with *recipe,* which can mean plan or system. "We have your letter" or "We received your letter" is better than "We are in receipt of your letter."

Receptionist. An office employee who receives telephone calls, greets inquirers and conferees, or makes appointments for executives or professional persons.

Regard, Regards. Say *in regard to,* and *with regard to;* but, *as regards.*

Respectively, Respectfully. *Respectively* means each in the order given; *respectfully,* in a worthy or considerate manner. Since they contributed $20 and $15 respectively, they must be treated respectfully.

Retel. Common abbreviation beginning a telegram sent in reply. Means regarding telegram.

Ring. Colloquial for telephone call.

Robot. A mechanical figure, automaton, hence an efficient but unfeeling person.

R.S.V.P. Means please reply. The expression, from the French *répondez s'il vous plaît*, requests an answer to an invitation.

Run. As a verb, colloquial for manage or conduct, to *run* a hotel. As a noun, a sudden panicky condition, a *run* on a bank; also a continued course, a *run* of good luck.

Same. Properly an adjective. Old-fashioned and unpardonable are such expressions as "We have received your letter and in reply to same."

Secondhand. Not *secondhanded*. Means not new, used previously, or derivative.

Set, Sit. Do not confuse the transitive *set, set, set, setting* with the intransitive *sit, sat, sat, sitting.* To *set* means to seat or cause to *sit.* Set the wastebasket in the corner. He sits at his desk all day.

So. One of the conjunctive adverbs, but is overused. Avoid the "so" habit, as in "They were so busy, and so they couldn't come; so we had to change our plans."

Some. Incorrect for *somewhat*, as in "Business is some better."

S O S. Radio distress signal used by ships and airplanes. In business, means urgent order or request.

Split infinitive. Not the crime it was once considered, but sometimes awkward. Say "He hardly ever seems to buy," not "He seems to hardly ever buy."

Stationary, Stationery. *Stationary* = fixed in place; *stationery* = writing supplies.

Stayed, Staid. *Stayed* is past tense and past participle of *stay*. *Staid* means sedate or settled; also an archaic form for *stayed*, in which sense it is seldom used.

Stratagem, Trick. *Stratagem* implies leadership in skillful management to attain an end; *trick* implies a crafty or fraudulent proceeding.

Than. See *different.*

Their, There. *Their* is the possessive pronoun; *there*, the adverb of place.

Therefore, Therefor. *Therefore* is used to mean "for that reason"; *therefor* is a rarely used legal term.

To, Too, Two. Be sure you use the right one of these. To misuse them betrays extreme carelessness or fuzzy-mindedness. *Too* means also.

Toward, Towards. Prepositions or adverbs identical in meaning. American usage prefers *toward*, British *towards*.

Trusting this will. Trite participial close. Use a fresh, positive statement.

Try and, Try to. *Try to* is correct.

Ult., Ultimo. Latin, *last, last month.* Avoid. Instead of 15th ult., name the month, May 15.

Under separate cover. Prefer *by parcel post,* or simply *separately.* Often "We are sending you" is sufficient.

Upon, On. *Upon* is stuffy unless you really mean to indicate position. *On* is generally better.

Uninterested, Disinterested. *Uninterested* means apathetic, lacking interest; *disinterested,* without bias or prejudice. He remained uninterested throughout the address. He will be a disinterested witness.

Unique. Means the only one of its kind, hence should not be used with *more* or *most.*

Unless, Except, Without. *Unless* is always a conjunction; *except* and *without* are always prepositions. Do not say "They will win without we do something to prevent."

Valued favor, Valued patronage. Too effusive in most contexts.

Waive, Wave. *Waive* means to forego a claim or pass up a point; *wave,* to signal, sway, or place undulations in. When the speaker agreed to waive that point, the chairman waved further discussion aside.

Ware, Wear. In compounds such as *hardware* and *neckwear* both mean goods. *Wear* is the word in general use as a verb or singular noun; *wares* is frequently used.

We, I. Use *we* when you speak for the company. Don't be afraid to use *I* when that is what you mean. Be natural—and consistent. You may sometimes use both in the same letter: "*We* have received a new shipment of sky hooks. . . . *I* plan to be in your city next Friday."

Who, Whom. Get these straight. *Who* is a subject, *whom* is an object. If you would say "he," use *who;* if you would say "him," use *whom.*

Who, Which, That. *Who* usually refers to persons only; *which,* to animals, ideas, or things; *that,* to persons, animals, ideas, or things.

Window dressing. The basic meaning is arranging objects in retail store windows for display purposes, or the resultant display. Now tends to signify hollow display or favorable reports that disguise undesirable conditions. Sometimes it means little more than putting one's best foot forward.

Wire. Colloquial for *telegram* (noun) and *telegraph* (verb).

Wirepulling. Colloquially the use of secret methods to influence persons or organizations, especially in politics.

Writer, The writer wishes to say. Don't be afraid to say *I;* to avoid it is often conspicuously awkward.

Yes man. Slang for an employee who always agrees with his superiors or associates through weakness or hope of advancement.

You claim, You state, You say. This seems to doubt what the other fellow says. Don't put him on the defensive.

Yours of recent date. Old, and the worse for wear. Avoid.

E

Copyreading and Proofreading

Preparation of Copy for the Press [1]

GENERAL SUGGESTIONS

1. **Copy should be prepared on single sheets of paper** of a uniform size, *one side only* being used. Sheets of the ordinary commercial letterhead size (8½ × 11 inches) are the most convenient. The sheets should be numbered, and plain white or neutral (gray, yellow, or brown) paper is best.

2. **Copy should be typewritten and double-spaced,** except that quotations and footnotes that go in smaller type may be single-spaced. A duplicate should be kept for reference and as a safeguard against loss in transmission, but no carbon or mimeographed copy should be sent to the printer. The first line of each page should begin not less than an inch from the top of the page, and there should be a blank margin of an inch and a half at the left side of the page. Sheets should be numbered consecutively. Any necessary insertions of more than a sentence should be on sheets of the same size as the rest of the copy, labeled 'Insert 41-A' or the like and included immediately after the page on which the proper point of insertion is marked 'Insert A.'

3. **Copy should embody the final ideas of the author.** Allowance must be made for some changes, but, to avoid expense, the copy as sent to the compositor should be as complete and perfect as possible.

4. **Footnotes.** A reference from the text of a work to a note that is to appear at the foot of the printed page should be indicated by a superior figure following the word to which the note refers and corresponding with the superior figure preceding the note. The figures should run consecutively through each chapter or article. The material constituting the footnote should be entered immediately below the line to which it refers and should be separated from the

[1] By permission. From *Webster's New Collegiate Dictionary,* copyright, 1961, by G. & C. Merriam Company.

text by lines running entirely across the page. Names of publications should be abbreviated in the references only after giving the full title and data at the first appearance of each title.

5. **All proper names, technical and scientific words, references, quotations, and figures** that appear in the MS should be verified.

6. **Spelling should be uniform.** For words that have two or more accepted spellings, one form should be adopted and adhered to throughout. When two spellings are shown in this dictionary, separated by a comma or by an italic *or*, the one printed first is in general to be preferred but the second is acceptable, sometimes equally acceptable with the first.

7. **Capitalization and punctuation should be used according to a uniform style.** For rules see the preceding sections on *Punctuation* and *Use of Capitals*.

8. **Paragraphing** should be indicated on copy, not left to the compositor or proofreader. To indicate a new paragraph the symbol ¶ is used.

9. **The title page, preface, table of contents, and list of illustrations or tables** should accompany the MS.

10. **The kind of type to be used,** if not ordinary roman, is indicated by underscoring. Underscore once for *italics*, twice for SMALL CAPITALS, three times for CAPITALS, and once with a wavy line for **bold-faced type.**

11. **Manuscript should be kept and mailed flat.** If necessary, it may be folded, but it should never be rolled.

CORRECTION OF PROOFS

12. **Corrections on proof sheets should be made by means of the standard proofreaders' marks** in the margins directly opposite the indicated errors, usually in the nearer margin. For every correction marked in the text there must be a

Proofreaders' Marks [2]

ℒ *or* ℐ *or* ℒ (L *dele*) dele *or* delete; take out or expunge	◯ (a ring drawn around an abbreviation, figure, etc.) spell out—used in the text	*bf* put in boldface type—used in the margin with _____ under text matter
ℒ take out a letter and close up	ⓢⓟ spell out—used in the margin	
⌢ print as a ligature; thus, a͡e (i. e., print æ); also, close up	⊙ period	⌐_____⌐ transpose
∨ *or* ⌣ less space	⌃ *or* ,/ comma	*tr* transpose—used in the margin.
◡ close up entirely; no space	:/ *or* ⊙ colon	*lc* lowercase—used in the margin with a slanting line drawn through the letter in the text
ꝰ turn a reversed letter	;/ semicolon	
∧ *or* > caret; insert at this point the marginal addition	⌄ apostrophe or single closing quotation mark	= *or* SC *or* sm caps put in small capitals—the double lines drawn under the letters or word
# *or* ⌗ space or more space	⌄⌄ double closing quotation mark	
Eq # space evenly—used in the margin		
L *or* ⌐ *or* [carry farther to the left	⌄ inverted comma or single opening quotation mark	≡ *or caps* put in capitals—the triple lines drawn under the letters or word
⌐ *or* ⌐ *or*] carry farther to the right	⌄⌄ double opening quotation mark	
⌐ elevate a letter or word		*ld* insert a lead between lines
⌐ sink or depress a letter or word	=/ *or* -/ hyphen	
☐ em quad space; or indent one em	[/] brackets	*stet* restore words crossed out—usually written in the margin (with dots under the words to be kept)
1/m, ⊢⊣, 1/em *or* ⊢⊔ *or* em one-em dash	(/) parentheses	
‖ straighten ends of lines	*wf* wrong font—used when a character is of a wrong size or style	∨ set as a superscript; thus, ꝯ (i. e., print 3)—used in the margin
≡ *or* /// *or* \\\ straighten a crooked line or lines	*ital* put in italic type—used in the margin with ____ under text matter	
⊥ *or* ⌣ push down a space which prints as a mark	*rom* put in roman type—used in the margin with _____ under text matter	∧ set as a subscript; thus, ꝯ (i. e., print 3)—used in the margin
✕ *or* + *or* ⊗ broken or imperfect type—used in the margin		? is this correct as set?—used in the margin
¶ make a new paragraph		

Proofs of Lincoln's Gettysburg Address with Corrections Marked (*above*) and Made (*below*) [3]

"Four score and 7 years ago our fathers brought forth on this continent a new nation, conceived in in liberty, and dedicated to the proposition, that all men are created equal. Now we're engaged in a great Civil War, testing whether that nation, or any nation conceived so and dedicated so, can long endure.

We are met on a great battle field of that war, we have come to dedicate a portion of this field, as a final resting place for those who here have given their lives that this nation might live, it is altogether proper and fitting that we should do this. But, in a larger sense, we can not dedicate—we cannot consecrate—we cannot hallow—this ground. The brave men, living and dead, who struggled here, have have consecrated it, far above our power to de-tract or add. The world will little note, nor long remember, what we say here, but it can never forget what we did here, It is for us, the living, rather, to be dedicated here to the great task remaining before us,—that from these honored dead we take increased devotion to that cause for which they gave the last full measure of devotion—that we now highly resolve that these dead shall not have died in vain—that this nation under God, shall have a new birth of freedom—and, government of the people, by the people, for the people, shall never perish from the earth.

"Fourscore and seven years ago our fathers brought forth on this continent a new nation, conceived in liberty, and dedicated to the proposition that all men are created equal. Now we are engaged in a great civil war, testing whether that nation, or any nation so conceived and so dedicated, can long endure. We are met on a great battle-field of that war. We have come to dedicate a portion of that field, as a final resting place for those who here gave their lives that that nation might live. It is altogether fitting and proper that we should do this. But, in a larger sense, we cannot dedicate—we cannot consecrate—we cannot hallow—this ground. The brave men, living and dead, who struggled here, have consecrated it, far above our poor power to add or detract. The world will little note, nor long remember, what we say here, but it can never forget what they did here. It is for us the living, rather, to be dedicated here to the unfinished work which they who fought here have thus far so nobly advanced. It is rather for us to be here dedicated to the great task remaining before us,—that from these honored dead we take increased devotion to that cause for which they gave the last full measure of devotion—that we here highly resolve that these dead shall not have died in vain—that this nation, under God, shall have a new birth of freedom—and that government of the people, by the people, for the people, shall not perish from the earth."

[3] By permission. From *Webster's Seventh New Collegiate Dictionary*, copyright, 1963, by G. & C. Merriam Company, publishers of the Merriam-Webster dictionaries.

corresponding direction or mark in the margin, either the same mark as is used in the text or an abbreviation representing the direction. These marks must be kept strictly in order of occurrence and marks in the same horizontal line separated from each other by a diagonal mark, or virgule (/), or a similar vertical mark. This mark is made after every punctuation mark inserted and is often made after every marginal mark.

13. **Queries on proof sheets must be answered.** If the proposal is approved, striking out the query mark is sufficient; otherwise write the answer.

14. **All final changes should be made on the galley proof** because changes on subsequent proofs are more expensive; subsequent proofs are for verification only. In making changes the author should keep in mind that the alteration of a few words at the opening of a paragraph may require the resetting of the whole paragraph, and in linotype work the alteration of a single comma requires the resetting of the whole line.

15. **The original manuscript should be returned** unchanged with the corrected galley proof.

16. **An index should be compiled**—if the book is likely to be used for reference—beginning with the arrival of the first page proofs and should be sent to the printer immediately following the final page proofs.

PRINTING TERMS

body.—The solid rectangular metal base supporting the face of a printing type. Sizes of type are determined by the measurement of the type body from the front (containing the nick) to the back. See TYPE, *Illust.*, in *Vocabulary*.

electrotype.—A facsimile plate, esp. for use in printing, made by taking an impression in a special kind of wax or a sheet of soft lead, depositing in this mold a thin shell of copper, nickel, or the like, by an electrolytic process, and backing this shell with molten metal. The wax mold is rendered conductive for electroplating by coating it with graphite.

em.—The portion of a line occupied by any square type body (formerly by the letter *m*, then a square type) used as a unit of measure for printed matter. The em, now usually an em pica, approximately ⅙ of an inch (see TYPE, in the *Vocabulary*), is the unit of measure for printed matter, esp. of column width.

en.—A type body, unit of measure, etc., one half the width of an em (which see).

end paper.—A sheet of paper folded and pasted to the first or last leaf of a book to give an extra flyleaf and a paste-down (that is, a leaf that is pasted to the inside of the cover to secure it to the book).

flush.—(Set) even with the edge of the type page, usually the left margin; without indention.

font.—A complete assortment of any particular size and style of type;—in British use often *fount*.

half title.—The name alone of a book, placed on a separate page or at the head of the first page of text; also, any similar sectional title.

indention.—The setting of a line or lines in from the margin; the beginning of a line or series of lines a little within the flush line of the text. In **hanging indention** all the lines of a paragraph except the first line are indented.

lead (lĕd).—A thin strip of type metal, used to separate lines of type in printing; hence, a similar strip of brass. Leads vary in thickness from one half point (¾₁₄₄ of an inch) to three points (½₂₄ of an inch) (from twenty-four to four to a pica). The commonest in use is the 2-point.

Linotype.—A trade-mark applied to a kind of typesetting machine which produces castings, or slugs, each of which corresponds to a line of separate types.

make-up.—Arrangement of type lines and illustrations into page form for printing.

Monotype.—A trade-mark applied to a typesetting machine consisting of two units. One, the keyboard, perforates a roll of paper which, when fed through the other, the caster, causes it to cast individual types and set them in justified lines.

pie *or* **pi.**—To upset or disarrange, as set type.

plate.—A page of stereotype, electrotype, or the like, to be printed from.

proof.—A trial impression from type, taken for correction or examination;—called also **proof sheet.—author's proof.** The clean proof sent to an author, after correction of the compositors' errors.—**galley proof.** A proof from type on a galley (the printer's steel tray holding type that has been set) before it is made up in pages. The first author's proof is generally a galley proof.—**page proof.** A proof of type that has been made up into page form.—**foundry proof.** A proof for a final reading before the electrotype or stereotype plates are made.—**plate proof.** A proof taken from a plate.

quad (**quadrat**).—A block of type metal lower than the letters, and half a one em, or two, or three ems in width,—used in spacing and in blank lines.

recto.—The right-hand (odd-numbered) page.

register.—Exact correspondence in position of lines, columns, or pages on the two sides of the sheet, or of the several impressions in a design printed in parts, as in process printing.

rule.—A thin type-high plate of type metal with a line or lines as its face. **Single rule** has one light line; **parallel rule,** two light lines; **double rule,** a light and a heavy line; **dotted rule,** a line of dots; **wave rule,** a wavy line.

run in.—To make (matter) continuous without a paragraph or break.

serif.—One of the fine lines of a letter, esp. one of the fine cross strokes at the top or bottom. See TYPE, *Illust.*, in the *Vocabulary.*

sidehead.—A subhead placed at or in the side of printed matter. In bookwork, it is usually placed in the left side of the first line of a paragraph.

signature.—(1) A letter or figure placed at the bottom of the first page of each sheet of a book or pamphlet, as a direction to the binder in arranging and folding the sheets;—called also **signature mark.** (2) A printed sheet containing a number of pages, as 4, 8, 12, 16, etc., folded as one unit and forming a section of a book or pamphlet; hence, in bookbinding, such a printed sheet or set of sheets folded into four, or some multiple of four, pages;—called also *section.*

small capital.—A letter in the form of, but about two thirds the size of, a capital. Small capitals are used chiefly to mark principal parts, plurals, and cross references (as, See TYPE, *n.*, 8 b). See § 10, p. 1197. Abbr. *s.c., s. caps.,* or *sm. cap.*

stereotype.—A plate made by taking a mold or matrix of a printing surface in plaster of Paris, paper pulp, or the like, and making from this a cast in type metal, commonly with more than the usual percentage of lead. Stereotypes are chiefly used in newspaper and magazine printing, electrotypes for printing books.

verso.—The left-hand (even-numbered), page.

F

Letters and the Law

The legal addressee of a letter is the person, persons, or firm named on the top line of the envelope address. Once the letter has been dropped in the mail it is the property of the legal addressee, though the writer of the letter retains all rights to publication.

Although the precedents and the interpretation of the law vary from state to state, certain principles relating to letters are generally accepted.

Fraud. If a sales letter includes intentionally misleading advertising, the writer of it may be held to be using the mails to defraud.

Warranties. An expressed warranty is a guarantee that is specifically stated in writing; the writer of a letter is legally bound by such a warranty in his letter.

An implied warranty is also legally binding upon the writer of a letter, even if he specifically states that no warranties other than the expressed warranties apply. The basic implied warranty is that the seller has free and clear title to what he is selling. An implied warranty exists also when the seller supplies merchandise to meet certain conditions or to do a certain job described by the buyer. For example, if A orders air conditioning unit #417 from B, there is no implied warranty except that the unit is B's to sell; but if A orders "an air conditioning unit which will cool my sixteen-by-twenty-four-foot room to 70 degrees Fahrenheit when the external temperature is 100 degrees Fahrenheit," B upon delivery of the unit implies a warranty that it will do the job.

Extortion. If a creditor threatens to collect a debt by using means above and beyond the due process of law, he may be held to be using extortion. Any threat of physical violence could be so construed. And since due process of law for collecting debts is through civil suit in the courts, a threat of criminal action against the debtor could be considered extortion. For example, if A threatens to have B put in jail unless he pays his debt, A is using extortion.

Libel. There are two types of libel suits, civil and criminal. In a civil suit the damaged person sues to recover damages because his credit standing, good name, position in the community, or job status has been hurt by the publication of libelous information about him. Publication occurs when one other person besides the writer sees the information before the damaged person receives it. Publication does not occur when the damaged person himself shows the information to others. Though ordinarily such libel cases develop from a letter only when the writer of the letter intentionally publishes the letter, good faith is not a sure defense against a civil suit for libel. It is important for the writer of a letter containing potentially damaging information to protect that information from publication by making sure that no one, not even a secretary, can read it before its legal recipient reads it. The recipient's secretary (if she regularly opens his mail), the postman (if the letter is left unsealed by mistake), even the recipient's wife (if the letter is sent to the home address) may read the letter and thus open the door for a libel suit. If potentially damaging information must be sent through the mail, therefore, it should be typed personally by the sender, sealed immediately in an envelope, and sent registered mail to be delivered to addressee only, return receipt requested. Though a civil suit for libel will not win if the damaging information is true, it is hard to be certain that every part of all potentially damaging letters is completely true.

Society protects its members against malicious attacks involving words as well as physical violence. If a person attempts to tear down another person's reputation by malicious spreading of damaging information about him, even if that damaging information is the truth, a criminal action for libel or slander may result (libel if written; slander if spoken). The damaged person cannot recover damages in such a case, but he can perhaps see his attacker sent to jail or fined by the state. The only defense against a criminal libel suit is good faith.

Privilege. If a person or firm seeks credit information in order to protect a real financial interest, damaging or potentially damaging facts about a third party may be sent in reply. The principle of privilege makes possible free exchange of information about credit as long as the information is needed to protect the interests of the inquirer. However, the principle of privilege does not protect credit information which is volunteered or which is handed out carelessly to satisfy curiosity. When the principle of privilege does not apply, the damaged party may sue for libel.

Contracts. An exchange of letters may under certain circumstances establish a contract. The first requirement for a contract is a firm offer; the second requirement is the acceptance of all the terms of that offer without qualification. Thus a letter which makes a firm offer and a reply which accepts the offer together make a contract. There is some uncertainty in the law about just when an acceptance becomes valid and just why it becomes valid at that time. In general, when an offer has been mailed, the acceptance becomes binding when the acceptance is dropped in the mail, but a telegram accepting a mailed offer does not become binding until it has been received by the person who made the offer.

Index